Issues in U.S. Immigration

Italian immigrants approaching Ellis Island on a ferry in 1905 (Library of Congress)

ISSUES IN
U.S. IMMIGRATION

Volume 1
Accent discrimination – Indentured servitude

Edited by
Carl L. Bankston III
Tulane University
Danielle Antoinette Hidalgo
Tulane University

Salem Press
A Division of EBSCO Information Services
Ipswich, Massachusetts

GREY HOUSE PUBLISHING

Some essays originally appeared in (in descending order of numbers): *Racial and Ethnic Relations in America* (1999), *Encyclopedia of Family Life* (1999), *Great Events from History: North American Series* (1997), *Great Events from History II: Human Rights* (1992), *Great Events: 1900-2001* (2002),*Women's Issues* (1997), *Magill's Legal Guide* (1999), *Encyclopedia of the U.S. Supreme Court* (2001), *Identities and Issues in Literature* (1997), *Criminal Justice* (2006), *American Justice* (1996), *The Bill of Rights* (2002), *Survey of Social Science: Sociology Series* (1994), and *Encyclopedia of American Immigration* (2010). New material has been added.

Publisher's Cataloging-In-Publication Data
(Prepared by The Donohue Group, Inc.)

Issues in U.S. immigration / edited by Carl L. Bankston III, Tulane
  University, Danielle Antoinette Hidalgo, Tulane University ; [edited by
  Salem Press]. -- [Second edition].

   volumes : illustrations ; cm

   Edition statement supplied by publisher.
   Previous edition titled: Immigration in U.S. history.
   Includes bibliographical references and index.
   ISBN: 978-1-61925-708-5 set

   1. United States--Emigration and immigration--History. 2. Immigrants--United States--History. I. Bankston, Carl L. (Carl Leon), 1952- II. Hidalgo, Danielle Antoinette. III. Salem Press.
IV. Title: Immigration in U.S. History.

JV6450 .I565 2015
304.8/7303

CONTENTS

COMPLETE LIST OF CONTENTS

VOLUME 1

VOLUME 2

Publisher's Note

In 1958, while campaigning in Congress for passage of amendments to the Refugee Relief Act, Senator John F. Kennedy published a little book titled *A Nation of Immigrants*. His immediate purpose was to call attention to the enormous contributions made to the United States by immigrants and thereby rally public support behind liberalization of the nation's immigration laws—a task in which he succeeded. At the same time, his book helped to fix in the public mind the fact that the United States was, and always had been, a nation of immigrants. During Kennedy's run for the presidency in 1960, much was made of his Irish ancestry and the fact that the great-grandson of humble Irish immigrants could be elected president of the United States. In 2003, more than a generation later, the public reacted with equal wonderment when Arnold Schwarzenegger—a first-generation Austrian immigrant—was elected governor of California. Schwarzenegger was not the first immigrant to be elected governor of an American state, but his elevation to that office seemed all the more remarkable because California, the nation's largest state by population, would rank as the world's seventh-largest economy, were it an independent nation. Indeed, its economy would dwarf that of Schwarzenegger's Austrian homeland. In 2006, Cuban-born Mel Martinez became the Chairman of the Republican Party–the first Latino to head a major political party.

Other notable immigrants outside the political arena include: Taiwanese Jerry Yang, founder of Yahoo; Indian Indra Nooyi, CEO of PepsiCo; and Hungarian Andy Grove, co-founder of Intel Corporation.

Of the 316,128,839 residents in the United States in 2013, 13.1% were foreign born. Of course, nearly 99% of all residents can trace their ancestry to immigrants who arrived in North America within the previous four centuries. Moreover, even Native Americans can trace their ancestry to immigrants who came thousands of years earlier. The United States is, indeed, a nation of immigrants.

Of the many themes that dominate U.S. history, immigration is one of the most constant and most pervasive. Since the first European and African immigrants began arriving in North America during the early seventeenth century, immigrants have steadily poured into what is now the United States. During the early twenty-first century, that flow has continued unabated—the major difference being that most immigrants now come from Latin America—especially Mexico and Central America—and Asia. Meanwhile, immigration remains as controversial a public issue as it has ever been. In 2014, President Obama's plan to ease the threat of deportation for the 4.7 million undocumented immigrants in the United States created intense controversy.

Because the United States is a nation of immigrants, it is obvious that most of the contributions to the building of the country have been made by immigrants and their descendants. Nevertheless, immigration has long been a subject of debate—and now more than ever, as Americans are increasingly feeling their security threatened by the constant flow of foreigners into the country.

Subject Matter The two volumes of *Issues in U.S. Immigration* (formerly *Immigration in U.S. History*) examine the many issues surrounding immigration—from the earliest settlement of British North America in the seventeenth century to the latest twenty-first century immigration legislation, including: Affordable Care Act and Undocumented Immigrants; DREAM Act; Real ID Act; and Secure Fence Act. The set's 215 essays explore immigration from a wide variety of perspectives, such as border control, law enforcement, court cases, demographics, discrimination, economic and labor issues, events, family issues, government and politics, illegal immigration, language and education, laws and treaties, literature, nativism and racism, refugees, religion, sociological theories, and stereotypes.

This second edition includes 75 new articles, including individual state essays, with current immigration statistics.

Issues in U.S. Immigration places special emphasis on the many ethnic communities that have provided American immigrants. Readers will find articles discussing: African immigrants, including Nigerian (NEW); Asian immigrants, including Bangladeshi (NEW), Cambodian (NEW), Chinese, Filipino, Hmong, Japanese, Korean, Laotian (NEW), Pacific islander, South Asian, Southeast Asian, Tibetan, and Vietnamese immigrants; Canadian immigrants (NEW), Latino and West Indian immigrants, including Cubans, Dominicans, Haitians, Jamaicans, and Mexicans; Middle Eastern immigrants, including Arabs, Iranians, Israelis, and Pakistani (NEW); European immigrants, including German, Irish, Italian, Jewish, Polish, Russian, and Scandinavian immigrants.

Issues in U.S. Immigration answers such questions as
- When did members of individual ethnic groups come to the United States?
- From what parts of the world have most immigrants come?
- Where have different immigrant groups settled in the United States?
- What contributions have immigrants made to the United States?
- How long has illegal immigration been a problem?
- How have U.S. immigration laws changed over time?
- How has U.S. immigration policy been influenced by events in other parts of the world?
- Which groups have been victims of discriminatory immigration laws?
- What is a "model minority"?
- What are "push and pull" factors?
- What are "mail-order brides" and "picture brides"?
- What is a green card?
- What do immigration lawyers do?
- How did Chinatowns get started?
- Why have there been conflicts among different immigrant groups?
- What has been the Supreme Court's role in American immigration law?

- Which immigrants were the first victims of segregation laws?
- What are the origins of ethnic stereotypes?
- How have immigrants organized to protect their rights and interests?
- What role have immigrants played in U.S. labor history?
- Did all African immigrants to North America come as slaves?
- What has been the impact of the September 11 terrorist attacks on U.S. immigration policy and border control?
- What was the "yellow peril"?
- What was the bracero program?
- What was American nativism?
- What was the role of immigrants in the political "machines" of big cities?
- Who are the "boat people"?
- How have bilingual education programs affected immigrants?
- What is "generational acculturation"?
- Is there a specifically immigrant literature?
- What state and federal agencies are responsible for enforcing immigration laws?

Volume One Volume 1 contains 114 articles, from Accent discrimination to Indentured servitude. Each of the alphabetically arranged articles opens with the type of ready-reference top matter for which Salem Press reference works are well known. Following the title is a brief **Definition** of the article's subject and a list of **Immigration Issues** it covers. Articles on events, court cases, organizations, and laws include **Dates** and **Places**, as relevant. Next is a paragraph on **Significance**, helping readers see at a glance the most essential information about the topic.

Boldface subheads help guide readers through longer articles, and all articles are followed by up-to-date, annotated **Further Reading** lists. Every article also includes **Cross-References** to other articles on closely related subjects. Readers are encouraged to follow the paths that these cross references provide.

Immigration provides a rich subject for illustration, and many articles include images – nearly 200 are placed throughout the volumes—of immigrants arriving in the New World, working, going to school, and adapting to life in America.

Volume Two The 101 articles in Volume 2 start with Indigenous superordination, and end with *Zadvydas v. Davis*. Following the last article is a section of individual **State Essays**, including New York City and Washington D.C., that offer specific insight into their specific immigration issues. Each essay includes a statistical table with numbers of immigrants, largest immigrant groups, with comparisons and rankings, based on 2013 numbers.

Following the State Essays, readers will find a comprehensive **Bibliography**, and detailed **Time Line of U.S. Immigration History**.

Next is a brand new feature to this second edition – a 100-page, 41-table section of **Immigration Statistics** from the U.S Department of Homeland Security Office of

Immigration Statistics. This section covers five broad categories: Legal Permanent Residents; Refugees and Asylees; Naturalizations; Non-immigration Admissions; and Enforcement Actions.

Issues in U.S. Immigration offers two helpful indexes. The first is a **Category Index of Topics** that carefully lists articles under one or more of 37categories, from African Americans to Women. The second index is a **Subject Index**.

Acknowledgments A number of articles in this set come from various Salem Press publications: *Racial and Ethnic Relations in America; Encyclopedia of Family Life; Great Events from History; Great Events from History II; Great Events: 1900-2001; Magill's Legal Guide; Encyclopedia of the U.S. Supreme Court; Identities and Issues in Literature; Criminal Justice; American Justice; The Bill of Rights; Survey of Social Science: Sociology Series*; and *Encyclopedia of American Immigration.* These articles and their Further Reading notes have all been updated, as necessary.

Grey House Publishing thanks the editors and contributors who made this reference work possible. See list following this Publiser's Note in Volume 1.

CONTRIBUTORS

Nobuko Adachi
Illinois State University

McCrea Adams
Independent Scholar

Carl Allsup
University of Wisconsin at Platteville

James A. Baer
Northern Virginia Community College

Barbara Bair
Independent Scholar

Carl L. Bankston III
Tulane University

Rosann Bar
Caldwell College

Graciela Bardallo-Vivero
Berkeley College

Alvin K. Benson
Utah Valley State College

Milton Berman
University of Rochester

Tej K. Bhatia
Syracuse University

Warren M. Billings
Louisiana State University at New Orleans

Cynthia A. Bily
Adrian College

Arthur Blaser
Chapman University

Steve D. Boilard
Independent Scholar

Aubrey W. Bonnett
State University of New York,
Old Westbury

Denise Paquette Boots
University of South Florida at Tampa

Anthony D. Branch
Golden Gate University

Michael Broadway
Independent Scholar

Mary Louise Buley-Meissner
University of Wisconsin at Milwaukee

Michael H. Burchett
Limestone College

William H. Burnside
Lenoir-Rhyne College

Edmund J. Campion
University of Tennessee

Brenda E. Reinertsen Caranicas
Fort Berthold Community College

José A. Carmona
Daytona Beach Community College

Peter E. Carr
Caribbean Historical and Genealogical
Journal

Irwin Halfond
McKendree College

Susan E. Hamilton
Independent Scholar

Sheldon Hanft
Appalachina State University

Keith Harper
Mississippi College

Peter B. Heller
Manhattan College

Arthur W. Helweg
Western Michigan University

Diane Andrews Henningfeld
Adrian College

Danielle Antoinette Hidalgo
Tulane University

Keith Orlando Hilton
University of the Pacific

Ronald W. Howard
Mississippi College

Heather Hummell
Independent Scholar

John Quinn Imholte
University of Minnesota at Morris

W. Turrentine Jackson
University of California at Davis

Robert Jacobs
Central Washington University

Duncan R. Jamieson
Ashland University

Kristine Kleptach Jamieson
Ashland University

Daniella Kleskovic
Independent Scholar

Kathleen Odell Korgen
William Patterson University

Melvin Kulbicki
York College of Pennsylvania

M. Bahati Kuumba
Buffalo State College

P. R. Lannert
Independent Scholar

Douglas Edward LaPrade
University of Texas—Pan American

Gregory A. Levitt
University of New Orleans

Thomas Tandy Lewis
Anoka-Ramsey Community College

Paul Madden
Hardin-Simmons University

Paul D. Mageli
Independent Scholar

Martin J. Manning
United States Department of State

Cecilia G. Manrique
University of Wisconsin at La Crosse

Carl Henry Marcoux
University of California at Riverside

Chogollah Maroufi
California State University at

Los Angeles

Rubén O. Martinez
University of Colorado

Hisako Matsuo
Southern Illinois University at
Carbondale

Daniel J. Meissner
University of Wisconsin at Madison

Randall L. Milstein
Lansing Community College

Christina J. Moose
Independent Scholar

Amy J. Orr
Linfield College

Maria A. Pacino
Azusa Pacific University

Gowri Parameswaran
Southwest Missouri State University

Pedro R. Payne
University of California at Riverside

David Peck
California State University at
Long Beach

Louis G. Perez
Independent Scholar

Wayne J. Pitts
University of Memphis

Marjorie J. Podolsky
Penn State University at Erie

R. Kent Rasmussen
Independent Scholar

William L. Reinshagen
Independent Scholar

Martha E. Rhynes
Independent Scholar

Silke Roth
University of Connecticut

Joseph R. Rudolph, Jr.
Towson University

Irene Struthers Rush
Independent Scholar

Wendy Sacket
Independent Scholar

Michael A. Scaperlanda
University of Oklahoma

Helmut J. Schmeller
Fort Hays State University

Kathleen Schongar
The May School

Stephen Schwartz
Buffalo State College

Larry Schweikart
University of Dayton

R. Baird Shuman
University of Illinois at Urbana-
Champaign

Donald C. Simmons, Jr.
Mississippi Humanities Council

Celia Stall-Meadows
Northeastern State University

James Stanlaw
Illinois State University

Francis C. Staskon
Independent Scholar

Susan A. Stussy
Neosho County Community College

Robert D. Talbott
University of Northern Iowa

Nancy Conn Terjesen
Kent State University

Leslie V. Tischauser
Prairie State College

Frank Towers
Clarion University

Paul B. Trescott
Southern Illinois University

Robert D. Ubriaco, Jr.
Spelman College

Jiu-Hwa Lo Upshur
Eastern Michigan University

Theodore M. Vestal
Oklahoma State University

Thomas J. Edward Walker
Pennsylvania College of Technology

Annita Marie Ward
Salem-Teikyo University

Major L. Wilson
Memphis State University

Richard L. Wilson
University of Tennessee, Chattanooga

Gene Redding Wynne, Jr.
Tri-County Technical College

George Yancey
University of Wisconsin at Whitewater

Philip Q. Yang
California Polytechnic State University
at San Luis Obispo

Cynthia Gwynne Yaudes
Indiana University

Clifton K. Yearley
State University of New York, Buffalo

Paul J. Zbiek
King's College

ISSUES IN
U.S. IMMIGRATION

ACCENT DISCRIMINATION

Definition: Employment discrimination based on the manner in which employees or prospective employees speak English

Immigration issues: Civil rights and liberties; Discrimination; Education; Language; Sociological theories

Significance: Under U.S. law, employers can discriminate against applicants for employment whom they believe to have accents that might impede their normal business activities. Immigrants, whose primary language is not English, therefore, may have to shed their accents to qualify for jobs that involve speaking with the general public.

A standard American English accent is commonly heard in schools and spoken on radio and television, but there are regional variations, especially in Hawaii, New England, and the southern states. Immigrants who learn English tend to speak the new language in accordance with the pronunciation and intonation patterns of their native tongues, which means that those unfamiliar with their accents may not understand them completely and may ask these immigrants to repeat what they are saying. At issue, therefore, is whether an employer can reject someone with an unfamiliar accent without discriminating against that person on the basis of ethnic group membership.

The Nature of Accents Vocal muscles develop so early in life that it is difficult for an adult native speaker of one language to learn a second language without carrying forward the accents of the primary language. In the United States, composed as it is of immigrants and their descendants, English is spoken with many accents. Some schools teach adult immigrants to speak without a noticeable accent, but these classes are expensive and not always accessible to newcomers, whose time is usually preoccupied with material adjustments to life in a new country.

The United States does not have an official standard of speech, although the informal standard is the American English accent spoken by newscasters at the national level. Accent is the result of speech patterns that differ from region to region or country to country. For example, Cuban speakers of Spanish speak more quickly than do Mexican speakers of Spanish. Variations also exist within countries. Because one characteristic of an ethnic group in the United States is the manner in which its members pronounce English, ethnic group membership is often identified by or associated with accent. It is this connection that makes accent a key issue of racial and ethnic relations.

Antidiscrimination Legislation and Litigation In the Civil Rights Act of 1964, Congress banned discrimination on the basis of a person's color, ethnicity, or race in education, employment, government services, public accommodations, public facilities, and voting. The law regarding employment discrimination prohibits not only obvious discrimination, such as signs that say "Blacks Need Not Apply," but also the use of neutral-sounding job qualifications that systematically place minorities or women at a disadvantage unless these qualifications are vital for the performance of the job. To refuse to hire a member of a minority group on the pretext that the person's accent is too strong, therefore, might violate the law unless the lack of a noticeable accent can be demonstrated to be necessary for the performance of the job.

In *Carino v. University of Oklahoma Board of Regents* (1984), the federal appeals court ruled that Donaciano Carino, a dental laboratory super visor, could not be terminated from his position because of his Filipino accent as his job did not involve communication with the general public.

In 1982, Manuel Fragante, a Filipino with a noticeable accent, applied for the position of applications intake clerk in the motor vehicle licensing division of the city and county of Honolulu. The hiring officer turned him down, claiming that Fragante's accent would make communication difficult; Fragante's lawyer argued that his client's accent was fully understandable and therefore was a mere pretext for a Japanese super visor to discriminate against a Filipino. In *Fragante v. City and County of Honolulu* (1987), the federal district court in Honolulu upheld the right of the employer to refuse to hire someone with a "heavy accent," ruling that Fragante's accent was not an immutable part of his Filipino ethnic group membership. The court of appeals upheld the ruling in 1989, and the Supreme Court refused to review the case in 1990.

In 1985-1986, James Kahakua and George Kitazaki applied for the position of weather-service broadcaster. Although they were native speakers of English, they spoke "pidgin" English, a decided accent local to Hawaii. The position involved broadcasting marine weather reports to ships at sea, and most of the vessels in the area were based in California, so the National Weather Service felt justified in refusing to hire the two men because their accents might prevent a clear transmission of information. Kahakua and Kitazaki sued the weather service for discrimination but lost.

Impact on Public Policy In the 1964 Civil Rights Act, Congress did not explicitly forbid discrimination on the basis of accent. For the present, clarity in speech is recognized as a bona fide occupational qualification for jobs involving considerable oral communication with the general public. The standards for determining whether an accent is unclear tend to be subjective, so the issue may be resolved by use of the Test of Spoken English (TESOL), a standardized test administered nationwide by the Educational Testing Service.

Michael Haas

Further Reading

Laughlin McDonald's *Rights of Racial Minorities: The Basic ACLU Guide to Racial Minority Rights* (2d ed. Carbondale: Southern Illinois University Press, 1993) is one of the publications sponsored by the American Civil Liberties Union that describes the laws governing employment discrimination.

A more focused study is Rosini Lippi-Green's *English with an Accent: Language,*

Ideology, and Discrimination in the United States (2nd ed; New York: Routledge, 2012).

For an analysis of the legal issues, see Mari J. Matsuda's "Voices of America: Accent, Antidiscrimination Law, and a Jurisprudence for the Last Reconstruction," in *Yale Law Journal* (100, 1991), and Beatrice Bich-Dao Nguyen's "Accent Discrimination and the Test of Spoken English: A Call for an Objective Assessment of the Comprehensibility of Nonnative Speakers," in *California Law Review* (81, October, 1993).

Other sources that touch on the subject of accent discrimination include *Portraits of Literacy Across Families, Communities, and Schools: Intersections and Tensions* (Mahwah, N.J.: L. Erlbaum Associates, 2005), by Jim Anderson and others; *Foreign Accent: The Phenomenon of Non-Native Speech* (Cambridge: Cambridge University Press, 2013) by Alene Moyer; Charmian Kenner's *Becoming Biliterate: Young Children Learning Different Writing Systems* (Sterling, Va.: Trentham Books, 2004); *Language and Cultural Diversity in U.S. Schools: Democratic Principles in Action* (Westport, Conn.: Praeger, 2005), edited by Terry A. Osborn; and Terrence G. Wiley's *Literacy and Language Diversity in the United States* (2d ed. Washington, D.C.: Center for Applied Linguistics, 2005).

See also Anglo-conformity; Bilingual education; Discrimination; English-only and official English movements; Proposition 227.

AFFORDABLE CARE ACT AND UNDOCUMENTED IMMIGRANTS

The Law: The Affordable Care Act, also known as ObamaCare, was President Barrack Obama's landmark action in his presidency. According to Healthcare. gov, only U.S. citizens and lawfully present residents are eligible for purchasing private health insurance through the Marketplace. "Lawfully present" includes immigrants who have:

- "Qualified non-citizen" immigration status without a waiting period (see the definition below)
- Humanitarian statuses or circumstances (including Temporary Protected Status, Special Juvenile Status, asylum applicants, Convention Against Torture, victims of trafficking)
- Valid non-immigrant visas
- Legal status conferred by other laws (temporary resident status, LIFE Act, Family Unity individuals)

Date: The 2010 Affordable Care Act (ACA)

Immigration Issues: While the Marketplace is meant for U.S. citizens and legal residents, there are some critics who argue that providing health care services would encourage more illegal immigration. Media Director Ira Mehlman of the the Federation for American Immigration Reform says in a Los Angeles Times interview, "County hospitals are overwhelmed with uninsured people, and they've been forced to come up with more money to accommodate these people—largely because they've encouraged them to come in."

Significance: The Affordable Healthcare Act, ObamaCare, and its policy changes limit immigrants' access to insurance and to health care. As such, there has been a reduction in noncitizen immigrants who have Medicaid or job-based insurance. Additionally, noncitizens and their children have poorer access to both regular ambulatory and emergency care, even if they are insured.

Background: The Affordable Care Act, also known as ObamaCare, was designed to give affordable health care coverage to everyone. However, the nearly 12 million undocumented immigrants currently living in the United States are excluded from benefiting. Under the federal health care law, undocumented immigrants are not eligible for any assistance. This keeps them from being able to receive federal subsidies to buy health insurance and from shopping for health insurance coverage in Marketplace.

Under the Affordable Care Act, lawfully present immigrants are able to buy private health insurance on the Marketplace. Additionally, they may be eligible for lower premiums and lower out-of-pocket costs based on income. Lawfully present immigrants are eligible for these reduced costs if:

- **Annual income is 400% of the federal poverty level or below:** This comes out to about $45,960 for an individual or $94,200 for a family of 4. Their eligibility for tax credits can be used immediately to reduce monthly premiums.
- **Annual household income is below 100% federal poverty level:** This comes out to $11,490 for an individual or $23,550 for a family of 4, who are not otherwise eligible for Medicaid, will be eligible for tax credits and lower out-of-pocket costs for private insurance through the Marketplace if they meet all other eligibility requirements.

Immigrants who are "qualified non-citizens" are commonly eligible for Medicaid and Children's Health Insurance Program (CHIP) coverage, if they are otherwise eligible for Medicaid and CHIP in the state.

The term "qualified non-citizen" includes those who are:

- Lawful Permanent Residents (LPR/Green Card Holder)
- Asylees
- Refugees
- Cuban/Haitian entrants
- Paroled into the U.S. for at least one year

- Conditional entrant granted before 1980
- Battered non-citizens, spouses, children, or parents
- Victims of trafficking and his or her spouse, child, sibling, or parent or individuals with a pending application for a victim of trafficking visa
- Granted withholding of deportation
- Member of a federally recognized Indian tribe or American Indian born in Canada

Under current law, there is a 5-year waiting period in order to qualify for Medicaid and CHIP coverage, most LPRs or green card holders. The 5 year waiting period begins after they receive "qualified" immigration status and before eligibility for Medicaid and CHIP. There are a few exceptions of LPRs who do not have to wait 5 years, such as people who are former refugees or asylees.

States have the option to waive the 5-year waiting period and cover lawfully residing children and/or pregnant women who would otherwise be eligible for Medicaid. In fact, this option is already in effect in 25 states, plus the District of Columbia and the Commonwealth of the Northern Mariana Islands. Additionally, twenty of these states cover lawfully residing children or pregnant women in CHIP. However, those who do not have eligible immigration status, and therefore aren't eligible for Medicaid, have the option of applying for Medicaid coverage for limited emergency services, but only if they meet all other Medicaid eligibility criteria in the state.

For those applying for Medicaid or CHIP, or for those who have assistance with health insurance costs in the Marketplace, it will not affect their chance of becoming a Lawful Permanent Resident or U.S. citizen. The one exception is for anyone who receives long-term care in an institution at the government's expense. They could face barriers when applying for their green card.

Legislation: The 2010 Affordable Care Act (ACA) includes a set of provisions that expands access to subsidized health insurance coverage to the non-elderly population, including immigrants.

Unauthorized immigrants are excluded from benefits of Medicaid or CHIP coverage or for exchange subsidies under the Affordable Care Act and are not be permitted to purchase unsubsidized coverage through the Marketplace. Additionally, they are not subject to the mandate and are excluded from temporary high-risk pools; however, they can remain eligible for emergency care under Medicaid, if they otherwise meet the eligibility criteria for Medicaid (NILC, 2010). The coverage of emergency services is meant to help hospitals providing services and to reduce medical billings to families with undocumented immigrants.

Some states may choose to continue covering undocumented children with state funds. While undocumented immigrants will not have access to subsidized coverage, they could however benefit from the fact that other family members, who are documented, will be able qualify for Medicaid or subsidized coverage. Additionally, their access to care could be dependent on safety net providers to serve them, to the extent that their medical services extend beyond screening and stabilizing treatments found in emergency medical conditions, which are situations that legally require hospitals to accept Medicare reimbursement.

While the Affordable Care Act provides additional funding for Community Healthcare Centers, a critical source for the uninsured to turn to, current budget cuts have limited these funds in the health reform bill (NCSL, 2011b). Additionally, because the number of uninsured in the U.S. is reduced following the healthcare reform, this may enable providers to cross-subsidize care for the remaining uninsured, a quarter of which will be undocumented immigrants. On the other hand, the reduction in disproportionate share hospital (DSH) spending may mean cutbacks with some providers on uncompensated care they provide to the uninsured.

While the ACA will expand the coverage options, not all immigrant groups will be included. In fact, undocumented immigrants, who are currently prohibited from enrolling in Medicaid or from purchasing coverage through the new health insurance exchanges, are projected to constitute 25 percent of the uninsured population after the major provisions of the ACA are fully implemented (Buettgens et al., 2010). The major provisions of the ACA include:

- The expansion of Medicaid up to 133 percent of the federal poverty level;
- New state-based health insurance exchanges combined with insurance market reforms;
- Premium subsidies for individuals with incomes below 400 percent of the Federal Poverty Limit (FPL) and cost-sharing subsidies for individuals with incomes below 250 percent FPL; and
- An individual requirement to obtain health insurance coverage.
- According to projections by the Congressional Budget Office, the ACA will reduce the uninsured rate by 11 percentage points, reducing the share without insurance coverage from 19 to 8 percent by 2017.

Heather Hummel

Further Reading

Emanuel, Ezekiel, *Reinventing American Health Care: How the Affordable Care Act will Improve our Terribly Complex, Blatantly Unjust, Outrageously Expensive, Grossly Inefficient, Error Prone System,* PublicAffairs; First Trade Paper Edition, March 3, 2015.

The author addresses the definitive story of American health care today—its causes, consequences, and confusions.

The Staff of the Washington Post, *Landmark: The Inside Story of America's New Health-Care Law-The Affordable Care Act-and What It Means for Us All (Publicaffairs Reports),* PublicAffairs; 1 edition (April 27, 2010)

A resource for understanding the Affordable Care Act written by the staff of the Washington Post.

Gruber, Jonathan and Schreiber, Nathan (illustrator), *Health Care Reform: What It Is, Why It's Necessary, How It Works,* Hill and Wang; 1 edition, December 20, 2011.

The author, a specialist in the industry, explains—in layman's terms that everyone can understand—the healthcare reform.

AFRICAN IMMIGRANTS

Identification: Voluntary and involuntary immigrants to North America from Africa

Immigration issues: African Americans; Civil rights and liberties; Slavery; West Indian immigrants

Significance: Africans began immigrating voluntarily to the United States in significant numbers only in the late twentieth century; however, involuntary African immigration to North America began during the early period of European settlement. Through slavery, members of this group made up one of the largest sources of migration to North America throughout early American history. Movement from Africa to the territory of the United States decreased sharply after the importation of slaves became illegal in the United States in 1808 and virtually ceased with the Civil War and the complete abolition of slavery during the 1860's.

During the late nineteenth and early twentieth centuries, immigration from Europe increased greatly. As a result, African Americans became a smaller proportion of the American population than they had been in earlier years. Nevertheless, throughout U.S. history, African Americans have constituted one of the nation's largest population groups.

Involuntary African Immigration The first people of African descent came to America with Spanish explorers during the early sixteenth century. During the late fifteenth century, the Portuguese had established trading posts in West Africa and had begun buying slaves from African leaders and selling these people to other Europeans. Spanish demand for workers in the New World in activities such as sugarcane cultivation and mining led to the development of the Atlantic slave trade during the first two decades of the sixteenth century.

Over the course of the sixteenth century, many European nations became active in West Africa and began to take part in the slave trade. The Dutch became the main carriers of slaves to North America in the earliest part of this period. In early 1619, a Dutch ship brought the first African slaves to the English colony at Jamestown, Virginia. The settlers exchanged goods and provisions for these slaves. The earliest Africans in Virginia were not clearly distinguished in status and treatment from European indentured servants, and the Africans were often able to earn their freedom. According to slavery scholar Ira Berlin, free people made up nearly 30 percent of the black population of Virginia's Northampton County by 1668.

Dutch involvement in the slave trade meant that many people of African ancestry arrived in the Dutch colony of New Netherland from about the 1620's onward. As in Virginia, however, the condition of these first slaves was generally better than that of slaves who arrived during later historical periods. These early slaves were allowed to own property, marry, and establish families. When the English took possession of New Netherland in 1664, the colony's capital, New

Imaginative depiction of the interior of a slave ship painted by Bernarda Bryson Shahn during the 1930s. (Library of Congress)

Amsterdam—renamed New York—contained about 300 slaves. These people constituted roughly one-fifth of New Amsterdam's entire population.

In the southern part of North America, African slaves began arriving in significant numbers somewhat later than in the northern part. The French Compagnie des Indes brought people of African ancestry to the port city of New Orleans, at the base of the Mississippi River, during the late seventeenth and early eighteenth centuries. As in New Amsterdam, slaves could generally own property and engage in economic activities of their own. The free black population also grew steadily, and the free black population of Louisiana became the largest in North America, continuing to exist even until the American Civil War.

Expansion of the Slave Trade The eighteenth century saw great increases in the numbers of African origin people arriving in North America. These changes were results of the growth of the plantation economy. The growth of the plantation system began in the Chesapeake region of Virginia and Maryland at the end of the seventeenth century, fueled by the cash crop tobacco. Big planters found African slaves a better source of labor for working this crop than indentured servants or hired hands. About 2,000 African slaves arrived in Virginia during the 1680's, and more than 4,000 during the 1690's. During the first decade of the eighteenth century, this figure increased again to almost 8,000 slaves newly imported to Virginia.

North American slaves came from all parts of West Africa, speaking different languages, so that it became difficult for them to maintain a common language or cultural identity. Achieving freedom became an increasingly rare occurrence. Treatment of slaves became harsher, and the lines separating black people, who were almost all slaves, from white people, who were all legally free, became sharper and deeper.

From Virginia and Maryland the plantation system spread to the ricegrowing regions of South Carolina and then Georgia during the first part of the eighteenth century. Before 1710, Africans had come to these regions at a rate of 300 or under per year. During the 1720's, however, this rate went up to about 2,000 new African arrivals each year, and the numbers continued to increase dramatically throughout the rest of the century.

Louisiana maintained the largest free population of people of African descent throughout the period of slavery. However, the cultivation of sugarcane promoted the expansion of the plantation system in the southwestern part of the state. After the vast expanse of territories along the Mississippi River was joined to the United States in 1803, plantation-style slavery and the demand for slaves increased throughout many southern lands.

With the growing importation of slaves during the eighteenth century, American shippers began to enter the trade along with the Europeans. Rhode Island became the most important center for shipping slaves, even though that colony never had a significant population of slave workers of its own. By the time the United States had adopted its Constitution in 1789, ships from Rhode Island had carried more than 100,000 Africans to the Americas.

End of the Legal Slave Trade   The Constitution of the United States implicitly recognized slavery—although it did not mention the word—but it also made provisions for the end of the slave trade. Although many of the founders of the U.S. were slave owners, the leaders of the new nation generally believed that the practice would gradually come to an end. Thus, the Constitution abolished the importation of slaves after the year 1808. In 1807, the British government had adopted a prohibition on the slave trade throughout its empire. Thus, laws in the early nineteenth century placed a brake on involuntary migration from Africa to North America.

Despite the ending of the slave trade, slavery itself did not begin to wind down after the foundation of the United States. A boom in the cotton trade, promoted by the invention of the cotton gin at the end of the eighteenth century, made plantation slavery increasingly profitable. This not only encouraged slave owners to keep and trade in slaves born in the United States, it also contributed to the smuggling of slaves into the nation.

It is difficult to estimate how many Africans were brought to the United States illegally between the prohibition of the importation of slaves in 1808 and the abolition of slavery in 1865. By some calculations, as many as 50,000 Africans may have entered the United States during that period. Official U.S. Census records show only 551 U.S. residents who had been born in Africa in 1850 and only

526 in 1860. However, it seems reasonable to assume that the illegality of the importation of slaves resulted in a great official undercounting of African origin people born after 1808. In addition, the 1870 census showed 2,657 people in the United States who had been born in Africa, and it is safe to assume that this did not reflect a great wave of arrivals from Africa during the Civil War and the early years of Reconstruction.

Most of the people of African descent who immigrated, voluntarily or involuntarily, to the United States during the first half of the nineteenth century were from other parts of the Americas, particularly the Caribbean. Reflecting this, U.S. Census figures showed that, in contrast to the small numbers of African-born black people, there were more than 4,000 officially reported foreign born blacks in total in 1850, more than 7,000 foreign-born blacks in 1860, and more than 9,600 in 1870. Again, the big jump in numbers in the first census after the Civil War is probably a reflection of underreporting of slave immigrants before the war.

From the beginnings of the transAtlantic slave trade until the American Civil War, an estimated 11.5 million people reached the shores of the Americas on slave ships from West Africa. Between 600,000 and 700,000 of these people probably reached the territories that became parts of the United States by the middle of the nineteenth century. The greatest numbers of those imported directly to U.S. lands came from the West African regions of Senegambia, Sierra Leone, the Windward Coast, and the Gold Coast. By 1860, this involuntary immigration had provided the basis for an African American population of nearly 4.5 million people.

Opposition to slavery provided the basis for a small amount of emigration of African Americans to Africa. The American Colonization Society sought to end slavery in the United States by freeing slaves and sending them back to Africa. The society helped to establish the colony of Liberia in 1822 and, over the following decade, sent 2,638 people to live there.

The End of the Era of Slavery   The Civil War brought an end to the legal institution of slavery in the United States. With the end of slavery came a long period of negligible immigration of people of African descent into the United States. Even with the illegal importation of slaves in the first half of the nineteenth century, most of the growth in the black population of the United States was a result of American births, rather than of immigration. From 1810 to 1860, the African American population of the United States grew from a reported 1,377,808 to 4,441,830. However, since immigration expanded other parts of the American population even more, the African American share of the total population decreased from 19 percent in 1810 to 14 percent in 1860.

After the end of slavery, direct African immigration to the United States was almost nonexistent, and there was little immigration of African origin people from the Caribbean and other areas. Between 1891 and 1900, only about 350 people are known to have entered the United States from Africa. Moreover, many of these late nineteenth century immigrants were theology students who were sponsored by Christian missionaries and were expected to return to their home countries after completing their studies in the United States. Meanwhile, after 1880, however, a great wave of immigrants began to reach the United States from Europe. Seeking economic opportunities in the industrial-izing economy of the United States, these new immigrants produced a great expansion of the size of the nation's population, and the African American share of the total shrank accordingly. By the time this great wave of European immigration had ended in the 1920's, the African American portion of the population had dropped 10 percent of the total.

The American occupation of Haiti from 1915 to 1934 brought some new immigrants from that Caribbean nation. Haiti was one of the main sources of the increase in the foreign-born black population of the United States from 40,339 people in 1910 to 98,620 in 1930. However, until the middle of the twentieth century, immigrants of African descent, from Haiti and all other places of origin, accounted for less than 1 percent of all new immigrants in the United States.

A rare example of an early African immigrant whose name is now well known is Phillis Wheatley, who was brought to Boston from the Senegal region of West Africa by a slave ship in 1761. While working as a servant for the family of John Wheatley, she was encouraged to develop her literary skills and became a published poet. (Library of Congress)

Modern African Origin Immigration Trends During the 1920's, the United States adopted an immigration policy based on the national origins quota system. This meant that immigrants were allowed to enter the United States in numbers proportional to their homelands' representations in the United States at the beginning of the twentieth century. Under this system, overall immigration decreased, and immigration of nonwhite people was particularly discouraged. In 1965, however, the United States again revised its immigration policy and removed most of its nationally and racially discriminatory policies.

The years following 1965 saw a steady increase in the numbers of African immigrants and immigrants of African descent from other parts of the world. The U.S. Census of 1960 showed 35,355 immigrants from Africa living in the United States. Only ten years later, this figure had more than doubled—to 80,143. The 2000 Census found that the African-born population in the U.S. had increased to 881,3000 by 2000, and the American Community Survey found that this population had increased to 1,606,919 by 2010; however, in 2010, African-born individuals constituted only a small fraction, 4 percent, of the foreign born population in the U.S. The states with the largest African foreign-born populations, as of 2010, were California (158,953), New York (158,878), Texas (136,112), Maryland (125,470), and Virginia (89,290).

Members of the African-born population were more likely to be naturalized citizens (46.1 percent) in 2010 than was the foreign-born population as a whole (43.7 percent), and over two-thirds indicated that they spoke English only (21.8

percent) or spoke English very well (49.1 percent). The African-born population was also more educated, on average, than the total U.S. population, with 16.1 percent of the African-born population holding a graduate degree, as compared to 10.4 percent of the total population; in addition 24.2 percent of the African born population held a bachelor's degree (and no further degrees) as compared to 17.7 percent of the total population, and only 12.1 percent of the African-born population was lacking a high-school diploma, as compared to 14.4 percent of the total population.

The preponderance of the African born population (74.3 percent) identified as Black, while 20.0 percent were White, and the remainder Asian, mixed race, or some other race. The most common countries of origin for the African foreign-born population in 2010 were Nigeria (219,309), Ethiopia (173,592), Egypt (137,799), Ghana (124,696), and Kenya (88,519).

The largest number of immigrants arriving from Africa in the late twentieth and early twenty-first centuries came from Nigeria, Africa's most populous nation. In 2003 alone, nearly 8,000 Nigerians immigrated to the United States, accounting for about one-sixth of all African immigrants to the United States during that year. The Nigerian immigrants to the U.S. in that and previous years were generally highly educated and settled in large cities. Ethiopia, in Northeast Africa, was the second-largest source of African immigration to the United States at the beginning of the twenty-first century. Many of these immigrants came to the United States during the 1980's and 1990's, when political and civil unrest made Ethiopia one of Africa's largest refugeeproducing nations. Other African nations sending significant numbers of immigrants to the United States at the beginning of the twenty-first century included Ghana, Egypt, Kenya, Morocco, Somalia, South Africa, Sudan, and Liberia. Political upheavals in Somalia and Sudan added to the flow of immigrants from Northeast Africa. From 1990 through 2003, nearly 115,000 refugees entered the United States from Africa, most of them from Northeast Africa.

Other Sources of Black Immigrants   Although African migration to the United States increased after 1965, the largest number of immigrants of African descent came from Latin America. In 2000, U.S. Census estimates showed that just under 513,000 black immigrants in the United States had been born in Africa. By contrast, over 1.5 million black immigrants had been born in Latin America. The Caribbean was the single-largest region of origin for these foreign born residents, with more than 1.25 million black immigrants from the Caribbean living in the United States in 2000. By 2009, there were about 3.5 million immigrants from the Caribbean residing in the U.S., an increase of more than 17 –fold in fifty years, with over 90 percent coming from Cuba, the Dominican Republic, Jamaica, Haiti, and Trinidad and Tobaco.

Afro-Caribbean immigrants have come from both Englishand Frenchspeaking island nations. The English-speakers have come mostly from Jamaica and Trinidad and Tobago, as well as from smaller nations, such as Antigua and Barbuda, Barbados, Dominica, St. Kitts and Nevis, St. Lucia, and St. Vincent and the Grenadines. The French-speakers have come primarily from Haiti, with smaller numbers from Guadeloupe and Martinique. Haiti was the single largest contributor of immigrants of African descent in the United States, and by the 1990's large Haitian communities had developed in New York, Miami, Boston, and other urban centers. Haitian immigration to the United States became a heated political issue during the late 1980's and

1990's, when large numbers of Haitian boat people began reaching the United States. The U.S. government classified the Haitians as economic immigrants, rather than political refugees, and generally followed a practice of refusing them political asylum.

Immigrants of African origin have complicated the debate over affirmative action in the United States. In 1978, the U.S. Supreme Court ruled that universities and other institutions could use race as a consideration in admissions decisions in order to promote the compelling national interest of diversity in schools and in the nation's leadership. Courts and institutions frequently assumed that the experiences of native-born African Americans were an important part of this diversity. Although the Supreme Court explicitly denied that affirmative action could be used to compensate the descendants of slaves, many supporters of affirmative action in the American public believed that making up for centuries of exclusion was also an important goal of affirmative action. However, foreign-born black Americans represented some of the highest achievers in the African American population, so that affirmative action policies in university and professional school admissions disproportionately benefited new immigrants and their children.

Carl L. Bankston III

Further Reading

Aarim-Heriot, Najia. *Chinese Immigrants, African Americans, and Racial Anxiety in the United States, 1848-82.* Urbana: University of Illinois Press, 2003. Study of the interrelationships among African Americans, Chinese immigrants, and others during the mid-nineteenth century.

Baker, Bruce E., and Brian Kelly, eds. *After Slavery: Race, Labor, and Citizenship in the Reconstruction South.* Gainesville: University Press of Florida, 2013. Essays on labor, race, and citizenship in the American South after the Civil War.

Bean, Frank D., and Stephanie Bell-Rose, eds. *Immigration and Opportunity: Race, Ethnicity, and Employment in the United States.* New York: Russell Sage Foundation, 1999. Collection of essays on economic and labor issues relating to race and immigration in the United States, with particular attention to the competition for jobs between African Americans and immigrants.

Berlin, Ira. *Generations of Captivity: A History of African-American Slaves.* Cambridge, Mass.: Belknap Press of Harvard University Press, 2003. Up-to-date and authoritative history of slavery in the United States. Provides an examination of the factors shaping the growth of the African American population during the years of slavery.

Coniff, Michael L., and Thomas J. Davis. *Africans in the Americas: A History of the Black Diaspora.* New York: St. Martin's Press, 1994. Survey of the distribution of Africans throughout the Western Hemisphere.

Conley, Ellen Alexander. *The Chosen Shore: Stories of Immigrants*. Berkeley: University of California Press, 2004. Collection of firsthand accounts of immigrants from more than twenty nations, including modern Ghana and Haiti.

Curtin, Philip D. *The Atlantic Slave Trade: A Census*. Madison: University of Wisconsin Press, 1969. Revisionist demographic study of the slave trade that went back to primary sources for data on the numbers of Africans transported to the New World and found that the actual numbers were radically less than those that had long been cited in historical literature.

Diouf, Sylvane A. *Slavery's Exiles: The Story of the American Maroons*. New York: New York University Press, 2014. A history of the maroons, escaped slaves who created settlements in regions such as the swamps of South Carolina and the Virginia mountains.

McKinnon, Jesse. *The Black Population: 2000*. Washington, D.C.: U.S. Census Bureau, 2001. The U.S. Census Bureau is the main source of demographic information on the United States, and McKinnon's book is the best place to begin an examination of the African American population. This short publication can be found in most libraries that contain census materials. It is also freely available online at the bureau's Web site.

Morgan, Kenneth. *Slavery and Servitude in Colonial North America: A Short History*. Washington Square, N.Y.: New York University Press, 2001. Survey of African American slavery during the colonial era of the United States.

Reitz, Jeffrey G., eds. *Host Societies and the Reception of Immigrants*. La Jolla, Calif.: Center for Comparative Immigration Studies, University of California, San Diego, 2003. Collection of articles on interactions between immigrants and other members of their new societies in countries around the world, including the United States and Canada. Emphasis is on large urban societies. Includes chapters on African Americans and immigrants in New York City.

Spear, John R. *The American Slave Trade: An Account of Its Origins, Growth and Suppression*. Williamstown, Mass.: Corner House, 1978. Well-researched and thoroughly documented book about the slave trade in general.

Stepick, Alex, et al. *This Land Is Our Land: Immigrants and Power in Miami*. Berkeley: University of California Press, 2003. Study of competition and conflict among Miami's largest ethnic groups—Cubans, Haitians, and African Americans.

Zéphir, Flore. The Haitian Americans. Westport, Conn.: Greenwood Press, 2004. Excellent over view of the Haitian experience in the United States.

See also Afro-Caribbean immigrants; Clotilde slave ship; Cuban immigrants and African Americans; Indentured servitude; Irish immigrants and African Americans; Jamaican immigrants; Korean immigrants and African Americans; Racial and ethnic demographic trends; Santería; Universal Negro Improvement Association; West Indian immigrants.

AFRO-CARIBBEAN IMMIGRANTS

Identification: Immigrants to North America of African descent from the **Caribbean** islands

Immigration issues: African Americans; Cuban immigrants; Demographics; Slavery; West Indian immigrants

Significance: African slaves imported to the Caribbean islands developed a unique Creole culture, rich in African heritage but infused with European notions of white supremacy that encouraged internal racism among AfroCaribbeans, who began immigrating to the United States even before the American Revolution.

The Caribbean islands were the birthplace of African slavery in the New World; between 1518 and 1860, millions of Africans were imported to the islands to work the extensive sugar plantations operated by European colonials. Around 43 percent of Africans transported to the Western Hemisphere were sold as slaves in the Caribbean; less than 5 percent of these Africans were imported to the United States and Canada.

Africans greatly outnumbered whites and native peoples on most Caribbean islands and therefore were able to forge their own cultural identities. These Creole cultures, which varied from island to island, combined Old World African folkways and elements of European and native language, religion, and customs to create a common framework from which to unite the diverse tribes of transplanted Africans. The harshness of Caribbean plantation life and the resultant high death rate among Caribbean slaves necessitated a constant flow of human cargo from Africa, ensuring the continued presence of strong African elements in island Creole cultures. Nevertheless, the influence of dominant European colonial societies continued to permeate the social, spiritual, and economic lives of Afro-Caribbeans long after slavery ended during the 1860's.

Modern Afro-Caribbeans The demoralizing effect of centuries of bondage and cultural alienation left Afro-Caribbean cultures susceptible to the influence of colonial value systems and social norms once the institution of slavery collapsed. Free Afro-Caribbean communities became structured along rigid lines of socioeconomic caste, based primarily upon the skin color and reputed ancestry of individuals and families. Many Afro-Caribbeans began to deny or downplay their African roots and to claim European colonial heritage and ancestry. Under this system, light-skinned Afro-Caribbeans of modest economic means were placed above their darker counterparts, and darkskinned individuals who attained wealth often gained entry into the whiter upper castes.

The system of "shading" that defined social hierarchy in Afro-Caribbean societies often affected these societies' perceptions of fellow Caribbeans. For example, residents of the Dominican Republic, although clearly of mixed European and African descent, traditionally identified themselves as "Spanish" while invariably classifying neighboring Haitians as "black." Economic and social discrimination against Haitian immigrants to the Dominican Republic is exemplary of the internal racism that accompanied massive internal and interisland migration in the Caribbean during the first half of the twentieth century. Rural (and often darker-skinned) Afro-Caribbeans migrating to urban areas and immigrants from poorer (and more Africanized) countries were often consigned to the most squalid living conditions and the least desirable employment.

In the aftermath of World War II, a new black political consciousness, influenced by labor and Civil Rights movements in the United States, began to emerge in the Caribbean in opposition to the old colonial social order. By this time, many Afro-Caribbeans had been exposed to strains of racial and economic protest from the United States, most notably in the teachings of black separatist Marcus Gar vey, who inspired the Rastafarian movement in Jamaica. By the postwar era, Afro-Caribbean workers and intellectuals had joined forces with Gar veyites to form labor unions; by the 1960's, many of these unions had been transformed into

Workers on a Puerto Rican sugarcane plantation around 1900. (Library of Congress)

black-dominated political parties, winning significant elections in British Guiana, Trinidad, and Jamaica.

Afro-Caribbeans in the United States Afro-Caribbean migration to North America predates the American Revolution. Slave trading between Caribbean and mainland colonies brought substantial numbers of AfroCaribbeans to North American port cities and exerted a palpable Caribbean influence upon slave and free black cultures; free Afro-Caribbean immigrants to North America attained notoriety in the black communities of New Orleans and other port cities.

The bulk of Afro-Caribbean immigration to the United States took place in the twentieth century, with more than five million people of African descent migrating from the Caribbean to the United States between 1945 and 1990. Among these immigrants were many thousands of "boat people" from Cuba and Haiti, who fled their native countries in search of political asylum or economic opportunity. Thousands more arrived by more conventional means, blending into the large Caribbean American communities in eastern urban areas. Although many established permanent residence in the United States, it is estimated that around 80 percent of Caribbean immigrants to the United States in the latter half of the twentieth century were seasonal workers who returned to their home countries.

In 2012, there were about 1.7 million Caribbean-born Black immigrants in the U.S., mainly from Jamaica, Haiti, Trinidad and Tobago, and the Dominican Republic; they represent about half of all Black immigrants in the country. About 80 percent of Caribbean-born Black immigrants are fluent in English, and 78 percent hold at least a high school diploma. Most live in one of two states: New York (38 percent) or Florida (28 percent).

Afro-Caribbean immigrants have exerted a profound influence on the cities and labor force of the United States, posing challenges to its social structure, educational system, and notions of assimilation and diversity. Homegrown racial prejudices have formed the crux of many of these challenges; many light-skinned Afro-Caribbeans, regarded as whites in their home countries, experienced racial discrimination for the first time in their lives upon migration to the United States. Immigrants from relatively homogenous Caribbean societies often encountered ethnic groups with whom they had had little or no previous contact, such as Mexican, Asian, and African American, sparking occasional cultural clashes and social tensions. Groups of AfroCaribbean immigrants have occasionally clashed with each other, as did Cuban Americans and Haitian Americans in Miami during the 1980's.

Despite occasional difficulties, various groups of Afro-Caribbeans established thriving communities in major metropolitan areas of the eastern and southern United States after World War II—most notably the Cuban American enclaves of Miami and the "Nuyorican" community of Puerto Ricans in New York City. These communities have contributed greatly to the cultural and political framework of eastern urban areas and the United States as a whole.

Michael H. Burchett

41

Further Reading

Black Identities: West Indian Immigrant Dreams and American Realities (Cambridge, Mass.: Harvard University Press, 1999), by Mary C. Waters, *Crosscurrents: West Indian Immigrants and Race* (New York: Oxford University Press, 1999), by Milton Vickerman,, and Afro-Caribbean Immigrants and the Politics of Incorporation: Ethnicity, Exception, or Exit (New York: Cambridge University Press, 2006) by Reuel Reuben Rogers all examine the West Indian immigrant experience in the United States.

Peter Winn, in *Americas: The Changing Face of Latin America* (New York: Pantheon Books, 1992), provides ample information on Afro-Caribbean migration to the United States and its effect on American society.

In *Africans in the Americas: A History of the Black Diaspora* (New York: St. Martin's Press, 1994), Michael L. Conniff and Thomas J. Davis compare and contrast the development of Afro-Caribbean and African American societies. Sidney W. Mintz and Richard Price discuss continuity between African and Afro-Caribbean cultures in *The Birth of African-American Culture* (Boston: Beacon Press, 1992).

For a discussion of the political and cultural impact of Afro-Caribbean literature, see Patrick Taylor's *The Narrative of Liberation* (Ithaca, N.Y.: Cornell University Press, 1989).

Other useful sources include Aubrey W. Bonnett's *Institutional Adaptation of West Indian Immigrants to America* (Washington, D.C.: University Press of America, 1982), Lorena Madrigal's *Human Biology of Afro-Caribbean Populations* (New York: Cambridge University Press, 2006), Philip Kasinitz's *Caribbean New York: Black Immigrants and the Politics of Race* (Ithaca, N.Y.: Cornell University Press, 1992), Ransford W. Palmer's *Pilgrims from the Sun: West Indian Migration to America* (New York: Twayne Publishers, 1995), Irma Watkins-Owens's *Blood Relations: Caribbean Immigrants and the Harlem Community, 1900-1930* (Bloomington: Indiana University Press, 1996), and Robert Carr's *Black Nationalism in the New World: Reading the African-American and West Indian Experience* (Durham, N.C.: Duke University Press, 2002).

Ellen Alexander Conley's *The Chosen Shore: Stories of Immigrants* (Berkeley: University of California Press, 2004) is a collection of firsthand accounts of modern immigrants from many nations, including Barbados, Cuba, and Haiti. A useful study of the employment of Afro-Caribbean immigrants is Melonie P. Heron's *The Occupational Attainment of Caribbean Immigrants in the United States, Canada, and England* (New York: LFB Scholarly Publications, 2001). *Ethnicities: Children of Immigrants in America* (Berkeley: University of California Press, 2001), edited by Rubén G. Rumbaut and Alejandro Portes, is a collection of papers on demographic and family issues relating to immigrants that includes chapters on Mexicans, Cubans, Central Americans, Haitians, and other West Indians. *This Land Is Our Land: Immigrants and Power in Miami* (Berkeley: University of California Press, 2003), by Alex Stepick et al., examines competition and conflict among Miami's largest ethnic groups—Cubans, Haitians, and African Americans.

See also Cuban immigrants and African Americans; Dominican immigrants; Haitian immigrants; Jamaican immigrants; Latinos; Santería; Universal Negro Improvement Association; West Indian immigrants.

ALIEN AND SEDITION ACTS

The Law: Four federal laws that ostensibly were passed to aid in avoiding war with France

Date: Became law June-July, 1798

Immigration issues: Citizenship and naturalization; Government and politics; Laws and treaties

Significance: The Alien and Sedition laws, three of which directly affected immigrants, led to further debate regarding the function of the Bill of Rights during wartime, the role of the federal government in legislating for the states, and the process of judicial review.

News of the XYZ affair, which almost brought the United States and France to war, descended upon the American people and their representatives in Congress like a thunderbolt. It galvanized the government into action on the high seas; it helped unite Americans against the French, just as the initial news of British seizures had united them against Great Britain; it seriously weakened the infant Republican Party, which was associated with Francophilism; and it firmly entrenched the Federalists in power. Even President John Adams, for a time, seemed to relish the thought of leading the United States against its newest antagonist, but Adams regained his sense of moderation in time to prevent a catastrophe. The same cannot be said of certain elements of the Federalist Party, which exploited the explosive situation to strike out at their political opponents.

Political Rivalries The Federalist Party, or at least its old guard, deeply resented gains made by the Republican opposition. Many of the Federalist leaders resented the very existence of the other political party. The High Federalists were by no means committed to a two-party system and rejected the idea of a loyal opposition. With the Republican tide at low ebb, these Federalists intended to strike a killing blow at two sources of Republican strength: the immigrant vote and the manipulation of public opinion through the use (and abuse) of the press.

In selecting these targets, the Federalists demonstrated an acute awareness of the impact of the press on the growth of political parties, and they intended to use their political power to muzzle the Republican press, while leaving the Federalist press intact. Furthermore, Federalists expressed a deep xenophobia, and they viewed people of foreign birth as threats to the fabric of ordered liberty that they believed the Federalists had built and must preserve.

Many Federalists had a long history of antiforeign sentiment. With the United States on the verge of war with France, the Federalists were apprehensive over the loyalty of thousands of French West Indian refugees who had flocked to the United States in an effort to escape the ferment of the French Revolution and its accompanying "Terror."

The Federalists were further concerned by the fact that the refugees who became U.S. citizens generally aligned themselves with the Republican Party. Much the same was true of the Irish, who supported anyone who opposed the English. Such conditions threatened the continued hold of the Federalists on political power in the national government. To deal with such potential subversives, foreign and domestic, the Federalist-controlled Congress passed a series of four acts, known collectively as the Alien and Sedition Acts.

Content of the Acts Three of the acts dealt specifically with aliens or immigrants. The Sedition Act declared speech or writing with the intent to defame the president or Congress to be a misdemeanor. The Alien Act permitted the president to deport allegedly dangerous aliens during times of peace. Neither act was enforced, however. The Naturalization Act struck at the immigrant vote. Previously, aliens could become naturalized citizens after residing for five years in the United States. The new act raised the probationary period to fourteen years.

The Sedition Act was by far the most notorious. It imposed heavy fines and imprisonment as punishment on all those found guilty of writing, publishing, or speaking against the federal government. By allowing a defendant to prove the truth of statements as a defense, the Sedition Act was a definite improvement over the English laws of sedition libel. The fact remains, however, that its intent was the repression of political opposition and the annoying Republican press, and the Sedition Act seemed plainly to ignore the First Amendment. Under the law, suits were initiated against the editors of eight major opposition presses.

John Adams, the second president of the United States. (Library of Congress)

The principal target was the Philadelphia *Aurora*, whose editor, William Duane, was prosecuted under the act. Congressman Matthew Lyon of Vermont received a jail sentence of four months and was fined one thousand dollars for disparaging remarks he had made about President Adams. Some of these suits gave a comic air to the gross abuse of power. One

44

gentleman was fined one hundred dollars for wishing out loud that the wadding of a salute cannon would strike President Adams in his backside.

Republican opposition to these laws was immediate. Vice President Thomas Jefferson, himself a Republican, believed that the Alien and Sedition Acts were designed to be used against such leading Republicans as the Swiss-born congressman from Pennsylvania, Albert Gallatin.

Republicans were convinced that the Sedition Act was designed to destroy them as an organized political party. The act had passed the House strictly along sectional-party lines. The vote was forty-four to forty-one, with only two affirmative votes coming from south of the Potomac River, where the Republicans were strongest.

Ineffectiveness of the Laws From the Federalist point of view, the acts were completely unsuccessful in suppressing the opposition. They were resented by many, and it soon became obvious even to those who first supported the new laws that they were as unnecessary as they were ineffective. The handful of "subversives" prosecuted under the Sedition Act hardly compensated for the fact that its existence gave the Republicans another campaign issue. Jefferson through the Kentucky legislature, and Madison through the Virginia legislature, penned immediate responses to the Alien and Sedition Acts. These remonstrances, known as the Virginia and Kentucky Resolves, aroused little enthusiasm at the time but did point out not only some of the basic principles of the Republican Party but also some striking differences between two streams of thought within the party.

Both resolutions maintained that the Constitution was a compact between sovereign states that granted to the federal government certain narrowly defined powers, while retaining all other enumerated powers. If the states created the Constitution, they had the power to decide when the federal government had overstepped its proper bounds.

Jefferson, in the Kentucky Resolves, went much further than Madison in assigning to the states the power to nullify a federal law—to declare it inoperable and void within the boundaries of a state. South Carolina was to do so in 1832, when it nullified the Tariff of 1828. The Virginia and Kentucky Resolves had no immediate effect, but they had spelled out the theoretical position that those advocating states' rights could, and ultimately did, take.

The Alien and Sedition Acts took their place among a growing list of grievances against the Federalist Party. The Alien Act expired in 1800 and the Sedition Act in the following year. The Naturalization Act was repealed by the Republican-controlled Congress in 1802. The only tangible effect of these measures was to contribute to the defeat of Federalism in 1800. However, the mood that led to their passage was to return in later days.

John G. Clark
Edward R. Crowther

Further Reading

Bradburn, Douglas. *The Citizenship Revolution: Politics and the Creation of the American Union, 1774-1804*. Charlottesville: University of Virginia Press, 2009. A study of how the concept of citizenship and nationhood developed over time in early days of American history.

Edelson, Chris. *Emergency Presidential Power: From the Drafting of the Constitution to the War on Terror*. Madison, Wisconsin: The University of Wisconsin Press, 2013. A historical study of presidential actions in times of crisis, from the Colonial period to the present day.

Elkins, Stanley, and Eric McKitrick. *The Age of Federalism: The Early American Republic, 1788-1800*. New York: Oxford University Press, 1993. Chapter 15 of this gracefully written document captures the motives and mentalities of the principals responsible for the acts.

LeMay, Michael C., and Elliott Robert Barkan, eds. *U.S. Immigration and Naturalization Laws and Issues: A Documentary History*. Westport, Conn.: Greenwood Press, 1999. The Alien and Sedition Acts are examined in their broader legal context in this work.

McCoy, Drew R. *The Elusive Republic: Political Economy in Jefferson's America*. Chapel Hill: University of North Carolina Press, 1980. Contains an excellent discussion of the competing theories of society and government bantered about by Federalists and Republicans.

Miller, John C. Crisis in *Freedom: The Alien and Sedition Acts*. Boston: Little, Brown, 1951. A thorough and judicious narrative of the passage of and response to the Alien and Sedition Acts.

Sharp, James Roger. *American Politics in the Early Republic: The New Nation in Crisis*. New Haven, Conn.: Yale University Press, 1993. Places the Alien and Sedition Acts in the context of paranoid politics during the 1790's.

Smith, James Morton. *Freedom's Fetters: The Alien and Sedition Laws and American Civil Liberties*. Ithaca, N.Y.: Cornell University Press, 1966. Contains the best discussion of the congressional debates over the passage of these laws.

See also Federal riot of 1799; Nativism; Palmer raids.

ALIEN LAND LAWS

Definition: State laws restricting the right of Asian immigrants to own land

Immigration issues: Asian immigrants; Chinese immigrants; Discrimination; Japanese immigrants; Laws and treaties

Significance: These state measures deprived Japanese Americans of their property rights.

Immigration from Japan to the United States increased significantly during the final decade of the nineteenth century, with most of the Asian immigrants settling in the Pacific states. As the number of Japanese laborers arriving in California increased substantially, however, a strong anti-Japanese sentiment developed: Their success threatened and antagonized the emerging labor unions. The Asiatic Exclusion League was formed in 1905, and a campaign to bar Japanese immigration was launched. Negotiations begun in 1906 between the United States and Japan resulted in the Gentlemen's Agreement of 1907, which limited immigration from Japan to nonlaborers and to families who were joining previously settled laborers. In 1907, an immigration bill was amended to prevent Japanese laborers from entering the United States via Hawaii, Mexico, and Canada.

The First Proposals The California legislature's attempts to pass alien land bills began in 1907 when it appropriated funds to investigate Japanese agricultural involvement. The California State Labor Commission's report, which was favorable to the Japanese, resulted in a reprimand for the commissioner. In 1910, twenty-seven anti-Japanese proposals were introduced in the legislature. Enactment of the proposed anti-Japanese legislation was prevented that year by influence from the White House and, in 1911, by President William Howard Taft's direct intervention.

On April 4, 1913, a California bill that would prohibit Japanese and other foreigners ineligible for citizenship from holding or leasing land in California prompted the Japanese ambassador, Viscount Chinda, to make an informal protest to the Department of State. The proposed bill in California was modeled on an 1897 federal law barring ownership of land by aliens ineligible for citizenship. The federal law, however, contained a proviso that it would not be applicable where treaty obligations conferred the right to own and hold land. The California bill included a clause prohibiting the leasing of land to Japanese, but the Japanese contended that this right had been conferred previously by the Treaty of 1894 and reenacted in the Treaty of 1911.

In Washington, D.C., the introduction of the 1913 California Alien Land bill was viewed seriously. The prevailing opinion was that its effect could be more sweeping than the problems of 1908 and could lead once again to talk of war. When Secretary of State William Jennings Bryan and Ambassador Chinda exchanged mutual assurances of continuing friendship between the United States and Japan on April 4, the Department of State expressed confidence that the matter would be resolved amicably. The following day, Bryan met with the California congressional delegation, which emphasized the necessity of the proposed legislation. Members of the delegation described how, in many parts of California, more than half the farms were operated by Japanese, and neither U.S. nor Chinese workers could compete with Japanese labor. They asserted that despite the Gentlemen's Agreement of 1907, "coolie laborers" were arriving continuously. The feeling in California was so strong, they reported, that people who leased land to the Japanese were ostracized by their neighbors. Members of the delegation intimated that violent protests against the increase in Japanese competition were imminent.

In Japan, the Tokyo press vehemently opposed the legislation. The Japanese government filed a formal protest on April 7. President Woodrow Wilson's position was to remain outside the conflict because he believed that the proposed legislation lay within the rights of a sovereign state.

The final draft of the new law was adopted by the California Senate on April 12. Ambassador Chinda presented his government's formal protest against the bill to the Department of State. Because of agitation in Tokyo, where the bill was denounced by the press and where demonstrators were calling for war, the California legislature, despite over whelming margins in both houses, delayed further action until May 20, when the Alien Land Law, known also as the Webb-Henley bill, was signed into law by Governor Hiram Warren Johnson. The statute barred all aliens ineligible for citizenship, or corporations with more than 50 percent ineligible alien ownership, from the legal right to own agricultural land in California, and it limited land-leasing contracts in the state to three years' duration.

U.S. secretary of state William Jennings Bryan around 1907. (Library of Congress)

Further Restrictions To prevent the Japanese from circumventing the law, a more restrictive alien land bill was introduced in the California legislature in 1920 to forbid the issei (first generation Japanese Americans) from buying land in the name of their U.S.-born children, the nisei. It also prohibited the transfer of land to noncitizens by sale or lease and established criminal penalties for aliens caught attempting to bypass the 1913 law. In a statewide ballot, California voters passed the 1920 Alien Land Law by a three-to-one margin. A number of cases to test the constitutionality of the new law were instigated by the Japanese. In 1923, the U.S. Supreme Court ruled against the issei in four of these cases. Further restrictions also were passed in a 1923 amendment, which, together with the 1924 Immigration Act, effectively denied further immigration and determined the status of Japanese immigrants in the United States. The alien land laws in California were not repealed until 1956.

During 1917, an alien land law was enacted in Arizona. In 1921, Washington, Texas, and Louisiana followed suit, as did New Mexico in 1922, and Oregon, Idaho, and Montana in 1923. Other states followed: Kansas in 1925; Missouri in 1939; Utah, Arkansas, and Nebraska in 1943; and Minnesota in 1945.

Susan E. Hamilton

Further Reading

Aarim-Heriot, Najia. *Chinese Immigrants, African Americans, and Racial Anxiety in the United States, 1848-82.* Urbana: University of Illinois Press, 2003. Study of the interrelationships among African Americans, Chinese immigrants, and European Americans in the United States during the mid-nineteenth century.

Chuman, Frank F. *The Bamboo People: The Law and Japanese-Americans.* Del Mar, Calif.: Publisher's Inc., 1976. Includes good coverage of the alien land laws.

Curr y, Charles F. *Alien Land Laws and Alien Rights.* Washington, D.C.: Government Printing Office, 1921. A contemporary account of the alien land laws.

Heinz, John, ed. *Analyzing Law's Reach: Empirical Research on Law and Society.* Chicago: American Bar Association, 2008. Essays on a variety of topics including alien rights.

Ichioka, Yuji. *The Issei: The World of the First Generation Japanese Immigrants, 1885-1924.* New York: Free Press, 1988. Includes discussion of the laborcontracting system and the exclusion movement.

Lee, Erika. *At America's Gates: Chinese Immigration During the Exclusion Era, 1882-1943.* Chapel Hill: University of North Carolina Press, 2003. Study of immigration from China to the United States from the time of the Chinese Exclusion Act to the loosening of American immigration laws during the 1960's.

McGovney, Dudley. "The Anti-Japanese Land Laws of California and Ten Other States." *California Law Review* 35 (1947): 7-54. A detailed discussion of alien land laws in relation to state, federal, and English common law up the time of publication.

Nomura, Gail M. "Washington's Asian/Pacific American Communities." In *Peoples of Washington: Perspectives on Cultural Diversity*, edited by Sid White and S. E. Solberg. Pullman: Washington State University Press, 1989. Provides specifics of Washington and Texas land laws.

Takaki, Ronald, ed. *Iron Cages: Race and Culture in Nineteenth Century America.* New York: Oxford University Press, 1990. Provides insight into the origin of anti-Asian sentiment and its connection to legislation such as the alien land laws.

See also Chinese Exclusion Act; Chinese exclusion cases; Chinese immigrants; Chinese immigrants and California's gold rush; Discrimination; Japanese American internment; Japanese immigrants; Japanese segregation in California schools; Ozawa v. United States; Page law; "Yellow peril" campaign.

AMERASIANS

Definition: Term coined by the American novelist Pearl S. Buck to describe children of U.S. servicemen and women born and raised in East Asia

Immigration issues: Asian immigrants; Chinese immigrants; Families and marriage; Japanese immigrants; Refugees

Significance: With U.S. participation in wars and occupations in Asia, American servicemen have fathered children with women in several Asian countries, posing the issue of immigration rights for both Amerasian children and their Asian mothers.

The Pearl Buck Foundation, set up in 1964 to help Amerasian children, continued its work after Buck's death in 1973. The existence of Amerasian children has posed knotty questions for judges and policy makers in the areas of immigration and citizenship law. The issues involved are not merely political. Amerasians were sometimes raised out of wedlock, sometimes adopted, and sometimes raised by both natural parents. Studying Amerasian children and youth in both East Asia and the United States permits sociologists and psychologists to assess the relative weights of different handicaps—their status as members of minorities, their foreign-language background, and their fatherlessness—impeding their progress toward healthy and productive adulthood.

Historical Background After Japan's defeat in World War II, U.S. servicemen occupied Japan. Within six years about 24,000 Amerasian children were born to Japanese women. After Japan regained sovereignty in 1952, several U.S. air bases remained on Japan's home islands, and Okinawa remained under U.S. occupation. Mixed marriages and the births of Amerasian babies continued into the first years of the twenty-first century, when the United States still stationed tens of thousands of troops in Asia. The U.S. occupation of South Korea during

Pearl Buck, author of The Good Earth *(1931),* The Dragon Seed *(1942), and other novels set in China. In 1938, Buck became the first American woman to receive the Nobel Prize in Literature. (Library of Congress)*

the late 1940's was followed by the Korean War. After the armistice in 1953, some U.S. soldiers remained. Hence, some South Korean women bore Amerasian babies into the early 1980's. Amerasian children were also born to women from Taiwan, which was protected by the U.S. Navy against the People's Republic of China after 1950.

After the French left Vietnam in 1954 and Vietnam was split into communist North Vietnam and anticommunist South Vietnam, the United States decided to defend the latter. About 30,000 Amerasian children were born to South Vietnamese women during U.S. involvement in the Vietnam War from 1964 to 1975. During this time some Amerasians were also born to women in Laos, Cambodia, and Thailand, which served as bases for U.S. air raids into Vietnam. When North Vietnam conquered South Vietnam in April, 1975, normal economic and diplomatic relations with the United States ceased, not to be restored until the mid-1990's. Hence, no Amerasian babies were born in Vietnam after 1976.

In the Philippines, Amerasian children were born soon after the United States acquired the islands in 1898. Although independence was granted in 1946, Amerasian births continued until 1992, when Clark Air Force Base and Subic Bay Naval Base were closed. By 1992 about 50,000 Amerasians lived in the Philippines. In 1993, Filipino prostitutes sued the U.S. government for financial aid in raising their Amerasian children. In November, 1997, Lorelyn Penero Miller, the Filipino daughter of a U.S. serviceman born out of wedlock, challenged the U.S. citizenship law in the U.S. Supreme Court.

Family, Citizenship, and Immigration Unlike France, which offered citizenship rights to its colonial Eurasians, the U.S. government recognized Amerasians as citizens only if they were born within the bonds of marriage. Amerasians born out of wedlock could be recognized as U.S. citizens only if specific American men recognized them as their children and provided documentary proof of fatherhood.

Out-of-wedlock births resulted from institutional obstacles to marriage as well as from individual irresponsibility. Until 1967 several American states prohibited white-Asian and black-Asian marriages. In 1945 U.S. immigration law still prohibited the entry of Japanese. Although the U.S. Congress twice gave Japanese war brides the opportunity to immigrate to the United States, many couples could not meet the deadlines. From the passage of the McCarran-Walter Act of 1952, which permitted all Asian spouses of U.S. servicemen to immigrate to the United States, until 1965, roughly half of all Korean and Japanese immigrants to the United States were servicemen's wives. Until 1992 many Filipino immigrants were the wives of servicemen. Despite the time-consuming requirement of approval by superior officers, which sometimes came through only after soldiers had been transferred back to the United States, more than 6,000 marriages between South Vietnamese women and U.S. servicemen occurred between 1965 and 1972.

Most Japanese and Korean Amerasians entering the United States were either preteen children of intact interracial families or preteen orphans adopted by American couples. Aside from twenty college-age Korean Amerasians sponsored yearly by Gonzaga University after 1980, relatively few Amerasian teenagers or young adults from Korea or Japan have ever immigrated to the United States.

Vietnamese Amerasians, by contrast, did not immigrate to the United States in large numbers until they were already late adolescents and young adults. Only a few Vietnamese Amerasian children, including many of the 2,000 orphans airlifted out of South Vietnam in April, 1975, left South Vietnam before the communist triumph. Although a 1982 U.S. law stipulated that Amerasians born between 1950 and 1982 from Vietnam, Thailand, Laos, Cambodia, and Korea (but not Japan) had priority in immigrating to the United States, it did little for Vietnamese Amerasians. Relatives were not allowed to accompany their children, and the United States had no diplomatic relations with Vietnam. Although well-publicized reunions between preteen Amerasian children and their fathers did occur in the United States in October, 1982, children claimed by their American fathers after 1975 were only a tiny percentage of all Vietnamese Amerasians.

From 1982 to 1988 about 4,500 Vietnamese Amerasians and 7,000 accompanying relatives entered the United States as refugees. The Amerasian Homecoming Act (1987) speeded up the exodus by permitting all Vietnamese Amerasians born between January 1, 1962, and January 1, 1977, to immigrate without proving that they had a specific American father and by permitting them to bring their mothers and siblings along. After 1991 Amerasians' spouses and children could come as well. By 1994 about 20,000 Vietnamese Amerasians and 60,000 relatives had settled in the United States.

Adjustments in Asia and the United States Because Amerasians usually had some of the physical features of their white or African American fathers, those raised in East Asian countries were usually discriminated against by their countries' racial majorities. However, being half white was socially acceptable in the Philippines. In Japan, Amerasians raised on U.S. military bases by intact two-parent families were shielded somewhat from prejudice. Most Amerasians raised in East Asia, however, grew up without fathers, in societies where fatherlessness was stigmatized. Their mothers sometimes abandoned them to the care of relatives or orphanages or even to the streets, while stepfathers mistreated them. In their mothers' countries, Amerasians had difficulty in receiving an education, finding jobs, and marr ying spouses. In post-1975 Vietnam they received on average no more than one to two years of schooling.

Fatherlessness was not confined to Amerasians reared in Asia; some Amerasians born in the United States, or taken there by their natural parents at an early age, saw their childhood disrupted by parental divorce. Of all Amerasians in the United States, those adopted by American couples at an early age and those whose natural parents' marriages remained intact throughout their childhood probably had an easier transition to adulthood than others. Thus, Vietnamese Amerasians airlifted to the United States as small children for adoption in 1975 and those reunited as preteen children with their natural fathers in 1982 faced fewer problems than post-1987 teenage and young adult Vietnamese Amerasian immigrants. The latter were usually accompanied by only one parent or by no parent at all and had to struggle to learn English while seeking to hold down a job.

Amerasian adolescents' search for an acceptable ethnic identity followed a different course in the United States than in East Asia. In the United States, Amerasians who were half white usually suffered less from majority prejudice than in East Asia, while half-black Amerasians suffered no more from majority prejudice than African Americans in general. The latter, however, were not always accepted by African Americans. Vietnamese Amerasians rejected in Vietnam were often also rejected by the Vietnamese refugee community in the United States.

Paul D. Mageli

Further Reading

Bass, Thomas A. Vietnamerica: The War Comes Home. New York: Soho Press, 1996. Benmayor, Rina, and Andor Skotnes, eds. Migration and Identity. New

Brunswick, N.J.: Transaction, 2005.

Conn, Peter J. Pearl S. Buck: A Cultural Biography. Cambridge, England: Cambridge University Press, 1996.

Field, Norma. In the Realm of a Dying Emperor: A Portrait of Japan at Century's End. New York: Pantheon Books, 1991.

McBee, Susanna. "The Amerasians: Tragic Legacy of Our Far East Wars." U.S. News and World Report 96 (May 7, 1984).

Spickard, Paul R. "Madam Butterfly Revisited." In Mixed Blood: Intermarriage and Ethnic Identity in Twentieth-Century America. Madison: University of Wisconsin Press, 1989.

Valverde, Kieu-Linh Caroline. "From Dust to Gold: The Vietnamese Amerasian Experience." In Racially Mixed People in America, edited by Maria P. P. Root. Newbury Park, Calif.: Sage Publications, 1992.

Westbrook, Peter. Harnessing Anger: The Way of an American Fencer. New York: Seven Stories Press, 1997.

Williams, Teresa. "Prism Lives: Identity of Binational Amerasians." In Racially Mixed People in America, edited by Maria P. P. Root. Newbury Park, Calif.: Sage Publications, 1992.

Yarborough, Trin. Surviving Twice: Amerasian Children of the Vietnam War. Dulles, Va.: Potomac Books, 2005.

See also Asian American education; Japanese immigrants; Mail-order brides; Southeast Asian immigrants; Vietnamese immigrants; War brides; War Brides Act; Women immigrants.

AMERICAN JEWISH COMMITTEE

Identification: Jewish rights and advocacy organization

Date: Founded in 1906

Immigration issues: Civil rights and liberties; Jewish immigrants; Religion

Significance: The American Jewish Committee is one of the oldest Jewish rights organizations.

The American Jewish Committee was founded in 1906 by a group of prominent American Jews in response to a series of anti-Jewish riots (pogroms) in Russia. It was to be a defense and advocacy group dedicated to the prevention of any "infraction of the civil and religious rights of Jews, in any part of the world." During and after World War I, its efforts were concentrated on aiding refugees and combating anti-immigrant and anti-Semitic sentiment in the United States.

During the late 1990's, the committee's work consisted mostly of analysis, advocacy, and legal action relating to issues such as immigration, civil rights, church-state relations, and social justice. In addition, it sponsors research in such areas as Jewish family life, intermarriage, and Jewish education, and the significance of Judaism in an age of modernity. Local chapters are encouraged to participate in legislative advocacy activities and involvement as amici curiae in litigation at the local and state levels. On the international scene, the committee has articulated a special commitment to Israel's security and to the support of democratic movements across the globe on the theory that the fate of Jews is inextricably bound to the fate of democracy.

Peter J. Haas

Further Reading

Cohen, Naomi Werner. *Encounter with Emancipation: The German Jews in the United States, 1830-1914.* Philadelphia: Jewish Publication Society of America, 1984.

Gerber, David, ed. *Anti-Semitism in American History.* Urbana: University of Illinois Press, 1986.

Harris, David A. *In the Trenches: Selected Speeches and Writing of an American Jewish Activist.* 2 vols. Hoboken, NJ: KTAV Pub. House, 2000-2002.

Sanua, Marianne Rachel. *Let Us Prove Strong: The American Jewish Committee, 1945-2006.* Waltham, MA: Brandeis University Press, 2007.

See also Ashkenazic and German Jewish immigrants; Eastern European Jewish immigrants; Israeli immigrants; Jewish immigrants; Jewish settlement of New York; Jews and Arab Americans; Sephardic Jews; Soviet Jewish immigrants.

ANGLO-CONFORMITY

Definition: Tendency of immigrants to North America to lose much of their native cultural heritage and conform substantially to an Anglo-Protestant core culture

Immigration issues: Language; Nativism and racism; Sociological theories

Significance: Anglo-conformity has a homogenizing effect that tends to obliterate non-Anglo cultures.

During the late nineteenth and early twentieth centuries, Anglo-conformity was practiced by immigrant groups who came from eastern and southern Europe—such as Poles, Italians, and Greeks. Although some members of those groups have maintained some of the distinctive elements of their native cultures, many others have become completely assimilated into the dominant American society.

As late as the early twenty-first century, many immigrant racial groups of non-European origin, such as Asian Americans and Hispanics, were still experiencing Anglo-conformity. For example, California's Proposition 227, which limits the

Editor of an Italian-language newspaper published in New York correcting proofs in 1943. Foreign language newspapers sprang up in virtually every major urban center to serve immigrant communities and made it easier for immigrants to avoid adapting to the dominant Anglo culture. (Library of Congress)

time elementary school students can spend in bilingual education, passed with a large amount of Mexican American political support in 1998. Since its passage, immigrants from Mexico, and their children, have faced strong social pressure to concentrate on English, the language of the dominant culture, at the expense of their own Spanish language. Anglo-conformity may also be experienced by non-immigrant racial minorities since they are generally expected to follow European American styles of dress and speech patterns when operating in the dominant American society.

George Yancey

Further Reading

Deveaux, Monique. *Cultural Pluralism and Dilemmas of Justice*. Ithaca, N.Y.: Cornell University Press, 2000.

Gabaccia, Donna R. *Immigration and American Diversity: A Social and Cultural History*. Malden, Mass.: Blackwell, 2002.

Kramer, Eric Mark, ed. *The Emerging Monoculture: Assimilation and the "Model Minority."* Westport, Conn.: Praeger, 2003.

Kwong, Peter. *Chinese America: The Untold Story of America's Oldest New Community*. New York: New Press, 2005.

Singh, Jaswinder, and Kalyani Gopal. *Americanization of New Immigrants: People Who Come to America and What They Need to Know*. Lanham, Md.: University

Press of America, 2002.

Wiley, Terrence G. *Literacy and Language Diversity in the United States.* 2d ed. Washington, D.C.: Center for Applied Linguistics, 2005.

See also Accent discrimination; Assimilation theories; Bilingual Education Act of 1968; British as dominant group; Euro-Americans; Immigration Act of 1924; Nativism; White ethnics.

Anti-Irish Riots of 1844

The Event: Nativist uprising against immigrant Irish-Catholic workers

Date: May 6-July 5, 1844

Place: Philadelphia, Pennsylvania

Immigration issues: Discrimination; European immigrants; Irish immigrants; Nativism and racism; Religion

Significance: This anti-Irish riot reflected nativist prejudice against immigrants and after ward moved Irish immigrants to band together more to protect themselves.

Rapid population growth, industrialization, and cultural conflict characterized urban America during the 1840's and helped produce bloody anti-Irish riots in Philadelphia's industrial suburbs of Kensington and Southwark in the summer of 1844. Already the second largest U.S. city in 1840, Philadelphia's population grew by more than one-third during the 1840's, from twenty-five thousand people to thirty-six thousand. Irish immigrants, hard-pressed by the Great Famine that had ruined the potato crops in their homeland, stimulated this growth, and they made up 10 percent of Philadelphia's population in 1844. Prior to commuter railroads and automobiles, most people lived near their workplace, and cities were densely populated. Low-income newcomers such as the Irish resided in cheap, substandard housing and symbolized the ill effects of disorderly urban growth to longtime Philadelphians.

The Irish Immigrants Lacking in job skills and capital, Irish immigrants filled the bottom rungs in the emerging industrial order's occupational ladder. As its population grew, Philadelphia expanded its involvement in large scale manufacturing. By 1840, half of Philadelphia's sixteen thousand working adults labored in manufacturing, and 89 percent of the workers in Kensington toiled in industrial trades. American-born whites predominated in such well-paying craft occupations as ship carpenter and ironmaker, leaving low paying jobs requiring less skill, such as weaving, for Irish newcomers. Perceiving immigrants and African

Americans as competitors for jobs and housing, many white American workers used violence to drive them from trades and neighborhoods.

During the 1830's, Philadelphia, like other major cities, hosted a strong working-class trade union and political movement. At its height, the General Trades Union of Philadelphia City and County (GTU) included more than ten thousand workers representing more than fifty different trades. Collective action in an 1835 general strike advocating a ten-hour workday succeeded in winning shorter hours and wage hikes in numerous workplaces. GTU activists voted against conservative Whigs who opposed strikes and Irish Catholic immigrants. The Panic of 1837 brought on a national economic depression and weakened the GTU and undermined the solidarity of its culturally and occupationally diverse constituency.

During the 1840's, native-born Protestant skilled workers fought for a dwindling supply of jobs and received little help from the financially weakened GTU. Evangelical Protestants from all social classes joined moral reform campaigns for temperance and strict observance of the Sabbath. Temperance and Sabbatarianism symbolized American-born white workers' efforts to sur vive hard times through personal discipline. Workers made up the majority of temperance societies in industrial suburbs such as Kensington and Southwark. Moral reforms often attacked immigrant cultural institutions, such as the Roman Catholic Church and Sunday tavern visits. Economic contraction and moral reform eroded the GTU's bonds of working-class solidarity, which might have prevented ethnic conflict in 1844.

Nativist Forces The American Republican Party, dedicated to eliminating the influence of Catholic immigrants in public life, best exploited the anxieties of native-born workers. The party flourished briefly in eastern cities during the mid-1840's, drawing support from Americanborn workers and middle-class professionals such as Philadelphia's Lewis Levin, a struggling lawyer and aspiring politician from South Carolina.

In the spring of 1844, American Republicans campaigned against Catholic voters' attempts to protect their children from Protestant religious instruction in the public schools. Protestant-dominated Philadelphia schools used the King James version of the Bible as a classroom textbook. Objecting that the King James version was not authoritative, Catholics preferred the Douay Bible, which included annotations written by the Vatican. Philadelphia's Catholic bishop, Francis Kenrick, wanted public schools to allow Catholic students to bring their Bibles to class or be exempted from Protestant religious instruction. American Republicans accused Philadelphia Catholics of plotting to remove the Bible from the schools entirely and to have priests take over classrooms.

In April, 1844, American Republicans staged rallies across the city to whip up support for their nativist program. Violence between the Irish and nativists broke out when nativists gathered near Irish neighborhoods. American Republicans scheduled a mass meeting for May 6 in Kensington's third ward, a neighborhood composed mainly of Irish weavers. On May 6, rain drove hundreds of nativists who traveled to the third ward rally to seek cover at the Nanny Goat Market, a covered lot of market stalls.

Title page of a Douay Bible—which was at the heart of the 1844 riots—features an illustration of St. Patrick's Cathedral in New York City. (Library of Congress)

Approximately thirty Irish waited at the market, and one yelled, "Keep the damned natives out of the market house; it don't belong to them. This ground is ours!" Samuel Kramer, editor of the pro-American Republican *Native American* newspaper (named for Anglo-American nativists, not American Indians), tried to finish his speech against the Catholic proposals for the Douay Bible, but Irish hecklers drowned him out. A shoving match escalated into fistfights and gunfire as nativists and Irish battled for control of the market house. Police arrived at dusk and temporarily restored order. Four men died, three of them nativists, and many more were wounded in the fighting.

Nativist Revenge The next day, nativists massed in Kensington for revenge. The *Native American* ran the headline: "Let Every Man Come Prepared to Defend Himself!" A parade of nativists marched through Kensington under a U.S. flag and a banner declaring, "This is the flag that was trampled underfoot by Irish Papists." Nativist mobs rampaged through Kensington for two more days, burning homes and invading two Catholic churches, where rioters defaced religious objects and looted valuables. Although Sheriff Morton McMichael tried to calm public disorder, police were too few in number to stop the violence. Needing reinforcements, McMichael called on General George Cadwalader, commander of the First Brigade of Pennsylvania state militia, stationed in Philadelphia. On May 10, state troops brought peace to the city and kept it under martial law for a week.

Tension prevailed in June, amid criticism of city officials and militia commanders for failing to prevent violence. American Republicans still had public support, and Catholics worried about more violence. Catholics feared that nativists would use July 4 patriotic celebrations as a pretext to riot. Parishioners at St. Philip's Catholic Church in Southwark, just south of Philadelphia, hoarded weapons inside the church in order to defend it.

Hearing of the arms cache, on July 5, Levin led thousands of nativists, including volunteer militia with cannons, to St. Philip's to demand the weapons. Stung by earlier criticism, Cadwalader's militia promptly seized the church and ordered nativists away. When the mob refused to move, Cadwalader opened fire and a pitched battle involving cannon and rifle fire ensued for a day and a half. The militia, helped by city police, prevailed in the fighting that left two rioters dead and dozens of state troops and civilians wounded.

The American Republican Party campaigned on the riots, attacking reigning politicians as the allies of Irish Catholics and making martyrs of the nativists killed in the riots. In October, Levin and another American Republican won election to the U.S. House of Representatives, and nativists captured several county offices, mostly on the strength of votes from working-class Kensington and Southwark. The American Republicans faded during the late 1840's, but nativists returned during the 1850's under the aegis of the American, or Know-Nothing, Party.

The riots forced Irish Philadelphians to band together as an ethnic group. The most prominent Irish opponent of the mobs was Hugh Clark, a master weaver and ward politician worth more than thirty thousand dollars in 1850. Clark had stridently opposed striking Irish journeymen weavers prior to 1844. Master weavers, some of them Irishmen like Clark, cut journeymen's wages in the wake of the Kensington riot, confident that few non-Irish workers would protest the cuts. Bishop Kenrick urged conciliation and softened his public position on the Bible controversy. American Republican anger at police and militia actions temporarily stalled police reform, but during the 1850's, Philadelphia and other cities established professional police departments to prevent more riots like those of 1844.

Frank Towers

Further Reading

Davis, Susan G. *Parades and Power: Street Theatre in Nineteenth-Century Philadelphia*. Philadelphia: Temple University Press, 1986. Examines public celebrations that frequently turned violent, such as the parade that became a riot in Kensington.

Feldberg, Michael. *The Philadelphia Riots of 1844: A Study of Ethnic Conflict*. Westport, Conn.: Greenwood Press, 1975. The most comprehensive account of the riots.

Gabaccia, Donna R. *Immigration and American Diversity: A Social and Cultural History*. Malden, Mass.: Blackwell, 2002. Survey of American immigration history, with attention to ethnic conflicts, nativism, and racialist theories.

Knobel, Dale T. *Paddy and the Republic: Ethnicity and Nationality in Antebellum America*. Middletown, Conn.: Wesleyan University Press, 1986. Study of nativistic stereotypes of the Irish that fed the riot.

Lannie, Vincent P., and Bernard C. Diethorn. "For the Honor and Glory of God: The Philadelphia Bible Riots of 1844." *History of Education Quarterly* 8, no. 1 (Spring, 1968): 44-106. Examines the Bible controversy in Philadelphia schools.

Laurie, Bruce. *Working People of Philadelphia, 1800-1850*. Philadelphia: Temple University Press, 1980. Provides background on workers and unions.
Montgomery, David. "The Shuttle and the Cross: Weavers and Artisans in the Kensington Riots of 1844." Journal of Social History 5, no. 4 (Summer, 1972):411-446. Analyzes the conflict in terms of social class.

Paulson, Timothy J. *Irish Immigrants*. New York: Facts On File, 2005. Broad sur vey of Irish immigration history.

Takenaka, Ayumi, and Mary Johnson Osirim, eds. *Global Philadelphia: Immigrant*

Communities Old and New. Philadelphia: Temple University Press, 2010. A study of the arrival of immigrants, their assimilation, and the changes they brought to the city.

Warner, Sam Bass, Jr. *The Private City: Philadelphia in Three Periods of Its Growth.* Philadelphia: University of Pennsylvania Press, 1968. Analyzes the riots in the context of other disturbances and police reform.

See also British as dominant group; Celtic Irish; European immigrants, 1790-1892; Federal riot of 1799; German and Irish immigration of the 1840's; Immigration and Nationality Act of 1965; Irish immigrants; Irish immigrants and African Americans; Irish immigrants and discrimination; Irish stereotypes; Know-Nothing Party; Nativism; Scotch-Irish immigrants.

ARAB AMERICAN INTERGROUP RELATIONS

Definition: Relationships among immigrants from different Arab countries

Immigration issues: Demographics; Middle Eastern immigrants; Religion; Stereotypes

Significance: Although Arab immigrants share the same language and many of them share the same religion, Islam, they are far from being a homogeneous group.

According to the American Community Survey, in 2010 the U.S. included almost 1.7 million Arab Americans, with a variety of national backgrounds including 190,078 with Egyptian ancestry, 105.981 with Iraqi ancestry, 61.664 with Jordanian ancestry, 501,988 with Lebanese ancestry, 82,073 with Moroccan ancestry, 93,438 with Palestinian ancestry, and 148,213 with Syrian ancestry, with the remainder simply self-identifying as "Arab" or having ancestry from other Arab countries. The Arab American population has increased substantially in the past several decades, including a 76.0 percent since 1990.

The definition of "Arab" may not be obvious or universal. The source for this data, the American Community Survey, which is conducted by the U.S. Census Bureau, includes a question on ancestry or ethnic origin. Responses to this question, which is based on an individual's self-identification, is used to classify larger ethnic categories. The Census Bureau considers a person to be of Arab ancestry if they report being Alberian, Bahraini, Egyptian, Emirati, Iraqi, Jordanian, Kuwaiti, Lebanese, Libyan, Morocan, Omani, Palestinian, Qatari, Saudi Arabian, Syrian, Tunisian, or Yemeni.

The Census Bureau does not collect information about religion, However, one Arab American group, the Arab Jewish Americans, part of the Sephardic Jewish population and believed to be sizable, is not counted by any official sources. They trace their ancestry predominantly to Syria, Egypt, Yemen, Iraq, Saudi Arabia, Tunisia, and Morocco. It is estimated that there are some 85,000 Arab Jews in the United States.

Demographics During the 1990's, about 48 percent of Arab Americans lived in twenty metropolitan areas. The largest populations were in the Detroit, Michigan (61,065), New York City (58,347), and Los Angeles-Long Beach (56,345) areas. In eight out of ten of the metropolitan areas with the highest Arab American populations during that period, the median household income for Arab Americans exceeded that of the overall population. For example, in the Los Angeles-Long Beach metropolitan area, the median income for Arab Americans was 130 percent of that of the general population.

In 2010, most Arab Americans (66.8 percent) lived in family households, and the average household size for those with Arab ancestry in the u.S. was 2.93, slightly above the U.S. average of 2.59. However, there was substantial variation among the different ancestry groups, with Yemenis having the largest average household size (4.34) and Lebanese the smallest (2.66).

Overall, Arab Americans tend to be better educated than the average American. They earn graduate degrees at a rate twice that of the general population. As might be expected given the level of educational achievement, in 1990, 80 percent of Arab Americans were employed versus 60 percent of all Americans. In 2010, the median household income for Arab Americans was $56,433, above the U.S. average of $51,914, but again with substantial variation among ancestry groups. Lebanese Americans had the highest median household income, at $67,264, and Iraqi Americans the lowest, at $32,075.

Most Arab immigrants to the United States seek permanent status. One exception has been Yemeni temporary male workers, who often want to earn large sums of money to take back to their families in Yemen. Some Arab Americans of higher educational and occupational status look down on these Yemenis because they are less educated and poorer and have adopted the dress and lifestyles of young working-class American men. This violation of traditional manners is irritating to non-Yemeni Arab Americans, especially those striving for acceptance by American society. They fear that non-Arab Americans with ambivalent attitudes toward Arab Americans and who hold negative stereotypes of Arabs fostered by their unfavorable portrayal in the mass media will think less of them because of the behavior of some of the young Yemeni men.

Arab Americans' fears are intensified by hate crimes against them, especially since the terrorist attacks of September 11, 2001. Nine days after those attacks, the attorney general of California reported that his office was investigating seventy separate incidents of possible hate crimes against Muslims in his state alone.

Arab American Women Many Arab American women have become strong and courageous feminists. Carol Haddad, of Lebanese and Syrian heritage, founded the Feminist Arab Network (FAN) in 1983. Its membership comprised about one hundred women, about one-third immigrants and the rest born in the United States. FAN organized panels, wrote articles for progressive feminist

The Arab American National Museum in Dearborn, Michigan. Since the late twentieth century, Michigan has had one of the largest concentrations of Arab residents in the United States. (Wikimedia Commons)

newspapers, magazines, and journals, and spoke to numerous groups about what Arab American women wanted for themselves, non-Arab American women, and women throughout the world. Although FAN did not last for more than a few years, it nevertheless brought together activist Arab American women and Jewish, Latina, Asian American, and Native American women to further feminist and progressive causes. In 1994, the South End Press published an anthology by Arab American and Canadian feminists entitled Food for Our Grandmothers. Thanks to FAN's efforts, women have served as chairs and presidents of the American-Arab Anti-Discrimination Committee (ADC).

The Multicultural Immersion Program The Arab American community is a diverse and successful one. Because of the turmoil in the Middle East, however, and the negative portrayal of Arabs in the mass media, Arab Americans have often felt the sting of prejudice and discrimination and the tragedy of violence and murder. At the 1984 Democratic National Convention, African American Jesse Jackson expressed empathy for the plight of Arab Americans, saying that "Arab Americans, too, know the pain and hurt of racial and religious rejection. They must not continue to be made pariahs."

During the Middle East turmoil in 1989, Arab American businesses in Chicago's black neighborhoods were frequently boycotted by African Americans. The boycotts were motivated by the anti-Arab defamation with which the mass media showered the nation and the failure of Americans to distinguish between Arab

Americans and overseas Arabs. All over the United States, Arab Americans became the targets of violence, property destruction, and even murder.

In 1996, to combat anti-Arab sentiment in Detroit, a social service agency called New Detroit launched the Multicultural Immersion Program. Directed by Sonia Plata, it consists of yearlong programs that bring together people from the major ethnic, religious, and racial groups in the metropolitan area to learn about one another through seminars presented by designated leaders from each of five major groups: African Americans, Arab Americans, Asian Americans, Latinos/Chicanos, and Native Americans. The key organizations that lend support to the groups are the Charles Wright African American Museum, the Arab Community Center for Economic and Social Services (ACCESS), American Citizens for Justice (an Asian American group), Casa de Unidad, and the American Indian Health and Family Services agency.

Milestones in Arab Immigration History

Year	Event
1870's	First Arab immigrants arrive in the United States.
1883	Kahlil Gibran, noted Lebanese immigrant and author, is born (dies 1931).
1892	First Arab American newspaper, Kawkab Amerika, is published.
1898	Maronites found newspaper called Al Hoda (the enlightener).
1948	The formation of the state of Israel creates a large Palestinian diaspora.
1961	Institute of Palestine Studies creates Maronite seminary (Lady of Lebanon) in Washington, D.C.
1967	Israeli victory in Six-Day War provides stimulus to Arab organizations to present their case to the American public.
1967	Professionals form Association of Arab American University Graduates.
1968	Sirhan Bishara Sirhan assassinates Senator Robert Kennedy.
1972	Lobbying group National Association of Arab Americans is founded.
Mid-1970's	Lebanese civil war divides Arab Americans.
1978	Lisa Najeeb Halaby marries King Hussein of Jordan and assumes the name Queen Noor.
1982	American-Arab Anti-Discrimination Committee (ADC), a civil rights activist group, is organized.
1985	West Coast ADC leader Alex Odeh is assassinated.
1989	Council of Lebanese American Organizations, umbrella organization lobbying for Lebanese freedom and sovereignty, is founded.
1991	Educational outreach group, Arab World and Islamic Resources and School Services, is created.
2001	Terrorist attacks on the United States raise American distrust of Arabs.

The first of the seven sessions in the annual program is an orientation, which is followed by five sessions that consist of seminars presented by members of each of the five major groups. Each group selects ten to fifteen of its leaders and members to organize and present an all-day, eight-hour program to members of the other four groups. These seminars feature lectures, discussions, presentation of audiovisual materials, dissemination of literature, and other creative efforts to foster communication, mutual understanding, and friendship among the program participants. The seventh session is a summing up of the program and graduation ceremonies. The program is under written by the Ameritech Corporation. Participants have access to Web sites that deal with multicultural issues.

The Multicultural Immersion Program has become a model for all American communities intent on fostering positive relations among minority groups and intergroup peace based on justice, mutual respect, and understanding. In 1997, the program had seventy graduates.

R. M. Frumkin

Further Reading

A comprehensive over view of Arab American background can be found in Gregory Orfalea's *The Arab Americans: A Quest for Their History and Culture* (Northampton, Mass.: Olive Branch Press, 2005).

Clear pictures of Arab Americans and their struggles for an American identity are presented in *The Development of Arab-American Identity*, edited by Ernest McCarus (Ann Arbor: University of Michigan Press, 1994), and in Yvonne Yazbeck Haddad's *Not Quite American? The Shaping of Arab and Muslim Identity in the United States* (Waco, Tex.: Baylor University Press, 2004). The former work deals with Arab images and stereotypes created by the mass media, antiArab racism and violence, including the murder of two Yemeni immigrant workers, and many other relevant topics.

Arab American women are discussed in Evelyn Shakir's *Bint Arab* (Westport, Conn.: Praeger, 1997) and Somaya Sami Sabry, Evelyn Alsultany and Nadine Naber's edited collection *Arab & American Feminisms: Gender , Violence, & Belonging* (Syracuse, NY: Syracuse University Press, 2011).

Barbara Aswad edited *Arab-Speaking Communities in American Cities* (New York: Center for Migration Studies of New York, 1974). Her book deals with Chaldeans, Arab Christians and Muslims, Lebanese and Syrian Arab Americans, and other significant topics related to Arab Americans. For additional titles, see Joan Nordquist's *Arab and Muslim Americans of Middle Eastern Origin: Social and Political Aspects—A Bibliography* (Santa Cruz, Calif.: Reference and Research Services, 2003).

Modern Arab American Fiction: A Reader's Guide (Syracuse, NY: Syracuse University Press, 2011) provides an overview of novels and short stories by Arab American authors.

See also Arab American stereotypes; Arab immigrants; Israeli immigrants; Jews and Arab Americans; Middle Eastern immigrant families; Muslims.

ARAB AMERICAN STEREOTYPES

Definition: North American perceptions and misperceptions about Arab immigrants

Immigration issues: Discrimination; Middle Eastern immigrants; Stereotypes; Women

Significance: American stereotypes of Arab immigrants are mostly negative and often confuse Arabs with other Middle Eastern peoples.

Social scientists have not studied stereotypes of Arab Americans in as much detail as those of some other ethnic groups, probably because of the relatively small number of Arab Americans in the United States. Arab American stereotypes are revealed mostly through an examination of media coverage of events such as the Israeli-Palestinian conflict, the 1970's civil war in Lebanon, and acts of terrorism involving Arabs—particularly since the terrorist attacks of September 11, 2001—and the depictions of Arabic-speaking people in American films and books. Although many stereotypes are of Arabs, not Arab Americans, the characteristics

Muslim women completing their prayers in a New Jersey park. The clothing worn by these women identifies them as Arabs in the eyes of many Americans; however, their apparel reflects the standards set by Islam and many of the women are, in fact, not Arabs. (Frances M. Roberts)

that are found in them are often attributed to Arab Americans.

The Arab stereotype is predominantly a negative image, revolving around a number of overgeneralizations and falsehoods. Arabs have been portrayed in the media as oil millionaires buying up the United States, white slavers, and uncivilized rulers of kingdoms. Palestinians have been depicted as terrorists and called derogatory names such as camel jockeys, ragheads, and sandsuckers. Common misconceptions include the belief that Iranians are Arabs and that all Arabs are Muslims.

Before 1930, Hollywood studios frequently portrayed Arabs as members of the French Foreign Legion or royalty, Egyptians, and sheiks. Films from 1961 through 1970 depicted Arabs as royalty, murderers, sheiks, slaves, and slaveowners and often featured harems. Many of the roles incorporated elements designed to show the foreignness of the Arab culture and its supposed lack of civilization in comparison with mainstream American culture. During the 1980's and 1990's, acts of terrorism and conflicts in the Middle East caused Hollywood and the media to add violence and barbarism to the Arab stereotype. Arabs, particularly Arab men, were seen as anti-American, greedy, oilrich, uncivilized foreigners who were abductors of Western women and, as Muslims, oppressors of women in general. In the media and in film, Islam has been equated with violence, terrorism, and suppression of women.

In order to counter the negative stereotyping, prejudice, and discrimination experienced by Arab Americans, numerous scholars have published papers on the topic, and several organizations such as the Association of Arab American University Graduates, the Institute of Middle Eastern and North African Affairs, and the American-Arab Anti-Discrimination Committee have been created to address these topics. One of the concerns about the negative stereotypes in the media is that they are not countered by positive portrayals. In particular, Arab American children are hardly present on television, and the Islamic religion is rarely depicted favorably.

Francis C. Staskon

Further Reading

Afzal-Khan, Fawzia, ed. *Shattering the Stereotypes: Muslim Women Speak Out.* New York: Olive Branch Press, 2005.

Alsultany, Evelyn. *Arabs and Muslims in the Media: Race and Representation after 9/11.* New York: New York University Press, 2012.

Cole, David. *Enemy Aliens: Double Standards and Constitutional Freedoms in the War on Terrorism.* New York: New Press/W. W. Norton, 2003.

Elaasar, Aladdin. *Silent Victims: The Plight of Arab and Muslim Americans in Post 9/11 America.* Bloomington, Ind.: Author House, 2004.

Haddad, Yvonne Yazbeck. *Not Quite American? The Shaping of Arab and Muslim Identity in the United States.* Waco, Tex.: Baylor University Press, 2004.

Nordquist, Joan. *Arab and Muslim Americans of Middle Eastern Origin: Social and Political Aspects—A Bibliography.* Santa Cruz, Calif.: Reference and Research Services, 2003.

Orfalea, Gregory. *The Arab Americans: A Quest for Their History and Culture.*

Northampton, Mass.: Olive Branch Press, 2005.

Sabry, Somaya Sami. *Arab-American Women's Writing and Performance: Orientalism, Race, and the Idea of the Arabian Nights.* New York: I.B. Tauris, 2011.

See also   Arab American intergroup relations; Arab immigrants; Israeli immigrants; Jews and Arab Americans; Middle Eastern immigrant families; Muslims.

ARAB IMMIGRANTS

Identification: Immigrants from Arabic-speaking nations of the Middle East

Immigration issues: Demographics; Middle Eastern immigrants; Religion

Significance: Arab Americans are an emerging group of U.S. citizens with an interest in the Middle East. The rise of Israel and Zionism have helped this group coalesce; however, Arab Americans have faced serious conflict with the influential American Jewish community.

Arab Americans are U.S. citizens who have roots in Arabic-speaking countries. Because Arab Americans are internally divided by religion and country of origin, reliable statistics on this group are difficult to obtain. Moreover, given the strong commitment of the United States to Israel, many individuals are reluctant to identify themselves as Arab Americans. Between one million and three million Americans are of Arabic or part-Arabic descent, but estimates vary greatly because of poor statistics.

Arab Americans are difficult to describe as a group because they often downplay or deny their ethnic origins in order to gain greater acceptance in an American mainstream that tends to stereotype them as "camel drivers" or probable terrorists and often compares their homelands unfavorably with the state of Israel. Arab Americans are generally included in the white category in U.S. Bureau of Census records, although on occasion some individuals may be classified as "other Asian." In key urban areas such as Detroit, Michigan, Arab American shopkeepers and entrepreneurs have experienced clashes with the African American community.

Definition and Overview   Arab Americans are all non-Jewish individuals claiming ancestral roots in Arabic-speaking countries from Morocco to Syria and Saudi Arabia or Yemen with minor exceptions such as Chaldean- and Kurdish-speaking individuals. Americans unfamiliar with the Middle East often assume that all Muslims native to the region are Arabs. Therefore, Turkish and Iranian (Persian) Americans, who are Muslims but not ethnically Arabs, are often mistakenly believed to be Arab Americans. Arab Americans are far more likely to be Christian than are natives of their home countries, although a majority of Arab immigrants since the 1960's have been Muslim. During the late 1990's, the Arab American community was believed to be about half Christian and about half Muslim, with

Christians being more acculturated and accepted in the United States. Arab American Christians often are indistinguishable from other Americans by the second generation, although Arab American Muslims form a more distinct group.

Middle Eastern problems such as the Lebanese civil war during the 1970's have pitted Arab American Christians against Arab American Muslims. However, since the Israeli victory in the Six-Day War in 1967, Arab Americans have begun to organize to confront hostile stereotypes in the press and discriminatory practices that often imperil their civil rights and employment opportunities. Arab American activists risk potentially serious conflict with the more established American Jewish community when they call on the U.S. government for an "even-handed" (that is, less pro-Israel) Middle East policy. However, both Arab Americans and American Jews may be able to serve as constructive bridges between the United States and the Middle East and help them return to the generally good relations enjoyed before 1948.

Early History Early Arab American immigrants came to the United States between 1870 and World War I. Most Arabic-speaking individuals who immigrated to the United States during this period were subjects of the Turkish Ottoman Empire, and immigration authorities often incorrectly called them Turks. Immigrants described as "other Asian" were in many cases Arabic-speaking.

Arab immigrants during this period were predominantly Orthodox or Eastern Catholic (Uniate) Christians. They often identified themselves by their religious loyalties or local origins, and very few of these pioneers stressed their Arab identity. Most came from the area that later became Israel, Jordan, Lebanon, and Syria, and they frequently called themselves Syrian. Some immigrants were urban artisans and skilled laborers, but most were peasants, less than half of whom were literate in their native Arabic.

Arab immigrants quickly became peddlers, and many participated very successfully in the free enterprise system. A minority among the Arab immigrant population turned to factory labor, but peddling allowed greater possibility for financial success and more opportunities to learn English and become acculturated. Some Arab American individuals established small businesses in cities and towns. Arab American communities grew in urban centers such as Boston, New York, and Detroit, and hard work produced success for many Arab Americans.

Early immigrants did not bring clergy with them from the Middle East. Therefore, Arab American community leaders worked to secure clergy to serve their compatriots. Most Arab immigrant clergy were marginally educated and prone to sectarian and ethnic factionalism. However, Maronite, Melkite, and Orthodox Christian churches were organized in New York toward the end of the nineteenth century.

Arab American newspapers thrived between 1892, when the first Arabic newspaper was established in New York, and the 1920's. By the late 1920's, the number of Arabic readers was in decline because immigration had been limited by the Immigration Act of 1924, and the children of earlier immigrants spoke only English. The children of both Christian and Muslim immigrants frequently married outside their ethnic groups, and many lost their Arab identity.

From the mid-1920's to World War II, immigration declined. After the passage of the Immigration and Nationality Act of 1965, the United States accepted significant although disputed numbers of Arab immigrants from all parts of the Arabic-speaking world. Most have been Muslims, and many have been educated professionals who originally entered the United States as students. New Arab groups, especially Egyptian Copts and Yemenites, have become important in the changing American cultural mosaic.

Arab American Organizations   Since the mid-1960's, an era emphasizing multiculturalism and the rediscovery of ethnic roots, Arab Americans have sought to foster pride in their Middle Eastern heritage. Significant Arab American organizations include the Association of Arab American University Graduates (formed in 1967), the National Association of Arab Americans (1972), the American-Arab Anti-Discrimination Committee (1982), Arab World and Islamic Resources and School Services (1991), the Council of Lebanese American Organizations (1989), the El Bireh Palestine Society of the USA (1981), and the Institute for Palestine Studies (1961).

Because the Arab American community includes many well-educated professionals, the Association of Arab American University Graduates (AAUG) has been very active since its founding in 1967. This tax-exempt educational and cultural organization promotes understanding between the American and Arab worlds through an annual convention, a strong publication program, speakers, and support of human rights in the Middle East and elsewhere. In its early years, the AAUG attracted post-1948 immigrants while the National Association of Arab Americans gained more U.S.-born individuals. By the 1990's, this distinction had largely disappeared.

The program of the twenty-ninth annual convention during October, 1996, in Anaheim, California, illustrates the diversity of concerns of Arab Americans. Both Democratic and Republican speakers were present. The cultural and legal status of the Arab American community as well as its demographic makeup provided the focus for several sessions. The group also scheduled sessions on Palestinian issues and their connection to Arab Americans, the status of Arab American women, and studies of Arab American urban communities in the United States.

The National Association of Arab Americans (NAAA) lobbies Congress concerning issues of concern to Arab Americans. A Februar y, 1996, statement by Khalil E. Jahshan, president of the NAAA, illustrates the group's public profile. Jahshan addressed the Near Eastern and South Asian Affairs Subcommittee of the Senate Foreign Relations Committee to request that the ban on the use of U.S. passports for travel to Lebanon be lifted for both humanitarian and business reasons. In his statement, Jahshan spoke with pride of the work of Lebanese Americans in Congress and praised Senator Spencer Abraham of Michigan and Representative Nick Joe Rahall of West Virginia for their support. The ban was lifted during the following year.

The American-Arab Anti-Discrimination Committee (ADC) confronts the civil rights issues facing the Arab American community. It has never had universal Arab American support because the head of the Maronite Catholic Church forbade its members from joining when the group did not support the Phalangist cause in the Lebanese civil war. However, since its founding by former South Dakota senator James Abourezk, a Lebanese American, the group has made significant progress on issues of concern to the Arab American community.

To protect the civil rights of Arab Americans, the ADC's department of legal services aids individuals who have experienced defamation and discrimination based on their Arab ethnicity. ADC wants the federal Office of Management and Budget to add a separate racial designation for Arab Americans to the record-keeping efforts of governmental agencies because it believes that Arab Americans are racially targeted and that anti-Arab hate crime is hard to document because it is difficult to separate relevant data regarding Arab Americans from data concerning other groups.

In an attempt to combat negative portrayals of Arabs in the media, the ADC media and publications department publishes a bimonthly newsletter, ADC Times, as well as special reports and "action alerts" on issues of concern. In addition, the organization's department of educational programs sponsors the ADC Research Institute, which encourages public school teachers to provide a balanced portrayal of Arab history and culture.

Arab World and Islamic Resources and School Services (AWAIR), founded in 1991, provides educational outreach at both the elementary and secondary school levels. To improve public understanding of the Arab world, this group conducts teacher training and provides a summer institute for teachers. To celebrate National History Day, this group donates an Arab and Islamic History Award. Book-length publications offer recommended curricula targeting both the elementary and the secondary school student.

The Council of Lebanese American Organizations (CLAO), an umbrella organization, lobbies for freedom and sovereignty for Lebanon and the withdrawal of all foreign troops, both Israeli and Syrian. It provides the monthly report Adonis as well as a monthly newsletter Lebanon File. In addition, this Lebanese American organization offers the annual Cadmus Award.

The El Bireh Palestine Society of the USA (EBPSUSA), founded in 1981, attempts to unite former residents of El Bireh now residing in the United States. It wishes to preserve traditional Arab culture and values in a new American environment and to facilitate contact among members. It offers educational and children's services. By focusing on remembered ties to a locality, this group strengthens the local allegiances of its members.

The Washington, D.C.-based Institute for Palestine Studies (IPS), founded in 1961, is a research-oriented, nonprofit, independent organization formed to study the Arab-Israeli conflict and status of the Palestinians. The best-known publication of IPS is the *Journal of Palestine Studies: A Quarterly on Palestinian Affairs and the Arab Israeli Conflict*. IPS also has an extensive list of publications in Arabic, English, and French.

Despite the existence of these organizations, Arab Americans have continued to experience significant civil rights problems in education, employment, immigration law, and public accommodations. Moreover, whenever crises develop in the Middle East or terrorist acts such as the bombing of the World Trade Center in New York in 1993 or the bombing of the Oklahoma City Federal Building in 1995,

Arab American boys in New York City. (R. Levine)

the Arab American community braces for significant hostility from the American population. At the time of the 1995 Oklahoma City bombing, members of the news media and others immediately speculated that Arab terrorists were the murderers but were later proved wrong.

Hate Crimes and Targeting Issues The ADC uses the Federal Bureau of Investigation (FBI) definition of a hate crime:

> a criminal offense committed against a person or property which is motivated, in whole or in part, by the offender's bias against a race, religion, ethnic/ national origin group, or sexual orientation group.

The situation after the devastating terrorist attacks of September 11, 2001, on the World Trade Center and the Pentagon building was much graver than any that had occurred before. The fact that the perpetrators of the attacks were Arabs was almost immediately known, and incidents of hate crimes against Arab and Muslim Americans increased dramatically. During the first days following the attacks, incidents were reported from all over the United States. Incidents included many violent attacks on mosques and Arab American community centers and assaults on people assumed to be from the Middle East—including many Asian Indians who were neither Middle Easterners nor Muslims.

Among the hundreds of incidents reported shortly after September 11, a Middle Eastern store clerk in Alabama was beaten. In Anchorage, Alaska, vandals did several hundred thousand dollars in damage to a print shop owned by an Arab American. In Chicago, a firebomb was thrown at an Arab American community center, and windows were broken in an Arab American-owned convenience store.

In Indiana, a man wearing a ski mask fired an assault rifle at a Denton gas station at which an American citizen from Yemen was working. Another Indiana man rammed his car into Evansville's Islamic Center. In California alone, more than seventy incidents of anti-Arab and anti-Muslim crimes were reported within the first ten days after the attacks. These incidents ranged from the painting of racist graffiti on schools and other locations and the stoning of several mosques to the burning down of a church with a predominantly Arab American congregation and violent assaults on individual persons.

Perhaps more serious than these hate crime incidents is evidence of governmental targeting of individuals perceived to be Arab American or Muslim. Although the Federal Aviation Administration (FAA) denies targeting Arab Americans or including Arab descent as part of its terrorist profile, Arab American individuals repeatedly face detention and interrogation at airports, an experience not shared by members of many other groups.

Arab Americans are often deported by the Immigration and Naturalization Service (INS) under unusual legal provisions that allow the use of secret and unreliable evidence not subject to challenge. In a November 8, 1995, decision of the U.S. Ninth Circuit Court of Appeals, eight Palestinians won a significant civil rights victory over INS efforts to deport them for their alleged ties to the Popular Front for the Liberation of Palestine. The court held that aliens had the same freedom-of-expression rights as United States citizens. Despite this success, Palestinian immigrants who protest Israeli actions such as the 1982 invasion of Lebanon remain vulnerable to deportation threats.

Media Bias *The Progressive Magazine* documents anti-Arab media bias in an August, 1996, article entitled "Up Against the Wall," detailing brutal U.S. Customs treatment of Arab women at the San Francisco airport. It also notes that both *U.S. News and World Report* and *The New Republic* incorrectly stated that the Prophet Muhammad advocated breaking treaties and broke the Treaty of Hudaybiah in 628. Only the first magazine retracted its error. Many Arab Americans see media bias against the Arab world and their poor treatment at the hands of U.S. government agencies as intertwined issues.

Prominent Arab Americans From assassin to peacemaker, from author to queen, Arab Americans have achieved prominence in many fields. One of the best-known Arab Americans is Lebanese-born artist and author Kahlil Gibran, who made a difficult cultural transition between a mountain village in late Ottoman Lebanon and turn-of-the-twentieth-century Boston. Although he was active in many cultural fields, Gibran is best remembered today as the author of *The Prophet* (1923).

Another well-known Arab American is Queen Noor of Jordan, the widow of King Hussein. She was born Lisa Najeeb Halaby in 1951, in the United States, to an Arab American family with Syrian roots. She received her B.A. in architecture and urban planning in 1974 as part of Princeton University's first coeducational class.

When she married King Hussein on June 15, 1978, she converted from Christianity to Islam. They had four children, two sons and two daughters. She has patronized many educational and cultural organizations in Jordan, and she has consistently exhibited an interest in work that enhances the welfare of women and children. Given her unique cross-cultural perspective, Queen Noor has attempted to serve as a bridge between American and Arab cultures. She supported the establishment of the Jordanian society in Washington in 1980 to promote better understanding and closer relationships between the United States and Jordan.

Two Arab Americans who have made their mark in politics are Spencer Abraham and George Mitchell. A conservative Republican, Abraham was elected to the U.S. Senate from Michigan in 1994. The Lebanese American Abraham received his bachelor's degree from Michigan State University in 1974 and his J.D. from Harvard in 1979. After teaching at the Thomas J. Cooley School of Law from 1981 to 1983, he became Michigan Republican chair in 1983. He served as chief of staff to Vice President Dan Quayle from 1990 to 1991 and was cochair of the Republican National Committee from 1991 to 1993. He failed in his bid for reelection to the Senate in 2001, but president George W. Bush made him secretary of energy in 2001. Although he does not stress his Arab ancestry outside Detroit's Arab community, Abraham has a strong interest in the Middle East. He values his family's immigrant past and has worked hard to fight severe restrictions on new immigration.

Mitchell, a Lebanese American born in Waterville, Maine, served as U.S. senator from Maine and Democratic majority leader during the 1980's. As a diplomat in Northern Ireland during the administration of Bill Clinton, he helped negotiate a peace agreement between Roman Catholics and Protestants in 1998.

Perhaps the most infamous Arab American is Sirhan Bishara Sirhan, born in Jerusalem on March 19, 1944. He became a resident of the United States in 1957 but remained an outsider who resented American economic and political aid to Israel. Angry over his family's losses in the War of 1948 and U.S. policy supporting Israel, Sirhan assassinated Senator Robert F. Kennedy on June 5, 1968, the day that Kennedy won the Democratic presidential primary in California. In addition to killing Kennedy, Sirhan assaulted five other people. After receiving a death sentence, Sirhan had his sentence commuted to life in prison. His assassination of Kennedy may have changed the course of U.S. political history because Kennedy appeared to have a realistic chance of receiving the 1968 Democratic presidential nomination. At the time, the press described Sirhan as a Jordanian because the term "Palestinian" had not yet come into use.

Arab American Churches   The Antiochian Orthodox Church is based in Syria, although it is now increasingly active in the United States. Metropolitan Philip heads the Antiochian Orthodox Christian Archdiocese of North America, headquartered in Englewood, New Jersey. Unlike most Arab Orthodox churches, the Antiochians do not focus solely on their own ethnic communities and Middle Eastern concerns. A notable example of Arab acculturation to life in the United States, this Arab-based church has sought and received the membership of many non-Arab Americans, including a significant number of former Episcopalians unhappy with what they perceive as liberal trends in belief and practice in the

Episcopal Church.

The Coptic Orthodox Patriarchate-Archdiocese of North America, an Egyptian-based group, owes allegiance to H. H. Pope Shenouda III of Alexandria and Cairo, Egypt. The North American bishop is H. G. Bishop Surial, who resides in New Jersey, home to a Coptic seminary. The Egyptian Copts practice a form of Eastern Orthodoxy that dates from antiquity. They are generally considered the descendants of the ancient Egyptians because Egypt was Coptic Christian before it became Muslim.

Maronite Catholics are an Eastern Rite church that has been in full communion with Rome since the sixteenth century. Lebanese immigrants have brought the Maronite Church to the United States from its native Lebanon. The Maronites are notable for their married clergy. Maronite parishes exist in Austin, Texas; Detroit; New York City; Washington, D.C.; and other U.S. cities. Our Lady of Lebanon Seminary in Washington, D.C., established in 1961, is the only Maronite Catholic seminary outside Lebanon. Priests from twentyfour American Maronite Catholic churches participated in the foundation of the seminary. During the Lebanese civil war in the 1970's, the Maronites in the United States and the Middle East allied with Israel. This caused severe conflict with other Arab American groups, especially those strongly supporting the Palestinian struggle for statehood.

Susan A. Stussy

Further Reading

A comprehensive over view of Arab American background can be found in Gregory Orfalea's *The Arab Americans: A Quest for Their History and Culture* (Northampton, Mass.: Olive Branch Press, 2005).

The Arab American Directory (2d ed. Alexandria, Va.: Arab Media House, 1997) provides a comprehensive view of the Arab American community in Washington, D.C.

"Up Against the Wall" in the August, 1996, issue of *The Progressive* illustrates media bias against Arabs and Muslims.

Michael W. Suleiman's "Arab Americans: A Community Profile," in *Islam in North America: A Sourcebook*, edited by Michael A. Koszegi and J. Gordon Melton (New York: Garland Publishing, 1992), surveys the nineteenth and twentieth century Arab American experience.

"Ninth Circuit: Aliens Have First Amendment Rights," in *The National Law Journal* (November 27, 1995), describes the Palestinian Los Angeles Eight's fight against the Immigration and Naturalization Service.

Jean Gibran and Kahlil Gibran's *Kahlil Gibran: His Life and World* (New York: Interlink Books, 1991) shows how an immigrant from an isolated and impoverished village in Lebanon became an important cultural figure in turn-of-thetwentieth-century Boston.

Issues of Arab American identity and challenges to their rights in post-September 11, 2001, America are discussed in Yvonne Yazbeck Haddad's *Not Quite American? The Shaping of Arab and Muslim Identity in the United States* (Waco, Tex.: Baylor University Press, 2004) and Aladdin Elaasar's *Silent Victims: The*

Plight of Arab and Muslim Americans in Post 9/11 America (Bloomington, Ind.: Author House, 2004), while Palestinian identity is discussed in Haim Gerber's *Remembering and Imagining Palestine: Identity and Nationalism from the Crusades to the Present* (New York: Palgrave Macmillan, 2008).

For studies of major Arab communities in two states, see Janice Marschner's *California's Arab Americans: A Prequel to California, An International Community Understanding Our Diversity* (Sacramento, Calif.: Coleman Ranch Press, 2003) and Rosina J. Hassoun's *Arab Americans in Michigan* (East Lansing: Michigan State University Press, 2003).

Arab American literature is the subject of *Dinar zad's Children: An Anthology of Contemporary Arab American Fiction* (Fayetteville: University of Arkansas Press, 2004), edited by Pauline Kaldas and Khaled Mattawa, and Steven Salaita's *Modern Arab American Fiction: A Reader's Guide* (Syracuse, NY: Syracuse University Press, 2011.

For additional titles, see Joan Nordquist's *Arab and Muslim Americans of Middle Eastern Origin: Social and Political Aspects—A Bibliography* (Santa Cruz, Calif.: Reference and Research Services, 2003).

See also Arab American intergroup relations; Arab American stereotypes; Israeli immigrants; Jews and Arab Americans; Middle Eastern immigrant families; Muslims.

ASHKENAZIC AND GERMAN JEWISH IMMIGRANTS

Identification: Jewish immigrants to North America from Germany and central and eastern Europe

Immigration issues: Demographics; European immigrants; Jewish immigrants; Religion

Significance: These earliest Jewish immigrants to the United States have formed the predominant part of the nation's Jewish American population.

During the second half of the seventeenth century, German and Ashkenazic Jews from the central and eastern European countries of Germany (Holy Roman Empire), Poland, and the Austro-Hungarian Empire came to North America by a variety of routes. Ashkenazic Jews are Jews from eastern Europe who spoke Yiddish and lived in separate enclaves, or ghettos, mainly in modern-day Russia and the Baltic countries outside Germany. Some came to America after the Dutch lost control of Brazil in 1654, and others came directly to New Amsterdam before it was added to the British Empire by the duke of York, after whom it was renamed New York City.

Immigrants reading sacred texts on the Jewish new year in 1907 in New York City. (Library of Congress)

New York City was the first to allow Jews to build a house of worship and purchase land for a cemetery. Although individual Jews and Jewish families can be found in the early colonial records of all of the thirteen original colonies, Charleston, South Carolina, was home to the largest Jewish community. Mediterranean Jews were predominant, although all of the colonial American Jewish congregations had large percentages of Ashkenazic and German Jews who came to the British North American colonies with the aide of London and Caribbean merchants.

After the American Revolution, immigration increased slowly, and by the 1830 U.S. Census, the Jewish population had reached nearly 3,000, predominantly Ashkenazic and German Jews. The European Enlightenment, the passage of laws preventing Jews from entering professions and leaving their ghettos, and new taxes, combined with the unsuccessful revolution in Poland and throughout central and eastern Europe in 1836, brought a dramatic increase in emigration by German-speaking Jews throughout the 1840's and 1850's. By the outbreak of the U.S. Civil War in 1861, there were 150,000 Jewish Americans, more than 90 percent of whom were Ashkenazic and German Jews.

During this era, large numbers of trained rabbis came to the United States, and denominational divisions followed. In 1834, German Jews seeking to anglicize the liturgical service founded Charleston's Society of Reformed Israelites. Isaac Leeser, the promoter of the Jewish Sunday School movement, anticipated the Conservative Jewish movement that emerged later in the century. This era also saw the publication of several Jewish periodicals, including one by Rabbi Isaac Meyer Wise, which became a springboard for the creation of the first Jewish seminary and the establishment of the reformed Union of American Hebrew Congregations.

From the middle of the nineteenth century to its final decade, the influence of German Jews in business and in Jewish social, cultural, and religious life reached its apex. The German Jewish community began to seek recognition of its expanding economic success, creating a separation between the German Jews and the later-arriving Ashkenazic Jews from Russia, which led to more sectarian and social divisions within the Jewish religious and secular communities.

As new immigration expanded the number of American Jews beyond the four million mark, American "popularism" and the reemergence of the Ku Klux Klan during World War I led to the passage of a series of immigration acts, the last of which (Immigration Act of 1924) changed the base year for computing national immigration quotas from 1920 to 1890 and had the greatest impact on Jewish immigration. The decrease in new immigration meant that the German and Ashkenazic Jewish groups would continue to be the dominant group in the Jewish American population. Jewish Americans numbered nearly six million during World War II, and in the second half of the twentieth century, their numbers did not increase.

Sheldon Hanft

Further Reading

Cohen, Naomi Werner. *Encounter with Emancipation: The German Jews in the United States, 1830-1914.* Philadelphia: Jewish Publication Society of America, 1984. Scholarly study of the reaction of this group to legal equality and citizenship.

Meltzer, Milton. *Bound for America: The Story of the European Immigrants.* New York: Benchmark Books, 2001. Broad history of European immigration to the United States written for young readers.

Sterba, Christopher M. *The Melting Pot Goes to War: Italian and Jewish Immigrants in America's Great Crusade, 1917-1919.* Ann Arbor, Mich.: UMI, 1999.

Straten, Jits van. *The Origin of Ashkenazi Jewry: The Controversy Unraveled.* New York: Walter de Gruyter, 2011. Using both demographic information and scientific techniques such as DNA analysis, van Straten discusses common assumptions regarding the origins of the Ashkenazi community and proposes a new answer.

See also American Jewish Committee; Eastern European Jewish immigrants; Israeli immigrants; Jewish immigrants; Jewish settlement of New York; Jews and Arab Americans; Sephardic Jews; Soviet Jewish immigrants.

ASIAN AMERICAN EDUCATION

Immigration issues: Asian immigrants; Chinese immigrants; Education; Japanese immigrants

Significance: Asian Americans have gained a reputation for high educational achievement. To some extent, this reputation reflects actual performance, and this performance has been part of the debate about why ethnic and racial groups vary in educational achievement.

The educational achievements of Asian Americans have attracted a great deal of scholarly and popular attention. Popular interest in Asian American educational performance often involves comparing this group with members of other minority groups, heightening the perception of Asian Americans as members of a so-called model minority, a stereotype that often makes Asian Americans uncomfortable. Scholars interested in immigrants, minority groups, and influences on education have studied the educational performance of various Asian American groups in order to obtain insight into how immigrant membership and minority group membership may be related to achievement in school.

Levels of Achievement   Although it is difficult to discuss the educational performance of such a diverse group, Asian Americans do seem to show overall levels of achievement that are quite high. Moreover, they begin to distinguish themselves educationally at fairly early ages. In an analysis of 1980 U.S. Census data presented in their book *Asians and Pacific Islanders in the United States* (1993), Herbert Barringer, Robert W. Gardner, and Michael J. Levin noted that Asian Americans showed high rates of preschool attendance. This was particularly true for Japanese, Chinese, Koreans, and Asian Indians. The 1990 U.S. Census showed this pattern continuing. About 24 percent of all Asian American children under six years of age were enrolled in school, compared with 21 percent of white children. Among Chinese, Taiwanese, Japanese, and Thai American children, rates of early school attendance were particularly high, with 27 percent of Chinese, 31 percent of Taiwanese, 31 percent of Japanese, and 30 percent of Thai children

Students of a Chinese school in New York City around 1910. (Library of Congress)

under six years of age enrolled in school.

School enrollment, however, is not the same thing as school performance. However, data from the 1988 National Educational Longitudinal Study show that as early as the eighth grade, Asian American children display higher levels of educational aspiration than other American children. According to these data, 43 percent of Asian American children reported that they aspired to education beyond a bachelor's degree, while only 25 percent of white eighth-graders wanted to pursue postgraduate education.

Asian American children are more likely than other American students to reach high school and stay in high school. Less than 6 percent of Asian Americans age sixteen to nineteen were high school dropouts in 1990, compared with nearly 7 percent of white Americans and 16 percent of African Americans. There were substantial variations among Asian groups; however, only the three most economically underprivileged Southeast Asian refugee groups (Cambodian, Hmong, and Laotian Americans) showed dropout rates that were higher than those of white Americans, and all of the Asian American groups had dropout rates that were lower than those of African Americans.

Standardized tests administered during elementary and secondary schools often show Asian children out-achieving other minority groups in the U.S., and sometimes White students as well. For example the 2007 TIMMS (Trends in International Mathematics and Science Study found that the average math score for 4th graders was 582, above the U.S. average of 529 as well as the average for White (550), Black (482) and Hispanic (504) 4th graders in the U.S. Similar results were seen in science scores for 4th graders: the average score for Asian American students was 573, as compared to the national average of 539, White students (567), Black students (488) and Hispanic students (502). Similar results were found in the math and science scores for 8th graders.

Schools that select students entirely or primarily through standardized testing often have disproportionately Asian student populations. For instance, several elite public high schools in New York city select students on the basis of a single exam. Although the student population of the city's public schools is 14 percent Asian, the student body of Stuyvesant, the most elite of the city's public schools, is 70 percent Asian. Two other elite public schools that admit students by examination only also have a student body that is more than half Asian: Bronx High School of Science (63 percent) and Brooklyn Technical High School (59 percent).

College entrance examinations are among the most commonly used indicators of high school performance. Although breakdowns by particular Asian groups are not available, the scores of Asian Americans in general were as high as the scores of any other racial group or higher. On the American College Test (ACT), for example, the average Asian American score was 21.7, equal to the average score for whites and higher than the average score for African Americans (17.1). The average Scholastic Aptitude Test (SAT) score for Asian Americans, 1056, was higher than that for members of any other racial or ethnic group, including white Americans (1052). Asian Americans tended to score much higher than white Americans on the math part of the test (560 for Asians, compared with 536 for whites) and substantially lower on the verbal part of the test (496 for Asians, compared with 526 for whites). This suggests that Asian American scores would have been even higher had many of them not been hampered by relatively weaker English proficiency.

Asian Americans were more likely than either white Americans or African Americans to be enrolled in college in 1990. Although 29 percent of whites and 23 percent of African Americans age eighteen to twenty-five were attending college in that year, 46 percent of Asian Americans in this age category were enrolled in higher education. Once again, there were substantial variations among Asian American groups, but only the Hmong and the Laotian Americans, two of the most recent and most economically underprivileged Asian American groups, showed lower rates of college enrollment than the majority white population.

Theories of Asian Educational Achievement   According to researchers Stanley Sue and Sumie Okazaki, in their 1990 article "Asian American Educational Achievement," published in the *American Psychologist*, theorists have usually attributed Asian American school achievement either to innate, genetic characteristics of Asians or to cultural characteristics. Genetic explanations address the problem by citing the performance of Asians on intelligence quotient (IQ) tests and other measures of ability as evidence of higher levels of innate intellectual ability among Asians. Psychologist Richard Lynn has argued that Asian scores on aptitude tests and IQ tests provide evidence for a genetic explanation of Asian academic achievement.

Cultural explanations of Asian American scholastic success have received wider acceptance than genetic explanations. From this point of view, Asian American families pass on cultural values that stress hard work and educational excellence. Looking at Vietnamese American children, Nathan Caplan, Marcella H. Choy, and John K. Whitmore maintained that Vietnamese families passed on cultural values to their children that enabled the children to do well in school. One difficulty with applying this explanation to Asian Americans in general is that the different Asian groups come from a variety of cultural backgrounds.

To address the difficulties raised by both the genetic and cultural explanations, Sue and Okazaki put for ward the theory of "relative functionalism" in their 1990 article. According to this theory, Asian success is to be explained by blocked mobility: As a result of barriers to upward mobility by other means, such as social networks, Asians tend to focus on education. Although blocked mobility may influence the life choices of Asians, it would not account for trends in other groups that also experience blocked mobility but do not show the levels of academic performance characteristic of Asians.

Sociologists Min Zhou and Carl L. Bankston III have argued that Asian American educational success may, to some extent, be a consequence of the types of social relations found in Asian American communities. They have claimed that tightly knit ethnic communities, such as Chinatowns or Southern California's Little Saigon, can promote the upward mobility of young people by subjecting them to the expectations of all community members and by providing them with encouragement and support from all community members. This explanation, though, does not tell us why Asian Americans who do not live in ethnic communities may sometimes be high achievers in school.

The precise causes of Asian American educational achievement, then, remain a matter of debate. In all likelihood, some combination of existing theories may account for the scholastic performance of this group, with some theories applying more to some specific groups than to others.

Carl L. Bankston III

Further Reading

James R. Flynn's *Asian Americans: Achievement Beyond IQ* (Mahwah, N.J.: Lawrence Erlbaum Associates, 1991) provides an over view of Asian American academic achievement and provides a useful introduction for those interested in this subject.

The variety and complexity within the Asian American community, and the unfair judgment that Asians aren't "really" minorities, is the focus of *The Misrepresented Minorities: New Insights on Asian Americans and Pacific Islanders, and the Implications for Higher Education* (Sterling, VA: Stylus Publishing, 2013), ed. by Samuel D. Museus, Dina C. Maramba, and Robert T. Teranishi.

Vivian S. Louie focuses on the academic achievements of Chinese Americans. *My Trouble Is English: Asian Students and the American Dream* (Portsmouth, N.H.: Boynton/Cook, 1995) offers insight into the importance of education as a means of upward mobility for Asian American students and into the challenges faced by many of these students.

Stacey J. Lee's *Unraveling the "Model Minority" Stereotype: Listening to Asian American Youth* (New York: Teachers College Press, 1996) investigates the motivations and problems of Asian American students.

The educational achievements of children of refugees from Southeast Asia are described in *Children of the Boat People* (Ann Arbor, Mich.: University of Michigan Press, 1991).

In *Growing Up American: How Vietnamese Children Adapt to Life in the United States* (New York: Russell Sage, 1998), Min Zhou and Carl L. Bankston III examine the experiences of Vietnamese children in American schools and compare Vietnamese American students with students of other Asian and non-Asian ethnicities.

Lynn Tsuboi Saito's *Ethnic Identity and Motivation: Socio-cultural Factors in the Educational Achievement of Vietnamese American Students* (New York: LFB Scholar Pub., 2002) looks at individual and group factors in educational success.

For broader studies of Asian American youth, see *Asian American Youth: Culture, Identity, and Ethnicity* (New York: Routledge, 2004), edited by Jennifer Lee and Min Zhou; Stacey J. Lee's *Up Against Whiteness: Race, School, and Immigrant Youth* (New York: Teachers College Press, 2005); and H. Mark Lai's *Becoming Chinese American: A History of Communities and Institutions* (Walnut Creek, Calif.: AltaMira, 2004).

For broader perspective on immigrant education, see *Educating New Americans: Immigrant Lives and Learning* (Mahwah, N.J.: L. Erlbaum Associates, 1999), by Donald F. Hones and Cher Shou Cha; *Overlooked and Underserved: Immigrant Students in U.S. Secondary Schools* (Washington, D.C.: Urban Institute, 2000), by Jorge Ruiz de Velasco and Michael Fix; and *Immigrants, Schooling, and Social Mobility: Does Culture Make a Difference?* (New York: St. Martin's Press, 2000), edited by Hans Vermeulen and Joel Perlmann. The latter volume is a collection of papers from a 1996 conference on culture and worldwide immigration that was held in Amsterdam.

See also Amerasians; Asian American literature; Assimilation theories; Bilingual education; Model minorities.

ASIAN AMERICAN LEGAL DEFENSE FUND

Identification: Asian American rights advocacy organization

Date: Founded in 1974

Immigration issues: Asian immigrants; Chinese immigrants

Significance: The Asian American Legal Defense Fund (AALDF) organization formed to defend and promote the legal rights of Asian Americans through litigation, legal advocacy, community education, leadership development, and free legal assistance for low-income and immigrant Asian Americans.

The Asian American Legal Defense Fund is headquartered in New York City, and the executive director in 1998 was Margaret Fung, an Asian American lawyer. The AALDF was organized to help relieve the effects of racial prejudice and social discrimination experienced by Asian and Pacific Americans.

Many individuals from the diverse Asian American population have attained middle-class status, and a select few have entered upper-level management within major United States corporations. However, in wages and career advancement, Asian Americans generally lag behind their white counterparts. The AALDF addresses these and other grievances by educating Asian American communities, particularly in the election process of the United States. Furthermore, to encourage voter participation, the AALDF has fostered the use of bilingual ballots and voter material in the United States. Asian Americans cast a significant number of votes in key electoral states such as California and major cities such as New York, Los Angeles, and San Francisco.

Alvin K. Benson

Further Reading

Chi, Tsung. *East Asian Americans and Political Participation: A Reference Handbook*. Santa Barbara, Calif.: ABC-Clio, 2005.

Segal, Uma Anand. *A Framework for Immigration: Asians in the United States*. New York: Columbia University Press, 2002.

See also Asian Pacific American Labor Alliance; Mexican American Legal Defense and Education Fund.

ASIAN AMERICAN LITERATURE

Definition: Fiction, essays, and other works written by Americans of Asian ancestry

Immigration issues: Asian immigrants; Chinese immigrants; Japanese immigrants; Literature

Significance: Asian American literature is usually based on themes that touch on the authors' cultural heritages. These works, which first appeared at the end of the nineteenth century, have enabled Asian Americans to identify with their own cultural heritage and have helped others to better understand their culture and experiences.

The first published Asian American writers were two sisters, Sui Sin Far (Edith Maud Eaton) and Onoto Watanna (Winifred Eaton), the daughters of British planter Edward Eaton and his Chinese wife, Lotus Blossom. Critics have accused Sui Sin Far of presenting stereotypical descriptions of the Chinese and of Chinatown, but in fact, through her collection of short stories *Mrs. Spring Fragrance* (1912), she portrayed the discrimination and psychic pain that Chinese immigrants endured. In novels such as *Heart of Hyacinth* (1904), Onoto Watanna wrote of love affairs between Asian women and white men in which her Asian women protagonists always accepted the superiority of their Western lovers. She chose a Japanese-sounding name for her pen name because at the time, although the American public discriminated against the Japanese, they viewed them more favorably than the Chinese, stereotyping them as harder working and more intelligent.

Before World War II, several Asian American writers described their experiences growing up in the United States. One book, Younghill Kang's *East Goes West* (1937), offers a humorous look at the life of a young Korean American and pokes fun at white people's prejudices.

After World War II, several Japanese Americans published books about the internment camps and other wartime experiences. In *The Two Worlds of Jim Yoshida* (1972), nisei (second-generation Japanese American) Jim Yoshida, who was in Japan when World War II broke out, relates how he was forced to serve in the Imperial Army and had to sue to regain U.S. citizenship after the war. In No-No Boy

(1957), John Okada, another nisei, writes about the hysteria that he experienced in wartime America, and in the award-winning book Obasan (1981), Joy Kogawa describes her life in a Canadian World War II internment camp.

The 1960's and 1970's During the 1960's and 1970's, the Civil Rights and women's movements inspired many minority groups to become active politically and to become more aware of their heritage. This heightened activity and awareness resulted in the publication of more works by Asian Americans, which helped others to understand and respect them.

In 1972, the first anthology of Asian American literature, *Asian-American Authors*, edited by Kai-Yu Hsu and Helen Palubinskas, was published. This anthology includes works from only three Asian American groups—Chinese, Japanese, and Filipino—and gives priority to writers born in America, such as Frank Chin, Jeffrey Paul Chan, Lawson Fusao Inada, and Shawn Wong. However, other anthologies soon followed, broadening the spectrum of Asian American writers to include Americans of Korean, Southeast Asian, and Indian ancestry and immigrants such as Chitra Divakaruni.

In 1972, *The Chickencoop Chinaman* was the first play by an Asian American, Frank Chin, to receive critical acclaim in New York. Asian American literature received widespread recognition with the publication in 1976 of Maxine Hong Kingston's *The Woman Warrior: Memories of a Girlhood Among Ghosts*. Kingston uses ancient Chinese stories to develop her best-selling novel around the character of Fa Mulan, a woman warrior. This work, like many others by Asian American writers, incorporates elements of traditional Asian mythology and culture.

Frank Chin, the author of The Chickencoop Chinaman, *the first play by an Asian American to be produced.* (Corky Lee)

84

It also illustrates the effect that the Civil Rights and women's movements have had on literature produced by members of minority groups.

Common Themes During the 1970's and 1980's, various demographic trends, such as increased immigration from Asia and Mexico, helped the United States become much more multicultural, and more Asian American writers felt encouraged to explore Asian themes. Although Asia is a large continent with many languages, cultures, and religions, certain themes and elements appear to be common in Asian American literature. These include the balance between dark and light and between masculine and feminine; conflicts between

Amy Tan, author of The Joy Luck Club. (Robert Foothorap)

ancient heritage, familial obligations, and contemporary (often Western) lifestyles; and the effects of immigration. After Kingston's work became popular, there was widespread appreciation for novelists, poets, dramatists, and essayists of Asian ancestry.

Many Asian American women have written of the cultural conflicts that women experience when they move from traditional Asian cultures to the more liberal American culture. Velina Hasu Houston explores this theme in a 1985 trilogy, *Asa ga Kimashita, American Dream*, and *Tea*, whose main characters are Japanese war brides who have to cross traditional boundaries in order to survive in their new environment. In *Arranged Marriages* (1995), Indian-born poet Divakaruni presents images of the adjustment problems that many women from traditional Indian backgrounds have in American society.

Asian American writers also have explored familial obligations and tensions. In "Seventeen Syllables" (1994), Hisaye Yamamoto explores the tensions created within Japanese American families when traditional cultural expectations clash with contemporary lifestyles. In *Clay Walls* (1986), a novel by Korean American Kim Ronyoung, the issue of obligation to family is explored as the wife and mother ruins her eyes doing embroidery work to support her family after her husband loses all their money gambling.

Some Asian American writers based their stories on the immigrant experience, as did Wakako Yamauchi in her novel *And the Soul Shall Dance* (1977) and Fred Ho in the play *Chinaman's Chance* (1987). In *Honey Bucket* (1979), Filipino American Mel Escueta explores the issue of identity, attempting to deal with the guilt he felt after killing Asians during the Vietnam War. Frank Chin uses stereotypes in the humorous novel *Donald Duk* (1991), as does David Henry Hwang in his Tony Award-winning play *M Butterfly* (1988).

Perhaps after Kingston, who made the American public aware of Asian American literature, Chinese American Amy Tan is the writer who has done the most to popularize the genre. Tan rose to public attention with the publication of her novel *The Joy Luck Club* in 1989. She won both the National Book Award and the *Los Angeles Times* book award that year. Tan turned her novel into a screenplay for the 1993 film *The Joy Luck Club*. She has objected to having her work described as Asian American literature because she believes that the themes in her work, which include male-female relationships and family obligations, are universal. Nevertheless, Tan's themes arise from an experience that may be termed Asian American: the balance between male and female; clashes between traditional cultures and contemporary lifestyles; struggles with familial obligations; and identity and spirituality issues.

Annita Marie Ward

Further Reading

The Greenwood Encyclopedia of Asian American Literature, ed. GuiyouHuang (Westport, CT: Greenwood Press, 2009) provides an overview of the subject.

King-kok Cheung edited *An Interpretive Companion to Asian American Literature* (Cambridge, England: Cambridge University Press, 1996).

Shirley Geok-lin Lim and Amy Ling edited *Reading the Literature of Asian America* (Philadelphia: Temple University Press, 1996).

Judith Caesar explored Asian American themes in "Patriarchy, Imperialism, and Knowledge in *The Kitchen God's Wife* " in *North Dakota Quarterly* (62, no. 4, 1994-1995).

Asian American literature is discussed in Sucheng Chann's *Asian Americans: An Interpretive History* (Boston: Twayne, 1991).

Klara Szmanko compares the use of the trope of invisibility in two American minority cultures in *Invisibility in African American and Asian American Literature: A Comparative Study* (Jefferson, NC: McFarland & Co., 2008).

For a discussion of the treatment of immigration in seventeen novels written for children, see Ruth McKoy Lowery's *Immigrants in Children's Literature* (New York: P. Lang, 2000).

Broader issues of Asian American identity are covered in *Migration and Identity* (New Brunswick, N.J.: Transaction, 2005), edited by Rina Benmayor and Andor Skotnes, and *Asian American Youth: Culture, Identity, and Ethnicity* (New York: Routledge, 2004), edited by Jennifer Lee and Min Zhou.

The six-volume *Asian American Encyclopedia* (New York: Marshall Cavendish, 1995), edited by Franklin Ng, covers all aspects of the Asian American experience, with many articles on individual writers and related topics.

See also Asian American education; Asian American stereotypes; Asian Indian immigrants; Asian Indian immigrants and family customs; Chinese immigrants; Chinese immigrants and family customs; Japanese immigrants; Literature; Southeast Asian immigrants.

ASIAN AMERICAN STEREOTYPES

Definition: North American perceptions and misperceptions about Asian immigrants and Asian Americans

Immigration issues: Asian immigrants; Chinese immigrants; Discrimination; Japanese immigrants; Nativism and racism; Stereotypes

Significance: The hard work and thriftiness that have contributed to the success of Asian Americans have, at times, caused members of other ethnic and racial groups to feel threatened. In the nineteenth and early twentieth centuries, Asian immigrants and their offspring were often called threats to American society and were viewed by white Americans as a group that could not be assimilated.

At the beginning of the twenty-first century, millions of Americans of Asian ancestry lived in the United States; however, some of the old negative stereotypes and attitudes about them persisted. Many fourth-generation Asian Americans were identified as Asian (Chinese, Japanese, and so on) rather than as "American."

The Chinese, who first immigrated to the United States during the mid-nineteenth century, were willing to work for low wages, which got them jobs but also made them the objects of white workers' jealousy and anger. On the West Coast, where many of the immigrants had settled, many white workers blamed Chinese immigrants for their economic woes. They called the Chinese laborers "coolies," a derogatory term, and claimed that they were of inferior character and could not be assimilated into American culture. This general climate of blame coupled with the desire of white nativists to limit immigration, and many discriminatory laws (such as the 1862 California law, An Act to Protect Free White Labor Against Competition from Chinese Coolie Labor) were passed against the Chinese immigrants. Many of these laws were later employed against immigrants from other Asian countries.

As the Chinese immigrants moved beyond California, white workers in area after area spoke out against them, claiming that their willingness to work for meager wages would ruin all Americans' standard of living. In 1885, in Rock Springs, Wyoming, a white mob drove Chinese workers out of town and burned their homes, killing twenty-eight Chinese immigrants in the process.

Transfer of Prejudice Although the Chinese were excluded from immigration by the 1882 Chinese Exclusion Act, other Asians—Japanese, Koreans, and Indians— did arrive in the United States. From 1900 to 1910, about 100,000 Japanese arrived on the West Coast. These immigrants tended to be better educated than the earlier Chinese immigrants had been. Nevertheless, white Americans on the West Coast, particularly in California, expressed alarm at their arrival, again claiming that the Japanese could never be assimilated into American society. The press and politicians claimed that a Japanese invasion was taking place and began to speak of the "yellow peril," which they said posed a threat to the American way of life and might result in the United States being taken over by the Japanese.

In 1924, Congress passed an immigration act that barred nearly all immigration from Asia. Only Filipinos were allowed to immigrate because as citizens of the Philippines, they could become U.S. citizens. However, during the late 1920's and during the Depression of the 1930's, trade unions wanted Filipino immigration banned, claiming the Filipino laborers' willingness to work cheaply was undercutting the American standard of living. Filipinos were called a "mongrel stream" that could not be assimilated. Union members urged the government to ship Filipinos back to the Philippines.

Asians During and After World War II By the time Japan bombed Pearl Harbor in December, 1941, two generations of Japanese Americans were living in the United States and Canada: the issei, the original immigrants, and their children, the nisei. Some Japanese American families had been in North America for more than fifty years. Nevertheless, both the Canadian and the United States governments assumed that these Japanese Americans would not be loyal to them and placed 120,000 Japanese Americans in internment camps until the end of World War II.

Immigrants who came to the United States under the quota system, established by the Immigration and Nationality Act of 1952 were often professionals, tending to be more affluent than earlier immigrants and far less likely to live in ethnic enclaves such as Chinatowns or Koreatowns. This new group of professional immigrants and their offspring gave the United States a new Asian American stereotype—the smart achiever.

In 1965, the quota system was abolished, allowing much more immigration from Asia. During the mid-1970's, large numbers of people from Cambodia, Laos, and Vietnam entered as refugees from the conflict in Southeast Asia. Many of these people, particularly the Hmong from Laos, were uneducated. Political leaders began to object to the entrance of refugees, claiming that their education and skill levels made it difficult for them to assimilate because they could not learn to read and write in English. It was also claimed that they took jobs away from Americans. Such stereotyping contributed to the English-only movement and passage of the 1986 Immigration Reform and Control Act.

Stereotypes and Resentment In the last decade of the twentieth century, household incomes for Asian American families and educational levels for Asian American adults were generally higher than those of the general American population. New resentments and stereotypes emerged. In the cities, this resentment was often directed toward shop owners and landlords of Asian ancestry. These shop owners were often stereotyped as mercenary and racist, particularly by some African Americans, such as the Nation of Islam's Louis Farrakhan, who likened the affluent Asian Americans to the Jewish landlords and shop owners of the mid-twentieth century. This resentment was portrayed in Spike Lee's movie *Do the Right Thing* (1989), which foreshadowed some of the violence directed toward shop owners of Korean ancestry during the Los Angeles riots of 1992.

Although people of Asian and Pacific islander heritage represented about 4 percent of the U.S. population in 1999, they made up 8 to 10 percent of enrollment in Ivy League institutions. Students of Asian heritage made up 35 to 40 percent of the student bodies at some universities in the University of California system, although the percentage of African American and Latino students fell from the early 1990's. This situation created resentment against Asian Americans and placed pressure on young Asian Americans to conform to the stereotype of Asian Americans as superior students.

Annita Marie Ward

Further Reading

The subject of stereotyping is discussed in *Asian American Youth: Culture, Identity, and Ethnicity* (New York: Routledge, 2004), edited by Jennifer Lee and Min Zhou.

William L. Tung's *The Chinese in America, 1820-1973* (Dobbs Ferry, N.Y.: Oceana Press, 1974) gives a detailed record and chronology of Chinese Americans' experiences from 1820 to 1973.

Other useful books include *The Japanese Americans, The Korean Americans, The Chinese Americans, The Filipino Americans*, and *The Indo-Chinese Americans*, all part of the Peoples of North America series, edited by Nancy Toff (New York: Chelsea House Publishers, 1989). Senator Daniel Patrick Moynihan served as senior consulting editor to the series.

Shilpa S. Davé looks at stereotyping of Asian Indians in American film and television in *Indian Accents: Brown Voice and Racial Performance in American Television and Film* (Urbana: University of Illinois Press, 2013).

Asian American Psychology: Current Perspectives, ed. by Nita Tewari and Alvin N. Alvarez (New York: Psychology Press, 2009), looks at a number of psychological issues, including stereotyping, in the lives of Asian Americans.

The six-volume *Asian American Encyclopedia* (New York: Marshall Cavendish, 1995), edited by Franklin Ng, covers all aspects of Asian American history and life.

See also Arab American stereotypes; Asian American literature; Asian American women; Asian Indian immigrants and family customs; Chinese immigrants; Chinese immigrants and family customs; Irish stereotypes; Japanese immigrants; Southeast Asian immigrants.

ASIAN AMERICAN WOMEN

Immigration issues: Asian immigrants; Chinese immigrants; Demographics; Families and marriage; Japanese immigrants; Women

Significance: During the 1990's, Asian American women belonged to the fastest-growing group of minorities in the United States and Canada.

According to 1999 projections by the U.S. Census, the total number of Asian Americans and Pacific islanders in the United States more than doubled from the 1980 census figure of 3.4 million. Despite this rapid population growth, Asians in the United States, as in Canada, accounted for less than 5 percent of the population.

Demographics There is growing awareness that Asian Americans come from many different backgrounds, not simply Chinese and Japanese ones. Although the 1990 census reported twenty-eight different Asian American groups, the focus of much of the literature has been on the eight largest or more recently controversial and influential groups: Chinese, Filipinos, Koreans, Asian Indians, Japanese, Vietnamese, Cambodians, and Hmong. Approximately 66 percent of Asian Americans in the United States live in five states: California, New York, Hawaii, Texas, and Illinois. They also have a tendency to congregate and concentrate in a few cities: Chicago, Honolulu, Los Angeles, New York, and San Francisco.

In general, Asian American men had higher rates of graduation from a high school or higher institution than women in 1990, 82 percent versus 74 percent. Among the various groups of women, however, disparities exist in terms of completion rates. A high school or higher educational level had been obtained by 86 percent of Japanese American women but only 19 percent of Hmong American women. Asian American women had a higher labor force participation rate than all women. In 1990, 60 percent of Asian American women were in the labor force, compared with 57 percent of all women in the United States.

The diversity in origins and cultural backgrounds of Asian Americans has made it difficult to speak of an Asian American culture that ties all these groups together. Nevertheless, common themes can be found in the experiences of women who must struggle constantly with the social burden not only of their race but also of their gender and their class.

Reasons for Coming to America Historically, it is difficult to speak of Asian American immigrant women, because there were relatively few of them. Restrictions on Chinese and Japanese men bringing their wives to American shores led to the phenomenon of bachelor men and picture brides. In addition to legal restrictions, cultural deterrents kept Asian women from venturing abroad: "Respectable" women did not travel far from home; the only women to do so were maids and prostitutes. Those Asian women who were able to immigrate labored under hard physical conditions and were often callously treated. In many cases, however, leaving their home country was these women's only alternative to poverty, war, and persecution. Some of the most recent arrivals to the United States—Southeast Asians from Vietnam, Cambodia, and Laos—came as refugees of wars in their homelands. Still other Asian women came in search of adventure and the excitement of living in a new country, especially those from more affluent families and those who were well educated.

Yet, no matter what their original status in their native countries, Asian American women have often encountered a hostile society in the West. Even those who have been living in the United States or Canada for many years or decades have not been spared this hostility. Moreover, Asian American women born in the West are not guaranteed fair treatment. Many immigrant Asian women are faced with financial hardships, violence, and social ostracism, forcing them to learn survival skills in order to adapt to life in a new country. Some have adjusted quite well to the new environment, while others have not.

Issues of Concern   Asian American women have to some degree helped perpetuate the myth of Asian Americans as a model minority since, as wives and mothers, they socialize their families—using a cultural emphasis on education, hard work, and thrift—to excel in earnings, education, and occupational status. Such goals often set Asian Americans apart from other ethnic groups and can lead to jealousy, resentment, and discrimination.

Despite the hard work and self-sacrifice of many Asian American women, however, disparity often exists between striving and achievement. Many newer immigrants must contend with a lack of communication because of poor English-speaking skills. Asian American women have acquired a reputation for being conscientious and industrious but docile, compliant, and uncomplaining as well. The necessity of a paycheck relegates some to work as hotel room cleaners, waitresses, cooks, shop clerks, and electronics assembly-line workers. Some postpone learning English and as a result may never leave their entry-level jobs.

In general, Asian American women with college educations are concentrated in limited, less prestigious rungs of the professional-managerial class. Professionally, Japanese women typically become elementary or secondary school teachers and Filipinas become nurses. In 1980, Asian American women with four or more years of college were most likely to find jobs in administrative support or clerical occupations, such as cashiers, file clerks, office machine operators, and typists. They are overrepresented in these jobs, many of which not only have low prestige, low mobility, and low public contact but also offer little or no decision-making authority. Executive managerial status is limited to such occupations as auditors and accountants. Asian American women are least represented in the more prestigious professions: physicians, judges, dentists, law professors, and lawyers. Thus, Asian American women in general are poorly represented in higher-level management and leadership positions and experience the "glass ceiling," which often prevents women and minorities from rising above a certain job level. The fact that Asian American women do not reap the income and other benefits one might expect given their high levels of educational achievement raises questions about the reasons for such inequality. To what extent is this situation attributable to self-imposed limitations related to cultural modesty, the absence of certain social and interpersonal skills required for upper-managerial positions, institutional factors beyond their control, or outright discrimination?

The number of Asian American women turning to mainstream politics, running for office, or working in politics is increasing. The Civil Rights and antiwar movements motivated many younger Asian American women to become politically active over issues of discrimination because of race, sex, or place of origin. During the 1960's, the first wave of Asian American feminism focused on empowering these women economically, socially, and politically. The second wave of activism during the 1980's focused on working with specific women's groups as support networks for women of color. Some Asian American women became involved in assisting the homeless and the poor (many of whom are elderly immigrants), nuclear disarmament efforts, and the international issues of freedom in the Philippines and Korea and the sex trade in Asia.

Many conflicts still need to be resolved. Some tension exists in the Asian American community between new arrivals and long-term residents or citizens, between native-born and foreign-born members, and between the professional and working classes. New arrivals still look to Asia for reference, while the U.S.-born tend to view the world from an American perspective. The established working class views the new arrivals as competitors for the same scarce resources. The established professionals look askance at those with limited English proficiency and their culturally ill-at-ease immigrant counterparts. Professionals dissociate themselves from the residents of ethnic ghettos in Chinatowns, Koreatowns, and Japantowns. Working-class Asian Americans view the professionals' tendency to speak for the community with suspicion.

The chasm between traditional Asian familial values and mainstream values has brought conflict for Asian American women. In order to be effective, they must be aggressive, but such an approach is contrary to traditional Asian feminine values of passivity and subordination. They must be highly visible and public, contrary to the values of modesty and moderation. Thus, the Asian American woman pressured to conform to traditional female roles must overcome a number of barriers in the attempt to adjust to the American environment.

Cecilia G. Manrique

Further Reading

George Anthony Peffer's *If They Don't Bring Women Here: Chinese Female Immigration Before Exclusion* (Urbana: University of Illinois Press, 1999) focuses on one major aspect of the experience of female Asian immigrants.

Ethnicities: Children of Immigrants in America (Berkeley: University of California Press, 2001), edited by Rubén G. Rumbaut and Alejandro Portes, is a collection of papers on demographic and family issues relating to immigrants that includes chapters on Filipino and Vietnamese immigrants.

Ye Le Espiritu's *Asian American Women and Men: Labor, Laws, and Love* (Lanham, MD: Rowman & Littlefield Pub., 2008), looks at how racism, immigration law, and gendered labor conditions have affected the relationships between Asian American men and women.

Additional sources of information about Asian Americans include Karin Aguilar-San Juan's *The State of Asian America* (Boston: South End Press, 1994), Harry H. L. Kitano and Roger Daniels's *Asian Americans: Emerging Minorities* (Englewood Cliffs, N.J.: Prentice Hall, 1988).

Asian/Pacific Islander American Women: A Historical Anthology, ed. Shirley Hune and Gail M. Nomura (New York: New York University Press, 2003) contains a series of essays about different aspects of Asian and Pacific Islander women's lives in America.

Tricia Knoll's *Becoming Americans: Asian Sojourners, Immigrants, and Refugees in the Western United States* (Portland: Coast to Coast Books, 1982), Ronald Takaki's *Strangers from a Different Shore: A History of Asian Americans* (Boston: Little, Brown, 1989), and William Wei's *The Asian American Movement* (Philadelphia: Temple University Press, 1993). *Making Waves: An Anthology of Writings by and About Asian American Women* (Boston: Beacon Press, 1989) is a collection of writings by Asian women edited by the Asian Women United of California.

The six-volume *Asian American Encyclopedia* (New York: Marshall Cavendish, 1995), edited by Franklin Ng, covers all aspects of Asian American society.

See also Amerasians; Asian American literature; Asian American stereotypes; Chinese immigrants; Chinese immigrants and family customs; Filipino immigrants; Garment industry; Japanese immigrants; Mail-order brides; Middle Eastern immigrant families; Page law; Picture brides; Southeast Asian immigrants; Thai garment worker enslavement; War brides; Women immigrants.

ASIAN INDIAN IMMIGRANTS

Identification: Immigrants to North America from the South Asian nation of India

Immigration issues: Asian immigrants; Demographics

Significance: The more than one million people of Asian Indian origin or descent living in the United States have contributed significantly to their adopted nation. The Asian Indian community contains a large proportion of well-educated, affluent, highly motivated people.

Emigration out of South Asia has been a dominant behavioral pattern since the Indus Valley civilization (2500-1700 b.c.e.). The impact of merchants and Buddhist missionaries from India is evident today in Central and East Asia, where Indian mythology, dance, and theater have had lasting effects. Movement from western India to Africa dates back to the second century c.e. Small-scale movement changed to mass emigration as Indians provided cheap labor for British colonies, many becoming indentured servants. The result was a diaspora of nine million Indians scattered throughout the British Empire but concentrated in places with labor-intensive economies, especially plantation systems, such as Mauritius, Fiji, Trinidad, and East Africa. Widescale migration to the United States, Australia, and Canada developed during the 1960's, largely because changes in immigration regulations removed existing racial barriers. The oil-rich Middle East has become a focus for South Asian immigration since 1970.

Coming to America Initially, Asian Indians came to the United States as sea captains and traders during the 1790's, actively pursuing trade between India and

North America. A very few came as indentured laborers. By 1900, the United States was home to about two thousand Indians, including about five hundred merchants, several dozen religious teachers, and some medical professionals. Six thousand Indians entered the United States through the West Coast between 1907 and 1917, but another three thousand were barred entry. Many of these immigrants came from Canada, where they had faced hostilities, only to meet with the same sort of treatment in the United States. Most immigrants from India during this period originated from Punjab and were adherents of the Sikh faith.

As Indian immigration increased, anti-Asian violence on the West Coast began to target Indians. Discriminatory laws were passed, prohibiting them from owning land and being eligible for U.S. citizenship. In fact, the Immigration Act of 1917 is sometimes referred to as the Indian Exclusion Act. The hostile environment, along with the Great Depression of the 1930's, resulted in several thousand immigrants returning to India. Therefore, in 1940, only 2,405 Asian Indians were living in the United States, mostly around Yuba City, California.

After World War II, new legislation gave Asian Indians the rights to become citizens and own land and established a quota of 100 immigrants per year, allowing for family reunification. Between 1948 and 1965, 6,474 Asian Indians entered the United States as immigrants. The Immigration and Nationality Act of 1965 removed the national origins clause in U.S. immigration legislation and gave preference to highly educated and skilled individuals. India had a ready pool of such

Sikh immigrants posing for a group portrait in 1910. (California State Library)

talent, and the mass movement from India to the United States began. Sixty-seven percent of the foreign-born Asian Indians in the United States have advanced degrees, as opposed to only 25 percent of the American-born. In addition, Asian Indians are highly represented in managerial positions and as sales/technical/clerical workers and have low representation in the service, blue-collar categories.

The post-1965 immigrants fall into three categories: initial immigrants, second-wave immigrants, and sponsored immigrants. The initial immigrants, who came soon after restrictions were lifted in 1965, are mainly very highly educated men—doctors, scientists, and academics—who migrated for better educational and professional opportunities. By the 1990's, most of these immigrants, now middle-aged, were earning more than $100,000 annually. Their wives typically had little more than a high school education and did not work outside the home, and their children were in their late teens or early twenties. This first wave of immigrants were concerned about retirement and their children. The second-wave immigrants, who came during the 1970's, were also highly educated professionals. However, these professionals tended to be couples, both of whom worked. Their children were mostly college-bound teenagers, and one of their main concerns was getting their children through college. The third group of immigrants were those individuals sponsored by established family members. They generally were less well educated and more likely to be running motels, small grocery stores, gas stations, and other ventures. Their concerns were to establish themselves in a successful business.

Profile The Asian Indian population in the United States—which consisted of about 7,000 people in 1970—grew to about one million by the late 1990's, making them the fourth-largest immigrant group. This group reached 815,447 in 1990, a 111 percent rise since 1980, when they numbered 387,000. The percentage of foreign-born was up from 70 percent in 1980 to 75 percent in 1990. As of 2010, 2.8 million Asian Indians lived in the U.S., constituting the third largest groups of Asian Americans; Most (87 percent) of Asian Indian adults (age 18 and older) were foreign born, a higher percentage than for Asian American adults overall (74 percent). Most (73 percent) say they speak English very well, and many are educated beyond high school: 32 percent of Indians hold a Bachelor's degree and 38 percent an advanced degree (the average for the U.S. population is 18% with a bachelor's degree and 10 percent for an advanced degree). The median household income for Asian Indians in the U.S. is $88,000, far above both the U.S. median household income of $49,800 as well as the Asian American median of $66,000.

The post-1965 immigrants flocked to the major metropolitan areas, where their skills were most marketable. By the mid-1990's, 70 percent of the Asian Indian population lived in eight major industrial-urban states: California, Illinois, Michigan, New Jersey, New York, Ohio, Pennsylvania, and Texas. However, the Asian Indians in the United States generally do not live in concentrated areas but are dispersed throughout the city. The vast majority speak English and are familiar with American ways, so they do not need to rely on their compatriots for help. In addition, because many of them are professionals, they are affluent enough to live where they choose.

Indian grocery store in Marysville, California. (California State Library)

The educational attainment of the Asian Indian population is very high: 73 percent of those age twenty-five or older have at least a high school education. A 1984 study showed that Asian Indians had a mean high school grade-point average of 3.8 on a scale of 4. Therefore, they form sizable proportions of the student bodies at the elite colleges in the United States. In 1998, they held more than five thousand faculty positions in American colleges and universities.

The Asian Indian population uses lobbying and campaign contributions to promote its special interests, which range from revisions of immigration policy to efforts to prevent or minimize Pakistan's military buildup.

One of the best-known areas of South Asian entrepreneurial behavior is the hotel and motel business. Hindus from the Gujarat region in India, most with the surname of Patel, began arriving in California during the late 1940's. They bought dilapidated hotels and motels in deteriorating neighborhoods and, with cheap family labor, turned the businesses into profitable enterprises. During the mid-1980's, the newsstand business in New York City was dominated by Indian and Pakistani immigrants who controlled 70 percent of the kiosks. However, ten years later, the Indians and Pakistanis were being replaced by immigrants from the Middle East. South Asians have also been prominently involved in laundries, gift shops, and the garment industry. During the early 1990's, 40 percent of the gas stations in New York City were owned by Punjabi Sikh immigrants.

Impact of Emigration on India India has benefited tremendously from emigration to the United States. Remittances, sent by immigrants to remaining family, have made areas such as Gujarat and Punjab relatively prosperous. Large amounts of capital from abroad have been invested in high technology, and new ideas from the United States and elsewhere are also evident. By the mid-1990's, many Asian Indians had returned from abroad to set up industries or work for international companies establishing a presence in India. The bicultural knowledge and skills of these returnees have contributed to Hyderabad's becoming the Silicon Valley of India. However, the impact is not limited to Hyderabad; it can be seen in Bombay, Calcutta, and Delhi as well as Punjab's prosperous agricultural Doab region.

Arthur W. Helweg

Further Reading

Arthur W. Helweg and Usha M. Helweg's *An Immigrant Success Story: East Indians in the United States* (Philadelphia: University of Pennsylvania Press, 1990) is a comprehensive study of the Asian Indian community in the United States.

Jagat K. Motwani's America and India in a *"Give and Take" Relationship: Sociopsychology of Asian Indian Immigrants* (New York: Center for Asian, African and Caribbean Studies, 2003) is a broad sociological study of Asian Indians to the United States.

Hugh Tinker's *A New System of Slavery: The Export of Indian Labour Overseas, 1830-1920* (Oxford, England: Oxford University Press, 1974) and *Separate and Unequal: India and the Indians in the British Commonwealth, 1820-1959* (Delhi: Vikas Publishing, 1976) chronicle South Asian migration.

Vivek Bald's *Bengali Harlem and the Lost Histories of South Asian America* (Cambridge, MA: Harvard University Press, 2013) looks at the history of working class Asian American immigrants to the U.S., beginning with the last decades of the nineteenth century.

Bruce La Brack's *The Sikhs of Northern California 1904-1974* (New York: AMS Press, 1988) sets forth the development of the Sikh community in California.

Sunaina Maira's *Missing: Youth, Citizenship, and Empire After 9/11* (Durham: Duke University Press, 2009), based on ethnographic research at one New England high school, looks at how cultural citizenship is produced for young South Asian Muslim immigrants.

The six-volume *Asian American Encyclopedia* (New York: Marshall Cavendish, 1995), edited by Franklin Ng, offers entries on a wide variety of topics relating to Asian immigrants.

Ellen Alexander Conley's *The Chosen Shore: Stories of Immigrants* (Berkeley: University of California Press, 2004) is a collection of firsthand accounts of immigrants from many nations, including Afghanistan, India, and Pakistan.

See also Asian American stereotypes; Asian Indian immigrants and family customs; Coolies; Sikh immigrants.

ASIAN INDIAN IMMIGRANTS AND FAMILY CUSTOMS

Immigration issues: Asian immigrants; Demographics; Families and marriage; Religion

Significance: Immigrants to the United States from the South Asian nations of India, Pakistan, and Bangladesh have had to struggle to maintain their cultural identities while striving to integrate successfully into mainstream American culture.

According to U.S. Census figures, slightly fewer than one million persons immigrated to the United States from India (including what is now called Pakistan) between 1820 and 2003. During the first three years of the twenty-first century, Indians continued to enter the United States at the rate of about 60,000 immigrants per year. The 1990 U.S. Census counted 1.4 million Asian Indians and a half million Pakistanis and Bangladeshis living in the United States. Even though the United States has far fewer immigrants from the Indian subcontinent than from several other Asian and Middle Eastern countries, the former became the fastest-growing immigrant group during the 1990's. The Indians and Pakistanis who have migrated to the United States and Canada since the 1960's represent a highly professional and educated class. Some 62 percent of them have earned undergraduate and graduate degrees. South Asians are concentrated primarily in several large urban centers, such as New York, Los Angeles, San Francisco, Philadelphia, and Chicago, although sizable numbers also live in smaller cities. Evidence has suggested that permanent communities of South Asians have established themselves in several big cities.

Family Size The size of the average East Indian and Pakistani family in the United States is small: 3.2 people per household. Families are usually nuclear, with parents and children living by themselves. However, groups of close relatives may live in the same area and maintain frequent contact with one another. Parents of Indian couples living in the United States quite commonly visit their children for several months, but they face relative isolation because they lack social contacts with persons with similar backgrounds.

Within families from the Indian subcontinent, husbands have remained the authority figures even in homes where wives have professional careers. Wives must often contend with the pressures of the "second shift" and their husbands' continuing demands for special privileges. Divorce has continued to be rare among all groups of South Asians. Only 4.5 percent of East Indian and Pakistani households lack husbands and only 1.3 percent are headed by unmarried couples. While these immigrants have a higher per-capita income than other Americans, they consume less than those in the same income brackets. They put a great premium on savings and investment.

East Indian food consumption has been highly resistant to change. Most Indian Hindus avoid beef and pork, while Pakistanis avoid pork and alcoholic beverages. In households with children, American style meals have become more frequent, but traditional Indian meals predominate.

Community Relations India is a culturally diverse country with sixteen major languages and several main religions. First-generation immigrants from the Indian subcontinent maintain the traditional values and rituals handed down to them as a way of preserving their identity. Most of them participate in organizations with others from their places of origin who speak the same language, practice the same religion, and eat the same foods.

Visiting friends and entertaining guests from similar backgrounds are major leisure-time activities among Indians and Pakistanis. Preparing lavish feasts for guests is a common traditional practice, and anything less is considered bad manners. Among those who practice Islam, regular Sunday schools exist in which children are taught to read the Quran and how to pray. Among Hindus, religious practice is less rigid and the major Hindu festivals are conducted in temples, usually presided over by priests.

Children South Asian children, both boys and girls, are usually indulged for the first five years of their lives. The age of five marks a transition in their lives; by then, they are expected to adhere to socially appropriate standards of behavior and to advance academically. The transition is more abrupt for boys than for girls. Indian and Pakistani immigrants' attitudes toward raising children have remained traditional.

Rigidly defined sex roles are taught and reinforced by adults. Girls are expected to become proficient at housework, take care of younger siblings, and be sensitive to social cues, while boys are expected to be strong and academically successful. Families from the Indian subcontinent have not emphasized athletic competence as much as other American families. Such attitudes have often been a source of conflict for young boys, whose parents have often not been willing to spend time or money in developing their children's athletic capacities to match those of their school peers.

Indian and Pakistani adolescents are expected by their families to excel in the sciences and enter science careers (preferably high-status and high-paying ones). Since mainstream American society places great emphasis on education, there is no conflict in this area. Yet, South Asian immigrants have not viewed education as the free, individualistic enterprise that the host society considers it. Children's educational achievements are regarded as contributing to families' social prestige.

Dating and Marriage Children of South Asian immigrants, especially when they reach adolescence, face immense conflicts between parental values and peer

Sikh families in New York City. (R. Levine)

pressure to conform to American customs, conflicts that have been especially pronounced in dating and marriage. Dating is usually forbidden, and arranged marriages are the preferred norm in most families. Girls are expected to remain virgins until they are married, and chastity is highly valued among Indian and Pakistani families when choosing brides for their sons. Parents consider sexual contact before marriage to be immoral and corrupt. There have been several reported cases in which lovers have eloped, married secretly, or even committed suicide, because their relationships were unacceptable to their parents.

Most men and women from the Indian subcontinent prefer to return to their homelands for arranged marriages. Relatives back home establish ties with several prospective partners and their families. Eventually, immigrant sons and daughters go to South Asia for short visits in order to select from among the chosen candidates and marry. Muslim parents usually tolerate interfaith marriages for boys, since offspring are expected to follow the father's faith. Daughters' choices are more limited, because children of daughters could lose their Islamic affiliation.

Religion and Religious Holidays When South Asians arrive in the United States and Canada, their religious attitudes become more lenient. Most Hindus fervently participate in religious activities, worshiping at home or at temples. Families with children practice their religions more often than families without children as a way of maintaining their children's sense of traditional consciousness.

Hindu and Muslim families celebrate most of their religious holidays as a way of keeping the heritage alive for their children. At such times, families renew social bonds and meet to discuss issues pertinent to their communities. East Indian children learn forms of classical (Indian) music and dance, and religious functions are a medium to display children's talents and skills. Hindu and Muslim schools have been opened in all areas with significant South Asian populations. Such schools are open on weekends and in the evenings to teach children basic religious practices.

A principal Hindu holiday is the Diwali, or the festival of lights, which celebrates the day Krishna, one of the principal gods in the Indian pantheon, killed the demon Kamsa. In India, streets and homes are usually lit up with oil lamps a month before the holiday. The night before the festival, firecrackers are lit and effigies of the demon Kamsa are burnt on street corners, while people sing praises to Krishna. The festivities continue the next day with more firecrackers, while friends and families exchange sweets and feast together.

Muslims' main holidays are Ramadan and aftar (breaking the fast at sunset). Prayers are held every evening followed by taravih (recital of Qur$3nic verses). Devout Muslims begin fasting a month before Ramadan. Adults and children refrain from eating or drinking water from sunrise to sunset. Special prayers are offered at Eid-ul-Fitr (marking the end of the month of Ramadan) and Eid-ul-Adha (commemoration of the pilgrimage to Mecca). After prayers, families often gather together for feasts.

Gowri Parameswaran

Further Reading

Abraham, Margaret. *Speaking the Unspeakable: Marital Violence Among South Asian Immigrants in the United States.* New Brunswick, N.J.: Rutgers University Press, 2000.

Conley, Ellen Alexander. *The Chosen Shore: Stories of Immigrants.* Berkeley: University of California Press, 2004.

Khandelwal, Madhulika S. *Becoming American, Being Indian: An Immigrant Community in New York City.* Ithaca, N.Y.: Cornell University Press, 2002.

Jain, Anapuma. *How to be South Asian in America: Narratives of Ambivalence and Belonging.* Philadelphia: Temple University Press, 2011.

Kurian, George, and Ram Srivastava. *Overseas Indians.* New Delhi, India: Viking Press, 1993.

Lal, Vinay. *The Other Indians: A Political and Cultural History of South Asians in America.* Los Angeles: Asian American Studies Center Press, University of California, 2008.

Lee, Jennifer, and Min Zhou, eds. *Asian American Youth: Culture, Identity, and Ethnicity.* New York: Routledge, 2004.

Motwani, Jagat K. *America and India in a "Give and Take" Relationship: Sociopsychology of Asian Indian Immigrants.* New York: Center for Asian, African and Caribbean Studies, 2003.

Saran, Parmatma. *The Asian Indian Experience in the USA*. New Delhi, India: Vikas Publishing House, 1985.

Vaidyanathan, Prabha, and Josephine Naidu. *Asian Indians in Western Countries: Cultural Identity and the Arranged Marriage*. Amsterdam: Swets & Zeitlinger, 1991.

See also Asian American education; Asian American literature; Asian Indian immigrants; Coolies; Immigration and Naturalization Service v. Chadha; Sikh immigrants.

ASIAN PACIFIC AMERICAN LABOR ALLIANCE

Identification: Asian American/Pacific islander advocacy organization

Date: Founded on May 1, 1992

Immigration issues: Asian immigrants; Civil rights and liberties; Labor

Significance: The Asian Pacific American Labor Alliance formed to address the needs of a growing Asian and Pacific islander community in the United States.

On May 1, 1992, the Asian Pacific American Labor Alliance (APALA) held its founding convention in Washington, D.C. That gathering drew five hundred Asian, American, and Pacific island unionists and laborers from around the United States, including garment factory workers from New York City, hotel and restaurant workers from Honolulu, longshore laborers from Seattle, nurses from San Francisco, and supermarket workers from Los Angeles. The establishment of APALA was the culmination of several decades of Asian American unionization activity.

Unionizing Since the mid-1970's, Asian American labor activists in California had worked to strengthen unionization attempts by holding organizational meetings in the larger Asian American communities within San Francisco and Los Angeles. Through the efforts of such neighborhood-based organizations as the Alliance of Asian Pacific Labor (AAPL), stronger ties between labor and the community were forged, and Asian union staff members were united more closely with rank-and-file labor leaders. Those too-localized efforts of the Alliance of Asian Pacific Labor, however, failed to organize significant numbers of Asian American workers. In order to begin unionizing on the national level, AAPL administrators, led by Art Takei, solicited organizational aid from the American Federation of Labor-Congress of Industrial Organizations (AFL-CIO), a key U.S. labor collective.

Upon the invitation of the AFL-CIO executive board, AAPL vice president Kent Wong attended the 1989 national AFL-CIO convention in Washington, D.C., to lobby for the establishment of a national labor organization for Americans of Asian and Pacific island descent. In addressing Wong's request, AFL-CIO president Lane Kirkland acknowledged the local accomplishments of the AAPL in California and recognized the organizing potential of the growing Asian American workforce. In 1991, Kirkland appointed a national Asian Pacific American labor committee. This group of thirty-seven Asian and American labor activists met for more than a year to create the Asian Pacific American Labor Alliance. In planning for the 1992 convention, the Asian Pacific American labor committee released a nationwide invitation for Asian, American, and Pacific island unionists, labor activists, and workers to gather in Washington, D.C., to take on the responsibility for bridging the gap between the national labor movement and the Asian Pacific American community.

APALA Is Born The response to that invitation exceeded the committee's expectations. At the May 1, 1992, convention, more than five hundred delegates participated in adopting an Asian Pacific American Labor Alliance constitution and in setting up a governmental structure with a national headquarters in Washington, D.C., and local chapters throughout the United States. Organized in this manner, APALA could receive recognition and control from a national administration guided by the AFL-CIO, while still using its powerful techniques of community organization at the local level.

During the convention, APALA organizers and delegates recognized and honored Asian Pacific American labor pioneers whose achievements they believed had melded national and local unionization efforts successfully. Among them was Philip Vera Cruz, the eighty-seven-year-old former vice president of the United Farm Workers Union. Vera Cruz had worked since the 1930's to create local unions for farmworkers in the southwestern United States, and continuously lobbied for national support of farmworkers' unionization.

With an eye toward the future, APALA drafted a Commitment to Organizing, to Civil Rights, and to Economic Justice, which called for empowerment of all Asian and Pacific American workers through unionization on a national level; it also called for the provision of national support for individual, local unionization efforts. APALA also promoted the formation of AFLCIO legislation that would create jobs, ensure national health insurance, reform labor law, and channel financial resources toward education and job training for Asian and Pacific island immigrants.

Toward that end, the group called for a revision of U.S. governmental policies toward immigration. APALA's commitment document supported immigration legislation that would promote family unification and provide improved immigrant access to health, education, and social services. Finally, the document promoted national government action to prevent workplace discrimination against immigrant laborers; vigorous prosecution for perpetrators of racially motivated crimes was strongly supported. To solidify their commitment, APALA delegates passed several resolutions, which they for warded to the AFL-CIO leadership. These documents decried the exploitative employment practices and civil rights violations alleged against several United States companies.

Convention delegates also participated in workshops that focused on individual roles in facilitating multicultural harmony and solidarity, enhancing Asian

American participation in unions, and advancing a national agenda to support more broadly based civil rights legislation and improved immigration policies and procedures. From these APALA convention workshops, two national campaigns were launched. The first involved working with the AFLCIO Organizing Institute to recruit a new generation of Asian Pacific American organizers, both at the national and local levels. The second campaign involved building a civil and immigration rights agenda for Asian Pacific American workers, based upon APALA's commitment document and its convention resolutions.

Through the legislative statement of its goals and in lobbying for their substantive societal implementation, the Asian Pacific American Labor Alliance was the first Asian American labor organization to achieve both national and local success. Although by the time of the 1992 APALA convention Asian Americans had been engaged in various forms of unionization activity for more than 150 years, establishment of APALA within the ranks of the AFLCIO provided it with more powerful organizational techniques. The Asian Pacific American Labor Alliance was able to solidly unite Asian Pacific workers, simultaneously integrating them into the larger U.S. labor movement.

Thomas J. Edward Walker
Cynthia Gwynne Yaudes

Further Reading

Aguilar-San Juan, Karin, ed. *The State of Asian America: Activism and Resistance in the 1990s*. Boston: South End Press, 1994. Explores the connection between race, identity, and empowerment within the workplace and the community. Covers Euro-American, African American, and Asian American cultures.

Chang, Edward, and Eui-Young Yu, eds. *Multiethnic Coalition Building in Los Angeles*. Los Angeles: California State University Press, 1995. Suggests ways to build multicultural harmony within the community and the workplace. Discusses labor union organization among African Americans, Chicanos, and Asian Americans in California.

Chi, Tsung. *East Asian Americans and Political Participation: A Reference Handbook*. Santa Barbara, Calif.: ABC-Clio, 2005. General reference source on Asian immigrants to the United States.

Espiritu, Yen Le. *Asian American Women and Men: Labor, Laws, and Love*. 2nd ed. Lanham, MD: Rowman & Littlefield, 2008. An historical analysis about how immigration laws, racism, and gendered labor have influenced gender relations in the Asian American community.

Friday, Chris. *Organizing Asian American Labor*. Philadelphia: Temple University Press, 1994. Analyzes the positive impact of Asian Pacific immigration upon the formation of industries on the West Coast and in the Pacific Northwest between 1870 and 1942.

Omatsu, Glenn, and Edna Bonacich. "Asian Pacific American Workers: Contemporary Issues in the Labor Movement." *Amerasia Journal* 8, no. 1 (1992). Discusses the advance in status that Asian American workers have achieved in recent decades; summarizes the political, economic, and social issues that still impede their progress.

Rosier, Sharolyn. "Solidarity Starts Cycle for APALA." *AFL-CIO News* 37, no. 10 (May 11, 1992): 11. Summarizes the AFL-CIO conference report on the establishment of the Asian Pacific American Labor Alliance.

Segal, Uma Anand. *A Framework for Immigration: Asians in the United States.* New York: Columbia University Press, 2002. Survey of the history and economic and social conditions of Asian immigrants to the United States, both before and after the federal immigration reforms of 1965.

Wong, Kent. "Building Unions in Asian Pacific Communities," *Amerasia Journal* 18, no. 3 (1992): 149-154. Assesses the difficulties of Asian American unionization and gives suggestions for overcoming those problems.

See also Asian American Legal Defense Fund; Asian American women; Chinese American Citizens Alliance; Garment industry; Hawaiian and Pacific islander immigrants.

ASSIMILATION THEORIES

Definition: Theories about the processes by which individuals or groups take on the culture of the dominant society, including language, values, and behavior, as well as the processes by which groups are incorporated into the dominant society

Immigration issues: Citizenship and naturalization; Families and marriage; Language; Sociological theories

Significance: Two major models of assimilation are the melting pot theory and Anglo-conformity.

Assimilationist theories suggest that the outcome of race and ethnic relations in society is assimilation: the ultimately harmonious blending of differing ethnic groups into one homogeneous society. A key question that emerges among assimilationist theorists concerns the basis of that homogeneity. The melting pot theory holds that distinct groups will each contribute to the building of a new culture and society that is a melting pot of all their differing values and behaviors, and the Anglo-conformity theory holds that (in North America) the varying groups will all adopt the values and behaviors of the dominant, Anglo-Saxon group.

Anglo-conformity According to Milton Gordon in his book *Assimilation in American Life* (1964), assimilation involves both acculturation and structural assimilation, wherein groups are fully incorporated into, and indistinguishable from, the larger society. Cultural assimilation, or acculturation, however, can proceed in either a melting pot pattern or an Anglo-conformity pattern. Gordon, who attributes the Anglo-conformity thesis to Stewart Cole, states that this pattern requires that immigrants completely abandon their cultural heritage in favor of Anglo-Saxon culture. According to Gordon, those who propose Anglo-conformity as a practical ideal of assimilation view the maintenance of the English language, institutions, and culture as desirable. Such views, in his estimation, are related to nativist programs that promote the inclusion of those immigrants who are most like the English as well as to programs that promote the acceptance of any immigrants willing to acculturate on the basis of Anglo-conformity.

According to Gordon, those espousing the Anglo-conformity ideal cannot be automatically labeled racist although, as he puts it, all racists in the United States can be called Anglo-conformists. Furthermore, Anglo-conformists tend to assume that English ways and institutions are better than others. Even those who do not support that view argue that these ways and institutions, regardless of their relative merit, do predominate in existing American society. Therefore, newcomers must adapt to what is already in place. Angloconformists also assume that once immigrants have acculturated based on Anglo-conformity, they will be found acceptable and will no longer be the targets of prejudice and discrimination.

Melting Pot Although the Anglo-conformity ideal has been the prevalent form of assimilation proposed, the melting pot ideal has also been an important and influential aspect of assimilationist thought. Particularly during the early twentieth century, those who viewed American society as a new experiment in which diverse peoples came together to forge a new culture saw Americans as a new "race" of people. In this view, the United States was a giant melting pot that received all immigrants, melting them—and their cultures— down into one homogeneous and unique group.

Patriotic poster published during World War I promoting the idea of cultural assimilation. (Library of Congress)

The melting pot theory of assimilationist theory was implied by sociologist Robert Ezra Park's theory of the race relations cycle, suggested during the 1920's. In that theory, Park presented the idea that assimilation involves both cultural and biological processes. In other words, Park conceived of assimilation as accomplished both by the "interpenetration" of distinct cultures, in which each group takes on some of the other's culture, and by amalgamation, or biological mixing through intermarriage and reproduction.

Gordon criticizes melting pot idealists for failing to discuss whether all groups can contribute equally to the final mixture. Furthermore, since Anglo-Saxons arrived chronologically before other immigrants, they were able to establish the social order into which newer immigrants are expected to "melt." Because of this difference in group influence on the American character and society, Gordon claims that the melting pot ideal masks the fact that nonAnglo-Saxons are the ones expected to change. Furthermore, although some differences, such as nationality, can be melted down among whites, other differences, such as race and religion, are either not willingly given up or cannot be melted away. African Americans and other people of color, according to Gordon, are prevented from melting down by racial discrimination.

Other Theories and Criticisms In their 1963 book *Beyond the Melting Pot*, Nathan Glazer and Daniel Patrick Moynihan review the melting pot theory in the light of continuing ethnic diversity and conflict in New York City. Glazer and Moynihan believed that ethnic groups could join society if they were willing to change, to acculturate. Unlike Gordon, Glazer and Moynihan do not view prejudice as the major obstacle to assimilation. They view internal group weaknesses as the major obstacle; they also cite the lack of a single American identity for immigrants to adopt. Glazer and Moynihan think that ethnic groups develop a new ethnic identity, thus remaining distinct— neither melted down nor conforming to the Anglo model.

In his 1981 book, *The Ethnic Myth*, Stephen Steinberg states that the early rise of nativism in the United States implies that Anglo-conformity dominated assimilationist views. Nativism is a term used for manifestations of the desire to maintain the given ethnic character of society or particular social institutions. Generally, nativists see themselves as the real Americans and are xenophobic, or fearful and hateful of foreigners. Anglo-Saxon settlers wished to preserve their cultural legacy in the face of massive immigration that labor shortages forced them to tolerate. Perhaps one of the greatest instruments for Anglo-conformity has been the centralized system of public education that was developed in the United States. Immigrants were and are taught English language skills, as well as citizenship, and are thus Americanized. According to Gordon, other forms of Anglo-conformity assimilation include political movements by nativists to exclude "foreigners" from social institutions, favoring immigration only by people similar in background and culture to Anglo-Saxons, and basing social inclusion on the adoption of Anglo-Saxon culture by immigrants.

Park, who supported the melting pot theory, held that the melting pot would emerge through amalgamation—accomplished through intermarriage across lines of ethnicity. Intermarriage then becomes an important measure of the extent to which groups are merging into one homogeneous group. Studies of intermarriage reveal that ethnic groups, in particular, are marr ying across group lines, though not always across religious or racial lines. For example, intermarriage has increased substantially between Jews and non-Jews, although in-marriage is still strong for Italian Americans and Irish Americans. Intermarriage still tends to be culturally prohibited across racial lines, reflecting important differences between race and ethnicity that melting pot theorists tended to downplay in their analyses.

Assimilationist theorists generally have not distinguished race from ethnicity. They have not ignored the significant differences between the levels of assimilation of white ethnic groups and groups of other races; they explain them either as a product of the greater prejudice held against people who look different or as a product of the failure of nonwhite minorities to conform to and embrace the dominant culture. Assimilationist theorists view prejudice as the product of the differences that minority group members present to the dominant society. As group members acculturate, these differences diminish, and the people are accepted by the dominant society. They then no longer experience discrimination.

Sharon Elise

Further Reading

Baghramian, Maria, and Attracta Ingram, eds. *Pluralism: The Philosophy and Politics of Diversity*. New York: Routledge, 2000. Collection of scholarly discussions of issues relating to assimilation and pluralism.

Barone, Michael. *The New Americans: How the Melting Pot Can Work Again*. Washington, D.C.: Regner y, 2001. Reconsideration of the melting pot theory in the context of early twenty-first century America.

Benmayor, Rina, and Andor Skotnes, eds. *Migration and Identity*. New Brunswick, N.J.: Transaction, 2005.

Bischoff, Henry. *Immigration Issues*. Westport, Conn.: Greenwood Press, 2002. Collection of balanced discussions about the most important and most controversial issues relating to immigration, including assimilation.

Chen, Ping. *Assimilation of Immigrants and Their Adult Children: College Education, Cohabitation, and Work*. El Paso: LFB Scholarly Pub., 2010. A study of the assimilation of the children of immigrants across three domains: college education, marriage, and work.

Cook, Terrence E. *Separation, Assimilation, or Accommodation: Contrasting Ethnic Minority Policies*. Westport, Conn.: Praeger, 2003. Sociological study of the dynamics of power relationships among different ethnic groups.

Faulkner, Caroline L. *Economic Mobility and Cultural Assimilation among Children of Immigrants*. El Paso: LFB Scholarly Pub., 2011. A test of segmented assimilation theory, using data from children of immigrants and later generations, while also taking into account additional factors including the intergenerational nature of assimilation, life course stage, starting points, gender, and comparisons with later generations.

Feagin, Joe R., and Clairece Booher Feagin. *Racial and Ethnic Relations*. 4th ed. Englewood Cliffs, N.J.: Prentice-Hall, 1993. Introductory text in the sociology of race relations that examines sociological theories against the background of extensive case history of both white ethnic groups and ethnic groups of other races.

Foner, Nancy, Rubén G. Rumbaut, and Steven J. Gold, eds. *Immigration Research for a New Century: Multidisciplinary Perspectives*. New York: Russell Sage Foundation, 2000. Collection of papers on immigration from a conference held at Columbia

University in June, 1998. Among the many topics covered are race, government policy, sociological theories, naturalization, and undocumented workers.

Glazer, Nathan, and Daniel Patrick Moynihan. *Beyond the Melting Pot.* 2d ed. Cambridge, Mass.: MIT Press, 1970. Controversial book that presents studies of African Americans, Jews, Puerto Ricans, Italians, and Irish Americans in New York to re-examine the melting pot thesis.

Gordon, Milton. *Assimilation in American Life.* New York: Oxford University Press, 1964. Presents the author's theory of assimilation, with chapters devoted to the Anglo-conformity model and the melting pot model.

Houle, Michelle E., ed. *Immigration.* Farmington Hills, Mich.: Greenhaven Press/ Thomson/Gale, 2004. Collection of speeches on U.S. immigration policies by such historical figures as Presidents Woodrow Wilson, Franklin D. Roosevelt, John F. Kennedy, and Bill Clinton. Includes a section on assimilation.

Kramer, Eric Mark, ed. *The Emerging Monoculture: Assimilation and the "Model Minority."* Westport, Conn.: Praeger, 2003. Collection of essays on a variety of topics relating to cultural assimilation and the notion of "model minorities," with particular attention to immigrant communities in Japan and the United States.

Singh, Jaswinder, and Kalyani Gopal. *Americanization of New Immigrants: People Who Come to America and What They Need to Know.* Lanham, Md.: University Press of America, 2002. Sur vey of the cultural adjustments through which new immigrants to the United States must go.

Vermeulen, Hans, and Joel Perlmann, eds. *Immigrants, Schooling, and Social Mobility: Does Culture Make a Difference?* New York: St. Martin's Press, 2000. Collected papers from a 1996 conference on culture and worldwide immigration that was held in Amsterdam.

See also British as dominant group; Cultural pluralism; Ethnic enclaves; European immigrant literature; Generational acculturation; History of U.S. immigration; Melting pot; Migrant superordination; Model minorities.

AU PAIRS

Definition: Immigrants—usually young Europeans—who do domestic work for families in exchange for room and board and opportunities to learn English

Immigration issues: Illegal immigration; Labor; Women

Significance: Au pairs help satisfy working parents' need to find care for their children at a reasonable cost, while making it easier for young foreigners to come to the United States.

During the late twentieth century, many American families with parents who worked outside their homes felt a pressing need for household help. For the wealthy, such services were often provided by children's nurses or nannies; however, a less costly alternative was au pairs, usually young foreign visitors who were treated as family members. Au pairs performed light domestic duties, including child care, cleaning, cooking, and laundering, in exchange for room and board, weekly stipends, and opportunities to learn the language of the families with whom they stayed.

Prior to 1986 it was a fairly common practice to hire illegal immigrants as au pairs, but the Immigration Reform and Control Act of 1986 increased the penalties that could be imposed on employers of such workers. Au pairs have continued to play an important role in the growth and development of children under their care and in helping to foster and maintain family unity, while giving young foreigners opportunities to come to North America.

Alvin K. Benson

Further Reading

Bloodgood, Chandra. *Becoming an Au Pair: Working as a Live-in Nanny*. Port Orchard, Wash.: Windstorm Creative, 2005.

Miller, Cindy F., and Wendy J. Slossburg. *Au Pair American Style*. Bethesda, Md.: National Press, 1986.

See also Indentured servitude; Mail-order brides; Women immigrants.

BANGLADESHI IMMIGRANTS IN THE UNITED STATES

Definition: Immigrants to the United States from the South Asian Nation of Bangladesh

Immigration issues: Asian immigrants; demographics

Significance: People have been emigrating to the United States from the region that became Bangladesh for over 100 years before that country was formed as an independent state in 1971. Education is highly valued in the culture of Bangladesh and many immigrants are immigrants and professionals.

Because Bangladesh became an independent state only in 1971, it is not possible to speak of Bangladeshi immigrants to the U.S. before that time, although individuals from the subcontinent of India, including the region that became Bangladesh, had been immigrating to the U.S. for over a century before the creation of the country of Bangladesh. Immigration from British India, which included the region that became Bangladesh, was particularly hampered by the 1917 *Asiatic Barred Zone Act* and the *Immigration Act of 1924*.

Early immigrants to the U.S. from the geographical area that became Bangladesh mainly settle in cities on the West Coast, such as San Francisco, Washington and

Oregon; therefore, most of them were located on the West Coast. These early immigrants were disproportionately male, and many were political activists, but their numbers remained relatively small, and increases in the size of the community gradual.

However, as the British occupation of Bengal (a region including present-day Bangladesh and West Bengal) progressed in the nineteenth and early twentieth centuries, so did the number of Bangladeshi immigrants. At the beginning of the twentieth century, many young students migrated to the States as did merchants who settled primarily in San Francisco and New York. Many of these migrants moved to the U.S. to escape poverty in their home region, and to seek a better life for themselves and their families.

Many of the migrants were male, and wanted to establish a life in America, including marrying and starting a family. However, discriminatory laws that placed obstacles in the way of the immigration of women from Asia, as well anti-miscegenation laws that prohibited that non-Caucasian immigrants from marrying Caucasian females, made it difficult for male immigrants from Asia to establish families. These laws remained in force until the mid-twentieth century.

Immigrants statistics In 1946, the *Luce-Cellar Act* allowed Asian Indians and Filipinos to become naturalized citizens, but also established a quota of 100 immigrants per year from each country who were allowed to enter the United States. However, the greatest reform affecting immigration came in 1965, when the *Immigration and Nationality Act of 1965* abolished the system of quotas based on national origins which had been in force since 1921.

In the following decades, the increase in immigrants from Bangladesh was remarkable. In 1973, only 154 immigrants from Bangladesh were recorded in the United States, but two years later, this number increased to 200, and in 1976, over 600 Bangladeshi immigrants were noted in the U.S. By 1980, over 3,500 immigrants from Bangladesh were present in the United States, including over 200 who had gained US citizenship. Most of these immigrants settled in urban areas, particularly in New Jersey, New York, and California.

Between in the 1982 and 1992, United Stated legally recognized over 28,000 Bangladeshi immigrants. However, it is important to incorporate the fact that there is also a large number of undocumented immigrants as well. Recent estimations are that there are about 150,000 individuals who entered the States without necessary documents. Moreover, over 50,000 of them have settled in the area of New York since most of them were focused on finding urban environment where they could create a new home for themselves.

Assimilation of Bangladeshi immigrants Immigrants from Bangladesh tend to maintain their cultural identity even after migrating to another part of the world. Their primary reasons for emigrating include escaping poverty and finding a better life for themselves and their families. It is also worth nothing that most immigrants from Bangladesh are fairly recent arrivals to the U.S., as compared to other nationalities who have had a longer period of time to settle in to the country and establish their identity. Many immigrants from Bangladesh are Muslims, and they are sometimes mistakenly identified as Arabs due to their religion, although they are primarily Dravidian and Indo-Aryan.

Originally, Bangladesh society followed a kinship system with extended households and status, with individuals referred to by terms such as aunt and uncle or grandmother and grandfather based on age and status, but not necessarily the specific blood relationships those terms imply in the U.S., a custom that sometimes caused confusion in their new country. Many traditional customs have been retained by Bangladeshi immigrants, including that of arranged marriage. For instance, if a young man from Bangladesh immigrates to the U.S, it is most likely that he will marry a girl from the same background from Bangladesh. Very often, individuals fly back home in order to meet their future spouse and perform the ceremony. Later on, both of them go back to the States as a newly married couple. The future bride is chosen by groom's parents and there are several "qualifications" that she has to have. In most of the cases the bride is younger than the groom; however, their financial and educational status is the considered to be the same. Moreover, both of the individuals practice common religion. After the parents have decided that given two individuals are the right match, soon to be husband and bride are allowed to talk and exchange photos in order to get to know each other before the ceremony. Furthermore, the fact that the groom lives in the United States is an additional bonus for the bride, since she will legally be able to enter the country and find opportunities for a development.

Professional qualifications of Bangladeshi immigrants Even though the statistical rate of uneducated individuals in Bangladesh is considered high, education is extremely valued in this culture. The educational system of Bangladesh was established during the British occupation, and Bangladesh currently has over 600 colleges. Currently, many young graduates are looking for the American visa during their studies in order to experience new culture as well as to continue their education and development. Looking at the professional qualifications of some of the first immigrants, it is noticeable that one third of them were classified as professional and experienced within a specific field, while the rest of the two thirds had lower level of education and were white collar employees. By observing the one third of educated individuals, their desire for further development and success in the United States is present. However, the migration of these educated individuals caused a brain drain in their native country.

Employment Taking in consideration previously mentioned fact that at the beginning of the immigration process, only skilled Bangladesh individuals who were mostly students, were capable of entering the country; there is no surprised that their professional capabilities were high. Many work in professions such as architecture, medicine, economics and engineering. However, in the past couple of years online green card lottery became extremely popular and many people took that opportunity as their way to the States. This route allowed people with lower educational and professional qualifications to have an equal chance to immigrate, and many newcomers have lower level of education and less professional skills than previous generations of immigrants. Many more recent immigrants from Bangladesh work as business owners, for instance manning newsstands in New York City. However, many are able to move up from these small enterprises and establish other businesses such restaurants and groceries stores.

Politics and Bangladeshi immigrants   The American community of Bangladeshi immigrants consists of approximately 150,000 individuals. As an independent entity, they do not wield any particular political clout, although they have greater political strength when allied with other Muslim Americans. Most immigrants from Bangladesh are allied with the Democratic Party, and many maintain concern for their economic and social situations. In addition, they tend to stay in touch with families who are still residents of their native country, and often they travel back home on an annual basis in order to maintain contact with their native culture and also to provide their extended families with support.

Daniella Kleskovic

Further Reading

Baum, S., & Flores, S. M. (2011). Higher education and children in immigrant families. *The Future of Children*, 21(1), 171-193.: Detailed description of second generations, their culture and traditional customs; moreover, a definition of education and professional development.

Lansford, J. E., Deater-Deckard, K. D., Bornstein, M. H., & ebrary, I. (2007). *Immigrant families in contemporary society*. New York: Guilford Press.: Portrays the assimilation process of various immigrants, while decribing the process of melting pot and acceptanc of the new culture and its values.

Niyogi, S. (2011). Bengali-american fiction in immigrant identity work. *Cultural Sociology*, 5(2), 243-262. doi:10.1177/1749975510378208: Examins the level of professional skills and development of Bangladeshi immigrants considering their educational process throughout time

Millman, J. (1997). *The other americans: How immigrants renew our country, our economy, and our values*. New York, N.Y., U.S.A: Viking.: Analysis of immigrants impact on the Western society and its culture.

Reimers, D. M., & ebrary, I. (2005). *Other immigrants: The global origins of the american people*. New York: New York University Press.: Portrays the amount of immigrant and the statistical perspective of various newcomers, including those from Bangladesh.

See also   Asian Indian immigrants; Immigration Act of 1924; Immigration and Nationality Act of 1965.

BILINGUAL EDUCATION

Definition: Education systems that involve the use of minority and majority languages for teaching schoolchildren whose primary language is not English

Immigration issues: Education; Language

Significance: Bilingual education, which combines language learning with teaching culture in meeting the educational goals of different minority groups, has become a controversial and highly politicized subject that is closely tied to immigration issues.

In 2011-2012, English Language Learners (ELL) comprised 9.1 percent (4.4 million students) of the students enrolled in public schools, a substantial increase from the 9.7 percent (about 4.1 million students) in 2002-2003. However, ELL students were unequally distributed throughout the country, with far more attending schools in large cities (where 14.2 percent of the students were ELL), and relatively lower percentage in suburban schools (9.4 percent), towns (6.2 percent), and rural areas (3.9 percent). The state with the highest percentage of ELL enrollment was California, and seven of the eight states with the highest percent of ELL students were in the West, while the state with the lowest percentage was West Virginia (0.7 percent).

One way to address the needs of ELL students, who are not yet proficient in English, is through bilingual education, However, bilingual education in the United States has had a turbulent history. On June 2, 1998, voters in California ended the thirty-year-old tradition of bilingual education in California public schools by passing Proposition 227, which gives immigrant children only one year to learn English before they enroll in regular classes. The passage of this initiative and the courts' response to the new law (which almost immediately became subject to court litigation) were seen as a critical test of the U.S. commitment to bilingual education; California, after all, represented the largest school system in the nation with the largest student population enrolled in bilingual classes. If California eliminated bilingual education, many other school systems in other states were hoping either to impose severe restrictions on bilingual instruction or to eliminate it totally by passing an English-only policy. In contrast, the Coral Way School in Miami, which became the first successful bilingual school in the United States in 1963, continued to offer a strong commitment to bilingual education. Although support was eroding in other parts of the United States, Miami support for bilingualism was gaining strength. These examples best represent the roller-coaster history of bilingual education.

Over the years, bilingual education has experienced a series of ups and downs as various immigrant groups have arrived in the United States. One of bilingual education's most significant moments was the passage of the Bilingual Education Act in 1968. The act promoted bilingualism as a way to address the educational needs of children whose primary language is not English. In 1974, the Supreme Court ruled in Lau v. Nichols that a school district was required to provide bilingual education. Subsequent court decisions further highlighted the need for solid bilingual education programs as a means of providing equal access to education. However, many schools did not comply with this ruling. Bilingual education underwent a series of setbacks during the administrations of Ronald Reagan and George Bush. By 1990, the tide was turning in favor of the English-only campaigns. The passing of Proposition 227 in California was intended to deliver the most severe blow yet to bilingual education in the United States.

Maintenance vs. Transitional Bilingualism The main problem that bilingual education attempts to address is how to respond to the need of minority children to learn the majority language, English. According to the U.S. Department of Education, more than five million children in public schools have limited English proficiency (LEP). If these children cannot understand what the teacher is saying, they obviously cannot learn academic subjects such as math, science, and reading. If their study of academic subjects is postponed until they are proficient in English, their progress in these subjects is seriously hampered. If the "sink-or-swim" approach is used and children are taught entirely in English, their performance in academic subjects will deteriorate. Bilingual education solves this problem by teaching academic subjects to LEP children in their native languages while teaching them English. Furthermore, studies show that improving cognitive skills in native

Classroom made up primarily of European immigrants in a Boston school in 1909. The question of how best to teach English to immigrant children is an old one, but attempts at bilingual education have generally been made more often in schools in which a single second language predominates than in schools whose pupils speak many different languages. (Library of Congress)

115

languages further facilitates the learning of academic subjects. However, studies such as those by Jim Cummins show that at least four to six years of instruction in native languages (called Late-Exit to English) are needed before optimal results are registered both on proficiency in English and on other subjects in terms of achieving or exceeding national norms.

Most bilingual programs in the United States can best be characterized as transitional bilingual programs because they encourage the maintenance of the native language as a transition toward the learning of English. This process is called subtractive bilingualism. In the first stage, students are monolingual, learning only in their native language. Then students enter a stage of transitional bilingualism, in which they are functional in both their native language and English. Finally, they become monolingual in English.

Maintenance programs are additive bilingual programs that maintain the students' native language as they learn English. At the beginning, students are monolingual, speaking only their native language, then they begin to become bilingual, adding English to their native language. In the end, the students become fully functional in English yet maintain their native language.

Proponents of additive bilingual programs claim that maintenance of the student's native language is critical for the child's linguistic and cognitive growth, school performance, psychological security, ethnic and cultural identity, self-esteem, and many other positive personality and intellectual characteristics. The supporters of transitional bilingual programs claim that these programs avoid unnecessary linguistic duality and confusion, which sometimes cause children to be unable to function well in either language; improve students' performance in school; and minimize social, ethnic, and political divisions. The latter view derives support from long-term bilingual programs that have been found to lack effectiveness. For example, in 1997, only 6.7 percent of LEP children moved into regular classes in California as compared with 15 percent in 1982. Other states exhibit the same trend, pointing to the low success rate of long-term bilingual programs aimed at maintaining both languages. Advocates of maintenance bilingual programs attribute these low success rates to factors that are not intrinsic to bilingual education, such as a lack of funding, trained teachers, and federal/state commitment to bilingual education; poorly structured classrooms (grouping large numbers of students with diverse and unrelated native languages); and not enough adequate pedagogical material. According to Jim Lyons, executive director of the National Association for Bilingual Education, a large number of bilingual programs are "not worthy of the name." Programs such as the Eastman school model (pioneered by Steven Krashen and Cummins), which is widely used in Los Angeles schools, have shown themselves to be effective. The model is notable for its effective use of the results of basic research in recent theories of language acquisition and its long-term bilingual and bicultural basis.

Alternatives to Bilingual Education Alternatives to bilingual programs generally take the shape of programs to teach children English. Instead of simply

Milestones in Bilingual Education

Period/Year	Event	Impact
1694-mid nineteenth century	Vernacular education schools	German-, French-, and Spanish-speaking schools in the East and South are common in spite of periodical attempts to replace German/Spanish with English.
1828	U.S.-Cherokee Treaty	Treaty recognizes language rights of the Cherokee tribe.
1848	Treaty of Guadalupe Hidalgo	Language rights of the new Spanish-speaking citizens of the United States are "guaranteed"—but rarely respected.
1868	Indian Peace Commission	Group concludes: "Their [native Indian] barbarous dialects should be blotted out and the English language substituted."
1889	American Protective Association proposal	Declares that English should be the sole language of instruction in all public and private schools.
1898	Spanish-American War	English becomes the medium of instruction in the new colonies, Puerto Rico, and Hawaii.
1917	World War II— Cox's bill	This bill, the product of anti-German sentiment, bans German from Ohio's elementary schools.
1930's	Decline of non-English languages	Bilingual education is wiped out, except in parochial schools in rural areas of the Midwest.
1964	Civil Rights Act	Language provision of this act becomes the legal basis for bilingual education.
1968	Bilingual Education Act	This act addresses the needs of students with limited English skills, promoting bilingualism and encouraging ways to help speed up children's transition to English.
1974	Lau v. Nichols decision	Establishes the principle that children have a right to instruction in a language that they can understand.
1998	Proposition 227	California voters pass Proposition 227, which gives immigrant children only one year to learn English before entering regular classes. Other school systems in other states watch this development with interest.

placing LEP children in ordinary classes, children are placed in English as a second language (ESL) or English language development (ELD) programs. The ELD approach follows a strategy that encourages students to first comprehend and then speak English. The lessons are delivered in a low-anxiety, small-group, and language-conducive environment. Students' errors are tolerated, and the focus is on the acquisition of interactive communicative skills. The teacher provides what is termed "comprehensible input" (expressions in English that make sense to children) by means of roleplaying, modeling, and pictures. After about six to twelve months of ELD instruction, a shift is made to "sheltered English" instruction, which includes simplified language with common vocabulary, frequent paraphrasing, clarification, comprehension checks, and the use of simple sentence structures to teach context-rich subjects such as art and music.

Researchers Keith A. Baker and Adriana A. de Kanter suggest the structured immersion program modeled after the St. Lambert French immersion program in Quebec as an alternative to bilingual education programs. However, the success of the Canadian program is attributed to community and parent support; the fact that language-majority students (English speakers) were immersed into a minority language (French); and that the program goals included additive bilingualism. Similarly structured immersion programs failed in the United States because they involved language-minority children, neglected their native language, and were based on subtractive bilingualism.

As political battles are being waged all over the United States concerning bilingual education, the nation's schools are still being over whelmed by never-ending waves of LEP children. However, the question of how best to teach these children English remains unanswered.

Tej K. Bhatia

Further Reading

James Crawford's *Bilingual Education: History, Politics, Theory, and Practice* (Trenton, N.J.: Crane, 1989) and Kenji Hakuta's *Mirror of Language: The Debate on Bilingualism* (New York: Basic Books, 1986) are two classic studies on the various facets (historical, political, and educational) of bilingual education.

James Cummins's *Empowering Language Minority Students* (Sacramento: California Association for Bilingual Education, 1989) deals with educational and other issues pertaining to minorities at risk.

A detailed treatment of language acquisition is presented in two volumes, *Handbook of Second Language Acquisition* (1996) and *Handbook of Child Language Acquisition* (1998), edited by William C. Ritchie and Tej K. Bhatia (San Diego: Academic Press). These two volumes contain several chapters dealing with the phenomenon of bilingualism, bilingual language acquisition, and bilingual education.

For more recent information see *Harnessing Linguistic Variation to Improve Education*, ed. Androula Yiakoumetti (New York: Peter Lang, 2012) and *Studies in Bilingual Education*, ed. Daniel Madrid & Stephen Hughes (New York: Peter Lang, 2012).

See also Anglo-conformity; Asian American Legal Defense Fund; Bilingual Education Act of 1968; Cultural pluralism; English-only and official English movements; Generational acculturation; Lau v. Nichols; Proposition 227.

BILINGUAL EDUCATION ACT OF 1968

The Law: Federal legislation that authorized federal assistance to schoolchildren of limited English-speaking ability
Date: 1968

Immigration issues: Civil rights and liberties; Cuban immigrants; Education; Language; Laws and treaties

Significance: In creating the Bilingual Education Act, Congress attempted to bend the will of the many to meet the needs of the few and provide a chance for the children of all people to share in the American Dream.

Although hailed as the world's melting pot, for most of its history the United States has been a nation of one language and culture. This conformist ethic maintained that as immigrants came to the United States they should give up their native customs and languages and assimilate as quickly as possible into the Anglo-American mainstream. Underlying this drive toward conformity was the unwritten rule in both Anglo and immigrant communities that to succeed, immigrants must bend to American culture instead of expecting American culture to bend to them. Although ethnic neighborhoods and enclaves did exist and in some areas even flourished, the mainstream of American society was one of English-derived Anglo tradition.

Bilingual Education: Theory vs. Reality It was believed by many educators that the best way to prepare the children of immigrant parents for life in American culture was to immerse them in the English language and customs as quickly as possible. In this process of immersion, it was thought that the children who could learn would; those who could not were obviously of inferior mental abilities and therefore were not capable of obtaining the American Dream. This philosophy, besides confirming the prevailing notion of Anglo-American superiority, also fit well with the notion of social Darwinism popular during the late nineteenth century.

The reality for most immigrant children during the late nineteenth and early twentieth centuries was that they were much more likely to sink than swim. In 1908, 13 percent of immigrant children enrolled in New York City schools at age twelve were likely to go on to high school, as opposed to 32 percent of the native-born. This trend was mirrored across the country, as non-English-speaking immigrant children, not understanding the language of instruction, fell further and further behind their native-born classmates.

While English dominance remained the rule across most of the United States in the years preceding World War I, certain areas of the country were forced by circumstance to provide limited native-language instruction. These areas included parts of Louisiana, where French was the language of the majority of the population, and the Northeast and Midwest, where there were substantial German American populations. These areas, as well as several Native American reservations, provided instruction in the language of the non-English-speaking population. With the advent of World War I, an intense wave of nationalism swept the country. It reinforced the negative reaction of many Americans to the large wave of immigration that had begun during the 1890's. Among the first casualties of this increase in "nativism" were programs for instructing schoolchildren in any language other than English.

State Legislation   By 1925, thirty-seven states had passed laws requiring instruction in English, regardless of what was the dominant culture of the region. This trend continued into the 1950's. By the end of that decade, however, there were growing indications that more and more students with limited English proficiency were falling through the cracks of the educational system and thereby becoming trapped in language-induced poverty and despair. For those children who attempted to stay in school, the outcome was often little better than if they had dropped out. During this period, the preferred method of dealing with those who spoke little or no English was to tag them as mentally retarded or learning impaired. Once so characterized, these children were placed in remedial instruction programs, where they were constantly reminded of how different they were from their native, English-speaking classmates.

For those who managed to avoid being tagged as retarded, the most likely educational track was vocational, foreclosing access to higher-paying professional occupations. Demographics began to force a change in the attitudes of many public officials by the early 1960's. As immigrant populations began to flood into the schools of the South, districts were forced to consider alternative means of instruction. The first to do so was Coral Way, Florida.

After the Cuban revolution of 1959, waves of Cuban refugees entered South Florida. Responding to the demand for quality bilingual instruction, the Coral Way school district implemented the first state-supported program to instruct students in their native language, thereby easing their transition to English. Since there was no U.S. precedent for the school district to draw upon, it turned to the American schools in Ecuador and Guatemala, which sought to develop fluency in both languages. The bilingual program was implemented for the first three grades of Coral Way schools and provided all students, Anglo and Cuban, instruction in both Spanish and English. Given the middle to upper-class background of much of the early Cuban immigrant population, there was no need for a compensatory component to the program to care for general language or learning deficiencies. With the success of the Coral Way project, the precedent for state and local government involvement in language assistance was set.

The Federal Government Becomes Involved   By the mid-1960's, there were indications that the federal government was ready to become involved as well. As the national government began to investigate poverty and discrimination, several pieces of legislation were enacted that paved the way for the eventual adoption of the Bilingual Education Act. Of these, the two most important were the 1964 Civil Rights Act, specifically Title VI barring discrimination in education, and the Elementary and Secondary Education Act of 1965, which established the precedent for federal involvement in aid to impoverished and educationally deprived students.

In 1968, the Elementary and Secondary Education Act would be the vehicle by which Congress funded bilingual education. By the time the Ninetieth Congress opened in 1967, bilingual education had become a popular topic. More than thirty-five bills on the subject were introduced during the session, as many members of Congress became aware of the injustice of forcing immigrant children to struggle to learn lessons in what was to them a foreign language.

President Lyndon B. Johnson saw no need to amend the Elementary and Secondary Education Act of 1965 but nevertheless eventually signed the Bilingual Education Act. (U.S. White House)

Of these bills, Senate Bill 428, introduced by Ralph W. Yarborough, was typical. It proposed amending the Elementary and Secondary Education Act to create a new section, Title VII, providing bilingual education for those students speaking Spanish at birth or whose parents had originated in either Mexico or Puerto Rico. The Yarborough bill thus was not universal in scope but rather a concession to the Hispanic community—by far the nation's largest non-English-speaking minority and a group that was increasingly vocal. Mexican Americans were of growing importance in Yarborough's home state of Texas. Yarborough's approach was immediately attacked by both the White House and members of Congress. President Lyndon B. Johnson had portrayed the Elementary and Secondary Education Act as the hallmark of his war on poverty and saw no need to modify it.

Commissioner of Education Harold Howe II formalized this position when he proposed that instead of creating a new Title VII, additional monies could be appropriated under the existing Title I of the act. This section earmarked funds for language programs in economically impoverished areas, although it did not require schools to use languages other than English in order to receive funding. In Congress, numerous members rose in opposition to the bill's limitation of bilingual education to one ethnic group, no matter how potentially powerful that group might be. It was argued that targeting one group for aid would unconstitutionally deny equal protection to myriad other ethnic groups and language minorities scattered across the country.

Representative James H. Scheuer of New York proposed a compromise that would provide funding for bilingual education to school districts with substantial non-Englishspeaking populations residing in economically disadvantaged areas. To receive funding, districts would be required to provide instruction in a student's native tongue until the child could demonstrate competence in English. Although Senator Yarborough resisted the expansion of the act's scope, he relented when the White House gave its grudging approval. With this political hurdle cleared, President Johnson signed the amendments adding Title VII to the Elementary and Secondary Education Act on January 2, 1968.

Although no money was appropriated for 1968, $7.5 million was appropriated for 1969, enough to fund bilingual education for some twenty-seven thousand students. Accompanying the political battle over the number of language groups to be served was a deeper philosophical struggle concerning the goals of bilingual education. Congress knew that it had to do something, but the "how" of bilingual education was unclear. The Bilingual Education Act created a framework for federal aid to schools with students of limited English ability but said little about whether the goal of the program should be a rapid transition to instruction in English or a slower approach allowing the maintenance of the child's native language and customs.

The act's only significant stipulation was that to obtain federal aid a district had to use native languages in instruction. This lack of clarity contributed to the creation of an ideological conflict that lasted into the twenty-first century and brought the overall impact and effectiveness of bilingual education into question.

Impact of Event The federal government's commitment to bilingual education grew into the hundreds of millions of dollars by the mid-1970's. Reauthorizations in 1972 and 1974 broadened the scope of the legislation and provided additional programs. These efforts were aided by both the federal courts and the Office of Civil Rights (then a part of the Department of Health, Education and Welfare).

***Lau v. Nichols* and Anglo Backlash** In 1974, the Supreme Court ruled in Lau v. Nichols that school districts with a substantial number of non-English-speaking students must take steps to overcome language difficulties. This provided the Office of Civil Rights with the backing needed to force recalcitrant school districts to initiate bilingual education plans. These Lau plans greatly expanded the number of native-language instructional programs available across the country. They also set standards for when students qualified for inclusion in a program and when they could be allowed (or forced) to exit. During this period, test scores repeatedly showed that students exiting from well-designed and well-implemented programs consistently performed at or above grade level and thus were on a par with their native English-speaking classmates.

By the 1980's, the ambiguities in the goals of bilingual education had begun to engender resentment in parts of the Anglo population. Some believed that the aim of bilingual education was not to speed immigrants into the mainstream but rather to maintain their culture through state-sponsored ethnic programs. Fueling this attack were several studies showing that some bilingual programs were allowing students to remain in bilingual classes longer than the three-year maximum and were not teaching them sufficient English to function in mainstream classrooms. With the election of Ronald Reagan to the presidency, the federal government began to retreat from aggressively promoting native-language instruction and instead encouraged districts to choose their own methods to develop capability in English.

Federal Reauthorization The 1984 reauthorization for the first time saw federal monies available for methods of instruction that did not utilize a student's native tongue but rather allowed for English immersion or submersion. Although this funding was limited in 1984, it was expanded in 1988. This change was amplified by a major retreat on the part of the Office of Civil Rights in its enforcement of Lau remedies. Under the Reagan administration, a school district was one-ninth as likely to be reviewed by the Office of Civil Rights as under the administrations of either Gerald Ford or Jimmy Carter. This change in government philosophy, while not signaling the end of bilingual education, did have a significant impact.

By the mid-1980's, several studies, including an influential one by the General Accounting Office, had shown that while there were problems in the implementation of some programs, the philosophy of instruction in students' native languages during the transition to English not only worked but allowed students to obtain grade-level standing much more quickly than English-only programs. Correspondingly, as the English-dominant approach became the program of choice for many districts, the performance of limitedEnglish students once again declined. As with any attempt to expand the rights of the few, the Bilingual Education Act was politically charged and buffeted by ideological storms. What was indisputable, however, was that the leap of faith that Congress undertook in 1968 was aimed at the future—a future in which the dominant Anglo-American culture would be forced to adapt to an increasingly diverse population.

Christopher H. Efird

Further Reading

August, Diane, and Eugene E. Garcia. *Minority Education in the United States: Research, Policy, and Practice*. Springfield, Ill.: Charles C Thomas, 1988. A fairly analytical work, this book provides a thorough discussion of the theoretical groundings of bilingual education as well as federal and state attempts to implement these programs. Well-indexed and referenced. Includes a particularly well-written chapter on specific types of bilingual education programs.

Crawford, James. *Bilingual Education: History, Politics, Theory, and Practice*. Trenton, N.J.: Crane Publishing, 1989. Written from a lay perspective, this book presents a good summary of the competing educational and political philosophies that characterize the debate over bilingual education. Although somewhat unsophisticated, the book touches on all aspects of bilingual education: political, practical, and philosophical.

Grant, Joseph H., and Ross Goldsmith. *Bilingual Education and Federal Law: An Overview*. Austin, Tex.: Dissemination and Assessment Center for Bilingual Education, 1979. As its name implies, this book summarizes and comments on the various federal laws pertaining to bilingual education. A particular strength is the author's excellent weaving together of the often conflicting priorities of the Congress, the president, and the courts to show how bilingual education has been affected.

Kenner, Charmian. *Becoming Biliterate: Young Children Learning Different Writing Systems*. Sterling, Va.: Trentham Books, 2004. Study of the technical aspects of bilingual education.

Leibowitz, Arnold H. *The Bilingual Education Act: A Legislative Analysis*. Rosslyn, Va.: InterAmerica Research Associates, National Clearing House for Bilingual Education, 1980. Provides a compact history both of the original 1968 amendments to the Elementary and Secondary Education Act that created the Title VII bilingual provisions and of the 1974 reauthorization. The discussions of the statutory provisions of each are thorough, but there is little discussion of impacts.

Osborn, Terry A., ed. *Language and Cultural Diversity in U.S. Schools: Democratic Principles in Action*. Westport, Conn.: Praeger, 2005. Consideration of bilingualism in the context of the role of multiculturalism and education.

Porter, Rosalie Pedalino. *Forked Tongue: The Politics of Bilingual Education*. New York: Basic Books, 1990. A fascinating presentation of the arguments opposed to bilingual education. Using both theoretical discussions and historical examples drawn from twenty years of bilingual practice, the author builds the argument that bilingual education has failed both the students it is supposed to help and the society that is paying for it.

Sandoval-Martinez, Steven. *How Much Bilingual Education? Educational vs. Legislative Considerations*. Los Alamitos, Calif.: National Center for Bilingual Research, 1984. A very short work, this paper is nevertheless useful for its discussion of the implications of legislative standards on bilingual program exit criteria. In looking at these criteria, the author demonstrates how standardized exit requirements are incongruent with the educational needs of most students.

Skutnabb-Kangas, Tove. "Multilingualism and the Education of Minority Students." In *Minority Education: From Shame to Struggle*, edited by T. SkutnabbKangas and J. Cummins. Philadelphia: Multilingual Matters, 1988. In keeping with the theme of the book, this chapter looks beyond the minority education problems in the United States and takes a more global perspective. The author investigates the impact that a multilingual population has on a society and the demands this imposes on the educational system to integrate language minorities into the mainstream.

Stein, Colman Brez, Jr. *Sink or Swim: The Politics of Bilingual Education*. New York: Praeger, 1986. Provides a good history of bilingual education policy from its modern inception in Coral Way, Florida, through the 1984 reauthorization. Contains a substantial discussion of state initiatives and how they worked to support or undermine federal programs.

Wiley, Terrence G. *Literacy and Language Diversity in the United States*. 2d ed. Washington, D.C.: Center for Applied Linguistics, 2005. Comprehensive study of language and literacy in American education.

See also Bilingual education; English-only and official English movements; *Lau v. Nichols*; Proposition 227.

BORDER PATROL, U.S.

Identification: Units of the federal agency that oversee the coastal and land boundaries of the United States
Date: Established in May, 1924
Place: Washington, D.C.

Immigration issues: Border control; Illegal immigration; Latino immigrants; Law enforcement; Mexican immigrants

Significance: Congress established the U.S. Border Patrol to prevent undocumented immigrants from Latin America and Canada from entering the United States. As a federal law-enforcement body under the aegis of the Department of Homeland Security since 2003, the U.S. Customs and Border Protection agency is responsible for controlling the entry of both people and substances into the United States.

The Customs and Border Protection (CBP) is one of the busiest law-enforcement agencies in the United States,. It is also one of the larger, and also one of the largest, including 21,391 border patrol agens for fiscal year 2013, a substantial increase from 2003, when CBP had 10,717 agents. On March 1, 2003, the Department of Homeland Security unified border personnel working in the immigration, customs, agriculture, and border patrol divisions under one agency. Formerly known as the U.S. Border Patrol under the Immigration and Naturalization Service, the border patrol was originally founded in 1924 after Congress passed strict limitations on legal immigration. With only several hundred mounted agents on horseback, there were challenges in patrolling all the areas between inspection stations in the United States. Over the next eighty years, the border patrols evolved into a technologically advanced and increasingly sophisticated workforce with nearly ten thousand uniformed agents.

Twenty-First Century Missions During the early twenty-first century, the CBP still maintained its primary mission to prevent the illegal entry of goods and immigrants into the United States. This duty, undertaken in cooperation with numerous other local and state law-enforcement agencies across the United States, resulted in approximately twelve million arrests between 1994 and 2004. This monumental task requires scrutiny from the land, air, and sea of more than 6,000 miles of international boundaries with Canada and Mexico and another 2,000 miles of coastal waters. Agents from twentyone sectors across the United States work in all weather conditions and terrains, twenty-four hours a day, 365 days a year.

Before 1924, a force of fewer than forty mounted inspectors rode the borders looking for Chinese migrants attempting to enter the country in violation of the 1882 Chinese Exclusion Act. Mexican workers proved so valuable to the economy of the American Southwest that little effort was made to prevent them from crossing the Rio Grande to work for cotton and sugar beet growers and as agricultural laborers. A literacy test passed in 1917 during World War I made it more difficult for farmhands to enter the United States, but the test could be avoided easily by sneaking into the country at night. Enforcement was lax because of protests from growers and farmers who depended on a cheap labor supply for their economic livelihood.

Dealing with Illegal Immigration During the early 1920's, illegal immigration from Mexico far exceeded the average of fifty thousand legitimate immigrants per year. In 1921, Congress adopted a restrictive immigration policy based on a

A small fence separates densely populated Tijuana, Mexico, right, from the United States in the Border Patrol's San Diego Sector in March 2007. Construction was underway at the time to extend a secondary fence over the top of this hill that would stretch to the Pacific Ocean. (U.S. Army/Gordon Hyde)

national quota system. Supporters argued for including the peoples of the Western Hemisphere in the limitations but did not succeed because of opposition from the State Department and agricultural interests in Texas, Arizona, and California. Secretary of State Charles Evans Hughes told Congress that limiting Latin American immigration would harm attempts to improve diplomatic relations with that part of the world, while farmers and growers claimed that a steady supply of migrants from south of the border was necessary to keep them in business. For these reasons, both the Senate and the House agreed to put no restrictions on New World peoples.

When Congress passed a law in 1924 establishing a national origins system for immigrants, it again excluded people from the Western Hemisphere. A proposal to include Latin Americans and Canadians under this more restrictive policy failed by large margins in the House and Senate. Hughes once again testified in opposition to the amendment and repeated his statement that the foreign policy of the United States demanded favorable treatment of migrants from Western nations.

A new element entered this debate in Congress, however, as several congresspeople, led by Representative John Box of Texas, emphasized what they perceived as the racial and cultural inferiority of the Mexican population. The discussion in Congress focused on Mexicans because they made up the largest portion of immigrants from the New World. Almost 100,000 had crossed the border legally in 1924. Thousands more had entered illegally to escape paying the eighteen-dollar visa fee required of all immigrants under the new law. The flow of Central and South Americans coming into the country numbered fewer than five thousand that year and was not perceived as a threat.

Opponents of Immigration Advocates of ending the flows of both legal and illegal immigration argued that Mexicans were taking away American jobs and working for star vation wages. The American Federation of Labor, under its new president, William Green, and the American Legion were major proponents of this viewpoint. "Scientific racists," who believed that white America was disappearing, argued about the dangers of "colored blood" polluting America and contaminating its way of life. Most Mexicans had Indian blood in them.

According to racial theorists of the time, Indians were inferior to Nordic types in intelligence and physical ability. The 1924 law was aimed at keeping the inferior races of southern and eastern Europe out of the country. It made no sense, therefore, to allow free access to inferiors from other parts of the world. These arguments had been successful in winning approval of the 1921 quota system, whereby each nationality group in the United States was limited in immigration each year to 3 percent of its total number in the United States according to the 1910 census. The 1924 law reduced the total to 2 percent of the population according to the census base of 1890. Congress decided to remove Latin America and Canada from these restrictions principally because of the belief that cheap Mexican labor was necessary to keep American farmers prosperous.

Labor unions had frequently challenged that view. During the 1921-1922 depression in the United States, they began a campaign to include Latin Americans under the quota system. They had a strong ally in Secretary of Labor James J.

Davis, a former union president. He ordered all unemployed Mexicans to leave the United States in 1922. Resentment and violence mounted because of the economic hard times, and in some Texas towns starving Mexicans were physically expelled. When the short depression ended and job opportunities opened, agricultural interests petitioned Congress to reopen the borders. Mexican labor was too valuable to the economy to exclude completely, because Mexicans did the jobs Americans simply would not do, and for wages Americans would not accept. The Spanish-speaking aliens would not become permanent residents, Congress was reassured, and they offered no political threat since the poll tax still in effect in Texas and other southern states prevented them from voting. The sugar beet growers and cotton farmers tried to appease the labor unions by arguing that the aliens were unskilled laborers and therefore were not a threat to American workers.

The same reasoning kept Canadians from inclusion in the new immigration system. These immigrants were mostly from French-speaking Quebec and worked in New England textile mills for very low wages. Most of the congressional debate centered on Mexicans, and there was little discussion of immigration from the north. Congress's major fear seemed to be that large numbers of "peons" from south of the border were entering the United States illegally and that they posed a threat to American values and customs because they were Roman Catholics and spoke a foreign language. Something had to be done to stop that flood, but the economic interests of southwestern farmers would also have to be protected. If, for foreign policy and economic reasons, Latin Americans could not be in the quota system, the reasoning went, perhaps the borders of the United States could be secured from illegal immigration by tighter controls. Smuggling of impoverished workers from south of the border was a major problem, and no agency of the American government existed to control it.

Birth of the Border Patrol Concern over the flow of laborers from the south led to the establishment of the U.S. Border Patrol on May 8, 1924. Congressman Claude Hudspeth of Texas, who owned a large farm in East Texas but who was not dependent on Mexican labor, proposed its creation and got Congress to provide $1 million for this new branch of the Bureau of Immigration and Naturalization in the Department of Labor. The Border Patrol had 450 officers, whose main job was to ride the Mexican border on horseback seeking out smugglers and the hiding places of illegal aliens. Opposition to the Border Patrol proved to be considerable. Ranchers and farmers protested and interfered with the arrests of their laborers. Patrol officers were told to expel any alien who could not prove that he or she had paid the visa fee.

The growers bitterly assailed the increasingly difficult requirements for legal immigration. The 1924 law mandated not only a ten-dollar visa fee, which had to be paid to an American consul in the nation of origin, but also a sixdollar head tax for each applicant. Few Mexicans could afford these fees because their average wage was twelve cents for a ten-hour day in their homeland. These fees thus encouraged illegal entry and the smuggling of laborers. For a small sum paid to smugglers, Mexican peasants could avoid the fees and the literacy test and easily find jobs paying $1.25 a day in Texas, Arizona, and California. In its first year of operation, the small Border Patrol staff reported turning back 15,000 aliens seeking illegal entry, although an estimated 100,000 farmworkers successfully evaded the border guards. For that reason, in 1926 Congress doubled the size of the Border Patrol and made it a permanent part of the Bureau of Immigration and Naturalization.

Impact of Event During its first three years of operation, the Border Patrol turned back an annual average of fifteen thousand Mexicans seeking illegal entry. It did not have enough personnel to end all illegal entr y, and Mexican workers were too valuable to the economy of the Southwest to eliminate completely. Ranchers and farmers who benefited greatly by using Mexican labor continued to oppose the picking up and deporting of field hands who preferred to deal with smugglers rather than paying the visa fee and head tax.

In 1926, the Immigration Service backed away from strict enforcement of the law and entered into a "gentlemen's agreement" with agricultural interests in California and Texas. This called for registration of all Mexican workers in the states. They would each receive an identification card that allowed them to work, in exchange for an eighteen-dollar fee payable at three dollars per week. When Congressman John Box heard about "immigration on the installment plan," he was outraged and called for an end to this "outlaw's agreement." He denounced Mexicans as racially inferior to white Europeans, since they were mainly Indian, and warned that their illegal influx had been so large that they threatened to reverse the results of the Mexican War of 1846-1848. After that conflict, the United States had acquired California, Arizona, and much of the Southwest, but now, according to Box, "blood-thirsty, ignorant" bandits from Mexico were becoming the largest population in those areas and retaking them.

Because of such fears, Congress, in 1929, voted to double the size of the Border Patrol and demanded a crackdown on illegal entry. Congress was also responding to union demands for increased border security. Steel corporations had recently begun to recruit Mexicans from the Southwest to work in places such as Chicago and Gar y, Indiana, where they would be paid less than Anglo-Americans. As European labor became more restricted because of the national origins requirement, Mexico and Latin America were seen by northern industrialists as new sources of cheap labor, much to the annoyance of labor unions. For many impoverished agricultural workers, the economic rewards seemed worth the risk. Many Mexicans moved north to Illinois, Michigan, and Ohio. In response, the Texas legislature passed a law charging a $1,000 fee for labor recruiters before they could begin operating in the state. The growers and farmers did not want all their cheap labor to move north.

A new law, suggested by the State Department, said that anyone caught entering the United States after having been deported previously would be charged with a felony and be liable for up to two years of imprisonment. This legislation greatly decreased illegal entry into North America. The Border Patrol was also authorized to cover the borders of Florida and Canada. The gentlemen's agreement was ended, and the full eighteen-dollar fee was again required. These measures, plus the economic insecurity brought about by the worldwide depression beginning in 1929, temporarily ended the conflict over illegal immigration from Mexico and other nations of the Western Hemisphere. The issue would not reemerge as an important problem until after World War II. The most important impact of the creation of the Border Patrol was to make illegal entry into the United States much more difficult than it ever had been before. A government agency now had the authority to arrest and deport illegal aliens.

Leslie V. Tischauser
Updated by the editors

Further Reading

Bischoff, Henry. *Immigration Issues.* Westport, Conn.: Greenwood Press, 2002. Collection of balanced discussions about the most important and most controversial issues relating to immigration. Among the specific subjects covered is the enforcement of laws regulating undocumented workers.

Crosthwaite, Luis Humberto, John William Byrd, and Bobby Byrd, eds. *Puro Border: Dispatches, Snapshots and Graffiti from La Frontera.* El Paso, Tex.: Cinco Puntos Press, 2003. This collage of illustrations and writings attempts to portray the various cultural and geographical considerations of those people who live on the line. Considers how the destitute of Mexico are ignored and forgotten.

Cull, Nicholas J., and David Carrasco, eds. *Alambrista and the U.S.-Mexico Border: Film, Music, and Stories of Undocumented Immigrants.* Albuquerque: University of New Mexico Press, 2004. Collection of essays on dramatic works, films, and music about Mexicans who cross the border illegally into the United States.

Hunter, Miranda. *Latino Americans and Immigration Laws: Crossing the Border.* Philadelphia: Mason Crest, 2006. Up-to-date study of Latino immigration that considers the changing role of the Border Patrol in the twenty-first century.

Krauss, Erich. *On the Line: Inside the U.S. Border Patrol.* New York: Kensington, 2004. A former border patrol agent details the five-month basic training regimen all agents must undergo and follows them into the field to give the reader a sense of how smugglers and drug dealers challenge these agents who work on the line every day.

LeMay, Michael C., and Elliott Robert Barkan, eds. *U.S. Immigration and Naturalization Laws and Issues: A Documentary History.* Westport, Conn.: Greenwood Press, 1999. History of U.S. immigration laws supported by extensive extracts from documents.

Moore, Alvin Edward. *Border Patrol.* Santa Fe, N.Mex.: Sunstone Press, 1991. Based on actual incidents, this fictional work describes a world of smugglers and illegal aliens and the dangerous nature of working on the U.S./ Mexico border.

Nevin, Joseph. *Operation Gatekeeper: The Rise of the "Illegal Alien" and the Making of the U.S.-Mexico Boundary.* New York: Routledge, 2002. Details the federal government's Operation Gatekeeper, which in the 1990's targeted the San Diego-Tijuana border in efforts to stop illegal immigration. The author argues that this assault on immigration did not effectively reduce unauthorized immigration and served to inflame anti-Hispanic racism in the United States.

Ngai, Mae M. *Impossible Subjects: Illegal Aliens and the Making of Modern America.* Princeton, N.J.: Princeton University Press, 2004. Scholarly study of social and legal issues relating to illegal aliens in the United States during the twenty-first century.

Perkins, Clifford A. *Border Patrol: With the U.S. Immigration Service on the Mexican Boundary, 1910-1954.* El Paso: Texas Western Press, 1978. The recollections and adventures of a former district officer. Discusses the founding, staffing, and organization of the Border Patrol and the contributions of some of its early members. Useful information on the education, attitudes, and responsibilities of officers. Told from the point of view of an officer who supported the mission of the Border Patrol. Many anecdotes concerning the methods used by enforcement officers. Has little to say in favor of open borders and free migration.

Shapira, Harel. *Waiting for José: The Minutemen's Pursuit of America.* Princeton: Princeton University Press, 2013. A study of the Minutemen, a group of individuals who, without official authority, have taken it on themselves to patrol the border between the U.S. and Mexico.

Staeger, Rob. *Deported Aliens.* Philadelphia: Mason Crest, 2004. Up-to-date analysis of the treatment of undocumented immigrants in the United States since the 1960's, with particular attention to issues relating to deportation.

Urrea, Luis Alberto. *The Devil's Highway: A True Story.* Boston: Little, Brown, 2004. Graphic, true story describes the harrowing journey of twenty-six Mexican men who attempted to enter the Arizona desert. The author argues that U.S. immigration policies are inhumane.

Urrea, Luis Alberto, and John Lueders-Booth. *Across the Wire: Life and Hard Times on the Mexican Border.* New York: Doubleday, 1992. The author describes his interactions with Mexicans who live on the border and the deplorable living conditions that many of them suffer.

Weber, Leanne. *Policing Non-Citizens.* Milton Park, Abingdon, Oxon: Routledge, 2013. A study of a newly-emerging form of policing, that of detecting non-citizens who are in the country unlawfully, with considerations for what this new responsibility means for criminology and policing

Williams, Mary E., ed. *Immigration: Opposing Viewpoints.* San Diego: Greenhaven Press, 2004. Various social, political, and legal viewpoints are given by experts and observers familiar with immigration into the United States.

See also Florida illegal-immigrant suit; Illegal aliens; Immigration and Naturalization Service; Immigration law; Justice and immigration; Operation Wetback.

BRACERO PROGRAM

Identification: U.S.-Mexico government program undertaken to facilitate the importation of Mexican farmworkers into the United States
Date: 1942-1964

Immigration issues: Border control; Economics; Illegal immigration; Labor; Latino immigrants; Mexican immigrants

Significance: The shortage of farm labor caused by U.S. entry into World War II prompted creation of the bracero program, but growing dependence of American farms on Mexican labor kept the program going nearly two decades after the war ended.

U.S. entry into World War II at the end of 1941 created an agricultural labor shortage in the United States. As early as 1942, American farmers were complaining about labor shortages farms faced and demanding that workers be brought in to help plant, harvest, and distribute their agricultural products. In response, the U.S. and Mexican governments created the bracero program, also known as the Mexican Farm Labor Program (MFLP). The program contained many provisions designed to protect both the farmers and the braceros (a term that comes from the Spanish word brazos, meaning "arms" or "helping arms").

Because many Mexicans were afraid of being forced into the U.S. military upon arrival in the country because of the war, one provision was that no Mexican contract workers could be sent to fight in the U.S. military. Another provision was that Mexican laborers were not to be subjected to discriminatory acts of any kind. The United States agreed that the contract laborers' round-trip transportation expenses from Mexico would be paid and adequate living arrangements would be provided for them in the United States. There was also a provision that the braceros would not displace local workers or lower their wages.

The braceros were to be employed only in the agricultural realm and on the basis of contractual agreements—written in English and Spanish—between the braceros

Housing for Mexican migrant workers in Edcouch, Texas. (Library of Congress)

and their employers. The farmers agreed to pay the braceros wages equal to those prevailing in the area of employment, and no less than thirty cents an hour, for a minimum of three-quarters of the duration of the contract. The braceros also were granted the right to organize. Ten percent of the braceros' earnings were to be deducted and deposited in savings funds, payable upon their return to Mexico. Finally, the braceros were to be given sanitary housing. In 1943, braceros would be granted the right to have a Mexican consul and Mexican labor inspectors intervene in disputes on their behalf. With these provisions and guidelines intact, on September 29, 1942, the first fifteen hundred braceros were transported to California by train.

Problems Arise   Braceros encountered a variety of problems in the United States. Although their contracts were explained to them before they signed them, many braceros did not have a basic understanding of the contracts' terms and conditions. Workers often understood little beyond the fact that they were going to work in the United States. Despite the difficulties of moving from one country to another, when the braceros arrived in the United States, they were not given time to orient themselves to their new surroundings but were required to report for work the day after their arrival.

Farmers were skeptical of the MFLP because they viewed it as infringing on their own welfare and traditional independence. The farmers wanted the federal government to provide workers, but they wanted it to be done on their own terms. However, the labor shortage crisis was so severe that the farmers consented to the government's program. Once the braceros were consigned to their employers, the binational agreement between Mexico and the United States was followed weakly, if at all, by the farmers. The farmers, who had much more power and control than the Mexican labor inspectors did, could basically do as they pleased with the workers and their contracts.

For example, as contract laborers, the bracero workers were expected to adapt to and stay on the job under adverse conditions from which local workers would have turned away. The bracero workforce was used for the heaviest and worst-paid jobs. This meant that the bulk of the imported workforce was used largely in the production and harvesting of crops that required large numbers of temporary, seasonal laborers for physically demanding stoop work. The braceros were considered a blessing, because local workers refused to do stoop labor. The farmers used the argument that Mexicans were better suited for back-bending labor than were the local workers to justify their claim that they could not continue farming without the braceros. Braceros frequently were treated as animals. Despite the ill treatment and harsh conditions, many braceros continued to migrate in order to find work and much needed money.

Dependency Develops   By entering into an agreement with Mexican workers and the federal government, agriculture began a dependency on braceros that continued after World War II had ended. Within a year of the program's inception, braceros had in many areas become a mainstay in farm production.

After World War II ended in 1945, the Migratory Labor Agreement was signed with Mexico to continue encouraging the seasonal importation of farmworkers.

Between 1948 and 1964, some 4.5 million Mexicans were brought to the United States for temporary work. Braceros were expected to return to Mexico at the end of their labor contract, but often they stayed. Although the United States government sanctioned this importation of Mexican workers, it shunned the importation of workers during times of economic difficulties. During the 1953-1954 recession, the government mounted a campaign called Operation Wetback to deport illegal entrants and braceros who had remained in the country illegally. Deportations numbered in excess of 1.1 million. As immigration officials searched out illegal workers, persons from Central and South America, as well as native-born U.S. citizens of Central or South American descent, found themselves vulnerable to this search. Protestations of the violation of their rights occurred, but to little effect.

Although the jobs reserved for the braceros were generally despised, they were nevertheless essential first links in the robust wartime food production chain. In this capacity, the Mexican workers made a vital and measurable contribution to the total war effort.

Kristine Kleptach Jamieson

Further Reading

Copp, Nelson Gage. *"Wetbacks" and Braceros: Mexican Migrant Laborers and American Immigration Policy, 1930-1960*. San Francisco: R and E Research Associates, 1971. Provides detailed accounts of emigration and immigration policies affecting migrant agricultural workers from Mexico.

Craig, Richard B. *The Bracero Program: Interest Groups and Foreign Policy*. Austin: University of Texas Press, 1971. Discusses the political agreement between the United States and Mexico regarding migrant laborers.

Galarza, Ernesto. *Merchants of Labor: The Mexican Bracero Story*. Santa Barbara, Calif.: McNally & Loftin West, 1978. Discusses the treatment of braceros and the effects of the bracero program in California.

Gamboa, Erasmo. *Mexican Labor and World War II: Braceros in the Pacific Northwest, 1942-1947*. Austin: University of Texas Press, 1990. A detailed history of the life, conditions, and social policy affecting migrant workers from Mexico in the United States.

Gonzalez, Gilbert G. *Guest Workers or Colonized Labor? Mexican Labor Migration to the United States*. Boulder, Colo.: Paradigm, 2005. Study of the state of Mexican labor immigration to the United States in the early twenty-first century.

Mitchell, Don. *They Saved the Crops: Labor, Landscape, and the Struggle over Industrial Farming in Bracero-Era California*. Athens, GA: University of Georgia Press, 2012. An analysis of the economic and social framework that created the bracero program and committed the U.S. to a system of agricultural production which remains active today.

Ngai, Mae M. *Impossible Subjects: Illegal Aliens and the Making of Modern America*. Princeton, N.J.: Princeton University Press, 2004. General history of the problem of illegal immigration in the United States that includes a chapter covering Operation Wetback and the bracero program.

Overmyer-Velasquez, Mark, ed. *Beyond la Frontera: The History of Mexico-U.S.*

Migration. New York: Oxford University Press, 2011. Essays about emigration from Mexico to the U.S in the 19th and 20th century, including the bracero program.

Valdes, Dennis Nodin. Al Norte: *Agricultural Workers in the Great Lakes Region, 1917-1970.* Austin: University of Texas Press, 1991. An in-depth discussion of the Mexican migration to and settlement in the upper Midwest regions.

See also Chicano movement; Farmworkers' union; Immigration Reform and Control Act of 1986; Mexican deportations during the Depression; Operation Wetback; Undocumented workers.

BRAIN DRAIN

The Law: The term "brain drain" was originally coined by the Royal Society of London. It was meant to describe the emigration of scientists and technologists to North America from post-war Europe. Yet it is also reported that the term was first used in the United Kingdom to describe the influx of Indian scientists and engineers. Naturally, the benefitting country is on the receiving end of the converse phenomenon, "brain gain," resulting in a large-scale immigration of technically qualified persons to their country. Although originally meant for technology workers leaving a country, the meaning has since been broadened by Merriam-Webster Dictionary into, "the departure of educated or professional people from one country, economic sector, or field for another, usually for better pay or living conditions."

Date: This phenomenon, often referred to as the "brain drain," was noticed as early as the 1960s

Immigration Issues: Most developing countries suffer brain drain because emigrant intellectuals refuse to return to their homeland.

A brain drain is effectively when an exceptional number of human resources emigrate from one country. Although these industry experts are leaving their homelands for better career options, it is important to note that the knowledge and wealth generated is twofold, both for the country of origin and the host country. A country of origin can benefit in two ways. One way is that when they export their skilled and highly educated workforce, they benefit by the substantial increase in the labor power they possess. The other way is based on the fact that when skilled migrants leave their homeland, an increased demand for higher level education amongst the population occurs.

Arguably benefitting the skilled individual more than society, brain drain is beneficial to a country on some level despite its inherent flaws. The problems that arise usually involve the loss of human capital in the form of a skilled labor force, which is vital to societal development and the country as a whole.

Significance: Skilled workers, especially in the medical, technical, and educational fields, are consistently being wooed by developed countries to migrate. In fact, in the case of healthcare, these employees are often critical to the survival of those in their countries of origin. Yet, rather selfishly, the developed countries don't necessarily give consideration to the impact on the originating countries who not only trained them in the first place, but depend on them for some level of survival.

Background: Brain Drain is a casual term that refers to the economics term "Human Capital Flight." Both refer to the somewhat controversial concept of emigration of well-educated, professional individuals who relocate to a developed country where they can earn better pay and live in better conditions than their home country.

One example of brain drain's impact is the Caribbean, which has one of the highest emigration rates globally. The International Monetary Fund (IMF) working paper suggests evidence of a brain-drain from the Caribbean, showcasing concerns that the region is losing more to emigration than it is gaining from remittances. Even though this region is the largest recipient of cash sent home from its nationals abroad, it has among the highest emigration rates in the world. Yet, according to the IMF working paper, remittances accounted for an average of only thirteen percent of the region's GDP in 2002. Regardless, they found that "emigration loss and external effects" and government expenditure on educating the migrants before they leave in the first place, outweighs the average recorded remittances for the Caribbean region. In other words, their residents are using the education system allotted to them to seek employment in other countries, leaving little to no benefit to their home country. The paper also states that the migration rate is high for the highly-skilled workers who have completed some form of tertiary education.

Even within the United States, there are examples of Brain Drain:

- Organizational: The flight of highly trained employees from large corporations that occurs when their employees sense that the direction and leadership of their employer has become unstable or stagnant.
- Geographical: The flight of highly trained individuals or college graduates from their locale, for instance, those migrating from small mid-western towns in the United States to the coastal states and large cities like New York, Los Angeles, and Miami.
- Industrial: The movement of traditionally skilled workers from one sector of an industry to another.

The social environment is considered to be a key reason migration to other countries. The reasons for these skilled workers wanting to leave their home countries range from lack of opportunities to political unrest or oppression to economic depression and health risks. Seeking employment in developed countries means the chance at enhanced opportunities, political stability, a flourishing economy. Let alone better living conditions.

Skilled workers, especially in the medical, technical, and educational fields, are consistently being wooed by developed countries to migrate. (Lisamarie Babik)

In the United States, the 2000 Census resulted in the release of a special report on worker migration within the borders of the United States. The report had a specific emphasis on the movement of young, single, college-educated migrants based on data that indicated a trend of these workers moving away from the "Rust Best" and northern Great Plains regions to the west coast, most specifically the San Francisco Bay Area, and the southeast.

On a global level, the United States is often the recipient of brain gain, and as a whole does not experience brain drain like many countries. However, the United States has been experiencing widespread rural depopulation over the past few decades. Many young rural graduates are moving to urban and suburban areas to seek career opportunities. This has negatively impacted rural communities within the United States. In an article with CNN Money, Danielle Guichard-Ashbrook, who directs the Massachusetts Institute of Technology's international students office, said legislative proposals are "trying to play catch-up" with the rest of the pro-business world. She adds, "We educate them, but then we don't make it easy for them to stay."

Ireland is one country that most would not think of when it comes to brain drain. Yet, based on 2013 numbers, the Official U.S. Immigration suggested a brain drain of talent from Ireland when they included 1,171 Irish people with "extraordinary abilities or achievements" as well as 1,259 athletes, artists and entertainers who left their homeland for opportunities in the United States. Separately, according to Ireland's Central Statistics Office (CSO), data showed a surge in those leaving the country in that 89,000 left in the 12 months to April 2013, almost 2,000 more than a year earlier.

Legislation: In President Barack Obama's 2013 State of the Union address, he noted attracting "the highly skilled entrepreneurs and engineers that will help create jobs and grow our economy" as a key tenet of immigration reform. Yet, the United States immigration structure requires these immigrants to enter through a visa system. Specifically, the government issues H-1B visas to foreign workers with specialized skills in science, technology and medicine. This visa allows them to legally reside and work in the United States, and is popular among large corporations who can afford to pay the fees to woo their foreign applicants. What most people don't necessarily realize is that while these corporations are paying the fees for these immigrant workers, it still works on their favor because they often net higher profits by paying their immigrant employees less than their U.S. citizen employees. It is reported that more than 80 percent of H-1B visa holders are paid lower wages than U.S. citizens in comparable positions.

The H-1B visa and brain drain effect continues to impact countries on a global level as technology advances and educational opportunities are available to those in developing countries who seek employment and better living conditions in developed countries.

Heather Hummel

Further Reading

Boeri, Tito; Bruker, Herbert; Doquier, Frederic; Rapoport, Hillel, *Brain Drain and Brain Gain: The Global Competition to Attract High-Skilled Migrants (Reports for the Fondazione Rodolfo Debenedetti)*, Oxford University Press, September 29, 2012. The authors explain who emigrates, why they emigrate, and the effects of emigration on both the sending and the receiving countries.

Collier, Paul, *Exodus: How Migration is Changing Our World*, Oxford University Press, October 1, 2013. The author, a world-renowned economist, lays out the effects of encouraging or restricting migration.

See also H1B Visa

British as dominant group

Immigration issues: Discrimination; European immigrants; Irish immigrants; Slavery

Significance: Beginning during the early seventeenth century and continuing unabated for more than three centuries, there was an immense flood of immigrants to North America from Great Britain. These people determined the linguistics, culture, religion, and politics of North America in ways that are still perceptible.

The seventeenth century was marked by a wave of English immigrants, including some who were indentured, to remote colonies in England's North American and Caribbean territories. These early arrivals were joined in the eighteenth century by Scotch-Irish and Scots settlers and, later, by Catholic Irish. In the first two centuries of settlement, African slaves were introduced to the New World. These later arrivals had an inestimable impact on North America, but certain factors help explain the British stamp.

The dominance of the English, both in the colonies and in Britain, was one factor. The British crown exerted control over immigration in the seventeenth century, with more than 70 percent of immigrants being English. Few Scots, Welsh, or Irish immigrated in the first decades of the colonial period, thus giving the English language and the Anglican (Episcopal) Church a commanding position in every day colonial life. When non-English groups arrived, they were confronted by a generally Anglicized society.

The changing dynamics of political and religious thought and the distance across the Atlantic Ocean helped make settlement a regional phenomenon. The land settled by various Britons was isolated and inwardly divided, often along religious lines. For example, in the northern colonies, where there was less arable land and farms were small, dissenters from within the Anglican Church, known as Puritans, were the dominant group, along with a few Dutch and German-speaking peoples. In the

Romanticized painting of the first Thanksgiving celebrated by English pilgrims in the New World in 1621. The event has traditionally been seen as a symbol of hope and cordial relations between the new settlers and Native Americans, but it may also be seen as a symbol of the first step toward British domination of North America. (Library of Congress)

southern colonies, particularly in the tidewater regions, the traditional Episcopal faith was observed. Other Protestants, such as the Presbyterian Scotch-Irish, were pushed to the frontier, where they raised large families to work small farm plots. The dominant Anglo-Americans with the best land settled onto large plantations.

It was in the coastal region, with its link to the Caribbean sugar centers, that African slavery took hold in British America. Slavery served as cheap labor that allowed for an almost aristocratic way of life that provided material benefit to the empire. Slaves contributed much to the way of life in the South but were in turn Anglicized. This continued until the British government made an effort to end the transatlantic (though not domestic) slave trade during the late eighteenth century.

British Domination of North America British domination of North America was seemingly ensured when the British defeated the French in the Seven Years' War (1756-1763) and with the decline of the Spanish in eastern North America. Ironically, these events precipitated the end of direct British rule in the colonies. Though the colonies remained divided on many issues, grievances against the British crown led to the American Revolution. Drawing from the ideas of leading Enlightenment theorists, especially Englishman John Locke, the American revolutionaries succeeded in overthrowing British rule and establishing a fledgling republic.

North America did not, however, become less British as a culture. The United States, and later Canada, essentially continued the same patterns of commerce, Indian affairs, and settlement begun in the colonial period. Subsequent non-British immigrants to North America thus entered a society defined by British roots but open to contributions from elsewhere.

Gene Redding Wynne, Jr.

Further Reading

Grigg, John A., ed. *British Colonial America: People and Perspectives*. Santa Barbara: ABC-CLIO, 2008.

Menard, Russell R. *Migrants, Servants, and Slaves: Unfree Labor in Colonial British America*. Burlington, Vt.: Ashgate, 2001.

Morgan, Kenneth. *Slavery and Servitude in Colonial North America: A Short History*. Washington Square, N.Y.: New York University Press, 2001.

Van Vugt, William E. *Britain to America: Mid-Nineteenth-Century Immigrants to the United States*. Urbana: University of Illinois Press, 1999.

Wepman, Dennis. *Immigration: From the Founding of Virginia to the Closing of Ellis Island*. New York: Facts On File, 2002.

See also Anglo-conformity; Assimilation theories; Euro-Americans; European immigrants, 1790-1892; European immigrants, 1892-1943; White ethnics.

BURLINGAME TREATY

The Treaty: Treaty between the United States and China
Date: July 28, 1868

Immigration issues: Chinese immigrants; Laws and treaties

Significance: The Burlingame Treaty established reciprocal rights between China and the United States, including respect for territorial sovereignty and bilateral immigration.

Formal American interest in China dates from the thirteen-thousand-mile voyage of the U.S. ship *Empress of China*, under the command of Captain John Green, which departed from New York City on February 22, 1784. The vessel returned from Canton in May, 1785, with tea, silks, and other trade goods of the Orient. Merchants in Philadelphia, Boston, Providence, and New York quickly sought profits in the China trade. By the late 1830's, "Yankee clippers" had shortened the transit time from America's Atlantic ports to Canton from a matter of many months to a mere ninety days.

Chinese Politics Political problems, however, hindered commercial relations. The Manchu, or Ch'ing, Dynasty (1644-1912), fearful of Western intentions,

Illustration from an August, 1869, issue of Harper's Weekly *depicting the completion of the Pacific Railroad, which employed large numbers of Chinese workers.* (Library of Congress)

restricted trade to one city, Canton, and sharply curtailed the rights of foreigners in China. Chafing at these limits, especially China's refusal to deal with Europeans on terms of equality, caused Great Britain to begin hostilities with the Manchu Dynasty, occasioned by the "unsavory issue" of England's trade in opium with China. The Opium War (1839-1842) resulted in the Treaty of Nanking (August 24, 1842), a triumph for the political and commercial interests of Great Britain in eastern Asia.

Britain obtained the cession of the island of Hong Kong and the opening of four additional cities—Amoy, Ningpo, Foochow, and Shanghai—to British trade. The U.S. government desired similar rights and obtained them in the Treaty of Wanghia (named for a village near Macao) on July 3, 1844; Commissioner Caleb Cushing, although not formally received by China as a minister, was permitted to negotiate this landmark agreement. The United States secured access to the newly opened ports and was extended the right of extraterritoriality; that is, U.S. citizens were to be tried for offenses committed in China under U.S. law by the U.S. consul.

Within the next twenty years, trade with China grew. The United States acquired Washington, Oregon, and California, and, with Pacific ports, had greater access to Chinese markets. The California gold rush (1849) and the construction of the Central Pacific Railroad (completed in 1869), with its need for labor, encouraged Chinese emigration to the United States. Meanwhile, U.S. missionaries, merchants, travelers, and adventurers were arriving in China. Conditions in "the Middle Kingdom," however, were not good. The authority of the central government had been challenged by the anti-Western Taiping Rebellion (1850-1864) and was suppressed only with outside help. Further European incursions into China, epitomized by the Anglo-French War with the Manchus (1854-1858), threatened to curtail U.S. cultural and commercial opportunities in China. If the United States did not act, it would face the prospect of being excluded from China by European imperialism.

American Diplomatic Representation Secretary of State William Henry Seward believed that it was time for the United States to have formal representation at the Manchu court. His fortunate choice was Anson Burlingame. Born on November 14, 1820, in rural New York, the son of a "Methodist exhorter," Burlingame had grown up in the Midwest, graduating from the University of Michigan. After attending Harvard Law School, Burlingame went into practice in Boston. With a gift of oratory and exceptional personal charm, Burlingame served in the U.S. House of Representatives (1855-1861) and was a pioneer of the new Republican Party. As a reward for his labor and in recognition of his talents, Burlingame was offered the post of U.S. minister to Austria, but the Habsburgs refused him because of his known sympathies with Louis Kossuth, the Hungarian revolutionary. As a second choice and a compensatory honor, Burlingame was given the assignment to China.

Because the United States was distracted with the Civil War, Burlingame was left on his own and could count on little U.S. military might to support his actions. Acquiring a great admiration for and confidence in the Chinese, Burlingame won the trust and respect of I-Hsin, known as Prince Kung, the co-regent of China with the dowager empress Cixi (Tz'u-hsi). When Burlingame resigned as the U.S.

minister to China, in November, 1867, the Imperial Manchu court asked him to head China's first official delegation to the West. The Burlingame mission toured the United States, being warmly received, and arrived in the United Kingdom as William Gladstone was assuming the prime ministership of that nation. Burlingame's brilliant career was cut short during a subsequent visit to Russia, where he contracted pneumonia, dying in St. Petersburg on February 23, 1870. Few had served their own country so well, and it was said that none had given China a more sincere friendship.

Anson Burlingame, the American diplomatic minister to China from 1861 to 1867. (NARA)

The most outstanding accomplishment of the Burlingame mission was the Burlingame Treaty, signed on July 28, 1868, in Washington, D.C. This document dealt with a variety of issues between China and the United States. The United States pledged itself to respect Chinese sovereignty and territorial integrity, a position in sharp contrast to that of the European powers and one that anticipated the subsequent U.S. "open door policy" (1899). The Burlingame Treaty accepted bilateral immigration between China and the United States, and by 1880 there were 105,000 Chinese living in the United States.

By the standards of the 1860's, the Burlingame Treaty was a landmark of fairness and justice. However, the United States did not honor its spirit or letter. Anti-immigrant feeling focused on a fear of Chinese "coolie" labor. The infamous Sandlot Riots in San Francisco, in June, 1877, were symptomatic of both the mistreatment of Asian immigrants and the rising sentiment for Asian exclusion. On March 1, 1879, President Rutherford B. Hayes vetoed a congressional bill limiting the number of Chinese passengers on board ships bound for the United States as a violation of the Burlingame Treaty. Hayes did, however, send a mission to China to work for the revision of the Burlingame Treaty. In 1880, China recognized the U.S. right to regulate, limit, and suspend, but not absolutely forbid, Chinese immigration.

Two years later, President Chester A. Arthur vetoed a twenty-year suspension of Chinese immigration as being a de facto prohibition, but on May 6, 1882, the Chinese Exclusion Act passed, suspending the importation of Chinese labor for a ten-year period. In 1894, another ten-year exclusion period was enacted; in 1904, exclusion was extended indefinitely. When, on December 17, 1943, Chinese immigration was permitted by an act of Congress, it was within the strict limits of the 1920's quota system, allowing the entrance of only 105 Chinese annually. Not until the mid-twentieth century did the United States depart from an immigration policy centered on ethnic origin, thus allowing the original intent of the Burlingame Treaty to be realized.

C. George Fry

Further Reading

Aarim-Heriot, Najia. *Chinese Immigrants, African Americans, and Racial Anxiety in the United States, 1848-82*. Urbana: University of Illinois Press, 2003. Study of the interrelationships among African Americans, Chinese immigrants, and European Americans in the United States during the mid-nineteenth century.

Dulles, Foster Rhea. *China and America: The Story of Their Relations Since 1784*. Princeton, N.J.: Princeton University Press, 1946. This brief, classic history places the Burlingame Treaty in the broad context of United States-Chinese trade and diplomacy over a period of 150 years.

Fairbank, John K. *China Perceived: Images and Policies in Chinese-American Relations*. New York: Alfred A. Knopf, 1974. A noted Harvard scholar compares the contrasting sensitivities, traditions, aims, and means of the United States and China as they have affected foreign policy.

Fairbank, John K., Edwin O. Reischauer, and Albert M. Craig. *East Asia: Tradition and Transformation*. Rev. ed. Boston: Houghton Mifflin, 1989. This profusely illustrated and thoroughly documented survey, a standard introduction to the history of Asia's Pacific Rim, illuminates the Chinese situation in 1868.

Miller, Stuart Creighton. *The Unwelcome Immigrant: The American Image of the Chinese, 1785-1882*. Berkeley: University of California Press, 1969. A succinct analysis that explains why the Chinese were the only immigrants other than Africans to be forbidden by law from entering the United States in the nineteenth century.

Mosher, Steven W. China *Misperceived: American Illusions and Chinese Reality*. New York: Basic Books, 1990. This combination of psychohistory and political analysis examines the varied U.S. perceptions of China, ranging from infatuation to hostility. Carefully annotated.

Peffer, George Anthony. *If They Don't Bring Women Here: Chinese Female Immigration Before Exclusion*. Urbana: University of Illinois Press, 1999. Scholarly study of the special problems faced by Chinese women who wished to come to the United States.

Tsai, Shih-shan Henry. *China and the Overseas Chinese in the United States, 1868-1911*. Fayetteville: University of Arkansas Press, 1983. Well-documented, concise, in-depth study of the key issue between the United States and China during the late nineteenth century: immigration.

Wang, Dong. *The United States and China: A History from the Eighteenth Century to the Present*. Lanham, MD: Rowman & Littlefield Pub., 2013. An historical examination of relations between the U.S. and China, from 1784 to the present day.

See also Chinese Exclusion Act; Chinese exclusion cases; Chinese immigrants; Chinese immigrants and California's gold rush; Coolies; Gentlemen's Agreement.

CABLE ACT

The Law: Federal law restricting citizenship rights of immigrants
Date: Became law on September 22, 1922

Immigration issues: Citizenship and naturalization; Families and marriage; Laws and treaties; Women

Significance: The Cable Act revoked the principle of allowing immigrant wives of American citizens automatically to assume the American citizenship of their husbands.

The Cable Act reformed the rules by which women lost or obtained U.S. citizenship through marriage to foreigners. Representative John L. Cable of Ohio noted when introducing his bill that "the laws of our country should grant independent citizenship to women." By this act, the United States took the lead among nations in the world in acknowledging the right of a woman to choose her citizenship rather than to lose or gain it upon marriage. During the early twentieth century, under the laws of virtually all nations, a woman automatically lost her citizenship and took that of her husband upon marriage to a foreigner. The Cable Act, supported by all major women's groups at the time, was viewed as an important piece of reform legislation aimed at protecting a woman's right to choose her citizenship. As Representative Cable noted upon the bill's passage into law: "Justice and common sense dictate that the woman should have the same right as the man to choose the country of her allegiance."

The effects of the Cable Act were varied. Although aimed primarily at rectifying cases in which American women, under the 1907 Expropriation Act, automatically lost their U.S. citizenship upon marriage to an alien, it also revoked provisions of an 1885 act that automatically conferred U.S. citizenship on alien women who married Americans. Therefore, a foreign woman could not automatically become an American citizen upon marriage to an American, even if that were her desire. Instead, like any other alien, she would have to undergo an independent process of naturalization. One effect of this aspect of the law was to discourage Chinese American men from marr ying immigrant women. For these reasons, the Cable Act has been considered antiimmigrant and anti-women by some latter-day observers. However, although an alien woman who married a U.S. citizen or whose husband became naturalized would no longer automatically be granted citizenship, she was not excluded from seeking U.S. citizenship. The act made the process of becoming an American citizen a matter of deliberate choice rather than an automatic effect of marriage. The Cable Act did not revoke the citizenship of any woman who before its passage had received American citizenship automatically by marriage.

The ultimate effect of the Cable Act was to treat women of all ethnic and racial backgrounds with complete equality insofar as the acquisition of U.S. citizenship was concerned. Modern human rights treaties generally follow this U.S. practice,

145

recognizing that acquisition of citizenship should be a matter of free and independent consent.

Robert F. Gorman

Further Reading

Bredbrenner, Candice Lewis. *A Nationality of Her Own: Women, Marriage, and the Law of Citizenship*. Berkeley: University of California Press, 1998.

Houle, Michelle E., ed. *Immigration*. Farmington Hills, Mich.: Greenhaven Press/Thomson/Gale, 2004.

LeMay, Michael C., and Elliott Robert Barkan, eds. *U.S. Immigration and Naturalization Laws and Issues: A Documentary History*. Westport, Conn.: Greenwood Press, 1999.

Shanks, Cheryl. *Immigration and the Politics of American Sovereignty, 1890-1990*. Ann Arbor: University of Michigan Press, 2001.

See also Chinese immigrants; Citizenship; Japanese American Citizens League; Naturalization; Naturalization Act of 1790; Ozawa v. United States; Wong Kim Ark case.

CALIFORNIA GOLD RUSH

The Event: Rapid influx of immigrants into California after the discovery of gold in the territory recently taken by the United States from Mexico
Date: January 24, 1848-September 4, 1849
Place: Western slope of the Sierra Nevada

Immigration issues: Chinese immigrants; Economics; European immigrants

Significance: Discovery of the precious metal invited a flood of eastern fortune seekers and global immigrants into the new U.S. territory, accelerating the development of the western territories of the United States and raising issues about the immigration of Asians that would not be fully resolved for more than a century.

On January 24, 1848, James W. Marshall discovered gold in the terrace of a mill that a group of men were erecting for John A. Sutter on the south fork of the American River, near Sacramento in Northern California. Despite Sutter's efforts to keep the news secret until he could secure and protect the vast estates he had obtained by Mexican land grants, California newspapers revealed the find in March. By May, the rush had started, and San Francisco, Monterey, San Jose, and other California communities were depopulated of men who headed for the streams flowing westward from the Sierra Nevada. During the first working season in the summer of 1848, Californians, joined by a few men from Oregon and Hawaii, searched for the precious metal without competition from the horde of gold seekers who would soon descend on the gold country.

The Rush Begins News of the discovery first reached the East in August, when the New York Herald published a report; the next month, official word arrived from Thomas O. Larkin, the U.S. consul in Monterey, who was alarmed at the impact of the event. After a tour of the diggings, Richard B. Mason, military governor of California, forwarded a report to Washington, D.C., accompanied by a small box of sample gold. In December, 1848, when President James K. Polk notified Congress of the gold discovery in his annual message, the United States and the whole world realized that earlier reports were true. Gold fever broke out in the eastern United States; thousands made arrangements to go to California in the spring. Some gold seekers planned to migrate and operate independently, while others organized cooperative groups or companies to share expenses, labor, and profits.

Many people living on the eastern seacoast elected to travel to California by sea. Within a month following the president's message, sixty-one ships had left the Atlantic seaports for a voyage of six months around Cape Horn, arriving at their destination in the summer months of 1849. It was possible to shorten the journey by taking a steamship to Chagres, crossing the Isthmus of Panama by land, and boarding another ship at Panama, bound for California, but passages were uncertain, even the most expensive accommodations were inadequate, and the isthmus was disease-ridden. When this route became overcrowded, some travelers chose a longer crossing through Nicaragua; however, they found greater difficulty obtaining passage on the Pacific side, because the vessels headed north already had been overloaded in Panama.

The largest number of gold seekers went to California overland, a shorter and cheaper trip. Warm weather permitted an early start on a journey across northern Mexico or New Mexico. Texas trails converged on El Paso, from which the adventurers headed west by way of Tucson and the Gila River into southern California, and then northward to regions in the Sierra where gold had been discovered. Santa Fe was another base, at which people arrived from Fort Smith, Arkansas, having ascended the valley of the Canadian River, or having come west from Missouri by way of the Santa Fe Trail.

At Santa Fe, some people elected to turn southward down the Rio Grande and west along the Gila River, following the route of Stephen Kearny's Army of the West into California. Others turned north and west in a greater semicircular path, known as the Old Spanish Trail, that went into southern California. The most popular route was the well-known Platte River Trail to the South Pass, then by way of Fort Hall or Salt Lake City to the California Trail, and across Nevada along the banks of the Humboldt River.

The Hazards of Migration The overland migration of 1849 along this route appeared to duplicate that of earlier years, but there were considerable differences. The danger from attacks by Native Americans was minimized because of the number of travelers, and parties were not nearly so likely to lose the route. The heavy

Chinese and white miners sluicing for gold at Auburn Ravine in Northern California's Placer County in 1852. (California State Library)

traffic exhausted the grass supply needed for animals, however, and water holes along the trail were infected with Asiatic cholera. Suffering was intense, because the immigrants knew nothing about traveling along plains or over mountains.

Guides were scarce, and many guidebooks and newspaper accounts were misleading. The trails were marked by the graves of those who had succumbed to cholera, dysentery, or mountain fever. Beyond the South Pass, much of the route was over hot and dusty alkali deserts. In the desert crossing between the sinks of the Humboldt and Carson Rivers, the ground was littered with abandoned wagons and carcasses of dead animals. Many weary immigrants resorted to pack animals or walked across the Sierra Nevada.

A relief society in Sacramento financed and delivered medical and food supplies to groups stranded in the desert, saving many lives. Conditions were equally bad in the desert west of the mouth of the Gila River. Those who wandered from the established routes encountered indescribable suffering; one party leaving the Colorado River to strike directly west into California left most of its members in a valley subsequently known as Death Valley.

San Francisco became the metropolis of the gold country, and supply towns grew at the strategic locations of Marysville, Sacramento, and Stockton. Hundreds of mining camps sprang up near the diggings, with picturesque names such as Poker Flat, Hangtown, Red Dog, Hell's Delight, and Whiskey Bar expressing the sentiments of a predominantly male society. Most of the "forty-niners" who migrated to California were young, unmarried, and male. However, thousands of women also made the voyage to California.

The High Cost of Living So many people came to California that the majority of gold seekers found it necessary to labor long, hard hours to obtain the gold necessary to provide shelter and food. The weak and the defenseless were quickly weeded out. As economic pressures mounted, prejudice against racial and national minorities increased. California mining camps were cosmopolitan, and the Euro-Americans from New England, the South, the Missouri frontier, and elsewhere used various devices to discriminate against such groups as the Chinese, Mexicans, and African Americans.

Native-born Euro-Americans constituted almost 80 percent of all the forty-niners. The second largest group was from Mexico and other countries of Latin America. Approximately 7 percent came from Europe and Asia. English and German immigrants were more successful at mining than were the French, most of whom returned to the supply towns and became shopkeepers. To escape the drudger y, miners occasionally spent days of recreation engaged in contests of strength, endurance, and speed to demonstrate their physical prowess. Many found amusement at night in the saloons, where they gambled at red dog or faro, or in dancehalls with women. Nevertheless, the miners were noted for their spontaneous humanitarianism in aiding the distressed.

When the gold rush began, California had a population of fourteen thousand; by the end of 1849, there were an estimated one hundred thousand in the former Mexican province. Exhibiting admirable leadership, some of these men laid plans for the calling of a constitutional convention to meet in September, 1849, to organize a new state seeking admission into the United States.

During the early days, mining in California was highly rewarding—an average miner obtained between ten and fifty dollars a day—but the rate of return declined rapidly as time passed. Nevertheless, until 1865 or thereabouts, an average of almost fifty million dollars of gold per year was mined in California. While the first fortunes were made in the more easily accessible placer deposits, the later fortunes generally were made by mining corporations that could afford the capital and machinery required to work the deeper deposits.

The Gold Rush in U.S. History The more than seventy-five thousand people who migrated to California in the hope of earning their fortunes had a significant effect on American history. The huge influx of people from the East displaced many Native Americans and highlighted racial tensions between the native-born and foreign-born. The notion of "manifest destiny" (a term that had surfaced three years earlier in an article by John L. O'Sullivan appearing in *The United States Magazine and Democratic Review*)—whereby expansionist interests held that it was the "fulfillment of our manifest destiny to overspread the continent allotted by Providence for the free development of our yearly multiplying millions"—had taken hold of the nation. Because of the large numbers of westward-moving fortune seekers, California was admitted as a state in 1850. California miners developed new mining technology that benefited mining in other regions of the country.

W. Turrentine Jackson
Judith Boyce DeMark

Further Reading

Aarim-Heriot, Najia. *Chinese Immigrants, African Americans, and Racial Anxiety in the United States, 1848-82*. Urbana: University of Illinois Press, 2003. Study of the interrelationships among African Americans, Chinese immigrants, and European Americans in the United States during the mid-nineteenth century that includes a discussion of the gold rush era.

Gordon, Mary M., ed. *Overland to California with the Pioneer Line*. Urbana: University of Illinois Press, 1984. Collection of memoirs of participants in various land expeditions to California during the 1840's.

Levy, Jo Ann. "Forgotten Forty-Niners." In *American History*. Vol. 1. Guilford, Conn.: Dushkin, 1995. Provides new information on the experiences of women in the California mining camps and surrounding towns.

Paul, Rodman W. *California Gold: The Beginning of Mining in the Far West*. Cambridge, Mass.: Harvard University Press, 1947. Covers several economic and social aspects of the gold rush era, including the impact on California, the contributions of the California miners to mining technology, and the regulation of mining society, particularly the growth of vigilante committees.

Richards, Leonard L. *The California Gold Rush and the Coming of the Civil War*. New York: Alfred A. Knopf, 2007. Richards examines the influence of the California Gold Rush as one of many civil crises that led up to the Civil War, including the contest over whether California would be a slave state.

Rohrbough, Malcolm J. *Rush to Gold: The French and the California Gold Rush, 1848-1854*. London: Yale University Press, 2013. An analysis of the role played by the approximately 30,000 French participants in the California Gold Rush, during a period when major changes were also taking place in French society.

Royce, Sarah. *A Frontier Lady: Recollections of the Gold Rush and Early California*. Lincoln: University of Nebraska Press, 1977. A diary that describes the author's experiences as a wife who took part in the California gold rush.

See also Burlingame Treaty; Chinatowns; Chinese Exclusion Act; Chinese immigrants; Chinese immigrants and California's gold rush; Chinese immigrants and family customs; Chinese Six Companies; Coolies; "Yellow peril" campaign.

CAMBODIAN IMMIGRANTS

Definition: Immigrants to the United States from the Southeast Asian Nation of Cambodia

Immigration issues: Asian immigrants; Demographics

Significance: Most Cambodian immigrants to the U.S. arrived in the 1980s, many from refugee camps where they fled following the Vietnam War and its aftermath. Cambodian immigrants place a high value on family and tend to have larger families than is average in the United States, and as a result the Cambodian population as a whole is substantially younger than the American population as a whole.

United States as a nation started accepting Cambodian immigrants from refugee camps in Thailand in 1979, with large numbers of immigrants from Cambodia arriving in the 1980s. According to the US Census, in 1990 there were over 118,000 Cambodian immigrants, while only 14% of those arrived before the 1980s. Due to the sudden increase of refugees, United States had to implement certain procedures in order to ease up the resettlement. Many voluntary agencies were created in order to help settle the immigrants, and individual and agency sponsors were sought to help financially support those who needed help the most. The original idea was that the sponsors would take care of the immigrant families for two years, in order to give them time to establish themselves in their new home, while other agencies provided classes in English and cultural matters to help the immigrants settle in to U.S. society.

Cambodian immigrant's assimilation   As a group, Cambodian immigrants are substantially younger than the average for the U.S., with a median age is 19 as compared to the U.S. average of almost 38. Over half of the Cambodians immigrants are under the age of 18, with about half being second generation, meaning that they were born in the United States. Cambodian immigrants tend to have large families, with an average of 5.03 members, as compared to 3.06 for the average U.S. family.

The process of adapting and assimilating the U.S. society was not easy for many Cambodian immigrants. Most migrated from rural areas and did not have a specific professional qualification most did not have extensive knowledge about the new culture they are joining. One of the major problems faced by Cambodian immigrants was the generation gap: the elder Cambodians wanted to preserve their identity, culture and language, while the younger generations had barely have any memory of their country of origin and were more interested in adapting to the U.S. In general, younger immigrants had an easier time adapting to his or her new culture and environment. However, some young Cambodians felt they were discriminated against because of their foreignness, and made changes like replacing their Cambodian name with an American name in order to try to fit in better. While many Americans were sympathetic toward Cambodian immigrants, particularly after news coverage of the difficulties they endured as refugees, there was also a tendency by Americans to stereotype the Cambodian refugee as passive and not willing to deal with confrontation.

Cambodian immigrants and their families   Even though they have migrated to another culture, Cambodians still tend to hold on to their wedding traditions.

151

Some immigrants retain customs such as wearing traditional Cambodian clothing for their wedding, while others are adopting Western-style wedding dresses and suits. (Thomas Wanhoff)

Although arranged marriages are still considered normal in Cambodian society, the younger generation of immigrants are starting to choose who they are going to marry on their own. Some immigrants retain customs such as wearing traditional Cambodian clothing for their wedding, while others are adopting Western-style wedding dresses and suits.

Family is one of the most important elements in Cambodian society. These ties have only been strengthened due to the immigration process, particularly for those who survived war and came through refugee camps, as the loss of or separation from some family members has tended to make the surviving members draw even more closely together. Although Cambodian families tend to be large, many are headed by a single woman, but this is due to the death of many Cambodian men during years of war, rather than to divorce.

According to the Cambodian culture, men are in charge of making sure their families have enough money to live properly, and their chief goals is to provide their family with the necessities of life. Only men are allowed to take on high-status roles such as becoming a monk, and traditionally higher education and professional training was primarily the preserve of men, while women were mostly trained and educated for home tasks. However, women hold high status and are treated with great care and admiration in traditional Cambodian culture. They are the ones who deal with the family budget and determine how money should be spent, and also have the primary responsibility for raising children, who are considered to be a family's greatest blessing and gift. However, these patterns are somewhat changing, and more Cambodian American women today are pursuing higher education and entering professions where they expect to have the same opportunities as do men.

Relationships of Cambodian immigrants with other ethnic groups Most Cambodians immigrants settled in urban areas in the U.S., where they came in contact with other cultures, something that they did not typically experience in Cambodia. However, there have been negative results from these culture encounters, including the fact that some young Cambodian men have become involved in gangs out of a perceived need to protect themselves. In part, this may be a reaction to the fact that Cambodian immigrants are well aware that their dark skin color, which sometimes results in prejudicial treatment from other Americans.

However, with the passage of time in American many Cambodians have become aware of how much in common they have with other ethnic groups such as Asians, Hispanics and African American. For instance, it has been observed that Cambodian immigrants located in Texas get along very well with Mexicans, and the two groups have cooperated successfully in business affairs. Numerous Cambodians work in Mexican markets, for instance, and have undertaken tasks such as learning Spanish in order to establish a better relationship with the Mexicans in their environment.

Cambodian immigrants and religion Many Cambodian refugees accepted Christianity as their religion, often as a result of their experiences in refugee camps. There are many reasons why individuals choose to change their religion, but one reason for the Cambodians was the tragedies they suffered during war, including the loss of their homes and families, and some felt that Buddhism failed them. During their time as refugees, some went through a spiritual crisis and were looking for something that will give them hope and faith for their children. Others changed religion as a sign of gratitude towards the volunteering agencies that help them during the settlement process. Very often those groups were connected with church and took their free time to help those who needed the help the most, and some financially supported the newcomers which through this time of crisis. Finally, some Cambodians felt that converting from Buddhism to Christianity would help them adjust better to life in America, and that U.S. society would be more welcoming towards the immigrants with whom they had something in common.

However, most Cambodians continue to practice Buddhism and observe traditional customs. As more refugees from Cambodia settled in the U.S., they established more houses of worship. At first, there were only 3 temples all over the United States; however, at the beginning of the 1990's over 50 of them were created throughout the country. Other religions became more accepted and aware of Buddhism existence which allowed the Cambodians greater freedom to practice their tradition. Even those who weren't living around the temples were given the opportunity to pray within the privacy of their homes or even at the public meeting halls, and many temples were located on private property (for instance, within a private home) while others were purpose-built building constructed in the traditional monastery style.

Employment level and economic situation of Cambodian immigrants The assimilation process was extremely difficult for Cambodian immigrants, in part because many had lived in rural areas and worked in agriculture in their home country, while in the U.S. most settled in urban areas. The unemployment rate for Cambodians is among the highest among ethnic immigrant groups, and many Cambodians had to work at low paid manual labor jobs, particularly when they first arrived in the U.S.

Looking at the overall condition of the given immigrants, their economic situation remains difficult. Over 40% of Cambodian families are living under the poverty line, while over 50% of Cambodian households receive public assistance. Their median income is slightly above $18,000 which is almost 50% lower than the average income for all U.S. families. The major handicap faced by Cambodian immigrants in the workplace is lack of education. Almost 90% of individuals among the given group has spent only 12 years in school, with older generations of women having even less education, with many only holding the equivalent of a sixth grade education.

Daniella Kleskovic

Further Reading

Alba, R. D., Nee, V., & ebrary, I. (2003). *Remaking the american mainstream: Assimilation and contemporary immigration.* Cambridge, Mass: Harvard University Press.; Detailed description of assimilation process concerning various immigrants, including Cambodian.

Bacon, J. L. (1996). *Life lines: Community, family, and assimilation among asian indian immigrants.* New York: Oxford University Press (US).: Extensive analysis of cultural values among newcomers and their children; the process of adapting while keeping the original culture present

Dahles, H. (2013). Cambodian returnees' entrepreneurial ventures. *Journal of Enterprising Communities: People and Places in the Global Economy,* 7(4), 383-396. doi:10.1108/JEC-03-2013-0009: Observation and detailed analysis of professional and entrepreneurial actions of Cambodian immigrants; furthermore, detailed comparison of the different society and their elements is presented.

Das, M., & ebrary, I. (2007). *Between two cultures: The case of cambodian women in america.* New York: P. Lang.: Comparison of different values and different images women portray in the given societies.

Faulkner, C. L., & ebrary, I. (2011). *Economic mobility and cultural assimilation among children of immigrants.* El Paso [Tex.]: LFB Scholarly Pub.: Detailed analysis of assimilation process as well as learning habits of second wave immigrants concerning their originated culture and traditions. Moreover, economic situation of various immigrants is portrayed.

See also Asian American Legal Defense Fund; Laotian immigrants; Vietnamese immigrants.

CANADIAN IMMIGRANTS

The Law: According to the Embassy of the United States in Ottawa, Canada, Canadian citizens are not required to have a visa to cross the border into the United States for the purposes of visiting or studying. However, as of January 23, 2007, other than a few exceptions to the law, all Canadians who enter the United States are required to show their valid passports. The exceptions include intending immigrants, fiancés, or investors who must obtain a visa prior to entry in the same manner as other nationalities. Other exceptions might include journalists, temporary workers or NAFTA professionals. These travelers are required to present all necessary supporting documentation and/or approved petitions directly to a U.S. Customs and Border Protection Officer at the Port of Entry.

Date: Updated 2007

Immigration Issues: For those Canadians seeking U.S. citizenship, it is required that they become a permanent U.S. resident for a certain period of time prior to becoming eligible through naturalization. Should a Canadian citizen obtain their permanent residency by marriage to a U.S. citizen, they have the option to apply for naturalization three years after becoming a permanent resident. However, if their residency is obtained by employment, they have to wait five years after becoming a permanent resident to apply for naturalization. Lastly, for those who have U.S. citizen parents, but are born in Canada, they could also qualify for citizenship in the U.S. through naturalization.

Significance: In order for a Canadian to seek U.S. citizenship, they must fulfill certain requirements, some of which can take up to five years.

Background One of the most known reasons that Canadians see citizenship in the U.S. is to seek opportunities that will further their careers in the arts. Many famous actors and actresses as well as musicians have crossed the border to the U.S. to not only pursue their craft, but to obtain citizenship. This list represents the most recognizable Canadians who crossed the border and subsequently became famous.

- **Pamela Anderson** – actress and animal rights activist, born in Ladysmith, British Columbia
- **Paul Anka** – teen idol in the late 1950s and 1960s, born in Ottawa, Ontario
- **Will Arnett** – actor who played George Oscar "G.O.B." Bluth II on the comedy series *Arrested Development*, born in Toronto, Ontario
- **Dan Aykroyd** – comedic actor in *Saturday Night Live*, where he was a writer and the youngest cast member for its first four seasons, from 1975 to 1979; starred in movies *The Blue Brothers*, *Trading Places*, *Ghostbusters* and *My Girl*, born in Ottawa, Ontario
- **Randy Bachman** – musician/songwriter, founding member of the bands *The Guess Who* and *Bachman–Turner Overdrive*, born in Winnipeg, Manitoba

- **Justin Bieber** – the R&B teen singer and performer, born in Stratford, Ontario
- **Michael Bublé** – contemporary jazz pop artist, born in Burnaby, British Columbia
- **Raymond Burr** – actor in the television dramas *Perry Mason* and *Ironside,* born in New Westminster, British Columbia
- **Neve Campbell** – actress in the 1990s television series *Party of Five,* film roles include the *Scream* horror film trilogy, born in Guelph, Ontario
- **John Candy** – comedic actor who played Del Griffith in the movie *Planes, Trains and Automobiles,* born in Newmarket, Ontario
- **Jim Carrey** – actor and comedian in films including *Dumb and Dumber, Batman Forever, How the Grinch Stole Christmas,* born in Newmarket, Ontario
- **Tommy Chong** – comedic actor in *Cheech & Chong* and Leo on the television sitcom *That '70s Show,* born in Edmonton, Alberta
- **Celine Dion** – singer-songwriter and composer, born in Charlemagne, Quebec
- **Percy Faith** – bandleader, orchestrator, composer and conductor, born and raised in Toronto, Ontario
- **Michael J. Fox** – actor in the television sitcom *Family Ties* and the *Back to the Future* trilogy, born in Edmonton, Alberta
- **Ryan Gosling** – actor in the movies *The Notebook, Blue Valentine* and *Lars and the Real Girl,* born in London, Ontario
- **Lorne Greene** – actor who played Ben Cartwright on the western *Bonanza,* and Commander Adama in the science fiction TV Series *Battlestar Galactica,* born in Ottawa, Ontario
- **Monty Hall** – host of the television game show *Let's Make a Deal,* born in Winnipeg, Manitoba
- **Peter Jennings** – anchor of ABC's *World News Tonight,* born in Toronto, Ontario
- **Stana Katic** – actress who played Detective Kate Beckett on the series *Castle,* born in Hamilton, Ontario
- **Margot Kidder** – actress who played Lois Lane in the *Superman* movies alongside Christopher Reeve, born in Yellowknife, Northwest Territories
- **Avril Lavigne** – pop-rock artist, born in Belleville, Ontario
- **Art Linkletter** – radio and television talk-show pioneer, famous for his interviews with children on the variety/talk show *House Party* in the 1950s and 1960s, born in Moose Jaw, Saskatchewan
- **Howie Mandel** – stand-up comedian, television host, and actor in the medical drama *St. Elsewhere* and host of the game show *Deal or No Deal,* born and raised in Willowdale
- **Rachel McAdams** – actress in the *The Notebook,* the hit comedy *Wedding Crashers* and the Sherlock Holmes movies, born in London, Ontario
- **Lorne Michaels** – creator and producer of *Saturday Night Live (SNL),* born in Toronto, Ontario
- **Joni Mitchell** – famous musician and singer in the folk rock movement; born in Fort Macleod, Alberta

- **Alanis Morissette** – the Grammy-winning singer-songwriter to include "You Oughta Know," "Ironic," "You Learn," "Hand in My Pocket," "Head over Feet," and "All I Really Want," born in Ottawa, Ontario
- **Mike Myers** – comedian famous for *Wayne's World, Austin Powers,* and *Shrek,* was born in Scarborough, Ontario
- **Leslie Nielsen** – actor and comedian in *The Naked Gun* film series, born in Regina, Saskatchewan
- **Sandra Oh** – actress who played Dr. Cristina Yang on the television series *Grey's Anatomy*; born in Ottawa, Ontario
- **Ellen Page** – actress in the film *Juno,* born in Halifax, Nova Scotia
- **Christopher Plummer** – actor who played Captain Georg von Trapp in *The Sound of Music,* other subsequent roles, and he holds the record as the oldest actor to ever win an Oscar at age 82 for Best Supporting Actor in the movie "Beginners," born in Toronto, Ontario

Monty Hall, former host of the television game show Let's Make a Deal, *born in Winnipeg, Manitoba.* (Public Domain)

- **Caroline Rhea** – comedic actress known for her role as Hilda Spellman in *Sabrina, the Teenage Witch,* and the voice of Linda Flynn in the animated show *Phineas and Ferb,* born in Montreal, Quebec
- **Seth Rogen** – actor in the movies *Knocked Up, Superbad, Monsters vs. Aliens* and *The Green Hornet,* born in Vancouver, British Columbia
- **Morley Safer** – television news magazine *60 Minutes,* born in Toronto, Ontario
- **Paul Shaffer** – musical director for David Letterman's late night talk shows, born in Thunder Bay, Ontario
- **William Shatner** – actor who played James T. Kirk, captain of the USS *Enterprise,* in the *Star Trek* television series and subsequent films, born in Montreal, Quebec
- **Martin Short** – comedic actor, *Saturday Night Live* alumnus, born in Hamilton, Ontario
- **Donald Sutherland** – actor with a film career spanning 50 years, born in Saint John, New Brunswick
- **Alan Thicke** – television personality who wrote the theme songs for *Diff'rent Strokes, The Facts of Life* and original theme to *Wheel of Fortune,* starred in the 1985-1992 television series *Growing Pains*; born in Kirkland Lake, Ontario
- **Alex Trebek** – host of the game show *Jeopardy!* born in Sudbury, Ontario

Legislation Canadians must be a permanent resident for three or five years, depending on their situation, prior to seeking U.S. citizenship. Additionally, they must also satisfy a continuous residence requirement, which means having to physically reside for a specific period of time in the U.S. for in the years prior to applying for citizenship.

In the cases of green cards via marriage, for those Canadians entering the U.S. as a Treaty Trader (and family), or to marry a U.S. citizen and reside in the U.S., Fiancés/Fiancées (and their children and spouses and children) are required to obtain a visa to enter the U.S. Canadian citizens must physically reside in the U.S. for a minimum of 18 months out of the 3 years prior to applying for citizenship while on a green card.

In the situations of obtaining green cards via the routes of employment or family, Canadian citizens must live in the U.S. for at least 30 months of the 5 years prior to applying for citizenship while on a green card.

In order to keep their continuous residence in the U.S., Canadians should not leave the U.S. for periods of more than six continuous months. Should they do so, they could break their continuous residence time unless there is demonstration of continuous to work and residency within the U.S. However, leaving the U.S. for a year or longer will result in the state of abandonment of permanent residency and the accumulated continuous residence is void. There are cases where if a Canadian expects to leave the U.S. for a year with plans to return, they may apply for a re-entry permit prior to departing in order to demonstrate the intention to return. This will benefit them in cases of not wanting to be tagged for abandonment.

In addition to showcasing physical residency, Canadian citizens must reside in the state or district from which they are applying for at least three months prior to seeking U.S. citizenship. Demonstration of good moral character, a good understanding of the English language, and loyalty to support and to defend the U.S. Constitution are added requirements.

According to U.S. Customs and Border Protection, Canadian citizen children of the ages of 15 years old and younger arriving by land or sea from contiguous territory may present an original or copy of his or her birth certificate or a Canadian Citizenship Card. Canadian Citizens 16-18 must have a valid passport, unless traveling as part of an organized group described below.

- Groups of Children: Canadian citizen children under age 19 arriving by land or sea from contiguous territory and traveling with a school group, religious group, social/cultural organization, or sports team, may also present an original or copy of his or her birth certificate, a Consular Report of Birth Abroad, a Naturalization Certificate, or a Canadian Citizenship Card.
- The group should provide, on organizational letterhead: The name of the group and supervising adult, a list of the children on the trip, the primary home address, phone number, date of birth, place of birth, and name of at least one parent or legal guardian for each child.

Additionally, a written and signed statement of the supervising adult certifying that they have obtained parental or legal guardian consent for each participating child is required.

Heather Hummel

Further Reading

Bray, Ilona, *Immigration Made Easy*, NOLO; Sixteenth Edition, January 31, 2013. A book that addresses every possible way to legally enter and live in the United States.

Brault, Gerald J., *The French-Canadian Heritage in New England*, UPNE; 1st edition, March 15, 1986. A comprehensive historical, sociological, and cultural introduction to the sizable Franco-American population the resides in and influences New England.

See also Border Patrol, U.S.; Green cards.

CELTIC IRISH

Identification: Immigrants to North America of southern Celtic Irish descent

Immigration issues: Demographics; European immigrants; Irish immigrants

Significance: The Celtic Irish were first brought to English colonies in North America as servants and laborers during the colonial era and long faced discrimination and abuse.

During the 1650's, the first immigrants from Ireland began to arrive in North America. It was not until the early eighteenth century that large numbers of people from throughout Ireland emigrated to North America. The majority of these immigrants were from northern Ireland and of Scottish ancestry; lesser numbers were from southern Ireland and identified themselves with traditional native peoples of Ireland and a Celtic heritage.

The Scotch-Irish immigrants to North America were fourth- or fifth-generation Scots in Ireland who had largely assimilated into the Irish culture except for their religious faith and their family names. The Scotch-Irish were predominantly Protestant rather than Roman Catholic, and their family names revealed a Scottish heritage. Scotch-Irish living in northern Ireland considered themselves Irish, not Scottish. Immigrants to North America from southern Ireland were predominantly Catholic and usually bore family names of Celtic origin.

Despite the common heritage of Ireland, these two groups of immigrants were regarded quite differently upon their arrival in North America. The Protestant Scotch-Irish shared a common faith with the large numbers of established

Protestant English settlers. The smaller numbers of southern Irish of Catholic and Celtic heritage became the focus of widespread ethnic discrimination.

Randall L. Milstein

Further Reading

Almeida, Linda Dowling. *Irish Immigrants in New York City, 1945-1995.* Bloomington: Indiana University Press, 2001.

Duffy, Jennifer. *Who's Your Paddy? Racial Expectations and the Struggle for Irish American Identity.* New York: New York University Press, 2014.

Meltzer, Milton. *Bound for America: The Story of the European Immigrants.* New York: Benchmark Books, 2001.

Miller, Kerby A. *Irish Immigrants in the land of Canaan: Letters and memoirs from Colonial and Revolutionary America, 1675-1814.* New York: Oxford University Press, 2003.

Paulson, Timothy J. *Irish Immigrants.* New York: Facts On File, 2005.

See also Anti-Irish Riots of 1844; European immigrants, 1790-1892; German and Irish immigration of the 1840's; Immigration and Nationality Act of 1965; Irish immigrants; Irish immigrants and African Americans; Irish immigrants and discrimination; Irish stereotypes; Scotch-Irish immigrants.

CENSUSES, U.S.

Definition: Official federal government enumerations of the nation's entire population—both citizens and noncitizens—taken every tenth year

Dates: Begun in 1790

Immigration issue: Demographics

Significance: Information collected by the U.S. Census includes each person's ethnic or racial background. This enables the size of each ethnic or racial group to be compared over time and allows governmental programs to take the size of an ethnic or racial group into account when determining policy.

The U.S. Constitution requires that population be the basis for determining the number of seats apportioned to each state in the U.S. House of Representatives. As the population of the country shifts, the decennial census permits a readjustment in the number of seats for each state. Census reports have also been used to calculate how many immigrants from particular countries are allowed admission into the United States as well as to determine what constitutes unlawful discrimination.

Censuses A population census is a complete count of all persons residing in a particular area. A census differs from a population sample, which scientifically selects a percentage of persons in an area in order to estimate characteristics of the entire population of the territory.

To undertake a population census, census takers must identify the dwelling units in the area to be covered; then they must go to each abode and obtain information from all persons residing therein. Inevitably, census takers miss some people because not everyone is at home when the census taker arrives, some people choose to evade being counted, others are homeless or transient, and not all dwelling units are easy to identify. Censuses, thus, generally undercount population, especially in areas where less affluent minorities reside. That is why, some argue, a method known as "statistical sampling" may be more accurate than an actual headcount, provided that the census has identified all dwelling units.

Legal Requirements The Constitution of the United States requires a population census every ten years. Because the Constitution requires that each state's representation in the federal House of Representatives be based on population, a major purpose of the decennial census is to increase or decrease the number of seats in the House of Representatives apportioned to each state in accordance with relative changes in the population of each state. The Constitution did not consider Native Americans to be citizens of the United States, so they were not originally counted in the census; those living on reservations did not affect the allocation of seats in the House of Representatives until after 1924, when they were granted American citizenship. Those of African descent were counted in each state, but before the Civil War (1861-1865), when they were not considered citizens, their number was multiplied by three-fifths for the purpose of reapportioning representation in the House of Representatives.

Beginning during the 1960's, affirmative action began to be applied to remedy employment discrimination in the United States. One aspect of the policy is that federal government employers and those with federal contracts are supposed to hire men and women of the various ethnic or racial groups in the same proportions as their relative availability in the workforce. To determine the composition of the workforce, employers usually rely on census data, which are disseminated by the U.S. Department of Labor.

Ethnic/Racial Categories In the first federal census of 1790, each individual was assigned membership in one of two racial groups: white and colored. The colored population was divided into free colored and slaves, and both categories were divided into black or mulatto. These census categories were used until 1860, when the Asiatic category was added and a count was made of the people in various Indian tribes. The 1870 census used four categories: white, colored, Chinese, and Indian. In 1880, Japanese became the fifth category, and the term "Negro" replaced "colored." These five categories remained on census reports through 1900. The 1910 census added several new categories: Filipinos, Hindus, and Koreans. A footnote in the census report noted that Hindus were "Caucasians" but still were counted separately from other categories of "whites."

The 1920 census added Hawaiians and part Hawaiians, but these two categories were removed from the national enumeration in 1930 and 1940. Mexicans joined

Census taker collecting information during the early twentieth century. Under the U.S. Constitution, the federal government is required to conduct a comprehensive census of the United States every ten years. (Library of Congress)

the category list in 1930 and 1940. In 1950, the only racial categories were white and nonwhite. In 1960, six categories were used: "white," "Negro," Japanese, Chinese, Filipino, and Indian. In 1970, Hawaiians and Koreans returned to the list, making eight categories. In 1980, the category "black" replaced "Negro," and the list of Asian and Pacific races expanded to include Asian Indians, Samoans, and Vietnamese. In 1990, nearly every country in Asia was represented as a separate category.

Although Mexicans appeared as a category in 1930 and 1940, they did not reappear in national statistics for forty years. In 1970, the census counted "Persons of Spanish Heritage," but in 1980, the census counted Cubans, Mexicans, and Puerto Ricans separately. In 1990, the census reported the number of persons from almost all countries in the Caribbean, Central America, and South America.

Census reports on the territories of Alaska and Hawaii used unique category schemes. For Alaska, the census counted Aleuts, Eskimos, and Alaskan Indians; Aleuts and Eskimos became national categories in 1980 and 1990, but Alaskan Indians were pooled with all other American Indians in both years. For Hawaii, the indigenous Hawaiians were counted, although up to 1930, they were divided into pure Hawaiians, Asiatic Hawaiians, and white Hawaiians.

From the beginning, the census had separate subcategories for European ethnic groups (British, French, German, and so on), all of which were counted as white. The breakdown was made to record the number of foreignborn individuals in the population. Due to concerns among the earlier immigrants from western and northern Europe that too many eastern and southern Europeans were arriving, Congress passed the Immigration Act of 1924. This act replaced a temporary immigration law, passed in 1921, which had restricted immigrants to 3 percent of each admissible nationality residing in the United States as of 1910.

According to the 1924 immigration act, known as the National Origins Act, the maximum from each European country was calculated as 2 percent of the nationality group already inside the United States as determined by the federal census of 1890. Most Asians, effectively, were barred from immigration under the law with the exception of Filipinos, as the Philippines was an American possession as of 1898. The restrictive 1924 immigration law imposed no quota on immigrants from the Western Hemisphere. With the Immigration and Nationality Act of 1965, Congress established equal quotas for all countries, regardless of hemisphere.

With the advent of affirmative action, a five-category scheme was developed by federal civil rights enforcement agencies. The so-called COINS categories stood for "Caucasian, Oriental, Indian, Negro, and Spanish." Later, the term "Oriental" was replaced by the term "Asian and Pacific islander," and the term "Hispanic" replaced the term "Spanish."

Census for the Year 2000 During the 1990's, considerable pressure was brought to bear to change the categories for the census for the year 2000. Some blacks wanted to be called "African Americans." Hispanics wanted to be counted as "Latinos" and as members of a race rather than an ethnic group. Native Hawaiians wanted to be moved from the category "Asians and Pacific islanders" and included with "American Indians and Native Alaskans." Middle Easterners, particularly those from Islamic countries, wanted separate status. Finally, some mixed-race or multi-ethnic people who spanned two or more of the categories wanted to be counted as "multiracial." Advocates of a society in which ethnic and racial distinctions would not be recognized officially wanted to drop all references to race and ethnicity in the census.

After many hearings and studies on the subject, the U.S. Office of Management and Budget decided to keep the previous categorizations with one modification: "Asians" would be counted separately from "Native Hawaiians and Other Pacific islanders." The proposal for a separate "multiracial" category was rejected, but persons with multiracial backgrounds would be allowed to check more than one category. Thus, data on ethnic backgrounds of people in the United States have been collapsed into five racial categories: African American or black, American Indian or Native Alaskan, Asian, Native Hawaiian or Other Pacific islander, and white. The census of the year 2000 permits a member of any of these five categories to also check "Hispanic or Latino."

Census for the Year 2010 One major change in the 2010 Census was that the long form, which collected detailed economic and social information from a subset of households in several previous census, was not used. Instead, a short form consisting of 10 questions, with the ability to enter information for up to 12 residents of a household, was the only form used to collect information. The American Community Survey (ACS), which began reporting official data in 2005, became the replacement for the information previously gathered by the long-form census. The ACS, which is administered annually to a sample of American households each year, collects more detailed information (e.g., on health insurance, disabilities, and the commute to work) than does the short Census form administered to all Americans every 10 years. Another change in 2010 was the acknowledgement of same-sex married couples. Although no choice was offered on the survey form for this category, same-sex couples could choose "husband" or "wife" or "unmarried partner," and information was tabulated by the Census Bureau for same-sex couples.

Impact on Public Policy The ethnic and racial diversity of the United States is best documented by the decennial federal census. The count of each ethnic or racial group is crucial in determining whether discrimination occurs, but questions about ethnic group membership or race on a census deeply affect the identity of many persons, who in turn may support efforts either to abolish ethnic and racial counts or to change categories.

Michael Haas

Further Reading

Anderson, Margo J. *The American Census: A Social History*. New Haven, Conn.: Yale University Press, 1988. Historical account of the taking of censuses that includes many of the associated controversies.

Anderson, Margo J., Constance F. Citro, and Joseph J. Salvo, eds. *Encyclopedia of the U.S. Census: From the Constitution to the American Community Survey*. 2nd ed. Thousand Oaks, CA: CQ Press, 2012. A comprehensive resources for the U.S. Census, covering history, politics, content and procedures from the beginnings through 2010.

Choldin, Harvey M. *Looking for the Last Percent: The Controversy over Census Undercounts*. New Brunswick, N.J.: Rutgers University Press, 1994. Critical study of the tendency of censuses to undercount minorities.

Kertzer, David I., and Dominique Arel, eds. *Census and Identity: The Politics of Race, Ethnicity, and Language in National Census*. New York: Cambridge University Press, 2002. Study of the counting of racial and ethnic minorities in the U.S. Census.

MacDonald, Heather I., and Alan Peters. *Urban Policy and the Census*. Redlands, CA: ESRI Press, 2011. Intended for researchers and policy analysts, this volume discusses ways to use Census and American Community Survey data for decision-making and planning.

Perlmann, Joel, and Mary Waters, eds. *The New Race Question: How the Census*

Counts Multiracial Individuals. New York: Russell Sage Foundation, 2002. Collection of critical essays on the U.S. Census's changing racial categories and the social and political effects of these changes.

Rodriguez, Clara E. *Changing Race: Latinos, the Census, and the History of Ethnicity*. New York: New York University Press, 2000. Study of the treatment of ethnic minorities in the U.S. Census, with special attention to the counting of Latinos.

Skerry, Peter. *Counting on the Census? Race, Group Identity, and the Evasion of Politics*. Washington, D.C.: Brookings Institution Press, 2000. Analytical study of the problems of accurately counting members of racial and ethnic groups in the U.S. Census.

Statistical Abstract of the United States, 2004-2005. 124th ed. Washington, D.C.: U.S. Census Bureau, 2005. Starting place for any research on demographics. Updated annually, this reference source is available on compact disc, and much of its information is freely available online on the U.S. Census Bureau's Web site.

See also Demographics of immigration; European immigrants, 1790-1892; European immigrants, 1892-1943; Immigration "crisis"; Justice and immigration; Racial and ethnic demographic trends.

CHICANO MOVEMENT

The Event: Period of Mexican American cultural and political awakening
Date: 1960's-1970's

Immigration issues: Civil rights and liberties; Latino immigrants; Mexican immigrants

Significance: During the era of the Chicano movement, Mexican Americans defined and took pride in their own identity, asserted their civil rights, and worked toward self-determination by improving their financial, social, and political circumstances.

The Chicano movement began during the early 1960's and peaked during the early 1970's. Many historians view the movement as a concise expression of the Chicano perspective on the Mexican American community's history. Chicano history begins with the indigenous peoples of what is now Mexico and the southwestern United States, proceeds with the Spanish conquest and colonization and the Mexican War (1846-1848), and continues during the subsequent expansion of European Americans into the American Southwest.

Historical Background According to Chicano analysts, Chicanos are a people who are indigenous to the Americas, originating from Aztlán, the Aztec homeland in Central and North America. After the Spanish conquest and colonization in the sixteenth century of what is now Mexico and the American Southwest, Chicano culture became a blend of Indian and Spanish customs and practices. Although the Spanish attempted to suppress the indigenous culture, the Indians' response to the influx of Spanish culture was to practice accommodation, outwardly accepting their "inferior" status to obtain concessions from the dominant group and occasionally rebelling.

In the eighteenth and nineteenth centuries, settlers from the United States began to arrive in the Southwest, then part of Mexico. These settlers, mostly of European ancestry, brought with them the concepts of white supremacy, patriarchy, Christianity, and capitalism. Under the 1848 Treaty of Guadalupe Hidalgo, which ended the Mexican War, Mexicans who remained in the new territories of the United States were designated as citizens with all constitutional rights and guarantees; land acquired under Mexican law was to be protected by U.S. law. However, by 1900, European Americans (called Anglos by Chicano historians) had seized 95 percent of Mexican-owned land.

The Mexican way of life gradually was replaced by the lifestyle of the Anglo settlers. Mexican farmers and ranchers were replaced by Anglos, who ran the farms and ranches differently, often along more capitalistic and less paternalistic lines. Some of the ranchers viewed Mexican Americans primarily as a reserve workforce. Across the Southwest, American businesses, courts, and law enforcement agencies replaced existing facilities. Schools were segregated; a triple system separated Mexican Americans, African Americans, and European Americans.

From approximately 1900 to 1930, millions of Mexican citizens migrated to the United States. Some fled to avoid the violent and economic dislocations of the Mexican Revolution; others came to fill the U.S. labor shortage caused by economic growth in industry and agriculture. Communities in the Southwest that historically had contained many Mexican Americans and industrial cities in the Midwest became destinations for those seeking employment, and migrant trails of Mexican and Mexican American workers developed throughout the United States.

Changing Generations   During the 1930's, the political and nationalistic loyalties of members of the Mexican American community under went profound change. The Mexican immigrants who arrived from 1900 to 1930 often did not think of themselves as citizens of the United States because of Mexico's geographic proximity and the ease of returning to their native country. Discrimination and anti-Mexican attitudes also made it hard for them to feel a part of their adopted country. However, in the post-World War I era, as millions of migrants moved into Mexican American communities and the U.S.-born generation began to grow up, more of the migrants began to think of themselves as Mexican Americans.

The Great Depression of 1930 resulted in the deportation of many Mexican immigrants. From 1930 to 1937, U.S. law officials and political authorities deported approximately 500,000 Mexican people (250,000 of whom were children born in the United States and therefore American citizens). The deportation demonstrates how many Americans viewed Mexican immigrants: as inexpensive and exploitable labor to be disposed of in times of economic distress.

This negative perception persisted even after World War II. From 1942 through 1945, several hundred thousand Mexican Americans were active in combat zones; several received the highest military honors. When the war ended and the veterans returned home, they discovered that their sacrifices had minimal effect on prewar attitudes toward and policies and structures affecting Mexican Americans. However, these veterans no longer accepted the status quo, and they joined with members of the community who had already rejected the ideas of gradualism and assimilation.

From 1946 through 1963, Mexican American veterans, believing in the American ideal of equality and equal opportunity and having proved their patriotism and loyalty, created new organizations to address what they perceived to be barriers to their reform-oriented strategies. However, despite these organizations' numerous successful efforts against economic, political, and social discrimination (including the legal defeat of the triple school system and a significant role in helping elect John F. Kennedy to the U.S. presidency), many members of the Mexican American community became disillusioned at the lack of substantive improvement for communities and individuals. The most prominent problems were the continued exploitation of agricultural workers, immigration issues, low levels of educational achievement, and limited economic opportunities.

Chicano Generation In the Southwest, many Mexican Americans, particularly young people, began to reexamine their identity, especially their experience as a mestizo (mixed race) people in a culture and society dominated by white European Americans. The election in 1963 of five Mexican Americans to the town council of Cr ystal City, Texas, a town where the majority of the population was Mexican American, marked the birth of a new political generation. This new generation rejected European Americans' definition of "Mexican American"; they saw themselves as Chicanos, an indigenous people with roots in the Aztec homeland of Aztlán and possessing their own mestizo culture.

"Chicano"

The origin of the term "Chicano" is uncertain; however, some experts believe that the word originated from an improper pronunciation or slang version of "Mexicano." Consequently, the user was viewed by middle-class Mexicans or Mexican Americans as uneducated, poor, and probably "Indian," a pejorative appellation from those of Mexican origin who rejected their indigenous roots. In the Chicano critique of Anglo society, the rejection of Anglo racial and ethnocentric designations also included the repudiation of those in Mexicano communities who accepted anti-Native American and capitalist belief systems. To call the self Chicano is to affirm that which is denounced by Anglo-created racial constructs and ethnocentric depictions. To be Chicano is to affirm and proclaim historic, indigenous origins and to understand that Chicano culture has Spanish-Indian roots in a land invaded and conquered by the European Americans.

The word chicano was appropriated from the denigratory use of "Mexicano" by whites who had stereotyped Mexican immigrants and citizens alike as lazy and dirty. Chicano came to connote ethnic pride, a defiant turning of the old hate language on its head. Members of the Chicano movement felt that to continue the previous (Mexican American) generation's strategy of reform was to practice accommodation and might even constitute an acceptance of European American constructions and a rejection of their mestizoindigenous history.

Four individuals form the core of the Chicano generation and movement: José Ángel Gutiérrez, Rodolfo "Corky" Gonzáles, Reies López Tijerina, and César Chávez. During the 1960's, Gutiérrez of South Texas organized young Chicanos into the Mexican American Youth Organization, which emphasized their right to cultural self-determination and had the development of bilingual/bicultural education for all Mexican American children as one of its principal goals.

In 1965, Gonzáles founded the Crusade for Justice in Denver, Colorado, to improve education, job opportunities, and police relations for Chicanos. He also organized the first Chicano Youth Liberation Conference in 1969, which brought together representatives from a number of Chicano organizations. At the first conference, the delegates adopted El Plan Espiritual de Aztlán, a manifesto of political and cultural nationalism. Tijerina of New Mexico formed La Alianza Federal de Mercedes in 1963 in an effort to reclaim land he and many Chicanos felt had been taken from the Mexican owners in violation of the 1848 Treaty of Guadalupe Hidalgo. He led a 1967 raid on the courthouse in Tierra Amarilla, New Mexico. Chávez, probably the best-known Chicano activist, led farmworkers in Delano, California, on a strike that developed into a grape boycott and lasted from 1965 to 1970. In many ways during these early years, the Chicano movement was integrated with Chávez's call for migrant farmworkers' rights because a huge proportion of the farmworkers were, and remain, Mexican or Mexican American.

These four men were the impetus for the Chicano movement and the core of its activities. Their concerns— improving the financial, social, and political status of Mexican Americans, gaining the respect due to Mexican Americans, claiming the right to self-determination, and building Chicano pride—were echoed in the goals of the many other Chicano organizations that were formed during the late 1960's and early 1970's. These and later organizations deal with additional issues such as the distinction between illegal workers and immigrants, legal problems involving the use of the Spanish language, the lack of mestizo-Chicano peoples in American history instruction, police brutality, lack of health and education services, lack of education, and structural poverty.

The final politicization of the Chicano generation grew out of the Vietnam War. Many Chicanos saw the overrepresentation of Mexican Americans in the combat zones of Vietnam as proof of the veracity of the Chicano view of European American society and as a further betrayal of Mexican American World War II veterans' beliefs and sacrifices. The Vietnam War and the older and younger generations' differing feelings about it produced great tension within Mexican American communities; some older Mexican Americans were compelled to question and adjust their basic beliefs about patriotism and reform. The 1970 Chicano Moratorium was the largest Chicano antiwar demonstration and also the most violent police riot involving Chicano protesters.

All of these events, issues, and concerns fueled an attempt by Gutiérrez and others to organize a national political party, La Raza Unida, during the early 1970's. Although some of the party's local efforts favorably altered political relations between Chicanos and European Americans, the party was not successful at the national level. After 1975, the Chicano movement no longer was a cohesive force in Mexican American communities, although Chávez's widow, Helen Chávez, continued his leadership of the fight for the rights of farm laborers. However, during its heyday, the Chicano movement did engage a new generation of Mexican Americans with a much more comprehensive and complete vision and understanding of the Mexican American/ Chicano experience in the United States.

Carl Allsup

Further Reading

Rodolfo Acina's *Occupied America: The Chicano Struggle for Liberation* (2d ed. New York: Harper & Row, 1976) presents the Chicano perspective on the Mexican American experience.

Mario Barrera's *Race and Class in the Southwest: A Theory of Racial Inequality* (Notre Dame: University of Notre Dame Press, 1976) looks at both class and race.

Arnoldo de Leon's *They Called Them Greasers: Anglo Attitudes Toward Mexicans in Texas, 1821-1900* (Austin: University of Texas Press, 1980) offers a history of the development of racial and ethnocentric constructs by European American society.

David Montejano's *Anglos and Mexicans in the Making of Texas, 1836-1986* (Austin: University of Texas Press, 1987) demonstrates the complex interaction of race, ethnicity, and class and the evolving response by Mexican Americans toward European Americans' efforts to control Mexican American people.

Charles M. Tatum's *Lowriders in Chicano Culture: From Slow to Show* (Santa Barbara, CA: Greenwood, 2011) and A. Gabriel Melendez's *Hidden Chicano Cinema: Film Dramas in the Borderlands* (New Brunswick, NJ: Rutgers University Press, 2013) look at two aspects of Chicano culture.

Alambrista and the U.S.-Mexico Border: Film, Music, and Stories of Undocumented Immigrants (Albuquerque: University of New Mexico Press, 2004), edited by Nicholas J. Cull and David Carrasco, is a collection of essays on dramatic works, films, and music about Mexicans who cross the border illegally into the United States.

See also Bracero program; Farmworkers' union; Latinos; Latinos and employment; Mexican American Legal Defense and Education Fund; Mexican deportations during the Depression; Operation Wetback; Undocumented workers.

Chinatowns

Definition: Ethnic enclaves outside traditional Chinese homelands in which Chinese immigrants are concentrated

Immigration issues: Asian immigrants; Chinese immigrants; Demographics; Ethnic enclaves

Significance: Chinatowns can be found in almost every major city with a high clustering of Chinese throughout Southeast Asia, South and North America, Europe, and Oceania.

The first significant Chinatown to emerge in the United States arose in San Francisco. It began to take shape in 1850 as large numbers of Chinese immigrants were lured there by the California gold rush. Initially called Little Canton, it was christened Chinatown by the press in 1853. In the next several decades, more than two dozen Chinatowns were established in mining areas, railroad towns, farming communities, and cities of California, as well as in Nevada, Utah, Colorado, Montana, Wyoming, Idaho, Oregon, and Washington. As the Chinese diaspora accelerated, especially after the 1882 Chinese Exclusion Act, Chinatowns gradually emerged in New York, Boston, Chicago, Philadelphia, Washington, D.C.,

Entrance to modern Los Angeles's Chinatown, which is a popular tourist attraction. (David Fowler)

Corner of Clay Street and Grant Avenue in San Francisco's Chinatown in 1927. Almost every major American city had a "Chinatown," but San Francisco's was to Chinese immigrants the one true center of Chinese culture in America. They called it Tangrenbu, the "port of the people of Tang ." Grant Avenue was used as the title of a song in Richard Rodgers and Oscar Hammerstein's musical about Chinatown, Flower Drum Song *(1958). (Library of Congress)*

Baltimore, Maryland, and other cities.

The formation of Chinatowns in the United States was an outcome of both voluntary and involuntary forces. In a foreign land and with language barriers, the Chinese needed their own communities for information sharing, lifestyle preservation, business transactions, cultural maintenance, kinship networking, and psychological support. Externally, hostility and violence against the Chinese, housing and employment discrimination, and institutional exclusion forced them to establish their own enclaves for self-protection and sur vival.

Over time, some Chinatowns have sur vived and continued to grow, whereas other Chinatowns, such as Pittsburgh's, have faded. Many important demographic, economic, social, and geographical factors have contributed to the growth or decline of a Chinatown, including the size of the city in which the Chinatown is located; the number of Chinese residents in the city; the sex and age distribution of the Chinese population in the Chinatown; the demand for Chinese labor in the area; the demand of the Chinese in the Chinatown for goods and services; the continuation of new Chinese immigration and settlement into the Chinatown; land-use patterns and land values in the Chinatown and its surrounding areas; changes in the socioeconomic status of Chinese residents; relationships between the Chinese and other groups; and adaptation strategies of the Chinatown.

During the 1990's, there were more than two dozen Chinatowns in the United States, of which New York's Chinatown was the largest. Modern Chinatowns have been transformed into tourist centers and Chinese shopping bazaars. They also serve as living Chinese communities, Chinese cultural meccas, commercial cores, suppliers of employment and entrepreneurial opportunities, historical education hubs, and symbolic power bases for political office holders and seekers. Nevertheless, there is some evidence that injustice and the exploitation of new Chinese immigrants also take place in some Chinatowns. Despite the existence of the three types of traditional social organizations in Chinatowns (*huiguan* or district associations, *zu* or clans, and *tongs* or secret societies), they have much less influence on the lives of Chinese residents than they did in the past.

Historically, all Chinatowns were located in urban centers, and residents tended to have a lower socioeconomic status. However, during the late 1970's, the first suburban Chinatown emerged in Monterey Park, located east of Los Angeles. Also dubbed the Chinese Beverly Hills or Little Taipei, it is home to mainly middle-class people. Chinese Americans are the dominant economic, social, and cultural force in the city. In November of 1983, Monterey Park elected the first Chinese American woman mayor, Lily Lee Chen. There are signs that suburban Chinatowns are multiplying in the San Gabriel Valley east of Los Angeles and in Silicon Valley, south of San Francisco, and they are likely to grow in the foreseeable future as a result of an influx of high-status Chinese immigrants.

Philip Q. Yang

Further Reading

Chen, Shehong. *Being Chinese, Becoming Chinese American*. Urbana: University of Illinois Press, 2002.

Guest, Kenneth J. *God in Chinatown: Religion and Survival in New York's Evolving Immigrant Community*. New York: New York University Press, 2003.

Jorae, Wendy Rouse. *The Children of Chinatown: Growing Up Chinese American in San Francisco, 1850-1920*. Chapel Hill: University of North Carolina Press, 2009.

Kwong, Peter. *Chinatown, New York: Labor and Politics, 1930-1950*. Rev. ed. New York: New Press, 2001.

Ling, Huping. *Chinese St. Louis: From Enclave to Cultural Community*. Philadelphia: Temple University Press, 2004.

Ma, L. Eve Armentrout. *Hometown Chinatown: The History of Oakland's Chinese*

Community. New York: Garland, 2000.

Shah, Nayan. *Contagious Divides: Epidemics and Race in San Francisco's Chinatown*. Berkeley: University of California Press, 2001.

Tsui, Bonnie. *American Chinatown: A People's History of Five Neighborhoods*. New York: Free Press, 2009.

Wong, William. *Oakland's Chinatown*. Charleston, S.C.: Arcadia, 2004.

Zesch,, Scott. *The Chinatown War: Chinese Los Angeles and the Massacre of 1871*. New York: Oxford University Press, 2012.

Zinzius, Birgit. *Chinese America: Stereotype and Reality—History, Present, and Future of the Chinese Americans*. New York: P. Lang, 2005.

See also Asian American stereotypes; Chinese immigrants; Chinese immigrants and family customs; Ethnic enclaves; Little Havana; Little Italies; Little Tokyos.

CHINESE AMERICAN CITIZENS ALLIANCE

Identification: Chinese American rights advocacy organization
Date: Founded on May 21, 1895
Place: San Francisco, California

Immigration issues: Asian immigrants; Chinese immigrants; Civil rights and liberties

Significance: The Chinese American Citizens Alliance became a major social and political force in the Chinese American community.

Chinese immigrants began arriving in the United States during the mid-nineteenth century. Most of the immigrants were young men who left their families behind in China and who intended to return home after they secured sufficient money to support their families comfortably. To secure passage to the United States, most of them indentured themselves to merchants or labor agents in a system called the credit-ticket arrangement whereby merchants advanced Chinese money for passage to the United States and kept collecting payments for years. Some Chinese left less willingly, emigrating because of famine and political and social unrest in southern China or falling victim to the so-called "Pig Trade," which replaced slavery after it was outlawed following the Civil War. They chose the United States because of exaggerated tales of wealth and opportunity spread by traders and missionaries.

Chinatowns Formed After the Chinese immigrants landed in the United States, labor agents, under the credit-ticket arrangement, gained almost complete domination of their indentured workers and kept them in isolated communities

Contemporary newspaper illustration of the anti-Chinese rioting in Denver, Colorado, in 1880. (Library of Congress)

that became known as Chinatowns. Many Chinese ultimately were unable to secure sufficient money for return passage to China; however, because they did not want to remain permanently in the United States, they had little incentive to assimilate. Their unwillingness or inability to become acculturated into the American "melting pot" became an indictment against all Chinese.

Life in California during the late nineteenth century was difficult at best for most Chinese. The Chinese communities organized *huiguan* (merchant guilds) that served as welcoming committees, resettlement assistance services, and mutual help societies for newly arrived immigrants.

Chinese immigrants were also organized by the Chinese Consolidated Benevolent Association (the Chinese Six Companies), originally agents of Chinese firms in Hong Kong that had established the "coolie trade" to San Francisco. The Six Companies kept traditional Chinese rules, customs, and values as the basis for

WHERE BOTH PLATFORMS AGREE.—NO VOTE—NO USE TO EITHER PARTY.

Editorial cartoon by J . A. Wales commenting on the convergence of anti-Chinese policies of the Democratic and Republican Parties in 1880. (Library of Congress)

appropriate behavior, helping protect Chinese from an increasingly antiChinese atmosphere.

Violence—External and Internal Anti-Chinese sentiments and violence against Chinese began almost as soon as they arrived in North America. These attitudes existed at the top levels of government and labor unions as well as being held by local citizens. During the mid- to late nineteenth century, various political parties, including the Know-Nothing Party, the Democratic Party, and the Republican Party, promoted anti-Chinese platforms. During this time, workers' unions organized anti-Chinese activities, and anti-Asian sentiments were propagated by newspapers in western states.

In 1871, twenty Chinese in Los Angeles were killed and their homes and businesses looted and burned. In 1877, a similar incident occurred in San Francisco. In Chico, California, five farmers were murdered. Anti-Chinese riots broke out in Denver, Colorado, and in Rock Springs, Wyoming. In 1885, Chinese workers, employed as strikebreakers, were killed at a Wyoming coal mine. Chinese residents in Seattle and Tacoma, Washington, were driven out of town, and thirty-one Chinese were robbed and murdered in Snake River, Oregon. In 1905, sixty-seven labor organizations, in order to prevent employers from hiring Asians, formed the Asiatic Exclusion League.

During the early 1890's, the Chinese Six Companies influenced Chinese not to sign documents required by the Geary Act (1892), an extension of the Chinese Exclusion Act of 1882, which required all Chinese residing in the United States to obtain certificates of eligibility with a photograph within a year. When the Geary Act was ruled legal, thousands of Chinese Americans became illegal aliens in the United States. The tongs, secret societies of criminals that originated in China, used this opportunity to take control of the Chinatowns. The result was a vicious and bloody civil war among Chinese Americans. Few first-generation Chinese Americans actively opposed the rule of the tongs.

Native Sons of the Golden State Many young American-born (second-generation) Chinese opposed these "old ways" of doing things. They accepted the idea that they were never going to return to China and wanted to adopt American ways and fit into American culture. These young, second-generation Chinese formed the Native Sons of the Golden State in San Francisco in an effort to assimilate into American mainstream culture. The Native Sons of the Golden State emphasized the importance of naturalization and voters' registration. All members were urged to become American citizens and to vote. The organization also encouraged active participation in the civic affairs of mainstream American life. The leaders thought that some of the anti-Chinese sentiments and discriminatory actions were, in part, caused by the traditional attitudes and behaviors of the Chinese immigrants who remained isolated, did not learn English, and did not take part in politics.

As the organization grew, it established chapters in Oakland, Los Angeles, San Diego, Chicago, Portland, Detroit, Pittsburgh, and Boston, eventually changing its name to the Chinese American Citizens Alliance (CACA). In 1913, CACA defeated a California law designed to prevent Chinese from voting. The group fought against the National Origins Act and sought the right for Chinese men to bring their wives to the United States. CACA helped defeat the Cinch bill of 1925, which attempted to regulate the manufacture and sale of Chinese medicinal products such as herbs and roots.

By promoting numerous social functions, CACA also helped keep Chinese American communities together and moved them toward assimilation. CACA fought against the stereotyped portrayals of Chinese in films, newspapers, and magazines as heathens, drug addicts, or instigators of torture. In 1923, for example, the organization attempted to block publication of a book by Charles R. Shepard, *The Ways of Ah Sin*, depicting negative images of Chinese. CACA has also supported other community organizations, such as Cameron House, Self-Help for the Elderly, and the Chinese Historical Society of America. The CACA has continued to speak out against stereotyping of Asians and Asian culture. For instance, in 2014, the CACA criticized the stereotyping of Asians in Gilbert and Sullivan's operetta *The Mikado*, both for the continuing "yellow-face" practice of using white actors in Asian roles, and the stereotyping of Japanese culture that might have been acceptable when the work premiered in 1885, but which the CACA argued should not be accepted today.

Gregory A. Levitt

Further Reading

Chi, Tsung. *East Asian Americans and Political Participation: A Reference Handbook.* Santa Barbara, Calif.: ABC-Clio, 2005. General reference work on Asian American political activism.

Chung, Sue Fawn. "The Chinese American Citizens Alliance: An Effort in Assimilation." Los Angeles: University of California, 1965. An unpublished doctoral dissertation, a rare secondary source devoted entirely to the organization.

Daniels, Roger. *Asian America: Chinese and Japanese in the United States Since 1850.* Seattle: University of Washington Press, 1988. Excellent overall account of Asian America that includes a brief description of the Chinese American Citizens Alliance.

Dillon, Richard H. *The Hatchet Men: The Story of the Tong Wars in San Francisco Chinatown.* New York: Coward-McCann, 1962. A dated but interesting account of the violence in San Francisco's early Chinatown under the rule of the tongs.

Junn, Jane. *New Race Politics in American: Understanding Minority and Immigrant Politics.* Leiden: Cambridge University Press, 2008. A collection of essays on immigrant and minority participation in American political life.

Lai, H. Mark. *Becoming Chinese American: A History of Communities and Institutions.* Walnut Creek, Calif.: AltaMira, 2004. Study of cultural adaptations of Chinese immigrants to the United States. Includes chapters on Chinese cultural and rights advocacy organizations.

Takaki, Ronald. *Strangers from a Different Shore: A History of Asian Americans.* Boston: Little, Brown, 1989. An account of Asians coming to live in America. Provides some discussion of the Chinese American Citizens Alliance during the 1940's and the late 1980's.

Yung, Judy, Gordon H. Change, and Him Mark Lai, eds. *Chinese American Voices: From the Gold Rush to the Present.* Berkeley: University of California Press, 2006. Documents written by Chinese Americans from the 1850s to the present day, placed into historical context by the editors.

See also Chinatowns; Chinese Exclusion Act; Chinese exclusion cases; Chinese immigrants; Chinese immigrants and California's gold rush; Chinese immigrants and family customs; Chinese Six Companies.

CHINESE DETENTIONS IN NEW YORK

The Event: When a Thai ship carrying 276 illegal émigrés from mainland China grounded off New York, federal authorities took the would-be immigrants into custody and prosecuted those responsible for transporting them to the United States

Date: June 6, 1993

Place: Rockaway Peninsula, Queens, New York

Immigration issues: Asian immigrants; Border control; Chinese immigrants

Significance: The federal government successfully prosecuted the persons responsible for attempting to smuggle unauthorized immigrants into the United States in this highly publicized case; however, the incident merely called attention to the fact that tens of thousands of Chinese immigrants were entering the country illegally during the early 1990's.

In the early morning hours of June 6, 1993, the *Golden Venture*, a 150-foot freighter, ran aground in the Atlantic Ocean a quarter of a mile off the coast of Queens, New York. On board were 285 Chinese people, most of them from China's southern coastal province of Fujian, who were attempting to enter the United States without proper authorization. The ship had left Bangkok, Thailand, in February, crossing both the Indian and Atlantic oceans before reaching the United States.

In the course of the arduous trip, at least five of the émigrés were thought to have contracted tuberculosis. Living conditions on board were squalid. Each passenger was given only one bottle of water a week and one meal a day, consisting primarily of rice.

The *Golden Venture* arrived in U.S. waters in May but, after two attempts, was unable to connect with the smaller ships that were to smuggle the Chinese passengers ashore. On May 17, an agent of New York's Fuk Ching gang, which ran the smuggling operation, wrested control of the freighter from its crew of seven Burmese and six Indonesians. In an act of desperation, the *Golden Venture* was purposely permitted to run aground on June 6.

As the ship foundered fifteen hundred feet off the New York coast, some of its human cargo dived into the cold water, attempting to swim through six-foot waves to the shore. A rescue effort involving hundreds of police officers, firefighters, and members of the Coast Guard was launched immediately. The rescuers were shocked by the appalling sanitary conditions aboard the grounded ship. By the time the rescue was completed, six of the Chinese émigrés had drowned. Of those remaining, 276 were remanded to the custody of the Immigration and Naturalization Service (INS) and dispatched to detention centers to await hearings on their requests for asylum. The INS announced its opposition to granting these requests.

Illegal Chinese Immigration Illegal immigration from China to the United States has occurred for more than a century, particularly from the southern province of Fujian, home of the Chinese aliens aboard the *Golden Venture*. As early as the 1849 gold rush in California, crime syndicates in China lured people

178

to the United States with promises of wealth and virtually limitless possibilities.

The system used in those early days differed little from the system employed by the current syndicates. They offer transportation to the United States, housing and jobs for people after they arrive, forged documents, and virtual immunity from deportation. In return, those who leave China pay a substantial down payment of the syndicate's fees and sign agreements to pay the remainder from the money they expect to earn upon arriving in New York City, San Francisco, or one of the other popular destinations for illegal aliens.

Once they reach their destinations, the Chinese usually realize that they have been deceived. They frequently work long hours in sweatshops, often for as little as a dollar an hour. Their income is barely enough to cover their living expenses, let alone repay the syndicate quickly and save enough money to bring other family members to the United States. They live in a condition of indentured servitude as virtual slaves, but they can do little to help themselves because of their tenuous legal status in the country.

An estimated fifty thousand to eighty thousand illegal Chinese aliens were smuggled into the United States each year during the late 1980's and early 1990's, paying fees of between $20,000 and $35,000 each. Only about 10 percent of these immigrants are apprehended by the INS and returned to China. In essence, then, the syndicates honor their claims of succeeding in helping people to escape from China. The rate of defection from China accelerated sharply in the years following the Tiananmen Square massacre in 1989.

Illegal immigration to the United States from China far exceeds such immigration from most other countries. Chinese immigrants enter the country by land, sea, and air. Some are smuggled into Mexico and make their way over the U.S.-Mexico border.

On July 6, 1993, the U.S. Coast Guard stopped three ships smuggling a total of 658 Chinese nationals, mostly young men, in international waters off Mexico's northern coast. Mexican immigration officials finally permitted these three dilapidated ships to dock in the Pacific port city of Ensenada, where the immigrants were held in custody. Eventually they were returned to China in a chartered Mexican jet aircraft. Crew members of these three ships were arrested and charged with violations of Mexican immigration laws. Most of the crew members of the *Golden Venture* were charged with violating American immigration laws.

Consequences An immediate consequence of the grounding of the *Golden Venture* was that nine crew members of the vessel were tried and convicted of smuggling. On December 3, 1993, they were each sentenced by the U.S. District Court in New York City to six months of imprisonment. These arrests and convictions did not, however, strike at the heart of the problem, the crime syndicates behind the smuggling. On August 27, 1993, Guo Liang Chi, leader of New York's Fuk Ching gang, was arrested in Hong Kong. That gang was thought to have been involved in the Golden Venture debacle. Charged in the January deaths of two of his New York accomplices, Guo Liang Chi faced extradition to the United States. The following day, federal investigators arrested fourteen other Fuk Ching gang members in New York City on charges of conspiring to smuggle immigrants, kidnapping, and extortion.

R. Baird Shuman

Further Reading

Bischoff, Henry. *Immigration Issues*. Westport, Conn.: Greenwood Press, 2002.

Segal, Uma Anand. *A Framework for Immigration: Asians in the United States*. New York: Columbia University Press, 2002.

Staeger, Rob. *Deported Aliens*. Philadelphia: Mason Crest, 2004.

Yoshikawa, Hirokazu. *Immigrants Raising Citizens: Undocumented Parents and Their Young Children*. New York: Russell Sage Foundation, 2011.

Zhao, Linda. *Financing Illegal Migration: Chinese Underground Banks and Human Smuggling in New York City*. Houndsmills, Basingstoke, Hampshire: Palgrave Macmillan, 2013.

See also   Border Patrol, U.S.; Chinese immigrants; Coast Guard, U.S.; Illegal aliens; Immigration and Naturalization Service; Justice and immigration.

Chinese Exclusion Act

The Law: Federal law restricting Asian immigration
Date: May 6, 1882

Immigration issues: Asian immigrants; Chinese immigrants; Citizenship and naturalization; Discrimination; Laws and treaties; Nativism and racism

Significance: The Chinese Exclusion Act was the first federal effort to exclude immigrants by race and nationality; it marked a turning point in what had been, until then, an open door to immigrants from around the world.

The Chinese Exclusion Act suspended immigration by Chinese laborers to the United States for a period of ten years and prohibited Chinese residents in the United States from becoming naturalized citizens. Merchants, students, and tourists, however, were still permitted to enter the United States for visits. Although the Chinese Exclusion Act was established as a temporary suspension of immigration by Chinese laborers, it was only the first of many laws designed to exclude Asians from entry into the United States.

This law was both a political and social reaction to increasing non-European immigration in the second half of the nineteenth century. As the country became more industrialized and its frontier began to disappear, Americans became increasingly apprehensive about employment and the role of immigrants. American labor organizations objected to what they perceived as unfair competition by Chinese laborers.

Background Chinese immigration to the mainland United States began in earnest after the Taiping Rebellion in 1848. Most Chinese immigrants headed for California, where the gold rush of 1849 led to an increased need for labor. In 1854, 13,100 Chinese came to the United States. This immigration, regulated by the Burlingame Treaty in 1868, was unrestricted; by 1880, the number of immigrants had risen to 105,465. The majority remained in California, where they were hired as laborers by the railroads, worked as domestics, and opened small businesses. San Francisco was the port of entry for many Chinese; the population of its Chinatown grew from two thousand to twelve thousand between 1860 and 1870.

Federal government photograph of Sun Yat-sen, the future first president of the Republic of China, that was made during his 1909-1910 visit to the United States. The photograph was kept in a file relating to Sun's entry into the United States under the restrictions of the Chinese Exclusion Act. (NARA)

The size and nature of this early Chinese immigration brought a long-lasting prejudice. Californians thought of Chinese laborers as "coolies"—that is, as cheap labor brought to the United States to undercut wages for American workers. Chinese workers were also accused of being dirty. Authorities in San Francisco suspected that crowded areas of Chinatown were the focus for disease and passed the Cubic Air Ordinance, prohibiting rental of a room with fewer than five hundred cubic feet of space per person. This municipal ordinance was later declared unconstitutional.

Discrimination and violence increased during the 1870's. In 1871, a mob attacked and killed nineteen Chinese people in Los Angeles. Dennis Kearney, a naturalized citizen from Ireland, organized the Workingmen's Party in 1877 to oppose Chinese immigrants. Shouting, "The Chinese must go!" Kearney threatened violence to all Chinese immigrants. In July, 1877, men from an "anti-coolie club" led workers into San Francisco's Chinatown on a rampage that lasted several days.

Because most local ordinances against the Chinese had been declared unconstitutional, people who opposed Chinese immigration turned to Congress for new legislation. Congress responded in 1879 with a bill to limit Chinese immigration by prohibiting ships from bringing more than fifteen Chinese immigrants at a time. The bill was vetoed by President Rutherford B. Hayes on the grounds that it violated the Burlingame Treaty. With popular sentiment against continuing Chinese immigration, however, the treaty was amended in 1880, allowing the United States to limit the number of Chinese immigrants.

Exclusionary Legislation   The Chinese Exclusion Act was a response to the intensity of anti-Chinese feelings in the West and to close political elections that made western electoral votes critical. As signed into law by President Chester A. Arthur, the act suspended immigration by Chinese laborers for ten years. The vote in the House of Representatives reflected the popularity of the measure. There were 201 votes in favor, 37 against, and 51 absent. Representatives from every section of the country supported the bill, with southern and western House members voting unanimously for the legislation.

Later laws were even more draconian. An amendment in 1884 excluded all Chinese and Chinese residents living in other countries from entering the United States except as students, merchants, or tourists. The Scott Act of 1888 prohibited outright the entry of Chinese laborers and denied reentry to those who traveled abroad, even if they held reentry visas. The law also placed additional restrictions on those who were still permitted to come to the United States. In 1892 the Geary Act extended for an additional ten years the exclusion of Chinese immigrants, prohibited the use of habeas corpus by Chinese residents in the United States if

Editorial cartoon depicting president Rutherford B. Hayes standing on an ice drift representing the United States as he vetoes the Chinese Exclusion bill of California. Senator Denis Kearney is shown standing a piece of the ice drift ("Kearneyfornee") that is breaking away from the United States. (Library of Congress)

arrested, and required all Chinese people to register and provide proof of their eligibility to remain in the United States. The act was renewed in 1902, and Congress made permanent the exclusion of Chinese immigrant laborers in 1904.

These exclusionary laws reflected a bias in American attitudes toward immigration by non-Europeans and increasing racial discrimination. Restrictions on intermarriage and land ownership by Chinese in many western states during the early nineteenth century led to a reduction in the number of Chinese residing in the United States from more than 100,000 in 1890 to 61,639 by 1920.

On December 17, 1943, the Chinese Exclusion Act was repealed. By then the threat of competition by Chinese labor was no longer an issue, and China was an ally of the United States in the war with Japan.

James A. Baer

Further Reading

Aarim-Heriot, Najia. *Chinese Immigrants, African Americans, and Racial Anxiety in the United States, 1848-82*. Urbana: University of Illinois Press, 2003. Study of the interrelationships among African Americans, Chinese immigrants, and European Americans in the United States during the mid-nineteenth century, up until the time of the Chinese Exclusion Act.

Barth, Gunther. *Bitter Strength: A History of the Chinese in the United States, 1850-1870*. Cambridge, Mass.: Harvard University Press, 1964. Although it does not treat events after 1870, this book is important to an understanding of anti-Chinese sentiment in California.

Chan, Sucheng, ed. *Entry Denied: Exclusion and the Chinese Community in America, 1882-1943*. Philadelphia: Temple University Press, 1991. Explores the legal ramifications of the Exclusion Act and the act's effects on Chinese who were living in the United States.

Lee, Erika. *At America's Gates: Chinese Immigration During the Exclusion Era, 1882-1943*. Chapel Hill: University of North Carolina Press, 2003. Study of immigration from China to the United States from the time of the Chinese Exclusion Act to the loosening of American immigration laws during the 1960's, with an after ward on U.S. immigration policies after the terrorist attacks of September 11, 2001.

LeMay, Michael C. *From Open Door to Dutch Door: An Analysis of U.S. Immigration Policy Since 1820*. New York: Praeger, 1987. Examines underlying causes of the anti-immigration movement in the United States in response to European and Chinese immigration since 1820.

LeMay, Michael C., and Elliott Robert Barkan, eds. *U.S. Immigration and Naturalization Laws and Issues: A Documentary History*. Westport, Conn.: Greenwood Press, 1999. General history of changing American immigration legislation.

Miller, Stuart Creighton. *The Unwelcome Immigrant: The American Image of the Chinese, 1785-1882*. Berkeley: University of California Press, 1969. Countering Coolidge's argument of an economic basis for the Exclusion Act, argues that racism was at the root of Californian and U.S. hostility toward Chinese immigrants.

Peffer, George Anthony. *If They Don't Bring Women Here: Chinese Female Immigration Before Exclusion.* Urbana: University of Illinois Press, 1999. Study of the special problems faced by female Chinese immigrants in the years leading up to the Chinese Exclusion Act.

Railton, Ben. *The Chinese Exclusion Act: What It Can Teach Us About America.* New York: Palgrave Macmillan, 2013. An examination of what the Chinese Exclusion Act can teach us about American immigration policy and American identity.

Shanks, Cheryl. *Immigration and the Politics of American Sovereignty, 1890-1990.* Ann Arbor: University of Michigan Press, 2001. Scholarly study of changing federal immigration laws from the late nineteenth through the late twentieth centuries, with particular attention to changing quota systems and exclusionary policies.

Soennichsen, John. *The Chinese Exclusion Act of 1882.* Santa Barbara: Greenwood, 2011. An examination of the Chinese Exclusion Act in historical context.

See also Asian American stereotypes; Burlingame Treaty; Chinatowns; Chinese American Citizens Alliance; Chinese exclusion cases; Chinese immigrants; Chinese immigrants and California's gold rush; Chinese immigrants and family customs; Chinese Six Companies; Coolies; Immigration Act of 1943; Migration; Page law; Wong Kim Ark case; "Yellow peril" campaign.

CHINESE EXCLUSION CASES

The Cases: Six U.S. Supreme Court rulings (*Chew Heong v. United States*; *United States v. Jung Ah Lung*; *Chae Chan Ping v. United States*; *Fong Yue Ting v. United States*; *Wong Quan v. United States*; and *Lee Joe v. United States*) addressing issues raised by the Chinese Exclusion Act of 1882

Dates: 1884-1893

Immigration issues: Asian immigrants; Chinese immigrants; Court cases; Discrimination; Nativism and racism

Significance: Using the Fourteenth Amendment, the Supreme Court first ruled in favor of challenges to laws excluding the Chinese from immigrating and becoming U.S. citizens, then succumbed to popular sentiment and upheld exclusionary statutes.

In 1882 Congress enacted the first Chinese Exclusion Act, prohibiting Chinese laborers and miners from entering the United States. An 1884 amendment required resident Chinese laborers to have reentry certificates if they traveled outside the United States and planned to return. The 1888 Scott Act prohibited Chinese laborers temporarily abroad from returning, thereby stranding thousands of Chinese. Merchants and teachers were exempted from the Scott Act if they had "proper papers," thereby beginning the practice of using "paper names" to create new identities so that Chinese could return. The 1892 Geary Act banned all future Chinese laborers from entry and denied bail to Chinese in judicial proceedings. All Chinese faced deportation if they did not carry identification papers. The 1893 McCreary Act further extended the definition of laborers to include fishermen, miners, laundry owners, and merchants. The 1902 Chinese Exclusion Act permanently banned all Chinese immigration.

The Supreme Court initially attempted to defend Chinese rights under the Fourteenth Amendment; however, as anti-Chinese sentiment grew more pronounced, the Court withdrew even its limited protections from Chinese immigrants. The Court defended the right of Chinese to reenter the United States in *Chew Heong* and *Jung Ah Lung*. In *Chae Chan Ping*, it found the Scott Act unconstitutional. However, in the three 1893 cases, it upheld a law retroactively requiring that Chinese laborers have certificates of residence or be deported.

Reentry documents carried by a Chinese immigrant in 1891. Under an amendment to the Chinese Exclusion Act of 1882, Chinese immigrants wishing to visit their homeland were denied reentry to the United States if they failed to secure such documents before returning to China. (National Archives)

Richard L. Wilson

Further Reading

Chan, Sucheng, ed. *Entry Denied: Exclusion and the Chinese Community in America, 1882-1943*. Philadelphia: Temple University Press, 1991.

Lee, Erika. *At America's Gates: Chinese Immigration During the Exclusion Era, 1882-1943*. Chapel Hill: University of North Carolina Press, 2003.

Railton, Ben. *The Chinese Exclusion Act: What It Can Teach Us About America*. New York: Palgrave Macmillan, 2013.

Shanks, Cheryl. *Immigration and the Politics of American Sovereignty, 1890-1990*. Ann Arbor: University of Michigan Press, 2001.

Soennichsen, John. *The Chinese Exclusion Act of 1882*. Santa Barbara: Greenwood, 2011.

See also Asian American stereotypes; Burlingame Treaty; Chinatowns; Chinese American Citizens Alliance; Chinese Exclusion Act; Chinese immigrants; Chinese immigrants and California's gold rush; Chinese immigrants and family customs;

Chinese Six Companies; Coolies; Immigration Act of 1943; Migration; Page law; Wong Kim Ark case; "Yellow peril" campaign.

Chinese immigrants

Identification: Immigrants to North America from mainland China

Immigration issues: Asian immigrants; Chinese immigrants; Demographics

Significance: The Chinese first came to the United States as laborers during the early to mid-nineteenth century, finding considerable prejudice and discrimination, which diminished after World War II.

Chinese people began to immigrate to the United States in 1820, but their

Chinese immigrants eating a meal aboard the crowded ship carrying them to the western United States. (Asian American Studies Library, University of California at Berkeley)

numbers remained small until the late 1840's, when the decaying empire of China was defeated in 1848 by Great Britain in the First Opium War. In 1849, gold was discovered in California, and the gold rush began. When word of the gold rush reached Canton, in the southeastern province of Kwangtung, many Cantonese peasants, who had made their living as laborers, farmers, and fishermen for centuries, began to leave their impoverished homeland for the chance of riches just across the Pacific.

According to U.S. Census figures, 1,477,680 people immigrated to the United States from China between 1820 and 2003. During the first three years of the twenty-first century, Chinese immigrants continued to enter the country at a rate of about 48,000 persons per year. According to the 1990 U.S. Census, Americans of Chinese ancestry from China, Hong Kong, and Taiwan numbered more than 1,700,000 persons.

Most of these early Chinese immigrants worked with exceptional diligence, industry, and enterprise and led a reticent existence in the mining camps and cities. These positive qualities earned the early Chinese immigrants acceptance among the California business community. Although their appearance set them apart from the rest of the townspeople, they were warmly welcomed as a valuable and respected segment of the citizenry. That goodwill wore thin as increasing numbers

Chinese fire-hose teams racing down the main thoroughfare of the notorious mining town Deadwood, Dakota, during a Fourth of July celebration around the end of the nineteenth century. (Library of Congress)

of Chinese arrived. In 1852 alone, more than twenty thousand Chinese landed at San Francisco, bringing the total number of Chinese on the coast to approximately twenty-five thousand. The flood of new arrivals severely taxed the city's resources, particularly in Chinatown, where most settled, at least temporarily. The white settlers' attitude toward the Chinese and Chinatown began to shift from curiosity to contempt.

Under the slogan "California for Americans," nativists began demanding legislation to restrict Chinese laborers and miners. In 1852, the California legislature responded by passing the state's first discriminatory tax law, the Foreign Miners' Tax. This law required all miners who were not citizens of the United States to pay a monthly license fee. Because the Chinese were the largest recognizable group of foreign miners and already were concentrated in easily accessible mining camps, they constituted the majority of those taxed. California governor John Bigler also began a crusade against Chinese immigration on the grounds that it constituted a danger to the welfare of the state. The efforts of California nativists culminated in the Chinese Exclusion Act of 1882, one of the earliest federal laws restricting immigration to the United States. Other legislation followed, including the alien land laws (1913-1923), the Cable Act (1922), and the National Origins Act (1924).

As a result of the exclusion, and because men far outnumbered women, the American Chinese population remained stable until the 1950's.

Chinese American Experiences The image of Chinese Americans improved during this period, which ranges from 1942, the first full year of U.S. war against Japan, to 1965, the year of the Immigration and Nationality Act. This improvement was in part the result of China's being an important ally of the United States in World War II. A public awareness of the difference between Chinese Americans and Japanese Americans began to develop, at the expense of the latter. The Chinese American literature of this period is dominated by two sentiments, a diplomatic sentiment, which seeks to explain the values and virtues of the Chinese heritage to the general reader, and a sentiment of belonging, of claiming America as home.

After 1965, the Chinese population of the United States rose from 250,000 in 1966 to 1.6 million in 1990. This gave rise to a debate over what, if any, distinctions should be drawn between the native-born and the foreign-born. Frank Chin and the other editors of *Aiiieeeee! An Anthology of Asian-American Writers* (1974) and *The Big Aiiieeeee! An Anthology of Chinese American and Japanese American Literature* (1991) attempt to differentiate between the native-born and the foreign-born, implying that Chinese American identity should be determined on the basis of an American, rather than Chinese, mindset. Newcomers (sometimes derided as "fresh off the boat," source of the title of David Henry Hwang's *FOB*, 1979) and more recent arrivals have brought with them significant resources and skills. These conditions render moot the American-centered definition of Chinese American identity. The increased diversity of the Chinese American community has made the issue of identity complex.

A common theme in twentieth century Chinese American literature is the critical representation of social issues. Cultural conflicts, generation gaps, and gender troubles are common to the experiences of many Chinese Americans from diverse backgrounds. This literature, including Maxine Hong Kingston's *The Woman Warrior* (1976) and *Tripmaster Monkey: His Fake Book* (1989), is essential to Chinese American identity and tends to problematize rather than resolve its dualities. This exploration of social issues has given rise to critiques of the American Dream (for example, Gish Jen's *Typical American*, 1991), of Western ideology regarding Asia (Hwang's *M. Butterfly*, 1988), and of the intricate complicities between American and Chinese ideologies. These thoughtful works epitomize the complex maturity of the Chinese American identity.

Compiled from essays by Balance Chow and Daniel J. Meissner

Further Reading

For comprehensive and up-to-date studies of Chinese immigrants, see H. Mark Lai's *Becoming Chinese American: A History of Communities and Institutions* (Walnut Creek, Calif.: AltaMira, 2004) and Birgit Zinzius's *Chinese America: Stereotype and Reality—History, Present, and Future of the Chinese Americans* (New York: P. Lang, 2005).

Victor R. Greene's *A Singing Ambivalence: American Immigrants Between Old World and New, 1830-1930* (Kent, Ohio: Kent State University Press, 2004) is a comparative study of the different challenges faced by members of eight major immigrant groups, including the Chinese.

Chinese Americans and the Politics of Race and Culture (Philadelphia: Temple University Press, 2008), ed. by Suecheng Chan and Madeliney Hsu, is a collection of essays on politics culture, and identity in the Chinese American community.

Gunther Barth's *Bitter Strength: A History of the Chinese in the United States, 1850-1870* (Cambridge, Mass.: Harvard University Press, 1964) describes the early years of Chinese immigration, providing a good examination of the development of anti-Chinese sentiment in California.

Bonnie Tsui's *American Chinatown: A People's History of Five Neighborhoods* (New York: Free Press, 2009) looks at contemporary life in Chinatowns in New York City, Los Angeles, Honolulu, San Francisco, and Las Vegas.

Stuart Creighton Miller's *The Unwelcome Immigrant: The American Image of the Chinese, 1795-1882* (Berkeley: University of California Press, 1969) examines Chinese immigration in terms of coolie labor and the fear that Chinese laborers would undermine labor and revive slavery.

Erika Lee's *At America's Gates: Chinese Immigration During the Exclusion Era, 1882-1943* (Chapel Hill: University of North Carolina Press, 2003) explores the period of limited Chinese immigration after the Chinese Exclusion Act and includes an afterword on U.S. immigration policies after the terrorist attacks of September 11, 2001.

Ellen Alexander Conley's *The Chosen Shore: Stories of Immigrants* (Berkeley: University of California Press, 2004) is a collection of firsthand accounts of modern immigrants from many nations, including China.

Studies of the adaptation of Chinese immigrants to life in the United States include Nazli Kibria's *Becoming Asian American: Second-Generation Chinese and*

Korean American Identities (Baltimore: Johns Hopkins University Press, 2002) and Lee-Beng Chua's *Psychosocial Adaptation and the Meaning of Achievement for Chinese Immigrants* (New York: LFB Scholarly Publications, 2002).

See also Asian American literature; Asian American stereotypes; Chinatowns; Chinese American Citizens Alliance; Chinese detentions in New York; Chinese Exclusion Act; Chinese exclusion cases; Chinese immigrants and California's gold rush; Chinese immigrants and family customs; Chinese Six Companies; Coolies; Immigration Act of 1943; *Lau v. Nichols*; Page law; Wong Kim Ark case.

CHINESE IMMIGRANTS AND CALIFORNIA'S GOLD RUSH

The Event: Participation of Chinese immigrants in California's gold rush
Date: 1849-1852
Place: San Francisco

Immigration issues: Asian immigrants; Chinese immigrants; Economics; Labor; Nativism and racism

Significance: A major impetus to immigration from East Asia, the California gold rush drew thousands of Chinese immigrants, who furnished hard labor and suffered nativist antipathy.

In 1848, the electrifying news that gold had been discovered in California was carried by every ship sailing from U.S. ports. Spread to every corner of the world, the word soon began to draw adventurers away from family and livelihoods to seek their fortunes in this distant land. In 1849, a tremendous number of pioneers—German, Irish, Scandinavian, Russian, Mexican, and others—streamed into San Francisco, doubling the population of the state within two years. Among these "forty-niners" was one group set apart by race, dress, and language—the Chinese. Drawn to the United States by the promise of golden wealth, the Chinese arrived in ever-increasing numbers, to the growing alarm of California residents.

Almost all the Chinese entering the United States at this time came from the area around Canton, in the southeastern province of Kwangtung. For centuries, Cantonese peasants had made their living as laborers, farmers, and fishermen. During the late 1840's, floods, famines, peasant revolts, and overpopulation forced many to leave their villages and seek work in nearby countries in the South China Sea. When word reached the province of gold mines opening in California, Cantonese were eager to leave their impoverished homeland for the chance of riches just across the Pacific. They were cautious, however—the journey was long, expensive, and uncertain. Only three Chinese made the trip in 1848.

Chinese immigrant panning for gold in a California stream. (Asian American Studies Library, University of California at Berkeley)

Gold Strikes in California In 1849, the news of larger and richer gold claims in California enticed 325 Cantonese to set sail for San Francisco. Most of these young, unskilled men were sojourners, hoping to prospect for a few years, acquire wealth, and return home. Like other new arrivals in the city, they outfitted themselves with supplies, including sturdy boots in place of their cotton shoes, and set out for the gold-bearing mountains around Sacramento. They often traveled and worked in groups for companionship and protection, taking over low-yielding claims that had been abandoned for more prosperous sites. Through diligence and frugality, honed by generations of marginal existence in China, they frequently turned abandoned claims into profitable ventures.

Not all Chinese immigrants, however, sought wealth in the gold mines. Some found work in the cities, particularly San Francisco, which offered abundant opportunity for unskilled laborers. Shops, restaurants, liveries, hotels, and other businesses grew desperately short of workers as able-bodied men abandoned their jobs to pan for gold. Chinese—newly arrived immigrants or disheartened miners—began filling these positions as general laborers, carpenters, and cooks. They also assumed jobs normally reserved for women—who were in short supply in this rugged frontier boomtown—such as seamstresses, launderers, and domestics. Their conscientious work style, quiet demeanor, and dependable service made them ideal employees. California businessmen soon began sending advertising notices to Canton, recruiting Chinese workers for their various enterprises.

Successful Chinese miners and workers also began opening their own businesses in the cities. In addition to equipping miners and supplying mining camps, they established restaurants, hotels, and various small businesses catering to both Chinese and Westerners. Norman As-sing, an English-speaking Chinese man who settled in San Francisco, managed his own candy store, bakery, and a popular restaurant in which he often entertained local politicians and policemen with lavish banquets. In December, 1849, his fellow countrymen elected him as the leader of the first Chinese mutual-aid society in the United States, an organization assisting newly arrived Chinese immigrants. This association filled an important role for the Chinese, who relied greatly on family and village relations for social and economic sufficiency.

Through letters and returning sojourners, news of profitable work in the cities and mines reached relatives and friends in Kwangtung. In 1850, approximately 450 more Chinese emigrated to California; the following year, the number jumped to more than 2,700. These new arrivals found assistance and familiar food and lodging in San Francisco's new Chinatown, a district in which Chinese had begun to settle for convenience and safety. After a short period of adjustment, most Chinese immigrants followed their predecessors into the mountains, joining one of the many Chinese mining camps operating around Sacramento. Others remained in the city to work as manual laborers. In general, these early Chinese immigrants worked with exceptional diligence, industry, and enterprise and led a reticent existence in the mining camps and cities.

Acceptance by the Business Community These positive qualities earned the early Chinese immigrants acceptance among the California business community. Although their waist-length braided hair, blue cotton pants and jackets, and broad-brimmed straw hats set them apart from the rest of the townspeople and "forty-niners," they were warmly welcomed as a valuable and respected segment of the citizenry. A San Francisco judge summed up the early goodwill of Americans toward the Chinese:

> Born and reared under different Governments and speaking different tongues, we nevertheless meet here today as brothers. . . . You stand among us in all respects as equals.

That goodwill wore thin as increasing numbers of Chinese arrived in the city. In 1852 alone, more than twenty thousand Chinese landed at San Francisco, bringing the total number of Chinese on the coast to approximately twenty-five thousand.

The flood of new arrivals severely taxed the city's resources, particularly in China-town, where most settled, at least temporarily. In packed Chinese boardinghouses, one cot was often rented to a number of workers who slept on it on a rotating basis. Overcrowding created sanitation problems, increased crime, and caused higher prices. Abundant cheap labor stimulated competition for unskilled work that, over time, drove down wages. The white settlers' attitude toward the Chinese and Chinatown began to shift from curiosity to contempt.

The attitude of white miners in the goldfields also changed. Prior to 1852, bandits and claim-jumpers had occasionally driven Chinese off successful excavations, but these attacks were generally motivated by greed, not racism. After 1852, antagonism and violence against Chinese miners increased. In Jacksonville, white miners drove Chinese miners off their claims and out of town. In Chili Gulch, a mob beat a Chinese miner to death. For protection, Chinese banded together in large mining camps, easily recognized by names such as China City, China Creek, China Flat, China Gulch, and China Town.

Nativist Backlash Under the slogan "California for Americans," nativists began demanding legislation to restrict Chinese laborers and miners. In 1852, the California legislature responded by passing the state's first discriminatory tax law, the Foreign Miners' Tax. This law required all miners who were not citizens of the United States to pay a monthly license fee. Since the Chinese were the largest recognizable group of foreign miners and already were concentrated in easily accessible mining camps, they constituted the majority of those taxed. The same year, California state senator George B. Tingley introduced a bill to eliminate "coolie labor"—contracts made with Chinese laborers for work in California—for a set number of years.

California governor John Bigler also began a crusade against Chinese immigration on the grounds that it constituted a danger to the welfare of the state. Tong K. Achick, a missionar y-schooled, English-speaking Cantonese who emigrated to San Francisco, represented the Chinese position before the California legislature. As leader of the Four Great Houses in San Francisco— forerunner of the famous Six Companies—he argued that these laws unfairly targeted law-abiding Chinese, who were an asset, not a liability, to the state.

The mood in California, however, had changed, and Tong and other Chinese advocates were unable to stop the growing anti-Chinese sentiment. California nativists continued to push for state and national legislation limiting Chinese immigration. Their efforts culminated in the Chinese Exclusion Act of 1882, the first federal legislation restricting immigration to the United States.

Daniel J. Meissner

Further Reading

Aarim-Heriot, Najia. *Chinese Immigrants, African Americans, and Racial Anxiety in the United States, 1848-82*. Urbana: University of Illinois Press, 2003. Study of the interrelationships among African Americans, Chinese immigrants, and European Americans in the United States during the mid-nineteenth century.

Barth, Gunther. *Bitter Strength: A History of the Chinese in the United States, 1850-1870.* Cambridge, Mass.: Harvard University Press, 1964. Describes the early years of Chinese immigration, providing a good examination of the development of anti-Chinese sentiment in California.

Miller, Stuart Creighton. *The Unwelcome Immigrant: The American Image of the Chinese, 1795-1882.* Berkeley: University of California Press, 1969. Examines Chinese immigration in terms of coolie labor and the fear that Chinese laborers would undermine labor and revive slavery.

Peffer, George Anthony. *If They Don't Bring Women Here: Chinese Female Immigration Before Exclusion.* Urbana: University of Illinois Press, 1999. Study of the special problems confronting female Chinese immigration to the United States during a period when the over whelming bulk of Chinese immigrants were men.

Takaki, Ronald. *Strangers from a Different Shore: A History of Asian Americans.* New York: Penguin Books, 1989. Chapter 3 succinctly examines the early years of Chinese immigration. Other chapters explore the Asian immigrant experience in detail.

Yung, Judy, Gordon H. Chang, and Him Mark Lai, eds. *Chinese American Voices: From the Gold Rush to the Present.* Berkeley: University of California Press, 2006. A collection of documents written by Chinese American and placed into context by the editors, from the 1850s to the present.

See also Burlingame Treaty; California gold rush; Chinatowns; Chinese Exclusion Act; Chinese immigrants; Chinese immigrants and family customs; Chinese Six Companies; Coolies; "Yellow peril" campaign.

CHINESE IMMIGRANTS AND FAMILY CUSTOMS

Immigration issues: Asian immigrants; Chinese immigrants; Families and marriage

Significance: Chinese Americans have drawn on a tradition of strong family relationships to help overcome discrimination and become one of the most successful immigrant groups in the United States.

Chinese Americans constitute the oldest and largest Asian American group in the United States. North Americans who identify themselves as Chinese are scattered throughout the fifty states and Canada with their largest concentrations in California, New York, Hawaii, Massachusetts, Illinois, British Columbia, and Ontario.

More than many other ethnic groups, Chinese Americans have labored to maintain the tradition of strong families and obedience to cultural traditions. While the roles of Chinese Americans under went great changes after World War II, most of them strongly desire to maintain traditions fostered by obedience to Confucian values.

Immigration and Discrimination Significant Chinese immigration to North America began in response to the California gold rush of 1848-1849. Seven thousand miles across the Pacific Ocean, China was a rapidly growing country plagued by foreign domination, political instability, and a weakened dynastic government. Before 1848, political and social stability in China had discouraged emigration to North America.

After news of American "mountains of gold" reached southern China, thousands of Chinese men joined Germans, Irish, Spanish, English, and other immigrants in the hunt for gold in Northern California. San Francisco was soon dubbed Jinshan, or "golden mountain," by newly arrived Chinese settlers. Mainly from southern China, Chinese immigrants were predominantly male. Most hoped to make money and return to their families in China. Like most gold seekers, these settlers became more frustrated than rich.

Reluctant to return home without money, most Chinese accepted positions in various trades that sought workers to offset severe labor shortages in the West. While typically paid less than non-Asian workers, Chinese immigrants were reluctant to return to the political instability and lower wages that awaited them in China. Chinese workers played an important part in the construction of the western section of the transcontinental railroad. Chinese immigrants working on the railroad were so valued for their dedication to hard work that the Central Pacific Railroad began to recruit workers in China. Even after the railroad was completed, immigration from China continued, and newly arrived Chinese immigrants were able to find jobs in factories and farms. Between 1860 and 1880 immigrants from China constituted more than 8 percent of California's population.

Scapegoating Chinese Immigrants As the North American economy entered a depression during the early 1880's, Chinese immigrants became convenient scapegoats for populist politicians, labor unions, and unemployed non-Asians. Even in Canadian British Columbia, the small Chinese population was blamed by many for the overall economic downturn. In response to growing anti-Chinese sentiments in the West, the United States moved to ban Chinese immigration with the passage of the Chinese Exclusion Act of 1882. The law suspended Chinese immigration and declared Chinese immigrants already in the United States ineligible for citizenship. While Chinese immigrants made up only an estimated 0.002 percent of the American population at the time, the act received wide support and severely limited Chinese immigration into the next century. In 1888 the Scott Act stiffened the 1882 law by prohibiting the entry of Chinese nationals into the United States. The Geary Act of 1892 extended the exclusion of Chinese immigrants by denying *habeas corpus* rights to persons of Chinese ancestry and requiring all persons of Chinese ancestry to register with local authorities. Immediate deportation threatened those Chinese immigrants who failed to comply with the requirement that they carry official permits. Despite a court challenge by

Family-run Chinese laundry operation around 1910. During the nineteenth and early twentieth centuries, Chinese immigrants became so closely associated with laundries that Chinese laundry workers became a popular stereotype. (California State Library)

American citizens of Chinese ancestry, the act was upheld by the U.S. Supreme Court. On the West Coast, numerous local laws were passed to limit the growth of Chinese businesses and settlements.

Severely hindered by discriminatory legal codes and racism, Chinese immigrants responded by constructing social structures to serve the needs of their existing population. So-called "Chinatowns" established schools, newspapers, businesses, and cultural institutions. For the most part, Chinese immigrants maintained a willingness to preserve family and cultural traditions despite the racism they experienced in North America. The 1906 San Francisco earthquake marked an important milestone in the growth of the Chinese American family. At that time, only 5 percent of the city's Chinese population were female. After the city's birth records were destroyed in the earthquake, thousands of Chinese claimed they had been born in the United States. Unable to refute their applications for naturalization, the U.S. government was forced to grant them citizenship and allow Chinese spouses to immigrate to the United States. After Chinese families were reunited, the traditional Confucian values of obedience and dedication to family remained an important element in Chinese American culture.

The Making of a "Model Minority" As discriminatory practices and laws were overturned in the twentieth century, Chinese Americans moved to integrate themselves into the mainstream of American culture. The U.S. alliance with China

Chinese woman with her five children in Hawaii in 1913. (NARA)

in its fight against Japan during World War II served as a major impetus to repeal barriers to immigration. As restrictions on immigration eased, families grew and typically worked hard to obtain educational opportunities for their children. The emphasis on education was so successful that by 1970, 56 percent of working Chinese held white-collar jobs, a figure above the national average.

Chinese Americans have generally attempted to maintain ties to their homeland and adhere to cultural traditions. Central to this effort is their use of the Chinese language as part of primary and secondary education. Knowledge of the Chinese language is a valued cultural tradition and a marketable job skill, particularly as North American trade with Asia has grown. In addition to preserving their language, most Chinese Americans observe traditional Chinese festivals. The most significant, the so-called Spring Festival, or Chinese New Year, is widely observed by Chinese Americans. This celebration is based upon the Chinese lunar calendar and is marked by a large family meal on New Year's eve. Children are presented with *hong bao*, red envelopes containing money, and fireworks are often used to scare off evil spirits. In 1993 the U.S. Postal Service issued a commemorative stamp in honor of the Chinese New Year.

Other major festivals include the mid-autumn Moon Festival to celebrate the annual harvest. Similar to the North American tradition of Thanksgiving Day, this festival celebrates the harvest and the good fortunes of the previous year. This holiday also centers on a large family dinner and is marked by the consumption of moon cakes stuffed with candied fruits. Other major festivals include the Dragon Boat Festival on the fifth day of the fifth moon according to the Chinese calendar. This festival is celebrated with sticky rice cakes and boat races.

Chinese immigration swelled during the 1980's and 1990's, so that in 2004, the Chinese American community included 49.1 percent who entered the U.S. before 1990, 34.1 percent who entered between 1990 and 1999, and 16.8 percent who entered in 2000 or later. With this new influx of immigrants, the role of the family in Chinese culture continued to change. As Chinese Americans became socially and economically diverse and obtained higher-paying jobs, the traditional commitment to the wishes of the family weakened. Because of the economic successes of some Chinese Americans, current stereotypes have also undergone radical change. Once denounced as "coolies" for their willingness to work hard for lower wages, many Chinese have been labeled a "model minority" for their perceived overcommitment to financial responsibility, education, and work.

For instance, in 2004, over half (50.2 percent) of Chinese Americans had at least a bachelor's degree, as compared to 27.0 percent of the U.S. population as a whole, and 52.0 percent of Chinese Americans worked in management, professional or related occupations, as compared with 34.1 percent of the U.S. population as a whole. On average, the Chinese also out-earned the general U.S. population: in 2004 the median household income for Chinese Americans was $57,433, well above the national average of $44,684. While it is significant that many Chinese Americans have college degrees and have achieved economic and professional success, many of them resent the model-minority stereotype, because it tends to overlook the discrimination toward Chinese Americans that has persisted in American culture.

Lawrence I. Clark

Further Reading

Brownstone, David M. *The Chinese-American Heritage*. New York: Facts On File, 1988. General sur vey of the Chinese immigrant experience in the United States.

Chen, Shehong. *Being Chinese, Becoming Chinese American*. Urbana: University of Illinois Press, 2002. Scholarly study of the sociological evolution of Chinese American communities since the early twentieth century.

Chua, Lee-Beng. *Psycho-social Adaptation and the Meaning of Achievement for Chinese Immigrants*. New York: LFB Scholarly Publications, 2002. Sociological analysis of the adaptative processes through which Chinese immigrants to the United States go, with a close examination of traditional Chinese belief systems.

Hoobler, Dorothy, and Thomas Hoobler. *The Chinese American Family Album*. New York: Oxford University Press, 1994. Exploration of the experiences of Chinese Americans that contains a broad range of first-person accounts— including personal recollections, diary entries, and letters—to accompany many photographs.

Kibria, Nazli. *Becoming Asian American: Second-Generation Chinese and Korean American Identities*. Baltimore: Johns Hopkins University Press, 2002. Comparative study of second-generation Chinese and Korean Americans.

Kuhn, Philip A. *Chinese Among Others: Emigration in Modern Times*. Lanham: Rowman & Littlefield, 2008. A study of how the Chinese as individuals and as families dealt with the demands of being emigrants in foreign lands.

Kwok-bun, Chan, ed. *International Handbook of Chinese Families*. New York: Springer, 2013. A comprehensive resource for understanding the Chinese family as a social institution, both in China and in other countries.

Lai, H. Mark. *Becoming Chinese American: A History of Communities and Institutions*. Walnut Creek, Calif.: AltaMira, 2004. Study of cultural adaptations of Chinese immigrants to the United States. Includes chapters on Chinese cultural and rights advocacy organizations.

Louie, Vivian S. *Compelled to Excel: Immigration, Education, and Opportunity Among Chinese Americans*. Stanford, Calif.: Stanford University Press, 2004. Sociological study of the largely family-driven Chinese drive to achieve success in education and business.

Peffer, George Anthony. *If They Don't Bring Women Here: Chinese Female Immigration Before Exclusion*. Urbana: University of Illinois Press, 1999. Study of female immigration during a period when the bulk of Chinese immigrants to the United States were young men.

See also Asian American stereotypes; Chinatowns; Chinese immigrants; Chinese immigrants and California's gold rush; Filipino immigrants and family customs; Korean immigrants and family customs; Southeast Asian immigrants; Vietnamese immigrants.

CHINESE SIX COMPANIES

Identification: Chinese immigrant protective association that merged several older organizations

Date: Begun in 1854

Place: San Francisco, California

Immigration issues: Asian immigrants; Chinese immigrants; Civil rights and liberties

Significance: Rising anti-Asian nativism prompted Chinese immigrants living on the West Coast to organize for political representation, social services, and physical protection.

News of the California gold rush of 1848-1849 was the first catalyst for large Chinese emigration across the Pacific to the United States. Most of the immigrants were young men who worked as laborers, often on the transcontinental railroads. The completion of the railroads and the Panic of 1873, which was brought on by an international financial crisis, had caused great economic difficulties in the West, and many white Americans and elements of organized labor began to blame the Chinese for the lack of jobs and the economic recession. Violence against Chinese became widespread. In October, 1871, crowds of whites burned and looted the Los

Angeles Chinatown after two white policemen were killed by Chinese assailants. Nineteen men, women, and children were killed and hundreds injured as angry whites randomly attacked crowds of Chinese.

Anti-Chinese Laws   Under intense political pressure from white voters in the West, Congress moved to exclude Chinese and other foreign-born Asians from obtaining citizenship. The 1870 Nationality Act denied the Chinese the possibility of becoming naturalized U.S. citizens. In 1878, California convened a constitutional convention that prohibited further Chinese immigration and granted local municipalities the right to exclude Chinese immigrants or confine them to specified areas.

Chinese immigrants were prohibited from owning property, obtaining business licenses, procuring government jobs, and testifying in any legal proceedings. At the urging of white voters in California, the U.S. Congress in 1882 passed the first of a number of Chinese exclusion acts that prohibited the entrance of Chinese into the United States. The Supreme Court upheld the exclusion acts, ruling in 1889 that the Chinese were "a race that will not assimilate with us [and] could be excluded when deemed dangerous to peace and security."

In San Francisco, anti-Chinese laws were supplemented to isolate its large Chinese community. Local laws and hostility from whites forced newly arrived Chinese to settle in Chinatown. Segregated by these discriminatory laws, Chinatown began to establish structures to govern and protect its residents. San Francisco's Chinatown, made up primarily of men as a result of the immigration control acts, had developed a reputation as a center of vice. Chinatown leaders moved to control the small criminal element that had begun to define Chinese society to the non-Chinese residents of San Francisco.

The Six Companies Form   Most of the early Chinese immigrants to San Francisco's Chinatown came from the southern provinces of Guangdong and Fujian. Early on, wealthy merchants in Chinatown had organized around clan groups and district associations in their hometowns in China. By 1854, there were six main associations in Chinatown. The first, formed in 1849, was the Gangzhou Gongsi, named after the district in Guangdong province that was the source of most of its members. The second, the Sany i Gongsi, consisted of immigrants from the administrative districts of Nanhai, Panyu, and Shunde. Immigrants from the districts of Yanging, Xinning, Xinhui, and Kaiping made up the third association, the Siy i Gongsi. Immigrants from the Xiangshan area formed the fourth association, the Yang He Gongsi. The fifth, the Ren He Gongsi, was made up of the so-called Hakka peoples from Guanxi province.

The formation in 1854 of the sixth association, the Ning Yang Gongsi, marked the informal beginnings of the Chinese Six Companies Association. The Six Companies served as a public association for leaders of the major associations in Chinatown to mediate disputes between its members and serve as a representative of the Chinese community as a whole. Newly arrived immigrants from China who were in need of assistance sought out these family or district associations. When business or personal disputes developed between members of

Unemployed men loitering on the "Street of the Gamblers" in San Francisco's Chinatown around the turn of the twentieth century, when San Francisco had the largest concentration of Chinese immigrants in North America. (Library of Congress)

different associations, the Six Companies would provide a forum for peaceful mediation of disputes.

The Role of the Companies The anti-Chinese legislation of the 1880's forced the Six Companies to move toward a more overt role as representatives of Chinese interests in San Francisco. On November 19, 1882, the group formalized its existence by establishing an executive body drawn from members of the existing associations. The Six Companies, formally known as the Chinese Consolidated Benevolent Association (CCBA), adapted some of the representative principles of U.S. political culture. The CCBA was recognized by the state of California in 1901. At the time, the Six Companies sought to create a body above family clans or associations that would resist the growing anti-Chinese movements in California and the western United States and would assume a more public role in its resistance to anti-Chinese legislation.

The Six Companies in San Francisco had limited success in challenging anti-Chinese legislation as violations of the Fourteenth Amendment to the U.S. Constitution. The Six Companies supported the 1886 case of *Yick Wo v. Hopkins*, which forced the Supreme Court to overturn San Francisco safety ordinances designed to harass Chinese laundrymen. Anti-Chinese attitudes in San Francisco and across the United States did not diminish after 1900. In 1902, an amendment to extend the Chinese Exclusion Act of 1882 indefinitely was passed by Congress without debate.

In the first half of the twentieth century, the Six Companies in San Francisco supported measures to improve the quality of life in Chinatown. In 1905, the Six Companies established a school in Chinatown to teach children Chinese culture and language. During the 1920's, it helped raise funds to construct the Chinese Hospital to serve the Chinatown community. The Six Companies also established block watch programs and night patrols to prevent crime in the Chinatown area. The group still worked to overturn antiChinese sentiment and was an increasingly powerful political force, able to deliver votes to local politicians sympathetic to the views of Chinatown citizens.

In 1943, Congress passed an Immigration Act that repealed the exclusion laws, and barriers to Chinese Americans in the United States began to fall. In California, many Americans of Chinese ancestry moved to white neighborhoods after anti-Chinese laws were overturned. In this period, one of the major activities of the Six Companies was the promotion of the Nationalist government in Taiwan. Because most of the residents of San Francisco's Chinatown had immigrated from mainland China, significant opposition to the historical leadership of the group appeared.

The Six Companies' promotion of social isolation from white society was very divisive during the 1960's. A longtime opponent of federal social programs to aid the poor, the Six Companies eventually embraced government assistance and even administered federal job training programs during the 1970's. As Chinese Americans became more involved in Chinese politics and gained access to higher-paying jobs, participation in Chinatown affairs decreased significantly. The Six Companies became less of a force in Chinese American politics on a national scale, but it continued to work from its base in San Francisco.

Lawrence I. Clark

Further Reading

Victor Nee and Brett de Barry Nee's "The Establishment," in Longtime Californ': A Documentary Study of an American Chinatown (New York: Pantheon Books, 1973), examines the founding of the Six Companies and its role in Chinatown in the twentieth century.

Thomas W. Chinn's Bridging the Pacific: San Francisco Chinatown and Its People (San Francisco: Chinese Historical Society of America, 1989) provides a detailed look at San Francisco from its founding to the late 1980's, by the cofounder of the Chinese Historical Association of America, while Bonnie Tsui's American Chinatown: A People's History of Five Neighborhoods (New York: Free Press, 2009) offers a current look at five American Chinatowns, including the one in San Francisco.

See also Burlingame Treaty; California gold rush; Chinatowns; Chinese American Citizens Alliance; Chinese Exclusion Act; Chinese immigrants; Chinese immigrants and family customs; Coolies; "Yellow peril" campaign.

CITIZENSHIP

Definition: Status of being a citizen—an inhabitant of a country who enjoys its full privileges and rights, such as the right to vote, to hold elective office, and to enjoy the full protections of government

Immigration issues: Citizenship and naturalization; Civil rights and liberties

Significance: Citizenship is a legal term recognizing certain rights and protections; it implies responsibilities as well as privileges. A large portion of immigrants to the United States seek citizenship, but not all qualify for it.

Residence in a particular place does not automatically give a person citizenship. Citizenship must be conferred by law or by constitution. The definition of a citizen was not spelled out in the U.S. Constitution until the Fourteenth Amendment was passed in 1868. That amendment states:

> All persons born or naturalized in the United States, and subject to the jurisdiction thereof, are citizens of the United States and of the State wherein they reside.

Birthright Citizenship and the English Heritage Americans are accustomed to the concept of automatic citizenship granted to persons born in the United States, who are called "natural-born citizens." Historically, this was not a common concept. Most nations were more like ancient Rome, which had different degrees of citizenship while the majority of people in the Roman Empire were merely "subjects" of Rome and did not have the rights of citizenship. Many were slaves of Rome. Rome had two classes of citizens: full citizens and those who could own property and engage in business but could not hold public office. The children of these "half citizens" received the same political status as their parents.

The concept of American citizenship grew from English roots. During the Middle Ages, political loyalties and protections came from the feudal system that operated in Europe for a thousand years. A characteristic of modern times was the development of the idea of nation-states and with that the concept of nationality. Both obligations and rights were intrinsic to the status of having a nationality.

The English common law held that people born within the royal dominions were automatically the "king's subjects." If one's parents were "naturalborn subjects," then one had an inherent claim to the "rights of Englishmen." As early as 1350 it was clear that in English law the place of birth was not so important as the citizenship of a child's parents. In legal terms, citizenship was affected by *jus soli* (birthplace) and *jus sanguinis* (descent).

Colonial Background The American colonists were merely English people residing in America, and they claimed all their rights as Englishmen. The Virginia Charter of 1606 recognized that situation, and in it the king granted to all his subjects living in the "Colonies and Plantations," as well as to any children born there, "all Liberties,

Franchises, and Immunities, within any of our other Dominions, to all intents and purposes, as if they had been abiding and born, within this our Realm of England."

In fact it was this very concept of equality of Englishmen, regardless of where in the realm they lived, that provided a philosophical basis for the American war for independence. The Americans demanded equal treatment and claimed that their own "American parliaments" (assemblies) should rule over them rather than the British Parliament in London. Not all American colonists were English, however, and that fact raised questions of citizenship. It was much easier to become naturalized citizens in America than in England. English Americans from the earliest days of settlement had accepted "foreigners" as equal subjects of the king.

Citizenship: Limited or Absolute? Are the obligations of citizenship and allegiance limited or absolute? This was a key question in the disputes between England and the American colonies before the American Revolution. In the Declaratory Act of 1766 the British Parliament claimed to have full authority "to make laws and statutes of sufficient force and validity to bind the colonies and people of America, subjects of the crown of Great Britain."

The Americans categorically rejected that idea of unlimited political authority over them. They claimed their rights as Englishmen to make their own laws within their colonial assemblies. They rejected the idea that the British Parliament could dictate to them and accepted the authority of the English king only in a limited constitutional sense. Citizenship required allegiance, but as freemen, not as slaves. Patrick Henry eloquently expressed the attitude of his countrymen:

> Is life so sweet and peace so dear as to be purchased at the price of chains and slavery? Forbid it, Almighty God! I know not what course others may take, but, as for me, give me Liberty or give me Death!

Contractual American Citizenship The result was an independent United States and a constitution that spelled out the limits of governmental authority. The government was to be strong enough to provide for the common defense and a stable society, but it was to be limited in its interference in the lives of the free citizens of the United States. Citizens owed obedience to governments only in exchange for the protection of their fundamental rights. It was essentially a contract with mutual obligations on both sides.

The new state governments had the authority to grant citizenship within their borders. They did so and welcomed many new immigrants. Typically the states required a year or two of residence within the state and an oath of allegiance and good moral character for a person to become a citizen.

After the U.S. Constitution went into effect, the Naturalization Act of 1802 required five years of residence, a loyalty oath accepting the principles of the Constitution, and proof of good character and behavior for a person to become a United States citizen. The law also required all immigrants to register with the government.

Citizenship Denied During the nineteenth century there were two classes of people born in the United States who were denied citizenship in that country: slaves and American Indians. Even the 250,000 free blacks in the United States did not have equal protection of the law and political opportunities associated with citizenship during the first half of the nineteenth century.

The conscience of many Americans was stirred, but it took a civil war and further political upheaval before these matters were addressed. Former slaves were—at least on paper—granted citizenship and guaranteed civil rights with the Thirteenth, Fourteenth, and Fifteenth Amendments to the Constitution (1865-1870). Some American Indians were granted citizenship with the Dawes Act of 1887; others had to wait until the Citizenship Act of 1924.

"Natural-born citizens" are either born in the United States or born in a foreign country of one or two parents who are United States citizens. A "certificate of citizenship" is issued to confirm that fact, but normally a five-year period of continuous residency in the United States is required between the ages of fourteen and twenty-eight years.

Naturalization A "naturalization paper" is issued for naturalized citizens when they acquire citizenship. They must have been lawful residents of the United States for five years and must demonstrate a knowledge of the fundamentals of American government and history, and they must be of good moral character. They must also

A newly naturalized American citizen from Japan. (NARA)

promise to obey the laws of the United States and defend its Constitution and laws and agree to serve in the United States military if required to do so. The process includes a hearing before a United States district court or certain state courts of record. That hearing is followed, at least thirty days later, by the administering of the oath of allegiance.

Foreign Visitors Aliens visiting the United States have certain rights and protections, but remaining in the United States is not one of them. Aliens are sometimes expelled from the United States for subversion, criminal or immoral behavior, violation of narcotics laws, or mental or physical defects. More often, however, expulsion is for failure to comply with conditions of non-immigrant status or for entering the United States without legal documents or by false statements.

The annual number of deportations from the U.S. has fluctuated over the year, from about 800,000 in 1982 to a high of about 1,800,000 in 2000, with about 700,000 deportations in 2011. One change over the years has been the increasing number of removals, as compared to returns: in a removal, the alien is barred from returning to the U.S. for a certain number of years and may face prison time if they try to return before the specified time is up, while a return does not carry those restrictions. In 1982, the proportion of deportations that were removals was negligible, while in 2011, about half the deportations were removals.

Expatriation American citizens have the right, if they choose, to relinquish their citizenship. This process is called "expatriation." They cannot, however, lose their citizenship simply by fleeing the country to avoid serving in the military or by serving in a foreign military without United States consent. A request to renounce citizenship can be accomplished in the United States only in time of war. In a foreign country a person can make the renunciation before a diplomatic officer or can take an oath of allegiance to another government.

Expatriation is a very rare occurrence among American citizens because citizenship is so highly prized. There are many millions of people in other parts of the world who would quickly take American citizenship if they had the opportunity. Many do immigrate to the United States, but American immigration laws slow the flow of naturalization, and many people must wait many years before becoming American citizens.

William H. Burnside

Further Reading

Becker, Aliza. *Citizenship for Us: A Handbook on Naturalization and Citizenship.* Washington, D.C.: Catholic Legal Immigration Network, 2002. Practical guide to U.S. citizenship laws for lay readers.

Hing, Bill Ong. *Immigration and the Law: A Dictionary.* Santa Barbara, Calif.: ABC-Clio, 1999. Detailed reference work on immigration law that addresses citizenship issues.

Kettner, James H. *The Development of American Citizenship, 1608-1870.* Chapel Hill: University of North Carolina Press, 1978. Offers a historical perspective on changing views and laws relating to citizenship in U.S. history.

Kondo, Atsushi, ed. *Citizenship in a Global World: Comparing Citizenship Rights for Aliens*. New York: Palgrave, 2001. Collection of essays on citizenship and immigrants in ten different nations, including the United States and Canada.

LeMay, Michael C., and Elliott Robert Barkan, eds. *U.S. Immigration and Naturalization Laws and Issues: A Documentary History*. Westport, Conn.: Greenwood Press, 1999. Broad sur vey of the history of changing federal legislation relating to immigration and naturalization.

Ostrander Susan A. *Citizenship and Governance in a Changing City*: Somerville, MA. Philadelphia: Temple University Press, 2013. A study of how immigration has impacted life in Somerville, a traditionally blue-collar suburb of Boston, MA.

Rubio-Marn, Ruth. *Immigration as a Democratic Challenge: Citizenship and Inclusion in Germany and the United States*. New York: Cambridge University Press, 2000. Comparative study of American and German laws concerning the naturalization of immigrants.

Yarwood, Richard. *Citizenship*. New York: Routledge, Taylor & Francis Group, 2014. An overview of the idea of citizenship, examining how the meaning of this term has changed over time and is interpreted differently in different contexts today.

See also Alien land laws; Cable Act; Immigration and Naturalization Service; Naturalization; Naturalization Act of 1790; Nguyen v. Immigration and Naturalization Service; Ozawa v. United States; Wong Kim Ark case.

CLOTILDE SLAVE SHIP

The Event: Last American ship to carry African slaves to the United States
Date: July, 1859
Place: Mobile Bay, Alabama

Immigration issues: African Americans; Slavery

Significance: Seizure of the *Clotilde* finally ended the importation of African slaves to the United States that had been illegal since 1808.

There are contradictory reports about slavers—ships especially built to transport slaves—during the period from 1858 to 1861. Historians, however, have managed to piece together an accurate account of the *Clotilde*, the last U.S. slave ship, which smuggled more than a hundred Africans into Alabama.

The Slave Trade The slave trade was outlawed by Congress in 1808. This brutal business continued without serious interference, however, until the early 1820's, when federal officials began capturing slavers and freeing their prisoners. Public sentiment, even in the South, did not favor revival of the trade. To annoy northern antislavery and abolitionist advocates, numerous rumors were spread by slave traders and sympathizers about slavers landing on the southeastern coast. For example, the *New York Daily Tribune* received many letters reporting landings of slavers in Florida and the Carolinas. There were even rumors during the 1860's of a prosperous underground slave-trading company operating in New Orleans. The *Clotilde's* history, however, has been confirmed by eyewitness accounts and careful reconstruction of events by historians.

Congress had revived laws against slave trading and declared that anyone convicted would be hanged. The United States had been later than almost every other civilized nation in the world in abolishing slave trading. Even New York City, bastion of abolitionists, became a refuge for eighty-five slave ships, many of them built and sent to Africa from that city. Much profit could be made in the $17,000,000-per-year business. According to one account, 15,000 Africans were smuggled to the United States in 1859 alone, the last 117 of whom were brought by the *Clotilde*. In contrast, the British government, after issuing its injunction against the slave trade in the eighteenth century, seized and destroyed 625 slave ships and freed their forty thousand prisoners. In the United States, only the abolitionists consistently confronted the government for its apathy toward slave smuggling.

The *Clotilde* Project Timothy Meagher, with brothers Jim and Byrns, masterminded the *Clotilde* project. Timothy, an imposing Irishman known for his adventurous character, was a plantation owner and captain of the steamboat *Roger B. Taney*, which carried passengers, cargo, and mail to and from Montgomery on the Alabama River. Apparently in a lighthearted argument with some passengers on his steamboat, Meagher made a thousand-dollar bet that within a year or two he would bring a ship full of slaves to Mobile Bay without being apprehended by federal officials. Meagher had many years' experience in cruising the Alabama River. He knew his way around every hidden bayou, swamp, canebrake, and sandbar better than anyone else in the South. For his operation, he needed a slave ship. He purchased a lumber schooner called the *Clotilde* for thirty-five thousand dollars in late 1858 and rebuilt it as a 327-ton slaver. He hired his friend Bill Foster, who was experienced in constructing and sailing the old slavers, as skipper.

Foster was to sail to the west coast of Africa and seek King Dahomey's assistance in procuring two hundred young slaves. The *Clotilde* was equipped with a crew, guns, and cutlasses. To control the prisoners, Meagher supplied the ship with iron manacles, rings, and chains. Foster hired his crew from all over the South, enticing them with liquor, money, and promises of adventure. In the dead of night, massive quantities of food, mainly yams and rice, and drinking water were transported to the ship from Meagher's plantation. To give the ship the look of a lumber schooner, some piles of lumber were placed on the deck. Captain Foster hired the infamous King Dahomey and his drunken thugs to raid villages and capture two hundred young, healthy men and women. The attacks must have taken place early one summer morning in May or early June of 1859. King Dahomey's band raided the two peaceful villages of Whinney and Ataka. They burned huts, injured women and children, and tied up more than 170 young Africans by their necks. The captives were forced into the hold of the *Clotilde.*

The return trip was an awful scene of helpless people, racked with convulsions, crammed into dark, damp quarters, lacking adequate food and water. Foster had as many as thirty-nine bodies thrown overboard before arriving back in the United States. The ship returned in July, 1859, and waited in front of Biloxi in the Mississippi Sound. Foster hired a friend's tugboat and in the dead of night, pulled the *Clotilde,* undetected by government vessels present in Mobile Bay, to a prearranged location in the swamps of the Tombigbee River. Meagher was the best man to maneuver the craft in the treacherous bayous. The sick, exhausted Africans were moved quietly to an out-of-the-way plantation belonging to Meagher's friend, John M. Dabney, who hid them in the canebrakes. From there, Meagher took charge of his steamer, the *Roger B. Taney,* and kept Foster and the *Clotilde* crew members hidden aboard her until they reached Montgomery, where they were paid off and whisked to New York City for dispersal.

Landing the Slave Cargo The slaver *Clotilde* was promptly burned at water's edge as soon as its African cargo had been removed. Meagher made elaborate preparations to throw townsfolk and government officials off the track. The Department of Justice was informed, however, and Meagher was arrested at his plantation and placed on trial in short order. Meagher's trial was a sham. He was released on bond for lack of evidence. His efforts to conceal all signs of the ship and its cargo had paid off, but he had to spend close to $100,000 in lawyers' fees and bribes. The prosecution was delayed, and the secessionists came to his rescue. News of the *Clotilde*'s landing and Meagher's trial was drowned by the presidential campaign and widespread talk of civil war.

Government officials finally learned where the Africans were hidden. They commissioned the steamer *Eclipse* for finding and transferring the Africans to Mobile. Meagher, learning of the government's decision, got the *Eclipse* crew and government passengers drunk, giving him and his men time to move the prisoners to a friend's plantation two hundred miles up the Alabama River.

Meagher's slave-smuggling venture was a financial disaster. He bought the Africans from King Dahomey for $8,460 in gold plus ninety casks of rum and some cases of yard goods. He was able to sell only twenty-five slaves; it is not clear exactly what happened to the rest. There were reports that Meagher later transferred the others to his plantation near Mobile. Some ended up marrying and living with local African Americans in the vicinity. Some were reported to have died of homesickness or other maladies. Many others settled in cabins behind the Meagher plantation house, which was burned in 1905.

The *Clotilde* in History In 1906, a journalistic account of the *Clotilde* episode appeared in Harper's Monthly Magazine. The author, H. M. Byers, had found several soft-spoken Africans who told of having been smuggled aboard the *Clotilde.* They still maintained some of their own culture and language, along with their African gentleness of demeanor. Most of their children were married to local black residents of Mobile and neighboring areas. Byers conducted extensive inter views with two who had endured the journey from Africa to Alabama: an old man named Gossalow, who had a tribal tattoo on his breast, and an old woman named Abaky, who had intricate tribal tattoos on both cheeks. Gossalow and his wife had been stolen from the village of Whinney, and Abaky from the town of Ataka, near King Dahomey's land. They had kept many of their old traditions in their original form with little modification. For example, they still buried their dead in graves filled with oak leaves. They spoke nostalgically of their peaceful West African farms, planted with abundant yams and rice.

The destruction of the *Clotilde* might be said to symbolize the end of one of the most despicable enterprises in modern history and the beginning of the infusion of the vibrant African culture into North American society.

Chogollah Maroufi

Further Reading

Byers, H. M. "The Last Slave Ship." *Harper's Monthly Magazine* 53 (1906): 742-746. A sensationalized journalistic version of the episode, but filled with valuable and accurate details. Especially valuable are the author's inter views with two surviving Africans who were smuggled into the United States aboard the *Clotilde.*

Howard, Warren S. "The Elusive Smuggled Slave." In *American Slavers and the Federal Law, 1837-1862.* Berkeley: University of California Press, 1963. Provides various accounts of the *Clotilde.*

Martinez, Jenny S. *The Slave Trade and the Origins of International Human Rights Law.* New York: Oxford University Press, 2012. Martinez argues that international admiralty courts, which among other things tried the crews of captured slave ships, played an important role in the establishment of international human rights law.

Sellers, James Benson. *Slavery in Alabama.* Birmingham: University of Alabama Press, 1950. Conveys the historical and social mood of the slave era and gives some details of the *Clotilde*'s smuggling operation.

Spear, John R. *The American Slave Trade: An Account of Its Origins, Growth and Suppression.* Williamstown, Mass.: Corner House, 1978. A well-researched and thoroughly documented book about the slave trade in general. Chapter 19 provides an account of the *Clotilde* voyage and its aftermath.

Wish, Harvey. "The Revival of the African Slave Trade in the United States, 1859-1860." *Mississippi Valley Historical Review* 27 (1940-1941): 569-588. A comprehensive account of various smuggling operations just before the Civil War.

See also African immigrants; Afro-Caribbean immigrants.

COAST GUARD, U.S.

Identification: Federal military service and law-enforcement agency that provides maritime support for the war on terror as part of the Department of Homeland Security

Date: Established in 1790 as the Revenue Marine

Immigration issues: Border control; Illegal immigration; Law enforcement

Significance: The nation's oldest maritime military service, the U.S. Coast Guard is responsible for protecting coastal boundaries and infrastructure and intercepting illegal drugs, goods, and aliens that are attempting to enter the United States.

The modern-day U.S. Coast Guard is the largest and most advanced maritime law-enforcement agency in the world and has a long and distinguished history as an autonomous military branch. In contrast to other branches of the U.S. military, the Coast Guard has never been part of the Department of Defense. The forerunner of the Coast Guard was established in 1790 as the Revenue Marine. Since then, the service has undergone major changes and restructuring.

In 2003, the Coast Guard became part of the Department of Homeland Security, and since then its primary mission has been to defend more than 95,000 miles of U.S. coastlines, 360 ports, 10,000 miles of interstate riverfronts, and 3.4 million square miles of ocean. This monumental responsibility requires the joint cooperation of local, state, and other federal agencies, as well as the private maritime industry and international entities.

The Coast Guard receives its law-enforcement statutory authority under Title 14 of the United States Code. Historically, the service has had three primary law-enforcement charges. These have included collection of tariffs for imported goods, protection of shipping from piracy on the high seas, and the interception of illegal goods and persons. Of these tasks, the primary goal of the Coast Guard prior to World War II involved the confiscation of material contraband. During the 1960's, however, the service began increasingly to limit the flow of illegal immigration coming from Cuba. After large numbers of Cuban refugees were intercepted during the early and mid-1960's, the numbers decreased until the landmark Mariel boatlift of 1980. That massive exodus of 125,000 Cuban refugees to the United States marked the largest Coast Guard peacetime operation to that date.

The 1970's saw a noticeable increase in the role of the Coast Guard in stemming the flow of illicit drugs into the United States. The service's drug-enforcement duties continued to increase throughout the first years of the twenty-first century, as the service seized large quantities of marijuana, cocaine, and other illicit drugs. Particularly notable were seizures of 13 tons of marijuana in San Diego in 1984, 20 tons of marijuana in Jamaica in 1987, and 13.5 tons of cocaine from a vessel 1,500 miles south of California in 2001.

The Coast Guard has also served in virtually every major military engagement since the founding of the United States. It has assisted U.S. Navy operations with personnel and equipment and has also been assigned special missions. It has a rich and well-documented history of recognized service during the Mexican War, the Spanish-American War, World War I, World War II, the Vietnam War, and the Persian Gulf War of 1991. As part of Operation Iraqi Freedom in early 2003, the Coast Guard continued to support other branches of America's armed services.

Current Day and Beyond On February 25, 2003, super vision of the Coast Guard was passed from the Department of Transportation to the newly founded Department of Homeland Security. The Homeland Security Act of 2002 lists five specific law-enforcement directives for the Coast Guard. These directives focus on securing ports, water ways, and coastal security; defense readiness and response; drug interdiction; illegal immigrant interdiction; other law-enforcement duties as needed.

Since the unprecedented loss of life and the disruption of domestic commerce that came with the terrorist attacks of September 11, 2001, the Coast Guard has faced significant challenges as it has defended ports, water ways, and maritime industries. Even before these attacks, however, the Coast Guard had a desperate need to replace its aging and technologically deficient fleet of equipment. The Coast Guard's increased responsibilities have made correcting those shortcomings a major area of concern for adequate domestic security.

To maintain the Coast Guard's state of preparedness and intelligence necessary to prevent and intervene in terrorist threats, a new generation of boats, cutters, fixed-wing aircraft, and helicopters was under development in 2005. This state-of-the-art system, known as the Integrated Deepwater System (IDS), was designed to integrate, link, and network all new equipment assets, both within the Coast Guard and between the Coast Guard and other military and government agencies. The new system promised to be a highly effective, efficient, and intelligent use of resources, equipment, and manpower by establishing a fully integrated communications system. After it is fully implemented, it is expected to provide a modern infrastructure to support the Coast Guard's increasingly complex operations.

In 2012, the Coast Guard included over 43,000 active duty members as well as over 8,000 reservists, 8,800 civilian employees, and 30,000 volunteer Auxiliarists. In that year, the Coast Guard screened more than 436,000 vessels, removed 107 metric tons of cocaine headed to the U.S., responded to 19,790 search and rescue cases, conducted 919 escorts and patrols, conducted over 25,000 container inspections and 1,424 boardings of vessels designated as posing greater than normal risk, and interdicted almost 3,000 undocumented migrants attempting to enter the U.S.

Denise Paquette Boots

Further Reading
Beard, Tom, Jose Hanson, and Paul Scotti, eds. *The Coast Guard*. Westport, Conn.: Hugh Lauter Levin, 2004. Containing a foreword by veteran broadcast journalist Walter Cronkite, this illustrated book covers the duty, history, life, and devotion of the Coast Guard and its people through a number of essays and contributors.

Birkler, John. *The U.S. Coast Guard's Deepwater Force Modernization Plan: Can It Be Accelerated?* Santa Monica, CA: Rand, 2004. An examination of the Coast Guard's efforts to modern its ships and aircraft to operate in a deepwater environment.

Johnson, Robert Erwin. *Guardians of the Sea: History of the U.S. Coast Guard, 1915 to the Present.* Annapolis, Md.: Naval Institute Press, 1987. Comprehensive and detailed account of the history of the Coast Guard from the early twentieth century through the 1980's. It offers explicit accounts of rescues, military operations, and more.

Krietemeyer, George. *The Coast Guardsman's Manual.* 9th ed. Annapolis, Md.: Naval Institute Press, 2000. Designed for members of the Coast Guard, this book offers a thorough over view of the Coast Guard history, uniforms, and operations, and is mandatory reading for recruits in boot camp.

Ostrom, Thomas. *The United States Coast Guard: 1790 to the Present.* Oakland, Oreg.: Elderberry Press, 2004. Written for serious scholars of American military and agency history, this book offers an exhaustive history of the Coast Guard.

White, Jonathan R. *Defending the Homeland: Domestic Intelligence, Law Enforcement, and Security.* Stamford, Conn.: Wadsworth, 2003. Sur vey of law enforcement in the United States discussing how the criminal justice system has changed since September 11, 2001.

See also Chinese detentions in New York; Cuban refugee policy; González rescue; Haitian boat people; Homeland Security Department; Mariel boatlift.

COOLIES

Definition: Pejorative term of the past for unskilled laborers from Asia, particularly those from the Far East

Immigration issues: Asian immigrants; Chinese immigrants; Labor; Slavery; Stereotypes

Significance: Already discriminated against and treated poorly by their American employers, Asian laborers who were regarded as "coolies" faced additional stigmatization and mistreatment.

"Coolie" derives from a Tamil word meaning hireling and was adapted by the British to refer to unskilled laborers in India and the Far East in the seventeenth century. The word was also used to describe unskilled five-year contract laborers, usually Indian or Chinese, working for low wages in exchange for free passage to British or Dutch colonies. Conditions were abysmal in the depots where the passengers waited and even worse on the ships, producing death rates comparable to those during the former slave trade. Horrid work conditions

Chinese mine workers traveling on a railroad handcart. Of ten called "coolie hats," the broad conical straw hats worn by Chinese laborers became one of the defining characteristics of "coolies." (Asian American Studies Library, University of California at Berkeley)

awaited the survivors.

With the influx of Chinese to the United States following the California gold rush of 1849, the pejorative term "coolie" was adapted to refer to any Chinese immigrant, creating the fiction that Chinese people were all slave laborers brought to the United States as part of a conspiracy to avoid paying decent wages to American workers. The racist coolie stereotype also connoted spreaders of disease, gambling, opium, prostitution, and heathenistic religious practices. As Chinese laborers helped build the railroads and worked in mines (often during strikes), this dehumanizing stereotype encouraged anti=Chinese riots and lynchings during the 1870's. Although only 105,000 Chinese had come to the United States by 1880, pressure from labor and western politicians resulted in the Chinese Exclusion Act of 1882, banning all Chinese immigration.

Irwin Halfond

Further Reading

Aarim-Heriot, Najia. *Chinese Immigrants, African Americans, and Racial Anxiety in the United States, 1848-82.* Urbana: University of Illinois Press, 2003.

Barth, Gunther. *Bitter Strength: A History of the Chinese in the United States, 1850-1870.* Cambridge, Mass.: Harvard University Press, 1964.

Miller, Stuart Creighton. *The Unwelcome Immigrant: The American Image of the*

Chinese, 1795-1882. Berkeley: University of California Press, 1969.

Ngai, Mae M., and John Gherde. *Major Problems in American Immigration History: Documents and Essays.* 2nd ed. Boston, MA: Wadsworth, Cengage Learning, 2013.

Zhu, Liping. *The Road to Chinese Exclusion: The Denver Riot, 1880 Election, and the Rise of the West.* Lawrence, KS: University of Kansas Press, 2013.

Zinzius, Birgit. *Chinese America: Stereotype and Reality—History, Present, and Future of the Chinese Americans.* New York: P. Lang, 2005.

See also Alien land laws; Asian American stereotypes; Burlingame Treaty; Chinese American Citizens Alliance; Chinese Exclusion Act; Chinese immigrants; Chinese immigrants and California's gold rush; Chinese immigrants and family customs; Page law; Wong Kim Ark case.

CUBAN IMMIGRANTS

Identification: Immigrants to North America from the Caribbean island of Cuba

Immigration issues: Cuban immigrants; Demographics; Latino immigrants; Refugees; West Indian immigrants

Significance: Large numbers of Cuban refugees entered the United States during the second half of the nineteenth century and during the 1960's and 1980's. Their tightly knit, prosperous communities, and later, their sheer numbers, caused racial tension and conflict, particularly with African American communities in Miami, into the twenty-first century.

In 1959, Fidel Castro led a popular revolt that toppled the government of Fulgencio Batista y Zaldívar in Cuba. A small number of Cubans who had sympathized with the Batista government fled to the United States. This tiny trickle of wealthy Cubans grew to torrential proportions as more and more people became dissatisfied with the new regime. The immigrants who came in this migratory wave, like those who came in the two that preceded it, met with discrimination and racial tensions in their new home.

Early Immigrants Twice before, large numbers of Cubans had sought refuge from war by traveling to the United States and various Latin American nations. The first group left Cuba between 1868 and 1878 during the battle for independence known in Cuba as the Ten Years' War. Most of the Cubans went to the Florida cities of Key West and Tampa, although some relocated in New York City and New Orleans. After the peace accord was signed in 1878, many Cubans returned to the island, although quite a large number remained in both Key West and Tampa (actually Ybor City) to work in the newly established tobacco factories.

These early immigrants—whose descendants still live in the area—formed tightly knit communities that revolved around the Roman Catholic Church and Spanish culture. Because the principal reason for the migration had been political, not economic, most Cubans viewed their time in the United States as temporary. Perhaps for this reason, they assimilated to a lesser extent than most immigrant groups and did not adopt many American norms or much of the culture. This was a major cause of tension between Cubans and the established population.

The end of the nineteenth century brought another large influx of Cubans. When the Cuban War of Independence started in February, 1895, and as conditions on the island deteriorated, large numbers of Cubans migrated to the United States and Latin America. As in the previous migration, Cubans settled mostly in Florida and other large eastern American cities. This time, the immigrants did not suffer as much culture shock because the Cubans who remained behind after the end of the Ten Years' War provided a ready-made Cuban American community where they could settle.

Twentieth Century The Cuban War of Independence, which in the United States became known as the Spanish-American War (1898), lasted three years, during which Cuban exiles lived in communities separated in many ways from the local population. Then, in 1953, Fidel Castro began a revolt against the corrupt government of Fulgencio Batistay Zaldívar that resulted in the Cuban Revolution and Castro's socialization of the economy under a communist-allied government. By the early 1960's, when the wave of Cubans fleeing the Castro regime arrived, many of the Cuban Americans were second- or third-generation Americans and did not have a lot in common with the newer arrivals. Therefore, the post-Castro Cubans had to contend with the criticisms of the older, established Cuban Americans.

The first wave of post-Castro Cubans arrived immediately after Castro took over. Shortly after the United States and Cuba broke diplomatic relations in January, 1960, the next migratory wave began. In this wave were more than fifty thousand children without their parents, who were brought to the United States by a former president of Cuba and other Cubans, the U.S. Catholic Welfare Bureau, and Senator George A. Smathers of Florida.

The next large wave was made up of refugees who arrived on the Freedom Flights initiated by President Lyndon B. Johnson during the mid-1960's. Two daily flights brought thousands of Cubans, straining the economy of Florida, where most of them settled. Working-class Americans, especially African Americans in Miami, suffered when jobs were lost to workers willing to work for any wage simply to have employment. During this time, many Cubans, formerly professionals, worked menial jobs while they attended night school in order to perfect their English and perhaps return to their chosen professions.

During the 1970's, the number of Cuban refugees fell, and many earlier arrivals began to move away from Miami's Little Havana to its suburbs or to other southern cities. By the time the Mariel boatlift of 1980 started, the early refugees were enjoying a high standard of living and were able to help the new arrivals establish themselves. However, the boatlift strained the public resources of southern Florida and created racial tensions. A riot broke out in the African American community

Fidel Castro at the time of his accession to power in Cuba in 1959. (Library of Congress)

in Miami after the acquittal of a Hispanic police officer who shot an African American. After much destruction, order was restored although the underlying tension did not go away. Congress passed the 1980 Refugee Act, which substantially lowered the number of Cuban refugees that could be admitted each year.

In 2010, about 1.9 million Hispanics of Cuban origin lived in the U.S., making them the third largest Hispanic group in the United States, after Mexican Americans and Puerto Ricans.

Because the earlier waves of Cuban refugees were composed of middle to upper-class Cubans, the south Florida area has experienced tremendous growth. Studies suggest that significant differences exist between refugees—like the Cubans—who migrate for political reasons and those who migrate for economic reasons. These differences are reflected in comparisons between Cuban Americans and Hispanic Americas as a whole. For instance, in 2010, compared to other Hispanic Americans, Cuban Americans are disproportionately foreign born (59 percent vs. 37 percent), are on average older (the median age of Cubans is 40, while the median age for all Hispanics is 27), and are more likely to speak English proficiently (42 percent of Cubans compared to 35 percent of all Hispanics). Cuban Americans are also more educated—24 percent have at least a bachelor's degree, compared to 13 percent of all Hispanics—and have higher incomes (the median personal earnings for Cubans age 16 and over was $25,000, compared to $20,000 for all Hispanics).

The Cuban American community is very tightly knit, although its members vary greatly in their cultural affiliations: Some members follow Cuban customs and traditions; others tend to live more or less typical American lifestyles. One attribute that separates Cuban Americans from other immigrant groups is their staunchly anti-communist stance. Although other immigrant groups have softened their stance on communists in China or Vietnam, the Cuban American community, especially in Miami, has tended to view this change in stance as a weakness. This attitude is likely to prevail until the community is predominantly second- and third-generation Cuban Americans.

Peter E. Carr

Further Reading

For a thorough review of Cuban Americans, see Thomas D. Boswell and James R. Curtis's *The Cuban American Experience* (Totowa, N.J.: Rowman & Allanheld, 1983), which Michele Zebich-Knos and Heather Nicol's *Foreign Policy Toward Cuba: Isolation or Engagement?* (Lanham, Md.: Lexington Books, 2005) helps to bring up-to-date.

Robert M. Levine and Moisés Asís's *Cuban Miami* (New Brunswick, N.J.: Rutgers University Press, 2000) explores the Cuban immigrant community of South Florida, which is home to the bulk of the nation's Cuban immigrants.

Other informative sources include John Crewdson's *The Tarnished Door: The New Immigrants and the Transformation of America* (New York: Times Books, 1983), Raul Moncarz and Jorge Antonio's "Cuban Immigration to the United States" in *Contemporary American Immigration*, edited by Dennis Laurence Cuddy (Boston: Twayne, 1982), and Norman Zucker's "Contemporary American Immigration and Refugee Policy: An Overview," in *Journal of Children in Contemporary Society* (15, no. 3, Spring, 1983).

Susan Eckstein's *The Immigrant Divide: How Cuban Americans Changed the US and Their Homeland* (New York: Routledge, 2009) looks at how Cuban immigrants to the U.S. influenced both the country in which they settled, and the country they left.

For other useful sources, see Lyn MacCorkle's *Cubans in the United States: A Bibliography for Research in the Social and Behavioral Sciences, 1960-1983* (Westport, Conn.: Greenwood, 1984).

Marco Rubio's *An American Son: A Memoir* (New York: Sentinel, 2012), is the autobiography of the Cuban-American politician who became Speaker of the House.

Ellen Alexander Conley's *The Chosen Shore: Stories of Immigrants* (Berkeley: University of California Press, 2004) is a collection of firsthand accounts of modern immigrants from many nations, including Cuba.

Ethnicities: Children of Immigrants in America (Berkeley: University of California Press, 2001), edited by Rubén G. Rumbaut and Alejandro Portes, is a collection of papers on demographic and family issues relating to immigrants that includes a chapter on Cubans.

See also Afro-Caribbean immigrants; Cuban immigrants and African Americans; Cuban refugee policy; Florida illegal-immigrant suit; González rescue; Latinos; Latinos and employment; Little Havana; Mariel boatlift; Santería.

CUBAN IMMIGRANTS AND AFRICAN AMERICANS

Immigration issues: African Americans; Cuban immigrants; Latino immigrants; West Indian immigrants

Significance: The tension that arose between African Americans and post-1959 Cuban refugees in the Miami area of Florida represents an illuminating case study of the effects of immigration on urban racial and ethnic relations during the late twentieth century.

During the late twentieth century, the attitude of African Americans and their organizations to immigration was one of ambivalence. As a minority group, African Americans could not consistently oppose immigration as a threat to some imagined American cultural or ethnic purity. Yet many African Americans, struggling against discrimination and disadvantage, feared immigrants as competitors for scarce jobs and public services. In Dade County, Florida, unrestricted immigration from Cuba after Fidel Castro took power in 1959 fed Miami African Americans' anxieties about economic displacement and political disempowerment. The black riots that erupted in Miami in 1980, 1982, and 1989, although ostensibly sparked by police brutality, were widely ascribed by contemporary commentators as resentment against Cuban refugees.

Cuban Refugees Tensions between African Americans and black immigrants from Jamaica and Haiti have been mitigated somewhat by a shared African heritage; with the refugee flow from Cuba, however, this factor did not come into play as much. When Castro took power in Cuba in 1959, people of full or partial African descent constituted nearly 40 percent of the total population of Cuba; yet 90 percent or more of the Cuban refugees of the 1960's and early 1970's were white. It was not until the Mariel boatlift of May to September, 1980, that the proportion of Afro-Cubans in the refugee flow came to approximate that of the island's population.

By the beginning of 1980, many of the Cuban refugees of the 1960's and early 1970's, who had arrived nearly penniless, had grown prosperous. Such success was due to the relatively high proportion of professionals and entrepreneurs among the earliest refugees, the refugees' hard work, and the generous financial assistance that the refugees, as defectors from a communist regime, received from the federal government to help defray the costs of vocational training and retraining, transportation, and resettlement. African Americans complained that the refugees received more assistance than either other immigrants or poor native-born Americans did. The Mariel boatlift refugees of May to September, 1980, and refugees who arrived after that year did not, however, receive as much government help as the earlier waves of immigrants.

African Americans also complained about the way refugees benefited from federal programs not specifically targeted at refugees. When affirmative action policies were implemented during the late 1960's to provide set-asides for minority businesses, Hispanics were considered to be a minority and Cubans were Hispanics; hence, refugee-owned businesses were judged to qualify as minority-owned businesses. Local African Americans resented what they saw as poaching by white newcomers on an entitlement originally intended for African Americans.

Some African-Americans also cite the treatment of persons of African descent within Cuba as a source of tension between the two groups. Although Fidel Castro proclaimed the ideal of a raceless society, many Blacks report being the victim of daily discrimination. In addition, the power structure in Cuba is predominantly white, while (as in the U.S.) Blacks are disproportionately present in prisons and tend to be poorer than white Cubans, in part because fewer receive remittances from relatives living abroad.

Cubans' Immigration Status as Bone of Contention From 1959 to 1980, few Cubans reaching U.S. shores were deported. The Cuban Adjustment Act of 1966 enabled all Cuban refugees to change their status to that of permanent resident after one year of living in the United States; other immigrants did not enjoy this privilege. After 1972, more and more Haitians, like Cubans, tried to reach the United States. Cubans fleeing by boat were always welcomed. In contrast, Haitians fleeing by boat were unceremoniously sent back to Haiti if intercepted at sea, detained in prison if they reached Florida, and often deported. Although the official justification for the disparity in treatment was ideological (Cuba was communist; Haiti was not), many Miami black activists perceived racism. Many Cuban escapees were white; almost all Haitian escapees were black. In May, 1995, U.S. president Bill Clinton officially ended the privileged status of Cuban refugees. When the first Cuban escapees were sent back to Cuba, on May 10, Miami Cubans staged a four-day action of civil disobedience; Miami's native-born African Americans stayed away from the protest.

Between 1968 and 1989, there were several episodes of rioting by black Miamians, the bloodiest of which took place in 1980. The riots of 1980, 1982, and 1989 were widely attributed by journalists and scholars to the resentment of Miami African Americans against Cuban refugees, although this was only one reason. All the riots stemmed from responses to alleged police misuse of force. In 1982 and 1989, the officers who used force were Hispanic, and Cubans did tend to rally around Hispanic police officers accused of brutality. Yet conflict between African Americans and police officers had existed even before the mass arrival of Cuban refugees. Although one victim of black violence during the 1980 riot was a

Cuban refugee, other victims were non-Hispanic whites: The mob was as much anti-white as anti-Cuban. Nor were native-born African Americans the only ones to complain about police brutality. In 1992, an incident of police violence against a Haitian in a Cuban-owned store aroused protest; and in 1990, Miami's Puerto Ricans also rioted against an alleged police abuse of force.

Whether Cuban refugees gained occupationally at the expense of Miami's African Americans is a controversial issue, although local black leaders lodged complaints about such displacement as early as the early 1960's. Allegations that Cubans ousted African Americans from service jobs in hotels and restaurants were met by counter-allegations that African Americans were themselves leaving such jobs voluntarily and that the percentage of Miami African Americans in white-collar jobs had increased by 1980. By founding many new businesses, Cuban refugees created jobs; many such jobs, however, went to fellow refugees rather than to African Americans. As the Hispanic population grew and trade links with Latin America expanded, native-born African Americans were hurt by the job requirement of fluency in Spanish. Although the Miami area economic pie grew during the 1960's and 1970's, African Americans' slice of that pie, scholars concede, was stagnant; compared with pre-1980 Cuban refugees, they suffered in 1980 from greater poverty and unemployment and had a lower rate of entrepreneurship.

Black-Cuban Conflict in Local Politics   From 1960 to 1990, the Hispanic percentage of Dade County's population (most, but not all of it, Cuban) rose from barely 10 percent to 49 percent; the black percentage of the county's population never rose above 20 percent. By the late 1970's, more and more Cuban refugees were becoming naturalized U.S. citizens, gaining both the right to vote and a decisive weight in local politics. In 1983, the Puerto Rican-born mayor dismissed the black city manager, replacing him with a Cuban. Cuban American candidates defeated African American candidates for the posts of mayor of Miami in 1985, Dade County Schools superintendent in 1990, Dade County district attorney in 1993, and mayor of Dade County in 1996. The Cuban influx into elective politics prevented a black takeover of city hall (as had taken place in Atlanta, Georgia, and Detroit, Michigan), thereby reducing the chances for black businesspeople to benefit from municipal contracts. Yet African Americans' powerlessness was relative: They could vote and affect the outcome of elections.

In spring of 1990, Mayor Xavier Suar persuaded the Miami city government to withdraw its official welcome to Nelson Mandela, the leader of the black liberation struggle in South Africa, who was then touring the United States. Mandela, in a television inter view, had praised Castro. Partly in response to this slap at Mandela, a Miami black civil rights leader, H. T. Smith, called for a nationwide boycott by black organizations of Miami-area hotels; this boycott was remarkably effective. It was ended in 1993 with an agreement promising greater efforts to employ African Americans in Miami's hospitality industry.

Complexities of Miami-area Interethnic Relations   Dade County's politics were not simply a Cuban-African American struggle. Sometimes African

Americans saw non-Hispanic whites as allies against the Cubans: In his losing bid for Congress against a Cuban American in 1989, the non-Hispanic white candidate won most of the black votes. Sometimes African Americans saw both Cubans and non-Hispanic whites as oppressors of African Americans. In a lawsuit that met with success in 1992, African Americans and Cubans cooperated in an effort to make the Dade County Commission more representative of ethnic minorities.

African Americans did not always form a united front against the Cubans: In a 1980 referendum ending the provision of Spanish-language documents and services by the Dade County government, black voters split, 44 percent for the proposition and 56 percent against. (Bilingualism was restored in 1993.) Haitians and native-born African Americans did not agree on all issues; among non-Hispanic whites, white ethnic migrants from the North did not always agree with white Anglo-Saxon Protestants of southern background; and some of Miami's non-Cuban Hispanics resented Cuban predominance.

In other major U.S. cities, Cubans were, if present at all, a smaller part of the larger Hispanic group. Only in Miami did Hispanics build up a powerful political machine; hence, black resentment of Hispanic political power played little role in race relations elsewhere. The police brutality issue also operated differently: in Compton, California, Washington, D.C., and Detroit, Michigan, for example, there were complaints, during the early 1990's, about alleged brutality by black police officers against Hispanics.

Paul D. Mageli

Further Reading

This Land Is Our Land: Immigrants and Power in Miami (Berkeley: University of California Press, 2003) by Alex Stepick and others is a study of competitition and conflict among Miami's largest ethnic groups— Cubans, Haitians, and African Americans.

In *Imagining Miami* (Charlottesville: University Press of Virginia, 1997), Sheila Croucher attacks the notion that either the black or the Cuban community is a monolith. Her analysis of the Mandela affair and the subsequent boycott is especially enlightening.

Marvin Dunn's *Black Miami in the Twentieth Century* (Tallahassee: University of Florida Press, 1997) is informative on the riots.

On the politics of bilingualism, consult Max Castro's essay in Guillermo J. Grenier and Alex Stepick's *Miami Now!* (Tallahassee: University Press of Florida, 1992).

The displacement thesis is presented most clearly in historian Raymond A. Mohl's "On the Edge: Blacks and Hispanics in Metropolitan Miami Since 1959," *Florida Historical Quarterly* (69, no. 1, July, 1990).

For rebuttals of this thesis, consult chapter 3 of Alex Stepick and Alejandro Portes's *City on the Edge: The Transformation of Miami* (Berkeley: University of California Press, 1993) and Alex Stepick and Guillermo Grenier's "Cubans in Miami," in *In the Barrios: Latinos and the Underclass Debate*, edited by Joan Moore and Raquel Pinderhughes (New York: Russell Sage Foundation, 1993).

A 2007 series in the *Miami Herald*, "A Rising Voice: Afro Latin Americans" includes substantial coverage of Afro-Cubans (http://www.miamiherald.com/multimedia/news/afrolatin/index.html").

City on the Edge is also informative on Miami's Haitians.

For a general study of racial issues relating to West Indian immigrants, see Milton Vickerman's *Crosscurrents: West Indian Immigrants and Race* (New York: Oxford University Press, 1999).

Immigration and Opportunity: Race, Ethnicity, and Employment in the United States (New York: Russell Sage Foundation, 1999), edited by Frank D. Bean and Stephanie Bell-Rose, is a collection of essays on economic and labor issues relating to race and immigration in the United States, with particular attention to the competition for jobs between African Americans and immigrants.

See also Cuban immigrants; Florida illegal-immigrant suit; Irish immigrants and African Americans; Little Havana; Mariel boatlift; Refugees and racial/ethnic relations; Santería.

CUBAN REFUGEE POLICY

Definition: Changing federal government policy regarding the immigration of Cuban refugees

Immigration issues: Cuban immigrants; Refugees; West Indian immigrants

Significance: In 1994, in a decision reflecting a broad shift in American attitudes toward immigration, President Bill Clinton ended the long-standing practice of automatically granting asylum to Cubans fleeing their country.

During the first half of August, 1994, thousands of Cubans, determined to flee their island nation's poverty and repression, set out from the port of Cojimar in makeshift rafts, braving shark-filled waters in an effort to reach southern Florida, ninety miles away. There, they assumed, freedom and a better life awaited them.

For almost three decades, the United States government had granted asylum automatically to virtually all Cubans who reached United States soil. As more and more Cuban refugees landed at Key West, Governor Lawton Chiles, Jr., of Florida pleaded with President Bill Clinton to do something about the influx. Chiles, running for reelection, feared that Florida taxpayers would rebel against the costs that a fresh wave of refugees might impose on the state.

On the evening of August 18, 1994, Clinton's attorney general, Janet Reno, announced at a hastily assembled news conference that Cuban refugees would no longer be entitled to automatic asylum. On the following afternoon, Clinton, in a televised press conference, repeated Reno's statement. He warned that Cubans intercepted at sea by the U.S. Coast Guard would henceforth no longer be taken to Florida; instead, they would be transferred to the U.S. naval base at Guantánamo Bay, at the eastern tip of Cuba, for detention for an indefinite period. In the future,

Clinton proclaimed, Cubans who claimed refugee status would have to prove that they were threatened by persecution. Each individual case would be examined by the American interests section of the Swiss embassy in Havana. On September 9, 1994, after negotiations between the Cuban and United States governments, Fidel Castro, Cuba's leader, promised to stop further attempts by rafters to flee Cuba. In return, the United States agreed to accept about twenty thousand immigrants from Cuba per year.

Anticommunism Versus Xenophobia In making his decision, Clinton responded to two strands of American public opinion: animosity toward immigrants and refugees in general, and a deep-rooted hostility to Cuba's leader, Castro. After taking power in January, 1959, Castro expropriated American-owned property without compensation and converted Cuba into a Communist state allied with the Soviet Union, America's archrival in the Cold War. In 1961, the United States broke diplomatic relations with Cuba, and in 1963, it imposed a trade embargo on the island nation. Castro's espousal of Communism was only one reason that so many Americans disliked him; another was the humiliation of having to tolerate an outspoken foe of the United States on an island that had been within the United States sphere of influence before 1959. The Cuban exile community that developed in Miami, Florida, provided a focus of anti-Castro sentiment on American soil.

From 1959 to 1962—when commercial airplane flights from the island were halted—about 200,000 Cubans fled their homeland. In late 1965, special "Freedom

Cuban refugees board a bus as they are taken to fly from Guantanamo, Cuba, to asylum in the United States in September 1996. (U.S. Department of Defense/Adrian Olguin)

Flights" were organized with Castro's cooperation. Although registration for these flights was closed in 1966, the flights themselves continued until 1973. The last mass influx of Cubans before 1994 was the Mariel boatlift of May to September, 1980, which took about 125,000 Cubans to American soil. Between 1980 and 1994, Castro forbade emigration.

During the economic boom years of the 1960's and early 1970's, neither the extreme liberality of the United States government's asylum policy toward Cubans nor the extensive financial assistance Washington offered Cuban refugees between 1962 and 1976 aroused much resentment among Americans. The Cuban refugees' flight to the United States was widely hailed as a propaganda victory for democracy in its worldwide struggle with communism, and their climb up the socioeconomic ladder in the United States was widely applauded as a triumph of hard work and determination.

As the American economy came to be beset by frequent short-term downturns and various long-term problems, many people in the United States came to view immigrants and refugees from Latin America as unwelcome competitors for jobs and public services. As president, Clinton heard widespread calls for cutbacks in legal immigration and witnessed widespread alarm over illegal immigration.

In 1994, Clinton still had bitter memories of the 1980 Mariel boatlift. President Jimmy Carter had ordered those refugees who lacked close relatives or other sponsors in the United States to be interned in camps across the United States until their fate could be determined bureaucratically. In June, 1980, a riot took place in a camp in Arkansas, where Clinton was then governor. Clinton later came to believe that popular indignation over the Mariel boatlift had cost him his chance of being reelected to the governorship in November, 1980, and had also contributed to the defeat of Carter's bid for reelection to the presidency in the same year.

In 1992, the U.S. Congress passed the Cuban Democracy Act, which further tightened a thirty-year-old embargo. Serious shortages of oil and of medicine began to be felt in Cuba. Signs of malnutrition began to appear among its people and, on August 5, 1994, a riot erupted in Havana. The riot persuaded Castro to permit limited emigration by those who wanted to leave. The need to keep already bad relations with the United States from becoming worse moved him to crack down on emigration once again in September, 1994.

Consequences In a second agreement with Castro, signed on May 2, 1995, Clinton promised that the Coast Guard would intercept at sea all Cubans fleeing their country and return them to Cuba. Those Cubans already interned in Guantánamo would be allowed to enter the United States. By early August, 1995, about half of the Guantánamo internees had been admitted to the United States, and the internment camp was slated to be closed by March, 1996.

The 1994 Cuban influx and Clinton's effort to stop it probably helped shift the debate in the U.S. Congress against advocates of free immigration and in favor of restrictionists. Proposals for reducing the total number of immigrants and refugees admitted to the United States, cracking down more severely on illegal immigration, and excluding legal aliens from certain welfare state benefits seemed to have better prospects of being enacted into law.

The "wet foot, dry foot" policy (so that a Cuban intercepted on the water ("wet food") would be returned, while a Cuban who made it on to U.S. soil ("dry foot") would be processed and have a chance to quality for residency and citizenship) has produced some interesting dilemmas in enforcement. For instance, in January 2006, 15 Cubans were discovered by the Coast Guard on the piling of a disused bridge in the Florida Keys. Although an argument could be made that this constituted making landfall, the Coast Guard interpreted their status as still being at sea, because they could not have walked to the U.S. from the piling. However, U.S. District Judge Federico Moreno later ruled that they should be counted as making landfall and thus be allowed to stay, and 14 of the 15 were granted visas (the 15th was believed to have a criminal record and thus was not granted a visa).

Paul D. Mageli

Further Reading

Bischoff, Henry. *Immigration Issues.* Westport, Conn.: Greenwood Press, 2002. Boswell, Thomas D. A Demographic Profile of Cuban Americans. Miami: Cuban American National Council, 2002.

Cohen, Steve. *Deportation Is Freedom! The Orwellian World of Immigration Controls.* Philadelphia: Jessica Kingsley, 2005.

Greenhill, Kelly M. *Weapons of Mass Migration: Forced Displacement, Coercion, and Foreign Policy.* Ithaca, NY: Cornell University Press, 2010.

Hamm, Mark S. *The Abandoned Ones: The Imprisonment and Uprising of the Mariel Boat People.* Boston: Northeastern University Press, 1995.

Legomsky, Stephen H. *Immigration and Refugee Law and Policy.* 3d ed. New York: Foundation Press, 2002.

Masud-Piloto, Felix R. *From Welcomed Exiles to Illegal Immigrants.* Lanham, Md.: Rowman & Littlefield, 1996.

Shemack, April Ann. *Asylum Speakers: Caribbean Refugees and Testimonial Discourse.* New York: Fordham University Press, 2011.

Zebich-Knos, Michele, and Heather Nicol. *Foreign Policy Toward Cuba: Isolation or Engagement?* Lanham, Md.: Lexington Books, 2005.

See also Cuban immigrants; Cuban immigrants and African Americans; Florida illegal-immigrant suit; Helsinki Watch report on U.S. refugee policy; Mariel boatlift; Model minorities; Refugees and racial/ethnic relations.

CULTURAL PLURALISM

Definition: Approach to cultural diversity that emphasizes intergroup tolerance and the maintenance of cultural distinctions among groups, in contrast to

assimilation

Immigration issue: Sociological theories

Significance: Cultural pluralism rejects the melting pot theory of cultural assimilation, with its emphasis on Anglo-conformity.

The concept of cultural pluralism has its origins in a 1915 essay by educator and social philosopher Horace Kallen, who argued—during an era rife with xenophobia, nativism, and anti-immigrant attitudes—that ethnic groups had a right to exist on their own terms, retaining their unique cultural heritage while enjoying full participation in, and the benefits of, a democratic society. *Beyond the Melting Pot* (1970), a controversial book by Nathan Glazer and Daniel Patrick Moynihan, expanded Kallen's early concept and revived the intense debate over the degree to which immigrant customs should, or would, survive with passing generations. In a new nation, Moynihan and Glazer argued, few vestiges of the immigrant culture would remain. Decades later, opinions of *Beyond the Melting Pot* still run a broad spectrum from praise to condemnation, but the book probably introduced one of the most important social science dialogues of the twentieth century.

Much of the debate over cultural pluralism has focused on the issues of bilingual (and multicultural) education in public schools and universities. The high point of disagreement appears to be over the concept of assimilationism versus multiculturalism. Arthur Schlesinger, Jr., and others have argued that different ethnic groups in the United States share a common culture, and that cultural pluralism is not a model for which the United States should strive. Critics respond that the melting pot paradigm is a fantasy, and that "vegetable soup" or "tossed

Growing evidence of multiculturalism in the United States is seen in this sign of a Miami merchant clock repair service that is patronized by both English and Spanish-speaking people. (Library of Congress)

salad" might be more accurate models. They also point out that if society blends itself into one culture, the cultural values of that finished product will probably be strongly European. Asiatic, African, and Hispanic cultures would not survive the meltdown.

Christopher Guillebeau

Further Reading

Baghramian, Maria, and Attracta Ingram, eds. *Pluralism: The Philosophy and Politics of Diversity*. New York: Routledge, 2000. Collection of scholarly essays on a wide variety of aspects of cultural pluralism.

Barone, Michael. *The New Americans: How the Melting Pot Can Work Again*. Washington, D.C.: Regnery, 2001. Reconsideration of the melting pot theory in the context of early twenty-first century America.

Bischoff, Henry. *Immigration Issues*. Westport, Conn.: Greenwood Press, 2002. Collection of balanced discussions about the most important and most controversial issues relating to immigration, including the impact of cultural diversity on American society.

Brooks, Stephen, ed. *The Challenge of Cultural Pluralism*. Westport, Conn.: Praeger, 2002. Collection of essays on cultural pluralism in modern world history. Includes chapters on theoretical aspects of the subject and on pluralism in Canada.

Buenker, John D., and Lorman A. Ratner, eds. *Multiculturalism in the United States: A Comparative Guide to Acculturation and Ethnicity*. Rev. ed. Westport, Conn.: Greenwood Press, 2005. Up-to-date collection of essays on aspects of pluralism.

Cook, Terrence E. *Separation, Assimilation, or Accommodation: Contrasting Ethnic Minority Policies*. Westport, Conn.: Praeger, 2003. Sociological study of the dynamics of power relationships among different ethnic groups.

Denton, Nancy A., and Stewart E. Tolnay, eds. *American Diversity: A Demographic Challenge for the Twenty-First Century*. Albany: State University of New York Press, 2002. Collection of papers presented at a conference on ethnic diversity in the United States.

Foner, Nancy, Rubén G. Rumbaut, and Steven J. Gold, eds. *Immigration Research for a New Century: Multidisciplinary Perspectives*. New York: Russell Sage Foundation, 2000. Collection of papers on immigration from a conference held at Columbia Unive3698888Mm rsity in June, 1998. Among the many topics covered are race, government policy, sociological theories, naturalization, and undocumented workers.

Norgren, Jill, and Serena Nanda. *American Cultural Pluralism and Law*. 3rd ed. Westport, CT: Praeger Publishers, 2006. An examination of the relationship between cultlural pluralism and the law, including challenges to the existing social order by groups ranging from recent immigrants to established racial and ethnic populations.

Vermeulen, Hans, and Joel Perlmann, eds. *Immigrants, Schooling, and Social Mobility: Does Culture Make a Difference?* New York: St. Martin's Press, 2000.

Collected papers from a 1996 conference on culture and worldwide immigration that was held in Amsterdam.

See also Assimilation theories; English-only and official English movements; European immigrant literature; Generational acculturation; Settlement house movement.

DEMOGRAPHICS OF IMMIGRATION

Definition: Characteristics of immigration populations that can be measured statistically

Immigration issues: Border control; Chinese immigrants; Demographics

Significance: Although the forces underlying immigration to North America have remained essentially unaltered throughout the histories of the United States and Canada as nations, the primary sources of immigrants to each country have changed. Until the late twentieth century, Europe supplied the over whelming majority of immigrants to both countries, but by the beginning of the twentieth century, Asia had become the principal supplier of immigrants.

The United States has experienced four major waves of immigration. In the first wave, between 1790 and 1820, most immigrants came from Great Britain and spoke English. During the second wave, from 1840 to 1860, the majority of immigrants were from northern and western Europe, most particularly Ireland and Germany. The third wave, from 1880 to 1914, is characterized by a transition in sources from northern and western Europe to southern and eastern Europe. This wave is associated with a peak period of U.S. immigration. In 1907, a record 1.3 million immigrants entered the country, with Italy accounting for more than 20 percent of this total. The outbreak of World War I effectively ended European immigration—numbers declined from 1 million in 1914 to 31,000 in 1918.

The transition in immigrant sources aroused nativist sentiments among older immigrant groups. Fear of Asian immigration, for example, led the U.S. Congress to enact the Chinese Exclusion Act in 1882. Other Asian groups were added to the exclusion list with the creation of the Asiatic Barred Zone in the 1917 Immigration Act. The justification for excluding these groups was found in racist theories of Anglo-Saxon superiority. The U.S. Congress responded to public pressure to curtail immigration from southern and eastern Europe by enacting the National Origins Quota system in 1924. Under this system, immigrant visas were apportioned for each country according to its contribution to the U.S. population in 1910.

Because Britain, Ireland, and Germany had provided the largest number of immigrants, they received the largest quotas. No restrictions were placed on immigration from the Western Hemisphere, largely in response to U.S. agricultural interests that wanted access to cheap Mexican labor that could be recruited when needed. In 1952, the so-called Texas Proviso was added to immigration law; the proviso exempted employers from sanctions for hiring undocumented workers. This had the effect of increasing illegal immigration after the United States ended its formal system of hiring agricultural workers, the bracero program, in 1964. The 1986 Immigration Reform and Control Act made it illegal for employers to hire undocumented workers.

Immigration levels declined from 1924 to 1945 as a result of the National Origins system, the Great Depression, and World War II. After 1945 U.S. concerns with immigrant origins (that is, worries about race) were replaced with concerns about immigrant skills and educational background (the United States, amply populated, began to wish only for immigrants who could contribute to the economy).

Changing U.S. Immigration Policies In 1965, the secretary of state testified before the House Judiciary Committee that the significance of immigration to the United States "now depends less on the numbers than on the quality of immigrants. . . . We are in the international market of brains." Restrictions on immigration from Asia and southern and eastern Europe were gradually removed during and after World War II. The National Origins system was formally replaced by the 1965 amendments to the Immigration and Nationality Act, which allocated an annual ceiling of 170,000 immigrants for the Eastern Hemisphere and 120,000 for the Western Hemisphere.

Within this overall ceiling, a system of priority categories was established based upon family reunification criteria and labor requirements, with the immediate relatives of U.S. citizens being exempt from the numerical cap. In 1990, a global quota of 714,000 immigrants was established for 1992 to 1994, and 675,000 beginning in 1995, with the majority of visas being allocated to spouses, children, and other relatives of U.S. citizens. In addition to this global quota are refugees, who are admitted under the 1980 Refugee Act, which had a 1992 ceiling of 142,000 persons and a series of smaller quotas designed for particular groups which have been adversely affected by earlier immigration laws.

These changes in legislation have coincided with a fourth wave of immigration. Since 1970 immigration has gradually increased to approach the record levels, in raw numbers, that were reached at the beginning of the twentieth century. The number of immigrants in the fourth wave relative to the rest of the population, however, is far less than at the beginning of the twentieth century. During the 1970's the United States admitted 4.4 million immigrants. The following decade this figure increased to 7.3 million. In 1993, a total of 904,300 immigrants legally entered the country. Concurrent with this boost in immigration has been a change in immigrant sources from the "developed" to the "developing" world.

During the 1960's, the six leading suppliers of U.S. immigrants were Mexico (443,300), Canada (286,700), Cuba (256,800), United Kingdom (230,500), Italy (206,700), and Germany (200,000). The comparable figures for the 1980's were: Mexico (1,653,300), the Philippines (495,300), Vietnam (401,400), China (388,800), Korea (338,800), and India (261,900). The six leading sources of immigration during the 1990's were Mexico (2,249,400), China and Hong Kong (529,000), the

Philippines (503,900), former Soviet republics (462,870), India (363,000), and the Dominican Republic (335,300).

This transformation in immigrant sources is also associated with a change in immigrant settlement patterns. During the third wave of immigration, the United States was undergoing industrialization, which meant a large demand for factory labor in cities. European immigrants settled in Northeastern and Midwestern industrial cities and transformed the urban landscape. Italian, Polish, and Greek neighborhoods, for example, grew up around Chicago's downtown district. Since the 1950's, factory closures in such traditional industries as textiles, automobiles, and steel have reduced the demand for labor and brought long-term economic decline to the region. Economic growth and the demand for labor have shifted to the rapidly growing service-based economies of the so-called Sun Belt states, which stretch from Southern California to Florida. Many of the new immigrant groups have settled in the rapidly growing cities of this region. The resulting ethnic diversity from this settlement can be seen in Los Angeles, Houston, and Miami.

Adding to the immigrant population during the early 1990's was an annual flow of an estimated 250,000 illegal immigrants. Illegal immigrants include those who overstay a visa (often a student visa) and those who simply walk across the border. Mexico is the leading source of these migrants, followed by El Salvador and Guatemala, two Central American countries torn, especially during the 1980's, by terrorism and warfare. California contains the largest number of illegal migrants. The net effect of the fourth wave of immigration has been to accelerate—not cause—the cultural transition of the United States from a predominantly white population rooted in western culture to a diverse society comprising many different ethnic and racial minorities.

As of 2010, 48 percent of foreign born population in the U.S. identified themselves White, 8 percent African American or Black, 25 percent as Asian, 16 percent as some other race, and 2 percent mixed race. In addition, 47 percent of the foreign-born population self-identified as Hispanic (an ethnic category: a Hispanic person can be of any race). Looking at the absolute number of immigrants in a state, California had by far the largest immigrant population (10.1 million), followed by New York (4.3 million), Texas (4.1 million), Florida (3.7 million), and New Jersey (1.8 million). However, the percent growth of immigrants as a share of the state's population was largest in Southern states, in part because they have historically had relatively small immigrant populations. In the decade beginning in 1990, North Carolina experienced a 274 percent growth in its immigrant population, followed by Georgia (233 percent) and Nevada (202 percent). In the decade beginning in 2000, Alabama had the largest percent growth in immigration (92 percent), followed by South Carolina (88 percent) and Tennessee (82 percent).

As of January 2011, according to the Office of Immigration Statistics, 11.5 undocumented immigrants were living in the U.S., with the greatest number residing in California (24 percent), Texas (16 percent) and Florida (6 percent). The greatest number of these undocumented immigrants come from Mexico (6.8 million, 59 percent of the total), while 660,000 (6 percent) come from El Salvador, 520,000 from Guatemala (5 percent), 380,000 (3 percent) from Honduras, 280,000 (2 percent) from China, and 270,000 fro the Philippines (2 percent).

Canadian Immigration In 1867, at the time of national confederation, Canada had a population of 3.2 million. During the following thirty years the young country struggled to obtain population growth as thousands of Canadians moved to the United States. The post-Confederation National Policy was designed to help establish the new country. Two aims of the National Policy were the construction of the transcontinental railroad and homestead settlement in the West.

The Canadian government was fearful of American northward expansion and annexation, and so viewed immigration to the prairies as an essential component of nation building. As in the United States, there were concerns about who immigrated. Chinese workers, for example, had been recruited to work on the railroad and in lumber camps, and their presence in British Columbia aroused racist fears. Opposition to the Chinese was particularly pronounced in Vancouver, where a dilapidated Chinatown had been established. The federal government responded to these nativist sentiments by taxing Chinese immigration. Later, the Canadian government pressured Japan into voluntarily limiting its emigrants to four hundred per year.

The beginning of the twentieth century was a boom period in Canadian immigration; 1.5 million immigrants entered the country between 1900 and 1914. In 1913 a record 400,000 arrived in the country. Many of these immigrants were from eastern and central Europe and were responding to the same factors that led their counterparts to settle in the United States. Instead of settling in urban areas, as in the United States, the Canadian immigrants generally settled on the prairies in rural ethnic communities. The relative isolation of these small towns and villages helped the immigrants sustain their cultural identity and in effect laid the foundation for the so-called Canadian mosaic and later multiculturalism.

After World War I, Canada established a national origins system, classifying prospective immigrants into ethnic categories: British and Northwest Europeans were classified as "preferred"; central and eastern Europeans "non-preferred," while in the "restricted" category were Italians, Greeks, and Jews. The responsibility for administering this system was transferred to the Canadian Pacific and Canadian National Railways in 1925. These companies owned vast tracts of land in the West and it was in their interest to sell off this land to new settlers. As a result, the preference categories were ignored. By the late 1920's, the majority of Canadian immigrants were from the non-preferred and restricted categories. The Great Depression and World War II all but ended immigration to Canada.

Canadian immigration policy changed after World War II. Non-Jewish displaced persons from Europe who had been made homeless by the war were admitted in 1946; Jews were allowed to immigrate two years later. The expanding industrial economies of Ontario and Quebec needed labor that could not be supplied from Britain, so the government began an active pro-immigration policy in 1949. Europe continued to supply most of Canada's immigrants during the 1950's and 1960's, but the majority of them came from Italy, Greece, and Portugal. Amendments to the 1952 Immigration and Nationality Act in 1962 and 1966 formally abolished the previous exclusions of particular racial groups and established a universalistic point system for admission into the country. Points were awarded for educational attainment, for the ability to speak the major languages, and for having Canadian family members. These reforms stemmed from the need to attract professionals to the expanding scientific, educational, governmental and health care sectors, from a reduction in racist attitudes, and from an increasing acceptance of Canada's multicultural character.

Since 1971, the federal government has actively promoted multiculturalism by providing grants for ethnic histories and promoting cultural heritage. The new admissions policy resulted in a shift away from Europe as the country's principal supplier of immigrants. Canadian support for diversity has also included the appointment in 1972 of the first Minister of State for Multiculturalism and the passage in 1988 of the Canadian Multiculturalism Act. In 1992, Hong Kong, Sri Lanka, India, and the Philippines were the four leading sources of Canadian immigrants. As of 2012, almost half (48.7 percent) of Canada's permanent residents (individuals with the right to live in Canada, but who are not citizens) came from Asia and the Pacific, with 22.6 percent from the Middle East, 14.7 percent from South and Central America, and 3.8 percent from the United States. The largest source countries for permanent residents in 2012 were China (33,018), the Philippines (32,747) and India (28,943), and all three countries were consistently among the largest home countries for Canadian permanent resident throughout the 2000s.

Michael Broadway

Further Reading

Allegro, Linda, and Andrew Grant Wood, eds. *Latin American Migrations to the U.S. Heartland: Changing Social Landscapes in Middle America*. Urbana: University of Illinois Press, 2013.

Barone, Michael, *Shaping Our Nation: How Surges of Migration Transformed America and Its Politics*. New York: Crown Forum, 2013.

Hughes, James W., and Joseph J. Seneca, eds. *America's Demographic Tapestry: Baseline for the New Millennium*. New Brunswick, N.J.: Rutgers University Press, 1999.

Kertzer, David I., and Dominique Arel, eds. *Census and Identity: The Politics of Race, Ethnicity, and Language in National Census*. New York: Cambridge University Press, 2002.

Massey, Douglas S. "The New Immigration and Ethnicity in the United States." *Population and Development Review* 21, no. 3 (September, 1995): 631-652.

Perlmann, Joel, and Mary Waters, eds. *The New Race Question: How the Census Counts Multiracial Individuals*. New York: Russell Sage Foundation, 2002.

Rumbaut, Rubén G., and Alejandro Portes, eds. *Ethnicities: Children of Immigrants in America*. Berkeley: University of California Press, 2001.

Segal, Uma A, Doreen Elliott, and Nazneen S. Mayadas. *Immigration Worldwide: Policies, Practices, and Trends*. New York: Oxford University Press, 2010.

Skerry, Peter. *Counting on the Census? Race, Group Identity, and the Evasion of*

Politics. Washington, D.C.: Brookings Institution Press, 2000.

See also Arab American intergroup relations; Asian American literature; Asian American women; Bilingual Education Act of 1968; Censuses, U.S.; Chinatowns; English-only and official English movements; Hawaiian and Pacific islander immigrants; Israeli immigrants; Jews and Arab Americans; Korean immigrants and family customs; Racial and ethnic demographic trends; Vietnamese immigrants.

DEPORTATION

Definition: Forcible removal of noncitizens from the territory of a country

Immigration issues: Border control; Citizenship and naturalization; Civil rights and liberties; Discrimination; Illegal immigration; Law enforcement

Significance: As a sovereign nation, the United States has always had the authority to deport noncitizens for any reason it chooses. During the 1990's, the federal government began using its deportation power on a larger scale as a weapon against illegal immigration.

During the 1990's, as the intensity of the debate over immigration in the United States steadily rose, church groups, civil libertarians, and immigration lawyers demanded severe limitations, in the interest of humanitarianism and due process, on the long-recognized power of the U.S. federal government to deport noncitizens. President Bill Clinton and the U.S. Congress, by contrast, insisted on the vigorous exercise of that power to promote greater control over immigration. From 1992 to 1997 the number of persons deported rose from 38,000 per year to more than 111,000 per year.

U.S. Citizens as Targets of Deportation Normally, U.S. citizens who have been born in the United States cannot be deported unless they renounce their U.S. citizenship or lose it as a result of desertion from the military in time of war. For example, the U.S.-born writer Margaret Randall, who lived in Mexico for more than twenty years, was a target of deportation when she returned to live in the United States for family reasons. Not until the early 1990's did the campaign to have her ousted from the United States finally cease. The pretext for the deportation proceedings was Randall's adoption of Mexican citizenship (she claimed, in order to make getting a job easier). Many suspected that her outspoken left-wing views were the real reason for the deportation effort.

Whether someone is an alien who is susceptible to deportation or a citizen is determined on legal rather than cultural grounds. Because citizenship was conferred by the U.S. Congress on Puerto Ricans in 1917, a Spanish-speaking Puerto Rican living on the mainland cannot be deported to Puerto Rico. On the other hand; a Spanish-speaking Mexican or an English-speaking Canadian or Australian may be deported to the lands of their birth.

Naturalized citizens are usually immune to deportation unless they are stripped of their citizenship for having concealed or distorted crucial information about themselves. Eastern Europeans or Germans suspected of having committed war crimes during World War II (1939-1945) have been the chief targets of such action. Conceivably, naturalized Americans of Bosnian or Rwandan background could be stripped of their new citizenship if it were discovered that they had committed war crimes in the past.

Aliens with Permanent Resident Status Aliens who have been granted permanent resident status may normally be deported only if they have committed certain types of crimes. The nature of the crimes that make a resident alien deportable has varied with changes in the immigration laws. Some of those deported for crimes have lived in the United States since childhood and may have few ties to the mother country.

After the passage of the Anti-Terrorism and Effective Death Penalty Act (AE-DPA) and the Illegal Immigration Reform and Immigrant Responsibility Act (IIRI-RA) in 1996, complaints arose that too many aliens were being deported for crimes that were relatively minor or that had been committed decades before deportation proceedings were begun. The new laws mandated deportation for certain kinds of felonies, but exactly what crime is a felony and how serious a felony it is can vary from one U.S. state to another. The post-1996 practice of retroactivity deporting individuals for crimes that would not have made them targets of deportation prior to the passage of the 1996 laws has also been sharply criticized by some legal scholars and by some judges in the federal court of appeals.

Nonimmigrant Aliens Those most vulnerable to deportation are foreigners residing in the United States who have never been granted permanent residence status. Such persons include those who entered the United States without submitting to inspection (the popular notion of "illegal aliens"); those who have overstayed temporary student, tourist, or work visas; applicants for asylum whose claims are denied; and even those who have fled strifetorn countries and been admitted to the United States on a temporary basis. In the latter case, such persons may be deported if the U.S. Congress decides that the emergency in their homeland has passed, a situation that afflicted Central Americans admitted to the United States in the turbulent 1980's who were threatened with deportation in the supposedly more peaceful 1990's. During the late 1990's most applicants for asylum wound up in deportation proceedings, although not all of them were actually deported.

Aliens sometimes think that they have permanent residence status when they actually do not. Marriage to an American citizen, if undertaken in good faith, can make it possible for an immigrant to gain resident alien status. However, acquisition of the status of permanent resident does not come automatically with marriage, however; an application for a change of status must be made, and getting a reply one way or the other can be time-consuming if the Immigration and

Detention pen at Ellis Island in which immigrants are waiting to be deported in 1902. (Library of Congress)

Naturalization Service (INS), the agency responsible for noncitizens, is under-staffed or overloaded with requests in any given year. During the late 1990's, some alien spouses of Americans found themselves barred from the U.S. after having briefly left the country. With their resident alien status not yet formally approved, they were still subject to deportation.

Deportation and Due Process The target of deportation efforts by the federal government does not usually enjoy quite the same level of rights as the target of criminal prosecution by a local government. Some deportations of aliens, particularly those who have entered without inspection, can take place without much protection of individual rights. In other instances, an alien threatened with deportation can get a hearing before an immigration judge and can appeal the judge's decision to the Board of Immigration Appeals (BIA). However, the judges in this system, unlike most federal judges, possess neither lifetime tenure nor salary guarantees.

Changes in the immigration law passed in 1996 seemed to aim toward reducing the barriers to deportation presented by due process. The right of the regular federal courts to review deportation decisions has long been a matter of controversy; legislation passed by the U.S. Congress in 1996 attempted to severely limit the scope of such judicial review. New restrictions were placed on those claiming the right of asylum; the window of opportunity to make a claim for asylum was narrowed, and the right of an official to order out of the country an alien whose claims seemed unconvincing was broadened.

If asylum applicants have recently arrived in the United States, they can find themselves detained in prison for a long time until their asylum claims are decided one way or the other by immigration judges or the Board of Immigration Appeals. Whether an asylum seeker is locked up or released into the community with permission to work depends on which INS district handles the matter, how many beds the nearest detention center has, and on prevailing attitudes toward immigrants. Before the mid-1990's most asylum seekers were released into the community; thereafter, the number of those detained rose sharply.

In criminal trials the accused have the right to cross-examine witnesses for the prosecution and to be informed of the exact nature of the evidence against them. Aliens who are targets of deportation on the grounds of alleged terrorist activities or any other political activities deemed dangerous to U.S. national security may be deported on the basis of evidence they are not allowed to see and testimony by witnesses they are not allowed to confront if it is deemed essential to U.S. national security to keep the evidence and the identity of the prosecution witnesses secret. During the late 1990's this problem often arose in the case of aliens from such Middle Eastern countries as Iraq.

Since, 1996, the term "deportation" has been replaced by the term "removal" which applies to both to individuals who were in the U.S. unlawfully and were removed from the country for that reason, and individuals who were denied entrance at the border (previously known as an "exclusion"). A new category, "returns" was developed to apply to Mexicans or Canadians apprehended at their own and simply prevented from entering the U.S. A removal carries harsh conditions including banning the individual from entering the U.S. for a number of years, while a return carries no such stipulation.

Aliens Expelled and Immigration Violations, 1985-1991

Item	1985	1986	1987	1988	1989	1990	1991
Aliens expelled	**1,062,000**	**1,608,000**	**1,113,000**	**934,000**	**860,000**	**1,045,000**	**1,091,000**
Deported	21,000	22,000	22,000	23,000	30,000	26,000	28,000
Required to	1,041,000	1,586,000	1,091,000	911,000	830,000	1,019,000	1,063,000
Prosecutions disposed of	**17,688**	**23,405**	**18,894**	**18,360**	**18,580**	**20,079**	**18,882**
Immigration violations	16,976	22,751	18,200	17,590	17,992	19,351	18,297
Nationality violations	712	654	694	770	588	728	585
Convictions	**9,833**	**15,259**	**11,996**	**12,208**	**12,561**	**12,719**	**11,509**
Immigration violations	9,635	15,104	11,786	11,929	12,379	12,515	11,392
Nationality violations	198	155	210	279	182	204	117

The Office of Immigration issued statistics applying the more recent terminology to prior years, and making it easier to see how patterns of enforcement have changed over the years. Looking at the past two decades, the peak year for removals and returns combined was 2000, with a total of 1,864,343 (118,467 removals and 1,675,876 returns). In more recent years, the total number of returns and removals has decreased, while the ratio of removals to returns has increased, due to an increasing number of removals and a decreasing number of returns. For instance, in 2011 there were 388,409 removals (54.7 percent of the total) and 322,164 returns, while in 2012, there were 419,384 removals (64.6 percent of the total) and 229,968 returns.

Deportation as Punishment There are two rationales for restricting aliens' rights. One is the notion that the U.S. Congress has, by law, nearly absolute control over who can migrate to the U.S. (the so-called plenary power doctrine); the other is the idea that deportation is not a criminal punishment. Because deportation proceedings are carried out under civil rather than criminal law, deportation is technically not considered to be a punishment. The reality can, however, diverge from legal doctrine. Unlike voluntary departure from the U.S., deportation severely limits deportees' rights to reenter the United States in the future. Individuals who have been in the United States only a short time and have been unable to make a living may welcome deportation to the home country. Persons who have lived in the United States for many years (sometimes since childhood), who have strong family and work ties to U.S. citizens and legal residents, and who have no family ties in the countries of their origin may view deportation as a catastrophe. Deporting aliens sometimes means sending them back to certain death at the hands of a brutal dictatorship.

Hence, immigration judges have, for a long time, been permitted to grant relief from deportation if an immigrant has sufficient ties (called "equities") to the United States. Such relief is not a right but a matter of judicial discretion. Aliens must show that they have lived in the United States a certain minimum number of years (at least seven), that they are of good character, and that the well-being of family members would be severely damaged if they were deported. For claimants to asylum, relief from deportation is a matter of right if they can prove to the satisfaction of an immigration judge or the BIA that they face a real threat of persecution upon returning to their home countries and that no other country besides the United States will admit them. Changes in the law in 1996 aimed at making such relief from deportation harder for individual aliens to obtain. Blanket relief from deportation for refugees from specific countries is a matter of congressional and executive whim. In a 1997 law, for example, such protection against deportation was extended by act of Congress to Nicaraguans but not to Haitians.

Paul D. Mageli

Further Reading

For an up-to-date analysis of the treatment of undocumented immigrants in the United States since the 1960's, see Rob Staeger's *Deported Aliens* (Philadelphia: Mason Crest, 2004), which gives particular attention to issues relating to deportation.

A good introduction to the subject of deportation can be found in Nadia Nedzel's "Immigration Law: A Bird's Eye View" in *Immigration: Debating the Issues*, edited by Nicholas Capaldi (Amherst, N.Y.: Prometheus Books, 1997).

A look at one protracted case, begun during the early 1970's and finally decided during the 1980's, Barbara Hinkson Craig's *Chadha: The Story of an Epic Constitutional Struggle* (New York: Oxford University Press, 1989) illuminates the relevant legal principles of political asylum and relief from deportation in language accessible to lay readers.

Journalist Debbie Nathan's "Adjustment of Status: The Trial of Margaret Randall" in *Women and Other Aliens: Essays from the U.S.-Mexico Border* (El Paso, Tex.: Cinco Puntos Press, 1991) discusses a rare late twentieth century deportation case involving a native-born American.

Paola Molina's *Re-immigration after Deportation: Family, Gender, and the Decision to Make a Second Attempt to Enter the U.S.* (El Paso: LFB Scholarly Publishing LLC, 2014), examines the cases of 70 individuals deported from the U.S. and living in a migrant shelter on the Mexican border.

The Social Political and Historic Contours of Deportation, ed. Bridget Anderson, Matthew J. Gibney and Emanuela Paoletti, is a collection of essays looking at the history and current practice of deportation in many countries around the world.

For an insightful study by a legal scholar of the effects of the AEDPA and the IIRIRA on the law of deportation, see Nancy Morawetz's "Rethinking Retroactive Deportation Laws and the Due Process Clause" *New York University Law Review*, 73 (April, 1998).

Allan Wernick, a lawyer who writes on immigration law for the *New York Daily News*, has written, for the English-literate immigrant *U.S. Immigration and Citizenship: Your Complete Guide* (Rocklin, Calif.: Prima, 1997), which offers tips on how to avoid deportation. Syed Refaat Ahmed's *Forlorn Migrants:*

An International Legal Regime for Undocumented Migrant Workers (Dhaka, Bangladesh: University Press, 2000) provides an international perspective on deportation issues.

See also Arab immigrants; Border Patrol, U.S.; Chinese Exclusion Act; Helsinki Watch report on U.S. refugee policy; Illegal aliens; Immigration and Naturalization Service; Immigration law; Mexican deportations during the Depression; Naturalization; Operation Wetback; Twice migrants; Zadvydas v. Davis.

Discrimination

Definition: Unequal or unfavorable treatment of persons on the basis of their membership in certain categories or groups, such as racial and ethnic minorities

Immigration issues: African Americans; Citizenship and naturalization; Civil rights and liberties; Discrimination

Significance: Responding to racial and ethnic discrimination and conflict has been particularly challenging for the U.S. government, given the immigrant nature of American society and the long-standing commitment to the principle of equality before the law in the country's political culture.

Within the founding documents of the United States are contradictory statements on equality and freedom—and hence on people's right not to be discriminated against. The Declaration of Independence calls it self-evident that "All men are created equal" and have "unalienable rights," yet prior to ratification of the Thirteenth Amendment in 1865, the Constitution upheld the institution of slavery, notably in a provision that fugitive slaves must be returned to their owners.

Any new country proclaiming equality while allowing slavery and thinking of an entire race as inferior is founded on an impossible contradiction, one that many of the founders undoubtedly realized would have to be faced in the future. Until the mid-twentieth century, however, the federal government generally avoided becoming involved in attempts to legislate against discrimination, allowing the states to establish their own policies. Many of the states, being closer to the people and their prejudices than the federal government was, were inclined to condone discrimination and even actively encourage it through legislation.

Discrimination existed in many different areas of life, including education, employment, housing, and voting rights. Two major pieces of legislation of the 1960's were designed to attack discrimination in these areas: the Civil Rights Act of 1964 and the Voting Rights Act of 1965. The primary avenue for fighting discrimination is through the courts, a fact which causes problems of its own. The Equal Employment Opportunity Commission (EEOC), for example, has the power to bring lawsuits involving employment discrimination; however, a huge number of charges of discrimination are brought before the agency. For that reason, by the mid-1990's it had a backlog of many thousands of cases awaiting its attention. In discrimination cases the courts have sometimes applied a standard of discriminatory intent and sometimes relied on a standard of discriminatory impact.

Some types of discrimination are easier to see and to rectify than others. A number of activists and legal experts had shifted their attention by the 1980's to a type of discrimination generally known as "institutional discrimination." Institutional discrimination is a type of discrimination that is built into social or political institutions, frequently in nearly invisible ways. Institutional discrimination is sometimes not even intentional.

Development of the American Nation The framework for the development of the United States and its treatment of ethnic minorities was established during the first half century of the nation's history. When the American Revolution ended in 1783, there were few people in the thirteen colonies who considered themselves "Americans," as opposed to Virginians, Pennsylvanians, New Yorkers, and so on. Nevertheless, the people who joined under the Articles of Confederation had much in common. They shared a common language, ethnic stock, and history as well as a philosophy of government that stressed individual rights over group rights. Given time and interaction, one would expect these former colonials to develop a common sense of national identity.

To a substantial extent, that integration occurred during the nineteenth century via such common endeavors as the successful wars against the Spanish in Florida, against Great Britain in 1812, and against various Indian tribes. As people moved westward to the frontier, the conquest of the continent itself also became a unifying national purpose.

Yet a major challenge to the development of this emerging sense of national identity also arose during the nineteenth century. Between 1830 and 1910, while the country was absorbing new territory, approximately forty-four million immigrants entered the United States, mostly Europeans with backgrounds differing from the white Anglo-Saxon prototype of the founders. Moreover, the Civil War resulted in the freeing of millions of African American slaves, who suddenly became American citizens. There was also a trickle of immigrants arriving from Asia. Finally, there were Jewish immigrants, primarily in the Northeast, and Hispanics, primarily in the Southwest. The country's citizenry was becoming multi-ethnic and multiracial.

Native Americans Adopted in 1789, the U.S. Constitution made Native Americans wards of the federal government. Treaties with the tribes, like all treaties, were to be federal affairs, and the Supreme Court has repeatedly affirmed the exclusive nature of this power of Congress (*Cherokee Nation v. Georgia*, 1831; *New York Indians v. United States*, 1898). The Supreme Court has also repeatedly upheld the federal government's right to rescind—by ordinary legislation or the admission of new states to the union—those rights accorded the tribes by prior treaties (the *Cherokee Tobacco* case, 1871; *United States v. Winans*, 1905). Even the rationale for the guardian-ward relationship existing between the federal government and the tribes has been elucidated in the opinions of the Court. Essentially, it involves three elements: the weakness and helplessness of Native Americans, the degree to which their condition can be traced to their prior dealings with the federal government, and the government's resultant obligation to protect them. Few of the federal policies adopted before World War II, however, can be described as protective or even benign toward Native Americans.

Policies toward Native Americans traditionally built on the pattern of relations with the tribes established by Europeans prior to the ratification of the Constitution. For hundreds of years, the French, Portuguese, Spanish, English, and Dutch subdued the tribes they encountered, denigrated their cultures, and confiscated their lands and wealth. Early U.S. actions continued the pattern, especially where tribes physically hindered western expansion. During the 1830's, the concept of Indian Territory (land for the Native Americans territorially removed from European settlers) gained favor among European Americans.

When even the most remote of areas were eventually opened to European immigrants, the Indian Territory policy was abandoned in favor of a reservation policy: relocating and settling tribes within contained borders. Meanwhile, contact with European diseases, combined with the increasingly harsh life forced on Native Americans, had devastating effects on the tribes in terms of disrupting their societies and dramatically reducing their numbers. Beginning during the 1880's, reservation policies were frequently augmented by forced assimilation policies: Many young Native Americans were taken from their reservations and sent to distant boarding schools. There, tribal wear and ways were ridiculed, and speaking native languages in class could mean beatings. Only with World War I did these policies soften.

Significant changes in government attitudes toward Native Americans did not come until the Indian New Deal was instituted by reform-minded commissioner of Indian affairs John Collier during the 1930's. During the late 1960's, another chapter opened as Indians began to demand their own civil rights in the wake of the predominantly African American Civil Rights movement. More enlightened federal policies toward Native Americans began to emerge, and since the 1960's considerable legislation has appeared, including the 1968 American Indian Civil Rights Act and the 1975 Indian Self-Determination and Education Assistance Act. A number of factors have worked against Native Americans in advancing their own cause, among them the small number of Native Americans (less than 1 percent of the American population), the assimilation of their most educated members into the general population, and the fact that Native Americans generally think of themselves not as "Indians" or "Native Americans" but as members of a specific tribe.

Discrimination in Immigration Policy Fulfillment of the U.S. self-determined manifest destiny to spread from the Atlantic to the Pacific Ocean required people, and early in the nineteenth century the government opened its doors wide to immigrants from Europe.

Yet even during this period, the door was open to few beyond Europe. Hispanic immigrants could enter the country fairly easily across its southern border, but American memories of Texas's war with Mexico made the country inhospitable toward them. More conspicuously, immigration policy was anti-Asian by design.

Sign on a Parker, Arizona, barbershop near a Japanese relocation center making it clear that persons of Japanese ancestry were not welcome inside. The term "Jap" arose around 1880 as a colloquial short form for "Japanese." It originally carried no negative connotations, but during World War II, it took on intensely pejorative meanings that now make it highly offensive, especially to Japanese Americans. (National Archives)

The Chinese Exclusion Act, for example, passed in 1882, prohibited unskilled Chinese laborers from entering the country. Later amendments made it even more restrictive and forced Chinese people living in the United States to carry identification papers. The law was not repealed until 1943. Beginning with the exclusion laws of the 1880's, quotas, literacy tests, and ancestry requirements were used individually and in combination to exclude Asian groups. Indeed, even after the efforts during the 1950's to make the immigration process less overtly discriminatory, preferences accorded to the kin of existing citizens continued to skew the system in favor of European and—to a lesser extent—African immigrants.

Meanwhile, Asians who succeeded in entering the country often became the targets of such discriminatory state legislation as California's 1913 Alien Land Bill, which responded to the influx of Japanese in California by limiting their right to lease land and denying them the right to leave any land already owned to the next generation. The most overtly discriminatory act against Asian immigrants or Asian Americans was perpetrated by the federal government, however, which under the color of wartime exigencies relocated tens of thousands of U.S.-born Japanese Americans living on the West Coast to detention camps during World War II. The Supreme Court upheld the relocation program in *Korematsu v. United States* (1944).

It was not until the 1960's and 1970's, during and following the Vietnam War and the collapse of a series of United States-supported governments and revolutionary movements in Asia and Latin America, that the United States opened its doors to large numbers of immigrants and refugees from Asia and the Hispanic world. The government went so far as to accord citizenship to children born of foreigners illegally living in the country.

African Americans Nineteenth century European immigrants generally were able to make the transition to American citizenship effectively. The urban political machines found jobs for them and recruited them into the political process as voters who, in turn, supported the machines. The prosperity of the country, manifested in the land rushes of the nineteenth century, the industrial revolution, and the postwar economic booms of the twentieth century, enabled the vast majority of these immigrants to achieve upward mobility and a share of the good life.

The citizens who were unable to fit into this pattern, apart from the reservation-bound American Indian tribes, were the African Americans. Enslaved in thirteen states prior to the Civil War (1861-1865) and kept in subservience by state laws and various extralegal arrangements for generations after ward, African Americans remained a social, economic, and political underclass with little expectation of progress until nearly eighty years after the Civil War Amendments were added to the Constitution to free and empower them.

The Thirteenth Amendment (1865) abolished slavery, the Fourteenth Amendment (1868) was designed to prevent states from interfering with the rights of former slaves, and the Fifteenth Amendment (1870) constitutionally enfranchised African Americans. By the end of the nineteenth century, however, Supreme Court opinions and state action had combined to minimize the impact of these amendments. In the *Slaughterhouse* cases (1873), the Supreme Court crippled the Fourteenth Amendment. The Court's decision limited the amendment's privileges and immunities clause only to those rights a citizen has by virtue of national citizenship, not state citizenship. Second, it interpreted the due process clause as a restraint only on how a state may act, not on what it can do. Only the equal protection clause of the Fourteenth Amendment, which the Court limited to issues of race, continued to offer protection to the newly freed slaves, and in two subsequent cases even that protection was substantially reduced.

First, in the *Civil Rights* cases of 1883, the Supreme Court ruled that the equal protection clause applies only to state action, not to private discrimination. Then, in the pivotal case *Plessy v. Ferguson* (1896), the Court held that states could satisfy the requirements of the equal protection clause by providing "separate-but-equal" facilities for African Americans and whites. In the meantime, the states began to employ literacy tests, poll taxes, and other devices and arrangements to restrict the ability of African Americans to vote.

Inclusion Policies Between 1896 and 1936, not only did the separate-butequal doctrine legitimize racial discrimination, but also the Supreme Court persistently sustained separation schemes as long as facilities of some kind were provided to a state's black citizens—even if the facilities were woefully inferior to those provided to the white community. During the mid-1930's, however, responding to cases being appealed by the National Association for the Advancement of Colored People (NAACP), the Supreme Court began to shift direction. Between 1936 and 1954, it began to demand that states provide equal facilities to both races and to adopt more demanding tests for measuring the equality of segregated facilities.

A Texas system providing separate law schools for African Americans and whites, for example, was ruled unconstitutional in 1950 in *Sweatt v. Painter* because the black law school lacked the "intangibles" (such as reputation and successful alumni) that confer "greatness" on a law school and hence was unequal to the long-established school of law for white students at the University of Texas. Likewise, during the same period the Supreme Court began to remove some of the state-imposed obstacles to African Americans voting in the South and to limit the use of state machinery to enforce private acts of discrimination. The separate-but-equal test itself was finally abandoned in 1954, when, in the landmark case *Brown v. Board of Education*, the Supreme Court ruled that segregated facilities are inherently unequal in public education.

The *Brown* decision led to a decade-long effort by southern states to avoid compliance with desegregation orders. With the Supreme Court providing a moral voice against segregated public facilities, however, these state efforts failed when challenged in court. Moreover, a powerful multiracial Civil Rights movement emerged to demand justice for African Americans in other areas as well. In response, Congress enacted such landmark legislation as the 1964 Civil Rights Act (outlawing discrimination in employment and in places of private accommodation), the 1965 Voting Rights Act, and a series of affirmative action laws designed to benefit groups traditionally discriminated against in American society. As a result of these laws, the profile of the United States as a multiracial society was irrevocably altered. This change occurred almost entirely as a result of action within the country's legal and constitutional channels. To be sure, prejudice cannot be legislated away even though discrimination can be made illegal. During the mid-1990's, most American cities continued to possess a large African American underclass even as affirmative action and Head Start programs were becoming controversial and being canceled. On the other hand, the policies that had been adopted during the 1950's and 1960's enabled a sizable African American middle and professional class to develop, and many American cities had elected African Americans to govern them by the 1990's.

It has been argued that the growing prosperity of a subgroup of the African American community undercut the power of the Civil Rights movement. By the 1990's, a number of successful and affluent African American leaders, such as Supreme Court justice Clarence Thomas, were themselves opposing further affirmative action plans as well as further efforts to finance welfare programs perceived as primarily benefiting a heavily minority urban underclass.

Joseph R. Rudolph, Jr.
McCrea Adams

Further Reading
For good short discussions of government policies toward Native Americans, see Edward H. Spicer, *The American Indians* (Cambridge, Mass.: Belknap Press of Harvard University Press, 1980), and Francis Paul Prucha, *Indian Policy in the United States: Historical Essays* (Lincoln: University of Nebraska Press, 1981).

Immigration and discrimination is well treated in Nathan Glazer, ed., *Clamor at the Gates: The New American Immigration* (San Francisco: Institute for Contemporary Studies, 1985); Ronald Takaki, ed., *From Different Shores: Perspectives on Race and Ethnicity in America* (2d ed. New York: Oxford University Press, 1994); and Nathan Glazer and Daniel Patrick Moynihan's classic, *Beyond the Melting Pot: The Negroes, Puerto Ricans, Jews, Italians, and Irish of New York City* (2d ed. Cambridge, Mass.: MIT Press, 1970).

For a social psychological perspective on the issue, see *Identity and Cultural Diversity: What Social Psychology Can Teach Us* by Maykel Verkuyten (Hove, East Sussex: Routledge, 2014), while Philip Kretsedamas' *Migrants and Race in the U.S.:Territorial Racism and the Alien/Outside* (New York: Routledge, 2014) looks at how individuals may classify immigrants in categories outside those already existent in a society.

Interesting works within the vast literature on the Civil Rights movement include Leon Friedman, *The Civil Rights Reader: Basic Documents of the Civil Rights Movement* (New York: Walker, 1968); Anna Kosof, *The Civil Rights Movement and Its Legacy* (New York: Watts, 1989); and Dennis Chong, *Collective Action and the Civil Rights Movement* (Chicago: University of Chicago Press, 1991).

Two books that look at issues of discrimination as they relate to immigrants are *Immigration: A Civil Rights Issue for the Americas* (Wilmington, Del.: Scholarly Resources, 1999), edited by Susanne Jonas and Suzanne Dod Thomas, and Donna R. Gabaccia's *Immigration and American Diversity: A Social and Cultural History* (Malden, Mass.: Blackwell, 2002).

See also Accent discrimination; Arab American stereotypes; Asian American Legal Defense Fund; Celtic Irish; Chinese Exclusion Act; Coolies; Immigration Act of 1990; Irish immigrants and African Americans; Irish immigrants and discrimination; Irish stereotypes; Lau v. Nichols; League of United Latin American Citizens; Mexican American Legal Defense and Education Fund; Nativism; Naturalization; *Plyler v. Doe*; Soviet Jewish immigrants.

DOMESTIC ABUSE AS A PROTECTED CATEGORY (ASYLUM)

The Law: Under the Asylum law, the United States grants legal status to qualifying individuals who are already living in the United States and who are fleeing persecution in their home countries. Whether in the United States legally or illegally, they fear harm if returned to their homeland or have been harmed in the past. Asylum is one form of relief from deportation for people who are otherwise clearly deportable. In the cases when asylum is denied, it is because the person has been proven to be not credible, has had a fundamental change in their circumstances where they no longer have a justifiable fear of persecution, or if they are able to avoid persecution by relocating to another part of their home country.

Date: 2009

Immigration Issues: Women's rights advocates are becoming hopeful due to significant changes in the United States immigration courts, which appear to being more open to helping battered women who submit asylum claims. They are starting to see that the laws set forth by the government are more commonly reflecting the social issues women face in their homelands, and are thereby seeking asylum and international protection.

Significance: There has been an ongoing debate within the international legal community regarding situations that involve battered women and whether or not they should be considered refugees. Now, victims of domestic violence in other countries have an increased chance of being granted asylum in a United States immigration court.

The 1951 United Nations Convention Related to the Status of Refugees, as amended by a 1967 Protocol, states a refugee as:

"A person who owing to a well-founded fear of being persecuted for reasons of race, religion, nationality, membership of a particular social group or political opinion, is outside the country of his nationality and is unable or, owing to such fear, is unwilling to avail himself of the protection of that country; or who, not having a nationality and being outside the country of his former habitual residence as a result of such events, is unable or, owing to such fear, is unwilling to return to it."

With some minor changes, this international definition was incorporated into United States law, via the Immigration and Nationality Act, 8 U.S.C. § 1101(a)(42).

Background: In April 2009, in the *Matter of L-R-*, the case of Ms. Alvarado and her two sons who sustained severe domestic violence, the Department of Homeland Security submitted a brief to the Board of Immigration Appeals. It was this case that led to the Department of Homeland Security's brief, which states, "Department of Homeland Security accepts that in some cases a victim of domestic violence may be a member of a cognizable particular social group and may be able to show that her abuse was or would be persecution on account of such membership."

Ms. Alvarado's case was one that changed the way people viewed asylum. She was just 19 years old when her school's 33 year old coach raped her at gunpoint. That was the opening event for the next two years of torment for Ms. Alvarado. The coach kept her in captivity where he repeatedly abused her physically and emotionally. His continuous threats to kill her and her family members were a ploy to keep her from leaving; however, in the times when she tried to escape, he reacted brutally. Despite risk of retaliation, she went to the police on a number of occasions, yet those pleas lead nowhere. To make matters worse, the coach prevented her from seeing her three children. Seeking assistance from a judge ended in his demand that he could help her see her sons if she had sex with him. Upon refusal, the judge informed her that she was a bad mother, because a "good mother" would do that if it meant seeing her children.

Ms. Alvarado fled to the United States in 1991, only to be found by her abuser, who forced her to return by the use of threats that he would kill her and her family. The next time she fled to the United States was in 2004 and with her children in tow.

Eventually, and at the urging of one of her sons, Ms. Alvarado sought legal counsel. 19 months after arriving back in the United States, she filed for asylum. The San Francisco Asylum Office referred her case to immigration court where the judge denied her claims. Regardless of the diagnosis of several experts that Ms. Alvarado suffered greatly from debilitating post-traumatic stress disorder (PTSD), the judge found her capable of working and caring for her children, which meant she should have been able to file within the one-year deadline, rather than the 19 months that it took her. He also stated that the persecution she suffered from did not qualify her for asylum under the current law. Ms. Alvarado's attorneys argued that she was indeed a member of a social group, a group defined by her gender and inability to leave an abusive domestic relationship. These arguments lead to the Department of Homeland Security's 2004 brief to Attorney General John Ashcroft. Department of Homeland Security argued that victims of domestic violence could fall into a particular social group due to the way in which the abuser and society perceive their domestic relationship position.

In the particular case of Ms. Alvarado, the Department of Homeland Security filed a brief arguing that Ms. Alvarado was a member of the social group "married women in Guatemala who are unable to leave the relationship," which was similar to the group, "Mexican women in domestic relationships who are unable to leave."

Six months later, in October 2009, the Department of Homeland Security indicated that Ms. Alvarado was "eligible for asylum and merits a grant of asylum as a matter of discretion." According to the Center for Gender & Refugee Studies, Documents and Information, two months later the immigration court issued a summary decision, granting Ms. Alvarado asylum.

Ms. Alvarado's case sheds light on the issue of spousal abuse, but it also plays a role in a larger effort to make the asylum regulations more lenient, resulting in higher numbers of immigrants entering the United States. It was a significant case in regards to clarifying the asylum standard —specifically in regards to further defining the "particular social group" and how "political opinion," however, the case is also a catalyst to broaden the definition of humanitarianism itself.

Legislation: Much of the legislative activity in regard to the Board of Immigration Appeals (BIA) and the Department of Homeland Security has been in the past few decades. Below is a timeline of critical events.

1985: Matter of Acosta The BIA decided on the Matter of Acosta, which required fundamental and immutable characteristics to form a cognizable particular social group.

1999: Matter of R-A- BIA decides *Matter of R-A-*, reversing a grant of asylum in the case of a Guatemalan woman who suffered years of domestic violence.

2000: Proposed Regulations The Department of Justice issued proposed regulations regarding asylum/withholding, including guidance on gender claims.

2001: Matter of R-A- Vacated Attorney General Janet Reno vacated *Matter of R-A-*, with order of remand to the BIA to decide the case when the Department of Justice regulations were finalized.

2004: R-A- DHS Brief After Attorney General John Ashcroft certified *Matter of R-A-* to himself again, the Department of Homeland Security filed a brief urging asylum for Ms. Alvarado, explaining that domestic violence related PSG meets the *Acosta* test.

2005: R-A- Remand to BIA Attorney General John Ashcroft remands the case to BIA, with order to decide when asylum regulations are finalized.

2008: R-A- Remand to IJ Attorney General Michael Mukasey certifies *R-A-* to himself, with order to not wait for the finalization of regulations, but rather to decide the case pursuant to BIA. The Board remanded the case back to the IJ.

2009: Matter of L-R- Brief, R-A- Grant In April, Department of Homeland Security files a brief in the case of Mexican woman, "L.R." explaining how domestic violence related PSG can meet the BIA's new requirements of "social visibility" and "particularity." In December, an immigration judge in San Francisco grants asylum to Ms. Alvarado.

2010: L-R- Grant An immigration judge in San Francisco grants asylum to L.R.

Heather Hummel

Further Reading

Chavez, Stella, *Yolanda's Crossing: A Girl's Journey from Abuse to the American Dream*, The Dallas Morning News; 1 edition, November 16, 2011. A book based on the reports in the *Dallas Morning News* about a young abused woman and her escape in America.

Villalon, Roberta, *Violence Against Latina Immigrants: Citizenship, Inequality, and Community*, NYU Press, June 2010. A book documenting the experiences of immigrant women and the policies both for and against them in seeking asylum.

Abraham, Margaret, *Speaking the Unspeakable: Marital Violence Among South Asian Immigrants in the United States*, Rutgers University Press; 1 edition, April 1, 2000. A book depicting domestic violence in immigrant communities, specifically with South Asian women.

See also Green cards; Illegal aliens; Justice and immigration.

DOMINICAN IMMIGRANTS

Identification: Immigrants to North America from the Caribbean island nation of the Dominican Republic

Immigration issues: Demographics; Latino immigrants; West Indian immigrants

Significance: Although the Caribbean's Dominican Republic has a comparatively tiny population, its emigrants make up one of the fastest-growing immigrant populations in the United States.

Situated between Cuba and Puerto Rico in the Caribbean Sea, the Dominican Republic shares the island of Hispaniola with its neighbor Haiti. The country is known primarily for its warm tropical climate, its sugarcane and tobacco exports, and its contributions to the international community in the personages of fashion designer Oscar de la Renta, musician Juan Luis Guerra, and major league baseball players such as Sammy Sosa, Juan Marichal, George Bell, and Pedro Guerrero.

According to U.S. Census figures, 915,274 Dominicans entered the United States between 1820 and 2003. During the 1990's, they arrived at an average rate of 33,500 immigrants per year. During the first three years of the twentyfirst century, that rate dropped significantly, to about 23,300 immigrants per year. Dominican

Dominican immigrants in New York City protesting the U.S. occupation of their homeland in early 1965. (National Archives)

immigrants are especially evident in New York City, where they ranked as the most populous immigrant group during the mid-1990's. Their significant presence in that city has led to the emergence of a Dominican American community.

During the early 1960's, after the assassination of Dominican dictator Rafael Léonidas Trujillo, the Dominican Republic was affected by political and economic turmoil. The ensuing unrest resulted in the outbreak of civil war on April 25, 1965, which led to a U.S. military occupation of the country in an effort to protect American economic interests. Following the U.S. inter vention, many political activists were granted visas to the United States in an effort to stem political dissent against the new U.S.-sponsored right-wing government of Dominican president Joaquín Balaguer. This marked the beginning of a continued pattern of Dominican emigration to North America that was fueled by political as well as economic reasons.

Following a brief period of industrial growth under the new leadership of President Balaguer, Dominicans saw their country's economy worsen. The middle class all but disappeared in the wake of escalating oil prices, a massive foreign debt, and a decline in exports that resulted in a 23 percent unemployment rate during the early 1990's. This factor, coupled with the increased sentiments of frustration by Dominicans toward the leadership of the country, led to a Dominican diaspora in search of a place in which to obtain political and economic freedom.

According to the U.S. Census, as of 2010, about 1.5 million Hispanics of Dominican origin resided in the U.S., accounting for 3 percent of the Hispanic population. Over half (57 percent) of Dominican Americans are foreign born, compared to 37 percent of the total Hispanic population and 13 percent of the total U.S population. Dominicans have higher levels of educational attainment than Hispanic Americans as a whole (15 percent of Dominican Americans have at least a bachelor's degree, as compared to 13 percent of all Hispanics) and the median annual personal earnings for Dominicans is the same as for Hispanics ($20,000).

A New Community The Dominican American community is made up of people who have obtained U.S. citizenship after their arrival to North America as well as those that are born in the United States of Dominican parents. So salient is the Dominican migratory pattern to the New York City area that it has earned Dominican Americans the nickname of Dominicanyorks. Mass migration into New York City has resulted in the "Dominicanization" of neighborhoods such as Washington Heights. However, Dominican Americans have found some challenges in adapting to their new environment. Some resistance from the established residents, as well as political challenges in their local community, has led many Dominican Americans to become more actively involved in the political and economic activities of their community.

Part of the acculturation of Dominican Americans into mainstream society has been brought about through active participation in their neighborhood schools. During the early 1980's, a campaign was mounted to gain greater control over the schools in Washington Heights in order to make them more responsive to the needs of the local community. In 1980, the Community Association of Progressive Dominicans confronted the school board to demand bilingual education for newly arrived immigrants. Their presence in the political arena was also established in

1991 with the election of Guillermo Linares, the first Dominican ever to sit on the New York City Council. However, as is often the case with newly arrived immigrant groups to the United States, the moderate success of Dominican Americans has been considered by some as a challenge to the established residents of Washington Heights (mainly Jews, Puerto Ricans, and African Americans).

Ethnic Relations As Steven Lowenstein explains in his 1989 work titled *Frankfort on the Hudson: The German-Jewish Community of Washington Heights, 1933-1983*, the move by Dominican Americans to gain greater control over the local schools came at the expense of the established Jewish population in that area. Some see this as a source of tension between the two groups. One Jewish leader is quoted as saying:

> In order to save our own congregation, we have to live with our neighbors, even if they are different from us, even if we don't like them. But we cannot help it. We have to live with the Blacks, with the Spanish.

During the initial migration years, Dominicans rented apartments in the mostly Jewish-owned tenements; however, as the years progressed, the Jewish population became increasingly sparse in the Washington Heights area.

The newly arrived Dominican immigrants found acceptance within the Puerto Rican community during the early 1960's. Many Dominican immigrants were able to find housing and employment through friendships with Puerto Ricans. Some argue that the preexisting presence of the Puerto Rican community was helpful to the newly arrived Dominicans in that it led both Jewish and African Americans to come to terms with the unavoidable reality of a Latin American presence in New York City. However, as more and more Dominicans began migrating to the area, tensions arose within the Puerto Rican community. The growing sentiment was that Dominican Americans were accepting low-wage jobs and undercutting the Puerto Ricans in the job market. Likewise, as the Dominican population grew, many Dominican Americans began to feel that the Puerto Rican agenda followed by most of the Latino community leaders was not representative of the ever-growing Dominican population.

Similarly, African Americans have found themselves in competition with Dominican Americans for jobs and housing. Some African American business owners have complained about the aggressive tactics of some of the Dominican business owners. According to Linda Chavez's study titled *Out of the Barrio: Toward a New Politics of Hispanic Assimilation* (1991), Dominicans own 70 percent of all Hispanic small businesses in New York. Although sociable relations between these two groups continue, they tend to reside in partially segregated neighborhoods, perhaps because of racial and ethnic preconceptions held by both groups. Not unlike their African American neighbors, Dominican Americans have also been subject to racial discrimination based on physical appearance. As Patricia Pessar pointed out in her 1995 book *A Visa for a Dream*, often Dominicans who are perceived as "white" by AngloAmericans are treated better and offered better jobs than Dominicans who are dark-skinned.

The mixture of races found among Dominicans has frequently led to many dark-skinned Dominican Americans being misidentified as African Americans and subsequently being subjected to the same kind of racism experienced by African Americans. In Sakinah Carter's 1994 work titled *Shades of Identity: Puerto Ricans and Dominicans Across Paradigms*, a twenty-two-year-old Dominican is quoted as saying:

> All we see on television when we arrive is how bad blacks are, so we cling to our difference, our Latino-ness, in order to say we are not those blacks that you hear about in the streets or see on the news. We aren't bad. But at the same time, it feels ridiculous not to embrace our blackness because many dark Dominicans do live as other blacks, treated as blacks by white people, and other Latinos who act like there is one Latino phenotype, like there's a way to look Latino.... I'm black and Latino, a black Latino—we exist, you know.

However, dating back to the initial wave of Dominican immigrants during the 1960's, and in spite of some social challenges, Dominicans, Puerto Ricans, Jews, and African Americans have all been able to coexist as productive members of their communities despite their cultural differences and racial preconceptions.

Pedro R. Payne

Further Reading

For a thorough study of the history of the Dominican Republic, see Frank Moya Pons's *The Dominican Republic: A National History* (New Rochelle, N.Y.: Hispaniola Books, 1995).

Luis E. Guarnizo writes a chapter on "Dominicanyorks" in *Challenging Fronteras*, edited by Mary Romero, Pierrette Hondagneu-Sotelo, and Vilma Ortiz (New York: Routledge, 1997), which explores the "binational interconnection" that has resulted from Dominican immigration into the United States.

Another good source for issues pertaining to Dominican migration and adaptation to American society is Ramona Hernandez and Silvio Torres-Saillant's chapter in *Latinos in New York*, edited by Gabriel Haslip-Viera and Sherrie L. Baver (Notre Dame, Ind.: University of Notre Dame Press, 1996).

Christian Krohn-Hansen's *Making New York Dominican: Small Business, Politics, and Everyday Life* (Philadelphia: University of Pennsylvania Press, 2013) traces the evolution of the New York City Dominican immigrant community from the 1960s to today.

Patricia Pessar, in *A Visa for a Dream* (Boston: Allyn & Bacon, 1995), manages to capture the Dominican immigrant experience as well as the cultural factors that affect Dominican acculturation into American society.

Debóra Upegui-Hernández's *Growing Up Transnational: Columbian and Dominican Children of Immigrants in New York City* (El Paso: LFB Scholarly Pub, 2014) compares how children of Columbian and Dominican immigrants manage the experience of living among multiple cultures, as well as how their experiences were shaped by factors such as class, skin color, and immigration history.

For a historical account of the African and European ancestry of Dominicans and other Latin Americans, see *Afro-Latin Americans Today: No Longer Invisible* (London: Minority Rights Group, 1995).

Works that discuss Dominican immigrants in the broader context of West Indian immigration include Melonie P. Heron's *The Occupational Attainment of Caribbean Immigrants in the United States, Canada, and England* (New York: LFB Scholarly Publications, 2001) and Milton Vickerman's *Crosscurrents: West Indian Immigrants and Race* (New York: Oxford University Press, 1999).

Immigration Research for a New Century: Multidisciplinary Perspectives (New York: Russell Sage Foundation, 2000), edited by Nancy Foner, Rubén G. Rumbaut, and Steven J. Gold, is a collection of papers on immigration from a conference held in 1998 that includes a chapter on Dominican immigrants.

See also Afro-Caribbean immigrants; Haitian immigrants; Immigration "crisis"; Latinos; Latinos and family customs; West Indian immigrants.

THE DREAM ACT

The Dream Act: 2012

The Law: DREAM Act: Development, Relief, and Education for Alien Minors. On June 15, 2012, President Barack Obama stated that his administration would no longer deport illegal alien youths who matched certain criteria previously proposed under the original DREAM Act.

Date: 2001

Immigration Issues: The DREAM Act is specifically meant to aid young immigrants who were brought illegally to the U.S. as children. It has been criticized as providing something like amnesty to people who are in the country illegally, thus possibly encouraging illegal immigration and rewarding those who broke the law, but has also been praised as helping to integrate young people brought to the country by their parents into U.S. society.

Significance: On August 1, 2001, the DREAM Act proposal was introduced in the United States Senate by Dick Durbin and Orrin Hatch, S. 1291. As of November 2013, 15 of the United States have incorporated their own addendums of the DREAM Act, most of which address tuition prices and financial aid availability through state universities. These 15 states include: Texas, California, Illinois, Utah, Nebraska, Kansas, New Mexico, New Jersey, New York, Washington, Wisconsin, Massachusetts, Maryland, Minnesota, and Oregon.

Background: The DREAM Act was meant to provide youth immigrants with conditional permanent residency based on good moral character and graduation from a U.S. high school. Those conditions apply to those who arrived in the United

States as minors, and who have lived in the country continuously for no less than five years prior to enactment of the bill. This stipulation includes undocumented aliens up to the age of 35 years old.

The 2009 version of the Senate bill proposed by Durbin and Hatch stated that beneficiaries must:

- Not have entered the United States on a non-immigrant Visa.
- Have proof of having arrived in the United States before age 16.
- Have proof of residence in the United States for at least five consecutive years since their date of arrival.
- If male, have registered with the Selective Service.
- Be between the ages of 12 and 35 at the time of bill enactment.
- Have graduated from an American high school, obtained a GED, or been admitted to an institution of higher education.
- Be of good moral character.

Students detained in Tucson, Arizona, after staging a sit-in at US Senator John McCain's office on May 17, 2010, in support of the DREAM Act. (Public Domain)

Those who completed two years in the military or two years at a four-year institution of higher learning, could obtain a six-year temporary residency. Within the six-year grace period, they become eligible for permanent residency if they have "acquired a degree from an institution of higher education in the United States or [have] completed at least two years, in good standing, in a program for a bachelor's degree or higher degree in the United States" or have "served in the armed services for at least two years and, if discharged, [have] received an honorable discharge".

"Any alien whose permanent resident status is terminated... shall return to the immigration status the alien had immediately prior to receiving conditional permanent resident status under this Act."

If an immigrant has met each of the requirements at the end of their six-year conditional period, they are granted permanent residency, which entitles them to becoming U.S. citizens. There are no formal statistics to indicate how many of those who are eligible continue on to complete the further citizenship requirements.

Legislation: Members of Congress in both the House of Representatives and the Senate introduced different versions of the bill. Members in the House passed one version of the bill on December 8, 2010 by a vote of 216-198; Senators debated an earlier version of the DREAM Act on September 21, 2010. A previous version of the bill, S. 2205, required 60 votes to gain cloture, failed by eight votes to pass on a 52-44 vote in 2007.

On April 25, 2001, an earlier version of the DREAM Act was introduced by Representative Luis Gutiérrez as the "Immigrant Children's Educational Advancement and Dropout Prevention Act of 2001" (H.R. 1582) during the 107th Congress. At the time, it received 34 cosponsors. The bill would have allowed undocumented immigrant students to first apply to be protected from deportation and secondly apply for lawful permanent residency if they met the following criteria, which is slightly different than the current bill:

- Good moral character;
- Enrollment in a secondary or post-secondary education program or current application to a college or junior college;
- Entered the United States by age 16 and were no older than 25;
- Resided continuously in the United States for a minimum of five years.

On May 21, 2001, just a month later, Gutiérrez's version of the bill was scrapped in favor of a more limited version titled "Student Adjustment Act of 2001" (H.R. 1918). This version of the bill garnered 62 cosponsors and also lowered its age eligibility to 21 years of age.

Senate by Republican Congressman Orrin Hatch introduced a mirror bill to the "Student Adjustment Act of 2001" on August 1, 2001. This legislation, S. 1291, was the first bill given the short title of "Development, Relief, and Education for Alien Minors Act" or "DREAM Act."

Ever since then, the DREAM Act has been introduced in both the Senate and the House at various times.

- In the Senate: S. 1545 (108th Congress), S. 2075 (109th Congress), S. 774 (110th Congress), and S. 2205 (110th Congress).
- In the House: H.R. 1684 (108th Congress), H.R. 5131 (109th Congress), and H.R. 1275 (110th Congress).

The DREAM Act was later incorporated into the National Defense Authorization Act for the Fiscal Year 2011. On November 16, 2010, President Barack Obama and top Democrats pledged to introduce the Dream Act into the House by November 29, 2010. The House of Representatives passed the DREAM Act on December 8, 2010; however, the bill failed to reach the 60-votes required to end debate on the Senate floor (55-41—Motion to invoke cloture on the motion to concur in the House amendment to the Senate amendment No. 3 to H.R. 5281).

It was on May 11, 2011 when Senate Majority Leader Harry Reid reintroduced the DREAM Act in the Senate. Some of the Republicans, including Sen. John Cornyn of Texas, Jon Kyl of Arizona, John McCain of Arizona, and Lindsey Graham of South Carolina, had previously supported the bill, and now withheld their votes. Their objection was that such a bill should only be granted if increasing immigration was also enforced.

Reid proposed the possibility of adding to the DREAM Act a workplace enforcement measure that would require employers to use the already in place E-Verify system, a government Internet-based verification system for work eligibility. President Obama supported the bill as one of his efforts to reform the US immigration system.

California enacted the California DREAM Act in July 2011, allowing illegal immigrant students access to private college scholarships for state schools. The next month, in August 2011, Illinois authorized a privately funded scholarship plan for children of immigrants both legal and illegal.

On June 15, 2012, President Barack Obama announced that his administration would stop deporting young illegal aliens who match certain criteria previously proposed under the DREAM ACT.

Heather Hummel

Further Reading

Perez, William, We Are Americans: *Undocumented Students Pursuing the American Dream*, Stylus Publishing, August 2009 An award-winning book about the millions of undocumented children (minors) who are brought into the United States by their parents.

Hernandez, Arnold, *The DREAM Act Explained*, Amazon Digital Services, Inc., July 18, 2013 A book that details the pending Immigration Reform Act of 2013 and its impact on students.

Suárez-Orozco, Carola, *Children of Immigration (The Developing Child)*, Harvard University Press, May 30, 2002 A book that addresses how "Americanization," long an immigrant ideals, has become difficult to define or to achieve.

Editorial Board, Second Act for the DREAM, The Washington Post [Internet article] http://www.washingtonpost.com/opinions/second-act-for-the-dream-act/2013/08/05/3085602a-f577-11e2-aa2e-4088616498b4_story.html (accessed

on August 5, 2013)

See also Deportation; Latinos and employment; Naturalization.

Eastern European Jewish immigrants

Identification: Jewish immigrants to North America from eastern European nations

Immigration issues: European immigrants; Jewish immigrants; Religion

Significance: Among Jewish immigrants to North America, eastern Europeans were relative latecomers and were not well received by either Christian Americans or other Jewish Americans.

The major emigration of eastern European Jews to the United States did not begin until the 1880's. Jews began to emigrate when the services they performed as small-scale merchants and artisans were rendered obsolete by the modernization of agriculture and the early impact of industrialization on the peasant economy of

Eastern European immigrants crossing the Atlantic in 1899. (Library of Congress)

Russia, Austria-Hungary, and the Polish territory held by Germany. The migration became a mass movement, however, when deadly state-sponsored riots left hundreds dead and thousands homeless in Russia and Russian Poland following the assassination of Czar Alexander II in 1881. About 250,000 Jews lived in the United States in 1880; by 1920, more than 2 million eastern European Jews had joined them.

They were not given a warm welcome. The American Jewish community re-acted with alarm, fearful that the up-surge in immigration would stimulate anti-Semitism and undermine the relatively comfortable position that Jews had attained in the country. Only as the magnitude of the problem became clear did the established Jewish community begin to organize an array of philanthropic institutions and establish defense organizations to combat anti-Semitism. The migration's size and the tendency of the new arrivals to cluster within the nation's largest cities, especially New York, made them particularly conspicuous. Crowded into slum areas where they transformed whole neighborhoods into regions where no English could be heard, they seemed particularly threatening to native-born Americans.

Many of the men, possessing few skills valuable to an industrial economy, became peddlers pushing carts or carrying packs filled with merchandise until they accumulated enough cash to open small retail stores. Many of the women and a significant proportion of the men found work in the garment industry. A few had previous experience in the needle trades, but of more importance was the willingness of owners to hire them. Manufacturing ready-to-wear clothing was a relatively new and risky industry that attracted Jewish entrepreneurs who were open to hiring and training Jewish workers.

Eastern European Jews settled in dense concentrations in their own neighborhoods and rarely interacted

One of the best-known Jewish immigrants in U.S. history was the magician and escape artist Harry Houdini. The son of a Hungarian rabbi, he was born Erik Weisz in Budapest in 1874 and came to the United States with his family as a boy. (Library of Congress)

with other ethnic groups. Those whom they displaced, especially the New York City Irish, often responded with small-scale street violence. In addition, the Jewish community experienced sharp internal divisions. Jews from a given area of Europe tended to settle near each other, build separate synagogues, and create self-help and burial societies designed to serve migrants from the specific city or region from which they had come. A hierarchy of prejudice separated Jewish groups and influenced the choice of marriage partners. German Jews looked down on Polish and Russian Jews. Russian Jews were reputed to view marriage with Galician Jews, who came from the most poverty-stricken region of the Austro-Hungarian Empire, as equivalent to marrying a Gentile, which was taboo.

Economic success increased the interaction of the eastern European Jews with the larger American society. In the affluent post-World War II years, they moved into the suburbs. Their children, fluent in English and increasingly college-educated, entered the professions as teachers, doctors, and lawyers. As the descendants of the eastern European Jews merged with the American middle class, relations with other ethnic and religious groups became easier and less antagonistic.

Further Reading

Milton Berman Cohen, Jocelyn, and Daniel Soyer, eds and transl. *My Future is in America: Autobiographies of Eastern European Jewish Immigrants*. New York: New York University Press, 2006.

Cohen, Naomi Werner. *Encounter with Emancipation: The German Jews in the United States, 1830-1914*. Philadelphia: Jewish Publication Society of America, 1984.

Gerber, David, ed. *Anti-Semitism in American History*. Urbana: University of Illinois Press, 1986.

Greene, Victor R. *A Singing Ambivalence: American Immigrants Between Old World and New, 1830-1930*. Kent, Ohio: Kent State University Press, 2004.

Howe, Irving. *World of Our Fathers*. New York: Harcourt Brace Jovanovich, 1976.

Sanders, Ronald. Shores of Refuge: *A Hundred Years of Jewish Immigration*. New York: Schocken Books, 1988.

Shapiro, Edward S. *Yiddish in American: Essays on Yiddish Culture in the Golden Land*. Scranton: University of Scranton Press, 2008.

Sterba, Christopher M. *The Melting Pot Goes to War: Italian and Jewish Immigrants in America's Great Crusade, 1917-1919*. Ann Arbor, Mich.: UMI, 1999.

See also American Jewish Committee; Ashkenazic and German Jewish immigrants; Israeli immigrants; Jewish immigrants; Jewish settlement of New York; Jews and Arab Americans; Sephardic Jews; Soviet Jewish immigrants.

ENGLISH-ONLY AND OFFICIAL ENGLISH MOVEMENTS

Definition: Attempts by federal and state governments, lobbyists, organizations, or private citizens to make English the "only" or "official" language in the United States

Immigration issues: Civil rights and liberties; Discrimination; Language; Nativism and racism

Significance: Although some Americans see English-only movements as patriotic or well-intended, others regard such efforts as anti-immigrant or racist.

Determining how many Americans cannot or do not use English for everyday activities is very difficult. According to the *1996 Statistical Abstract of the United States*, more than thirty-two million Americans, or more than 13 percent of the population, speak a language other than English at home. Of these, around 44 percent, or about fourteen million people, do not speak English "very well." Figures such as these are cited by many Americans as evidence of national unity eroding under a wave of linguistic diversity and cultural strife.

During the 1980's, organizations such as U.S. English began pressing for state, local, and federal legislation to make English the only official language in various parts of the country. Several attempts have been made to pass a U.S. constitutional amendment mandating English as an official national language, but they have all failed.

However, eighteen states have passed some form of official English legislation. In response to these activities, other organizations, such as English Plus, have worked to maintain linguistic and cultural pluralism in the United States. Four states have passed some kind of mandate supporting such sanctions.

Historical Precedents Although two-thirds of Americans believed that English already was the official language of the United States during the 1990's, the Founders did not establish an official language, perhaps because they felt no need to address the issue. Although the United States has always had a large number of non-English speakers on its soil, English has been the dominant language in the land since the first settlements in the original thirteen colonies. In 1790 after the Revolutionary War—when the nation was perhaps at its height of linguistic diversity—the population was still 76 percent English-speaking, apart from many slaves.

The second most commonly spoken language in the new nation was German, spoken in states such as Pennsylvania, originally a bilingual English and German state. However, by 1815, the German speakers had largely merged linguistically and culturally with the English-speaking majority. English became the de facto national language.

Although some of the nation's leaders occasionally complained about non-English speakers (for example, Theodore Roosevelt once said that Americans should not be "dwellers in a polyglot boarding house"), and the issue was occasionally raised, the official language debate did not receive much thought until the mid-1980's. The debate reached the national level in 1986 when California's Proposition 63, which made English the official state language, passed with 73 percent of the vote.

The Debate   Those who argue for an official language policy say that to live successful and fruitful lives in the United States, immigrants and non-English speakers must learn English: Without fluency in English, they will forever remain in a linguistic underclass, economically and educationally deprived. They believe that bilingual education and multilingual voting ballots and driver's license exams serve only to foster and perpetuate these people's dependence on other languages. They say that the situations in pluralistic countries such as Canada, India, or Belgium, where linguistic wars have been fought, demonstrate the need for a single language to unify the country. English-only supporters cite statistics showing that immigrants want to learn English and argue that, therefore, their efforts are not anti-immigrant.

Probably the most organized and outspoken English-only group is U.S. English, which was established in 1983 and by the year 2005 claimed a membership of 1.8 million. The original board of directors and advisers included many well-known and respected individuals, including Nobel Prize-winning author Saul Bellow,

Immigrants in an English-language class being conducted in a Ford Motor Company plant in Detroit during the early twentieth century. (Library of Congress)

State Language Policies

State	Year	Action
States Where English Has Become the "Official" Language		
Alabama	1990	by constitutional amendment
Arizona	1988	by constitutional amendment
Arkansas	1987	by legislative statute
California	1986	by constitutional amendment
Colorado	1988	by constitutional amendment
Florida	1988	by constitutional amendment
Georgia	1986	by legislative statute
Hawaii	1978	by constitutional amendment
Illinois	1969	by legislative statute
Indiana	1984	by legislative statute
Kentucky	1984	by legislative statute
Mississippi	1987	by legislative statute
Nebraska	1920	by constitutional amendment
North Carolina	1987	by legislative statute
North Dakota	1987	by legislative statute
South Carolina	1987	by legislative statute
Tennessee	1984	by legislative statute
Virginia	1981	by legislative statute
States Supporting "English Plus," Official Linguistic Pluralism		
New Mexico	1989	by legislative resolution
Oregon	1989	by legislative resolution
Rhode Island	1992	by legislative statute
Washington	1989	by legislative resolution
Other Policies		
All U.S. states	1990	Native American Language Act gives American Indian languages special rights and status.
Arizona	1999	Grade 1 through 8 foreign-language instruction is mandated by statute.

social critics Alistair Cooke and Jacques Barzun, former university president and senator S. I. Hayakawa, actor and California governor Arnold Schwarzenegger, and newscaster Walter Cronkite (who resigned in 1988).

The organization has argued that English is the common bond that unites all Americans and that the United States shoud take active steps to avoid language segregation to avert some of the bitter linguistic conflicts that have plagued many pluralistic nations. They advocate adopting a constitutional amendment establishing English as the official language in the United States, restricting or eliminating bilingual education programs, requiring English competency for all new citizens, and expanding opportunities for learning English.

The storm over official English surprised many people when Senator Hayakawa, a Republican from California, during the early 1980's introduced a constitutional amendment to make English the official language. The amendment also would have eliminated many foreign-language supplementary materials in both the public and private sector and, therefore, appeared to be aimed at ending bilingual education. Many people perceived the English-only movement as an attempt to disfranchise immigrants or nonnative English speakers by depriving them of access to basic social services and education. Many people felt that the amendment would only splinter the country into even more divisive interest and ethnic groups and foster xenophobia and intolerance.

English Plus One of the groups that formed to combat English-only initiatives was English Plus, established in 1987. The group is a coalition of more than fifty prestigious educational and civil rights organizations, including the American Civil Liberties Union, the Center for Applied Linguistics, and the National Council of Teachers of English. The organization's stated goals are to strengthen the vitality of the United States through linguistic and cultural pluralism.

English Plus recognizes that English is, and should be, the primary language of the United States; however, the group argues that the equal protection clause of the U.S. Constitution requires that language assistance be made available to all who require it in order for them to enjoy equal access to essential public services, education, and the political process. Their efforts include advocating the acquisition of multiple language skills to foster better foreign relations and U.S. competitiveness in the global economy, encouraging people to retain their first language, working to develop and maintain language assistance programs such as bilingual education in elementary and high schools, and launching campaigns against legislative initiatives or actions that would make English the official language.

The Future Many Americans feel threatened by rising immigration and changing demographics. Others see little reason to oppose English-only or official-English amendments or statutes since English is so necessary to life in the United States. These feelings are reflected in official actions such as the attempt to add language referring to English as a "common and unifying language" to immigration bills at the national level in 2006 and 2007, and the attempt in Nashville, Tennessee to prohibit the government from using any language other than English (the attempt failed). Some Americans, however, believe that these amendments and statutes are really a form of racism. These people ask why proponents of English-only want to pass a law to enforce what is already in effect, unless they have a hidden agenda. However, regardless of what legislators or voters do, American identity, culture, and intellectual achievement will continue to be influenced by immigrants, who no doubt will be making their contributions in English.

James Stanlaw

Further Reading

Fernando de la Peña's *Democracy or Babel: The Case for Official English* (Washington, D.C.: U.S. English, 1991) makes the argument that English should be the official language in the United States.

S. I. Hayakawa, the most influential spokesperson for the English-only movement, argues for amending the U.S. Constitution in *The English Language Amendment: One Nation... Indivisible?* (Washington, D.C.: Washington Institute for Values in Public Policy, 1985) and states his case in "Why English Should Be Our Official Language" in *The Educational Digest* (52, 1987).

Arguments against official English are found in *Not Only English: Affirming America's Multilingual Heritage*, edited by Harvey Daniels (Urbana, Ill.: National Council of Teachers of English, 1990), and *Official English/English Only: More Than Meets the Eye* (Washington, D.C.: National Education Association of the United States, 1988).

Bill Piatt's *¿Only English? Law and Language Policy in the United States* (Albuquerque: University of New Mexico Press, 1990) discusses the legal downsides to making English the national language.

Political scientist Raymond Tatalovich's *Nativism Reborn? The Official English Language Movement and the American States* (Lexington: University of Kentucky Press, 1995) examines the state legislatures and legislators who passed English-only measures and suggests that such sentiment is closely tied to anti-immigration politics.

Deborah J. Schildkraut's *Press One for English: Language Policy, Public Opinion, and American Identity* (Princeton, NJ: Princeton University Press, 2005) looks at how concepts of national identity can fuel debates such as the English-only movement.

English: Our Official Language?, edited by Bee Gallegos (New York: H. W. Wilson, 1994), and *Language Loyalties: A Source Book on the Official English Controversy*, edited by James Crawford (Chicago: University of Chicago Press, 1992), present articles on the English-only controversy that appeared in the popular media and scholarly journals.

Other works offering broader perspective on language include *Language and Cultural Diversity in U.S. Schools: Democratic Principles in Action* (Westport, Conn.: Praeger, 2005), edited by Terry A. Osborn; *Portraits of Literacy Across Families, Communities, and Schools: Intersections and Tensions* (Mahwah, N.J.: L. Erlbaum Associates, 2005), edited by Jim Anderson and others; Charmian Kenner's *Becoming Biliterate: Young Children Learning Different Writing Systems* (Sterling, Va.: Trentham Books, 2004); and Terrence G. Wiley's *Literacy and Language Diversity in the United States* (2d ed. Washington, D.C.: Center for Applied Linguistics, 2005).

See also Accent discrimination; Anglo-conformity; Bilingual education; Bilingual Education Act of 1968; British as dominant group; Generational acculturation; Hansen effect; *Lau v. Nichols*; Proposition 227.

Ethnic enclaves

Definition: Isolated ethnic communities, free from contact from the majority population, that are usually intended to maintain customs and traditions that are under attack by outsiders

Immigration issues: Discrimination; Ethnic enclaves

Significance: Ethnic enclaves—such as Chinatowns, Little Tokyos, and Koreatowns—are usually created by groups that feel oppressed or discriminated against by outside forces.

Ethnic enclaves are territories inhabited by a distinct group of people who are separated from the dominant population by differences in language, religion, social class, or culture and who are frequently subjected to prejudice and discrimination. An ethnic group has a shared history based on a sense of difference from others resulting from several factors, including a unique set of experiences (such as being enslaved or defeated in a war), skin color or other physical differences (such as height), or geography.

Reasons for Formation Enclaves are established for two major reasons. Some are found in nations and among groups where a distinct sense of injustice exists between peoples. This sense of discrimination prevents communication and results in isolation and a sense of inferiority within the minority group. The dominant group persecutes persons deemed inferior who then withdraw into isolated communities to protect themselves from attack. Enclaves can also be built because of a sense of ethnic superiority, or ethnocentrism. In this case, one group sees itself as being far superior to any others and deliberately separates itself from the rest of society. This self-imposed isolation results from the view that the way of life being lived by group members should not be contaminated by "inferior" outsiders.

Ethnic enclaves result from the failure of groups to accommodate, acculturate, or assimilate. Accommodation is a reduction of conflict among groups as they find ways of living with one another based on mutual respect for differences. Groups maintain their differences but agree to live with one another. In places where enclaves develop, only physical separation lessens conflict: Groups continue to hate and discredit one another but geography keeps them apart.

Acculturation, meaning taking over some of the attitudes and beliefs of the other group, fails to take place in these situations because contact between different peoples is rare, and they stick to their traditional values. Instead of becoming more alike, as would be true under the process of assimilation, the groups become more and more different. A common culture fails to develop, and frequently misunderstandings and miscommunication can lead to violent conflicts. It is as if each group lives in a different world, with memories, sentiments, feelings, and attitudes that are totally unknown to the other. The more divergent peoples are or become, the more difficult assimilation will be. This situation is evident among the peoples of southeastern Europe, especially in areas of the former Yugoslavia, such as Bosnia, Croatia, and Serbia. It is also true in African states such as Burundi, Nigeria, and South Africa.

In a few situations, enclaves develop as a defense against attacks by physically or numerically superior outsiders. If the group does not retreat and separate from the dominant society, it will be annihilated. In this case, cutting off the community from contact with others serves the function of preserving traditions, customs, and beliefs. Most often, this is done by withdrawing into the wilderness beyond the reach of the persecutors. In the United States during the 1840's, members of the Church of Jesus Christ of Latter-day Saints (Mormons) adopted this strategy to save themselves from mob attacks in the East. Brigham Young, the successor to the group's founder Joseph Smith, deliberately chose to settle his people by the Great Salt Lake, then part of Mexico, because it seemed far enough away from the United States that no one would bother them. The Mormons lived in this isolated area free from contact with others well into the 1880's and preserved their distinct religious beliefs.

Development of the Concept The concept of ethnic identity and ethnic enclaves developed in the nineteenth century, though different words and phrases such as "immigrant group," "foreign stock," and "race" were used in place of "ethnic." The term "ethnic" was first used by social scientists during the 1920's to differentiate the supposedly less fervent attachments based on language and history in comparison to the supposedly more fundamental biological attachments based on racial inheritance. Many social scientists were interested in the question of how people of different linguistic and historical traditions would become part

Vietnamese American community center in the Little Saigon district of Garden Grove, California, which has one of the largest concentration of Asian immigrants in the United States. (David Fowler)

of modern, specifically American, society. Robert Ezra Park of the University of Chicago developed a theory of intergroup relations based on an inevitable process of contact, competition, accommodation, and, finally, full assimilation. As group members moved upward in the American class system, they would gradually lose their ethnic attachments and ultimately be accepted as true citizens.

The more different groups were from the white, Anglo-Saxon, majority, however, the longer and more difficult the process would be (as in the case of American Indians and African Americans). Gunnar Myrdal, the great Swedish sociologist, supported this view in his classic *An American Dilemma* (1944), a study of race relations in the United States. Park's analysis of assimilation has been mostly accepted by sociologists, though Milton Gordon, in *Assimilation in American Life* (1964), pointed out that assimilation takes much longer than has been assumed and is frequently marred by conflict and disorder. Most sociologists and historians writing on the subject since then have agreed with Gordon and have detailed the difficulties experienced by various American ethnic groups. Most observers have agreed that retreating into enclaves is sometimes necessary for group survival but always makes cooperation between groups more difficult.

Leslie V. Tischauser

Further Reading

Broad studies of ethnic enclaves in American cities include Susan K. Wierzbicki's *Beyond the Immigrant Enclave: Network Change and Assimilation* (New York: LFB Scholarly Publications, 2004), Michel S. Laguerre's *The Global Ethnopolis: Chinatown, Japantown, and Manilatown in American Society* (New York: St. Martin's Press, 1999), and Stephanie Bohon's *Latinos in Ethnic Enclaves: Immigrant Workers and the Competition for Jobs* (New York: Garland, 2000).

Yoonmee Chang looks at ghettoization and class inequalities in Asian American communities in *Writing the Ghetto: Class, Authorship, and the Asian American Ethnic Enclave* (New Brunswick, NJ: Rutgers University Press, 2010, while Michael E. Martin looks at patterns of residential segregation in the Latino community in *Residential Segregation Patterns of Latinos in the United States, 1990-2000: Testing the Ethnic Enclave and Inequality Theories* (New York: Routledge, 2007).

Nathan Glazer and Daniel Patrick Moynihan's *Beyond the Melting Pot: The Negroes, Puerto Ricans, Jews, Italians, and Irish of New York City* (Cambridge, Mass.: MIT Press, 1963) is a classic study of the long-term persistence of ethnic identities in the United States.

Milton M. Gordon's *Assimilation in American Life* (New York: Oxford University Press, 1964) outlines the factors involved in the process of assimilation.

Martin N. Marger's *Race and Ethnic Relations: American and Global Perspectives* (Belmont, Calif.: Wadsworth Press, 1985) surveys ethnic problems from a worldwide perspective.

See also Chinatowns; Little Havana; Little Italies; Little Tokyos; Machine politics.

EURO-AMERICANS

Identification: Also known as European Americans, a pan-ethnic identity that encompasses all Americans of European ancestry, ranging from descendants of the earliest colonizers to recent immigrants

Immigration issue: European immigrants

Significance: "Euro-American" is a problematic group label in that it is less widely used than other pan-ethnic identities.

In *Ethnic Identity: The Transformation of White America* (1990), Richard Alba observed that the emergence of a Euro-American group has been shaped by the decline of individual European ethnic affiliations, the creation of a common historical narrative of immigration, struggle, and mobility, and the increasing Euro-American reaction to political challenges from peoples of color and post-1965 immigrants.

As a group label, "Euro-American" is less widely used than other panethnic identities, such as Asian American, Hispanic, and Native American. Dominant identities tend to be "hidden" in intergroup interactions, and the lack of awareness or use of the Euro-American label reflects the dominant status of the group in the United States. This process is compounded by the existence of competing labels for Euro-Americans: "white," "Caucasian," and Anglo-American—the latter term reflecting the historical dominance of British Americans within the group. The future role of Euro-American group identity will be determined by both the political and social strategies of the group itself, and the external and structural forces that mold all pan-ethnic identities.

Ashley W. Doane, Jr.

Further Reading

Alba, Richard D. *Ethnic Identity: The Transformation of White America*. New Haven, Conn.: Yale University Press, 1990.

Benmayor, Rina, and Andor Skotnes, eds. *Migration and Identity*. New Brunswick, N.J.: Transaction, 2005.

Cohn, Raymond L. *Mass Migration Under Sail: European Immigration to the Antebellum United States*. New York: Cambridge University Press, 2009.

Meltzer, Milton. *Bound for America: The Story of the European Immigrants*. New York: Benchmark Books, 2001.

See also European immigrant literature; European immigrants, 1790-1892; European immigrants, 1892-1943; Generational acculturation; German and Irish immigration of the 1840's; German immigrants; Gypsy immigrants; Irish immigrants; Italian immigrants; Melting pot; Nativism; Polish immigrants; Scandinavian immigrants; White ethnics.

EUROPEAN IMMIGRANT LITERATURE

Definition: Fiction, essays, and other works written by immigrants of European ancestry

Immigration issues: European immigrants; Literature; Nativism and racism

Significance: The literature produced by European American writers has, to a great extent, reflected the struggles of assimilation, the loss of identity in that process, and the pain of being torn between different cultures.

As part of the graduation ceremonies at the Ford Motor Company English school in Detroit during World War I, students climbed to the stage wearing the native dress of their European homelands, carrying signs that read Greece, Syria, Italy, and so on. They then entered a giant cardboard cauldron labeled "Melting Pot" and emerged dressed in coats and ties and carrying their diplomas and small American flags. Assimilation was dramatically complete.

This stage show is symbolic of a much larger (and usually more subtle) process that millions of immigrants to the United States in the nineteenth and twentieth centuries under went. Between 1820 and 1990, more than fifty million immigrants entered the United States, and three-quarters of them came from Europe. Before 1890, the majority of these immigrants were—in descending numbers—German, Irish, and English. Between 1890 and 1914 fifteen million Europeans arrived in the

German American farmers in Nebraska during the mid-twentieth century. (Library of Congress)

United States, and most of them came from southern and eastern Europe: Greece, Italy, Hungary, Poland, and Russia. By 1980, individuals of European origin composed the bulk of the United States population (approximately 75 percent) and Europeans continued to immigrate to the United States in large numbers.

Demographics Although many European American immigrated to the U.S. several generations ago, many still identify their heritage or ancestry as coming from a particular country. For instance, the American Community Survey for 2009 found that 50.7 million American self-identified as having German ancestry, 36.9 million with Irish ancestry, 27.7 million with English ancestry, 18.1 million with Italian ancestry, 10.1 million with Polish ancestry, 9.4 million with French Ancestry, 5.8 million with Swedish ancestry, and 5.0 million with Dutch ancestry.

Such distinctive and over whelming national identification has often been blurred in American cultural consciousness by the peculiar assimilative process of the United States. Economic and social discrimination, on one hand, pushed immigrants into early and often involuntary assimilation. The dedication of the Statue of Liberty in 1886—where the Jewish American poet Emma Lazarus's words "Give me . . . your huddled masses yearning to breathe free" are inscribed—was not unanimously endorsed. In the press and on the streets

---

The Statue of Liberty

Poet Emma Lazarus wrote this sonnet in 1883 in support of the fund organized to raise money to build the pedestal on which the Statue of Liberty was placed three years later. The sonnet now appears on a bronze plaque at the base of the statue. In 1972, the American Museum of Immigration was opened inside the base of the statue.

The New Colossus

Not like the brazen giant of Greek fame,
With conquering limbs astride from land to land;
Here at our sea-washed, sunset gates shall stand
A mighty woman with a torch, whose flame
Is the imprisoned lightning, and her name
Mother of Exiles. From her beacon-hand
Glows world-wide welcome; her mild eyes command
The air-bridged harbor that twin cities frame.
"Keep, ancient lands, your storied pomp!" cries she
With silent lips. "Give me your tired, your poor,
Your huddled masses yearning to breathe free,
The wretched refuse of your teeming shore.
Send these, the homeless, tempest-tost to me,
I lift my lamp beside the golden door!"

there were attacks on immigrants from southern and eastern Europe. When not changed by officials at the government's Ellis Island reception center, the names of many European immigrants often quickly were changed by the immigrants themselves, who as foreigners were greeted with hostility and suspicion but who as Americans were welcome. The Polish name Sciborski might become Smith; the Italian name Pina, Pine; the Jewish name Greenberg, simply Green.

European Americans during the late nineteenth century were drawn by the lure of the American Dream, which promised equal access to wealth and possibility to all. Supporting this dream was the dominant ideological construct of the melting pot, which, like the symbolic cauldron in the Ford Motor Company graduation ceremonies, encouraged immigrants to give up their native heritage and take on a narrower American identity. Behind the melting pot theory was the belief in homogeneity over heterogeneity, assimilation over pluralism. The term itself was first popularized in a play, *The Melting-Pot*, by the English Jewish writer Israel Zangwill in 1908. As Werner Sollors noted in *Beyond Ethnicity: Consent and Descent in American Culture* (1986):

> More than any social or political theory, the rhetoric of Zangwill's play shaped American discourse on immigration and ethnicity, including most notably the language of self-declared opponents of the melting-pot concept.

Opponents of immigration have a long history in the United States, and the objects of their attacks have kept changing. The first nativist expression was an anti-Catholic sentiment, aimed mainly at the millions of Irish who immigrated after 1820. By the end of the nineteenth century, xenophobic feelings had shifted and were aimed at Slavic, Italian, Greek, and other eastern and southern European immigrants. The height of nativist opposition to immigration came during World War I. The literacy test of 1917 marked the beginning of the end of the open-door immigration policy of the United States. Legislation during the 1920's closed the door.

Assimilation vs. Ethnic Identity   The process of assimilation during the nineteenth and twentieth centuries had a profound effect not only on European American identity but also on the literature and culture that different European American ethnic groups produced. In many cases forced by discrimination, loss of language, loss or change of name, and the ideological impetus of Americanization to give up ethnic roots, many European Americans ended up torn between American and European ethnic identities. If the members of an ethnic culture did not assimilate, they faced the danger of becoming ghettoized, forced into an almost secretive, subcultural status.

Writers in the twentieth century, in common with the cultures they represented, were often afraid to exhibit their ethnic identity. As late as 1969, when Mario Puzo published *The Godfather*, for example, critics within the Italian American community argued that the work would only confirm the worst stereotypes of Italians in the United States. In another novel of the same year, Philip Roth was condemned by Jewish community leaders for his characters in *Portnoy's Complaint*. Ethnic writers were hindered by their own ethnic communities from revealing too much, which made it easier for them to make the sometimes Faustian bargain with the dominant culture to trade their ethnic consciousness for entrance into the literary mainstream.

The dominant culture of the earlier twentieth century was clearly white, Anglo-Saxon, and Protestant, and the ideology of the melting pot reinforced the dominant culture's hold on the popular mind. All writers should be American, this theory held, and ethnic cultural and literary artifacts were exotic and suspect. One perhaps could go folk-dancing as a cultural curiosity, but European American ethnic identification was discouraged on a number of ideological and institutional levels.

The dominant literature and literary culture were Anglo; students in different parts of the country all read the most famous works that had been written in England and New England, but they had little knowledge of works in other languages—including their native languages. High school students from New York City to rural New Mexico, from Seattle to Maine, might know the nineteenth century English novelist George Eliot's *Silas Marner: The Weaver of Raveloe* (1861) by the time they finished high school but nothing of their own ethnic literary heritage. Sociological theory supported the notion that ethnic identification was an insignificant factor in success in American life.

During the 1960's, however, this cultural history changed. Nathan Glazer and Daniel Patrick Moynihan, in *Beyond the Melting Pot: The Negroes, Puerto Ricans, Jews, Italians, and Irish of New York City* (1963), as James A. Banks has written in *Teaching Strategies for Ethnic Studies* (1991):

> presented one of the first theoretical arguments that the melting pot conception... was inaccurate and incomplete. They argued that ethnicity in New York was important and that it would continue to be important for both politics and culture.

Similarly, Michael Novak's The Rise of the *Unmeltable Ethnics: Politics and Culture in the 1970's* (1971) helped to fuel the growth of the "new ethnicity" and the new ethnic consciousness during the 1970's, a consciousness that used not the melting pot metaphor but rather metaphors of a patchwork quilt, a salad bowl, or a kaleidoscope to explain the pluralistic nature of ethnicity in the United States. This theoretical underpinning worked to support the massive search that members of many ethnic groups were making for their history. Alex Haley's *Roots: The Saga of an American Family* (1976), which traces his ancestors back to Africa (and which became a popular television miniseries), helped to encourage similar rediscoveries in other ethnicities—and not only in those which had experienced the most recent discrimination (African American, Asian American, Latino, and Native American) but also in those European American communities that had supposedly been dominant through the twentieth century but that actually had been downplaying their ethnicity.

Although American culture was decidedly European American in essence and influence from its beginnings, the assimilative process often meant that individual European identities—Scandinavian as well as Slavic—were lost. The multicultural movement of the 1970's and 1980's helped to recover and reinvigorate a number of ethnic identities and literatures, and the last quarter of the twentieth century saw the publication of many literary works reflecting the change: ethnic autobiographies, accounts of the search for ethnic roots, studies of ethnic culture and ethnic literatures, and novels and plays about the ethnic experience. The European American experience was at the center of this ethnic renaissance.

European American Identity and Literature Critics and scholars began to talk about ethnic literature only at the end of the period of unrestricted immigration, when the closed doors into the United States threw the assimilative process into a sharper, harsher focus. Probably the keystone work in this regard is Abraham Cahan's *The Rise of David Levinsky*, published in 1917. As David M. Fine has written in *The City, the Immigrant, and American Fiction, 1880-1920* (1977), the novel:

> occupies a pivotal position in the history of American literature. It... stands at the head of a long line of twentieth-century novels which would portray modern urban America from the eyes of the city's non-Anglo component. The novel's ambitious mixture of material success and spiritual failure, its insistence on the high cost of assimilation, and its concern with the identity crisis bred by the Americanization process place it squarely in the forefront of twentieth-century "minority voice" fiction.

The themes that Fine lists permeated all immigrant literature, in nonfiction (essay, autobiography) and in fiction (short story, novel), through the twentieth century. Repeatedly after 1917, European American writers depicted in depth and detail the painful process of assimilation, the pull between native and adoptive cultures, the mixed feelings of insecurity and hope. Where does my identity come from—the protagonists of dozens of plays and novels and autobiographies asked—from which of my two selves? A whole range of replies were given, from full assimilation to marginality, but under the hegemonic hold of melting-pot theory, more often than not the replies were unclear and confused.

In 1916, the critic Randolph Bourne posed the basic problem in his essay "Trans-National America" by citing the failure of the melting pot. "We are all foreign-born or the descendants of foreign-born," the Anglo-Saxon Bourne argued, and assimilation has clearly failed. "Assimilation, in other words, instead of washing out the memories of Europe made them more and more intensely real." Bourne's call for a truly multicultural and pluralistic "TransNational America" would not be heeded for more than half a century.

Mary Antin's *The Promised Land* (1912) is a sensitive and touching account of a young Jewish woman's journey from rural Russia to urban America, and represents one end of the assimilative continuum, since it is an autobiography arguing for total Americanization. Her vivid description of the assimilation process is told through stories like the one of her father accompanying his children to their first day of school—and following his dream

> The boasted freedom of the New World meant to him far more than the right to reside, travel, and work wherever he pleased; it meant the freedom

to speak his thoughts, to throw off the shackles of superstition, to test his own fate, unhindered by political or religious tyranny.

Other autobiographers of the period were less sure of the truth of the American Dream. The Danish-born journalist Jacob Riis, who in *How the Other Half Lives* (1890) describes the terrible conditions in New York City tenements, narrates the struggles of his own life in *The Making of an American* (1901) and urged his fellow Danish Americans to remain loyal to Denmark and its traditions. Louis Adamic's *Laughing in the Jungle: The Autobiography of an Immigrant in America* (1932) and *My America* (1938) describe his journey from Slovenia to America, criticize several aspects of American democracy, and conclude that immigrants must take pride in the customs and qualities of their lands of origin. Autobiography has often been a more common and powerful literary genre than fiction, especially for ethnic writers, who could use the form to wrestle with their immigrant history and try to figure out their own identity. Ludwig Lewisohn's *Mid-Channel* (1929) and Edward Bok's *The Americanization of Edward Bok* (1920), the one German Jewish and the other Dutch, are two other examples of European American autobiography from this period.

Perhaps the most poignant and powerful literary representative of early European immigration was Anzia Yezierska, who traveled from Russian Poland to New York's Lower East Side. Writing under her European name (rather than Hattie Mayer, the name which she had been given at Ellis Island), she was the only Jewish woman from eastern Europe of her generation to produce a real body of fiction. Her novels and short stories, including *Hungry Hearts* (stories, 1920) and *Bread Givers* (novel, 1925), depict the lives of marginalized Americans, especially immigrant women.

These histories—of immigration and assimilation, of the hope and failure of the American Dream—would be told again and again through the Great Depression of the 1930's, and in spite of the restrictions facing European American writers. Carl Sandburg (a second-generation Swede) produced some of the most powerful poetry about urban America written during the middle of the twentieth century, in addition to writing a multivolume biography of a true American hero, Abraham Lincoln. Sandburg never lost the workingclass perspective of his immigrant family. Likewise, William Saroyan produced some of the most poignant descriptions of life in his Fresno, California, Armenian community (*The Daring Young Man on the Flying Trapeze*, 1934, and *My Name Is Aram*, 1940), and wrote plays, including *The Time of Your Life* (1939), and novels, such as *The Human Comedy* (1943), that capture his genial spirit.

Other European American writers were depicting the struggles of life for immigrants on the margin. Henry Roth in *Call It Sleep* (1934) follows a young Austrian Jewish immigrant through his harrowing adventures in New York City. Thomas Bell, in *Out of This Furnace* (1941), a novel of immigrant labor in America, details the hardships that faced his Slovak family in the western Pennsylvania steel mills. The two novels are comparable to a number of other Depression-era works—Roth in his implied criticism of capitalist society, and Bell in his argument that his characters should be able to retain their native heritage.

The immigrant story was told by non-immigrant writers as well. Upton Sinclair, in *The Jungle* (1906), depicts the horrendous working conditions which his Lithuanian characters and other eastern European immigrants faced in the stockyards of Chicago. Willa Cather, in another classic of American literature, *My Ántonia* (1918), told the story of a Bohemian family struggling to make a living on the Nebraska prairie. The dying grandmother in Tillie Olsen's powerful story "Tell Me a Riddle" (1961) was once an orator during the 1905 Russian revolution.

In spite of the melting-pot theory that prevailed through the middle of the twentieth century, in other words, writers continued to tap the rich vein of their ethnic and immigrant roots. Many of the best descriptions of immigrant life—Roth's and Olsen's and Lewisohn's, or Michael Gold's *Jews Without Money* (1930)—came from Jewish American writers whose sense of community was so strong that they could more easily dip into that heritage. Saul Bellow and Bernard Malamud tapped that source after World War II, and Isaac Bashevis Singer, who was born in Poland and emigrated to the United States in 1935, and Cynthia Ozick have also explored it.

Immigration did not cease during the twentieth century for European writers. Polish American writer Jerzy Kosinski, in the secretive style that characterized so much of his life, fled his native Poland for America in an elaborate scheme during the 1950's and wrote about his childhood there during World War II in the vivid novel *The Painted Bird* (1965). Vladimir Nabokov, who was born in Russia and educated in England, lived and wrote in Germany and France. In 1940, he came to the United States and produced some of his most important novels after that date. Aleksandr Solzhenitsyn, on the other hand, who emigrated to the United States from the Soviet Union during the 1970's, never matched the literary power he had achieved when he was writing in his native Russia.

William Saroyan, the most prominent literary voice of Armenian Americans. (D.C . Public Library)

Irish American Literature Irish American literature is one of the oldest and largest collections of writing produced by a European American group. Before the Revolutionary War, the English were the majority of migrants to America. After independence, it was the Irish: Between 1820 and 1930, more than 4.25 million Irish immigrants came to the United States. For their first decades, life was hard, and they faced constant discrimination. The sign "No Irish Need Apply" could be seen on businesses into the twentieth century. The people Henry David Thoreau mentions in *Walden* (1854) at the bottom of the socioeconomic ladder are Native Americans, black slaves, and the Irish.

In spite of their tremendous difficulties, the Irish produced a cultural legacy in the United States second to none. A number of major nineteenth century writers—Henry James, Edgar Allan Poe, and William Dean Howells among them—had Irish ancestry that played no part in their literature, but dozens of writers used that heritage in their literary work. The first Irish American writer to gain national prominence was Peter Finley Dunne, the turn-of-twentieth-century newspaperman whose fictional Irish bartender Mr. Dooley became the most popular figure in American journalism. Up until World War I, Mr. Dooley commented in Dunne's columns on every important American political or social event—including immigration:

> As a pilgrim father that missed the first boats, I must raise me clar yon voice again' the invasion iv this fair land be th' paupers an' arnychists iv effete Europe. Ye bet I must—because I'm here first.

Dunne's sharp, often fatalistic humor was characteristic of much later Irish American literature.

Several of the major twentieth century American modernists were Irish. F. Scott Fitzgerald boasted of his Irish heritage, and a number of minor Irish American characters figure in his romantic novels and short stories. In Fitzgerald's

Play wright Eugene O'Neill with his third wife, Carlotta, in 1933. (Library of Congress)

unfinished *The Last Tycoon* (1941) Irish characters play major roles, and Fitzgerald seems in that book to be grappling with his own Irishness. Perhaps the most important playwright of the American stage, Eugene O'Neill, was the son of an Irishman who had come to America after the great potato famine. Some of O'Neill's masterpieces feature Irish American characters. O'Neill wrote about his family and troubled childhood late in his career in *Long Day's Journey into Night* (1956).

James T. Farrell, in his *Studs Lonigan: A Trilogy* (1935) and in the later four novels centering on the character of Danny O'Neill (including *My Days of Anger*, 1943), describes Irish families struggling on Chicago's South Side to overcome economic and personal oppression, often holding on to their ethnic and religious prejudices. John O'Hara was much less sympathetic to his Irish characters, and in his novels set in the fictional Gibbsville (resembling his native Pottsville, Pennsylvania), such as the 1934 *Appointment in Samarra*, the Irish characters are usually outsiders and often contemptible.

Other writers in mid-century continued to add to the Irish American heritage. Betty Smith, who was not Irish herself but who had grown up in the Irish American Williamsburg section of Brooklyn, wrote one of the best novels about the Irish experience in America in *A Tree Grows in Brooklyn* (1947). Mary McCarthy's novels occasionally contain Irish characters, and her *Memories of a Catholic Girlhood* (1957) is a compelling account of growing up in America during the early decades of the twentieth century. The Southerner Flannery O'Connor's novels and short stories are greatly influenced by her Irish Catholic heritage.

Many Irish American writers, as might be expected, deal with the Irish in the cities. Edwin O'Connor paints a masterful portrait of Boston Irish political bosses in *The Last Hurrah* (1956), and William Kennedy's novels about Albany, New York (including *Ironweed*, 1983) have been critical and commercial successes. Maureen Howard's *Natural History* (1992) deals with the Irish power structure in Bridgeport, Connecticut, early in the twentieth century.

Late twentieth century Irish American writers include the novelists Mary Gordon, J. F. Powers, J. P. Donleavy, and T. Coraghessan Boyle, poets from Frank O'Hara to Tess Gallagher, and journalists from the streetwise Jimmy Breslin, Pete Hamill, and Joe Flaherty to the elegant Brendan Gill of *The New Yorker*.

Italian American Literature The largest immigrant groups to arrive in the latter part of the nineteenth century were southern and eastern Europeans. Between 1820 and 1930, more than 4.5 million Italians arrived in the United States, and, like the Irish Americans, they produced a number of writers whose work expressed particular awareness of their background.

Pietro di Donato's *Christ in Concrete* (1939) depicts the squalid world of Italian construction workers, and is the classic expression of the Italian American experience. John Fante wrote a number of novels and short stories about the Italian American experience: *Wait Until Spring, Bandini* (1938) tells of family life in his native Colorado. *Ask the Dust* (1939) follows the hero, Arturo Bandini, to Los Angeles, and *Dago Red* (1940) includes a number of family sketches. Jerre Mangione in *Monte Allegro* (1943) tells of a son who returns to Sicily and feels a mystical sense of being at home. The list of successful and popular Italian American novelists runs from Paul Gallico through Mario Puzo and Evan Hunter to Don De Lillo.

Italian American writers have in fact contributed to every literary genre. Bernard DeVoto was one of the most important literary critics during the middle of the twentieth century, and John Ciardi was a preeminent American poet and translator. Lawrence Ferlinghetti and Gregory Corso were leading members of the Beat movement of the 1950's, and later poets include Helen Barolini, Rose Basile Green, Diane DiPrima, and Dana Gioia. Finally, Italian Americans have become prominent journalists. Philip Caputo's *A Rumor of War* (1977) is one of the best accounts of the Vietnam War, for example, and Gay Talese has written a number of volumes of note,

Betty Smith, author of A Tree Grows in Brooklyn, *a novel about the Irish experience in America.*

including *Unto the Sons* (1992), about the Italian American immigrant experience.

Immigrant literature has often dealt with the American Dream, with its promise as well as with its collapse. More than most literatures, the body of work produced by European American writers has reflected the struggles of assimilation, the loss of identity in that process, and the pain of being split between two cultures. The heroes and heroines of European American literature—David Levinsky, Studs Lonigan, and Arturo Bandini among them—are often filled with self-doubt and search blindly for their identity. In those characters and their struggles, their creators helped to expand the definition and the canon of American literature.

David Peck

Further Reading

Banks, James A. *Teaching Strategies for Ethnic Studies.* Newton, Mass.: Allyn & Bacon, 1991. Useful for the student as well as the teacher; relates key themes and concepts to texts.

Benmayor, Rina, and Andor Skotnes, eds. *Migration and Identity.* New Brunswick, N.J.: Transaction, 2005. Collection of essays on the theme of ethnic identity and its expression among immigrant communities.

Bourne, Randolph. *The Radical Will: Selected Writings.* Edited by Olaf Hansen. Berkeley: University of California Press, 1992. An over view of Bourne's ideas.

Floreani, Tracy. *Fifties Ethnicities; The Ethnic Novel and Mass Culture at Midcentury.* Albany, NY: State University of New York Press, 2013. A study of how immigrants were presented in popular culture in 1950s America, including in print, television, and film.

Fine, David M. *The City, the Immigrant, and American Fiction, 1880-1920.* Metuchen, N.J.: Scarecrow Press, 1977. A starting place for study of immigrant fiction.

Fuchs, Lawrence H. *The American Kaleidoscope: Race, Ethnicity, and the Civic Culture.* Hanover, N.H.: University Press of New England, 1990. Comprehensive review of American culture, in the context of a non-melting-pot metaphor.

Glazer, Nathan, and Daniel Patrick Moynihan. *Beyond the Melting Pot: The Negroes, Puerto Ricans, Jews, Italians, and Irish of New York City.* Cambridge, Mass.: MIT Press, 1963. A landmark of ethnic studies, centered on New York City but with implications for ethnic studies in all America.

Greeley, Andrew. *Ethnicity in the United States: A Preliminary Reconnaissance.* New York: John Wiley & Sons, 1974. Ethnicity of European origin is the focus.

Lowery, Ruth McKoy. *Immigrants in Children's Literature.* New York: P. Lang, 2000. Examination of the depictions of immigrants in children's fiction that focuses on seventeen novels.

Meltzer, Milton. *Bound for America: The Story of the European Immigrants.* New York: Benchmark Books, 2001. Broad history of European immigration to the United States written for young readers.

Novak, Michael. *The Rise of the Unmeltable Ethnics: Politics and Culture in the 1970's.* New York: Macmillan, 1971. Central work in the revival of interest in ethnicity during the 1970's and after.

Sollors, Werner. *Beyond Ethnicity: Consent and Descent in American Culture.* New York: Oxford University Press, 1986. Argues that ethnic literature is the prototypical American literature.

Tamburri, Anthony Julian. *Re-reading Italian Americana: Specificities and Generalities on Literature and Criticism.* Madison: Fairleigh Dickinson University Press, 2014. Surveys Italian American literature, including influences and reception, as well as examining the current state of criticism of Italian American Literature.

See also Euro-Americans; European immigrants, 1790-1892; European immigrants, 1892-1943; Generational acculturation; German and Irish immigration of the 1840's; Gypsy immigrants; Irish immigrants; Italian immigrants; Melting pot; Nativism; Polish immigrants; Scandinavian immigrants; White ethnics.

EUROPEAN IMMIGRANTS, 1790-1892

The Event: The first century of immigration after the ratification of the U.S. **Constitution**
Date: 1790-1892

Immigration issues: European immigrants; Irish immigrants

Significance: Between 1790 and 1892, more than sixteen million Europeans migrated to the United States. Because they constituted nearly one-third of the total population and 53 percent of the urban residents, European immigrants played a disproportionately important role in the development of American intergroup relations.

In 1790, the initial U.S. Census was conducted and Congress passed the first uniform naturalization law. For the next 102 years, more than 90 percent of the immigrants came from Germany, Great Britain, Ireland, and Scandinavia ("Old Immigrants"). In 1892, for the first time, more arrivals were from eastern and southern Europe (new immigrants) than from northern Europe. During that same year, Ellis Island replaced the Castle Garden as the major receiving center for immigrants landing in New York when the federal government took control of the process.

From 1821 to 1892, approximately 4.5 million German Protestants, Roman Catholics, and Jews; 3.5 million Irish Catholics; 2.7 million British Protestants; and 1 million Scandinavian Protestants emigrated, with more than two-thirds coming to the United States. The Irish gravitated toward unskilled labor in the eastern cities; the English, Welsh, and Scots often found work as skilled laborers in this same region. Germans tended to find positions as skilled craftspeople or in the trades in both eastern and midwestern cities. Many Germans, Scandinavians, and Dutch became farmers in the Midwest.

Relations with the Dominant Culture At the onset of large-scale immigration, the descendants of the early colonists, who were mostly Protestants of English and Scotch-Irish descent, dominated the United States in numbers and control over society. They resented and discriminated against the new arrivals for a variety of reasons. As a group, they were generally satisfied with their lives in the United States and had established an "American culture" separate from that of Europe. A new wave of Europeans could disrupt this. Consequently, many Americans became nativists, hoping to prevent what they viewed as an immigrant "takeover" of the nation.

The hierarchical structure of Roman Catholicism, which they considered at odds with the tenets of democracy, negatively affected the large Irish and German Catholic population. Jews were still blamed for the death of Christ, and many people overestimated their influence in the financial world. Although American Protestants increasingly embraced temperance and prohibition of alcoholic beverages, many Irish and German immigrants saw spirits as a part of their culture. Irish, Welsh, and English laborers often believed that organized labor was the key to better pay and working conditions; however, many native stock Americans felt that labor unions were in opposition to American individualism and free labor capitalism. Germans and Scandinavians, who desired to maintain Old World languages and traditions, were chastised for being un-American. All of these factors were responsible for divisions between colonial-stock Americans and the immigrants.

Relations Among Old Immigrants Despite commonalties of the ethnic experience, the old immigrants never viewed themselves as a unified group. Conflict

Cartoon in an 1881 issue of Frank Leslie's Illustrated Newspaper showing Columbia—the symbol of the United States—welcoming refugees from German oppression to the "asylum of the oppressed." (Library of Congress)

between the groups was more apparent than cooperation. These differences often had European roots that combined with American circumstances.

Religious differences continued to separate people in the United States as they had in Europe. Almost all the British, Scandinavians, and Dutch were Protestants, as were half of the Germans. Like their American counterparts, the British Protestants were at odds with Irish Catholics. The religious differences in the German states were also brought to the United States. Individual Germans viewed themselves as German Protestants, German Catholics, or German Jews rather than as members of a single culture.

Political issues also divided the old immigrants. Catholics and urban laborers, especially the Irish, gravitated toward the more open Democratic Party.

Protestant skilled workers and midwestern farmers believed that the Whigs, and later the Republicans, reflected their interests of upward socioeconomic mobility and conservative social values. Catholics and the less conservative German Protestants objected to any laws restricting alcohol. Conversely, many English, Welsh, and German Pietist Protestant immigrants abstained from liquor and favored its prohibition. In regard to slavery, unskilled Irish laborers feared that emancipation could bring about competition with African Americans for low-paying jobs; English, Welsh, and German skilled workers and tradespeople believed that the extension of slavery would damage the freelabor, capitalist economy.

The Assimilation Process The Americanization process for the older group of immigrants was hastened because all ethnic groups began to enjoy increased social and economic mobility by the latter part of the nineteenth century and because the arrival of the new immigrants lifted them to a higher level of social status.

The various ethnic groups achieved social and economic mobility differently. The English, Welsh, and Scots often moved from their skilled labor positions to become bosses, super visors, and managers in corporate America. They used the school systems to educate their children, who moved into professional positions.

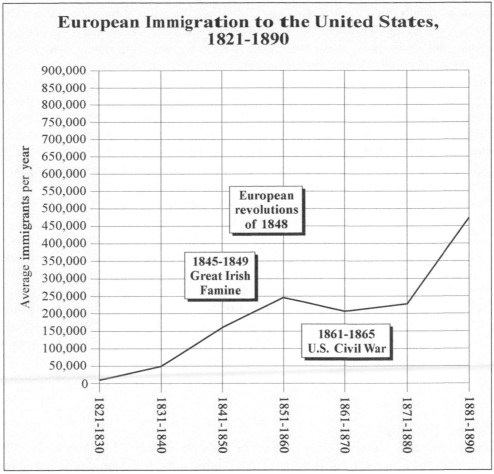

European Immigration to the United States, 1821-1890

Source: U.S. Census Bureau.

Many descendants of the Welsh and English immigrants became teachers and administrators in elementary and secondary education systems, giving those groups a tremendous impact upon education in the United States.

Working from positions as unskilled laborers, the Irish moved through the corporate ranks. Politics was also a means of Irish mobility. Colonial-stock Americans found local politics disdainful; however, the Irish recognized an opportunity to gain political power in the growing urban areas. By the late nineteenth century, many eastern cities were under the control of political machines dominated by the Irish. Although colonial stock and other old immigrants criticized boss politics, the machines served the rapidly expanding urban-ethnic community at a time when official government agencies were lacking. The Irish were also able to gain mobility through their leadership in the Roman Catholic Church. The church became a major force in American life with the arrival of numerous Catholic immigrants. The Irish church hierarchy was instrumental in sponsoring a vast educational network that educated all Catholics from elementary school through the university.

Germans and Scandinavians were perhaps less inclined to use higher education as a means of mobility. However, as the United States rapidly expanded, the services of German tradespeople and farmers were all the more needed. This, in turn, brought about a growth in German businesses and farms, resulting in the upward mobility of shipowners and workers alike. German Jews, many of whom began as peddlers and small shopkeepers, were able to expand their businesses to meet the increasing consumer demand. This economic success combined with a strong emphasis upon education was responsible for a remarkable degree of socioeconomic mobility for German Jews. The arrival of ten million eastern and southern Europeans resulted in a higher socioeconomic status for the old immigrants. The new arrivals provided a large labor pool to fill unskilled positions. The old immigrants could move into the more lucrative skilled and management jobs or expand their businesses to serve the growing population. Also, many of the values of the northern European immigrants were more identifiable as American ideals. To both colonial stock and old immigrants, the new immigrants appeared to be considerably different. Consequently, the colonial stock found the old immigrants more acceptable.

By the mid-twentieth century, the descendants of the old immigrants were less commonly viewed as distinct ethnic groups. The British found their heritage largely assimilated into the larger American culture, and Germans' ethnic identification diminished during the two world wars. Certain groups, such as the Welsh and Scandinavians, still maintain ethnic institutions. However, these institutions are intended more to preserve the vestiges of the cultures than to help immigrants deal with challenges in the United States. To most observers, the descendants of the old immigrants are firmly entrenched in mainstream American culture.

Paul J. Zbiek

Further Reading

Baylin, Bernard. *The Barbarous Years: The Peopling of British North America: The Conflict of Civilizations, 1600-1675*. New York: Alfred A. Knopf, 2012. A study of the first immigrants to America, including their origins, their reasons for emigrating, and their adaptations to their new home.

Berthoff, Rowland. *British Immigrants in Industrial America, 1790-1950*. Cambridge, Mass.: Harvard University Press, 1953. Classic study of British immigration to the United States.

Dolan, Jay. *The Immigrant Church: New York's Irish and German Catholics, 1815-1965*. Baltimore: Johns Hopkins University Press, 1975. Chronicles how the Irish and Germans established Roman Catholicism in America.

Greene, Victor R. *A Singing Ambivalence: American Immigrants Between Old World and New, 1830-1930*. Kent, Ohio: Kent State University Press, 2004. Comparative study of the different challenges faced by members of eight major immigrant groups: the Irish, Germans, Scandinavians and Finns, eastern European Jews, Italians, Poles and Hungarians, Chinese, and Mexicans.

Handlin, Oscar. *The Uprooted: The Epic Story of the Great Migrations That Made the American People*. 2d ed. Boston: Little, Brown, 1973. Work by one of the pioneering scholars on ethnic history that deals extensively with the old immigrant period.

Meltzer, Milton. *Bound for America: The Story of the European Immigrants*. New York: Benchmark Books, 2001. Broad history of European immigration to the

United States written for young readers.

Van Minnen, Cornelis A, and Manfred Berg, eds.. *The U.S. South and Europe: Translatlantic Relations in the Nineteenth and Twentieth Centuries*. Lexington, KY: University Press of Kentucky, 2013. Essays on the relationship between the American South and Europe, including the experiences of German immigrants in the South.

Van Vugt, William E. *Britain to America: Mid-Nineteenth-Century Immigrants to the United States*. Urbana: University of Illinois Press, 1999. Scholarly study of nineteenth century immigrants to the United States from Great Britain.

Wepman, Dennis. *Immigration: From the Founding of Virginia to the Closing of Ellis Island*. New York: Facts On File, 2002. History of immigration to the United States from the earliest European settlements of the colonial era through the mid-1950's, with liberal extracts from contemporary documents.

See also European immigrant literature; European immigrants, 1892-1943; German and Irish immigration of the 1840's; German immigrants; Italian immigrants; Jewish immigrants; Know-Nothing Party; Migration; Nativism.

EUROPEAN IMMIGRANTS, 1892-1943

The Event: The last major phase of European immigration to the United States
Date: 1892-1943

Immigration issues: European immigrants; Nativism and racism

Significance: A new wave of southern European immigrants met with nativist resentment and federal controls.

In 1808, the U.S. government purchased Ellis Island from the state of New York for ten thousand dollars. The new federal property, located in New York Harbor about one mile from the southern tip of Manhattan Island, served first as a fort and later as an arsenal. Until 1882, the state of New York had guided the influx of immigration from the old Castle Garden station at the tip of Manhattan. The opening of Ellis Island on January 1, 1892, as the first federal immigration station symbolized a new era for the United States as well as the beginning of the end of free immigration to the New World. San Francisco Bay's Angel Island later served a similar role for immigrants entering the United States on the West Coast.

Congress had begun the selective process of excluding undesirable elements among those emigrating to the United States with the passage of the federal Immigration Act in 1882. That measure was designed to prevent the immigration of persons who had criminal records and those who were mentally incompetent or indigent. That same year, Congress also passed the Chinese Exclusion Act (later extended to all Asians), barring an entire nationality from entry as racially undesirable for a period of ten years. In 1904 the act's provisions were extended indefinitely, to be repealed only in 1943.

Immigration Patterns Shift Most immigrants before the 1890's had come from northern and western Europe. During the 1880's a fundamental change occurred. In addition to the traditional immigrants, who shared common language patterns with persons already in the United States, people from Mediterranean and Slavic countries began to arrive in increasing numbers. One may measure the change more dramatically by comparing two peak years in U.S. immigration. In 1882, 87 percent of the 788,000 immigrants came from northern and western Europe. In 1907, only 19.3 percent were from northern and western Europe, while 80.7 percent came from southern and eastern Europe.

A great impetus to immigration was the transportation revolution engendered by the steamship. In 1856, more than 96 percent of U.S. immigrants came aboard sailing ships, on trips that took between one and three months. By 1873, the same percentage came by steamships, which took only ten days. The new steamships were specifically designed for passengers, and while still subject to overcrowding and epidemics, they were a major improvement over the sailing ships. Steamship companies competed for immigrant business and maintained offices in Europe. The Hamburg-Amerika line, for example, had thirty-two hundred U.S. agencies throughout Europe. More than half of the immigrants in 1901 came with prepaid tickets supplied by relatives in the United States.

As the older agricultural economy of Europe was replaced by an industrial one, many former farmers moved to European cities in search of employment; often unsuccessful in that search, they were easily persuaded to try the New World, where jobs were said to be plentiful. The same railroad-building process that opened the American West to the immigrant made it easier and cheaper for the Europeans to reach their coastal areas and embark for the United States.

Most of the emigration from southern Europe was occasioned by economic distress. Southern Italy's agriculture was severely affected by competition from Florida in oranges and lemons, as well as by a French tariff against Italian wines. The Italian emigration began with 12,000 in 1880 and reached a peak of nearly 300,000 in 1914. After immigration restriction laws took full effect, Italian immigration fell to 6,203 in 1925.

From Russia and the Slavic areas, emigration was also caused by political and religious problems. Jews fled in reaction to the riots set off by the assassination of Czar Alexander II in 1882, the pogroms of 1881-1882 and 1891, and the 1905-1906 massacres of thousands of Jews. Jewish immigration to the United States began with 5,000 in 1880 and reached a peak of 258,000 in 1907. Some two million Roman Catholic Poles also arrived between 1890 and 1914. In 1925, however, the Immigration Service recorded only 5,341 entrants from Poland and 3,121 from Russia and the Baltic states.

Nativist Fears Two issues caused the greatest concern to American nativists during the 1890's: the tendency of the new immigrants to congregate in the cities, and the fact that they spoke seemingly unassimilable languages. One of the first

Immigrants arriving at Ellis Island in 1902. Through this reception center, New York City was the principal port of entry for European immigrants from 1892 until 1954. (Library of Congress)

articulate spokesmen against unrestricted immigration, the Reverend Dr. Josiah Strong, was alarmed by the concentration of foreign peoples in cities. Strong's famous book, Our Country, published in 1885, clearly stated what many other U.S. citizens feared: that the new influx of immigrants would create permanent slums and perpetuate poverty.

The urban nature of the settlement was unavoidable. U.S. agriculture was suffering from the same shocks that had disrupted European agriculture, and the populist movement in the country made clear that the myth of utopia in the western United States was no longer believable. Most of the new immigrants were attracted by the pull of U.S. industry and opportunity, and they came to the United States with the express purpose of settling in a city. In addition, new industrial technology had reduced the demand for skilled labor, while the need for unskilled and cheap factory help increased. To add to the social clash between the new and old immigrants, the arrival of a new labor force in great numbers probably allowed some older laborers to move up to more important supervisory and executive positions.

Many new immigrants did not share the optimism and enthusiasm of established Americans. Some tended to be pessimistic and resigned, distrustful of change, and unfamiliar with democratic government after having lived in autocratic situations. At the height of the new immigration occurred the Panic of 1893, followed by a depression that lasted until 1897, which seemed to confirm the fears of persons already settled in the United States that the country and the system were failing. The new immigration, however, was but one of the major social, cultural, and economic changes taking place in the turbulent United States of the 1890's.

European immigrants being processed inside Ellis Island's vast reception center around 1904. (Library of Congress)

In 1907, Congress created the Dillingham Commission to investigate the problems of immigration. Many of the commission's findings reflected the fears of citizens concerning the new immigration and led to the passage of restrictive legislation during the 1920's. Unrestricted immigration ended with the passage of the National Origins Act of 1924, which restricted immigrants in any year to 154,277. Each country's quota could be no more than 2 percent of the number of its native inhabitants counted in the 1890 census, a year in which few born in southern and eastern Europe were part of the U.S. population.

When Ellis Island closed as a reception center in 1954, few immigrants still arrived by ship, and the Immigration Service could handle all arrivals at Manhattan's docks. When the Atlantic reopened after World War II, planes began to replace ships as vehicles of immigration, and there was no need for Ellis Island. By that time, much of the fear of the "new" immigration had evaporated. Italian, Slavs, and Jews had not remained in permanent slums, mired in perpetual poverty, as Strong had feared, and their descendants had fought side by side with U.S. soldiers of British and German ancestry against the Nazis and the Japanese.

During the 1940's, there was much criticism of the rigidity of the immigration restriction legislation that hampered attempts to deal with the problems of refugees. Not until 1965, however, would the rigid quota system established in 1924 be replaced with a more flexible system. When that reform opened the door to increased entry by Asians and Latin Americans, complaints about the new "new immigrants" began to echo nineteenth century uneasiness about the former "new immigrants."

Richard H. Collin
updated by Milton Berman

Further Reading

Barone, Michael. *Shaping Our Nation: How Surges of Migration Transformed America and its Politics.* New York: Crown Forum, 2013. A study in how waves of immigration, from the Scots-Irish in the 18th century to recent influxes of Hispanics and Asians, as well as internal migration, have shaped American society and politics.

Briggs, Vernon M. *Mass Immigration and the National Interest.* Armonk, N.Y.: M. E. Sharpe, 1992. An economist argues that nineteenth and early twentieth century immigration aided the U.S. economy but the post-1965 immigration does not.

Brownstone, David M., Irene M. Franck, and Douglas L. Brownstone, eds. *Island of Hope, Island of Tears.* New York: Penguin Books, 1986. Inter views with elderly people who went through Ellis Island during the early years of the twentieth century provide highly personal accounts of the "new" immigrants. Many photographs.

Carnevale, Nancy C. *A New Language, A New World: Italian Immigrants in the United States, 1890-1945.* Urbana: University of Illinois Press, 2009. An historical case study of Italian immigrants in America, with particular focus on their experience with language in the process of negotiating their relationship with the dominant culture.

Daniels, Roger. *Coming to America: A History of Immigration and Ethnicity in American Life.* New York: HarperCollins, 1990. A well-written, scholarly account of U.S. immigration from the colonial period through the 1980's.

Dinnerstein, Leonard, Roger H. Nichols, and David H. Reimers. *Natives and Strangers: Blacks, Indians, and Immigrants in America.* 2d ed. New York: Oxford University Press, 1990. A comparative study of immigrant and minority groups in the United States.

Fleegler, Robert L. *Ellis Island Nation: Immigration Policy and American Identity in the Twentieth Century.* Philadelphia: University of Pennsylvania Press, 2013. Fleegler argues that "contributionism,"the belief that immigrants from eastern and southern Europe made important contributions to American society, as a key factor in the acceptance of individuals from those backgrounds.

Gabaccia, Donna R. *Immigration and American Diversity: A Social and Cultural History.* Malden, Mass.: Blackwell, 2002. Sur vey of American immigration history, from the mid-eighteenth century to the early twenty-first century, with an emphasis on cultural and social trends, with attention to ethnic conflicts, nativism, and racialist theories.

Greene, Victor R. *A Singing Ambivalence: American Immigrants Between Old World and New, 1830-1930.* Kent, Ohio: Kent State University Press, 2004. Comparative study of the different challenges faced by members of eight major immigrant groups: the Irish, Germans, Scandinavians and Finns, eastern European Jews, Italians, Poles and Hungarians, Chinese, and Mexicans.

Handlin, Oscar. *The Uprooted: The Epic Story of the Great Migrations That Made the American People.* 2d ed. Boston: Little, Brown, 1973. Dramatic narrative focusing on the life experiences of immigrants.

Higham, John. *Strangers in the Land: Patterns of American Nativism, 1860-1925.* New Brunswick, N.J.: Rutgers University Press, 1955. Analyzes the nativist movements that led to the passage of immigration restriction.

Meltzer, Milton. *Bound for America: The Story of the European Immigrants.* New York: Benchmark Books, 2001. Broad history of European immigration to the United States written for young readers.

Reimers, David M. *Still the Golden Door: The Third World Comes to America.* New York: Columbia University Press, 1985. Study of twentieth century immigration to the United States, primarily after World War II.

Sandler, Martin W. *Island of Hope: The Story of Ellis Island and the Journey to America.* New York: Scholastic, 2004. History of the most important immigrant reception, from 1892 through 1954. Written for younger readers.

Vought, Hans Peter. *Redefining the "Melting Pot": American Presidents and the Immigrant, 1897-1933.* Ann Arbor, Mich.: UMI, 2001.

Wepman, Dennis. *Immigration: From the Founding of Virginia to the Closing of Ellis Island.* New York: Facts On File, 2002. History of immigration to the United States from the earliest European settlements of the colonial era through the mid-1950's, with liberal extracts from contemporary documents.

See also Eastern European Jewish immigrants; European immigrant literature; European immigrants, 1790-1892; German and Irish immigration of the 1840's; German immigrants; Immigration Act of 1917; Immigration Act of 1924; Italian immigrants; Jewish immigrants; Migration; Polish immigrants; War brides.

E-Verify Employment Verification System

The Law: Illegal Immigration Reform and Immigrant Responsibility Act (IIRIRA)
Date: 1996

Immigration Issues: The E-Verify program is an internet-based employment-verification program that is part of several immigration-reform proposals in Congress. As of August 2014, employer use of E-Verify is not required nationally, although some states are using it, but proposed new legislation might make it mandatory throughout the U.S. E-Verify impacts every employee hired by a business with the goal of discovering undocumented immigrants in the workforce.

Significance: E-Verify is an electronic program used by employers to verify an employee's employment eligibility after hire. By laws already in place, employers must complete a Form I-9; however, participation in E-Verify remains a voluntary program for most employers. Through E-Verify, participating employers submit information taken from a new hire's Form I-9 (Employment Eligibility Verification Form) to the Social Security Administration and to the U.S. Citizenship and Immigration Services (USCIS) to determine if the provided information matches government records, which determines whether or not the new hire is authorized to work in the United States.

Background Established in 1997, along with two other programs, E-Verify was originally a pilot program designed to prevent illegal aliens from getting jobs in the U.S. The program is administered by the U.S. Department of Homeland Security, USCIS, Verification Division, and the Social Security Administration. While the other two programs were later discontinued, the Immigration and Customs Enforcement finalized regulations that require electronic storing and generating I-9 records.

E-Verify provides employers with instant verification of an employee's employment eligibility via an Internet-based system. The system compares information given on an employee's Employment Verification Eligibility Form (Form I-9) to the data found on file with the U.S. Department of Homeland Security and Social Security Administration records.

Migrant farmworkers pick cucumbers on a Virginia farm. Farmers are worried that their workers may disappear if they are required to use the E-verify system since 80 percent of their workforce are undocumented immigrants. (U.S. Dept. of Agriculture)

"The new system will rely more heavily on 'photo-matching.' The E-Verify system will contain a vast database of photographs, and workers applying for jobs would need to present identification with photographs that match those in the database to prove they are who they say they are and that they are in the country legally," reports Rosalind S. Helderman via the Washington Post.

Used nationwide by more than 1.4 million hiring sites and over 500,000 companies, both small and large, E-Verify is a free service that offers speedy and accurate employee verification. Being an online service, it is readily accessible to companies. The system is used to verify employees' data against millions of government records, providing employers with results in as little as 3 to 5 seconds.

Employers that enroll in E-Verify are required to submit electronic employee information to a government database in order to participate. If the results indicate that an employee's information conflicts with the information in the database, the employee is unable to work until the matter is resolved.

Each week, nearly 1,400 new participating companies join E-Verify to utilize their services, which has earned the spot of being one of the federal government's highest rated services in customer satisfaction.

Those who oppose the system argue that by expanding mandatory E-Verify, the jobs of thousands of U.S. citizens would be threatened. In addition, U.S. businesses would be liable for additional costs that many cannot afford, resulting in the backfiring of the goal to create a stronger workforce and that it would slow America's economic recovery. The USCIS Verification Division provides employers and their employees with program support by administering customer service. By using innovative technological solutions, they initiate and instill community outreach programs that serve to further the E-Verify mission.

Legislation The mission of the USCIS Office of Chief Counsel (OCC) is to provide legal advice to immigration officials concerning issues that arise in conjunction with their performance of their official duties. (8 CFR 100.2(a)(1) and 103.1(b)(1).) There have been rare cases in which a particular program is of such general interest and importance that the OCC has rendered a formal legal opinion. As a matter of policy, we have determined that providing legal opinions to private parties in matters that may come before immigration officials is inappropriate. For this reason, we are unable to express an opinion on the issues submitted by the public.

The general provisions of laws enacted by Congress are interpreted and implemented by regulations issued by various agencies. These regulations apply the law to daily situations. After regulations are published in the Federal Register, they are collected and published in the Code of Federal Regulations, commonly referred to as the CFR. The CFR is arranged by subject title and generally parallels the structure of the United States Code. Thus, Title 8 of the CFR deals with "Aliens and Nationality", as does Title 8 of the U.S. Code (www.uscis.gov.laws).

By September 2007, most of the federal government was not using the E-Verify system. However, an Office of Management and Budget directive mandated that all federal government agencies had to sign up to use E-Verify by October 1, 2007.

Heather Hummel

Further Reading

U.S. Citizenship and Immigration Services E-Verify [website]. http://www.uscis.gov/e-verify (accessed Aug. 6, 2014). Website created by the Department of Homeland Security to provide information about the E-Verify program to employers, employees, Federal contractors, and the public.

American Immigration Council, *How Expanding E-Verify Would Hurt American Workers and Business* [Internet article] http://www.immigrationpolicy.org (accessed March 2, 2010). An article that depicts the downsides of the E-Verify system.

Helderman, Rosalind S, "Inside the Immigration Bill: E-Verify Draws Fire", *The Washington Post* [Internet article]. http://www.washingtonpost.com/blogs/post-politics/wp/2013/04/16/inside-the-immigration-bill-e-verify-expansion-draws-fire-from-civil-libertarians/ (accessed April 16, 2013) An article that discusses the opposition and concerns around photographs and their use in the E-Verify system.

Krainin, Todd, "The Problem with E-Verify" *Reason Magazine* [Internet article] http://reason.com/reasontv/2013/02/12/the-problem-with-e-verify-the-aclus-chri (accessed February 12, 2013) The ACLU's Chris Calabrese discusses immigration reform.

Marquardt, Marie Friedmann; Steigenga, Timothy J; Williams, Philip J.; Vasquez, Manuel A. *Living "Illegal": The Human Face of Unauthorized Immigration,* The New Press, 2011 A book that recommends suggestions for immigration reform.

Kaye, Jeffrey, Moving Millions: How Coyote Capitalism Fuels Global Immigration, Wiley, 2010 A book authored by a PBS correspondent that addresses immigration reform.

Marks, Alexandra, "With E-Verify, too many errors to expand its use?" *Christian Science Monitor* [Internet article] http://www.csmonitor.com/USA/2008/0707/p02s01-usgn.html (accessed July 7, 2008) An article about the impact of misinformation in the E-Verify system and how it hurts legitimate employees.

See also H1B visa; Illegal aliens; Undocumented workers.

FAMILY BUSINESSES

Definition: Commercial enterprises owned and operated by individual families

Immigration issues: Chinese immigrants; Cuban immigrants; Economics; Families and marriage; Labor

Significance: Family businesses, which represent the oldest form of business enterprise in the world, continue to affect the U.S. economy during the twenty-first century, and they play a special role in many immigrant communities.

From ancient pottery makers of Mesopotamia to the family farm of nineteenth century America, a natural form of business organization consisted of using the varied talents of family members to achieve efficiency. Indeed, the very concept of "home economics" implies that all families had to operate—at times—like businesses in their allocation of scarce resources and utilization of labor. The rise of the modern corporation during the mid-nineteenth century reduced the overall influence of family firms on the economies of nations but did not eliminate family businesses or reduce their popularity.

Prior to the mid-nineteenth century, most business organizations, especially in the United States, were family firms. These included farms, plantations, small shops, and factories and covered areas of endeavor as varied as banking, mining, textile manufacturing, bookselling, and rice planting. In family firms on farms or plantations, husbands generally oversaw "outdoor" activities, such as planting, harvesting and mining. In the case of artisans or merchants, husbands managed the shop floor or store office. On farms, wives managed purchases for personnel, and on larger plantations they managed the "inside" work related to the plantation houses and slave quarters, such as clothing and feeding the people in residence as well as their own family members.

In cities, wives helped clean stores, keep books, take orders, and—in cases of illness or death of their husbands—they actually managed the businesses. Children were viewed as a source of unpaid labor, with the understanding that they were learning a trade as well as earning their keep. In some cases, parents sent male children to other merchants or artisans as apprentices to "learn the business," as was the case with the American banker J. P. Morgan. The division of labor allowed the family to retain as profits all the money they would have had to spend paying laborers and training employees.

Immigrants and Family Businesses   For generations, immigrants have constituted an important segment of family businesses, from Italian restaurants to Japanese gardening services. Beginning during the 1960's and 1970's, new waves of Cuban, Vietnamese, Lebanese, and Mexican immigrants came to the United States. More than 200,000 Cubans arrived in Florida in the first two years after Fidel Castro came to power, creating 25,000 new businesses in Dade County alone. Michael Zabian, a Lebanese refugee who settled in Lee, Massachusetts, developed a family-run business that eventually encompassed a grocery store and a department store.

Numerous studies of Haitian, Jamaican, and Vietnamese families in the United States have shown that they capitalize on family labor to achieve business success. As a result, they have higher per-capita incomes than many white families. Proportionally, far more black Jamaicans, Haitians, and Dominicans in the United States run businesses than American-born whites.

Child labor laws and compulsory education have limited the extent to which immigrants have been able to utilize family labor to expand family wealth. Moreover, not all immigrants have the same cultural perspectives. Adult Chinese immigrants, for example, sometimes work extra hours so that their children can concentrate on their education. Immigrant couples often run businesses as a team.

Members of a Chinese family posing in front of their New York City grocery store. (Smithsonian Institution)

More often, however, immigrant wives manage their households while their husbands concentrate on their family businesses.

The key to these immigrants' success—and that of previous generations of European immigrants—is their commitment to hard work through harnessing the efforts of their extended families. Lebanese businesses, for example, stay open between sixteen and eighteen hours a day. A study of Korean family businesses in Atlanta found that they worked an average of sixty hours a week. The work habits of Jamaican immigrant families were so pronounced that they were spoofed in many of the skits performed on the cutting-edge variety series *In Living Color.* However, most statistics concerning wealth accumulation in the United States have not accounted for the labor or on-the-job experience gains of family members, thus dramatically underestimating the value and influence of family-owned companies. Ironically, legislation designed to limit part-time work and require minimum wages has reinvigorated family businesses paying no detectable wages at all, for families' children have become the only labor that many low-profit operations can afford.

Government Regulations and Family Businesses As immigrants have quickly learned, many of the regulations enacted between 1960 and 1990 have enhanced the desirability of owning small businesses predominantly operated by family members. Small dry cleaners, independent restaurants, or tanning salons cannot hire many employees at the increasing minimum wage rates and stay competitive.

People hoping to develop and sell new products and needing employees to operate telephones and offices cannot afford the rising taxes required by the government. Very few small businesses can begin to comply with the blizzard of regulations related to employee health and protection, sexual harassment, disabilities acts, and dozens of other expensive laws and regulations. As a result, small firms have increasingly turned to family members to help operate their businesses. There is no way of determining how many of the 28.2 small businesses operating in the U.S. in 2013 (including 22.5 million without employees) but evidence suggests that the number was large and growing, as witnessed by the fact that "microbusinesses" (firms with fewer than five employees) constituted the most rapidly growing category of all enterprises.

The arrival of widespread computer technology and the Internet, with its commercial operations on the World Wide Web, have accelerated the expansion of microbusinesses and broadened the appeal of the family firm. A family of four, with a capable teenager who is computer competent, can operate a thriving Web-based business from the home, thus avoiding government regulations that apply to hired employees. This is seen in the fact that most corporations have less than $100,000 in total assets. Yet while the U.S. economy has continued to grow, the sales of the top corporations has fallen steadily as a share of gross national product (GNP), buoyed only by the spectacular rise of a few companies such as Microsoft.

One of the most rapidly rising new areas of family business—again, populated by immigrants—are nail salons. By 1996 nail salons constituted a $6 billion business (equal to that of the video game market dominated by Japanese corporations such as Nintendo), a figure that industry analysts suggest underestimates the level of activity. Family-owned salons have appeared in "upscale" malls, and in Los Angeles County alone the number of nail technicians rose from 9,700 to 15,200 in five years, with more than 80 percent being Vietnamese-born. During the 1980's virtually no economist predicted the growth of such family businesses, and the Bureau of Labor Statistics did not even track the listing for manicurists as late as 1979. This has changed with the growth of the nail salon industry, and the Bureau of Labor Statistics reports that 86,900 individuals worked as manicurists and pedicurists in 2012, and that the occupation was expected to grow by 16 percent (faster than average) over the decade 2012-2022.

A significant problem facing small business family firms, which has implications for the entire family, is that nearly half of the 800,000 new firms launched annually fail. The central fact of entrepreneurial life is that of risk, and every family enterprise confronts the competition of the market each day. Unlike arrangements whereby family members might be employed by different companies and are thus somewhat protected against layoffs or business failures, family business failures can imperil the structure of the family itself.

Yet, virtually all of the founders of successful family businesses have failed at least once. Automobile manufacturer Henry Ford, banker A. P. Giannini, and retailer Sam Walton all either declared bankruptcy or were kicked out of companies they created.

In general, most small firms have small annual incomes hovering around $16,000, as compared to General Motors' annual sales of $126 billion. Nevertheless, many family-owned small businesses remain small deliberately, with adults choosing to work fewer hours or to be less aggressive at expanding their enterprises in order to focus on nonbusiness family relationships. The number of individual family businesses that become large, however, represents an ever-increasing share of all business activity, because the overall pool of small businesses and family firms continues to swell.

Expansion of the Internet can further accelerate the advantages already enjoyed by home-based, family-run operations, and the Small Business Administration provides guideslines for those wishing to establish an online business (http://www.sba.gov/content/start-online-business). Businesses can take and ship orders, determine customer satisfaction, and maintain all records without expanding their employee base outside the family. The economic cost of regulation and taxation facing large firms with many employees, combined with the computer/Internet revolution, can accelerate the increasing number of family businesses and their influence on the market. Mandatory retirement ages and the desperate need for reliable employees by small businesses means that retirees will increasingly be approached by family members for part-time employment. Finally, family farms—the essence of the family business in previous eras—still exist and even thrive in modern society.

Larry Schweikart

Further Reading

Bean, Frank D., and Stephanie Bell-Rose, eds. *Immigration and Opportunity: Race, Ethnicity, and Employment in the United States.* New York: Russell Sage Foundation, 1999. Collection of essays on economic and labor issues relating to race and immigration in the United States, with particular attention to the competition for jobs between African Americans and immigrants.

Bruchey, Stuart, ed. *Small Business in American Life.* New York. Columbia University Press, 1980. Essay collection that features an excellent over view by the author and contains a number of specialized, highly useful essays on small business growth and operations.

Foner, Nancy, Rubén G. Rumbaut, and Steven J. Gold, eds. *Immigration Research for a New Century: Multidisciplinary Perspectives.* New York: Russell Sage Foundation, 2000. Collection of papers on immigration from a conference held at Columbia University in June, 1998. Among the many topics covered is immigrant businesses.

Gilder, George. *Recapturing the Spirit of Enterprise.* San Francisco: C. S. Press, 1992. An updated version of Gilder's The Spirit of Enterprise (1984), this work approaches entrepreneurship with attention to analysis of macroeconomic data and to numerous case studies.

Kretsedemas, Philip, and Ana Aparicio, eds. *Immigrants, Welfare Reform, and the Poverty of Policy.* Westport, Conn.: Praeger, 2004. Collection of articles on topics relating to the economic problems of new immigrants in the United States, with particular attention to Haitian, Hispanic, and Southeast Asian immigrants.

Melin, Leif, Mattias Nordqvist, and Pramodita Sharma, eds. *The SAGE Handbook of Family Business*. Thousand Oaks, CA: SAGE Publications, 2014. A reference work with sections covering topics such as the theoretical, managerial, behavioral and organizational aspects of running a family business today.

Min, Pyong Gap. *Ethnic Business Enterprise: Korean Small Business in Atlanta*. New York: Center for Migration Studies, 1988. Excellent source dealing with the situation of Korean small businesses.

Neff, Alixa. "Lebanese Immigration into the United States: 1880 to the Present." In *The Lebanese in the World: A Century of Emigration*, edited by Albert Hourani and Nadim Shehadi. London: Taurus, 1992. Details the history of Lebanese immigration to the United States.

Park, Lisa Sun-Hee. *Consuming Citizenship: Children of Asian Immigrant Entrepreneurs*. Stanford, Calif.: Stanford University Press, 2005. Cultural study of Asian immigrants who operate family businesses.

Schweikart, Larry. "Business and the Economy." In *American Decades: The 1950's*, edited by Richard Layman. Detroit: Gale Publications, 1994. Includes material dating to World War II dealing with such business developments as franchises, the revival of the family firm, and the dominance of large corporations.

Sharma, Pramodita, ed. *Exploring Transgenerational Entrepreneurship: The Role of Resources and Capabilities*. Northampton, MA: Edward Elgar Pub., 2014. A collection of essays about family businesses, drawing on longitudinal studies of 26 companies in 12 countries.

Sowell, Thomas. *Race and Culture: A World View*. New York: Basic Books, 1994. Synthesizes a great array of data on immigrants to various nations, emphasizing their contributions to the economies in their new homes.

Yoon, In-Jin. *On My Own: Korean Businesses and Race Relations in America*. Chicago: University of Chicago Press, 1997. Study of the highly entrepeneurial Korean immigrants.

See also Jews and Arab Americans; Korean immigrants; Korean immigrants and African Americans; Korean immigrants and family customs.

Farmworkers' unions

The Event: Formation of the National Farm Workers Association (NFWA)— a predecessor to the United Farm Workers of America (UFW), the first permanent agricultural workers' union in the United States
Date: September 30, 1962
Place: Fresno, California

Immigration issues: Civil rights and liberties; Economics; Labor; Mexican immigrants

Significance: The organization of farmworkers brought the plight of both American and immigrant farmworkers to the attention of the public and called attention to the suffering and indignities farmworkers endured.

Throughout the twentieth century farmworkers struggled to organize themselves against a politico-agribusiness complex that has been rather successful at resisting them. Only after the mid-1960's did working conditions for farmworkers begin to improve substantially. Improvements in income and working conditions have been the direct results of the termination of the bracero program as well as the struggles for union recognition and collective bargaining by the United Farm Workers of America (UFW) and its organizational predecessors, the National Farm Workers Association (NFWA) and the United Farm Workers Organizing Committee (UFWOC). The September, 1962, founding of the NFWA in Fresno, California, by César Chávez, Dolores Huerta, and others signaled a new era in the efforts by farmworkers to unionize and bargain collectively with their employers, mostly large agricultural growers.

In 1966, Chicanos and Mexicanos in the NFWA and Filipino farmworkers in the Agricultural Workers Organizing Committee (AWOC), an affiliate of the American Federation of Labor-Congress of Industrial Organizations (AFL-CIO), merged organizations to form the UFWOC. In February of 1972, the UFWOC became a full-fledged affiliate of the AFL-CIO and formed the UFW. In 1975, straggles by the UFW culminated in the passage of the Agricultural Labor Relations Act (ALRA) by the California legislature. Led by Chávez and Huerta, the NFWA brought years of community organizing experience to bear on the problems of farmworkers. These problems included economic hardship, general powerlessness against employers, and the lack of adequate facilities in the fields.

Establishment of the NFWA The NFWA was established as an independent, service-oriented, Chicano farmworkers' labor organization that provided credit, burial, and other family services. It sought to organize farmworkers one by one. Prior to the 1960's one important factor hindering the unionization of farmworkers was the bracero program, which was established under the Emergency Labor Program of 1942 to ease the labor shortage brought on by World War II. The bracero program super vised the recruitment of Mexican nationals to meet U.S. growers demands for labor. It was continued by Public Law 78 after the end of World War II and was maintained until 1963, when PL 78 expired.

During the 1950's, Mexican braceros greatly influenced the unionization of U.S. farmworkers. By serving as alternate sources of cheap labor, they often were used as strikebreakers by growers. In 1947, the newly founded National Farm Labor Union (NFLU) led a strike against the powerful Di Giorgio Fruit Corporation at Ar vin, California. The union demanded an increase in wages, seniority rights, grievance procedures, and recognition of the union as sole bargaining agent. Robert Di Giorgio refused the demands and launched an assault on the NFLU. He used braceros as strikebreakers and manipulated both the press and politicians in his favor. The U.S. Senate Committee on Un-American Activities set upon investigating the union.

In 1949, a special subcommittee of the House of Representatives' Education and Labor Committee held hearings on the Di Giorgio strike. The committee supported the growers and Di Giorgio won the strike. This particular strike taught Ernesto Galarza, one of the strike leaders, an important lesson in the struggle between farmworkers and growers. In his view, farmworkers could not be organized until growers' access to exploitable immigrant labor groups was halted. Braceros, as international migrant workers, were more exploitable than American workers. If they tried to organize, they were labeled as communists and deported.

Federal Government Involvement Those braceros seen by growers as causing unrest among farmworkers were often reported to the Immigration Service, the Department of Labor, and the Department of Justice, each of which would investigate the "leaders" for violations of U.S. laws. Consequently, during the 1950's, there was not a single strike by braceros, although the NFLU continued to organize strikes among other farmworkers. In 1960, when the NFLU surrendered its charter, the AWOC replaced it. AWOC was the AFL-CIO's new organizational effort to organize farmworkers. With the aid of the United Packinghouse Workers (UPWA), AWOC quickly initiated farmworkers' strikes in the lettuce fields of the Imperial Valley in California.

The AWOC-UPWA effort was based on the enforcement of federal regulations that prohibited the use of braceros on ranches where there were strikes. Although these initial strikes were successful, competition from the International Brotherhood of Teamsters led to the demise of the AWOC-UPWA effort. In the period following these strikes, AWOC membership declined as a result of disillusionment, leaving only a group of Filipino agricultural workers as members. By 1962, the year the NFWA was founded, economic conditions for farmworkers had worsened as a result of increased mechanization on farms and the continued negative impact of the bracero program on unionization efforts. In 1965, farmworkers in Tulare County, California, lived in dilapidated labor camps condemned by the Tulare Housing Authority. The labor camps had been built by the U.S. Farm Security Administration near the end of the Great Depression to provide temporary shelters for Dust Bowl migrants. Condemnation led to rent increases meant to yield the necessary revenue to build new housing.

Strikes Late in the summer of 1965, the NFWA led rent strikes among farmworkers. The rent strike at Woodville, one of the labor camps, evolved into an employment strike at the nearby J. D. Martin Ranch. Strikers complained about low pay, the lack of toilets in the fields, and a peeping crew boss. The strike failed. Within two weeks, however, the NFWA became involved in a strike for higher wages initiated by the Filipino membership of the AWOC local at Delano. On September 16, 1965, the NFWA formally joined the Delano Grape Strike. Four days later NFWA picket leaders asked farmworkers to walk off the fields. The AWOC-NFWA strike spread throughout the DelanoEarlimart-McFarland area, affecting approximately thirty ranches and involving several hundred farmworkers. Hundreds of college students, civil rights workers, and religious groups joined the farmworkers within days of the onset of the strike. Civil rights organizations quickly sent members of their staff to help with the strike.

In October, under the charismatic leadership of Chávez, the NFWA launched a grape boycott. Supporters quickly started picketing stores and piers throughout California. In response, growers began to bully picketers, often in the presence of law enforcement officials who did nothing to stop them. Growers also resorted to spraying sulfur near the picket lines. The strike continued to gain momentum, and within two weeks nearly four thousand farmworkers were out of the fields. Many growers were not economically hurt because they were able to import workers from neighboring cities who were willing to cross picket lines to work. Strike leaders began to spread word of the strike to farmworkers in neighboring areas. In March, 1966, the U.S. Senate Subcommittee on Migratory Labor conducted public hearings in Delano and other nearby cities.

At the Delano hearings, Senator Robert F. Kennedy, a member of the subcommittee, reminded the local sheriff to brush up on the rights of all people, including farmworkers. In 1966, some growers slowly began to settle with the strikers; others continued to hold out, turning instead to the International Brotherhood of Teamsters Union for "sweetheart contracts." The strike continued through the years 1966 and 1967.

In 1968, the union, now called the United Farm Workers Organizing Committee (UFWOC), extended its boycott to include every California grower of table grapes. Slowly, more individual growers agreed to recognize the union, but many powerful others continued to hold out. Finally, in July of 1970, UFWOC scored the largest victory in the history of farm-labor organizing when several of the most powerful growers agreed to the union's demands, thereby officially ending the strike. Several other victories by the UFWOC followed during the next several months. Farmworkers had finally achieved union recognition among growers and begun to participate in the collective bargaining process. Conflict with the Teamsters, however, continued to thwart the union, which had again changed its name and was known as the United Farm Workers of America (UFW). In 1975, the UFW was instrumental in the passage of the Agricultural Labor Relations Act (ALRA) in California. The ALRA brought some order to the rivalry between the UFW and the Teamsters.

The Union's Impact The major consequences stemming from the founding of the National Farm Workers Association in 1962 were the eventual establishment of a permanent farmworkers' labor union and passage of the ALRA in California. The farmworkers forced growers to recognize their union and to agree to collective bargaining. This meant improvements in wages and working conditions for farmworkers. The ALRA eliminated "sweetheart contracts," permitted union organizers on the property of employers, and established a California Agricultural Labor Relations Board that, among other things, conducted elections, determined bargaining units, and investigated unfair labor practices.

The ALRA also prohibited secondary boycotts, which stop the delivery of goods from primary employers (growers) to secondary employers (retail stores),

Protestors marching in Modesto, California, in support of a boycott called against the Gallo wine company's vineyards in 1975. (Lou Dematteis)

but permitted unions to organize consumer boycotts by discouraging the public from trading with stores. Within a few months of the passage of the ALRA, over four hundred union representation elections were held. Mexican immigrants, Chicanos, and other poor groups have provided a steady supply of cheap labor to agribusiness, especially in the Southwest. In order to maintain access to cheap labor and to thwart unionization efforts, growers have generally been highly supportive of unrestricted immigration from Mexico.

Efforts by farmworkers to organize unions and bargain collectively have been brutally suppressed by growers, who often have had local criminal justice systems and federal immigration agencies on their side during periods of labor disputes. Growers' use of sheriffs, police officers, judges, strikebreakers, and private armies against farmworkers were common. Indeed, the U.S. government itself, through the bracero program, was a "labor contractor" for growers.

The NFWA brought the plight of the farmworkers to the forefront of America's conscience and highlighted the suffering and indignities farmworkers were forced to endure. It also marked the inception of the farmworkers' first permanent, broad-based organization. Chicano and Filipino farmworkers, long neglected by labor legislation and traditional trade unions, organized their own independent labor union and assumed their rights to organize and bargain collectively with their employers. The Delano Grape Strike, begun in September of 1965, propelled César Chávez and the NFWA to the front of the civil and labor rights struggles.

Chávez turned the strike into a crusade by promoting the view that farmworkers are human beings who deserve respect and a living wage. In 1968, he fasted for twenty-five days in order to gain support for the farmworkers' struggle. He ended the fast by "breaking bread" with Senator Robert Kennedy, then a candidate for the U.S. presidency. Chávez's nonviolent approach and charismatic qualities brought dignity and strength to the farmworkers and greatly influenced the consciousness of Americans. Through use of the consumer boycott, farmworkers were able to involve the American public in their struggle for human and union recognition. As a result, Americans "discovered" the farmworkers, who through their own efforts affirmed and reclaimed their humanity. Their struggles did not end, however. Pro-grower politicians and bureaucrats have continued to pose problems, and widespread use of toxic pesticides by growers has continued to affect the health and well-being of farmworkers.

Rubén O. Martinez

Further Reading

Acuña, Rodolfo. *Occupied America: A History of Chicanos.* 3d ed. New York: Harper & Row, 1988. General history of Chicanos. It includes detailed sections on Chicano agricultural labor organizing, tracing Chicano labor struggles to the turn of the century. It also details labor struggles in other sectors of the economy.

Araiza, Lauren. *To March for Others: The Black Freedom Struggle and the United Farm Workers.* Philadelphia: University of Pennsylvania Press, 2014. A study of how five Black organizations---SNCC, the NAACP, the Natural Urban League, the Southern Christian Leadership Conference, and the Black Panther Party— came to support and be involved in the struggle of the United Farm Workers.

Bean, Frank D., and Stephanie Bell-Rose, eds. *Immigration and Opportunity: Race, Ethnicity, and Employment in the United States.* New York: Russell Sage Foundation, 1999. Collection of essays on economic and labor issues relating to race and immigration in the United States, with particular attention to the competition for jobs between African Americans and immigrants.

Bender, Steven W. *One Night in America: Robert Kennedy, César Chavez, and the Dream of Dignity.* Boulder, CO: Paradigm Publishers, 2008. A study of the friendship betwee Robert Kennedy and César Chávez, and how their shared vision shaped the battle for the rights of migrant farm workers.

Briggs, Vernon M. *Immigration and American Unionism.* Ithaca, N.Y.: Cornell University Press, 2001. Scholarly sur vey of the dynamic interaction between unionism and immigration. Covers the entire sweep of U.S. national history, with an emphasis on the nineteenth century.

Cull, Nicholas J., and David Carrasco, eds. *Alambrista and the U.S.-Mexico Border: Film, Music, and Stories of Undocumented Immigrants.* Albuquerque: University of New Mexico Press, 2004. Collection of essays on dramatic works, films, and music about Mexicans who cross the border illegally into the United States.

Dunne, John Gregory. *Delano.* Rev. ed. New York: Farrar, Straus & Giroux, 1971. Description of the events leading up to the formation of the United Farm Workers of America. It also describes the union's organizing efforts during the 1960's.

Galarza, Ernesto. *Merchants of Labor: The Mexican Bracero Story.* Charlotte, N.C.: McNally & Loftin, 1964. Excellent historical analysis of the bracero program from its inception to 1960. Examines the structure of control affecting the lives of Mexican nationals and American agricultural workers in the fields.

Gonzalez, Gilbert G. *Guest Workers or Colonized Labor? Mexican Labor Migration to the United States*. Boulder, Colo.: Paradigm, 2005. Historical study of Mexican farmworkers in the United States that examines the subject in the context of American dominance over Mexico.

Hernandez, Donald J., ed. *Children of Immigrants: Health, Adjustment, and Public Assistance*. Washington, D.C.: National Academy Press, 1999. Collection of papers on issues of public health and welfare among immigrants to the United States, with extensive attention to immigrant farmworkers.

Kretsedemas, Philip, and Ana Aparicio, eds. *Immigrants, Welfare Reform, and the Poverty of Policy*. Westport, Conn.: Praeger, 2004. Collection of articles on topics relating to the economic problems of new immigrants in the United States, with particular attention to Haitian, Hispanic, and Southeast Asian immigrants.

Kushner, Sam. *Long Road to Delano*. New York: International Publishers, 1975. Provides a class analysis of the development of agribusiness in California. It describes farmworkers' working conditions and their struggles against exploitation. There is a chapter on the organizing efforts of the Communist Party during the 1930's among farmworkers. The foreword is by Bert Corona, a major Chicano community leader.

Milkman, Ruth, ed. *Organizing Immigrants: The Challenge for Unions in Contemporary California*. Ithaca, N.Y.: ILR Press, 2000. Broad study of unionism and immigrants in the nation's most populous state.

Nelson, Eugene. *Huelga: The First Hundred Days of the Great Delano Grape Strike*. Delano, Calif.: Farm Worker Press, 1966. Brief account of the events that led up to the Delano Grape Strike and details the activities up to December, 1965. Written by one of the organizers of the strike, the book captures the mood and views of the farmworkers. Contains several photographs, including some of law enforcement officials and strikebreakers.

Taylor, Ronald B. *Chávez and the Farm Workers: A Study in the Acquisition and Use of Power*. Boston: Beacon Press, 1975. Provides a sympathetic description of the César Chávez-led farmworkers' struggles during the 1960's and early 1970's. In particular, the book details some of the struggles the farmworkers had with the Teamsters union. Contains some photographs, including one of Chávez and Robert Kennedy.

See also Asian Pacific American Labor Alliance; Bracero program; Chicano movement; Latinos; Latinos and employment; Mexican American Legal Defense and Education Fund; Mexican deportations during the Depression; Undocumented workers.

FEDERAL RIOT OF 1799

The Event: Public riot in protest of the federal government's passage of the Alien and Sedition Acts
Date: February 10, 1799
Place: Philadelphia, Pennsylvania

Immigration issues: Government and politics; Irish immigrants

Significance: A turning point in intergroup relations in the United States, the federal riot became a symbol of conflict between an established, dominant group and an incoming immigrant population.

A riot at Saint Mar y's Church in Philadelphia in Februar y, 1799, was the direct result of the passage of the Alien and Sedition Acts of 1798. These four laws—the Naturalization Act, the Alien Act, the Alien Enemies Act, and the Sedition Act—had been passed in June and July and sought collectively to limit the rights of immigrants and to silence criticism of the new U.S. government. Two main political factions dominated at the time, the conservative Federalists and the Jeffersonian Republicans. Federalists were mainly the wealthy and established, and Roman Catholics as well as Protestants were among this group.

Saint Mary's Church, considered one of the most venerable and well-respected Catholic congregations in the United States, counted many of these Federalists among its members and included both established Anglo-Americans and Irish Americans. Republicans were made up largely of immigrants, including many new Irish immigrants, and these less affluent and newer Americans felt the impact of the Alien and Sedition Acts most sharply. They circulated petitions protesting the acts and gathered signatures throughout Philadelphia without incident. They intended to present the petitions to Congress.

Four of these immigrant Republicans—James Reynolds, Samuel Cummings, Robert Moore, and William Duane—posted fliers protesting the Alien and Sedition Acts at Saint Mary's, again requesting signatures from the Irish members of the congregation. Following the February 10, 1799, Sunday service at Saint Mary's, a violent confrontation took place between these men and members of the congregation.

The four were tried on February 21, 1799, for causing the riot. Saint Mary's Father Leonard Neale, who had accused the men, strongly condemned the actions of the Republicans, while Father Matthew Carr testified that it was a long-honored tradition in Ireland to post notices and seek support for petitions following church services. The jury delivered a verdict of "not guilty" to the charge of causing a riot.

The riot signified a turning point during the early history of intergroup relations in the United States. Although the short-range effect of this conflict was to weaken the Federalist hold within Saint Mary's congregation, the "Irish riot" became a symbol of conflict between an established, dominant group and an incoming immigrant population. Such conflicts would characterize much of U.S. history.

Kathleen Schongar

Further Reading

Elkins, Stanley, and Eric McKitrick. The Age of Federalism: The Early American Republic, 1788-1800. New York: Oxford University Press, 1993.

Miller, John C. Crisis in Freedom: The Alien and Sedition Acts. Boston: Little, Brown, 1951.

Sharp, James Roger. American Politics in the Early Republic: The New Nation in Crisis. New Haven, Conn.: Yale University Press, 1993.

See also Alien and Sedition Acts; Anti-Irish Riots of 1844; Irish immigrants; Irish immigrants and discrimination.

Filipino immigrants

Identification: Immigrants to North America from the Philippines, an archipelago nation located across the China Sea from mainland Southeast Asia

Significance: Filipino Americans rank as the second-largest Asian American group in the United States, after Chinese Americans, and substantial numbers of Filipino immigrants also live in a few parts of Canada. There are several large Filipino American communities in California and Hawaii, and Filipinos can be found throughout North America, often thoroughly integrated into American neighborhoods and workplaces.

The Philippines has long had close ties to the United States because it was a U.S. possession or territory from 1898 to 1946. The United States established English as the language of instruction in high schools and colleges in the Philippines, and Filipinos have long been familiar with American movies and other media. Filipinos began settling in North America soon after the Philippines became part of the United States, and the numbers of Filipino Americans began to increase greatly during the late 1960's.

History of Filipino American Settlement Filipino settlement in North America falls into three major periods. The first period, from 1906 to the beginning of World War II in 1941, resulted from the U.S. demand for cheap agricultural labor. Sugar plantations dominated the economy of Hawaii early in the twentieth century, and plantation owners were interested in finding hardworking field hands who would work for low wages. The Hawaii Sugar Planters Association began recruiting in the Philippines, and by 1946, the association had brought more than a quarter of a million Filipinos to Hawaii. California, which also had a need for seasonal

Roadside stand of a fruit seller in San Lorenzo, California, during World War II. This picture was taken in May, 1942—three months after President Franklin D. Roosevelt signed an executive order to intern all persons of Japanese descent living on the West Coast. At a moment of anti-Japanese hysteria in California, Asian entrepreneurs such as this Filipino farmer advertised their non-Japanese ethnic identities in order to do business safely. (National Archives)

agricultural workers, was the home of more than thirty-one thousand of the forty-six thousand Filipinos living on the mainland in 1940. Filipino Americans continue to make up part of the migrant farm labor force of California and other western states, but the numbers of migrant Filipino workers are steadily decreasing.

The second migration period began in 1946, when the Philippines became politically independent of the United States. Large U.S. military bases had been established in the Philippines, and many of the Filipinos admitted to the United States were women married to American servicemen. At the same time, Filipinos who had become naturalized American citizens after the war were able to petition to have family members enter the United States. Because of these two factors, most immigrants in this period came as a result of marriage or family connections.

The United States maintained military bases in the Philippines until 1991, so Filipinos who married U.S. military personnel continued to arrive in the United

States. Another form of migration through marriage is the phenomenon of mail-order brides, women who meet and marry American men through correspondence. During the 1990's, approximately nineteen thousand mail-order brides were leaving the Philippines each year to join husbands and fiancés abroad, with the United States as the primary destination. In 1997, social scientist Concepcion Montoya identified Filipina mail-order brides, who often establish social networks among themselves, as a rapidly emerging American community.

The third migration period began in 1965, when the United States passed a new immigration law that ended the discrimination against Asians present in all previous immigration laws. The result was a rapid growth in the Asian American population in general and in the Filipino American population in particular. The number of Filipinos living in the United States grew by roughly 100 percent in each ten-year period from 1960 to 1990: from 176,000 in the census of 1960 to 343,000 in that of 1970, to 775,000 in 1980, to more than 1,400,000 in the 1990 census. Between 1971 and 2003, new immigrants entered the United States from the Philippines at an average of 45,000 persons per year.

The third period of Filipino immigration differs greatly from the earlier periods. Although immigrants before 1965 were mostly laborers from the rural Philippines, immigrants after 1965 tended to be highly educated professionals (such as doctors, nurses, teachers, and engineers), and they often came from cities. Migration to the United States became a goal for many Filipino professionals because economic opportunities were much greater in the United States. During the 1970's, one out of every five graduates of nursing schools in the Philippines left for the United States, and the majority of those nurses did not return to the Philippines. This may have created "brain drain" problems for the Philippines, because it lost many of its medical professionals, executives, and technicians to the United States, but this migration has been a benefit to the American economy. Filipino doctors and nurses are on the staffs of many U.S. hospitals, and teachers from the Philippines are employed in many U.S. schools.

Filipinos in American Society According to the Census Bureau, in 2010, 2.5 million people of Filipino descent lived in the U.S., making them the second largest Asian American group after the Chinese (4.0 million). Over two-thirds (69 percent) of Filipino Americans age eighteen and older were born outside the U.S., a slightly lower percentage than for all Asian American adults (74 percent). Most Filipino adults (69 percent) say they speak English very well, a much higher percentage that for all Asian Americans (53 percent), and they are more likely (47 percent) to hold a bachelor's or advanced degree than is the American population as a whole (28 percent), although slightly less likely than Asian Americans as a whole (49 percent). The median household income for Filipino Americans is also higher ($75,000) than for all Asians ($66,000 or the U.S. as a whole ($49,800).

Women outnumber men among foreign-born Filipinos, largely because marriage to U.S. citizens has continued to be a major source of migration from the Philippines. In 2011, in the foreign-born Filipino American population, 60 percent were female and 40 percent male, while for the native born Filipino population,

Filipino farm workers. (Library of Congress)

the male and feemale populations were approximately equal (which would be expected in any population in which migration did not play a role).

The most common occupations for Filipino-born men in 2011 were service and personal care (16.7 percent), manufacturing, installation and repair (12.8 percent) administrative support (12.4 percent). For Filipino-born women, the most common occupations were registered nursing (18.3 percent), administrative support (15.8 percent), and service and personal care (15.3 percent). Both Filipino men and women are far more likely to work as registered nurses than is the foreign born population as a whole: for men, 5.0 percent of Filipinos as compared to 0.5 percent of the total foreign born population work as registered nurses, while for females, 18.3 percent of Filipino women compared to 3.7 percent of the total immigrant population work as registered nurses.

Almost half (45 percent) of Filipino immigrants lived in California in 2011 (811,900 individuals), while the state with the second-highest number of Filipino immigrants was Hawaii (6 percent; 112,200 individuals). Other states with large Filipino-born populations include New Jersey (5 percent; 86,600 individuals), Texas (5 percent, 86,400 individuals), Illinois (5 percent, 84,800 individuals) and New York (5 percent, 84,400). The Los Angeles metro area had the largest number of Filipino immigrants (388,400), followed by San Francisco (156,400) and New York (150,500).

Many Filipino Americans, especially the early agricultural laborers in California, experienced discrimination. However, modern Filipinos usually report relatively few problems in their relations with members of other racial and ethnic groups. Familiarity with the English language and with mainstream American culture, high levels of marriage with white and black Americans, and a concentration in skilled occupations and white-collar professions tend to help Filipino Americans in interethnic relations.

One reflection of the high degree of integration of Filipino Americans into American society is the high percentage of foreign-born Filipino Americans who take on U.S. citizenship. More than one-fourth of the Filipinos who arrived in the United States during the 1980's had been naturalized as citizens by 1990. More than 80 percent of those who had arrived before 1980 had become citizens. By contrast, fewer than 15 percent of all people who had immigrated to the United States during the 1980's had become citizens, and only 61 percent of foreign-born people who had immigrated before 1980 had become citizens.

Carl L. Bankston III

Further Reading

For broad surveys of Filipino American history and communities, see Veltisezar B. Bautista's *The Filipino Americans: From 1763 to the Present—Their History, Culture, and Traditions* (Farmington Hills, Mich.: Bookhaus, 1998) and Barbara Mercedes Posadas's *The Filipino Americans* (Westport, Conn.: Greenwood Press, 1999).

Yen Le Espiritu's *Filipino American Lives* (Philadelphia: Temple University Press, 1995) presents the narratives of thirteen Filipino Americans who tell the stories of their lives.

Filipino Americans: Transformation and Identity (Thousand Oaks, Calif.: Sage Publications, 1997), edited by Maria P. P. Root, is a collection of essays that consider immigration from the Philippines to the United States, Filipino American communities and community institutions, mixed-heritage Filipino Americans, and Filipina mail-order brides in the United States.

Luciano Mangiafico's *Contemporary American Immigrants: Patterns of Filipino, Korean, and Chinese Settlement in the United States* (New York: Praeger, 1988) describes major waves of migration, locations of large communities of these three ethnic groups, and contemporary social conditions of the groups.

Michel S. Laguerre's *The Global Ethnopolis: Chinatown, Japantown, and Manilatown in American Society* (New York: St. Martin's Press, 1999) is a study of Asian ethnic enclaves that considers Filipino communities.

Linda España-Maram's *Creating Masculinity in Los Angeles's Little Manila: Working-Class Filipinos and Popular Culture, 1920-1950s* (New York: Columbia University Press, 2006) looks at the role of leisure activities, including those officially considered shady or even illicit (gambling, boxing, dancing with white women) in creating male Filipino identity.

Jose V. Fuentecilla's *Fighting from a Distance: How Filipino Exiles Helped Topple a Dictator* (Urbana: University of Illinois Press, 2013) looks at the role played by Filipinos in America in overthrowing Filipino dictator Ferdinand Marcos. For a more general study of Asian immigrants, see Uma Anand Segal's *A Framework for Immigration: Asians in the United States* (New York: Columbia University Press, 2002), which survey the history and economic and social conditions of Asian immigrants, both before and after the federal immigration reforms of 1965.

See also Asian American stereotypes; Censuses, U.S.; Filipino immigrants and family customs; Hawaiian and Pacific islander immigrants; Mail-order brides; Refugee fatigue.

FILIPINO IMMIGRANTS AND FAMILY CUSTOMS

Immigration issues: Asian immigrants; Families and marriage

Significance: Immigrants of Filipino ancestry have a number of distinctive values and customs regarding family, and there are large Filipino populations in the United States and Canada.

In 2010 there were 2.5 million people of Filipino descent lived in the U.S., and as of 2013, about half a million in Canada. Both countries experienced a continuous flow of immigrants from the Philippines from the 1970's through the 1990's, while Canada experienced an increased number of Filipino immigrants in recent years and the Philippines has produced the most new immigrants to Canada from 2006 to 2013. Almost half (45 percent, 811,900 individuals) of the U.S. Filipino population lived in California, followed by Hawaii (6 percent, 112,200 individuals) and More than half of all Canadian Filipinos lived in Ontario (218,660 individuals) , primarily in Toronto (185,085 individuals). The large numbers of Filipinos, the continuing flow of new arrivals, and the existence of large ethnic communities all helped to maintain distinctive Filipino American family customs. In general, Filipino American families who live in areas where there are few other people from the Philippines retain few distinctive family characteristics. In the large Filipino concentrations, such as Los Angeles, continual contact among Filipinos has helped members maintain cultural continuity.

Cultural Values and Family Relations Four widely recognized key cultural values guide Filipino family relations and family customs. These are *utang na loob* (moral debt), *hiya* (shame), *amor proprio* (self-esteem), and *pakikisama* (getting along with others). Children, from the Filipino perspective, owe an eternal debt to their parents, who gave them life. Children are therefore expected to show

311

obedience and respect to parents and grandparents.

The cultural value *hiya* dictates that individuals feel ashamed when they fail to behave according to expected social roles, which are often thought of in terms of family relations even when they involve people who are not actually family members. Younger people are expected to show respect for their elders at all times. When children greet an older person, such as a grandparent, they show respect by taking the elder's hand and bowing slightly to touch the back of the hand with the forehead.

Older brothers and sisters are not to be treated as equals but are addressed as *kuya* ("big brother") and *ate* ("big sister"). Moreover, older friends are often called *kuya* or *ate*. Children call unrelated adults *tita* ("aunt") or *tito* ("uncle"). People who do not seem to recognize or care about these types of social relations may be referred to as *walang hiya* ("shameless"), a term that expresses very strong disapproval.

Even when people violate social expectations, others will be reluctant to criticize them openly out of fear of offending their sense of *amor proprio*. Criticisms must be indirect, and they depend on individuals' own sense of shame. *Pakikisama*, or getting along with others, dictates that people avoid direct confrontation. In terms of the family, it also means that individuals should always place the interests of the family and the maintenance of relations within the family first and consider their own interests and desires as secondary.

In respect to these customs and values, life in North America has often led to tension within Filipino families. Children raised in the United States, for example, sometimes feel that it is humiliating to place the hands of elders against their foreheads. Adults, in turn, feel frustrated if children refuse to follow accepted customs, and they sometimes see their children as rude or even *walang hiya*. Young people exposed to American ideas of individualism also find it difficult to place the interests of the family before their own, which parents may find disturbing.

Baptism and Sponsors Godparents or sponsors are virtual members of Filipino families, a cultural practice known as *compadrazgo*. When children are due to be baptized into the Roman Catholic Church, mothers and fathers ask a number of men and women to stand as sponsors or godparents for their children. Two of the sponsors are recognized by the Church as the children's godparents, but Filipinos rarely distinguish between these two primary sponsors and the other secondary sponsors; all are referred to as the children's *ninongs*, if they are men, and *ninangs*, if they are women. Sponsors are regarded as being close to additional parents, and they are expected to help the children in any way they can. They give the children presents on birthdays and other major occasions and they play key roles in baptisms, religious confirmation, and wedding ceremonies.

Since sponsors have an obligation to help children, people in the Philippines often seek out powerful or influential persons to play this role. In the United States and Canada, however, it is much more common for close friends to act as sponsors, creating formal, customary ties among people who refer to each other as *compadre* or *copare* and *comadre* or *comare* (literally "co-father" and "co-mother").

Friends, even if they are not actually sponsors of one another's children, often shorten these terms and address each other simply as *pare* or *mare*.

Wedding Customs Since the majority of Filipino Americans are Roman Catholics, the Roman Catholic Church is usually central to wedding ceremonies. Even when Filipinos marry in civil ceremonies, they almost always get married again in the church. In the Philippines, grooms' families traditionally pay all wedding expenses. Some Filipino families native to the United States or Canada have adopted the North American custom in which brides' families pay wedding expenses, but most either continue to follow Filipino ways or compromise and share costs.

Weddings in the Philippines, especially in the countryside, are often lavish events in which families spend far beyond their means providing food and entertainment for large numbers of guests. Filipino Americans rarely go to these extremes, however, and most restrict their guest lists to friends and relatives. Nevertheless, food remains an important part of wedding ceremonies, and guests at Filipino American marriages can expect to find a large array of Filipino dishes.

Wedding rites among Filipino Americans often retain many Spanish Catholic customs not seen in other North American Catholic weddings. During weddings in which couples adhere strictly to Filipino traditions, bridegrooms give brides silver coins, known as *aras*, which symbolize wives' control of household finances. This type of traditional wedding includes the brides' and grooms' sponsors as well as the maid of honor and the best man. One set of sponsors holds the veil, one holds a rope, and one holds a candle. Brides wear gowns that are very similar to those worn in other American weddings, but instead of tuxedos grooms and the best man may wear the *barong tagalog*, the formal Filipino shirt.

Carl L. Bankston III

Further Reading
Almirol, Edwin B. *Ethnic Identity and Social Negotiation: A Study of a Filipino Community in California.* New York: AMS Press, 1985.
Bandon, Alexandra. *Filipino Americans.* New York: New Discovery Books, 1993.
Bautista, Veltisezar B. *The Filipino Americans: From 1763 to the Present—Their History, Culture, and Traditions.* Farmington Hills, Mich.: Bookhaus, 1998.
Espiritu, Yen Le. *Filipino American Lives.* Philadelphia: Temple University Press, 1995.
_____. *Home Bound: Filipino American Lives Across Cultures, Communities, and Countries.* Berkeley: University of California Press, 2003.
Jamero, Peter. *Growing Up Brown: Memoirs of a Filipino America.* Seattle: University of Washington Press, 2006.
Laguerre, Michel S. *The Global Ethnopolis: Chinatown, Japantown, and Manilatown in American Society.* New York: St. Martin's Press, 1999.
Mangiafico, Luciano. *Contemporary American Immigrants: Patterns of Filipino, Korean, and Chinese Settlement in the United States.* New York: Praeger, 1988.
Posadas, Barbara Mercedes. *The Filipino Americans.* Westport, Conn.: Greenwood Press, 1999.

Rodriguez, Evelyn Ibatan. *Celebrating Debutantes and Quinceneras: Coming of Age in American Ethnic Communities.* Philadelphia: Temple University Press, 2013.

Root, Maria P. P. *Filipino Americans: Transformation and Identity.* Thousand Oaks, Calif.: Sage Publications, 1997.

Rumbaut, Rubén G., and Alejandro Portes, eds. *Ethnicities: Children of Immigrants in America.* Berkeley: University of California Press, 2001.

See also   Asian American stereotypes; Censuses, U.S.; Filipino immigrants; Hawaiian and Pacific islander immigrants; Mail-order brides; Refugee fatigue.

FLORIDA ILLEGAL-IMMIGRANT SUIT

The Event: Florida state lawsuit against the federal government demanding restitution for state expenditures on illegal immigrants, who were principally from Cuba

Date: April 11, 1994

Place: Miami, Florida

Immigration issues: Border control; Cuban immigrants

Significance: Although the state's lawsuit was ultimately unsuccessful, it helped to focus national attention on the inadequacy of federal funding of the Immigration and Naturalization Service.

After claiming that illegal immigration to Florida was out of control, Governor Lawton M. Chiles, Jr., filed a lawsuit against the federal government demanding more than $884 million reimbursement for education, health, and prison expenditures incurred by the state of Florida. These expenses were related to illegal aliens who entered the state during 1993. To emphasize the serious economic pressures on local governments caused by illegal immigration, both the Dade County Public Health Trust and the county's school board joined Governor Chiles as plaintiffs in the suit. The lawsuit named as defendants commissioner of the Immigration and Naturalization Service (INS) Doris Meissner and U.S. attorney general Janet Reno, along with regional and district officials of the INS.

The complaint was filed on April 11, 1994, as *Chiles v. United States*. It alleged that the federal government, through the defendants and their predecessors, had since before 1980 "abdicated its responsibility under the immigration laws and the Constitution to enforce and administer rational immigration policies." The suit also pointed out that, according to the INS's own figures, at least 345,000 undocumented aliens resided in Florida in 1991. That number constituted at least 36 percent of all immigrants in the state. The lawsuit stated that Florida is a victim of an ongoing immigration emergency that endangers the lives, property, safety, and economic welfare of the residents of the state.

On December 20, 1994, Federal District Judge Edward B. Davis threw out the lawsuit. In his decision, Davis said that he recognized the financial burden to Florida resulting from "the methods in which the Federal Government has chosen to enforce the immigration laws" but ruled that this did not give the state the right to recover money. He concurred instead with the federal government's argument that the case represented a political rather than a legal question over "the proper allocation of Federal resources and the execution of discretionary policies" dealing with immigration.

A National Immigration Crisis? In November, 1994, Governor Chiles faced a reelection campaign in a state in which much of the electorate was tired of successive waves of refugees from Cuba and Haiti. Political considerations were important in his decision to file the lawsuit early in the campaign year.

Judge Davis, in denying the suit, admitted that Florida faced "a Hobson's choice." His written decision stated that if Florida chose not to provide services to illegal aliens, including closing schools, emergency rooms, and other service providers, the impact on the health, safety, and welfare of its citizenry could be devastating. If, on the other hand, Florida chose to provide the services, the costs could cripple the state.

In the meantime, Governor Chiles's lawsuit and other pressures pushed the Bill Clinton administration to ask Congress later that year for $350 million to help governors pay the costs of imprisoning illegal aliens convicted of felonies. In November, 1994, Attorney General Reno and INS commissioner Meissner promised a 40 percent increase in border patrol resources along the Mexico-U.S. border within the next six months.

Such moves were clearly in response to the popular perception—in the other politically powerful border states of Texas and California as well as in Florida—that the federal government was not meeting its responsibility for controlling immigration. Many citizens were concerned that illegal immigration diminished the number of jobs available in an already tight job market. California's Proposition 187, a ballot initiative passed by a large majority in November, 1994, threatened to cut off most public services to illegal immigrants. These services, according to Governor Pete Wilson of California amounted to more than $3 billion annually in a state with increasingly serious budget problems.

More than simple economics was at work. Both the Florida lawsuit and California's Proposition 187 reflected a growing public backlash against large numbers of illegal immigrants and perhaps even against the relatively high rate of legal immigration. Not only was Chiles reelected in Florida, but Wilson also was re-elected, by a substantial margin. Most observers attributed Wilson's margin of victory in large part to his tough stance on illegal immigration. Some immigrant-rights advocates accused Wilson of pandering to racial and ethnic divisions in a state with the highest unemployment rate in the country.

Consequences Illegal immigration clearly remains a politically volatile issue.

315

During the year following Florida's unsuccessful lawsuit, a new Republican-controlled Congress gave evidence of responding to growing public concern over illegal immigration. In March, 1995, House Speaker Newt Gingrich formed a bipartisan task force to consider strategies to crack down on illegal immigration. That same month, Senator Dianne Feinstein of California, a Democrat, assailed the Clinton administration for lax enforcement of immigration laws. Political pressures indicated the likelihood of much larger appropriations for INS enforcement of immigration laws.

Increased funding for the INS eventually materialized. The service's 2001 budget was set at $4.8 billion—a figure roughly triple its 1994 budget. In 2003, the INS was subsumed into the Department of Homeland Security, and Border Patrol activities were subsumed within the Customs and Border Patrol agency. As of 2012, the budget for the Customs and Border Patrol agency was $11.7 billion, the largest budget among Department of Homeland Security agencies.

Anthony D. Branch

Further Reading

Hernandez, Donald J., ed. *Children of Immigrants: Health, Adjustment, and Public Assistance.* Washington, D.C.: National Academy Press, 1999. Collection of papers on issues of public health and welfare among immigrants to the United States.

Levine, Robert M., and Moisés Asís. *Cuban Miami.* New Brunswick, N.J.: Rutgers University Press, 2000. Broad study of Cuban immigrants in Miami, which is the center of the largest Cuban community in the United States.

Stepick, Alex, et al. *This Land Is Our Land: Immigrants and Power in Miami.* Berkeley: University of California Press, 2003. Study of competition and conflict among Miami's largest ethnic groups—Cubans, Haitians, and African Americans.

Zebich-Knos, Michele, and Heather Nicol. *Foreign Policy Toward Cuba: Isolation or Engagement?* Lanham, Md.: Lexington Books, 2005. Critical study of changing U.S. policies toward Cuba.

See also Cuban immigrants; Cuban refugee policy; González rescue; Haitian immigrants; Illegal aliens; Justice and immigration; Mariel boatlift; Proposition 187.

GARMENT INDUSTRY

Definition: Clothing-manufacturing businesses in urban centers

Immigration issues: Economics; Labor; Women

Significance: The decentralized structure of the garment industry, with its small and medium-sized firms and varying degrees of labor specialization, has always offered respectable but poorly paid wage labor for unskilled female workers, especially immigrants.

In 1818, two-thirds of all clothing in the United States was homemade. The mechanization of the textile industry at the beginning of the nineteenth century provided cheap cloth, which needed to be processed to be marketable. The textile industry was therefore interested in speeding up the production process through the mechanization of the garment industry and the creation of a market of ready-made clothes. The introduction of the Singer sewing machine in 1852 and the mass production of paper patterns during the 1860's were stepping stones on the way to the ready-made industry.

Ready-made clothing was first produced for men, especially sailors, miners, lumbermen, soldiers, and plantation owners, who demanded cheap clothing for slaves. In the second half of the nineteenth century, a growing middle class emerged, which increased the market for ready-to-wear men's clothing. The immigration of skilled and unskilled workers from southern and eastern Europe beginning during the late nineteenth century provided the needed labor force for the expansion of the garment industry. The market for ready-made women's clothing increased because of the growing number of women in clerical and sales jobs, as well as in light manufacturing. In the first decade of the twentieth century, the women's garment industry expanded tremendously, and, by 1914, the women's clothing sector had surpassed that for men's clothing.

During the 1920's, the garment industry lost importance as a result of shifts in spending patterns away from clothing and toward personal transportation. Consequently, in search of cheap labor, manufacturers moved from the unionized cities in the Northeast—such as New York City, Philadelphia, Baltimore, and Chicago—to smaller Appalachian communities in Pennsylvania as well as to Connecticut, the Southwest, and the Southeast. During the 1960's, these so-called runaway shops started to go overseas, especially to Southeast Asia. Chinese immigrants, Puerto Ricans, and other minority groups continue to provide a cheap labor force in the sweatshops of the American garment industry.

Gender Division of Labor in the Industry Before the mechanization of the garment industry, men produced custom-made men's clothing, while women made cheap clothing for women and children. Men worked as skilled tailors, while many women found work as seamstresses. Skilled female dressmakers under went a "de-skilling" process during the modernization process of the garment industry. Dressmakers became "operatives," while male workers could secure skilled work.

In the second half of the nineteenth century, the division of labor shifted from the types of garments that were produced to the types of tasks that were performed. During the 1870's, male skilled and semiskilled workers invaded the women's clothing industry, which had been a predominantly female domain. Male tailors continued to perform the skilled tasks, such as pattern making and cutting. The sewing machine opened the men's clothing industry for female workers, who found work as poorly paid finishers.

Seamstresses, who represented the majority of female garment workers, did piecework for clothing manufacturers or contractors. They received precut garments and finished them in their homes. Seamstresses not only received the lowest wages of all workers but also had to pay for rent, fuel, candles, and even needles in order to do their work. Low wages were the result of a huge labor supply: The seamstresses competed with prison labor, poorhouse labor, farmer's wives and daughters, and church women's sewing circles who did not depend on this income.

Before 1880, Irish, English, German, and Swedish immigrant women worked in the garment industry. Between 1880 and 1890, Jewish and Italian immigrant women began to replace them. By 1890, about 40 percent of New York City's garment workers were Russian Jews and 27 percent came from Southern Italy. In Chicago, Eastern Jews, Italians, Bohemians, Poles, Lithuanians, and Moravians worked in the garment industry. In 1911, a fire in the Triangle Shirtwaist Company factory in New York City killed 146 garment workers, most of them European immigrant women. The public outrage caused by the tragedy led to the formation of the New York Factory Investigation Commission and paved the way for industrial regulations.

Unionization of the Garment Industry   Before 1900, the unionization of garment workers was mainly restricted to the organization of skilled male workers in the craft unions. This situation changed as a result of the militancy of immigrant garment workers. One of the most famous chapters in the history of immigrant women's organizing is the "Uprising of the Twenty Thousand." In November, 1909, 20,000 New York City waistmakers (factory-employed seamstresses) went on strike. The vast majority of the strikers were Russian Jewish women, joined by Jewish men, Italian women, and native-born women. Women became some of the most dedicated and idealistic participants in the labor movement. Militant and with a socialist background, they helped to form the new unionism—labor unions that organized throughout the industry.

The International Ladies' Garment Workers' Union (ILGWU) and the Amalgamated Clothing Workers were the first unions to organize female workers on a large scale and the first to employ women as organizers. Rose Schneiderman was a socialist activist and union leader who fled the pogroms in Russian Poland in 1891. She organized her first union in the United States at the age of twenty-one and was the first female vice president of the United Cloth Hat and Cap Makers Union. Schneiderman, an organizer of the ILGWU, later became president of the National Women's Trade Union League (NWTUL), an alliance of immigrant women workers and upper-class white women that was supporting women's unionization and lobbying on behalf of women's concerns, such as protective legislation. Fannia Cohn, also an organizer with the ILGWU, established the education department of the union, which laid the cornerstone of workers' education.

Silke Roth

Further Reading

Bean, Frank D., and Stephanie Bell-Rose, eds. *Immigration and Opportunity: Race, Ethnicity, and Employment in the United States*. New York: Russell Sage Foundation, 1999.

Blicksilver, Jack. "Apparel and Other Textile Products." In *Manufacturing: A Historiographical and Bibliographical Guide*, edited by David O. Whitten and Bessie E. Whitten. Vol. 1 in Handbook of American Business History. Westport, Conn.: Greenwood Press, 1990.

Briggs, Vernon M. *Immigration and American Unionism*. Ithaca, N.Y.: Cornell University Press, 2001.

Chin, Margaret M. *Sewing Women: Immigrants and the New York City Garment Industry*. New York: Columbia University Press, 2005.

Glenn, Susan A. *Daughters of the Shtetl: Life and Labor in the Immigrant Generation*. Ithaca, N.Y.: Cornell University Press, 1990.

Jensen, Joan M., and Sue Davidson, eds. *A Needle, a Bobbin, a Strike: Women Needleworkers in America*. Philadelphia: Temple University Press, 1984.

Karas, Jennifer. *Bridges and Barriers: Earnings and Occupational Attainment Among Immigrants*. New York: LFB Scholarly Publishing, 2002.

Levine, Louis. *The Women's Garment Workers: A History of the International Ladies' Garment Workers' Union*. New York: B. W. Huebsch, 1924.

Pastorello, Karen. *A Power Among Them: Bessie Abramowitz Hillman and the making of the Amalgamated Clothing Workers of America*. Urbana: University of Illinois Press, 2008.

Waldinger, Roger, ed. *Strangers at the Gates: New Immigrants in Urban America*. Berkeley: University of California Press, 2001.

See also Asian Indian immigrants; Asian Pacific American Labor Alliance; Eastern European Jewish immigrants; Thai garment worker enslavement; Triangle Shirtwaist Company fire; Women immigrants.

GAY LESBIAN TRANSGENDER IMMIGRANTS AND ASYLUM SEEKERS

The Law: In the United States, asylum is granted to those who qualify as a particular social group; however, by definition, a group must have a common characteristic that either cannot change or should not have to change due to its fundamental identities or consciences. The size of the social group is immaterial; what matters is that there is social visibility. Therefore, a list of affected groups such as: race, religion, national origin, or political opinion does not qualify as sufficient enough to satisfy all affected refugees that the United States seeks to help. Instead, the asylum laws in the United States protect particular social groups. Under the Lesbian, Gay, Bisexual or Transgender (LGBT), asylum is granted under the particular social group category. LGBT candidates fit these categories under the section of common characteristic. While there are those who argue that their characteristic could be changed, it is something fundamental to one's identity; therefore, it should not be changed.

Date: In the United States, asylum on the basis of sexual orientation was first granted in 1994.

Immigration Issues: There are two issues surrounding how an LGBT can qualify for asylum. The key to qualifying as a social group is the group's social visibility. If the group is seen to exist in and by their culture, then it is likely to be considered a social group for asylum purposes. Therefore, the first instance is to showcase that the LGBT community in their homeland is sufficiently visible. The second instance is to showcase that ones treatment amounts to persecution on account of their LGBT identity.

Significance: The Williams Institute at UCLA, which researches sexual-orientation and gender-identity law and public policy, estimates that there are at least 267,000 LGBT individuals who comprise the over 11 million undocumented immigrants. It is also recognized that the actual number of LGBT individuals is likely much higher since its estimate does not account for the undocumented LGBT children or the adults who have openly identified themselves as LGBT. Legalizing the identified 267,000 of undocumented LGBT immigrants living in America and giving them a type of roadmap to citizenship would provide them with the legal certainty of not being separated from their families or communities. They would be able to seek work legally and to earn higher wages, which in turn allows them to become full and equal members of society.

Background Known as the "Gang of 8," four Senate Democrats—Chuck Schumer (NY), Dick Durbin (IL), Bob Menendez (NJ), and Michael Bennet (CO)—and four Senate Republicans—John McCain (AZ), Lindsay Graham (SC), Marco Rubio (FL), and Jeff Flake (AZ)—spent several months developing a proposal to fix the failing immigration system in the United States.

In April 2013, the "Gang of 8" filed a bill to reform the immigration system. On May 21, 2013, the Senate Judiciary Committee voted in favor of sending the Border Security, Economic Opportunity, and Immigration Modernization Act of 2013 to the Senate floor. The concepts within the bill offered immigration reform that secures the United States borders, eliminates immigration backlogs, and provides the more than 11 million undocumented people living in the United States a chance at citizenship.

Yet, this bill offers critical reform that would put undocumented immigrants—including the estimated 267,000 lesbian, gay, bisexual, and transgender, or LGBT, undocumented individuals—on a path toward obtaining the full rights and protections afforded to United States citizens.

Beyond offering undocumented immigrants a road map to citizenship, the bill before the Senate also offers critical safeguards to LGBT asylums seeking protection in the United States from the dozens of countries that criminalize homosexuality.

It also helps protect LGBT individuals in immigration detention facilities, who are often at a high risk for abuse, mistreatment, and physical and sexual violence.

Asylum for LGBT Immigrants Since the asylum laws speak to groups of people, increased visibility to the LGBT community and their rights have come into play whether or not the culture sufficiently considers them to be a separate group from other people. This is a step forward in the right direction for their community.

In fact, immigration courts have granted claims based on LGBT status for candidates from countries all over the globe, including: Albania, Argentina, Guyana, Indonesia, Jamaica, Lebanon, Morocco, and Uganda. At the same time, the immigration courts have rejected claims for candidates coming from Mexico, Peru, Nigeria, and Zimbabwe. With this in mind, just because asylum has not been granted to those countries' claims does not limit the possibility of accepting them in the future.

LGBT refugees in those cases need to showcase ample evidence that their particular government holds discriminatory attitudes towards their group. Additionally, LGBT asylum seekers also have to demonstrate persecution by their country on account of their sexual orientation or identity. For example, a country that deems it illegal for an LGBT person to have sex, then prosecution for could be

Performance by Rainbow Singers, a group of LGBT asylum seekers. (Ross Burgess)

321

evidence enough to demonstrate persecution. LGBT asylum seekers must consider that each case is taken as an individual one, and that while it is easier than it used to be to be granted asylum, theirs still may or may not result in such an outcome.

One other form of persecution that has resulted in successful asylum outcomes that impacts the LGBT community is persecution on account of an HIV/AIDS diagnosis, which qualifies as its own social group. There have been several cases in which people have been ostracized, and even denied medical treatment, in their countries due to their HIV positive status. Although the United States used to deny entry to anyone who was HIV positive, changes have been made that now support their arrivals and asylums.

Legislation In the United States, the Immigration Act of 1917 excluded individuals who were found "mentally defective" or who had a "constitutional psychopathic inferiority." A similar Public Health Service definition of homosexuals was determined by the Immigration and Naturalization Service (INS) to reinforce the language of the Immigration Act of 1917, which effectively banned all homosexual immigrants who disclosed their sexual minority status.

The enactment of the 1952 Immigration and Nationality Act (INA) continued the ban against the LGBT community. which prohibited entry into the country by "aliens afflicted with a psychopathic personality, epilepsy, or a mental defect." The INA did not specifically state whether or not the term "psychopathic personality" included homosexuality. However, in 1965 an amendment was made by Congress that added "sexual deviation" as a "medical ground for denying prospective immigrants entry into the United States."

It wasn't until 1990, a quarter of a century later, when Congress passed the Immigration Act of 1990 that finally withdrew the phrase "sexual deviation" from the INA. Four years later, in 1994, asylum was first granted on the basis of sexual orientation.

Since then, and through the supportive actions of the Department of Homeland Security, the LGBT has recently experienced administrative changes that were put in place to ensure that the LGBT asylum seekers are treated with dignity and are given a fair asylum hearing.

These policies are noted as significant steps forward. However, even with the new changes and when you consider that—according to estimates from the United Nations High Commissioner for Refugees—since 1998, the United States has processed approximately 46,000 asylum applications annually, only 62% of applicants were successful. While the laws have come a long way, there is still always room for improvement.

Heather Hummel

Further Reading

Yarbrough, Susan, *Bench-Pressed: A Judge Recounts the Many Blessings and Heavy Lessons of Hearing Immigration Asylum Cases*, iUniverse, March 22, 2013. A book that looks at asylum and immigration law as written by a former

United States immigration judge. She shares five significant asylum cases that profoundly changed her not only as a judge, but also as a person.

Grussendorf, Judge Paul Esq., *My Trials: Inside America's Deportation Factories*, CreateSpace, June 18, 2012. An account of the immigration court system as written by an immigration judge and based on his two decades of experience.

See also Cultural pluralism; Domestic abuse as a protected category (asylum); Refugees and racial/ethnic relations.

GENERATIONAL ACCULTURATION

Definition: Different degree and speed of changes in cultural patterns of groups when two or more ethnic and racial groups interact over a series of generations

Immigration issues: Chinese immigrants; Japanese immigrants; Language; Religion; Sociological theories

Significance: Although assimilation and acculturation are used interchangeably by sociologists and anthropologists, acculturation is a part of the assimilation process.

Since its colonial period, America has received immigrants from all over the world and created a mosaic of ethnic groups of various races, religions, and national origins. However, Anglo-Saxons from England had the greatest impact on American culture, particularly in American language, religion, and cultural values. Many ethnic and racial groups have gone through voluntary and involuntary acculturation processes over time to conform to this AngloSaxon culture. Members of the second generation (children of foreign-born parents) are more acculturated than their parents, and members of the third generation (children of native-born parents) are more acculturated than theirs. The concept of generational acculturation assumes that the foreign cultures that immigrants bring with them will be attenuated over generations.

Generational Difference The first generation of many immigrant groups established ethnic enclaves, such as Little Italies, Little Tokyos, Chinatowns, and Jewish communities, and provided new immigrants of the same national origin with elements of their old culture, including ethnic grocery stores, cafés, and restaurants, and protection from societal hostility. First-generation immigrants were able to function in their own ethnic enclaves without speaking English and without changing their religious faith or cultural values. These immigrants were structurally and culturally separated from each other and from the core society, thus creating what scholar Horace Kallen called "structural pluralism."

Members of the second generation (American-born children) in general, however, achieved English competence and acquired American values through the public school system and the mass media. Because of societal hostility toward immigrants who possessed cultural traits not derived from Euro-American culture, native-born children, who witnessed their parents' hardships, tended to abandon their parents' culture. The second generation's relinquishment of distinctive cultural traits frequently created a gap between them and their parents, who retained the cultural values of their nation of origin.

This poster issued by the federal government during World War II to remind Americans of the positive contributions made to the nation by immigrants draws upon the concept of the "melting pot"—one of the underpinnings of generational acculturation. (NARA)

Linear Model Historians often cite a theory of second-generation rejection, as if there were ironclad laws that dictated the cultural changes undergone by immigrant children. Generational acculturation tends to assume linear assimilation of immigrants to the core culture over generations. Members of the third generation (American-born children of American-born parents) are more acculturated than their parents. According to this linear model of generational acculturation, newer generations will either eventually be absorbed into Euro-American culture or contribute to creating the American melting pot.

Since the 1960's, scholars have frequently conducted research on Chinese and Japanese Americans to study generational differences in acculturation processes. Unlike most European immigrants, the first generations of Chinese and Japanese entered the mainland of the United States during a short and distinctive span of time;

then immigration was blocked. Chinese first entered the U.S. mainland as unskilled cheap labor during the 1850's, and their immigration was blocked by the Chinese Exclusion Act in 1882. After the exclusion of Chinese, the demand for cheap labor attracted the Japanese, and their immigration continued until it was restricted by the Immigration Act of 1924. For both groups, the second generation was born during a rather distinctive span of time, and even the third generation can be fairly well defined by span of years of birth. The three generations were also rather discrete birth cohorts and experienced distinctive acculturation processes in the change of cultural and behavioral patterns, in integration with whites, and in intermarriage with other racial and ethnic groups.

Nonlinear Model   In 1952, scholar Marcus Lee Hansen described a renewed interest in ethnicity among members of the third generation: "What the second generation tries to forget, the third generation tries to remember." He argued that there may be internal social and psychological forces rather than external social forces that explain the persistence of white ethnicity. Members of the second generation, who observed the hardships that their foreign-born parents had experienced, tended to de-emphasize their ethnicity and cultural traits to avoid prejudice and discrimination from the larger society. Hansen found that members of the third generation, who are more acculturated in terms of English skills and American values and are free from severe discrimination, try to reconnect with their grandparents and their ethnic roots.

Ethnogenesis theory, set forth by Andrew M. Greeley in *Ethnicity in the United States* (1974), also argues that ethnic identity and acculturation are situational. Although newer generations of immigrants share cultural traits with the host group, they also retain distinctive characteristics. This process of rejection and maintenance of original cultural traits is situational and contextual according to an ethnic group's nationality, mode of entrance to the United States, political and economic climate at the time of entrance, and a host of other factors. Therefore, according to Greeley, acculturation is neither linear nor accelerated over generations.

Scholars during the late twentieth century criticized the linear acculturation model, which assumed an Anglo-conformist perspective to analyze the acculturation process of ethnic and racial minority groups. These scholars argue that acculturation of these groups was a forced and involuntary process in order for them to be accepted as members of the host society. These processes are reflected in the episodes of boarding schools for Native American children, a different taxation system for Roman Catholics, prohibition of Spanish in public education, and so forth.

Acculturation Process for Later Immigrants   Generational acculturation of immigrants since the late 1980's is different from the patterns mentioned above. Recent immigrants tend to retain their distinctive cultural traits over generations because of the emphasis on cultural diversity in the workplace and in the educational system in American society. The motives behind cultural maintenance are also related to the social class of recent immigrants. Immigrants who lack English skills retain their own language out of necessity, but immigrants who possess English skills and high socioeconomic status retain their language and culture out of desire. These immigrant parents hope their children will become bilingual and bicultural—able to speak two languages and live in two cultures. With an increasing number of immigrants expected in the twenty-first century and a continuing appreciation of diversity, more and more immigrants are expected to retain their distinctive cultural traits.

Hisako Matsuo

Further Reading

Bratina, Michele P. *Acculturation and Attitudes Toward Violence Among Latinos.* El Paso: LFB Scholarly Publishing LLC 2013. A study of how attitudes toward violence among Latino men change with assimilation, and what role is played by other factors.

Gordon, Milton. *Assimilation in American Life: The Role of Race, Religion, and National Origins.* New York: Oxford University Press, 1964. Seminal work that remains the standard reference on the assimilation process.

Greeley, Andrew M. *Ethnicity in the United States: A Preliminary Reconnaissance.* New York: John Wiley & Sons, 1974. Exposition of Greeley's ethnogenesis theory, which argues that ethnic identity and acculturation are situational. Hansen, Marcus Lee. "The Third Generation in America" Commentary 14 (1952). Presentation of Hansen's theories on third-generation immigrants.

Kallen, Horace. *Culture and Democracy in the United States.* New York: Boni & Liveright, 1924. Presents Kallen's views on structural pluralism.

Lai, H. Mark. *Becoming Chinese American: A History of Communities and Institutions.* Walnut Creek, Calif.: AltaMira, 2004. Study of cultural adaptations of Chinese immigrants to the United States. Includes chapters on Chinese cultural and rights advocacy organizations.

Ling, Huping. *Voices of the Heart; Asian American Women on Immigration, Work, and Family.* Kirksville, MO: Truman State University Press, 2007. A study of the acculturation process of Asian American women living in the Midwest.

Matsuo, Hisako. "Identificational Assimilation of Japanese Americans: A Reassessment of Primordialism and Circumstantialism." *Sociological Perspectives* 35 (1992). Examination of the assimilation process among Japanese Americans.

Rumbaut, Rubén G., and Alejandro Portes, eds. *Ethnicities: Children of Immigrants in America.* Berkeley: University of California Press, 2001. Collection of papers on demographic and family issues relating to immigrants. Includes chapters on Mexicans, Cubans, Central Americans, Filipinos, Vietnamese, Haitians, and other West Indians.

Singh, Jaswinder, and Kalyani Gopal. *Americanization of New Immigrants: People Who Come to America and What They Need to Know.* Lanham, Md.: University Press of America, 2002. Sur vey of the cultural adjustments through which new immigrants to the United States must go.

Waldinger, Roger, ed. *Strangers at the Gates: New Immigrants in Urban America.* Berkeley: University of California Press, 2001. Collection of essays on urban aspects of immigration in the United States, particularly race relations, employment, and generational acculturation.

See also Assimilation theories; Ethnic enclaves; Hansen effect; Melting pot.

GENTLEMEN'S AGREEMENT

The Treaty: Treaty between the United States and Japan that limited immigration from Japan to the mainland United States to nonlaborers, laborers already settled in the United States, and their families

Date: March 14, 1907

Place: United States and Japan

Immigration issues: Asian immigrants; Government and politics; Japanese immigrants; Laws and treaties

Significance: As a consequence of this 1907 agreement between the U.S. and Japanese governments, immigration from Japan to the mainland United States was limited to nonlaborers, laborers already settled in the United States, and their families.

The first Japanese immigrants who arrived in California in 1871 were mostly middle-class young men seeking opportunities to study or improve their economic status. By 1880, there were 148 resident Japanese. Their numbers increased to 1,360 in 1891, including 281 laborers and 172 farmers. A treaty between the United States and Japan in 1894 ensured mutual free entry although allowing limitations on immigration based on domestic interests. By 1900, the number of Japanese recorded in the U.S. Census had increased to 24,326. They arrived at ports on the Pacific coast and settled primarily in the Pacific states and British Columbia.

An increase in the demand for Hawaiian sugar in turn increased the demand for plantation labor, especially Japanese labor. An era of government-contract labor began in 1884, ending only with the U.S. annexation of Hawaii in 1898. Sixty thousand Japanese in the islands then became eligible to enter the United States without passports. Between 1899 and 1906, it is estimated that between forty thousand and fifty-seven thousand Japanese moved to the United States via Hawaii, Canada, and Mexico.

Tensions Develop On the Pacific coast, tensions developed between Asians and other Californians. Although the Japanese immigrant workforce was initially welcomed, antagonism increased as these immigrants began to compete with U.S. labor. The emerging trade-union movement advocated a restriction of immigration. An earlier campaign against the Chinese had culminated in the 1882 Chinese Exclusion Act, which suspended immigration of Chinese laborers to the United States for ten years. This act constituted the first U.S. law barring immigration based on race or nationality. A similar campaign was instigated against the Japanese. On March 1, 1905, both houses of the California state legislature voted to urge California's congressional delegation in Washington, D.C., to pursue the limitation of Japanese immigrants. At a meeting in San Francisco on May 7, delegates from sixty-seven organizations launched the Japanese and Korean Exclusion League, known also as the Asiatic Exclusion League.

President Theodore Roosevelt, who was involved in the peace negotiations between Japan and Russia, observed the developing situation in California. George Kennan, who was covering the Russo-Japanese War, wrote to the president:

> It isn't the exclusion of a few emigrants that hurts here... it's the putting of Japanese below Hungarians, Italians, Syrians, Polish Jews, and degraded nondescripts from all parts of Europe and Western Asia. No proud, high spirited and victorious people will submit to such a classification as that, especially when it is made with insulting reference to personal character and habits.

Roosevelt agreed, saying he was mortified that people in the United States should insult the Japanese. He continued to play a pivotal role in resolving the Japanese-Russian differences at the Portsmouth Peace Conference.

Anti-Japanese feeling waned until April, 1906. Following the San Francisco earthquake, an outbreak of crime occurred, including many cases of assault against Japanese. There was also an organized boycott of Japanese restaurants. The Japanese viewed these acts as especially reprehensible. Their government and Red Cross had contributed more relief for San Francisco than all other foreign nations combined.

Tension escalated. The Asiatic Exclusion League, whose membership was estimated to be 78,500 in California, together with San Francisco's mayor, pressured the San Francisco school board to segregate Japanese schoolchildren. On October 11, 1906, the board passed its resolution. A protest filed by the Japanese consul was denied. Japan protested that the act violated mostfavored-nation treatment. Ambassador Luke E. Wright, in Tokyo, reported Japan's extremely negative feelings about the matter to Secretary of State Elihu Root. This crisis in Japanese American relations brought the countries to the brink of war. On October 25, Japan's ambassador, Shuzo Aoki, met with Root to seek a solution. President Roosevelt, who recognized the justification of the Japanese protest based on the 1894 treaty, on October 26 sent his secretary of commerce and labor to San Francisco to investigate the matter.

President Theodore Roosevelt. (Library of Congress)

In his message to Congress on December 4, President Roosevelt paid tribute to Japan and strongly repudiated San Francisco for its antiJapanese acts. He encouraged Congress to pass an act that would allow naturalization of the Japanese in the United States. Roosevelt's statements and request pleased Japan but aroused further resentment on the Pacific coast. During the previous twelve months, more than seventeen thousand Japanese had entered the mainland United States, two-thirds coming by way of Hawaii. Roosevelt recognized that the basic cause of the unrest in California—the increasing inflow of Japanese laborers—could be resolved only by checking immigration.

U.S. and Japan Negotiate Negotiations with Japan to limit the entry of Japanese laborers began in late December, 1906. Three issues were involved: the rescinding of the segregation order by the San Francisco school board, the withholding of passports to the mainland United States by the Japanese government, and the closing of immigration channels through Hawaii, Canada, and Mexico by federal legislation. The Hawaiian issue, which related to an earlier Gentlemen's Agreement of 1900, was the first resolved through the diplomacy of Japan's foreign minister, Tadasu Hayashi, ambassadors Wright and Aoki, and Secretary of State Root.

Before Japan would agree to discuss immigration to the mainland, it was necessary for the segregation order to be withdrawn. In February, 1907, the president invited San Francisco's entire board of education, the mayor, and a city superintendent of schools to Washington, D.C., to confer on the segregation issue and other problems related to Japan. On February 18, a pending immigration bill was amended to prevent Japanese laborers from entering the United States via Hawaii, Mexico, or Canada.

Assured that immigration of Japanese laborers would be stopped, the school board rescinded their segregation order on March 13. An executive order issued by the president on March 14 put into effect the restrictions on passports.

Japanese sugar plantation workers in Hawaii around 1890. (Hawaii State Archives)

Subsequently, the Japanese government agreed to conclude the Gentlemen's Agreement. In January, 1908, Foreign Minister Hayashi agreed to the terms of immigration discussed in December, 1907. On March 9, Secretary of State Root instructed Ambassador Wright to thank Japan, thus concluding the negotiations begun in December, 1906.

As reported by the commissioner general of immigration in 1908, the Japanese government would issue passports for travel to the continental United States only to nonlaborers; laborers who were former residents of the United States; parents, wives, or children of residents; and "settled agriculturalists." A final provision prevented secondary immigration into the United States by way of Hawaii, Mexico, or Canada.

When the Gentlemen's Agreement of 1907 cut off new supplies of Japanese labor, Filipinos were recruited to take their place, both in Hawaii and in California, as well as in the Alaskan fishing industry. As U.S. nationals, Filipinos could not be prevented from migrating to the United States.

Susan E. Hamilton

Further Reading

Esthus, Raymond A. *Theodore Roosevelt and Japan*. Seattle: University of Washington Press, 1967. Extensive, detailed examination of President Theodore Roosevelt's relationship with Japan.

Kikumura, Akemi. *Issei Pioneers: Hawaii and the Mainland, 1885 to 1924*. Los Angeles: Japanese American National Museum, 1992. Brief but well-researched text, with photographs that accompanied the premiere exhibit of the Japanese American National Museum.

LeMay, Michael C., and Elliott Robert Barkan, eds. *U.S. Immigration and Naturalization Laws and Issues: A Documentary History*. Westport, Conn.: Greenwood Press, 1999. Comprehensive history of American immigration policy.

Ngai, Mae, and Jon Gjerde. *Major Problems in American Immigration History: Documents and Essays*. 2nd ed. Boston: Wadsworth, Cengage Learning, 2013. A collection of essays and documents covering the history of immigration in U.S. history.

Shanks, Cheryl. *Immigration and the Politics of American Sovereignty, 1890-1990*. Ann Arbor: University of Michigan Press, 2001. Scholarly study of changing federal immigration laws from the late nineteenth through the late twentieth centuries, with particular attention to changing quota systems and exclusionary policies.

United States Department of State. *Report of the Hon. Roland S. Morris on Japanese Immigration and Alleged Discriminatory Legislation Against Japanese Residents in the United States*. 1921. Reprint. New York: Arno Press, 1978. Contemporary correspondence relating to the Gentlemen's Agreement.

See also Alien land laws; Border Patrol, U.S.; History of U.S. immigration; Immigration Act of 1921; Japanese immigrants; Japanese segregation in California schools; Picture brides; Women immigrants; "Yellow peril" campaign.

German and Irish immigration of the 1840's

The Event: Period during which more than one million Germans and Irish immigrated to the United States

Date: 1840's

Immigration issues: European immigrants; Irish immigrants; Nativism and racism

Significance: The years before the Civil War, during which there was an influx of Germans and Irish into the United States, was one of the most significant periods in U.S. immigration history.

Of the 31,500,000 persons counted in the 1840 U.S. Census, 4,736,000 were of foreign birth. That year's census also showed that the greatest number of immigrants had come from two countries: 1,611,000 from Ireland and 1,301,000 from Germany (principally from the southwestern states of Württemberg, Baden, and Bavaria). The migration, which had gained momentum in the years following the Napoleonic Wars, reached large numbers by the 1840's and grew dramatically during the 1850's, when more than one million Germans and Irish came to the United States. The Crimean War, the Panic of 1857, and the Civil War were among the events that brought an end to this wave of immigration.

When seen in broad perspective, the migration reflected the process of economic and social change that had gathered force in the period of peace after 1815. The rapid increase in the population of Europe served to magnify the evils that the factory system had brought about by displacing old societal patterns and swelling the army of paupers. Of far greater importance at the time, however, was the disruption of life for the agricultural masses. In Ireland, population pressures had led to a continuing subdivision of land and to a structure of paying rent to absentee landowners that amounted to economic persecution.

The remarkably fecund potato made this complex system possible, but events would soon uncover its tragic limitations. Dependence on the potato was not as great in southwestern Germany, but the process of subdividing the land there had grown considerably. Moreover, the encumbrance of ancient tithes and dues was compounded by a web of mortgages, as debts were incurred to improve farming practices. In both countries, tenant farmers constituted the bulk of emigrants before the 1840's. Yet their departure, inspired chiefly by the fear of losing status and not by immediate need, revealed that a long-run process of adjustment was in the making.

The potato famine precipitated this process. The blight began in 1845 and assumed devastating proportions by the following year. Untold suffering and death marked the movement of the Irish to the coast, where ship fever took its toll in 1847. Although the potato famine extended to Germany, there was less actual misery in the country. The rumor that the United States was about to close its gates, however, created a situation approaching panic among the many who were desperately seeking to emigrate before it was too late. The great exodus enabled a process of land consolidation to begin; consolidation, in turn, stimulated further emigration after the famine had passed. Repression in the wake of Europe's Revolution of 1848 also added political exiles to the tide of migration from Germany, but their numbers were small. The over whelming mass of people were driven by economic, rather than political, forces.

Patterns of commerce that had developed between North America and Europe made cheap transportation available and helped to determine the way the newcomers settled in the United States. Irish immigrants came by two major routes. Ships carrying timber from Canada to Ireland made the return trip with cargoes of emigrants, most of whom then began the trek southward to New England. Another route lay through Liverpool, where the cotton ships from Southern ports returned to Boston and New York. Once in the new land, the mostly unskilled Irish took whatever jobs were available. It was common for male immigrants to start in canal and railroad construction and then move into the mill towns to take on more permanent work in large urban areas.

Among the unique aspects of Irish immigration in the nineteenth century was that more women emigrated than men; thus, there were more Irish women than men in the United States throughout the century. Although female Irish immigrants have often been stereotyped as maids, they worked in many of the same occupations as other U.S. women in the nineteenth century and were often able to see their daughters move into higher-paying or more prestigious positions, such as that of schoolteacher.

Germans, on the other hand, were unique because of the large number of family groups that emigrated. Approximately two-thirds of the Germans who emigrated came as family groups. The first large group of German Jews came during the 1840's, as thousands fled social and economic persecution in Bavaria. The Germans, like the Irish, came by two basic routes, but greater diffusion and diversity characterized their settlement.

Many chose to stay in the East, while others moved westward along the Erie Canal through Buffalo and out to Ohio. By the 1840's, a larger contingent came to New Orleans on the cotton ships from Le Havre. Some remained in the South, notably in Texas, but the majority of German immigrants moved to the valleys of the Upper Ohio and Mississippi Rivers. There, as in the East, they brought a range of craft and professional skills into the urban centers. The vast number who settled on the land, meanwhile, generally preferred to buy farms already cleared by earlier settlers.

The reception of the newcomers was somewhat mixed. The abundance of space and the ideal of asylum generally tended to make the reception of immigrants favorable. Persons of influence, such as Governor William H. Seward of New York, added to this positive viewpoint by recognizing the contributions that immigrants had made to the development of the country. Opposition arose on several grounds, however. The influx of immigrants undoubtedly increased the problems of crime, poverty, unemployment, and disease, particularly in large urban areas. Bloc voting and the fear of political radicalism made many fear the newcomers.

The different customs of the Irish and Germans, such as German beer gardens and Irish wakes, offended many Americans. The belief that there was a papal plot among Irish and German Catholics to subvert Protestantism and democracy provided the greatest focus to nativist sentiments. During the 1850's, a nativist movement known as the Know-Nothings attempted to harness such feelings; its timing and rapid demise reflected less a fear of foreign influences than the internal tensions engendered by the conflict of slavery and the disruption of the Whig Party. Few people in the United States called for anything more than closing the gate on any undesirable immigrants, and the lengthening of the probationary period of citizenship from five to twenty-one years.

The significance of German and Irish immigration in the two decades prior to the Civil War lies in the cultural diversity they gave to the United States and the assistance they gave to the building of their new country.

Major L. Wilson
Judith Boyce DeMark

Further Reading

Clark, Dennis. *Hibernia America: The Irish and Regional Cultures.* Contributions in Ethnic Studies 14. Westport, Conn.: Greenwood Press, 1986. Discusses the Irish in the United States from the colonial era through the nineteenth century, with emphasis on the push/pull factors of immigration.

Diner, Hasia. *Erin's Daughters in America: Irish Immigrant Women in the Nineteenth Century.* Baltimore: Johns Hopkins University Press, 1983. Wellbalanced portrayal of Irish immigrant women, describing their lives in Ireland and their successes and failures in the United States.

Duffy, Jennifer Nugent. *Who's Your Paddy? Racial Expectations and the Struggle for Irish American Identity.* New York: New York University Press, 2014. A study of the development of a group identity among immigrants from Ireland.

Gabaccia, Donna R. *Immigration and American Diversity: A Social and Cultural History.* Malden, Mass.: Blackwell, 2002. Sur vey of American immigration history, from the mid-eighteenth century to the early twenty-first century, with an emphasis on cultural and social trends and attention to ethnic conflicts, nativism, and racialist theories.

Greene, Victor R. *A Singing Ambivalence: American Immigrants Between Old World and New, 1830-1930.* Kent, Ohio: Kent State University Press, 2004. Comparative study of the different challenges faced by members of eight major immigrant groups: the Irish, Germans, Scandinavians and Finns, eastern European Jews, Italians, Poles and Hungarians, Chinese, and Mexicans.

Griffin, William D. *A Portrait of the Irish in America.* New York: Charles Scribner's Sons, 1981. Photographic essay of Irish immigration, with detailed captions. Includes an introductory text with many drawings and photographs from the nineteenth century.

Levine, Bruce. *The Spirit of 1848: German Immigrants, Labor Conflict, and the Coming of the Civil War.* Urbana: University of Illinois Press, 1992. Discusses the relationship of Germans in Europe and the United States. Compares the Revolutions of 1848 and the American land debates that led to war.

Meltzer, Milton. *Bound for America: The Story of the European Immigrants*. New York: Benchmark Books, 2001. Broad history of European immigration to the United States written for young readers.

Ngai, Mae, and Jon Gjerde. *Major Problems in American Immigration History: Documents and Essays*. 2nd ed. Boston: Wadsworth, Cengage Learning, 2013. A collection of essays and couments coering the history of immigration in U.S. history.

Paulson, Timothy J. *Irish Immigrants*. New York: Facts On File, 2005. Brief sur vey of Irish immigrant history for young adult readers.

Rippley, LaVern J. *The German-Americans*. Boston: Twayne, 1976. Focuses on Germans in the United States in the nineteenth century. Discusses German American contributions to U.S. culture.

Wepman, Dennis. *Immigration: From the Founding of Virginia to the Closing of Ellis Island*. New York: Facts On File, 2002. History of immigration to the United States from the earliest European settlements of the colonial era through the mid-1950's, with liberal extracts from contemporary documents.

See also Anti-Irish Riots of 1844; Celtic Irish; European immigrants, 1790-1892; German immigrants; Irish immigrants; Irish immigrants and African Americans; Irish immigrants and discrimination; Irish stereotypes; Scotch-Irish immigrants.

GERMAN IMMIGRANTS

Identification: Immigrants to North America from Germany

Immigration issues: Demographics; European immigrants; Native Americans

Significance: Since the early nineteenth century, German Americans have constituted a major ethnic group in the United States. These early immigrants— Roman Catholic, Protestant, Separatist, and Jewish—assimilated relatively easily and completely and dispersed throughout the country. In contrast to other immigrant groups, such as the Irish, Italians, and Poles, few negative characteristics were attributed to Germans.

The first German colony was established in Germantown, Pennsylvania, in 1683 by Mennonites, an Anabaptist sect. (The Amish later separated from the Mennonites.) However, individual Germans were already present in the English colonies and in the Dutch colony of New Amsterdam. The Hutterites, another Anabaptist sect, came to America in 1874, settling in South Dakota. Although pacifists, they were subjected to conscription during World War I. Most of the community migrated to Canada, but many later returned. Two Hutterites who were sentenced for refusing conscription died from maltreatment.

Methodism developed a following among German Americans in the nineteenth century, and although the Methodist Church began phasing out the German branch in 1924, some congregations of the German Methodist Church persisted throughout the twentieth century. Germans also set up Baptist and Presbyterian Churches. By 1890, nearly half of German Americans were Roman Catholic. Catholics and Lutherans did not mix much, which tended to divide German American political influence. The German and Irish wings of the American Catholic Church experienced some conflict during the 1880's and 1890's, and before World War I, German, Irish, and Polish congregations attended separate Catholic churches. Similarly, German and Scandinavian congregations often established separate Lutheran churches, and German American and eastern European Jews generally formed separate worship groups, although the eastern European Jews commonly spoke Yiddish, which is more than 80 percent German. German American Jews maintained cultural ties with Germany until the Nazi period.

Relations with American Indians The Germans seemed to have less trouble with American Indians than other settlers in the eighteenth century, and in Texas, where thriving German settlements were established during the 1830's and 1840's, the Meusenbach-Comanche Treaty of 1847, negotiated between John Meusenbach and Comanche leaders Buffalo Hump, Santana, and Old Owl, was never broken by either side.

German emigrants embarking for the United States at the port of Hamburg. (National Archives)

Two German travelers and a German American made significant contributions to American Indian ethnology. Alexander Philipp Maximilian, Prince of Wied-Neuwied, visited the United States in 1832 and produced a comprehensive study of the Mandan tribe, which later became extinct. Friedrich Gerstäcker, who visited the United States from 1837 to 1843 and again in 1849 and 1867, created a detailed ethnography of American Indian culture. German American Gustavus Sohon, born in Prussia, served in the U.S. Army as a surveyor in the Northwest. There he became familiar with several American Indian tribes along the Columbia River and made numerous sketches of their lives, which are a valuable part of the anthropological record.

German Americans and Slavery Various German American groups spoke out against slavery in the United States. The Mennonites of Germantown, Pennsylvania, made the first protest in 1688. The Salzburger Protestant colony of Ebenezer in Georgia, founded in 1734, also opposed slavery.

The failed Revolution of 1848, during which reactionary authorities in Berlin and Vienna suppressed attempts at constitutional reform, resulted in thousands of liberal intellectuals migrating to the United States. These new immigrants, who were particularly active in establishing newspapers, had a major impact on the cultural life of German American communities. The Forty-eighters, as they were known, were strongly opposed to slavery, and under their influence, a strong alliance formed between abolitionist forces and the German press in the United States.

Among the Forty-eighters was Mathilde Franziska Anneke-Giesler, an early champion of women's rights who came to the United States in 1850. Although she wrote almost exclusively in German, she was in close contact with suffragists Susan B. Anthony and Elizabeth Cady Stanton and often lectured in English. Antagonism to her feminist and antislavery attitudes caused her to go to England in 1860, where she lectured against slavery, returning to the United States in 1865.

In 1854, Germans meeting in San Antonio, Texas, declared their opposition to slavery, and German Americans fought on the North's side during the Civil War. In a battle with Confederate soldiers, one German American guard of sixty-five men lost twenty-seven people and had nine of its wounded murdered by opposition forces.

Relations with Anglo-Saxon Society During the early nineteenth century, the German community in New York was significant enough to be courted by both political parties. A German Democratic Party organization was created in 1834, and eventually a German language newspaper was established to reflect the party's platform.

The years before the Civil War saw the rise of nativism, and anti-Catholicism was rampant. In 1855, murderous rioters in Louisville, Kentucky, attacked German Americans because many of them were Catholic and foreign-born and tended to be politically radical. The German Americans' opposition to slavery also created hostility in several regions.

German Americans experienced some friction with Anglo-Saxon Protestants of a puritanical bent, who disdained frivolity, especially on Sunday, and disliked some German customs associated with Christmas because they appeared to be pagan in origin. This immigrant group also clashed with the growing temperance movement in the nineteenth and twentieth centuries. The breweries founded by Germans in cities such as Cincinnati, Ohio; Milwaukee, Wisconsin; and St. Louis, Missouri, contributed to the economic development of these cities, and German Americans largely controlled the American brewing industry.

German Americans in Texas kept that state from becoming a dry state until national Prohibition went into effect. One of the major purposes of the German American Alliance was to oppose Prohibition. The German American Alliance (Deutsch-Amerikanische Nationalbund) was formed in 1901 as a national, sectarian, politically nonpartisan German American organization. It reached a membership of three million by 1916 to become the largest ethnic organization in U.S. history. Congress abrogated the organization's charter in 1918. Germans were also active in the labor movement that began after the Civil War and in radical politics, which caused some conflict with the dominant society.

World War I U.S. entry into World War I unleashed a tremendous irrational hostility toward anything German, including music—not just folk or popular music but classical music and opera. German Americans were harassed and subjected to physical assault, vandalism, and even murder. This hysteria existed even in areas where German Americans constituted more than onethird of the population or

German immigrants celebrating at a folklore festival in Washington, D.C. The slogan on the banner translates as "A Toast, a toast to happiness: One, two, three, drink up!" (Smithsonian Institution)

337

even a majority.

Laws in various states forbade teaching German in schools and speaking German in public, and thousands were convicted. Such laws were declared unconstitutional by the U.S. Supreme Court in 1923. Anti-German attitudes lingered for a few years after the war and accelerated Anglicization of churches, social organizations, and newspapers.

World War II In 1936, the Deutschamerikanische Volksbund, the German American Bund, replaced an earlier organization intended to represent the Nazi Party in the United States. The membership was believed to be only sixtyfive hundred, and 40 percent were not actually of German stock, but the organization's posturing, arrogance, and hostility in effect mobilized public opinion against the Nazis and complicated diplomatic relations between the United States and Germany. The Steuben Society, the most prestigious German American organization, and other German organizations felt it necessary to repudiate the Bund, and German American antifascist organizations were formed.

After World War II, German American ethnic identity became increasingly tenuous as the population moved to the suburbs, and changes in recreational tastes weakened ties to German culture. Postwar German immigrants were less inclined to take part in German cultural organizations.

In 1948, the Russian blockade of the land routes to West Berlin made that city, and by extension West Germany, a symbol of freedom and democracy, giving Americans a more positive attitude toward Germany. West Germany became a military ally, and during the second half of the century, became increasingly integrated into the pan-European identity of the European Union. Similarly, German Americans came to identify more with the broader European American culture.

William L. Reinshagen

Further Reading

Victor R. Greene's *A Singing Ambivalence: American Immigrants Between Old World and New, 1830-1930* (Kent, Ohio: Kent State University Press, 2004) is a comparative study of challenges faced by members of eight major immigrant groups including Germans.

LaVern Ripley's *The German-Americans* (Boston: Twayne, 1976) is a well-written history of Germans in the United States from colonial times to the U.S. Bicentennial, explaining contemporaneous events in German Europe and mentioning prominent German Americans.

Alfred Llau's *Deutschland––United States of America, 1683-1983* (Bielefeld, Germany: Univers-Verlag, 1983) covers three hundred years of immigration and German-American relations.

Gerard Wilk's *Americans from Germany* (New York: German Information Center, 1976) focuses particularly on the experiences of German Americans over the years, and Irene M. Franck's *The German American Heritage* (New York: Facts On File, 1988) provides details and statistical information.

German Culture in Texas, edited by Glen E. Lich and Dona B. Reeves (Boston:

Twayne, 1980), is a collection of articles on various aspects of the German regions of Texas.

Barbara Schmitter Heisler's *From German Prisoner of War to American Citizen: A Social History with 35 Interviews* (Jefferson, NC: McFarland & Company, 2013) studies the experience of German POWs during World War II who became American citizens.

The University of Wisconsin publishes *The Yearbook of German American Studies* and annotated bibliographies.

See also Ashkenazic and German Jewish immigrants; English-only and official English movements; Euro-Americans; European immigrants, 1790-1892; German and Irish immigration of the 1840's; Jewish immigrants; War brides; War Brides Act.

GONZÁLEZ RESCUE

The Event: Rescue of Elián González, a young Cuban boy who survived the sinking of a refugee boat off the coast of Florida
Date: November 25, 1999
Place: Miami, Florida

Immigration issues: Border control; Cuban immigrants; Families and marriage; West Indian immigrants

Significance: González's rescue and transportation to Florida touched off a long battle between his relatives in Miami and his father in Cuba that influenced U.S. immigration policy and altered American images of Cuban Americans and their place in American society.

On November 22, 1999, a five-year-old Cuban boy named Elián González and thirteen other Cubans left Cardenas, Cuba, bound for the United States on a sixteen-foot motorboat. At 10 p.m., their boat capsized and Elián's mother, Elizabeth Brotons, and at least ten other passengers drowned. Three days later, Elián was found floating on an inner tube three miles from Ft. Lauderdale, Florida, and was taken to Hollywood Regional Medical Center. He was later released to his great-uncle, Lázaro González, by the Immigration and Naturalization Service (INS) until his immigration status could be determined.

Lázaro González and Elián's cousin Marisleysis González wanted to keep the boy in the United States, but Elián's father, Juan Miguel González, demanded that the boy be returned to him in Cuba. After González and his wife had divorced, Elián had lived with his mother, although the father, who had remarried, maintained a relationship with the boy. González believed that he had the right to claim his son, who was allegedly taken out of Cuba without his knowledge. Elián's stateside relatives argued that his mother had died bringing her son to the United States in search of freedom and that she would have wished for her child to live in the United States.

On December 8, Cuban president Fidel Castro demanded that Elián be returned to Cuba. After Castro's statement, Lázaro González submitted Elián's political asylum application to the INS. A policy created in 1994 grants any Cuban who makes it to land the right to apply for asylum and to stay in the United States. However, anyone caught before reaching land is sent back to Cuba.

Political Battle On January 5, the INS announced that Elián belonged with his father and must be returned to Cuba. However, Elián's Miami relatives' attorneys pleaded for the attorney general to reconsider the case. In Miami, in response to the INS statement, hundreds of Cuban American protesters blocked intersections and cut off access to the port. Many were arrested.

Following the protests, Lázaro González filed petitions for temporary custody of Elián in a Florida state court. Attorney General Janet Reno denied González's request to overturn the decision of the INS commissioner. On January 22, Elián's Cuban grandmothers came to the United States and met with Reno to appeal for Elián's return to Cuba. They also met with Elián but returned to Cuba without the boy.

One of the most dramatic moments in the Elián González case occurred during the early morning of April 22, 2000, when local police officers and agents of the Immigration and Naturalization Service burst into the home of the boy's Miami relatives and seized him.

Subsequently, Elián's Miami relatives argued for an asylum hearing. U.S. district judge K. Michael Moore was assigned to hear the case, and U.S. government lawyers asked Moore to dismiss the asylum lawsuit. Demonstrators tied up traffic outside the court, and others gathered outside the González home in support of the family. Judge Moore dismissed the lawsuit, and the INS informed the Miami relatives that it would revoke Elián's legal status in the United States and strip them of their right to care for him if they did not hand over the boy once the appeals were exhausted.

In March, Castro announced that he would send Juan Miguel González to the United States to pick up his son. The U.S. State Department approved visas for González, his wife, and their infant son as well as Elián's cousin, his teacher, and his pediatrician to travel to the United States. On April 6, the Cubans arrived in Washington, D.C. Following more demonstrations, Miami Dade mayor Alex Penelas called on the Cuban American community for peace.

Reno met with Elián's Miami relatives and ordered them to surrender the boy. However, the relatives defied the order and obtained a court order to keep Elián in the United States. The federal appeals court extended the court order until a May hearing. Nevertheless, on April 22, after long negotiations with Elián's Miami relatives and their lawyers, Reno gave orders for federal agents to seize Elián from their home. In response to the surprise 5:15 a.m. raid in which Elián was removed from the home, people in Miami rioted in the streets for two days. More than 268 people were arrested.

On May 11, the Eleventh U.S. Circuit Court of Appeals in Atlanta heard oral arguments from lawyers for Elián's father and Miami relatives. However, on June 1, the Atlanta federal court ruled Elián was not entitled to a political asylum hearing and upheld a Miami federal judge's ruling that Elián's father had the right to speak on his behalf. After several requests from the Miami relatives' attorneys, the court advised them that the injunction preventing Elián from leaving the United States would expire at 4 p.m. on June 28, and on that day, Elián, his father, and the rest of his family and friends returned to Cuba.

Consequences For Castro and his people, Elián represented a kidnapped child who should be returned to his father. The streets of Cardenas, Elián's place of birth, were filled with posters demanding Elián's return to Cuba. Castro's ultimatums and his handling of the situation may have enhanced his stature among his followers. However, some Cuba experts suggested that Castro used the situation to distract human rights advocates from political and human rights problems during 1999 in Cuba and his own people from severe economic problems during 2000. For Cuban Americans in Miami, Elián was a symbol of Cuban suffering and a poster child for the anti-Castro movement. They felt that he would have access to a more prosperous life in the United States and that once he returned to Cuba, he would live a life of communist brainwashing.

Although many Cuban Americans thought that trying to keep the boy in the United States was the right thing to do, influential voices questioned whether they should have made a five-year-old child a symbol of the battle against Castro. Others thought that the Elián saga weakened the influence of Cuban Americans in the U.S. government. Finally, the case raised an important question of who should decide a child's future—parents or government officials.

José A. Carmona

Further Reading

Coffey, Kendall. *Spinning the Law: Trying Cases in the Court of Public Opinion.* Amherst, NY: Prometheus Books, 2010.

Dubinsky, Karen: *Babies Without Borders: Adoption and Migration Across the Americas.* New York: New York University Press, 2010.

Levine, Robert M., and Moisés Asís. *Cuban Miami.* New Brunswick, N.J.: Rutgers University Press, 2000.

Stepick, Alex, et al. *This Land Is Our Land: Immigrants and Power in Miami.* Berkeley: University of California Press, 2003.

Zebich-Knos, Michele, and Heather Nicol. *Foreign Policy Toward Cuba: Isolation or Engagement?* Lanham, Md.: Lexington Books, 2005.

See also Coast Guard, U.S.; Cuban immigrants; Cuban refugee policy; Haitian boat people; Mariel boatlift; Refugees and racial/ethnic relations.

Green cards

Definition: Identification documents carried by immigrants in the United States certifying that they are legal residents

Immigration issues: Border control; Citizenship and naturalization; Illegal immigration; Labor; Law enforcement

Significance: Crucial possessions to resident aliens in the United States, green cards have come to symbolize the aspirations of many immigrants.

The formal name of the plastic identity cards certifying that their bearers are legally admitted resident aliens is Alien Registration Receipt Cards. First used during the 1940's, when the United States began registering and fingerprinting aliens as a wartime security precaution, the cards were originally green. They have continued to be known as "green cards," even though their color and design have been changed several times to deter forgery. They were blue during the 1960's and 1970's, white during the 1980's, and pink during the 1990's.

The cards are issued by the Immigration and Naturalization Service (INS) to aliens who have fully complied with the provisions of the immigration laws governing their admission to the United States as permanent residents eligible for naturalization. Each card contains the alien's name, photograph, thumbprint, date of birth, registration number, and an expiration date. Cards issued since 1989 expire after ten years.

The cards are highly valued, because they permit holders to legally seek gainful employment and to live undisturbed anywhere in the United States. Illegal aliens violate the immigration laws if they accept employment and are subject to deportation when discovered living in the United States. Students and visitors temporarily resident in the country are also barred from working and are subject to deportation if they overstay the visitor's period specified in their entrance visas.

Because of the value of green cards, a whole industry has sprung up to forge them. On occasion, INS employees have succumbed to the temptation to sell cards for substantial payments. Prices vary widely. In 1990, for example, an INS manager was accused of accepting more than

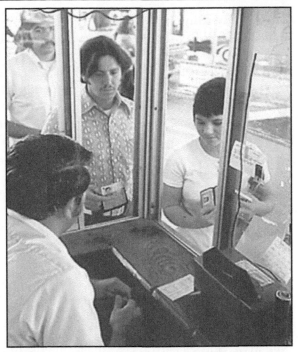

Mexican farmworkers presenting their green cards as they cross the border into the United States at Calexico to shop in American stores. (National Archives)

$100,000 in bribes from Colombian drug smugglers for supplying false official documents that authorized the issuance of authentic green cards. Reportedly, false green cards could be purchased for as little as twenty dollars in central Los Angeles. Even if crude, the cards permit employers to hire cheap labor while appearing to comply with the letter of the law, which prohibits them from knowingly hiring illegal aliens.

Green card holders are entitled to apply for naturalization as United States citizens after five years of residence provided they have not engaged in criminal activity, can read and write simple English, and demonstrate a basic knowledge of the history and government of the United States. They must pay income tax on all money earned anywhere in the world and cannot remain outside the country for more than one year without special permission. Aliens enjoy the civil rights, liberties, and due process of law guaranteed by the U.S. Constitution, as well as the protections of the Fifth and Sixth Amendments in criminal matters. When conscription is in force, green card holders can be drafted into the armed forces and may be required to register with the Selective Service. However, unlike American citizens, they are not entitled to U.S. passports or the protection of U.S. consulates when traveling abroad.

Milton Berman

Further Reading

Baldwin, Carl R. *Immigration: Questions and Answers.* New York: Allworth Press, 1995.

Becker, Aliza. *Citizenship for Us: A Handbook on Naturalization and Citizenship.* Washington, D.C.: Catholic Legal Immigration Network, 2002.

Kimmel, Barbara B., and Alan M. Lubiner. *Immigration Made Simple: An Easy Guide to the U.S. Immigration Process.* Rev. ed. Chester, N.J.: Next Decade, 1996.

LeMay, Michael C., and Elliott Robert Barkan, eds. *U.S. Immigration and Naturalization Laws and Issues: A Documentary History.* Westport, Conn.: Greenwood Press, 1999.

Lewis, Loida Nicolas. *How to Get a Green Card.* 6th ed. Berkeley, Calif.: Nolo, 2005.

Menjivar, Cecilia and Daniel Kanstroom, eds. *Constructing Immigrant 'Illegality': Critiques, Experiences, and Responses.* New York: Cambridge University Press, 2014.

Schoenholtz, Andrew Ian, Philip G. Schrag, and Jaya Ramji-Nogales, eds. *Lives in the Balance: Asylum Adjudication by the Department of Homeland Security.* New York: New York University, 2014.

See also Border Patrol, U.S.; Illegal aliens; Immigration law.

Gypsy immigrants

Identification: Immigrants to North America from various European countries who call themselves Rom

Immigration issues: European immigrants; Stereotypes

Significance: The United States is home to an estimated quarter of a million to one million people of Gypsy ancestry. Nevertheless, Gypsies are one of the least assimilated and most misunderstood ethnic groups in North America.

Most scholars believe that the Gypsies are descended from a caste of entertainers in ancient India. No one knows precisely why they left their original home, but ancient historical records report that thousands of these entertainers were sent to Persia in the ninth century b.c.e. From Persia, they apparently migrated to various parts of the Middle East, North Africa, and Europe.

Some Gypsies migrated to North America and Latin America during colonial times from the British Isles and from Spain and Portugal. The French emperor Napoleon Bonaparte deported hundreds of Gypsies from France to the then-French colony of Louisiana, which became part of the United States in 1803. During the late nineteenth and early twentieth centuries, North America received large waves

Gypsies living in Chicago's South Side in 1941. (Library of Congress)

of immigrants from southern Europe, and many Gypsies arrived at this time. The fall of European communism during the early 1990's led to another wave of Gypsy migration from eastern Europe.

Despite their long history in the United States, Gypsies have retained a distinctive ethnic identity and resisted assimilating into mainstream American culture. They frequently avoid census takers, and because of the negative stereotypes often attached to them, many Gypsies are somewhat secretive about their ethnic identity. Therefore, there is no precise count of the Gypsies in the United States, although estimates run from 250,000 to 1 million. The two largest Gypsy American groups are those who trace their ancestry to southern and eastern Europe and refer to themselves as the Rom and those who trace their ancestry to the British Isles and refer to themselves as Romnichals. Gypsies from Mexico, who migrated to the Americas from Spain, often call themselves Gitanos. Most Gypsy Americans speak some branch of the Romani language as well as English.

Modern Gypsies are less nomadic than their ancestors were, but Gypsies still move around much more often than most other Americans do. They tend to make their homes in large cities, where employment is available. The largest concentrations are found in Los Angeles, San Francisco, New York, Chicago, Boston, Atlanta, Dallas, Houston, Seattle, and Portland.

Relations between Gypsy Americans and other ethnic groups are often troubled by a lack of trust and understanding. Gypsy Americans do voluntarily remain separate from non-Gypsies, and traditional Gypsy belief even teaches that

345

non-Gypsies are ritually unclean. They prefer to avoid public schooling and often educate their children within their own families, which perpetuates their distinctiveness. Popular images of Gypsies stereotype them as romantic wanderers or as career criminals preying on all outsiders. Despite the latter stereotype, though, the conviction rates of Gypsy Americans for serious crimes such as rape and murder are actually lower than comparable rates of other Americans. Gypsy American conviction rates for theft, moreover, are no higher than those of the American population in general.

Carl L. Bankston III

Further Reading

Bhopal, Lawant, and Martin Myers. *Insiders, Outsiders, and Others: Gypsies and Identity*. Hatfield, Hertfordshire: University of Hertfordshire Press, 2009.

Meltzer, Milton. *Bound for America: The Story of the European Immigrants*. New York: Benchmark Books, 2001.

Sutherland, Anne. *Gypsies: The Hidden Americans*. London: Tavistock, 1975. Sway, Marlene. Familiar Strangers: Gypsy Life in America. Urbana: University of Illinois Press, 1988.

Tong, Diane, ed. *Gypsies: An Interdisciplinary Reader*. New York: Garland, 1998.

See also European immigrants, 1790-1892; European immigrants, 1892-1943; White ethnics; Xenophobia.

H-1B VISA

The Law: Because many companies seek experts from all over the world to fulfill certain, specialty positions at their companies, the H-1B visa is a solution for bringing in these employees on a temporary basis to complete the job. The H-1B is a United States granted, non-immigrant visa that falls under the Immigration and Nationality Act, section 101(a)(15)(H).

Date: 1990s

Immigration Issues: Under 8 U.S. Code § 1184 - Admission of non-immigrants, the H-1B is limited to those in "specialty occupations." These occupations are defined as requiring "theoretical and practical application of a body of highly specialized knowledge in a field of human endeavor including but not limited to biotechnology, chemistry, architecture, engineering, mathematics, physical sciences, social sciences, medicine and health, education, law, accounting, business specialties, theology, and the arts, and requiring the attainment of a bachelor's degree or its equivalent as a minimum (with the exception of fashion models, who must be 'of distinguished merit and ability')."

Significance: H-1B work-authorization is strictly limited to employment by sponsoring employers. In addition, the foreign employee cannot count on experience alone. They must also possess at least a bachelor's degree—or its equivalent—and state licensure, if required to practice in that field. Should foreign workers in H-1B status leave their position either by their choice or by the decision of the sponsoring employer, they must either apply for and be granted a change of status to another non-immigrant status, find another employer (subject to application for adjustment of status and/or change of visa), or leave the United States.

Background H-1B visas were put in place to grant international employees with specialty occupations to live and work in the United States in their chosen career for a temporary time period.

H-1B visa holders are considered to hold a non-immigrant visa, it is one of the few visa categories recognized as "dual intent," which means they can have legal immigration intent (apply for and obtain the green card) while still a holder of the visa.

Previously, the employment-based green card process took only a few years, less than the duration of the H-1B visa itself. Amazingly, the current process of the legal employment-based immigration is so backlogged and retrogressed that in most cases it takes many years for guest-work visa holders from certain countries to obtain their green cards.

However, because the period of time allotted for the H-1B visa remains the same, all too many H-1B visa holders have been forced to renew their visas in one or three-year increments in order to keep their legal status while their green card application is processed.

Duration of Stay The standard duration of stay for an H-1B visa holder is three years, at which time is extendable to six years. An exception to maximum length of stay applies in certain circumstances, as follows:

- If a visa holder has submitted an I-140 immigrant petition or a labor certification prior to their fifth year anniversary of having the H-1B visa, they are entitled to renew their H-1B visa in one-year or three-year increments until a decision has been rendered on their application for permanent residence.
- If the visa holder has an *approved* I-140 immigrant petition, but is unable to initiate the final step of the green card process due to their priority date not being current, they may be entitled to a three-year extension of their H-1B visa. This exception originated with the American Competitiveness in the Twenty-First Century Act of 2000.
- The maximum duration of the H-1B visa is ten years for exceptional United States Department of Defense project related work.

In some cases, H-1B holders want to remain working in the U.S. when the six years comes to conclusion; however, if they have not obtained permanent residency status, they must remain outside of the U.S. for one year before given the opportunity to reapply for another H-1B visa.

Known as the H-1B portability or transfer, there is no condition that requires the individual to remain for any specific period of time in the original position. The only stipulation is that the new employer sponsors another H-1B visa, which could possibly be subjected to the quota. Under current law, H-1B visa has no stipulated grace period should the employer-employee relationship ceases to exist.

Congressional Yearly Numerical Cap Under current law, the limit to the number of foreign nationals who can receive an H-1B visa is 65,000 per fiscal year. However, there are laws that exempt up to 20,000 foreign nationals who have a master's or higher degree from a U.S. university. Also excluded from the 65,000 ceiling are all H-1B non-immigrants who are either employees or contractors for universities, non-profit research facilities associated with universities or government research facilities.

Each year on the first business day in April, the United States Citizenship and Immigration Services starts accepting applications for visas that count against the fiscal year starting in October. USCIS accepts H-1B visa applications no more than 6 months prior to the requested start date. Beneficiaries not subject to the annual cap are those who currently hold cap-subject H-1B status or have held cap-subject H-1B status at some point in the past six years.

American Competitiveness in the Twenty-First Century Act of 2000 The American Competitiveness in the Twenty-First Century Act of 2000 (AC21) and the U.S. Department of Labor's PERM system for labor certification erased most of the earlier claimed arguments for H-1Bs as indentured servants during the green card process.

Due to AC21, H-1B employees can change jobs if they have the following requirements in place:

- An I-485 application pending for six months
- An approved I-140
- The position they move to must be substantially comparable to their current position

However, many people are ineligible to file I-485 at the current time due to the widespread retrogression in priority dates. Therefore, it is possible that they will be unable to change jobs for many years, leaving them at the mercy of the sponsoring employer.

American Recovery and Reinvestment Act of 2009 On Feb. 17, 2009, President Obama signed into law the American Recovery and Reinvestment Act of 2009 ("stimulus bill"), Public Law 111-5. Section 1661 of the ARRA incorporates the Employ American Workers Act ("EAWA") by Senators Sanders (I-Vt.) and Grassley (R-Iowa) which puts limits on certain banks and other financial institutions from hiring H-1B workers unless they first offered positions to U.S. workers who were equally or better-qualified. The goal is to keep banks from hiring H-1B workers in occupations they had laid off U.S. workers from.

Changes in USCIS policy In a USCIS Interoffice Memorandum from Michael Aytes, Associate Director, Domestic Operations, to all Regional Directors and Service Center Directors, dated December 5, 2006, and upon policy review, the USCIS determined that individuals who spent more than one year outside of U.S. and did not exhaust their entire six-year term could then choose to be re-admitted for the "remainder" of initial six-year period without being subject to the H-1B cap.

The USCIS clarified that, "Any time spent in H-4 status will not count against the six-year maximum period of admission applicable to H-1B aliens."

Four years later, USCIS issued a memorandum dated January 8, 2010, which stated a clear "employee employer relationship" must exist between the petitioner (employer) and the beneficiary (prospective visa holder). It states the steps that must be taken by the employer to be considered in compliance, and it showcases the documentation requirements to back up the employer's assertion that a valid relationship exists.

In the memorandum, there were three stated examples of what is considered a valid "employee employer relationship":

- A fashion model
- A computer software engineer working off-site/on-site
- A company or a contractor which is working on a co-production product in collaboration with DOD

In the case of the software engineer, the petitioner must agree to do all or a portion of the following:

- Supervise the beneficiary on and off-site
- Maintain such supervision through calls, reports, or visits
- Have a "right" to control the work on a day-to-day basis *if such control is required*
- Provide tools for the job
- Hire, pay, and have the ability to fire the beneficiary
- Evaluate work products and perform progress/performance reviews
- Claim them for tax purposes
- Provide (some type of) employee benefits
- Use "proprietary information" to perform work
- Produce an end product related to the business
- Have an "ability to" control the manner and means in which the worker accomplishes tasks

Heather Hummel

Further Reading
Back, James and Werner, Robert G., *How to Secure Your H-1B Visa: A Practical Guide for International Professionals and Their U.S. Employers*, Apress; 1

edition, January 22, 2013. A book penned by authors from Silicon Valley who are immigration lawyers with a combined 60 years of experience in handling professional work visas.

Beaudry, Dan, *Power Ties: The International Student's Guide to Finding a Job in the United States*, Lulu, October 22, 2009. The author, former head of campus recruiting at Monster.com, and former Associate Director of Corporate Recruiting at the Boston University School of Management, shares information from the job search system he has used to help many international students find employment in the United States.

See also Brain drain; Demographics of immigration; Undocumented workers.

HAITIAN BOAT PEOPLE

Definition: Haitian refugees who attempt to reach the United States on small boats

Immigration issues: African Americans; Border control; Illegal immigration; Refugees; West Indian immigrants

Significance: During the mid-1980's, increasing numbers of Haitians attempted to reach the United States by boat to escape the political chaos in their homeland. U.S. policy toward these illegal immigrants has varied between receiving the Haitians as refugees and treating them as unwanted illegal aliens.

On January 31, 1992, the U.S. Supreme Court voted, by a vote of six to three, with Justices Clarence Thomas, Harry A. Blackmun, and John Paul Stevens dissenting, to grant the government's motion to stay an injunction prohibiting the forcible return of Haitians who had fled their country. Attorney General William Barr stated that the government now had clear authority to return the more than nine thousand Haitian refugees held at Guantánamo Naval Base in Cuba. That authority would remain in force until a decision on repatriation could be made by the United States Court of Appeals of the Eleventh Circuit in Atlanta, and that decision appealed to the Supreme Court.

In the weeks preceding the lifting of the injunction, the number of refugees fleeing Haiti had increased dramatically. When the government could no longer accommodate the refugees aboard the Coast Guard cutters patrolling the waters between Haiti and the United States, the naval base at Guantánamo was prepared for them. The base quickly became overcrowded as more refugees arrived daily. The U.S. State Department estimated that only one-third of the refugees qualified for political asylum. The remaining refugees were fleeing economic conditions.

Hours after the Supreme Court lifted the injunction, the Coast Guard cutter Steadfast, with 150 Haitians on board, sailed from Guantánamo on the ten- to twelve-hour voyage to Port-au-Prince, the Haitian capital. Additional Haitians were sent back in the next two days. Previously, about four hundred Haitians had returned voluntarily through the United Nations High Commissioner for Refugees.

President George Bush had strongly condemned the growing political violence in Haiti. On January 25, 1992, he recalled Ambassador Alvin P. Adams, Jr., following an attack by police officers in civilian clothes on a political meeting called by Communist Party leader René Theodore, who had been nominated prime minister in a compromise concluded several weeks before the meeting. President Bush believed that chances for a political settlement in Haiti were decreasing and was concerned that the increasing number of Haitian refugees would be too large for the United States to handle. Opposition to the administration's repatriation policy was raised by civil rights groups and others who charged that the policy was racist. Their attempt to stop the program by injunction had delayed the return of the boat people but did not stop it.

The Refugee Problem In February of 1986, the military seized power in Haiti after a thirty-year rule by the Duvalier family. François Duvalier had ruled from 1956 to 1971 and his son Jean-Claude Duvalier ruled from 1971 to 1986. After 1986, the military continued the extremely repressive and brutal policies of the Duvaliers. In 1990, popular demonstrations and a general strike brought about the downfall of the military, followed by open elections in December. Jean-Bertrand Aristide, a Roman Catholic priest, was elected president. He advocated far-reaching political reforms and social changes. He was able to remain in office not quite a year before being overthrown by the military.

Amnesty International reported that under military rule the Haitian people were living in a climate of fear and repression and that hundreds of people were extrajudicially executed or were detained without warrant and tortured. Many were brutally beaten in the streets. Freedom of the press was severely curtailed, and property was destroyed by members of the military and the police.

The nations of the Organization of American States, including the United States, imposed an embargo to pressure Haiti for the return of the duly elected president to power. The embargo added to the problems of the Haitian people, who were the poorest in the Western Hemisphere. Shortages of fuel, food, medicines, and potable water developed, and unemployment increased because factories had to close when they ran out of fuel. More than

140,000 Haitians fled after the coup. During the month of January, 1992, 6,653 were picked up at sea. The Bush administration felt compelled to return those Haitians it regarded as economic, rather than political, refugees.

The United States government had begun returning Haitians in November, 1991, but at the end of the year had been restrained by the injunction obtained by civil rights advocates in Miami, Florida. The Bush administration feared that at least an additional twenty thousand Haitians would flee the island. The lifting of the injunction in January, 1992, gave the administration a victory. The return of refugees resumed with the voyage of the Steadfast.

Consequences The Supreme Court again refused, on February 11, 1992, to end the return of the refugees, and the repatriation program continued. When opponents failed to stop the program by court order, they turned to Congress. Representative Charles E. Summer, a member of the House Subcommittee on International Law, Immigration, and Refugees, introduced legislation granting Haitians protected status that would permit them to stay in the United States until Haiti's military government was overthrown. The proposed legislation also granted a quota of two thousand refugees from Haiti. The legislation was not passed.

The repatriation problem was solved in September, 1994, when President Bill Clinton sent former president Jimmy Carter, General Colin L. Powell, and Senator Sam Nunn to negotiate an agreement with General Raoul Cédras, the ruler of Haiti, for the return of Aristide to serve the remainder of his term. United States forces temporarily occupied Haiti to ensure an orderly transition of political power and the development of democratic government. The United States obtained a foreign policy victory in 1994 with the return of Aristide to the presidency in Haiti—where he was again ousted in 2004. At the same time, the problem of Haitians fleeing to the United States was solved. Civil rights groups in the United States and abroad, however, criticized U.S. policy on the basis of humanitarian and civil rights concerns. Others charged the United States with racism. Overall, the gamble by President Clinton when he sent troops into Haiti redounded to his credit and gave a boost to his foreign policy.

Robert D. Talbott

Further Reading

Blake, Nicholas J., and Razan Husain. *Immigration, Asylum and Human Rights.* New York: Oxford University Press, 2003.

Laguerre, Michel S. *Diasporic Citizenship: Haitian Americans in Transnational America.* New York: St. Martin's Press, 1998.

Legomsky, Stephen H. *Immigration and Refugee Law and Policy.* 3d ed. New York: Foundation Press, 2002.

Okpewho, Isidore, and Nkiru Nzweghu, eds. *The New African Daspora.* Bloomington: Indiana University Press, 2009.

Shaw-Taylor, Yoku, and Steven A. Tuch, eds. *The Other African Americans Contemporary African and Caribbean Immigrants in the United States.* Lanham: Rowman & Littlefield, 2007.

Stepick, Alex. P*ride Against Prejudice: Haitians in the United States.* Boston: Allyn & Bacon, 1998.

Yoshida, Chisato, and Alan D. Woodland. *The Economics of Illegal Immigration.* New York: Palgrave Macmillan, 2005.

Zéphir, Flore. *The Haitian Americans.* Westport, Conn.: Greenwood Press, 2004.

See also González rescue; Haitian immigrants; Helsinki Watch report on U.S. refugee policy; Mariel boatlift; Refugees and racial/ethnic relations.

HAITIAN IMMIGRANTS

Identification: Immigrants to North America from the Caribbean island nation of Haiti

Immigration issues: African Americans; Demographics; Refugees; West Indian immigrants

Significance: Primarily of African descent, Haitians have immigrated to the United States, particularly New York and Florida, in significant numbers since the 1950's. In general, U.S. policy toward Haitians has been unreceptive since the 1970's, treating them as economic migrants rather than refugees.

During the 1980's and early 1990's, many Haitians seeking asylum in the United States were intercepted at sea and forced to return to Haiti. This treatment contrasts with that of Cuban asylum seekers, who have generally received a generous welcome to U.S. shores as legitimate refugees. The U.S. government's differential treatment of Cubans fleeing the Marxist-dominated Fidel Castro government and of Haitians fleeing a very poor country governed by right-wing repressive leaders caused many to question U.S. refugee policy. In addition, Haitians speak Creole and are black, leading some to suggest latent racist motivations for the U.S. government's actions.

The Haitian Immigration Experience Haitians, like citizens of most Caribbean countries, have for many decades participated in labor-based migration throughout the Caribbean region, including the United States. Haiti's economy is among the poorest in the Western Hemisphere, providing a significant reason for migration. However, authoritarian regimes also contributed to migration, as some people fled political repression. During the 1950's and 1960's, skilled Haitian professionals legally entered the United States and Canada as permanent or temporary immigrants. Although many left Haiti in part because of political repression, they were treated as routine immigrants rather than refugees. Legal immigration continued throughout the 1970's and 1980's, but larger numbers of much poorer people also began to leave Haiti by boat.

For many years, Haiti was governed by the authoritarian regimes of François "Papa Doc" Duvalier and his son, Jean-Claude "Baby Doc" Duvalier, who finally fled the country in 1986. A series of repressive regimes continued to rule the country until Haiti's first democratically elected government, that of Jean-Bertrand Aristide, was established in 1990. This government was overthrown by a military coup in 1991, however, and had to be reinstalled by the international community in 1994, after three years of devastating economic sanctions imposed by the United Nations that, coupled with domestic political repression, precipitated large flows of refugees. The refugee flows subsided once the military regime gave up power, the U.N. peacekeeping forces were deployed, the Aristide government was reestablished, and the economic sanctions were removed. However, another military coup overthrew Aristide a second time in early 2004.

353

Thousands of Haitians have immigrated to the United States since the early 1970's. Many thousands more were deported because they were judged to be lacking legitimate asylum claims. In 2009, according to data from the American Community Survey, about 830,000 people of Haitian ancestry were living in the U.S. (0.3 percent of the total U.S. population). Most lived in Florida (376,000) or New York (191,000). The Haitian American population was younger, on average, than the U.S. population as a whole, with a median age of 30 compared to 37 for the entire population. Haitians were more likely to live in family households (79 percent) as compared to the total U.S. population (67 percent), and were involved in the labor market at a higher rate (71 percent of those aged 16 or over) than the total population (65 percent).

Reactions to the Immigrants Reactions to the Haitian migration varied considerably. Generally, the earlier and more skilled migration out of Haiti was uncontroversial. As larger numbers of poorer Haitians, especially the "boat people," sought entry into the United States, however, concern about the economic implications of these undocumented migrants arose. Local politicians, especially in southern Florida, under pressure from their constituents, including elite members of the Cuban exile group, along with others concerned about the potentially disruptive Haitian flow, put pressure on Congress and successive presidents to deter the Haitian migration.

However, steps by the federal government to staunch the Haitian migratory flows eventually prompted political opposition by second-generation Cubans, voluntary agencies, human rights groups, and the Congressional Black Caucus. Many of these groups charged that the discriminatory treatment of Haitians was based at least in part on race. Efforts to detain Haitians in the United States were successfully challenged in court, and advocates for Haitians won a number of court-related victories to ensure fairer treatment for Haitian asylum seekers. The interdiction programs instituted by President Ronald Reagan, however, continued under the presidencies of George Bush and Bill Clinton. Only with the return of democracy to Haiti in 1994 did the migration pressures from Haiti to the United States ease.

Future Prospects The return of stability to the Haitian political system and the application of considerable international economic assistance holds out hope that Haiti will benefit from economic development, thus encouraging investment at home and further reducing pressures for migration abroad. The booming economy in the United States during the 1990's and the reduction in illegal and undocumented migration from Haiti helped to reduce the controversy surrounding Haitian migration.

Robert F. Gorman

Further Reading

Three books that discuss the Haitian experience in the United States are Flore Zéphir's *The Haitian Americans* (Westport, Conn.: Greenwood Press, 2004), Michel S. Laguerre's *Diasporic Citizenship: Haitian Americans in Transnational America* (New York: St. Martin's Press, 1998), and Alex Stepick's *Pride Against Prejudice: Haitians in the United States* (Boston: Allyn & Bacon, 1998). Stepick's *Haitian Refugees in the U.S.* (London: Minority Rights Group, 1982) and

Jake Miller's *The Plight of Haitian Refugees* (New York: Praeger, 1984) provide critiques of the Haitian predicament in the United States.

To set the Haitian situation into the wider immigration experience, see Alejandro Portes and Rubén G. Rumbaut's *Immigrant America: A Portrait* (Berkeley: University of California Press, 1990).

For a contrast of the Cuban and Haitian refugee and resettlement experience, see Felix R. Masud-Piloto's *From Welcomed Exiles to Illegal Immigrants* (Lanham, Md.: Rowman & Littlefield, 1996).

On the foreign policy implications of U.S. Haitian policy, see *Western Hemisphere Immigration and United States Foreign Policy* (University Park: Pennsylvania State University Press, 1992), edited by Christopher Mitchell.

Ellen Alexander Conley's *The Chosen Shore: Stories of Immigrants* (Berkeley: University of California Press, 2004) includes a firsthand account of an immigrant from Haiti.

Flore Zéphir's *Trends in Ethnic Identification Among Second-Generation Haitian Immigrants in New York City* (Westport, Conn.: Bergin & Garvey, 2001) examines the Haitian community of New York City.

Ethnicities: Children of Immigrants in America (Berkeley: University of California Press, 2001), edited by Rubén G. Rumbaut and Alejandro Portes, is a collection of papers on demographic and family issues relating to immigrants that includes chapters on Haitians and other West Indians.

The New African Daspora, edited by Isidore Okpewho, and Nkiru Nzweghu (Bloomington: Indiana University Press, 2009) and *The Other African Americans Contemporary African and Caribbean Immigrants in the United States*, ed. Yoku Shaw-Taylor and Steven A. Tuch (Lanham: Rowman & Littlefield, 2007) look at the Haitian American population in the larger context of Black immigrants to the U.S.

This Land Is Our Land: Immigrants and Power in Miami (Berkeley: University of California Press, 2003), by Alex Stepick and others, is a study of competition and conflict among Miami's largest ethnic groups—Cubans, Haitians, and African Americans.

See also Afro-Caribbean immigrants; Cuban immigrants and African Americans; Dominican immigrants; Florida illegal-immigrant suit; Haitian boat people; Refugees and racial/ethnic relations; Santería; West Indian immigrants.

HANSEN EFFECT

Definition: Sociological theory relating to the experiences of immigrants in the United States

Immigration issue: Sociological theories

Significance: In The Problem of the Third Generation Immigrants (1937), sociologist Marcus Lee Hansen found that immigrants have more similar experiences in adjusting to life in the United States within generations than across the generations.

Hansen reported that the first generation of immigrants, often finding it difficult to learn English and seek gainful employment, remained oriented to the home country. The first generation tended to observe customs of the home country in matters of dress, food, language spoken at home, recreation, and cultural values.

The second generation, whether born in the United States or brought to the new country at a very early age, attended school with non-immigrant children and attempted to assimilate because of peer pressure, which often ridiculed old-fashioned habits and values. The second generation, thus, rejected an identification with the parents' home country in order to be accepted and prosper in the new country.

The third generation, in contrast, has been eager to rediscover the traditions of the root cultures from which they came. Cultural pride, in short, emerged as the third generation's reaction to the efforts of the second generation to neglect its origins and cultural heritage.

The Hansen effect was postulated primarily with reference to European Americans, however. The culture of African Americans was thoroughly suppressed, and the various generations of Asian Americans and Hispanic Americans have tended to retain the values of their ancestors.

Michael Haas

Further Reading
Bischoff, Henry. *Immigration Issues.* Westport, Conn.: Greenwood Press, 2002.
Zølner, Mette. *Re-imagining the Nation: Debates on Immigrants, Identities and Memories.* New York: P.I.E.-P. Lang, 2000.

See also Assimilation theories; Ethnic enclaves; Generational acculturation; Melting pot.

Hawaiian and Pacific islander immigrants

Identification: Immigrants to North America from the Polynesian, Melanesian, and Micronesian islands of the South Pacific

Immigration issues: Demographics; Native Americans

Significance: The ethnically diverse peoples from the South Pacific maintain relatively harmonious relationships while negotiating inclusion in the U.S. labor market and European American and Asian American institutions and exploring their rights as indigenous peoples.

Hawaiian Americans are individuals with Hawaiian ancestry who are American citizens. Pacific islander Americans are American Samoans, Guamanians, and people of the Northern Mariana Islands and Pacific atolls who reside on their islands, in Hawaii, or on the mainland United States. Pre-1980 census publications did not differentiate Pacific islander groups except for Hawaiians. Pacific islanders sometimes move to the mainland United States because of the mainland's better economic prospects and educational opportunities. Generally, they adapt more easily to suburban and rural areas than to large urban areas. During the 1990's, Asian and Pacific islander Americans were the fastest-growing minority group in the United States, with the Hawaiian group being the largest.

Guam and the Northern Mariana Islands The territory of Guam and the U.S. commonwealth of the Northern Mariana Islands are believed to have been inhabited as early as 2000 b.c.e. by ancient Chamorros of MayoPolynesian descent. Colonized by Spanish missionaries in 1668, Guam was annexed by the United States in 1898 and ceded to the United States in 1919. Guam was occupied by the Japanese during World War II and retaken by the United States in 1944. In 1950, Guam's inhabitants were given U.S. citizenship. When the 1962 Naval Clearing Act allowed other ethnic groups to make Guam their home, Filipinos, Europeans, Japanese, Chinese, Indians, and Pacific islanders moved there, joining the Carolinians and present-day Chamorros.

Guam's 1990 census recorded a population that was 47 percent Chamorro, 25 percent Filipino, and 10 percent European, with Chinese, Japanese, Korean, and others making up the remaining 18 percent. Ninety percent are Roman Catholics. Guam is a self-governing, organized unincorporated territory, and policy relations between Guam and the United States are under the jurisdiction of the U.S. Department of the Interior. A 1972 U.S. law gave Guam one nonvoting delegate to the U.S. House of Representatives. Guam remains a cosmopolitan community retaining customs and traditions from many cultures and has a flourishing tourist industry.

Saipan, Tinian, and Rota, the principal islands of the Mariana Islands, have a long history of foreign occupation, by the Spanish from 1521 to 1899, the Germans from 1899 to 1914, and the Japanese from 1914 to 1944. From 1947 to 1978, the area was recognized as a trust territory of the United Nations with the United States as the administering authority. In 1978, the islands became self-governing in political union with the United States. When the United Nations Trusteeship Council concluded that the United States had discharged its obligations to the Mariana Islands, the United States conferred citizenship upon individuals who met the necessary qualifications. The Security Council of the United Nations voted to dissolve the trusteeship in 1990.

American Samoa The Samoans' heritage is Polynesian. European visitors, traders, and missionaries arrived in the eighteenth century. In 1872, Pago Pago harbor was ceded to the United States as a naval station. An 1899 treaty among Great Britain, Germany, and the United States made Samoa neutral, but when kingship was abolished the following year, the Samoan islands east of 171 degrees were given to the United States. American Samoa remains an unincorporated territory administered by the U.S. Department of the Interior. The 159,358 people (as of 2010), who live in Guam are American nationals. Although unable to vote in federal elections, American Samoans can freely enter the United States and, after fulfilling the residency requirements, can become citizens. Their language is Samoan but many speak English. In 1995, it was estimated that 65,000 Samoans had migrated to the United States, living mainly in California, Washington, and Hawaii. In Hawaii, they have experienced "cultural discrimination" before a public housing eviction board and have been called a stigmatized ethnic group.

Hawaii It is estimated that the final migration of Hawaiians from Polynesia occurred about 750 c.e. Hawaii's early social system consisted of the ali'i (nobility), who imposed hierarchical control over the *maka'ainana* (commoners), whose labor supported a population that, by the mid-eighteenth century, had increased to at least 300,000. England's Captain James Cook, who reached Kauai in 1778, named Hawaii the Sandwich Islands. King Kamehameha first unified the islands of Maui, Oahu, Hawaii, Lanai, and Molokai under a single political regime in 1795. Kauai and Niihau joined the union in 1810. The first Congregationalist

missionaries arrived from New England in 1820, followed by European and American merchants and Yankee traders. With Western contact came diseases for which the Hawaiians had no immunity or treatment. By 1853, the native population had fallen to seventy-one thousand.

Chinese, Japanese, and Portuguese immigrants arrived to provide labor for the sugar plantations. Workers coming from Korea, Puerto Rico, Europe, Scandinavia, Russia, Micronesia, Polynesia, and the Philippines considered themselves temporary immigrants. By 1890, Hawaii was a multi-ethnic society in which non-Hawaiians made up most of the population. Hawaii's independence was recognized by the United States from 1826 until 1893, when American and European sugar plantation owners, descendants of missionaries, and financiers deposed the Hawaiian monarchy, established a provisional government, and proclaimed Hawaii a protectorate of

Queen Liliuokalani, the last monarch of the Hawaiian kingdom, around 1893. (Hawaii State Archives)

the United States. Annexed by Congress in 1898, Hawaii became a U.S. territory in 1900 and the fiftieth state in 1959.

During the 1970's, a Hawaiian rights and sovereignty movement emerged. Viewed, at first, as a radical grassroots minority, the movement gained momentum after a series of demonstrations and acts of civil disobedience. In 1977, representatives from many organizations and individual Hawaiians met in Puwalu sessions to discuss Hawaiian issues. State Supreme Court justice William Richardson advised Hawaiians to use the courts to redress grievances, challenge laws, and assert gathering, access, and water rights. A constitutional convention, primarily concerned by the state's improper use of lands ceded to the United States after annexation and transferred to the state in 1959, reviewed and revised the functions and responsibilities of Hawaii's government in 1978. The following year, the legislature created the Office of Hawaiian Affairs (OHA) to provide and coordinate programs, advocate for Hawaiians, and serve as a receptacle for reparations.

Throughout the succeeding ten years, sovereignty groups strongly criticized the OHA. In 1993, the U.S. Congress officially acknowledged and apologized for the actions a hundred years earlier (U.S. Public Law 103-150). That same year, the sovereignty groups Ka Laahui and Hui Na'auao were awarded education grants, and Governor John Waihee formed the Hawaiian Sovereignty Advisory Commission, which was renamed in 1996 as Ha Hawaii. The most radical sovereignty group, the Oahana Council, declared independence from the United States in January, 1994. In 1997, a number of workshops were conducted by *kupuna* (elders) who emphasized unity among the various factions. When Governor Benjamin Cayetano resolved in his 1998 state-of-the-state address "to advance a plan for Hawaiian sovereignty," he echoed the words of former governor Waihee. Waihee had also ventured his concern that while establishing self-determination, Hawaiians would tear apart the "multicultural fabric" of contemporary Hawaiian society.

Hawaii's population, which had doubled after the islands gained statehood, fell during the 1990's, partly because of the slow growth that resulted from an economic recession and the vast reduction of the military presence on the islands, and also because of the high cost of living on the Islands. As of 2013, the population of Hawaii was 1.4 million, of which about 10 percent were Native Hawaiian or Pacific Islanders and 37.7 percent Asian.

Hawaiians living on the mainland remain connected with their heritage and values through social, university, and cultural associations that promote cultural events and regularly publish newsletters. Hula halaus exist in many states, and Hawaii's music industry brings musicians to the mainland for live performances. Local Hawaiian newspapers are available on the Internet. Pacific islanders confront various integration difficulties after moving to the United States. Because federal and state statistics combine Pacific islanders and Asian Americans, it is impossible to obtain reliable demographics. Such statistical reporting complicates the interpretation of data on household configuration, earned income, and educational and professional attainment.

The U.S. government's *Current Population Report* (1992) noted that the Asian American and Pacific islander population was not homogeneous; a population analysis of the group as a whole masked the diversity present. Pacific islanders do not identify with Asian Americans but with other island peoples. This issue becomes pertinent when Pacific islanders request funding from the Administration for Native Americans. Unlike Asian Americans, Pacific islanders qualify as Native Americans. Newly arriving Asian Americans are often placed in migrant programs. They then create businesses and quickly move out of poverty. Research at the University of Utah showed that Pacific islanders largely work in the service sector and their family businesses mostly involve unskilled labor.

As of 2010, 1.2 million people in the United States were Native Hawaiians or other Pacific Islander (alone or in combination with other races). The median agefor this population was 26.2 years, with 34.6 percent age 18 or younger. Of the 197,977 individuals who were born outside the United States, just under half (97,282) were naturalized U.S. citizens. The median family income for Native Hawaiians and other Pacific Islanders was $59,521, with the most common spheres of employement management, business, science and arts occupations (28.3 percent), sales and office occupations (27.8 percent), and service occupations (23.5 percent).

Susan E. Hamilton

Further Reading

Asians and Pacific Islanders in the United States, by demographers Herbert Barringer, Robert W. Gardner, and Michael J. Levin (New York: Russell Sage Foundation, 1995), addresses the adaptation of immigrants into American society.

In his essay "The Hawaiian Alternative to the One-Drop Rule," in *American Mixed Race: The Culture of Microdiversity*, edited by Naomi Zack (Lanham, Md.: Rowman & Littlefield, 1995), F. James Davis discusses the history of the one-drop rule and the mixed-race experience on the islands.

Lawrence H. Fuchs's *Hawaii Pono: An Ethnic and Political History* (Honolulu: Bess Press, 1961) is a classic study of the diverse cultural contributions to Hawaii and the impact of American settlement from 1893 to 1959.

Michael Haas's *Institutional Racism: The Case of Hawaii* (Westport, Conn.: Praeger, 1992) is a well-researched inquiry into racism and ethnic relations.

From a Native Daughter: Colonialism and Sovereignty in Hawaii (Monroe, Maine: Common Courage Press, 1993) is a collection of essays by Haunani-Kay Trask, a spokesperson for Hawaiian rights.

Decolonizing Native Histories: Collaboration, Knowledge, and Language in the Americas, ed. Florencia E. mallon (Durham, NC: Duke University Press, 2012) includes an essay on Hawaiian self-determination and nationhood, while Camilla Fojas's *Islands of Empire: Pop Culture and U.S. Power* (Austin: University of Texas Press, 2014) looks at the image of Hawaii in in U.S. popular culture.

See also Asian American stereotypes; Asian American women; Asian Pacific American Labor Alliance; Censuses, U.S.

HEAD MONEY CASES

The Cases: U.S. Supreme Court rulings on the taxing of immigrants
Date: December 8, 1885

Immigration issues: Court cases; Economics; Laws and treaties

Significance: The Supreme Court approved a statute allowing Congress to levy a head tax on immigrants, thereby establishing congressional power over immigration and taxes imposed for other purposes.

Early immigration in the United States was handled by the individual states, some of which imposed head taxes on every immigrant whom shippers delivered to the United States. They used the revenue from those taxes to create funds to alleviate the financial distress of immigrants. In 1849, the U.S. Supreme Court struck down these state laws as an interference with congressional power in the Passenger Cases.

To help the states deal with the financial burden of indigent immigrants, Congress passed a federal per capita tax on immigrants, which it collected and gave to the affected states. Litigants challenged the tax, claiming that Congress could not impose a tax unless it was for the common defense or general welfare of the people. Justice Samuel F. Miller wrote the unanimous opinion rejecting their claim. He maintained that immigration was a form of commerce over which Congress had broad authority, and the tax in this case was really a fee associated with regulating commerce.

Richard L. Wilson

Further Reading

LeMay, Michael C., and Elliott Robert Barkan, eds. *U.S. Immigration and Naturalization Laws and Issues: A Documentary History.* Westport, Conn.: Greenwood Press, 1999.

Shanks, Cheryl. *Immigration and the Politics of American Sovereignty, 1890-1990.* Ann Arbor: University of Michigan Press, 2001.

Williams, Mary E., ed. *Immigration: Opposing Viewpoints.* San Diego: Greenhaven Press, 2004.

See also Chinese Exclusion Act; Chinese exclusion cases; European immigrants, 1790-1892; Immigration and Naturalization Service; Immigration law; Page law.

HELSINKI WATCH REPORT ON U.S. REFUGEE POLICY

The Event: Critical report of an international human rights organization on U.S. treatment of political refugees
Date: June, 1989
Place: New York, New York

Immigration issues: Government and politics; Laws and treaties; Refugees

Significance: The Helsinki Watch report documented ways in which the U.S. Immigration and Naturalization Service's treatment of asylum seekers violated laws and international conventions and made specific recommendations for correcting abuses.

Wars, dictatorial regimes. and natural disasters generated large numbers of refugees during the 1970's and 1980's. Many of the refugees sought residence in the United States. Some groups of newcomers stood excellent chances of receiving political asylum and resettlement assistance. Others, particularly those fleeing Haiti, Guatemala, and El Salvador. Faced detention, deportation, and an uncertain future in their homelands. Concerned citizens responded by forming human rights groups such as Helsinki Watch.

Helsinki Watch was founded in 1979, in the context of increased world concern for the status of refugees. New legal instruments and standards had been drafted. These included the Final Act of the Conference on Security and Cooperation in Europe (also called the Helsinki Declaration). Under its provisions, thirty-five countries pledged respect for security and human rights considerations. They also pledged that it would be their aim to "facilitate freer movement and contacts . . . among persons, institutions, and organizations of the participating States." Helsinki groups in many of the member states (including notably the former Soviet Union) assumed responsibility for monitoring their governments' compliance with the Helsinki Declaration and other humanitarian standards.

Human rights increasingly came to be viewed as a global concern. The focus of rights activists was no longer solely on how their governments treated their own citizens. It was extended to any government's policies which threatened the human dignity of any country's nationals. In the United States, the Helsinki Watch Committee and Americas Watch were soon joined by Asia Watch, Africa Watch, and Middle East Watch, which all combined forces as Human Rights Watch. Human rights ideals were promoted in a pragmatic manner, with specific recommendations addressed to policy makers. Some human rights advocates were criticized for "solving" problems by issuing reports and declarations for an undefined audience, but the Watch Committees' reports were straightfor ward, compassionate, and subject to implementation in the near future.

Helsinki Watch Helsinki Watch was founded in 1979 by a group of publishers, lawyers, and other activists to promote domestic and international compliance with the human rights provisions of the 1975 Helsinki accords. The Watch Committees enlisted one of America's leading civil liberties attorneys, Ar yeh Neier, as Human Rights Watch executive director. Random House publisher Robert Bernstein served as Helsinki Watch chair. Human Rights Watch compiled reports on human rights conditions on every continent. In particular, it advocated "continuation of a generous and humane asylum and refugee policy . . . , toward all nationalities." An exemplary report was *Detained, Denied, Deported: Asylum Seekers in the United States*, dated June, 1989.

The report explores concepts that are well defined in international law. The United Nations Convention Relating to the Status of Refugees (1951) and the U.S. Refugee Act of 1980 define a "refugee" as one who is outside his or her country "because of persecution or a well-founded fear of persecution on account of race, religion, nationality, membership in a particular social group, or political opinion." Asylum is a protected status which may allow refugees into a foreign country. In the United States, refugees may apply for permanent residency after one year. Legislation in the United States provides that refugees may (not must) be granted asylum. It also provides that if there is a clear probability of persecution, an individual is not (with few exceptions) to be deported to his or her homeland.

Detained, Denied, Deported was the work of lawyer and Human Rights Watch intern Karin König, among others. It drew on the work of leading experts on asylum law, including Arthur Helton of the Lawyers' Committee on Human Rights. König's introduction notes that poor countries, such as Malawi and Pakistan, have assumed the biggest burden in providing asylum to refugees from neighboring countries. In contrast, such wealthy countries as the United States assert that most of those seeking asylum are not refugees entitled to protection, but "economic migrants" subject to deportation.

International standards are succinctly and accurately described in the report. The principle of *nonrefoulement* prohibits return of refugees to situations in which they would be imperiled because of their race, religion, nationality, social group, or political opinion. It applies only to refugees already present in a country; it does not create a right of entry. Article 14 of the United Nation's Universal Declaration of Human Rights (1948) provides the right to seek and enjoy asylum. (An earlier draft included a right to seek and be granted asylum.) A United Nations High Commission for Refugees (UNHCR) conference in 1977 sought a treaty containing an individual right to asylum. The conference was adjourned indefinitely for fear that protections would be reduced rather than enhanced.

U.S. Asylum Policies A history of U.S. asylum policies identifies a new group of "spontaneous" asylum seekers from Central America and the Caribbean. Their treatment has been less generous than that accorded refugees from southeast Asia. The Refugee Act of 1980 is associated with improvements—withholding of deportation where refugees would face a "clear probability" of persecution was declared mandator y, no longer left to the discretion of the attorney general.

The report gradually shifts from dispassionate description of refugee policies to ardent advocacy of reform. It notes discrimination in treatment of refugees from different regions. Applicants for asylum from U.S. allies such as Guatemala and El Salvador had to provide more extensive evidence and establish a higher level of persecution. The claim is bolstered by citing statistics: In fiscal year 1988, Salvadorans' and Guatemalans' applications were approved at rates of only 3 and 5 percent respectively, compared to 75 percent for Iranians and 77 percent for Ethiopians.

The U.S. Department of State claimed that Salvadorans and Guatemalans sought asylum in the United States for economic (and therefore illegitimate) reasons rather than because of persecution. The Watch Committee report includes telling case studies of government insensitivity to human feelings, drawn from immigration lawyers and nongovernmental organizations. The State Department is castigated for its analysis of asylum applicants' petitions, which is often superficial and tailored to foreign policy objectives.

Recommendations in the Report The report offered five recommendations for the executive branch of the U.S. government. First is an end to policies that deter asylum seekers from appealing negative decisions or from applying in the first place. Specific mention is made of the Haitian Interdiction Program and of practices whereby individuals who present no threat to society are detained. The next two recommendations address the role and training of immigration agents and judges. Immigration and Naturalization Service (INS) agents should receive special training so that they can properly follow national and international law.

To eliminate political bias, independent organizations' human rights reports should be given greater emphasis than State Department analyses. An agency independent from the State and Justice Departments should be involved in asylum adjudication. Although asylum seekers present in the United States receive the most extensive publicity, many more apply through the Overseas Admission Program (OAP). The Watch recommends that the OAP include a formal right of appeal, and that its activities ensure generous and nondiscriminatory admission from areas where the UNHCR determines a need. Finally, decisions of judicial and administrative bodies (many of which assure protection to the asylum applicant) need to he fully implemented.

Congress is prodded as well. It is urged to take appropriate action and to enact legislation to control the attorney general's discretion to ensure consistent and impartial application. When immigration authorities are expected to enforce and adjudicate immigration laws, the former task overshadows and distorts the latter. Although not in the Recommendations section, the text includes a specific plea for granting extended voluntary departure status (or "safe haven") to Salvadorans and Guatemalans.

Detained, Denied, Deported is part of an ongoing research program. Helsinki Watch pays close attention to U.S. refugee issues, and Americas Watch monitors repression in El Salvador and Haiti. Human Rights Watch played a key role in another 1989 report. *Forced Out: The Agony of the Refugee in Our Time*, which sought to "awaken, alarm, shock, and horrify," in order to counter "compassion fatigue" in addressing global dimensions of the refugee issue. Efforts such as the

Helsinki Watch group's encountered opposition. Well-funded lobbies sought to limit immigration and would make exceptions for very few of those who feared persecution. It would be up to other nongovernmental groups, Congress, and the courts to promote reform.

Aftermath The Helsinki Watch report did not produce immediate change in U.S. policies and received minimal press coverage. By acting in combination with other advocates for the refugee, however, the Watch Committee helped encourage steps to make American policy more humane. A diverse movement advocating refugee concerns hoped to ensure humane treatment through three channels.

First are reforms instituted by the executive branch and Congress. The Immigration Act of 1990 contained important new provisions. Cognizance of the plight of Salvadoran refugees was reflected in "safe haven" provisions (they were eligible for an eighteen-month period of safe haven if they could prove their nationality and show that they had arrived in the United States prior to September 19, 1990). The justification is that during a civil war protection is justified, but not asylum. Safe haven is to be temporary; applicants are expected to return to El Salvador eventually. Immigration rights activists welcomed this step, but they criticized stiff fees for applicants, higher than for applicants under similar programs for Libyan, Liberian, and Kuwaiti refugees. They also noted other measures such as the "investor visas," which provided special access for rich would-be immigrants.

Second are court decisions and settlements. In *Orantes-Hernandez v. Meese* a federal district court concluded that INS practices constituted coercion of Salvadoran asylum applicants. The court noted that applicants' access to counsel was often frustrated and ordered remedial steps. In another case, the Center for Constitutional Rights, a public-interest law firm, charged the United States with ideological bias in processing Guatemalan and Salvadoran asylum requests, contrary to the Refugee Act. The government agreed under a settlement to allocate $200,000 for a publicity campaign to notify refugees of their rights. The INS agreed to review 150,000 applications that it had denied in the last ten years. Another 1991 case broadened protection for children who were detained. A federal appellate court was persuaded that due process was violated by refusing to release immigrant children to nonrelatives or social service agencies.

A third area is growth of the lobby which promotes the rights of refugees. Activists are drawing connections between human rights of a country's own citizens and rights of refugees. The American Civil Liberties Union and Amnesty International have determined that important aspects of asylum and refugee issues fall within their limited mandates.

Refugee studies are drawing attention from scholars in law and the policy sciences. Many of their efforts provide data which can be used by advocates for the potential asylum applicant. Key figures in the media and entertainment industry also help call attention to the plight of refugees.

Aliens view the United States as a land with an open door to the oppressed, but that door might more aptly he described as guarded. Nongovernmental organizations such as Helsinki Watch will continue to play a major role in opening America to the persecuted. A useful instrument in this effort will be the issuance of reports such as *Detained, Denied, Deported*, reports that describe U.S. obligations under national and international law and identify policies that advance human dignity.

Arthur Blaser

Further Reading

Allport, Alan. *Immigration Policy*. Philadelphia: Chelsea House, 2005. Study of U.S. immigration and refugee policies written for young-adult readers.

Bischoff, Henry. *Immigration Issues*. Westport, Conn.: Greenwood Press, 2002. Collection of balanced discussions about the most important and most controversial issues relating to immigration. Among the specific subjects covered are the economic contributions of immigrants, government obligations to address humanitarian problems, and enforcement of laws regulating undocumented workers.

Blake, Nicholas J., and Razan Husain. *Immigration, Asylum and Human Rights*. New York: Oxford University Press, 2003. Study of human rights issues relating to immigration throughout the world. Includes a postscript on the challenges of protecting human rights after the terrorist attacks of September 11, 2001.

Detained, Denied, Deported: Asylum Seekers in the United States. New York: U.S. Helsinki Watch Committee, 1989. Well-organized, readable description of asylum law, with application to U.S. practices. Includes a useful statistical appendix.

Frelick, Bill. *Refugees at Our Border: The U.S. Response to Asylum Seekers*. Washington, D.C.: U.S. Committee for Refugees, 1989. Brief report on a fact-finding trip which raises many of the same issues as the Helsinki Watch study. Urges improved access for asylum seekers to attorneys and nonprofit agencies.

Hollenbach, David, ed. *Driven from Home: Protecting the Rights of Forced Migrants*. Washington, DC: Georgetown University Press, 2010. A collection of essays on the rights of forced migrants and the best ways to meet their needs.

Human Rights Watch. *Human Rights Watch Annual Report*. New York: Author, 1987-. Summary of the Watch Committee's work. It reports on the variety of studies which identify and analyze human rights violations. Also monitors each U.S. administration's compliance with human rights standards.

Lawyers Committee for Human Rights and Helsinki Watch. *Mother of Exiles: Refugees Imprisoned in America*. New York: Author, 1986. Readable description of the plight of eleven detainees, published to coincide with the centenary celebrations for the Statue of Liberty. Arthur Helton's essay identifies violations of U.S. and international law.

Legomsky, Stephen H. *Immigration and Refugee Law and Policy*. 3d ed. New York: Foundation Press, 2002. Legal textbook on immigration and refugee law.

Loescher, Gil, and John A. Scanlan. *Calculated Kindness: Refugees and America's Half-Open Door, 1945 to the Present*. New York: Free Press, 1986. An excellent review of the history and politics of U.S. refugee policies. Notes and explains patterns of discrimination and the "unprecedented harshness" of the Reagan administration. Draws on extensive inter views and archival research.

MacEoin, Gar y, and Nivita Riley. *No Promised Land: American Refugee Policies and the Rule of Law*. New York: OXFAM America, 1982. Thoughtful analysis conducted for a nongovernmental organization with an emphasis on refugees from Haiti, El Salvador, and Guatemala. Discussion of INS procedures concludes that the INS violates U.S. and international law.

Schoenholtz, Andrew I., Philip G. Schrag, and Jaya Ramji-Nogales. *Lives in the Balance; Asylum Adjudication by the Department of Homeland Security*. New York: New York University Press, 2014. A study of how and why the Department of Homeland Security grants or rejects asylum requests, based on analysis of a database of 383,000 cases.

Silk, James. *Despite a Generous Spirit: Denying Asylum in the United States*. Washington, D.C.: U.S. Committee for Refugees, 1986. Pamphlet describing the asylum process, with an analysis of growing restrictiveness of U.S. policies. It recommends that Congress play a greater role in ending programs designed to deter people from seeking asylum in the United States.

Yarnold, Barbara M. *Refugees Without Refuge: Formation and Failed Implementation of U.S. Political Asylum Policy in the 1980's*. Lanham, Md.: University Press of America, 1990. Scholarly analysis of U.S. policies which finds bias and a failure to implement the Refugee Act. Examines nongovernmental groups which have represented refugees. Concludes that nongovernmental groups have enjoyed success in widening availability of asylum. Tables and appendices report interesting data.

Zolberg, Aristide R., and Peter M. Benda, eds. *Global Migrants, Global Refugees: Problems and Solutions*. New York: Berghahn Books, 2001. Collection of articles on international dimensions of refugee policies.

See also Cuban refugee policy; Haitian boat people; Refugee fatigue; Refugee Relief Act of 1953; Refugees and racial/ethnic relations.

HISTORY OF U.S. IMMIGRATION

Definition: Survey of immigration in American history

Immigration issues: Chinese immigrants; Demographics; European immigrants; Irish immigrants

Significance: Immigration to the North American continent began during the early sixteenth century, when settlers from the British Isles established the dominant culture of what is now the United States. Immigrants who have arrived since then have faced conflict and discrimination before being accepted into American society.

The movement of people from Europe to the Americas began at the end of the fifteenth century with the urge to explore new lands and to take their riches back to the Old World. The desire to settle permanently in the Americas was caused by upheavals in European society that saw a doubling of the population, battles over agricultural land, and the Industrial Revolution, which threw craftspeople and artisans out of work. While some immigrants came to escape religious persecution, most came with the hope of bettering their economic position. The labor of these immigrants made possible the development of the United States as an industrial nation.

British Dominance The dominant culture of the early colonies in North America was established by immigrants from the British Isles, and this cultural tradition still prevails in American life. Nevertheless, it was the Spanish who achieved the first permanent settlement, founding St. Augustine (in what is now Florida) in 1565. Other early Spanish settlements included Santa Fe (now New Mexico) and the missions in California founded by Father Junípero Serra.

The Spanish political role in early American life ended with the cession of part of Florida to the British in 1763, the return of Louisiana to the French in 1800, a treaty that ceded the remainder of Florida to the United States in 1819, and Mexican independence from Spain in 1821. Yet these early settlements, combined with twentieth century immigration from Mexico, Latin America, and the Caribbean, continue to influence American culture. Spanish is the second most frequently spoken language in the United States.

The Virginia colonies in 1607 were the first British settlements in North America. The British immediately saw the need for laborers to develop the new land. They considered American Indians (the Indian population in the seventeenth century has been estimated at from four to eight million) to be an inferior race. Whereas the Spanish colonists had attempted to integrate the American Indians into the life of their settlements (while exploiting their labor), the British colonists first tried, unsuccessfully, to use them as slave labor, then forced them to move off whatever land the colonists wanted for themselves. Through the years, the Indian population was reduced by war and European diseases. A large number of immigrants in the seventeenth century came from the British Isles as indentured servants or convicts. These immigrants usually were assimilated into the general population after their servitude, often prospering in their own enterprises.

African Immigrants Black explorers had accompanied the French and Spanish during early explorations of the North American continent. Landowners in the West Indies had been importing slaves from Africa to work on their plantations for many years before the first Africans were brought to the Virginia colony in 1619. Slavery quickly took hold in America as the solution to the insatiable demand for labor to develop the new land, especially in the South with its economy based on rice, indigo, and tobacco.

Estimates of the numbers of slaves who sur vived the brutal conditions of the Atlantic passage in the seventeenth and eighteenth centuries range from hundreds of thousands to millions. This forced migration constituted one of the largest population movements in the history of the world.

Nineteenth Century Immigration Emigration from Europe in the seventeenth and eighteenth centuries was stimulated by political and economic forces that had been building for hundreds of years. Early settlers in addition to the British included significant numbers of Dutch and French people. The voyage by sailing ship, which could take from one to three months, was fraught with hardship—disease, overcrowding, and deprivation of food and water. Nevertheless, the population of the colonies was approximately 2.5 million by the beginning of the Revolutionary War. By the early eighteenth century, most Americans were native born.

The greatest wave of immigrants, an estimated thirty million, came from Europe between 1815 and World War I. During the mid-nineteenth century, the Irish, victims of British land laws and several years' failure of the potato crop, became the largest group of immigrants. The second-largest group, German middle-class artisans and landless peasants, came as a result of an increase in population and the upheaval of the Industrial Revolution. Others emigrated from Belgium, Denmark, France, the Netherlands, and the Scandinavian countries. Ellis Island in New York was the port of entry for most immigrants from 1892 until 1954.

On the West Coast, an estimated 100,000 Chinese laborers were imported. These immigrants, considered a threat by native workers, were often treated like slaves. Between 1890 and 1924, a wave of immigrants began coming from Italy, eastern and central Europe, and Russia. A number of European Jews also came to escape religious persecution. Smaller groups came from the Balkan countries and the Middle East. These people, with different appearances and customs, were not as easily assimilated as had been the people of western or northern Europe.

Twentieth Century Immigration Until the early twentieth century, the United States government welcomed most newcomers. While some local and state laws restricted the entry of lunatics, the illiterate, anarchists, or people with communicable diseases, there was little regulation of immigration, apart from the federal Chinese Exclusion Act of 1882. The late nineteenth century, however, saw an upsurge of demands for restrictive legislation born of the fear that the quality of American life was being eroded by the newcomers. During the early 1920's, in response to this fear, the federal government began to regulate immigration.

There was little immigration during the Great Depression of the 1930's. Following World War II, however, and in the years since, a new wave of immigrants has come to the United States, many of them from Asia, Mexico, the Caribbean, and South America. According to one estimate, by 1990, 6 percent of the population of the United States had been born in a foreign country. The increasing entrance of unknown numbers of undocumented immigrants since the 1970's had, by the late 1980's, created a sentiment for new restrictive legislation.

Ethnic and Racial Conflict The history of immigration to the United States is, in many ways, a record of ethnic and racial conflict. Almost all new immigrant groups have faced a degree of resistance, ranging from quiet disapproval to blatant discrimination and violence, before being accepted as part of the American population. History books have traditionally romanticized the idea of the American "melting pot" in which the cultures of all ethnic groups combine into a new,

Immigration inspectors examining the eyes of European immigrants passing through Ellis Island during the early twentieth century. Between 1892 and 1954, most of the immigrants to the United States from Europe arrived by ship and passed through Ellis Island. The development of inexpensive transatlantic air traffic was one of the reasons Ellis Island was closed as a reception center. (Library of Congress)

unique American culture. More recently, however, many scholars have argued that becoming an American essentially entails adopting the ways of a dominant culture that is strongly based on Anglo-Saxon traditions and ideals; this phenomenon of adaptation has been termed "Anglo-conformity." Nevertheless, immigrant groups have affected the culture of the United States in many ways, great and small.

As for the immigrants themselves, far from being the poor and oppressed people celebrated in myth and poetry, most were healthy, ambitious young men and women. The weak and hopeless did not have the necessary energy to pull up stakes and take the risks required to start again in a new land. Identifying with their national origins and seeking to protect their own traditions, these immigrant groups often struggled against one another and against the larger society to find a place in American society.

Immigrants during the colonial period, faced with immediate threats to their sur vival on the frontier and the backbreaking labor needed to develop the land, apparently gave little heed to ethnic identification or cultural difference. These early settlers (disregarding the fact that people were already living there) believed that divine providence had given them this new land, and they achieved a political unity that welcomed newcomers. During the late eighteenth century, however, Congress, fearing foreign-born political dissidents, passed the short-lived Alien Act in 1798 to expel suspected foreign spies. Although local and state controls on immigration had attempted to prohibit "undesirables" from entering, the first major federal immigration legislation excluded prostitutes and convicts in 1875.

Nativism, a political and social movement that pits native-born Americans (themselves descendants of earlier immigrants) against newer arrivals, has been a persistent theme in American history. The movement was particularly strong during the mid-nineteenth century during the massive influx of Irish Catholics escaping famine in Europe. These Irish immigrants were persecuted by native Protestants fearing political domination by the Roman Catholic pope.

These religious quarrels often ended in violence. In Charlestown, Massachusetts,

British cartoon from about 1912 lampooning American hypocrisy in criticizing Russian exclusion of Jewish American immigrants at the same time the United States had a law excluding Chinese immigration. (Library of Congress)

in 1834, a mob burned the Ursuline convent in the belief that the nuns had kidnapped young women and were forcing them into the Roman Catholic sisterhood. In 1844 a series of riots in Philadelphia between Catholic and Protestant workers left many dead and injured and resulted in extensive destruction of property. This xenophobia, directed against the Germans and other "foreigners" as well as the Irish, culminated in formation of the Know Nothing Party, a political organization that attempted to influence the elections of 1854 and 1855 but ultimately declined as the nation headed toward civil war.

Anti-Asian Discrimination On the West Coast, a similar pattern of persecution was directed against Asians. Chinese immigrants began coming during the gold rush of 1848. Unlike the Irish, who immigrated in family groups, most Chinese were men who did not plan to stay; they intended to make money and return to their homeland. Chinese workers were employed by the thousands in building the railroads, as well as on farms and in many menial occupations. Bigotry against the Chinese took many forms, including broad accusations of vice and idolatry. Considered inferior and a threat to native-born Americans, Asians became the target of increasing resentment and violence. In 1882 the Chinese Exclusion Act was passed by Congress; it remained in force until 1943.

Japanese immigrants began to enter the United States during the early twentieth century and were blamed for taking away jobs by providing cheap labor. A "gentlemen's agreement" between the governments of Japan and the United States in 1907 limited the number of Japanese immigrants. By 1924 all Asians were excluded from entering the United States. Discrimination against Asians after the Japanese attack on Pearl Harbor in 1941 resulted in the unconstitutional internment of more than 100,000 Japanese Americans, most of them citizens, and the confiscation of their property. In 1988 Congress offered an apology and partial financial restitution to the families of these Japanese Americans.

Late Twentieth Century Backlash A new form of nativism intensified during the 1980's and 1990's, based on the realization that there was a large and increasing population of undocumented immigrants, most of whom had entered or were remaining in the United States illegally. The majority of these undocumented immigrants were from Mexico, but there were also many from Asia, Latin America, and the Caribbean. The problem, many people began to believe, was that these workers and their families were taking jobs away from American citizens and were placing a financial strain on government educational and welfare programs.

The economic downturn of the late 1980's deepened such concerns. Considerable debate occurred concerning the reality or fantasy of this "threat" and concerning the actual costs versus benefits of the undocumented population; it was noted, for example, that many do pay taxes and that many perform jobs that most native-born Americans do not want.

Immigrant Adjustments Immigrants to the United States, despite their many cultural differences, have shared the common experience of being uprooted from

President Lyndon B. Johnson signing the Immigration and Nationality Act of 1965, which substantially changed U.S. immigration policy toward non-Europeans. Johnson made a point of signing the legislation near the base of the Statue of Liberty, which has always stood as a symbol of welcome to immigrants . Lower Manhattan can be seen in the background. (LBJ Library Collection/Yoichi R. Okamoto)

372

their familiar ways of life and of having to adjust to the lifeways of a new culture. As these immigrants become assimilated, they begin to think of themselves as Americans; ironically, members of assimilated groups may then begin to distrust more recent immigrant groups as being threats to the "American way of life" to which the older immigrants feel they belong. The traditional pattern of assimilation is for first-generation immigrants to begin at the bottom of the economic ladder and work their way upward. They often settle in ethnic neighborhoods and continue to speak their native language. The second generation, having been educated in the public schools, tends to reject the "foreign" language and customs of their parents. Members of the third generation often return to their heritage, seeking both to be acculturated Americans and to recover their roots.

The most glaring exception to this pattern has been the lack of true assimilation of African Americans. Because they were brought involuntarily to the United States and because the vast majority lived in slavery for more than three hundred years, they have faced unique handicaps. Following the Civil War, African Americans in the South experienced a brief period of political power during Reconstruction, but the backlash of the white supremacy movement put an end to this hope. The rise of the terrorist Ku Klux Klan, voting restrictions that kept African Americans from voting, Jim Crow segregation laws, and a Supreme Court decision that gave approval to segregated facilities (*Plessy v. Ferguson*, 1896) were among the factors that stood in the way of assimilation following slavery. Slavery has left a legacy that still haunts the social, political, and cultural life of the United States.

Several social and political movements during the late nineteenth century created a national demand to restrict immigration. Nativism was strong; the Ku Klux Klan's activities were directed against "foreigners" as well as against African Americans. The fact that the appearance and customs of eastern and southern Europeans were different from other European Americans made them easy to identify, and this made them easy targets for discrimination. So-called scientific theories about race were prevalent among white Europeans and Americans at the time, and these theories assumed the superiority of Anglo-Saxon and Nordic peoples. This belief led to the eugenics movement. Racial purity was believed to be desirable, and there was a fear that "inferior" races would breed with the native-born European Americans and would lead to a morally debased American population.

In the Immigration Act of 1924, Congress established quotas for immigrants based on a complex set of rules about national origin, favoring northern Europeans. The first significant deviation from this policy came when President Harry S. Truman used his executive powers to grant asylum to European refugees fleeing World War II. The McCarran-Walter Act (the Immigration and Nationality Act of 1952) revised the quota system used to determine immigration; it maintained the exclusion of immigration from Asia. The Immigration Act of 1965 finally ended the system of quotas based on national origin.

Marjorie J. Podolsky

Further Reading

Conley, Ellen Alexander. *The Chosen Shore: Stories of Immigrants.* Berkeley: University of California Press, 2004. Collection of firsthand accounts of modern immigrants from many nations.

Gonzales, Alfono. *Reform Without Justice: Latino Migrant Politics and the Homeland Security State.* New York Oxford University Press, 2014. A study of the Latino rights movement and its general lack of effectivenss in countering anti-immigration sentiments.

Greene, Victor R. *A Singing Ambivalence: American Immigrants Between Old World and New, 1830-1930.* Kent, Ohio: Kent State University Press, 2004. Comparative study of the different challenges faced during the peak era of immigration to the United States by members of eight major immigrant groups: the Irish, Germans, Scandinavians and Finns, eastern European Jews, Italians, Poles and Hungarians, Chinese, and Mexicans.

Houle, Michelle E., ed. *Immigration.* San Diego: Greenhaven Press, 2004. Collection of speeches on U.S. immigration policies by such historical figures as Presidents Woodrow Wilson, Franklin D. Roosevelt, John F. Kennedy, and Bill Clinton.

Meltzer, Milton. *Bound for America: The Story of the European Immigrants.* New York: Benchmark Books, 2001. Broad history of European immigration to the United States written for young readers.

Roleff, Tamara, ed. *Immigration.* San Diego: Greenhaven Press, 2004. Collection of articles arguing opposing viewpoints on different aspects of immigration, such as quotas and restrictions, revolving around questions of whether immigrants have a positive or negative impact on the United States.

Roman, Ediberto. *Those Damned Immigrants: America's Hysteria over Undocumented Immigration.* New York: New York University Press, 2013. A data-based study of Latino immigration that seeks to counter charges made by the anti-immigrant movement.

Sandler, Martin W. *Island of Hope: The Story of Ellis Island and the Journey to America.* New York: Scholastic, 2004. History of the most important immigrant reception, from 1892 through 1954. Written for younger readers.

Vought, Hans Peter. *Redefining the "Melting Pot": American Presidents and the Immigrant, 1897-1933.* Ann Arbor, Mich.: UMI, 2001. Study of the role of U.S. presidents in American immigration policy through an era of heavy European immigration and fundamental changes in American immigration policy.

Wepman, Dennis. *Immigration: From the Founding of Virginia to the Closing of Ellis Island.* New York: Facts On File, 2002. History of immigration to the United States from the earliest European settlements of the colonial era through the mid-1950's, with liberal extracts from contemporary documents.

Williams, Mary E., ed. *Immigration: Opposing Viewpoints.* San Diego: Greenhaven Press, 2004. Various social, political, and legal viewpoints are given by experts and observers familiar with immigration into the United States.

See also Demographics of immigration; European immigrants, 1790-1892; European immigrants, 1892-1943; Illegal aliens; Immigration and Naturalization Service; Immigration "crisis"; Immigration law; Justice and immigration; Migration; Push and pull factors; Undocumented workers.

HMONG IMMIGRANTS

Identification: Immigrants to North America from a minority community living in several Southeast Asian nations

Immigration issues: Asian immigrants; Demographics; Refugees

Significance: Laotian mountain tribespeople from a preliterate society experienced culture shock when they migrated to the United States as refugees, beginning in 1976. Their adjustment difficulties contradict the stereotype of Asian Americans as a highly educated, successful "model minority."

The Hmong (pronounced "mong") people have a long history of escaping adversity. For centuries the Hmong were an ethnic group persecuted in China. During the early nineteenth century, they moved to Burma (Myanmar), Thailand, Vietnam, and Laos. In Laos, the Hmong settled in the isolated highlands. During the political turmoil of the 1950's and 1960's, many Hmong fought for the anticommunist army under General Vang Pao. The U.S. Central Intelligence Agency (CIA) secretly ran and financed this Vietnam War effort in which Laotian men served in rescue missions and guerrilla operations. When the communists took power in Laos in 1975 and the United States withdrew, there were reprisals against the Hmong. To escape persecution, many Hmong fled to United Nations refugee camps in Thailand. In Ban Vinai and other refugee camps, Hmong families waited to establish political refugee status so that they could emigrate to the United States.

Refugees on the Move The first Hmong refugees arrived in the United States in 1976, assisted by world relief organizations and local organizations such as churches. Between 1976 and 1991, an estimated 100,000 Hmong came to the United States. Because of their high birthrate, the population increased substantially, and in 2010 260,076 Hmong lived in the U.S.

Areas of second settlement were selected based on climate, cheap housing, job availability, state welfare programs, and family unification. As of 2010, the greatest number of Hmong (91,224) lived in California, followed by Minnesota (66,181), Wisconsin (49,240) and North Carolina (10,864). The reception the Hmong received varied from hearty welcome to ethnic antagonism on the part of some Americans who were ignorant of Hmong bravery and sacrifices in the Vietnam War and who did not grasp the difficulty of Hmong adjustment to life in the United States.

Culture Shock Three branches of the Hmong came to the United States: the Blue Hmong, the White Hmong, and the Striped Hmong. They spoke different dialects and wore distinct traditional clothing but shared many cultural traditions that made it difficult to adjust to life in a modern society. Most refugees had never experienced indoor plumbing, electricity, or automobiles. For many Hmong, their only work experience before coming to the United States was as soldiers and as farmers. The traditional crops of rice and corn were raised on fields so steep that sometimes farmers tethered themselves to a stump to keep from falling off their fields. For the Hmong who tried farming in the United States, adjustment was difficult. Their slash-and-burn method of clearing land was not permitted. They were unfamiliar with pesticides and chemical fertilizers. Refugees worked as migrant farmworkers and in many low-paid urban positions that did not require English proficiency. The

Hmong girl in a Sacramento, California, school. (Eric Crystal)

unemployment rate was very high for many Hmong communities. In 1988, 70 percent of the Fresno Hmong depended on welfare and refugee assistance.

Education was another area of difficult cultural adaptation. During the 1990's, many Hmong children struggled in U.S. schools. Many attended English-as-a-second-language classes, and many were placed in vocational tracks. Hmong children often had low scores on standardized tests of vocabulary and reading comprehension. When large numbers of Hmong children entered certain school systems during the late 1970's and 1980's, administrators and teachers were completely unprepared. Learning English proved difficult, especially for the older Hmong who had never attended school in Laos. Special training programs first taught Hmong language literacy, then English.

Hmong beliefs about religion and medicine are very different from common attitudes in the United States. Traditional Hmong religion is a form of animism, a belief that spirits dwell in all things, including the earth, the sky, and animals. Hmong attempted to placate these spirits in religious rituals that often included animal sacrifice. In medical ceremonies, a shaman or healer tried to locate and bring back the patient's runaway soul. Many bereaved Hmong refused autopsies, believing they interfered with reincarnation.

Hmong family traditions often put them at odds with U.S. culture. The Laotian practice was to arrange marriages, usually interclan agreements in which a bride price was paid. Women married as teenagers, then derived their status from being a wife and mother of many children. Marriage by capture was part of Hmong tradition but led to U.S. criminal charges of kidnapping and rape. Divorce was discouraged but possible in Laos, and children could be kept by the husband's family. Such practices conflict with many U.S. laws and folkways.

Other conflicts arose over U.S. laws that the Hmong did not understand. Carrying concealed weapons was common in Laos but led to arrest in the United States. Zoning laws stipulating where to build a house or plant a field were unfamiliar to the Hmong. Disputes arose over Hmong poaching in wildlife refuges.

Culture shock seems to have taken a toll on the Hmong. During the 1970's and early 1980's, many apparently healthy Hmong men died in their sleep in what was labeled Sudden Unexplained Death Syndrome. Possible explanations were depression, "survivor guilt," and the stress of a new environment in which the men lacked control of their lives. The peak years for the syndrome were 1981 and 1982.

Strengths of the Hmong Not all aspects of Hmong tradition handicapped their adjustment to life in the United States. Some members possess fine-motor skills honed in their intricate needlework. Without sewing machines or patterns, Hmong women embroider and appliqué to produce marketable products that also preserve their cultural memories. Flower cloths are square designs with symmetrical patterns. Story cloths are sewn pictures depicting past events, including war brutality and refugee camp life. Hmong developed memorization skills as part of their oral tradition of elaborate folktales. Hmong women are credited with admirable parenting skills, especially in their sensitivity to their children's needs. The Hmong typically possess a fierce independence and will to survive.

The Hmong appear to be adjusting to the new culture in which they find themselves, especially the younger generation. Hmong youth typically adopt American ways, wearing Western dress and enjoying rock music and video games. The group shows resilience in adapting traditions to changed circumstances. The Hmong have devised a custom of group support as clans form communities for mutual aid. Seamstresses have adapted their needlework patterns to satisfy Western markets. Crowded city dwellers often plant impromptu gardens in the narrow spaces between buildings.

Nancy Conn Terjesen

Further Reading
I Begin My Life All Over: The Hmong and the American Immigrant Experience, by Lillian Faderman with Ghia Xiong (Boston: Beacon, 1998), combines thirty-five narratives and emphasizes generational differences.

Another collection of Hmong immigrant narratives is Sue Murphy Mote's *Hmong and American: Stories of Transition to a Strange Land* (Jefferson, N.C.: McFarland, 2004).

Diversity in Diaspora; Hmong American in the Twenty-first Century, ed. Mark Edward Pfeifer, Monica Chiu, and Kou Yang (Honolulu: University of Hawai'I Press, 2013) is a collection of essays about the Hmong community in the U.S., including gender issues, arts and literature, and political participation.

For a recent account of the plight of Hmong refugees, see Linda Barr's *Long Road to Freedom: Journey of the Hmong* (Bloomington, Minn.: Red Brick Learning,

2004).

Anne Fadiman's *The Spirit Catches You and You Fall Down: A Hmong Child, Her American Doctors, and the Collision of Two Cultures* (New York: Farrar, Straus & Giroux, 1997) looks at how cultural differences affected the treatment of a young epileptic Hmong American girl.

Paul Hillmer's *A People's History of the Hmong* (St. Paul: Minnestoa Historical Society Press, 2010), tells the story of Hmong refugees around the world, based on over 200 interviews.

Wendy Walker-Moffat's *The Other Side of the Asian American Success Story* (San Francisco: Jossey-Bass, 1995) is a research report explaining negative educational experiences.

Spencer Sherman's "The Hmong in America: Laotian Refugees in the Land of the Giants," in *National Geographic* (October, 1988), describes communities in North Carolina and California.

Ronald Takaki's *Strangers from a Different Shore: History of Asian Americans* (Boston: Little, Brown, 1989) includes a chapter on post-1965 immigrants.

Lan Cao and Himilce Novas use a question-answer format to describe seven nationalities in *Everything You Need to Know About Asian American History* (New York: Plume, 2004).

Julie Keown-Bomar's *Kinship Networks Among Hmong-American Refugees* (New York: LFB Scholarly Publications, 2004) is a sociological study of Hmong immigrants.

See also Asian American education; Asian American stereotypes; Asian American women; Model minorities; Southeast Asian immigrants; Vietnamese immigrants.

HOMELAND SECURITY DEPARTMENT: 2003

The Law: Homeland security is an American term referring to the nationwide effort to prevent terrorist attacks within the borders of the United States, reduce the terrorism vulnerability, and minimize damage from attacks, as stated by the Secretary of the Air Force in 2006.

Date: 2002

Immigration Issues: Following the attacks of September 11 (aka 9/11), the United States Federal Government put in place a security framework designed to protect the U.S. from further large-scale attacks directed from abroad. In addition, this framework was developed to enhance federal, state, and local capabilities to better prepare for, respond to, and recover in the event of future threats and disasters. Thus became the creation of the Department of Homeland Security (DHS) in March, 2003, and its collaboration of twenty-two separate agencies and offices into a single, Cabinet-level department.

Significance: After the September 11 attacks, the term "Homeland Security" came into play following reorganization in 2003 of many U.S. government agencies in order to form the United States Department of Homeland Security. The term is most often used to refer to the actions of the Department of Homeland Security, the United States Senate Committee on Homeland Security and Governmental Affairs, or the United States House of Representatives Committee on Homeland Security. Homeland defense (HD), on the other hand, is the protection of United States territory, sovereignty, domestic population, and critical infrastructure against external threats and aggression.

Background: Homeland Security is officially defined by the National Strategy for Homeland Security as "a concerted national effort to prevent terrorist attacks within the United States, reduce America's vulnerability to terrorism, and minimize the damage and recover from attacks that do occur". What most don't realize is that even prior to these attacks, the term Homeland Security had been used in limited policy circles. It wasn't until after the September 11th attacks that it became a prominent household term. In fact, the phrase "security of the American homeland" appeared in the 1998 report *Catastrophic Terrorism: Elements of a National Policy* by Ashton B. Carter, John M. Deutch, and Philip D. Zelikow.

Homeland security is coordinated at the White House by the Homeland Security Council, currently headed by John Brennan. Homeland security is also used to indicate the civilian aspect of this effort; "homeland defense" refers to the military component, led chiefly by the U.S. Northern Command headquartered in Colorado Springs, Colorado.

The George W. Bush administration consolidated many actions under the United States Department of Homeland Security (DHS), a cabinet department established as a result of the Homeland Security Act of 2002. However, much of the nation's homeland security activity remains outside of Department of Homeland Security; for example, the FBI and CIA are not part of the Department, and other executive departments, such as the Department of Defense and Department of Health and Human Services, play an important role in certain aspects of homeland security.

The concept of "Homeland Security" in the United States extends and recombines the responsibilities of different government agencies and entities. According to Homeland Security research, the U.S. federal Homeland Security and Homeland Defense includes 187 federal agencies and departments, including the United States National Guard, the Federal Emergency Management Agency, the United States Coast Guard, U.S. Customs and Border Protection, U.S. Immigration and Customs Enforcement, United States Citizenship and Immigration Services, the United States Secret Service, the Transportation Security Administration, the 14 agencies that constitute the U.S. intelligence community and Civil Air Patrol. Although many businesses now operate in the area of Homeland Security, it is a government function.

Because the U.S. Department of Homeland Security includes the Federal Emergency Management Agency, it also has responsibility for preparedness, response, and recovery to natural disasters.

According to the U.S. Office of Management and Budget Analytical Perspectives, Budget of the United States Government, Fiscal Year 2011, and Homeland Security Research Corporation, DHS Homeland security funding constitutes only 20-21% of the consolidated U.S. Homeland Security - Homeland Defense funding, while approximately 40% of the DHS budget funds civil, non-security activities, such as the U.S. coast guard search and rescue operations and customs functions. The U.S. Homeland Security is the world's largest Homeland counter terror organization, having 40% of the global FY 2010 homeland security funding.

The scope and duties of Homeland Security includes:

- Emergency preparedness and response (for both terrorism and natural disasters), including volunteer medical, police, emergency management, and fire personnel;
- Domestic and International intelligence activities, largely today within the FBI;
- Critical infrastructure and perimeter protection;
- Investigation of people making and distributing child pornography;
- Border security, including both land, maritime and country borders;
- Transportation security, including aviation and maritime transportation;
- Biodefense;
- Detection of radioactive and radiological materials;
- Research on next-generation security technologies.

Dust clouds enveloping Lower Manhattan after the collapse of the World Trade Center towers on September 11, 2001. (www.bigfoto.com)

Legislation: Just eleven days after the September 11, 2001, terrorist attacks, Pennsylvania Governor Tom Ridge was appointed as the first Director of the Office of Homeland Security in the White House. The office oversaw and coordinated a comprehensive national strategy to safeguard the country against terrorism and respond to any future attacks.

Due to the passage of the Homeland Security Act by Congress in November 2002, the Department of Homeland Security officially became a stand-alone, Cabinet-level department. Opening its doors on March 1, 2003, its purpose remains to further coordinate and unify national homeland security efforts.

From the *Department of Homeland Security June 2002*, George W. Bush, "The President proposes to create a new Department of Homeland Security, the most significant transformation of the U.S. government in over half-century by largely transforming and realigning the current confusing patchwork of government activities into a single department whose primary mission is to protect our homeland. The creation of a Department of Homeland Security is one more key step in the President's national strategy for homeland security."

Title I - Department of Homeland Security
Sec. 101. Executive Department; Mission
(a) Establishment. - "There is established a Department of Homeland Security, as an executive department of the United States within the meaning of title 5, United States Code.
(b) Mission
　　(1) In General. - The primary mission of the Department is to
　　　　(A) prevent terrorist attacks within the United States;
　　　　(B) reduce the vulnerability of the United States to terrorism; and
　　　　(C) minimize the damage, and assist in the recovery, from terrorist attacks that do occur within the United States."

On February 15, 2005, Secretary Michael Chertoff took office and initiated a Second Stage Review (2SR) to evaluate the department's operations, policies, and structures. More than 250 members of the department and 18 action teams participate in this effort. The teams also consulted public and private partners at the federal, state, local, tribal, and international levels. On July 13, 2005, Secretary Chertoff announced a six-point agenda, based upon the findings, which included a significant reorganization of the department.

The President's fiscal year 2010 budget requested the transfer of the Federal Protective Service (FPS) from U.S. Immigration and Customs Enforcement (ICE) to the National Protection and Programs Directorate (NPPD)—streamlining decision-making and aligning the protection of federal buildings with DHS' broader critical infrastructure protection mission and the provision was included in the DHS appropriations bill President Obama signed into law on Oct. 28, 2009. It also elevated the Office of Intergovernment Programs from NPPD to a direct report to the Secretary and renamed it to the Office of Intergovernmental Affairs.

In 2010, Secretary Janet Napolitano led the completion of the first-ever Quadrennial Homeland Security Review (QHSR), which established a unified, strategic framework for homeland security missions and goals. Subsequently, DHS conducted a Bottom-Up Review (BUR) to align our programmatic activities and organizational structure to better serve those missions and goals. The QHSR reflects the most comprehensive assessment and analysis of homeland security to date. DHS worked closely with the White House, National Security Staff, other Federal departments and agencies, and our state, local, tribal and territorial partners to represent the whole-of-government approach to national security envisioned by the Administration.

Heather Hummel

Further Reading

Kamien, David, *McGraw-Hill Homeland Security Handbook: Strategic Guidance for a Coordinated Approach to Effective Security and Emergency Management*, Second Edition, McGraw-Hill; 2 Edition, November 12, 2012. A book that emphasizes its focus as a "one-stop guide" for professionals or students who are involved in counterterrorism, homeland security, business continuity, or disaster risk management.

Bullock, Jane, Haddow, George, Coppola, Damon P., *Introduction to Homeland Security*, Fourth Edition: Principles of All-Hazards Risk Management, Butterworth-Heinemann; 4 Edition, January 17, 2012. A textbook in which the authors showcase their experience and analysis, offering additional research-based data that gives balance to the "field-tested practical information included in each chapter."

Bullock, Jane, Haddow, George, Coppola, Damon P., *Homeland Security, The Essentials*, Butterworth-Heinemann; 4 Edition, November 2, 2012. A book in which the authors describe the risks the United States faces and the infrastructures that are in place to address them. They delineate the principles put upon Homeland Security in order to prepare for, mitigate, manage, and recover from terrorists, emergencies, and disasters.

HULL-HOUSE

Identification: Settlement house founded by Jane Addams and Ellen Gates Starr
Date: Established in September, 1889
Place: Chicago, Illinois

Immigration issues: Families and marriage; Women

Significance: Hull-House represented an attempt on behalf of middle-class

Hull-House. (University of Illinois at Chicago, University Library, Jane Addams Memorial Collection)

American women to address the needs of Chicago's inner city, many of whose residents were poor immigrants.

Inspired by Toynbee House in London, Jane Addams and Ellen Gates Starr purchased a dilapidated mansion on South Halsted in Chicago and created Hull-House. Addams and Starr believed that the urban poor, particularly immigrants, had been victimized by industrialization. Consequently, they tried to improve their lot by providing a variety of services, including English classes, a day nursery for working mothers, a kindergarten, an employment bureau, and a health class. Hull-House soon became the best-known settlement house in the United States. Addams also advocated specific legal reforms, such as a juvenile court system, workers' compensation laws, and child labor legislation. However, she ran afoul of machine politics and urban bosses who saw settlement house workers as a threat to their own power.

From its inception, Hull-House was an endeavor geared primarily to meet women's needs. Addams conformed to nineteenth century gender roles, in that she saw women as natural nurturers. Consequently, she shaped HullHouse's outreach to reflect this perception. The settlement house attracted numerous individuals as volunteers, especially educated, middle-class women who were interested in helping slum dwellers. Likewise, Hull-House provided an outlet for their benevolent impulses and served as a harbinger for later Progressive Era reform and regulation.

In 2012, the Jane Adams Hull House Association announced that it was filing for bankruptcy, but Hull House continues to operate as a museum.

Keith Harper

Further Reading

Addams, Jane. *The Jane Addams Reader*. Edited by Jean Bethke Elshtain. New York: Basic Books, 2002. Selection of writings by Jane Addams, the founder of Hull-House.

_____. *Twenty Years at Hull House*. Edited by Victoria Bissell Brown. Boston: Bedford/St. Martin's, 1999. Scholarly edition, with additional autobiographical materials, of a book that Addams first published in 1911. Provides detailed account of the establishment, operation, and philosophy of Hull-House.

Bryan, Mary Lynn McCree, and Allen Davis, eds. *One Hundred Years at HullHouse*. Bloomington: Indiana University Press, 1990. A compendium of primary sources about Hull-House, including numerous photographs.

Carson, Mina. *Settlement Folk: Social Thought and the American Settlement Movement, 1885-1930.* Chicago: University of Chicago Press, 1990. An extensively documented examination of the contribution of U.S. settlement house workers to the development of social welfare. Provides a historical and ideological context for the work of Hull-House.

Deegan, Mary Jo. *Race, Hull-House, and the University of Chicago: A New Conscience Against Ancient Evils*. Westport, Conn.: Praeger, 2002. Study of HullHouse, from 1892 to 1960, in the context of racial and ethnic issues.

Glowacki, Peggy, and Julia Hendry. *Hull-House*. Charleston, S.C.: Arcadia, 2004. Well-illustrated study of Hull-House, which is discussed in the context of its surrounding community.

Knight, Louise W. *Jane Addams: Spirit in Action*. New York: W. W. Norton, 2010. A biography of Jane Addams, emphasizing her role as a progressive political force.

See also Machine politics; Settlement house movement; Women immigrants.

HUMAN SMUGGLING (OR HUMAN TRAFFICKING)

The Law: The "Trafficking Victims Protection Act of 2000" provides tools to combat trafficking in persons both worldwide and within the United States. Section 107(c)(3) reads: "Authority to Permit Continued Presence in the United States. Federal law enforcement officials may permit an alien individual's continued presence in the United States, if after an assessment, it is determined that such individual is a victim of a severe form of trafficking and a potential witness to such trafficking, in order to effectuate prosecution of those responsible, and such officials in investigating and prosecuting traffickers shall protect the safety of trafficking victims, including taking measures to protect trafficked persons and their family members from intimidation, threats of reprisals, and reprisals from traffickers and their associates."

Date: 2000

Immigration Issues: The immigration issues surrounding human trafficking and smuggling are multiple. Illegal aliens enter the United States illegal by either their own willingness through smuggling or by illegal force through trafficking.

Significance: Spanning numerous crimes from country to country, trafficking affects an increasing number of victims, creating a comparison to modern-day slavery. The United Nations defines human trafficking and smuggling as one of the "fastest growing areas of international criminal activity." The United States Government estimates that there are between 600,000 and 800,000 victims annually. Additionally, between 14,500 and 17,500 are trafficked into the United States. The large majority of victims are women and children, especially since trafficking is commonly known to be used for sexual exploitation or labor exploitation purposes.

Background Using exploitation through tactics that use both physical and emotional abuse such as brutal force, coercion, threats, and deception, trafficking is not only illegal, but violent. Additionally, human rights abuse, to include illegal and heinous tactics such as: debt bondage, deprivation of liberty, and lack of control over freedom and labor.

As will be described below, there are significant and notable differences in the definitions of human trafficking and human smuggling; however, the illegal activities and the characteristics and trends of those involved are similar. For example, extreme poverty, civil unrest, lack of economic opportunities, and political uncertainty, are common factors in both human smuggling and trafficking in persons. Note that even though trafficking is often perceived as crossing borders to different countries, it is also true that trafficking occurs within the same country. Often times victims are moved within the same borders, but sold to another organization.

The differences between trafficking and human smuggling are significant in that smuggling is agreed upon by the two parties, whereas trafficking is involuntary by the victim. In fact they are distinct enough that there are significant statutory differences between trafficking and human smuggling.

Key issues that decipher the difference between trafficking and smuggling are: fraud, coercion, and force. In addition, under United States law, if the victim is under 18 years old and is forced to perform a commercial sex act, then it is considered trafficking, regardless of whether or not fraud, coercion, or force is involved. Below are further definitions of each.

Human Smuggling The definition of human smuggling is: "The facilitation, transportation, attempted transportation or illegal entry of a person(s) across an international border, in violation of one or more countries laws, either clandestinely or through deception, such as the use of fraudulent documents."

Typically, human smuggling results in the smuggler gaining financial or other material benefits, even though these benefits may not comprise of the crime. People who are smuggled willingly enter into agreements with their smugglers to "work off a smuggling debt." For example, people will engage in smuggling because it becomes the only way for them to reunite with their families. Therefore, human smuggling is generally with the consent of the person(s) being smuggled, who often pay large sums of money. The vast majority of people who are assisted in illegally entering the United States are smuggled, rather than trafficked. Even still, it is not uncommon for smuggled people to become victims of other crimes.

With the advantage of being reunited with family members often comes a steep emotional or physical price to be paid. Those being smuggled endure unsafe conditions and are subjected to physical and sexual abuse and are held hostage until their "debt" is paid by whoever is coming to retrieve them. There is always an added risk that they never make it to their destination and, instead, become a trafficking victim.

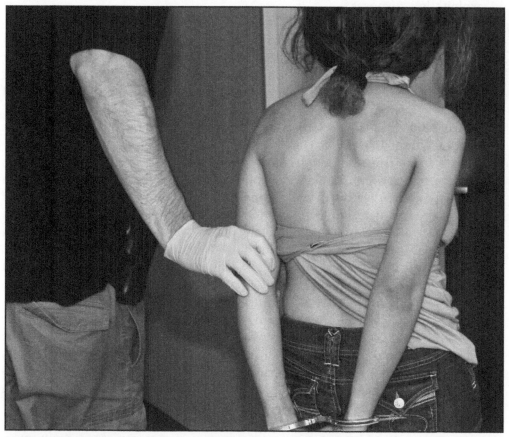

An FBI agent leading away an adult suspect arrested in the Operation Cross Country II, when 105 children were rescued from forced prostitution in October 2008. (U.S. Department of Justice)

Trafficking in Persons (TIP) Trafficking is different from smuggling in that it specifically targets the victim, who is used as an object of criminal exploitation. Trafficking results in a profit from exploitation of the victim, and by use of force, fraud, and coercion, it brings to surface many additional illegal actions.

Despite the differences from smuggling, trafficking can still resemble the act of smuggling, especially in the form of the illegal border crossing. Already vulnerable, trickery by a trafficking organization can result in the coercion of those being smuggled into becoming trafficking victims.

Coercing the victims into believing they would have a better life is the greatest known tactic in trafficking. TIP use manipulation tactics to coerce victims who are then used for sexual exploitation. Noted cases involve women who were trafficked for sexual exploitation, who may at first agreed to the sex industry, but naively believed they would earn a decent wage and be given livable conditions. Their reality quickly shifted to the traffickers keeping the majority of or even their entire income while the women were kept in bondage and subjected to physical abuse and sexual violence. Additional tactics involved the victims believing they would be given a reputable job in the United States once they were smuggled in, when the truth was they were deceived and also forced into the sex industry.

Debunking the Myths There are many myths around both human trafficking and human smuggling. One example, as mentioned previously, is that human trafficking is not limited to crossing country borders. It can be done within the same country and does not require transportation of the victims, whereas smuggling does. Another myth is that victims are illegal aliens, whereas the truth is, many citizens of the United States are victims of trafficking. Lastly, the myth that all victims are women is false, as there are adult, male victims as well.

Profiting by Trafficking Those who engage in the criminal act of trafficking are commonly using their victims for profit in business ranging from factory sweatshops; domestic, restaurant, and agricultural labor; and for prostitution and sexual entertainment. Though it may be hard to believe, oftentimes victims are unaware that they are being victimized, or may be forced into protecting their exploiters.

Legislation According to the "Trafficking Victims Protection Act of 2000," severe forms of trafficking in persons always includes the recruitment, harboring, transportation, provision, or obtaining of a person for one of the three following purposes:

- Labor or services, through the use of *force, fraud or coercion*, AND resulting in involuntary servitude, peonage, debt bondage, or slavery; OR
- Commercial sex act, through the use of *force, fraud or coercion*; OR
- If the person is under 18 years of age, any commercial sex act, whether or not force, fraud or coercion is involved.

Smuggling The Immigration and Nationalization Act, Section 274(a)(1), (2), provides for criminal penalties under Title 8, United States Code, Section 1324, for acts or attempts to bring unauthorized aliens to or into the United States, transport them within the U.S., harbor unlawful aliens, encourage entry of illegal aliens, or conspire to commit these violations, knowingly or in reckless disregard of illegal status.

Trafficking in Persons (TIP) On October 28, 2000, Congress passed the Victims of Trafficking and Violence Protection Act of 2000 ("VTVPA"), a statute that addresses the ongoing and significant problem of trafficking of persons for the purpose of committing commercial sex acts, or to subject them to involuntary servitude, peonage, debt bondage, or slavery.

Heather Hummel

Further Reading

Lloyd, Rachel, *Girls Like Us: Fighting for a World Where Girls Are Not For Sale: A Memoir*, Harper Perennial, Reprint Edition, February 28, 2012. A book with the author's account of her survivor story about her hard-won escape from the commercial sex industry and her bold founding of GEMS, New York City's Girls Education and Mentoring Service.

Bowley, Mary Frances, *The White Umbrella: Walking with Survivors of Sex Trafficking*, Moody Publishers, New Edition, September 14, 2012. A book that tells vignettes of survivors and the heroes who helped them to recovery.

Hodge, Sibel, *Trafficked: The Diary of a Sex Slave*, CreateSpace, 2010. A story told by an international bestselling and award winning author about a woman named Elana, a victim of trafficking in persons.

See also Border Patrol, U.S.; Mail-order brides; Women immigrants.

ILLEGAL ALIENS

Definition: Colloquial term for foreign-born persons who enter the United States without legal authorization and those who enter legally but violate the terms of their admission or fail to acquire permanent residence status

Immigration issues: Border control; Economics; Illegal immigration; Law enforcement; Mexican immigrants

Significance: The steady increase in the population of undocumented aliens in the United States presents a variety of challenges to the American criminal justice system. In addition to the federal government's monumental problem of enforcing the nation's immigration laws, state and local law enforcement agencies face a growing problem of criminal activities by illegal aliens.

In 1994, the U.S. Immigration and Naturalization Service (INS) produced the first detailed national estimates of the numbers of illegal aliens in the United States. The INS estimated that 3.4 million unauthorized residents were in the country in October, 1992. Later, the INS estimated the number to be about 7 million in the year 2000. The U.S. Census Bureau's estimate for that same year 8 million. Since the early 1990's, the annual growth rate of the illegal alien population has ranged between 350,000 and 500,000. At that rate, the number of illegal residents in the United States was about 9 million in 2004. By January 2011, according to estimates by the Office of Immigration Statistics of the Department of Homeland Security, there were 11.5 million unauthorized immigrants living in the U.S. Twenty-five percent of these unauthorized immigrants were estimated to live in California, with 16 percent in Texas, and 6 percent in Florida. Some states that have had relatively small numbers of immigrants (both legal and illegal) in the past experienced a large increase in the number of unauthorized immigrants in the early 21st century—for instance, Georgia's population of unauthorized immigrants increased by 95 percent from 2000 to 2011, from 220,000 to 440,000 individuals.

According to Office of Immigration Statistics estimates, most (8.9 million) authorized immigrants come from North America (including Mexico, Central America, the Caribbean, and Canada), with 1.3 million from Asia, 0.8 million from South America, 0.3 million from Europe, and 0.2 million from other parts of the world. By far the most common country of origin for unauthorized immigrants was Mexico (59 percent of the total), followed by El Salvador (6 percent) and Guatemala (5 percent). According to the Pew Hispanic Center, in 2010 at least 5.5 million children had at least one parent who was an unauthorized immigrant; of these children, most (82 percent) were born in the U.S. and thus were U.S. citizens.

The U.S. Criminal Justice System The standard American response to illegal immigration has been increased border enforcement through the authority of the federal government. Throughout the 1990's, the numbers of both illegal border crossings and illegal aliens in the United States increased incrementally. Among the strategies to stem illegal immigration were Operation Gatekeeper in California, Operation Hold-the-Line in Texas, and Operation Safeguard in Arizona. All were attempts to deter illegal border crossings.

The U.S. Department of Justice allocated unprecedented resources to these innovative strategies, including additional Border Patrol agents, advanced computer systems, and improved security fences, lighting, and support vehicles. As a result, by 1998, the numbers of attempted border crossings and apprehensions dropped to their lowest levels in almost twenty years. However, human rights activists and researchers criticized these efforts and argued that increased sur veillance along the border were not preventing illegal entries but were instead forcing undocumented immigrants to seek riskier methods of entering the United States. In response to these charges, U.S. president George W. Bush and Mexican president Vicente Fox later pledged to pursue immigration reform policies to address border enforcement and human rights concerns.

The fact that the terrorist attacks on the United States of September 11, 2001, were perpetrated by illegal aliens made countering illegal immigration a top

priority of the Bush administration. After that date, new federal laws and policies were adopted, including the Patriot Act of 2001, the Homeland Security Act of 2002, and the Enhanced Border Security and Visa Entry Reform Act of 2002. In March, 2003, the Immigration and Naturalization Service was divided into three bureaus within the newly created Department of Homeland Security: the Bureau of Immigration and Customs Enforcement (ICE); the Bureau of Customs and Border Protection (CBP); and U.S. Citizenship and Immigration Services (USCIS).

Although the federal government is primarily responsible for securing the nation's borders, the impact of illegal aliens on the criminal justice system reaches far beyond the federal system. Indeed, the problem and its required solutions may have an even deeper impact on state and local jurisdictions. At state and local levels, the costs of arresting, prosecuting, sentencing, and super vising illegal aliens who commit criminal offenses have become a major issue. Some states have filed suits to force the federal government to reimburse them for the costs of criminal justice actions against aliens for whom the federal government is responsible.

The federal government does reimburse states for some costs associated with criminal acts by illegal aliens. Section 510 of the Immigration Reform and Control Act of 1986 (IRCA) authorizes the U.S. attorney general to reimburse states for the criminal justice costs attributable to undocumented persons. The Bureau of Justice Assistance, a branch of the Office of Justice Programs, administers the State Criminal Alien Assistance Program (SCAAP), in conjunction with ICE of the Department of Homeland Security. SCAAP provides federal payments to states and localities that incur correctional officer salary costs for incarcerating undocumented aliens who have committed at least one felony or two misdemeanor convictions for violations of state or local law and are incarcerated for at least four consecutive days during a reporting period. During the fiscal year 2004, the total appropriation was approximately $297 million. SCAAP payments are calculated with a formula that provides pro rata shares of the funds to jurisdictions that apply, based on the total number of eligible criminal aliens as determined by ICE.

Criminal illegal aliens pose considerable challenges to law-enforcement efforts in part due to the highly criticized stance of many cities and counties that have adopted "sanctuary laws." Such laws are local ordinances adopted in attempts to reduce victimizations of aliens and to improve crime reporting rates among immigrant populations. The National Council of La Raza and other advocacy groups have defended sanctuary laws by arguing that they promote community-oriented policing efforts and protect against racial profiling, police misconduct, and civil rights violations. Critics against the policy contend that such laws allow illegal aliens who commit crimes to circumvent federal law and avoid identification and deportation.

Future Trends The number of illegal aliens residing in the United States grew steadily throughout the 1990's. More than half of all unauthorized visitors in the country were born in Mexico. According to the Center for Immigration Studies, about 9 percent of living people born in Mexico now reside in the United States. Additional resources to deter illegal border crossings as a result of laws implemented following the September 11, 2001, attacks have done little to slow the influx of illegal aliens and there is no evidence to suggest that current levels of

illegal entry into the United States will decrease significantly.

Barring major changes in the nation's legal immigration policy or enforcement strategies it is likely that immigration will continue at roughly current levels. More and more people will continue to enter this country lawfully. At the same time, however, it can be expected that many will enter the United States illegally. Controlling the national borders, thwarting organized alien smuggling rings, and identifying and deporting people who are in the United States illegally, especially those who commit crimes, will be priorities.

Wayne J. Pitts

Further Reading

Ahmed, Syed Refaat. *Forlorn Migrants: An International Legal Regime for Undocumented Migrant Workers*. Dhaka, Bangladesh: University Press, 2000. An international perspective on the problem of illegal immigrants by a Bangladeshi scholar.

Bischoff, Henry. *Immigration Issues*. Westport, Conn.: Greenwood Press, 2002. Collection of balanced discussions about the most important and most controversial issues relating to immigration, including laws regulating undocumented workers.

Cull, Nicholas J., and David Carrasco, eds. *Alambrista and the U.S.-Mexico Border: Film, Music, and Stories of Undocumented Immigrants*. Albuquerque: University of New Mexico Press, 2004. Collection of essays on dramatic works, films, and music about Mexicans who cross the border illegally into the United States.

Daniels, Roger. *Guarding the Golden Door: American Immigration Policy and Immigrants Since 1882*. New York: Hill & Wang, 2004. Study of the impact of ignorance, partisan politics, and unintended consequences in immigration policy during the post-Nine-Eleven war on terrorism.

Gonzales, Alfono. *Reform Without Justice: Latino Migrant Politics and the Homeland Security State*. New York Oxford University Press, 2014. A study of the Latino righs movemenst and its general lack of effectivenss in countering anti-immigration sentiment.

Kretsedemas, Philip, and Ana Aparicio, eds. *Immigrants, Welfare Reform, and the Poverty of Policy*. Westport, Conn.: Praeger, 2004. Collection of articles on topics relating to the economic problems of new immigrants in the United States, with particular attention to Haitian, Hispanic, and Southeast Asian immigrants.

Menjivar, Cecilia and Daniel Kanstroom, eds. *Constructing Immigrant 'Illegality': Critiques, Experiences, and Responses*. New York: Cambridge University Press, 2014. A collection of essays examining the concept of illegal immigration and how it is shaped by immigration law.

Nevins, Joseph. *Operation Gatekeeper: The Rise of the "Illegal Alien" and the Making of the U.S.-Mexico Boundary*. New York: Routledge, 2002. Critical history of federal efforts to control the influx of undocumented immigration across the border with Mexico.

Ngai, Mae M. *Impossible Subjects: Illegal Aliens and the Making of Modern*

America. Princeton, N.J.: Princeton University Press, 2004. Scholarly study of social and legal issues relating to illegal aliens in the United States during the twenty-first century.

Staeger, Rob. *Deported Aliens.* Philadelphia: Mason Crest, 2004. Informative study of immigration of illegal aliens to the United States and Canada since the 1960's, with attention to changes in immigration law.

Yoshida, Chisato, and Alan D. Woodland. *The Economics of Illegal Immigration.* New York: Palgrave Macmillan, 2005. Analysis of the economic impact of illegal immigration in the United States.

See also Border Patrol, U.S.; Chinese detentions in New York; Coast Guard, U.S.; Florida illegal-immigrant suit; Green cards; Immigration and Naturalization Service; Immigration "crisis"; Immigration Reform and Control Act of 1986; Justice and immigration; Operation Wetback; Plyler v. Doe; Proposition 187; Undocumented workers.

IMMIGRANT ADVANTAGE

Definition: Sociological term for a set of distinctions among minority groups that reside within a society and those peoples who immigrate to these societies voluntarily from other nations

Immigration issue: Sociological theories

Significance: Immigrant members of ethnic minorities often have advantages over already resident members of their ethnic groups.

Resident minority groups are often "marginalized," living on the fringe of society, often in poverty, lacking education, occupational skills, political power, or the means to integrate into the mainstream. These marginalized groups, like the immigrants, are frequently made up of ethnic and racial minorities. However, compared with marginalized groups, immigrants have numerous advantages and often become successful, productive members of a society. One of the primary advantages is that immigrants choose to move to a new country and are therefore motivated to succeed. Another advantage is that they often have the resources needed to relocate to a new country. National immigration services work hard at keeping out low-skilled and poorly educated immigrants.

A third advantage is that immigrants to the United States tend to believe in the "great melting pot" ideal and want to join the mainstream society and learn the new language. To become citizens of the United States, for example, immigrants must speak, read, and write English and pass an exam on U.S. history and government. Therefore, although immigrants may start on the lowest rungs of the economic ladder, they often move up quickly, unlike marginalized resident minorities.

Rochelle L. Dalla

Further Reading

Barone, Michael. *The New Americans: How the Melting Pot Can Work Again.* Washington, D.C.: Regnery, 2001.

Cook, Terrence E. *Separation, Assimilation, or Accommodation: Contrasting Ethnic Minority Policies.* Westport, Conn.: Praeger, 2003.

Foner, Nancy, Jan Rath, Jan Willem Duyvendak, and Rogier van Reekum, eds. *New York and Amsterdam: Immigration and the New Urban Landscape.* New York: New York University Press, 2014.

Jacoby, Tamar, ed. *Reinventing the Melting Pot: The New Immigrants and What It Means to Be American.* New York: Basic Books, 2004.

See also Accent discrimination; Chicano movement; Generational acculturation; Hansen effect; Machine politics; Naturalization.

IMMIGRANTS IN SPORTS

The Law: There are two available visas for athletes that are covered under 8 CFR 214.2 (o)(2)(i) and 8 CFR 214.2 (p)(2)(i). Only a United States employer or agent can file an O or P petition, with the exception of a foreign employer who files through a U.S. agent.The O-1 visa includes, but is not limited to athletes. It is known as the Extraordinary Ability Individuals Visa, and the international beneficiaries who receive it are those who exhibit exceptional and extraordinary abilities in a myriad of industries. These include: the arts, athletics, business, education, sciences, and those who are in the motion picture or television industry. Under this visa, they are entitled to temporarily come to the United States to perform for a U.S. employer the temporary services that they are qualified to perform for an event or number of events. In order to qualify for this visa, the applicant must demonstrate an extraordinary ability of their skill through sustained or international acclaim. Alternatively, the P-1 visa is granted uniquely to athletes and artists and is usually the easier of the two for an athlete to qualify for. Internationally recognized artists, entertainers, or athletes can petition to enter the United States in order to participate in a sporting event or a performance for an American employer. They may also qualify under an international employer that is working through an American agent. Though it is renewable, it is issued for the length of the season or a contract that expires in up to five years.

Date: The current nonimmigrant alien statutes were enacted in 1990 and became effective in 1992.

Immigration Issues: There are three levels of accepting immigrants in sports. They are minor amateur athletes, collegiate athletes who are transitioning to the professional level (usually in the age group of 18-22), and professional athletes over the age of 18. Each is required to fulfill stringent criteria in order to be granted immigrant in sports visas and status.

393

Significance: The United States allows qualifying immigrants into the United States to join and compete with teams and in other individual athletic endeavors as long as the visa requirements are met. Immigrant athletes during the 2012 London Olympics made up of more than 40 of the 600 Olympians. The presence of immigrant athletes is especially recognized in the baseball leagues. For example, 25% of the All-Star teams are comprised of immigrant players.

Background: In examining the three types of immigrant athletes, there are: amateur youths, collegiate in transition, and professional over 18 years old.

Amateur Youth Athletes There are two types of amateur athletes who apply for visas. One is the amateur athlete who wants to come to the United States for a short term training program as a visitor. The other is the minor amateur athlete (under the age of 18) seeking long term training that extends past a six month period who apply for the F-1 Student Visa.

Additionally, other amateur athletes can qualify for a P-1 visa. In this case, the athlete must show international recognition status. The amateur athlete must have a U.S. sponsor that is willing to submit the P-1 visa petition on the athlete's behalf. The government also has a list of six criteria for showing international recognition and the amateur athlete or team must meet at least two of these six criteria that include:

- Evidence of having participated in international competition with a national team;
- A written statement from an official of the governing body of the sport which details how the alien or team is internationally recognized;
- A written statement from a member of the sports media or a recognized expert in the sport which details how the alien or team is internationally recognized;
- Evidence that the individual or team is ranked if the sport has international rankings; or
- Evidence that the alien or team has received a significant honor or award in the sport.

Collegiate Transition-Aged Athletes (18 to 22 years old) These athletes' goal is to focus full time on their chosen sport rather than attend college. In which case, they cannot qualify for an F-1 student visa. Yet, they often don't have ample success to qualify for a P-1 visa as a professional athlete; therefore, their options are limited. In some cases these transitional athletes are able to qualify for a P-1 visa if they are regarded as internationally recognized in their sport. This visa allows them to live and work in the United States for up to five years in order to compete in the sport.

The criteria for these athletes to establish international recognition are:

- Evidence of participation in international competition with a national team;

- Evidence of participation to a significant extent for a U.S. college or university in intercollegiate competition in a prior season;
- A written statement from an official of the governing body of the sport which details how the alien or team is internationally recognized;
- A written statement from a member of the sports media or a recognized expert in the sport which details how the alien or team is internationally recognized;
- Evidence that the individual or team is ranked if the sport has international rankings; or
- Evidence that the alien or team has received a significant honor or award in the sport

In addition, an employer or agent must submit the P-1 application on behalf of the athlete.

College Graduates Alternatively, immigrant students who complete graduation from a college or university in the United States often qualify for Optional Practical Training (OPT). The OPT allows them to live and work in the United States for up to 12 post-graduation months.

At the time their OPT expires, their visa options include:

- H-1B visa is for workers in specialty fields or occupations. This visa is a three year option and is renewable for a second three-year period.
- O-1 visa is for those with an extraordinary ability. This visa is also a three year option, and the athlete must demonstrate having received sustained national or international acclaim and recognition for achievement in their chosen sport.
- P-1 visa is for internationally recognized athletes. This visa is a five year option that allows internationally recognized athletes to compete in their chosen sport in the United States.
- P-3 visa is for culturally unique performers/Q-1 visa for participates in cultural exchange programs. For example, an athlete who participates in a sport in which their country or culture is particularly renowned, then they can sometimes qualify for a P-3 or Q-1 visa to teach or coach in that sport.

Professional Athletes Professional athletes are allowed to come to the United States to participate in tournaments or competitions via one of two ways. The first is by using a visa waiver, which is permitted if they are from a visa waiver country. The second is by using a B-1 visitor visa. However, athletes who qualify for either a visa waiver or B-1 visas are not permitted to earn money other than prize money from tournaments.

Professional athletes who have the goal of becoming a U.S. citizen, and are therefore able to earn money beyond prize money, are generally required qualify for either the P-1 or the O-1 visas. These athletes' options are many, and the first two listed are "self-petition" options, therefore they do not require an agent or employer. The other three require the petition by an employer or sponsor. In addition, many of these are applicable because the USCIS states that the "arts" include athletics. The options include:

- EB-1 alien with extraordinary ability. Self-petition.
- EB-2 alien with exceptional abilities in the arts, sciences or business and a national interest waiver. Self-petition.
- EB-2 alien with exceptional ability or advanced degreed professional and pre-certification under Schedule A Group II (exceptional ability in the arts and sciences).
- EB-2 alien with exceptional ability in the arts, sciences or business or advanced degreed professionals.
- EB-3 skilled or professional worker. An athlete or coach can be viewed as a skilled or professional position.

Coaches and Other Supporting Individuals Immigration options extend to those who support athletes, such as coaches, trainers, mental conditioning consultants, nutritional advisors, and more. Their visa options include:

- H-1B visa for workers in specialty occupations.
- O-1 visa for aliens with extraordinary ability.
- O-1 visa for aliens with extraordinary ability.
- O-2 accompanying alien visa.
- P-1 visa for internationally recognized athletes.
- P-1S essential support worker.
- P-3 visa for culturally unique performers/Q-1 visa for participates in cultural exchange programs.

Famous Immigrant Athletes and Coaches These once immigrant athletes came to the United States and became word-renowned in sports, including: tennis, race car driving, body-building, basketball, and more.

- **Freddy Adu, Ghana:** Freddu Adu was born in Ghana in 1989. In 1997, when he was just eight years old, his mother won the Diversity Immigrant Visa Program, also known as the "green card lottery," which grants permanent residence to randomly selected applicants from certain countries. They moved to the United States and settled in Maryland. At the age of 14, he signed with Major League Soccer and played for D.C. United. In 2003, Adu signed a $1 million endorsement deal with Nike.
- **Mario Andretti, Italy:** Mario Andretti was born on February 28, 1940. He watched the Italian Grand Prix at Monza as a small child and was hooked. He later left war-torn Italy in 1955 with his family and moved to Pennsylvania. Andretti began racing cars with his twin brother, Aldo, who later quit after serious injury. Mario went on to win NASCAR's Daytona 500 in 1967 and later became one of only two drivers to win races in: Formula One, IndyCar, World Sportscar Championship and NASCAR. In total, he had 109 career wins on major circuits.

- **Mikhail Baryshnikov, USSR:** Mikhail Baryshnikov was born in 1948 in Latvia, which at the time was part of the Soviet Union. In 1966, he debuted with the Kirov Ballet. He later defected to the West in 1974 while on tour in Canada and went on to dance for the American Ballet Theatre and the New York City Ballet. He is often referred to as the greatest living male dancer. He also held the titles of artistic director of ABT and a choreographer and actor. He earned an Oscar nomination for his role in the 1977 film The Turning Point and stared in the famed tv show Sex and the City from 1998 to 2004.

- **Patrick Ewing, Jamaica:** Patrick Ewing was born in Kingston, Jamaica on August 5, 1962. He moved to the United States with his family at the age of 13. As a high school senior, he not only grew to 7' tall, but that was when he learned to play basketball. He attended Georgetown, after receiving many offers for college, from 1981-1985. He was the only player to win the consensus All-American award three times (1983, '84, '85) and was named Outstanding Player in 1984 when Georgetown won the NCAA. He also starred on the U.S. Olympic team that won in 1984. In 1985, Ewing was drafted by the New York Knicks, where he was a starter for 14 seasons. Later, in 1996, Ewing was named one of the top 50 players in NBA history.

- **Dikembe Mutombo, Congo:** Dikembe Mutombo was born in 1966 in the Democratic Republic of the Congo (which was then Zaire). The 7'2" athlete earned an academic USAID scholarship to attend Georgetown University (1988-1991), where he interned for the U.S. Congress and the World Bank. The Denver Nuggets drafted him in 1991. He later played center for the Houston Rockets, and when he was 40 years old, he was the oldest player in the National Basketball League. In 1997 Mutombo launched a foundation to improve health and education in Congo.

- **Knute Kenneth Rockne, Norway:** Knute Kenneth Rockne was born in Voss, Norway on March 31, 1931. He became both a football player and coach for the University of Notre Dame. Rockne is regarded as one of the greatest coaches in college football history, and, in fact, his biography at the College Football Hall of Fame calls him "without question, American football's most-renowned coach." As Norwegian American, Rockne earned his degree as a

Arnold Schwarzenegger was born in Austria in 1947. He moved to the U.S. and won the title Mr. Universe in body-building. In 2003, Schwarzenegger was elected 38th governor of California. (Bob Doran)

chemist at the University of Notre Dame and popularized the forward pass, which made Notre Dame a major factor in collegiate football.

- **Arnold Schwarzenegger, Austria:** Arnold Schwarzenegger was born in Austria in 1947. He moved to the United States in his twenties after competing in and winning the title Mr. Universe in body-building. He graduated from the University of Wisconsin and went on to become a famous movie star, staring in films such as Conan the Barbarian and the Terminator trilogy. Later, in 2003, Schwarzenegger was elected 38th governor of California, and was re-elected in 2006.

- **Maria Sharapova, Russia:** Maria Sharapova was born in Nyagan, Russia on April 19, 1987. She moved to the United States as a child with her father, escaping the fallout at Chernobyl. Separated from the rest of her family for 2 years, she couldn't reunite with her mother until her mother could gain a visa to join them. Maria began playing tennis at 4 years old and by 6 was in Moscow for an exhibition featuring Martina Navratilova. She grew to become a 6' tennis star who, in 2004 and at just 17 years old, defeated reigning tennis champion Serena Williams in the Grand Slam at Wimbledon.

- **Sammy Sosa, Dominican Republic:** Sammy Sosa was born in 1968 in the Dominican Republic. He began playing baseball at the age of 14, and two years later was recruited by the Texas Rangers at the age of 16. He went on to play for the Chicago White Sox, Chicago Cubs and Baltimore Orioles before resigning with the Texas Rangers. He was named a sportsman of the year by Sports Illustrated in 1998.

Legislation Recent legislation includes: October 7, 2009, the United States Citizenship and Immigration Services (USCIS) issued a clarification in regards to agents who file as a petitioner for the O and P visa classification. The clarification limited agent-based petitions to "those in the business as an agent." This clarification precludes one employer from filing an athlete's petition on behalf of other employers, with the exception of the petitioning employer exhibiting proof that they are in business as an agent and the other employers is its clients.

Two years later, on November 20, 2009, Acting Associate Director, Domestic Operations Donald Neufeld issued a Memorandum stating the Requirements for Agents and Sponsors Filing as Petitioners for the O and P Visa Classifications. His Memorandum retracted this component, permitting the petitioning employer to act as the agent for the other employers for "the purpose of filing the petition."

Heather Hummel

Further Reading

Schwarzenegger, Arnold, *Total Recall: My Unbelievable Life Story*, Simon & Schuster, October 1, 2012. An autobiographical look at the successes, and even failures, of immigrant athlete, movie star, and politician, Arnold Schwarzenegger.

Aria, Barbara, *Misha!: The Mikhail Baryshnikov Story*, St. Martins Press, 1998. A freelance writer's biographical take of the life of Mikhail Baryshnikov.

Sosa, Sammy and Breton, Marcos, *Sammy Sosa, An Autobiography*, Grand Central Publishing, May 4, 2000. A coauthored autobiographical book at the life of Dominican Republic born immigrant athlete, Sammy Sosa.

See also H1B visa; Naturalization; Visas.

IMMIGRATION ACT OF 1917

The Law: Restrictive federal legislation on immigration
Date: May 1, 1917

Immigration issues: Asian immigrants; Discrimination; Language; Laws and treaties; Nativism and racism

Significance: In an effort to exclude as immigrants those of ethnic origin considered incompatible with the racial stock of the country's founders, the U.S. Congress enacted this law to require literacy as a condition of admission to the United States.

During the late nineteenth century, the U.S. government for the first time began to accept the responsibility for restricting immigration. As long as there had been no question that people were welcome to enter and to become citizens of the United States—as had been the case since the American Revolution—each state was at liberty to regulate the flow of foreign nationals within its borders. After 1830, however, because of a large increase in the numbers of immigrants, especially from Catholic Ireland, where famine had motivated huge numbers to emigrate, a somewhat different public attitude emerged.

It became a matter of public anxiety, especially in the eastern United States, not only that the increased immigration was likely to create an oversupply of labor (a major concern of labor unions) but also that there were many entering the country who were deemed undesirable. Many people came to believe that laws should be made and enforced that would restrict the numbers and the kinds of people who would be allowed to enter the United States. In their party platforms, politicians of the period included promises to enact laws restricting immigration of criminals, paupers, and contract laborers—largely unskilled workers who were promised free transportation to America contingent upon repayment once admission was obtained and wages were earned. Others vowed themselves in favor of preventing the United States from becoming a place where European countries could conveniently rid themselves of their poor and of their criminal elements and stated their preference for what they would consider to be worthy and industrious Europeans—to the particular exclusion of laborers from China.

Beginning in 1875, numerous acts dealing with the problem of immigration were passed by Congress. Effective enforcement, however, was the problem with the earliest provisions for exclusion. Many began to believe that large

Senator Henry Cabot Lodge of Massachusetts was one of the most outspoken advocates of literacy tests for immigrants. (Library of Congress)

numbers of those who were not wanted could be refused admission by virtue of the fact that they would be unlikely to pass a simple literacy test. A senator from Massachusetts, Henry Cabot Lodge, was an early and influential advocate of a literacy test. In one of his congressional speeches, Senator Lodge proposed to exclude from admission any individual who could neither read nor write. (Literacy in any language was to be qualifying; knowledge of English was not to be required.)

It was believed, according to the senator, that the test would prevent immigration of many Italians, Russians, Poles, Hungarians, Greeks, and Asians, and that it would cause the exclusion of fewer of those who were English-speaking or who were Germans, Scandinavians, or French. Lodge insisted, in his argument, that the latter were more closely kin, racially, to those who had founded and developed the United States, and that therefore they would be more readily appreciated. (The senator made allowance for the Irish, even though he saw them as being of different racial stock, because they spoke English and had been associated with the English peoples for many centuries.)

Lodge further argued that the northern European immigrants were the ones most likely to move on to the West and South, where population was needed, whereas the southern Europeans—those intended to be excluded by the test— tended to stay in the crowded cities of the North and East, creating slums and placing a disproportionate financial burden on local charitable institutions. He categorized as also unlikely to pass the test those who intended only temporary stays—those who came to earn money that would not be used to further the country's development but whose purpose was to work and live in the poorest of conditions until their savings were adequate to return to and to make life better for a family in their country of origin.

In 1896, a Senate bill that included provision for the literacy test was sponsored by Lodge. The same bill was introduced in the House of Representatives. Congress passed the bill, but it was vetoed by President Grover Cleveland. The House was able to override the veto, but the Senate took no action.

In his veto message, President Cleveland indicated his extreme displeasure with the intent of the bill, reminding Congress of the fact that many of the country's best citizens had been immigrants who may have been deemed inferior. His opinion of the literacy test was that it would be no true measure of the quality of an applicant for admission, and that illiteracy should not be used as a pretext for exclusion when the real reasons were obviously different.

The controversy over the literacy test went on for approximately twenty-five years. Meanwhile, the idea became more popular. In 1907, the Joint Commission on Immigration was funded by Congress and charged to investigate U.S. immigration policy. In 1911, the commission released its forty-one-volume report. The literacy test was adopted as a provision of the Comprehensive Immigration Act of 1917—which was based primarily on recommendations of the commission—but only after similar attempts had been vetoed by President William Howard Taft in 1913 and by President Woodrow Wilson in 1915. Wilson twice vetoed the act of 1917 as well, only to have Congress pass it over his objections after his second veto.

President Wilson argued, in his first veto message to Congress, that the literacy test was an unprincipled departure from the nation's policy toward immigrants. He expressed concern that the literacy test, rather than being a test of character or of fitness to immigrate, was instead a penalty for not having had the opportunity for education and would exclude those who sought that very opportunity in order to better their circumstances.

The 1917 act provided that all persons seeking admission who were over sixteen years of age and who were physically capable of reading were to be tested. Those who were unable to read a few dozen words in some language were to be excluded from admission as immigrants. There were numerous exceptions, and in many cases illiteracy could be overlooked. Those seeking escape from religious persecution were excepted, as were those formerly admitted who had resided in the United States for five years and who had then departed but had returned within six months. Illiterate relatives of those passing the test were admissible if other wise qualified.

Impact of Event The main objective of the literacy test—to exclude those of certain ethnic origins or traditions—failed to reduce immigration in general and from the countries of southern and eastern Europe in particular. Other provisions had effectively discouraged emigrant Asians from choosing the United States as their intended destination. Instead, immigration increased in the four fiscal years that followed enactment of the 1917 law; 1,487,000 applicants were admitted in that period. Of that number, only 6,142 aliens (less than 0.5 percent) were deported for having failed the literacy test. Most of these were from Mexico, French Canada, or Italy.

Case studies of aliens who were unable to pass the literacy test indicate

President Woodrow Wilson, with his second wife, Edith, at his second inauguration in 1917. Wilson twice vetoed the Immigration Act of 1917, only to see Congress pass it over his objections. (Library of Congress)

that humane attempts were made by immigration authorities to ensure that the 1917 law was not cruelly enforced. Admission for a limited period could be granted, under bond, for those who other wise qualified but who were unable to pass the test. Applicants were given a chance to take classes in reading and writing a language of their choice, and more than one opportunity to pass the literacy test could be granted for those who appeared capable of sustaining themselves. Canadian immigration often was the alternative for those whose cases could justify no further extensions of time in which to pass the test and for whom deportation was no longer avoidable.

The racist attitudes of leaders such as Lodge were to dominate U.S. immigration policies until much later in the twentieth century, after the United States had participated in two world wars and after there had been refutation of earlier studies that attributed superior intellect and character to the northern European stock. The fact that the Spanish had colonized the Southwest considerably before northern Europeans began populating the eastern seaboard seems not to have been considered.

P. R. Lannert

Further Reading

Abbott, Edith. *Immigration: Select Documents and Case Records*. New York: Arno Press, 1969. Contains extracts of immigration acts and relevant court decisions as well as social case histories from the files of Illinois immigration officials. Indexed.

Gabaccia, Donna R. *Immigration and American Diversity: A Social and Cultural History*. Malden, Mass.: Blackwell, 2002. Sur vey of American immigration history, from the mid-eighteenth century to the early twenty-first century, with an emphasis on cultural and social trends, and with attention to ethnic conflicts, nativism, and racialist theories.

Legomsky, Stephen H. *Immigration and Refugee Law and Policy*. 3d ed. New York: Foundation Press, 2002. Legal textbook on immigration and refugee law.

LeMay, Michael C., and Elliott Robert Barkan, eds. *U.S. Immigration and Naturalization Laws and Issues: A Documentary History*. Westport, Conn.: Greenwood Press, 1999. History of U.S. immigration laws supported by extensive extracts from documents.

Shanks, Cheryl. *Immigration and the Politics of American Sovereignty, 1890-1990*. Ann Arbor: University of Michigan Press, 2001. Scholarly study of changing federal immigration laws from the late nineteenth through the late twentieth centuries, with particular attention to changing quota systems and exclusionary policies.

See also Cable Act; Chinese Exclusion Act; Immigration Act of 1921; Immigration Act of 1924; Immigration Act of 1943; Immigration Act of 1990; Immigration and Nationality Act of 1952; Immigration and Nationality Act of 1965; Immigration and Naturalization Service; Immigration law; Immigration Reform and Control Act of 1986; Naturalization Act of 1790; Page law; War Brides Act.

IMMIGRATION ACT OF 1921

The Law: Federal legislation on immigration that imposed a quota system
Date: May 19, 1921

Immigration issues: Asian immigrants; Chinese immigrants; Discrimination; Laws and treaties; Nativism and racism

Significance: This restrictive legislation created a quota system that favored the nations of northern and western Europe and put an end to the ideal of the United States as a melting pot.

Throughout most of the nineteenth century, immigration to the United States was open to anyone who wanted to enter. By the 1880's, however, this unlimited freedom was beginning to disappear. The first law restricting immigration came in 1882, when Chinese were excluded from entering American territory. Hostility to Chinese workers in California sparked Congress to pass a bill amid warnings that Chinese worked for lower wages than whites and came from such a culturally inferior civilization that they would never make good Americans. The law became permanent in 1902. Five years later, under a gentlemen's agreement with the Japanese government, citizens of that country were added to the excluded list. The only other people barred from entering the United States were prostitutes, insane persons, paupers, polygamists, and anyone suffering from a "loathsome or contagious disease." Under these categories, compared to more than a million immigrants per year from 1890 to 1914, less than thirteen thousand were kept out annually.

The small number of those excluded troubled anti-immigrant groups, such as the American Protective Association, founded in 1887, and the Immigration Restriction League, created in Boston in 1894. Both organizations warned of the "immigrant invasion" which threatened the American way of life. These opponents of open immigration argued that since 1880, most new arrivals had come from different areas of Europe from that of the pre-1880 immigrants, who came largely from Germany, England, Ireland, and Scandinavia. The "new" immigrants—mainly Slavs, Poles, Italians, and Jews—came from poorer and more culturally "backward" areas of Europe.

Many of these immigrants advocated radicalism, anarchism, socialism, or communism, and were unfamiliar with ideas of democracy and progress. Furthermore, they preferred to live in ghettos in cities, where they strengthened the power of political machines and corrupt bosses. Those who considered themselves guardians of traditional American values found support for their position among trade unionists in the American Federation of Labor (AFL), whose president, Samuel Gompers, argued that the new immigrants provided employers with an endless supply of cheap labor, leading to lower wages for everyone.

Advocates of restriction found their chief congressional spokesperson in Senator Henry Cabot Lodge, a member of the Immigration Restriction League, who sponsored a bill calling for a literacy test. Such a law, which called upon immigrants to be able to read and write in their native language, was seen as an effective barrier to most "new" immigrants. Congress passed the bill in

1897, but President Grover Cleveland vetoed it, arguing that it was unnecessary and discriminatory. Cleveland believed that American borders should remain open to anyone who wanted to enter and that there were enough jobs and opportunities to allow anyone to fulfill a dream of economic success. Advocates of this vision of the American Dream, however, were lessening in number over time.

The assassination of President William McKinley in 1901 led to the exclusion of anarchists and those who advocated the violent overthrow of the government of the United States. A more important step to a quota system, however, came in 1907, when the House and Senate established the U.S. Immigration Commission, under the leadership of Senator William P. Dillingham. The commission issued a forty-two-volume report in 1910, advocating a reduction in immigration because of the "racial inferiority" of new immigrant groups. Studies of immigrant populations, the commission concluded, showed that people from southern and eastern Europe had a higher potential for criminal activity, were more likely to end up poor and sick, and were less intelligent than other Americans. It called for passage of a literacy test to preserve American values. Congress passed legislation in 1912 calling for such a test, but President William Howard Taft vetoed it, saying that illiteracy resulted from lack of educational opportunity and had little to do with native intelligence. Open entrance to the United States was part of American history, and many of America's wealthiest and hardest working citizens had come without knowing how to read and write. If the United States barred such people, Taft argued, America would become weaker and less wealthy.

In 1915, Woodrow Wilson became the third president to veto a literacy bill, denouncing its violation of the American ideal of an open door. Two years later, in the wake of American entrance into World War I and growing hostility against foreigners, Congress overrode Wilson's second veto and the literacy test became law. Along with establishing a reading test for anyone over age sixteen, the law also created a "barred zone" which excluded immigrants from most of Asia, including China, India, and Japan, regardless of whether they could read. As it turned out, the test that asked adults to read a few words in any recognized language did little to reduce immigration. Between 1918 and 1920, less than 1 percent of those who took it failed. Representative Albert Johnson, chair of the House Committee on Immigration, had been a longtime advocate of closing the borders of the United States. In 1919, he called for the suspension of all immigration. Johnson's proposal was defeated in the House of Representatives.

In 1920, however, immigration increased dramatically, as did fears that millions of refugees from war-torn Europe were waiting to flood into the United States. Much of the argument for restriction was based on ideas associated with scientific racism. The Republican candidate for the presidency, Warren G. Harding, advocated restriction in several speeches, warning of the dangers inherent in allowing open admission. He called for legislation that would permit entrance to the United States only to people whose background and racial characteristics showed that they could adopt American values and principles. The next year, Vice President Calvin Coolidge authored a magazine article claiming that laws of biology proved that "Nordics," the preferred type, deteriorated intellectually and physically when allowed to intermarry with other races. These views reflected the growing influence of eugenics, the science of improving the human race by discouraging the birth of the "unfit." Madison Grant, a lawyer and secretary of the New York Zoological Society, and later an adviser to Albert Johnson's Immigration Committee, wrote the most influential book advocating this racist way of thinking, The Passing of the Great Race in America (1916). In it, he described human society as a huge snake. Nordic races made up the head, while the inferior races formed the tail. It would be this type of scientific argument, more than any other, that would provide the major rationale for creation of the 1921 quota system. The tail could not be allowed to rule the head.

President William Howard Taft around 1908. Taft was chief justice of the United States when the Immigration Act of 1921 was enacted, but he vetoed legislation making literacy a requirement for immigration while he was president. (Library of Congress)

Early in 1921, the House debated and passed Johnson's bill calling for a two-year suspension of all immigration. The Senate Committee on Immigration, chaired by Senator LeBaron Colt, held hearings on a similar proposal but refused to support a total ban after hearing arguments from business groups fearful that complete exclusion would stop all access to European laborers. Representatives from the National Association of Manufacturers testified on the need to have access to inexpensive labor, even though some business leaders were beginning to fear that too many in the immigration pool were influenced by communism and socialism, especially after the communist victory in Russia in 1918. The possibility of thousands of radical workers with a greater tendency to strike coming into the country seemed too high a price to pay in return for lower wages. Unions, especially the AFL, continued to lobby for strict regulation of immigration. To keep wages high, Samuel Gompers told Congress, foreign workers had to be kept out. By 1921, the only widespread support for free and open immigration came from immigrant groups themselves. Although a few members of Congress supported their position, it was a distinctly minority view.

Senator William Dillingham, whose report in 1910 had renewed efforts to restrict immigration, offered a quota plan which he hoped would satisfy business and labor. He called for a policy in which each nation would receive a quota of immigrants equal to 5 percent of that country's total population in the United States according to the 1910 census. Dillingham's suggestion passed the Senate with little opposition and gained favor in the House. Before its final approval, however, Johnson and his supporters of total suspension reduced the quota to 3 percent and set 350,000 as the maximum number of legal immigrants in any one year. Woodrow Wilson vetoed the bill shortly before leaving office, but it was passed with only one dissenting vote in the Senate during a special session called by President Harding on May 19, 1921. The House approved the Emergency Quota Act the same day without a recorded vote. The only opposition came from representatives with large numbers of immigrants in their districts. Adolph Sabath, a Democratic congressperson from Chicago, led the dissenters, arguing that the act was based on a "pseudoscientific proposition" that falsely glorified the Nordic nations. His comments had little effect on the result. One of the most important changes in American immigration history went into effect in June of 1921.

Impact of Event The Emergency Quota Act of 1921 severely reduced immigration into the United States. In 1922, its first full year of operation, only 309,556 people legally entered the country, compared with 805,228 the previous year. Quotas for Europe, the Middle East, Africa, Australia, and New Zealand were generally filled quickly, although economic depressions in England, Ireland, and Germany kept many potential immigrants at home. Less than half the legal number of immigrants came to America the first year; the southern and eastern Europeans filled almost 99 percent of their limit. No limits existed for Canada, Mexico, and other nations of the Western Hemisphere. To keep an adequate supply of cheap agricultural labor available to farmers in Texas and California, Congress refused to place a quota on immigration from these areas of the world. Japan and China were the only countries with a quota of zero, as Congress continued its policy of exclusion for most areas of Asia.

The 1921 act provided for "special preferences" for relatives of U.S. citizens, including wives, children under eighteen, parents, brothers, and sisters. The commissioner of immigration was to make it a priority to maintain family unity; however, this was to be the only exception to the strict quota policy.

Congress extended the "emergency" law in May, 1922, for two more years. This move, however, did not satisfy Representative Johnson and others supporting complete restriction. Johnson's Immigration Committee continued to hold hearings and gather evidence supporting an end to all immigration. Johnson became increasingly interested in eugenics and remained in close contact with Madison Grant. In 1923, Johnson was elected president of the Eugenics Research Association of America, a group devoted to gathering statistics on the hereditary traits of Americans. He seemed especially interested in studies showing a large concentration of "new" immigrants in mental hospitals, prisons, and poorhouses. Such information led him to call for a change in the law. A reduction in the quota for "new" immigrants was necessar y, he claimed, to save the United States from even larger numbers of paupers, mental patients, and criminals. The Immigration Committee voted to change the census base from 1910 to 1890, when there were far fewer southern and eastern Europeans in the country, and to reduce the quota from 3 percent to 2 percent. Congress would adopt those ideas in 1924.

Under the 1921 law, boats filled with prospective immigrants were returned to their homelands. These actions, however, were only the beginning, and the guardians of racial purity in Congress were already moving toward even tighter controls. Restrictionists had gotten most of what they wanted.

Leslie V. Tischauser

Further Reading

Bennett, Marion T. *American Immigration Policies*. Washington, D.C.: Public Affairs Press, 1963. Although written from a prorestriction point of view, this book contains useful information on all immigration laws up to 1962 and their effects on the numbers of people entering the United States. Contains a brief but useful summary of arguments for and against the 1921 act.

Divine, Robert. *American Immigration Policy, 1924-1952*. New Haven, Conn.: Yale University Press, 1957. Interesting and detailed account of the congressional movement toward restriction. Although mainly concerned with the 1924 law and its aftermath, there is a summary of attitudes in Congress and the rest of the United States that led to the 1921 act. Written from an antirestriction point of view.

Higham, John. *Strangers in the Land: Patterns of American Nativism, 1860-1925*. New York: Atheneum, 1975. Classic account of anti-immigrant hostility in the United States from the Civil War to the final victory for restriction during the 1920's. Presents a full account of the arguments for and against quotas, and contains an extensive discussion of the 1921 bill and the congressional debate on the subject.

Lee, Erika. *At America's Gates: Chinese Immigration During the Exclusion Era, 1882-1943*. Chapel Hill: University of North Carolina Press, 2003. Study of immigration from China to the United States from the time of the Chinese Exclusion Act to the loosening of American immigration laws during the 1960's.

Legomsky, Stephen H. *Immigration and Refugee Law and Policy*. 3d ed. New York: Foundation Press, 2002. Legal textbook on immigration and refugee law.

LeMay, Michael C., and Elliott Robert Barkan, eds. *U.S. Immigration and Naturalization Laws and Issues: A Documentary History*. Westport, Conn.: Greenwood Press, 1999. History of U.S. immigration laws supported by extensive extracts from documents.

Menjivar, Cecilia and Daniel Kanstroom, eds. *Constructing Immigrant 'Illegality': Critiques, Experiences, and Responses*. New York: Cambridge University Press, 2014. A collection of essays examining the concept of illegal immigration and how it is shaped by immigration law.

Ngai, Mae, and Jon Gjerde. *Major Problems in American Immigration History: Documents and Essays*. 2nd ed. Boston: Wadsworth, Cengage Learning, 2013. A collection of essays and couments coering the history of immigration in U.S. history.

Shanks, Cheryl. *Immigration and the Politics of American Sovereignty, 1890-1990*. Ann Arbor: University of Michigan Press, 2001. Scholarly study of changing federal immigration laws from the late nineteenth through the late twentieth centuries, with particular attention to changing quota systems and exclusionary policies.

Solomon, Barbara. *Ancestors and Immigrants*. Cambridge, Mass.: Harvard University Press, 1956. A study of the Immigration Restriction League of Boston. Asserts that restrictionists perceived their world as crumbling under the influx of vast numbers of immigrants who knew nothing of democracy and liberty and were inferior intellectually and physically. Most of the study looks at attitudes before 1921.

See also Cable Act; Chinese Exclusion Act; Immigration Act of 1917; Immigration Act of 1924; Immigration Act of 1943; Immigration Act of 1990; Immigration and Nationality Act of 1952; Immigration and Nationality Act of 1965; Immigration and Naturalization Service; Immigration law; Immigration Reform and Control Act of 1986; Naturalization Act of 1790; Page law.

IMMIGRATION ACT OF 1924

The Law: Federal legislation on immigration that made the quota system more restrictive
Date: May 26, 1924

Immigration issues: Asian immigrants; Chinese immigrants; Discrimination; Laws and treaties; Nativism and racism

Significance: Also known as the National Origins Act, the Immigration Act of 1924 restricted immigration by means of a quota system that severely restricted immigration from central and eastern Europe.

There was no clearly defined official U.S. policy toward immigration until the late nineteenth century. The United States was still a relatively young country, and there was a need for settlers in the West and for workers to build industry. Chinese immigrants flowed into California in 1849 and the early 1850's, searching for fortune and staying as laborers who worked the mines and helped to build the transcontinental railroad.

The earliest immigration restriction focused on Asians. In 1875, the federal government restricted the number of Chinese and Japanese coming into the country. The push for restriction of Asian immigrants was led by U.S. workers. After the depression of 1877, Denis Kearney, an Irish-born labor organizer, helped found the Workingman's Trade and Labor Union of San Francisco, an anti-Chinese and anticapitalist group. Kearney and others believed that lower-paid Chinese workers took jobs away from white workers, and they agitated for expulsion of the Chinese and legal restrictions on future immigrants. Their efforts were successful in 1882, when the Chinese Exclusion Act was passed. The act exempted teachers, students, merchants, and pleasure travelers, and remained in effect until 1943. With the act of 1882, the federal government had, for the first time, placed restrictions on the immigration of persons from a specific country. More specific policy toward European immigration began during the 1880's. In 1882, the federal government excluded convicts, paupers, and mentally impaired persons. Organized labor's efforts also were successful in 1882, with the prohibition of employers' recruiting workers in Europe and paying their passage to the United States.

Restrictive Changes   Federal law became more restrictive during the early twentieth century, with the passage of the Immigration Act of 1903, which excluded epileptics, beggars, and anarchists. In 1907, the U.S. Immigration Commission was formed. This group, also known as the Dillingham Commission, published a forty-two-volume survey of the impact of immigration on American life and called for a literacy test and further immigration restriction. Although several presidential vetoes had prevented a literacy requirement, in 1917, the U.S. Congress overrode President Woodrow Wilson's veto and passed a law requiring a literacy test for newcomers. The test was designed to reduce the number of immigrants, particularly those from southeastern Europe, where the literacy rate was low.

   The marked change in official policy and in the view of a majority of people in the United States was caused by several factors. A strong nativist movement had begun after World War I with such groups as the American Protective Association,

U.S. Health Service officers inspecting Japanese immigrants arriving on the West Coast of the United States several months before the U.S. Congress passed the restrictive Immigration Act of 1924. (National Archives)

an organization that began in the midwest during the 1880's and focused on prejudice against aliens and Roman Catholics. Senator Henry Cabot Lodge organized the Immigration Restriction League in Boston, indicating the addition of U.S. leaders and intellectuals to the restriction movement. The war had brought the United States into position as a major world power, with a resultant view that the United States should be a nation of conformity. Political and economic problems in Europe, including the war and a postwar economic depression, had led to fear of too many immigrants fleeing Europe. Changes in the U.S. economy reduced the need for manual labor, thus creating a fear of lack of job security.

The push for restriction coincided with the most intensive era of immigration in United States history. From the late 1880's until the 1920's, the nation experienced

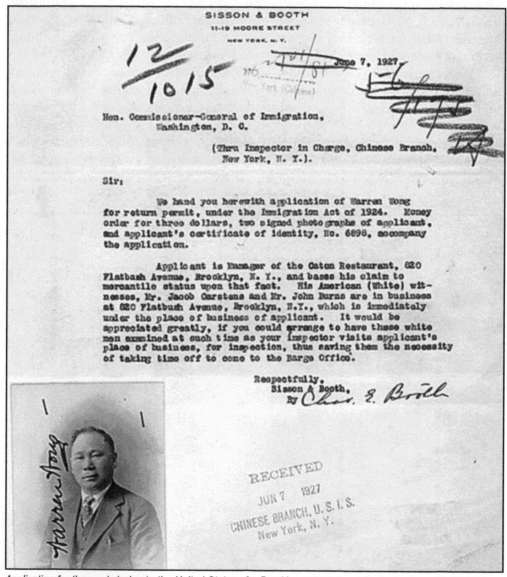

Application for the readmission to the United States of a Brooklyn restaurateur who had returned to China for a visit. The letter cites the terms of the Immigration Act of 1924. (NARA)

wave after wave of immigration, with millions of persons coming into the country each decade. The growth of new physical and social sciences that emphasized heredity as a factor in intelligence led many people to believe that persons such as Slavs or Italians were less intelligent than western Europeans such as the Norwegians or the English. The belief in genetic inferiority gave credence to the immigration restriction movement and helped sway the government.

At the same time that millions of newcomers were entering the United States, a spirit of reform, the Progressive Era, had grown throughout the country. Americans who saw themselves as progressive and for ward-looking pushed for change in politics, society, and education, particularly in the crowded urban areas of the Northeast. Europeans had emigrated in large numbers to the cities, and newer groups, such as Italians and Poles, were seen by many progressive-minded reformers as the root of urban problems. Thus it was with the help of progressive leaders that a push was made at the federal level to restrict the number of immigrants.

Quota System   In 1921, Congress passed a temporary measure that was the first U.S. law specifically restricting European immigration. The act established a quota system that held the number of immigrants to 3 percent of each admissible nationality living in the United States in 1910. Quotas were established for persons from Europe, Asia, Africa, Australia, and New Zealand. Although only a temporary measure, the Immigration Act of 1921 marked the beginning of a permanent policy of restricting European immigration. It began a bitter three-year controversy that led to the Immigration Act of 1924.

The U.S. Congress amended the 1921 act with a more restrictive permanent measure in May of 1924, the Johnson-Reid Act. This act, which became known as the National Origins Act, took effect on July 1, 1924. It limited the annual immigration to the United States to 2 percent of a country's population in the United States as of the census of 1890. With the large numbers of northern and western Europeans who had immigrated to the country throughout the nation's history, the act effectively restricted southern and eastern European immigrants to approximately 12 percent of the total immigrant population. Asian immigration was completely prohibited, but there was no restriction on immigration from independent nations of the Western Hemisphere.

The new law also changed the processing system for aliens by moving the immigration inspection process to U.S. consulates in foreign countries and requiring immigrants to obtain visas in their home countries before emigrating to the United States. The number of visas was held to 10 percent in each country per month and thus reduced the number of people arriving at Ellis Island, leading to the eventual closing of the facility.

The Immigration Act of 1924 reflected a change in the controversy that occurred in the three-year period after the act of 1921. By 1924, the major factor in immigration restriction was racial prejudice. By using the U.S. Census of 1890 as the basis for quotas, the government in effect sharply reduced the number of southern and eastern Europeans, who had not begun to arrive in large numbers until after that census year. The passage of the act codified an official policy of preventing further changes in the ethnic composition of U.S. society, and it was to remain in effect until passage of the Immigration and Nationality Act of 1965.

Judith Boyce DeMark

Further Reading

Curran, Thomas J. *Xenophobia and Immigration, 1820-1930.* Boston: Twayne, 1975. Basic over view of the reasons for immigration restriction throughout U.S. history, focusing on nativism and such groups as the Ku Klux Klan.

Divine, Robert A. *American Immigration Policy, 1924-1952.* New Haven, Conn.: Yale University Press, 1957. Reprint. New York: Da Capo Press, 1972. One of the most comprehensive treatments of the history of immigration restriction from the 1924 act through the mid-1950's.

Hirobe, Izumi. *Japanese Pride, American Prejudice: Modifying the Exclusion Clause of the 1924 Immigration Act.* Stanford, Calif.: Stanford University Press, 2001. Scholarly study of the impact of the Immigration Act of 1924 on Japanese immigrants.

Lee, Erika. *At America's Gates: Chinese Immigration During the Exclusion Era, 1882-1943.* Chapel Hill: University of North Carolina Press, 2003. Study of immigration from China to the United States from the time of the Chinese Exclusion Act to the loosening of American immigration laws during the 1960's.

LeMay, Michael C., and Elliott Robert Barkan, eds. *U.S. Immigration and Naturalization Laws and Issues: A Documentary History.* Westport, Conn.: Greenwood Press, 1999. History of U.S. immigration laws supported by extensive extracts from documents.

Menjivar, Cecilia and Daniel Kanstroom, eds. *Constructing Immigrant 'Illegality': Critiques, Experiences, and Responses.* New York: Cambridge University Press, 2014. A collection of essays examining the concept of illegal immigration and how it is shaped by immigration law.

Ngai, Mae, and Jon Gjerde. *Major Problems in American Immigration History: Documents and Essays.* 2nd ed. Boston: Wadsworth, Cengage Learning, 2013. A collection of essays and documents covering the history of immigration in U.S. history.

Seller, Maxine S. "Historical Perspectives on American Immigration Policy: Case Studies and Current Implications." In *U.S. Immigration Policy*, edited by Richard R. Hofstetter. Durham, N.C.: Duke University Press, 1984. Contains a chronology of the series of events leading up to the Immigration Act of 1924, with a discussion of how those events relate to recent immigration history.

Shanks, Cheryl. *Immigration and the Politics of American Sovereignty, 1890-1990.* Ann Arbor: University of Michigan Press, 2001. Scholarly study of changing federal immigration laws from the late nineteenth through the late twentieth centuries, with particular attention to changing quota systems and exclusionary policies.

See also Cable Act; Chinese Exclusion Act; Immigration Act of 1917; Immigration Act of 1921; Immigration Act of 1943; Immigration Act of 1990; Immigration and Nationality Act of 1952; Immigration and Nationality Act of 1965; Immigration and Naturalization Service; Immigration law; Immigration Reform and Control Act of 1986; Naturalization Act of 1790; Page law; War Brides Act.

IMMIGRATION ACT OF 1943

The Law: Federal legislation on immigration that loosened restrictiions
Date: December 17, 1943

Immigration issues: Asian immigrants; Chinese immigrants; Citizenship and naturalization; Laws and treaties

Significance: The Immigration Act of 1943 repealed Asian exclusion laws, opening the way for further immigration reforms.

The passage by Congress of the Immigration Act, also known as the Magnuson Act, and President Franklin D. Roosevelt's signing it into law ended the era of legal exclusion of Chinese immigrants to the United States and began an era during which sizable numbers of Chinese and other Asian immigrants came to the country. It helped bring about significant changes in race relations in the United States.

The first wave of Chinese immigrants came from the Pearl River delta region in southern China. They began coming to California in 1849 during the gold rush and continued to come to the western states as miners, railroad builders, farmers, fishermen, and factory workers. Most were men. Many came as contract laborers and intended to return to China. Anti-Chinese feelings, begun during the gold rush and expressed in mob actions and local discriminatory laws, culminated in the Chinese Exclusion Act of 1882, barring the immigration of Chinese laborers for ten years. The act was rcnewed in 1892, applied to Hawaii when those islands were annexed by the United States in 1898, and made permanent in 1904. Another bill, passed in 1924, made Asians ineligible for U.S. citizenship and disallowed Chinese wives of U.S. citizens to immigrate to the United States. As a result, the Chinese population in the United States declined from a peak of 107,475 in 1880 to 77,504 in 1940.

The passage of the Magnuson Act of 1943, which repealed the Chinese Exclusion Act of 1882, inaugurated profound changes in the status of ethnic Chinese who were citizens or residents of the United States. It made Chinese immigrants, many of whom had lived in the United States for years, eligible for citizenship. It also allotted a minuscule quota of 105 Chinese persons per year who could enter the United States as immigrants.

The 1943 bill was a result of recognition of China's growing international status after 1928 under the Nationalist government and growing U.S. sympathy for China's heroic resistance to Japanese aggression after 1937. It also was intended to counter Japanese wartime propaganda aimed at discrediting the United States among Asians by portraying it as a racist nation.

Post-World War II Changes World War II was a turning point for ChineseU.S. relations. After Japan's attack on Pearl Harbor in December, 1941, China and the United States became allies against the Axis Powers. Madame Chiang Kai-shek, wife of China's wartime leader, won widespread respect and sympathy for China during her visit to the United States; she was the second female foreign leader to address a joint session of Congress.

In 1943, the United States and Great Britain also signed new treaties with China that ended a century of international inequality for China. These events and the contributions of Chinese Americans in the war favorably affected the position and status of Chinese Americans. The 1943 act also opened the door for other legislation that allowed more Chinese to immigrate to the United States. In the long run, these laws had a major impact on the formation of Chinese families in the United States.

The War Brides Act of 1945, for example, permitted foreign-born wives of U.S. soldiers to enter the United States and become naturalized. Approximately six thousand Chinese women entered the United States during the next several years as wives of U.S. servicemen. An amendment to this act, passed in 1946, put the Chinese wives and children of U.S. citizens outside the quota, resulting in the reunion of many separated families and allowing ten thousand Chinese, mostly wives, and also children of U.S. citizens of Chinese ethnicity, to enter the country during the next eight years. The Displaced Persons Act of 1948 granted permanent resident status, and eventually the right of citizenship, to 3,465 Chinese students, scholars, and others stranded in the United States by the widespread civil war that erupted between the Chinese Nationalists and communists after the end of World War II.

The Refugee Relief Act of 1953 allowed an additional 2,777 refugees to remain in the United States after the civil war ended in a communist victory and the establishment of the People's Republic of China. Some Chinese students from the Republic of China on Taiwan, who came to study in the United States after 1950 and found employment and sponsors after the end of their studies, were also permitted to remain and were eligible for naturalization.

The four immigration acts passed between 1943 and 1953 can be viewed as a result of the alliance between the United States and the Republic of China in World War II and U.S. involvement in the Chinese civil war that followed. In a wider context, they were also the result of changing views on race and race relations that World War II and related events brought about. Finally, they heralded the Immigration and Nationality Act of 1965, which revolutionized U.S. immigration policy in ending racial quotas. Its most dramatic consequence was the significant increase of Asian immigrants in general, and Chinese immigrants in particular, into the United States.

The new immigrants changed the makeup of Chinese American society and caused a change in the way the Chinese were perceived by the majority groups in the United States. Whereas most of the earlier immigrants tended to live in ghettoized Chinatowns, were poorly educated, and overwhelmingly worked in low-status jobs as laundrymen, miners, or railroad workers, the new immigrants were highly educated, cosmopolitan, and professional. They came from the middle class, traced their roots to all parts of China, had little difficulty acculturating and assimilating into the academic and professional milieu of peoples of European ethnicity in the United States, and tended not to live in Chinatowns. The latter group was mainly responsible for revolutionizing the way Chinese Americans were perceived in the United States.

Jiu-Hwa Lo Upshur

Further Reading

Chan, Sucheng, ed. *Entry Denied: Exclusion and the Chinese Community in America, 1882-1943.* Philadelphia: Temple University Press, 1991. Articles from nine scholars on different facets of Chinese immigration to the United States during the era of exclusion.

Lee, Erika. *At America's Gates: Chinese Immigration During the Exclusion Era, 1882-1943.* Chapel Hill: University of North Carolina Press, 2003. Study of immigration from China to the United States from the time of the Chinese Exclusion Act to the loosening of American immigration laws during the 1960's.

LeMay, Michael C., and Elliott Robert Barkan, eds. *U.S. Immigration and Naturalization Laws and Issues: A Documentary History.* Westport, Conn.: Greenwood Press, 1999. History of U.S. immigration laws supported by extensive extracts from documents.

Menjivar, Cecilia and Daniel Kanstroom, eds. *Constructing Immigrant 'Illegality': Critiques, Experiences, and Responses.* New York: Cambridge University Press, 2014. A collection of essays examining the concept of illegal immigration and how it is shaped by immigration law.

Min, Pyong Gap, ed. *Asian Americans: Contemporary Trends and Issues.* Thousand Oaks, Calif.: Sage Publications, 1995. Collection of essays that gives an overall picture of Asian American issues. A new edition was scheduled for 2006 publication.

Ngai, Mae, and Jon Gjerde. *Major Problems in American Immigration History: Documents and Essays.* 2nd ed. Boston: Wadsworth, Cengage Learning, 2013. A collection of essays and couments coering the history of immigration in U.S. history.

Riggs, Fred W. *Pressure on Congress: A Study of the Repeal of Chinese Exclusion. 1950.* Reprint. Westport, Conn.: Greenwood Press, 1972. Detailed account of the reasons for the repeal of the exclusion law.

Shanks, Cheryl. *Immigration and the Politics of American Sovereignty, 1890-1990.* Ann Arbor: University of Michigan Press, 2001. Scholarly study of changing federal immigration laws from the late nineteenth through the late twentieth centuries, with particular attention to changing quota systems and exclusionary policies.

See also Cable Act; Chinese Exclusion Act; Immigration Act of 1917; Immigration Act of 1921; Immigration Act of 1924; Immigration Act of 1990; Immigration and Nationality Act of 1952; Immigration and Nationality Act of 1965; Immigration and Naturalization Service; Immigration law; Immigration Reform and Control Act of 1986; Naturalization Act of 1790; Page law; War Brides Act.

IMMIGRATION ACT OF 1990

The Law: Federal legislation on immigration that imposed new restrictions
Date: November 29, 1990

Immigration issues: Discrimination; Laws and treaties

Significance: Congress passed this legislation in response to a widespread belief among legislators and the general public that many of the economic and social ills of the United States were caused by large populations of poor, non-English-speaking immigrants and in response to a growing need for skilled workers in technical fields in an increasingly international marketplace.

One of many immigration laws passed during the twentieth century, the Immigration Act of 1990 set numerical limits for immigrants to the United States and established a system of preferences to determine which of the many applicants for admission should be accepted. Under the terms of the 1990 act, only 675,000 immigrants, not including political refugees, were to be admitted to the United States each year. These immigrants were eligible for preferential admission consideration if they fell into one of three groups: immigrants who had family members already legally in the country; employment-based immigrants who were able to prove that they had exceptional ability in certain professions with a high demand; and those from designated underrepresented nations, who were labeled "diversity immigrants."

Because the new law nearly tripled the annual allotment of employment-based immigrants from 54,000 to 140,000, business and industry leaders heralded their increased opportunity to compete internationally for experienced and talented engineers, technicians, and multinational executives. Others believed that the preference for certain kinds of workers masked a preference for whites over non-whites, and wealthier immigrants over poorer. Divisions over the law between racial and political groups intensified when successful lobbying led to refinements in the law making it easier for fashion models and musicians, especially from Europe, to gain visas, while efforts to gain admittance for more women fleeing genital mutilation in African and Arab nations failed.

The act made it easier for certain people—contract workers, musicians and other artists, researchers and educators participating in exchange programs—to perform skilled work in the United States on a temporary basis, with no intention of seeking citizenship. At the same time, the new law made it more difficult for unskilled workers, such as domestic workers and laborers, to obtain immigrant visas.

Finally, the Immigration Act of 1990 attempted to correct criticism of the 1986 Immigration Reform and Control Act by increasing that act's antidiscrimination provisions and increasing the penalties for discrimination. In a significant change in U.S. immigration law, the act revised the reasons a person might be refused immigrant status or be deported. After 1952, for example, communists were denied permission to enter the country on nonimmigrant work visas and were subject to deportment if identified, and potential political refugees from nations friendly to the United States were turned away as a matter of foreign policy. Under the new law, a wider range of political and ideological beliefs became acceptable.

Cynthia A. Bily

Further Reading

Legomsky, Stephen H. *Immigration and Refugee Law and Policy*. 3d ed. New York: Foundation Press, 2002. Legal textbook on immigration and refugee law.

LeMay, Michael C., and Elliott Robert Barkan, eds. *U.S. Immigration and Naturalization Laws and Issues: A Documentary History*. Westport, Conn.: Greenwood Press, 1999. History of U.S. immigration laws supported by extensive extracts from documents.

Ngai, Mae, and Jon Gjerde. *Major Problems in American Immigration History: Documents and Essays*. 2nd ed. Boston: Wadsworth, Cengage Learning, 2013. A collection of essays and couments coering the history of immigration in U.S. history.

Shanks, Cheryl. *Immigration and the Politics of American Sovereignty, 1890-1990*. Ann Arbor: University of Michigan Press, 2001. Scholarly study of changing federal immigration laws from the late nineteenth through the late twentieth centuries, with particular attention to changing quota systems and exclusionary policies.

See also Cable Act; Chinese Exclusion Act; Immigration Act of 1917; Immigration Act of 1921; Immigration Act of 1924; Immigration Act of 1943; Immigration and Nationality Act of 1952; Immigration and Nationality Act of 1965; Immigration and Naturalization Service; Immigration law; Immigration Reform and Control Act of 1986; Naturalization Act of 1790; Page law; War Brides Act.

IMMIGRATION AND NATIONALITY ACT OF 1952

The Law: Federal law relaxing restrictions on immigration
Date: June 27, 1952

Immigration issues: Asian immigrants; Citizenship and naturalization; Laws and treaties; Refugees

President Harry S. Truman objected to some parts of the Immigration and Nationality Act but nevertheless signed it into law. (Library of Congress)

Significance: Also known as the McCarran-Walter Act, the Immigration and Nationality Act of 1952 eased restrictions on Asian immigration and consolidated federal immigration statutes.

During the early 1950's, as it had periodically throughout the twentieth century, immigration again became the subject of intense national debate, and a movement arose to reform immigration law. At the time, there were more than two hundred federal laws dealing with immigration, with little coordination among them.

Reform Efforts   The movement toward immigration reform actually began in 1947, with a U.S. Senate committee investigation on immigration laws, resulting in a voluminous report in 1950 and a proposed bill. The ensuing debate was divided between a group who wanted to abandon the quota system and increase the numbers of immigrants admitted, and those who hoped to shape immigration law to enforce the status quo.

Leaders of the latter camp were the architects of the Immigration and Nationality Act of 1952: Patrick McCarran, senator from Nevada, Francis Walter, congressman from Pennsylvania, and Richard Arens, staff director of the Senate Subcommittee to Investigate Immigration and Naturalization. McCarran was the author of the Internal Security Act of 1951, which provided for registration of communist

418

organizations and the internment of communists during national emergencies; Walter was an immigration specialist who had backed legislation to admit Europeans from camps for displaced persons; Arens had been staff director for the House Committee on Un-American Activities. Each looked upon immigration control as an extension of his work to defend the United States against foreign and domestic enemies.

McCarran was most outspoken in defending the concept of restrictions on the basis of national origin, stating in the Senate:

> There are hard-core indigestible blocs who have not become integrated into the American way of life, but who, on the contrary, are its deadly enemy. . . . this Nation is the last hope of Western civilization; and if this oasis of the world shall be overrun, perverted, contaminated, or destroyed, then the last flickering light of humanity will be extinguished.

Arens branded critics of the proposed act as either communists, misguided liberals enraptured by communist propaganda, apologists for specific immigrant groups, or "professional vote solicitors who fawn on nationality groups, appealing to them not as Americans but as hyphenated Americans." Among the bill's critics, however, were Harry S. Truman, the U.S. president in 1952, and Hubert H. Humphrey, senator from Minnesota and future Democratic presidential nominee. One liberal senator, Herbert Lehman, attacked the national origins provisions of the existing immigration code as a racist measure that smacked of the ethnic purity policies of the recently defeated German Nazis. Truman vetoed the bill, but his veto was overridden, 278 to 113 in the House, and 57 to 26 in the Senate.

In several areas, the 1952 law made no significant changes: Quotas for European immigrants were little changed, no quotas were instituted for immigrants from North and South American countries, and the issue of illegal immigration was given scant attention. There were significant changes in some areas, however: reversal of the ban on Asian immigration, extension of naturalization to persons regardless of race or sex, and the first provision for refugees as a special class of immigrants.

Provisions The Asiatic Barred Zone that had been established in 1917 was eliminated by providing for twenty-five hundred entries from the area—a minuscule number for the region, but the first recognition of Asian immigration rights in decades. This small concession for Asians was offset partially by the fact that anyone whose ancestry was at least half Asian would be counted under the quota for the Asian country of ancestry, even if the person was a resident of another country. This provision, which was unlike the system of counting quotas for European countries, was specifically and openly designed to prevent Asians living in North and South American countries, which had no quota restrictions, from flooding into the United States.

The Immigration and Nationality Act of 1952 also ensured for the first time that the "right of a person to become a naturalized citizen of the United States shall not be denied or abridged because of race or sex." The provision of not denying citizenship based on sex addressed the issue of women who had lost their U.S. citizenship by marrying foreign men of certain categories; men who had married women from those categories had never lost their citizenship.

The issue of refugees was a new concern resulting from World War II. More than seven million persons had lost their homelands in the aftermath of the war, as a result of the conquering and reorganization of countries primarily in Eastern Europe. The 1952 act did not present a comprehensive solution to the problem of refugees but did give the attorney general special power, subject to congressional over view, to admit refugees into the United States under a special status. Although this was expected to be a seldom-used provision of the law, regular upheavals throughout the world later made it an important avenue of immigration into the United States.

Finally, the Immigration and Nationality Act also included stringent security procedures designed to prevent communist subversives from infiltrating the United States through immigration. Some of these harsh measures were specifically mentioned by Truman in his veto message, but the anticommunist Cold War climate made such measures hard to defeat.

Over the objections of Congress, President Truman appointed a special commission to examine immigration in September, 1952. After hearings in several cities, it issued the report *Whom Shall We Welcome?*, which was critical of the McCarran-Walter Act. Some liberal Democrats attempted to make the 1952 presidential election a forum on immigration policy, but without success. Dwight D. Eisenhower, the victorious Republican nominee for president, made few specific statements on immigration policy during the campaign. After his election, however, he proposed a special provision for allowing almost a quarter of a million refugees from communism to immigrate to the United States over a two-year period, couching his proposal in terms of humanitarianism and foreign policy. The resulting Refugee Relief Act of 1953 allowed the admission of 214,000 refugees, but only if they had assurance of jobs and housing or were close relatives of U.S. citizens and could pass extensive screening procedures designed to deter subversives. Several similar exceptions in the following years managed to undercut the McCarran-Walter Act, which its many critics had been unable to overturn outright.

Irene Struthers Rush

Further Reading

Dimmitt, Marius A. *The Enactment of the McCarran-Walter Act of 1952.* Lawrence: University Press of Kansas, 1971. Written as a doctoral dissertation, this study provides one of the most thorough analyses of the 1952 immigration bill.

Legomsky, Stephen H. *Immigration and Refugee Law and Policy.* 3d ed. New York: Foundation Press, 2002. Legal textbook on immigration and refugee law.

LeMay, Michael C. *From Open Door to Dutch Door: An Analysis of U.S. Immigration Policy Since 1820.* New York: Praeger, 1987. A comprehensive over view of the forces behind and results of changing U.S. immigration policy. Chapter 5 opens with a discussion of the Immigration Act of 1952.

_____, ed. *The Gatekeepers: Comparative Immigration Policy.* New York: Praeger, 1989. Compares immigration policy and politics in the United

States, Australia, Great Britain, Germany, Israel, and Venezuela. Helpful in understanding overall immigration issues.

LeMay, Michael C., and Elliott Robert Barkan, eds. *U.S. Immigration and Naturalization Laws and Issues: A Documentary History*. Westport, Conn.: Greenwood Press, 1999. History of U.S. immigration laws supported by extensive extracts from documents.

Ngai, Mae, and Jon Gjerde. *Major Problems in American Immigration History: Documents and Essays*. 2nd ed. Boston: Wadsworth, Cengage Learning, 2013. A collection of essays and couments coering the history of immigration in U.S. history.

Reimers, David M. "Recent Immigration Policy: An Analysis." In *The Gateway: U.S. Immigration Issues and Policies*, edited by Barry R. Chiswick. Washington, D.C.: American Enterprise Institute for Public Policy Research, 1982. Discusses immigration policies and laws from the 1920's through the 1970's. Includes information on Senator Patrick McCarran's role in immigration law.

Shanks, Cheryl. *Immigration and the Politics of American Sovereignty, 1890-1990*. Ann Arbor: University of Michigan Press, 2001. Scholarly study of changing federal immigration laws from the late nineteenth through the late twentieth centuries, with particular attention to changing quota systems and exclusionary policies.

See also Cable Act; Chinese Exclusion Act; Immigration Act of 1917; Immigration Act of 1921; Immigration Act of 1924; Immigration Act of 1943; Immigration Act of 1990; Immigration and Nationality Act of 1965; Immigration and Naturalization Service; Immigration law; Immigration Reform and Control Act of 1986; Naturalization Act of 1790; Page law; War Brides Act.

IMMIGRATION AND NATIONALITY ACT OF 1965

The Law: Federal legislation that eased restrictions on Asian immigration
Date: October 3, 1965

Immigration issues: Asian immigrants; Citizenship and naturalization; Laws and treaties; Refugees

Significance: The Immigration and Nationality Act of 1965 removed restrictions on non-European immigration, significantly altering the ethnic makeup of U.S. immigrants.

The Immigration and Nationality Act of 1952 codified legislation that had developed haphazardly over the past century. Although it liberalized some areas, it was discriminatory in that quotas were allotted according to national origins.

This resulted in western and northern European nations receiving no less than 85 percent of the total allotment. The Immigration and Nationality Act of 1965 allowed non-Europeans to enter the United States on an equal basis with Europeans. Before the 1965 legislation, U.S. immigration policies favored northern and western Europeans.

Reform Begins With the election of John F. Kennedy in 1960, circumstances for meaningful immigration reform came into being: Kennedy believed that immigration was a source of national strength, the Civil Rights movement had promoted an ideology to eliminate racist policies, and the U.S. position during the Cold War necessitated that immigration policies be just. Thus, Kennedy had Abba Schwartz, an expert on refugee and immigration matters, develop a plan to revise immigration policy.

In July of 1963, Kennedy sent his proposal for immigration reform to Congress. His recommendations had three major provisions: the quota system should be phased out over a five-year period; no natives of any one country should receive more than 10 percent of the newly authorized quota numbers; and a seven-person immigration board should be set up to advise the president. Kennedy also advocated that family reunification remain a priority; the Asiatic Barred Zone be eliminated; and nonquota status be granted to residents of Jamaica and Trinidad and Tobago, as it was to other Western Hemisphere residents.

Ceremony under the Statue of Liberty at which President Lyndon B. Johnson (standing to the left of the chair) signed the Immigration and Nationality Act. The Ellis Island reception center is visible at the upper left corner of the picture, to the west of Manhattan Island. (Lyndon B. Johnson Library/Yoichi R. Okamoto)

Last, the preference structure was to be altered to liberalize requirements for skilled people.

After the assassination of President Kennedy, President Lyndon B. Johnson took up the cause of immigration. Although immigration was not a major issue during the 1964 campaign, both sides had courted diverse ethnic communities, whose will now had to be considered. The Democratic Party's landslide victory gave Johnson a strong mandate for his Great Society programs, of which immigration reform was a component. Secretary of State Dean Rusk argued the need for immigration reform to bolster U.S. foreign policy. Rusk, Attorney General Robert F. Kennedy, and others criticized the current system for being discriminatory and argued that the proposed changes would be economically advantageous to the United States. Senator Edward Kennedy held hearings and concluded that "all recognized the unworkability of the national origins quota system."

Outside Congress, ethnic, voluntary, and religious organizations lobbied and provided testimony before Congress. They echoed the administration's arguments about discrimination. A few southerners in Congress argued that the national origins concept was not discriminatory—it was a mirror reflecting the U.S. population, so those who would best assimilate into U.S. society would enter. However, the focus of the congressional debate was on how to alter the national origins system, not on whether it should be changed. The most disputed provisions concerned whether emphasis should be on needed skills, family reunification, or limits set on Western Hemisphere immigration. Family unification prevailed.

Provisions The new law replaced the national origins system with hemispheric caps, 170,000 from the Old World and 120,000 from the New. Spouses, unmarried minor children, and parents of U.S. citizens were exempt from numerical quotas. Preferences were granted first to unmarried adult children of U.S. citizens (20 percent); next, to spouses and unmarried adult children of permanent resident aliens (20 percent). Professionals, scientists, and artists of exceptional ability were awarded third preference (10 percent) but required certification from the U.S. Department of Labor. Married children of U.S. citizens had fourth preference (10 percent). Next were those brothers and sisters of U.S. citizens who were older than twenty-one years of age (24 percent), followed by skilled and unskilled workers in occupations for which labor was in short supply (10 percent). Refugees from communist or communist-dominated countries or the Middle East were seventh (6 percent). Nonpreference status was assigned to anyone not eligible under any of the above categories; there have been more preference applicants than can be accommodated, so nonpreference status has not been used.

The law had unexpected consequences. The framers of the legislation expected that the Old World slots would be filled by Europeans. They assumed that family reunification would favor Europeans, because they dominated the U.S. population. However, those from Europe who wanted to come were in the lower preference categories, while well-trained Asians had been coming to the United States since 1943 and were well qualified for preference positions. Once they, or anyone

423

else, became a permanent resident, a whole group of people became eligible to enter the country under the third preference category. After a five-year wait—the residential requirement for citizenship—more persons became eligible under the second preference category. As a result, many immigrants were directly or indirectly responsible for twenty-five to fifty new immigrants.

The law set forth a global ceiling of 290,000, but actual totals ranged from 398,089 in 1977 to 904,292 in 1993. Refugees and those exempt from numerical limitations were the two major categories that caused these variations. The refugee count had varied according to situations such as that of the "boat people" from Cuba in 1981. In 1991, refugees and those seeking asylum totaled 139,079; in 1993, they totaled 127,343. Persons in nonpreference categories increased from 113,083 in 1976 to 255,059 in 1993. Total immigration for 1991 was 827,167 and for 1993 was 904,292—well above the global ceiling.

The Immigration and Nationality Act of 1965 enabled some of the most able medical, scientific, engineering, skilled, and other professional talent to enter the United States. The medical profession illustrates this trend. In the ten years after the enactment of the 1965 act, seventy-five thousand foreign physicians entered the United States. By 1974, immigrant physicians made up one-fifth of the total number of physicians and one-third of the interns and residents in the United States. Each immigrant doctor represented more than a million dollars in education costs. In addition, they often took positions in the inner-city and rural areas, which prevented the collapse of the delivery of medical services to those locations.

Arthur W. Helweg

Further Reading

Daniels, Roger. *Coming to America: A History of Immigration and Ethnicity in American Life.* New York: HarperCollins, 1990. Good general history of U.S. immigration. Analyzes the causes and consequences of the Immigration and Nationality Act of 1965.

Glazer, Nathan, ed. *Clamor at the Gates: The New American Immigration.* San Francisco: ICS Press, 1985. Superb evaluation of the "new immigration" that resulted from the Immigration and Nationality Act of 1965.

Legomsky, Stephen H. *Immigration and Refugee Law and Policy.* 3d ed. New York: Foundation Press, 2002. Legal textbook on American immigration and refugee law.

LeMay, Michael C., and Elliott Robert Barkan, eds. *U.S. Immigration and Naturalization Laws and Issues: A Documentary History.* Westport, Conn.: Greenwood Press, 1999. History of U.S. immigration laws supported by extensive extracts from documents.

Ngai, Mae, and Jon Gjerde. *Major Problems in American Immigration History: Documents and Essays.* 2nd ed. Boston: Wadsworth, Cengage Learning, 2013.

A collection of essays and couments coering the history of immigration in U.S. history.

Reimers, David M. *Still the Golden Door: The Third World Comes to America.* 2d ed. New York: Columbia University Press, 1992. Detailed historical study of the significant political and social events and personages leading to and implementing the passage of the Immigration and Nationality Act of 1965.

Segal, Uma Anand. *A Framework for Immigration: Asians in the United States.* New York: Columbia University Press, 2002. Sur vey of the history and economic and social conditions of Asian immigrants to the United States, both before and after the federal immigration reforms of 1965.

Shanks, Cheryl. *Immigration and the Politics of American Sovereignty, 1890-1990.* Ann Arbor: University of Michigan Press, 2001. Scholarly study of changing federal immigration laws from the late nineteenth through the late twentieth centuries, with particular attention to changing quota systems and exclusionary policies.

See also Cable Act; Chinese Exclusion Act; Immigration Act of 1917; Immigration Act of 1921; Immigration Act of 1924; Immigration Act of 1943; Immigration Act of 1990; Immigration and Nationality Act of 1952; Immigration and Naturalization Service; Immigration law; Immigration Reform and Control Act of 1986; Naturalization Act of 1790; Page law; War Brides Act.

IMMIGRATION AND NATURALIZATION SERVICE

Identification: Former federal government agency that until 2003 administered laws relating to the admission, exclusion, and deportation of aliens and the naturalization of aliens lawfully residing in the United States

Date: Established in 1891; functions transferred to Department of Homeland Security in 2003

Immigration issues: Border control; Citizenship and naturalization; Illegal immigration; Law enforcement

Significance: The Immigration and Naturalization Service (INS) is the most important agency in the enforcement of U.S. immigration law.

On March 3, 1891, the U.S. Congress passed an immigration law that gave the federal government the sole responsibility for the enforcement of immigration policy and created a Bureau of Immigration as part of the Treasury Department. Soon after ward, the Bureau was transferred to the newly created Commerce Department and then, in 1913, to the Department of Labor. The Bureau expanded greatly during and after World War I, when the passport system was instituted and the Bureau placed agents at all major points of entry. In 1933 an executive order changed the name of the Bureau to the Immigration and Naturalization Service. Seven years later, the INS was transferred from the Department of Labor to the Department of Justice. On March 1, 2003, the functions of the INS were transferred to U.S. Citizenship and Immigration Services within the newly created Department of Homeland Security.

The INS had five primary duties. First, it inspected people who were not citizens of the United States, or aliens, to determine if they could be legally admitted into the country, either as residents or visitors. Second, it made judgments regarding requests of aliens for benefits under American immigration law. Third, it guarded against illegal entry into the United States. Fourth, it investigated, apprehended, and deported aliens who were in the country illegally. Fifth, it examined noncitizens who wished to become citizens.

Law Enforcement   Since the Immigration and Naturalization Service was responsible for admitting those who were permitted legally to enter the United States and for excluding or deporting those who were not, it was the chief agency for enforcing the nation's immigration laws. The enforcement missions of the INS were carried out by four divisions: the Border Patrol, Investigations, Intelligence, and Detention and Deportation.

The Border Patrol was made up of uniformed officers who guarded the country's borders in order to prevent illegal entry. Most of these officers patrolled the border between the United States and Mexico, where the greatest number of illegal entries occurred. As popular concern over illegal immigration from Mexico grew during the 1980's and 1990's, Border Patrol officers found themselves under pressure to stem the flow. During the early 1990's the entire Border Patrol consisted of only 3,700 agents. Although these agents caught over one million illegal immigrants per year, an estimated 300,000 to 400,000 immigrants succeeded in crossing into the country annually. In addition, the Border Patrol faced the problem of distinguishing among noncitizens from Mexico and Central America and U.S. citizens of Hispanic ancestry.

As a result of the pressures and unique challenges of its law-enforcement mission, the Border Patrol was in a position to receive a great deal of criticism. A study by the American Friends Service Committee, conducted during the early 1990's, found nearly four hundred victims of abuse by the Border Patrol. Half of these victims were U.S. citizens.

The 1996 Illegal Immigration Reform and Immigrant Responsibility Act attempted to enhance the Border Patrol's enforcement power by authorizing that additional border guards control the U.S.-Mexico border. It also provided funds for a fence along the border between California and Mexico. Nevertheless, controlling the border continued to be an over whelming challenge.

The Investigations Division of the INS was in charge of enforcing immigration laws in the interior of the United States. Investigation agents investigated places of employment where they suspected that illegal aliens were working. They attempted to apprehend aliens for deportation and prosecute employers who knowingly hired individuals who were in the country illegally. Investigations agents also worked with other law-enforcement agencies to arrest noncitizens who were involved in criminal activities such as drug trafficking and organized crime. A special Anti-Smuggling Branch of the Investigations Division concentrated on breaking up smuggling rings run by noncitizens. During the early 1990's the INS employed about 1,600 investigations agents, and the 1996 law authorized the hiring of an additional 1,200 agents.

The Intelligence Division was in charge of gathering, analyzing, and communicating information relevant to all INS operations, and it directed the headquarters command center. The Detention and Deportation Division took custody of illegal aliens and aliens arrested for criminal activities in the United States. This division was in charge of setting deportation procedures in motion. When aliens could not be immediately deported, they could be placed in detention facilities run by this division of the INS in nine Service Processing Centers around the United States. The Detention and Deportation Division could also place its detainees in institutions run by the Federal Bureau of Prisons.

In addition to enforcing immigration law, the INS also cooperated with other enforcement agencies in attempting to stop the flow of drugs into the United States. From 1988 until early 2003, the Border Patrol was the chief agency for intercepting illegal drugs coming from foreign countries. INS agents in the interior worked with other agencies attempting to stop drug-trafficking organizations.

Inspections and Citizenship In addition to immigration law enforcement, the INS was responsible for examining people from other countries who want to come to the United States temporarily or permanently and for enabling qualified resident aliens to become U.S. citizens.

These tasks were handled by three sections: Adjudication and Nationality, Inspections, and Legalization and Administrative Appeals. Adjudication and Nationality received applications for immigration benefits and petitions for citizenship. In 1995 the INS naturalized 500,000 new citizens, a staggering number considering that only 2,800 INS officers worked with both citizenship and immigration benefits cases that year.

The Inspections office had the task of inter viewing all travelers entering the United States by air, land, or sea. In 1996 the two thousand inspections agents processed about 484 million travelers. Legalization and Administrative Appeals is in charge of the petitions of immigrants whose applications for immigration have been refused.

Other INS Activities The Immigration and Naturalization Service was the primary source of federal government information on migration and on procedures for acquiring citizenship. The service's Information Resources Management prepares records and databases. The INS issued a wide variety of publications, including an annual Statistical Yearbook of the Immigration and Naturalization Service and an INS Fact Book. As a part of its naturalization services, the service provided advice, information, and textbooks to those who wanted to prepare for citizenship examinations.

Billboard erected by the Immigration and Naturalization Service in Atlanta, Georgia, to remind Americans of the rights of immigrants. (Jean Higgins)

Twenty-first Century Changes During the late twentieth century, changes in world migration patterns, the ease of international travel, and a growing emphasis on controlling illegal immigration fostered the growth of the INS. Following the terrorist attacks of September 11, 2001, the INS was one of several existing federal agencies that were incorporated into the new U.S. Department of Homeland Security, a cabinet department of the federal government that is concerned with protecting the American homeland and the safety of American citizens.

Since the creation of the Department of Homeland Security, most INS functions have been divided into two bureaus: the U.S. Citizenship and Immigration Services (USCIS) and the Bureau of Immigration and Customs Enforcement. The Executive Office for Immigration Review and the Board of Immigration Appeals, which review decisions made by the USCIS, remain under the jurisdiction of the Department of Justice.

Immigration officers now specialize in inspection, examination, adjudication, legalization, investigation, patrol, and refugee and asylum issues. The USCIS continues to enforce laws providing for selective immigration and controlled entry of temporary visitors such as tourists and business travelers. It does so by inspecting and admitting arrivals at land, sea, and airports of entr y, administering benefits such as naturalization and permanent resident status, and apprehending and removing aliens who enter illegally or violate the requirements of their stay. Like its

428

predecessor, the INS, the USCIS has been criticized for downplaying its mission of social service and cultural assimilation while overemphasizing its law-enforcement role in ways that may produce human rights abuses.

Carl L. Bankston III
Updated by Theodore M. Vestal

Further Reading

Cohen, Steve. *Deportation Is Freedom! The Orwellian World of Immigration Controls.* Philadelphia: Jessica Kingsley, 2005. Critical analysis of the implementation of U.S. immigration laws, with particular attention to the work of the Immigration and Naturalization Service.

Cole, David. *Enemy Aliens: Double Standards and Constitutional Freedoms in the War on Terrorism.* New York: New Press/W. W. Norton, 2003. Critical analysis of the erosion of civil liberties in the United States since September 11, 2001, with attention to the impact of federal policies on immigrants and visiting aliens.

Daniels, Roger. *Guarding the Golden Door: American Immigration Policy and Immigrants Since 1882.* New York: Hill & Wang, 2004. Study of the impact of ignorance, partisan politics, and unintended consequences in immigration policy, including during the post-September 11, 2001, war on terror.

Gomez, Iris D. *Representing Non-citizens and INS Detainees: Resolving Problems in the Current Climate of Uncertainty.* Boston: MCLE, 2003. Legal guide for attorneys who represent aliens facing legal problems with the Immigration and Naturalization Service.

Legomsky, Stephen H. *Immigration and Refugee Law and Policy.* 3d ed. New York: Foundation Press, 2002. Legal textbook on American immigration and refugee law.

LeMay, Michael C., and Elliott Robert Barkan, eds. *U.S. Immigration and Naturalization Laws and Issues: A Documentary History.* Westport, Conn.: Greenwood Press, 1999. History of U.S. immigration laws supported by extensive extracts from documents.

Ngai, Mae, and Jon Gjerde. *Major Problems in American Immigration History: Documents and Essays.* 2nd ed. Boston: Wadsworth, Cengage Learning, 2013. A collection of essays and couments coering the history of immigration in U.S. history.

Staeger, Rob. *Deported Aliens.* Philadelphia: Mason Crest, 2004. Up-to-date analysis of the treatment of undocumented immigrants in the United States since the 1960's, with particular attention to issues relating to deportation.

Weissinger, George. *Law Enforcement and the INS: A Participant Observation Study of Control Agents.* Lanham, Md.: University Press of America, 1996. A look inside the daily lives of INS officers.

Welch, Michael. "The Role of the Immigration and Naturalization Service in the Prison-Industrial Complex." *Social Justice* 27 (Fall, 2000): 73-89. Critical analysis of the INS in administering policies that produce human rights abuses rather than cultural assimilation.

See also Cable Act; Chinese Exclusion Act; Immigration Act of 1917; Immigration Act of 1921; Immigration Act of 1924; Immigration Act of 1943; Immigration Act of 1990; Immigration and Nationality Act of 1952; Immigration and Nationality Act of 1965; Immigration law; Immigration Reform and Control Act of 1986; Naturalization Act of 1790; Page law; War Brides Act.

IMMIGRATION AND NATURALIZATION SERVICE V. CHADHA

The Case: U.S. Supreme Court ruling on a deportation case that had important political ramifications

Date: June 23, 1983

Immigration issues: Asian immigrants; Court cases; Government and politics

Significance: By overturning congressional use of the legislative veto, the Supreme Court, in this single decision, overturned more combined laws than it had in its entire history.

During the 1960's, Jagdish Chadha, a Kenyan of Asian Indian descent carr ying a British passport, entered the United States on a student visa. When his student visa expired, he was denied reentry into either Great Britain or Kenya and applied for permanent residence in the United States. After lengthy deliberations, the Immigration and Naturalization Service (INS) granted his application to stay, only to have the House of Representatives veto the INS decision, leaving Chadha to face deportation.

Both liberals and conservatives saw the case as a chance to overcome the burgeoning practice of Congress passing laws containing legislative veto provisions. These enactments allowed one or both houses of Congress to act jointly or independently to cancel executive branch regulations made pursuant to some vague delegation of power.

Liberal public interest groups played the more public role as Ralph Nader's consumer advocate litigation group took over Chadha's case in the Supreme Court. The liberal public interest group's interest in the case stemmed from the explosion of congressional enactments of legislative vetoes. After having fought for the passage of regulatory legislation on the environment, consumer protection, worker safety, or similar causes, these liberal groups often were frustrated by the bureaucratic regulatory process. If they succeeded in the bureaucracy, they then were frustrated by the actions of their more wealthy opponents, who would persuade one or both houses of Congress to kill offending regulations with a legislative veto. Those conservatives who opposed both excessive delegations of power and legislative vetoes had no apparent vehicle for participation.

Conservative chief justice Warren E. Burger wrote the Court's 7-2 majority opinion, which cut across liberal and conservative opinion and ended the use of the congressional veto. A moderate Lewis F. Powell, Jr., concurred. Moderately conservative justice Byron R. White dissented, upholding the use of legislative vetoes, and conservative justice William H. Rehnquist also dissented. The diversity of opinion continues. The Court seemed willing to push further in the direction of Chadha in *Bowsher v. Synar* (1986), but seemed to withdraw from Chadha's advanced stand in *Morrison v. Olson* (1988) and *Mistretta v. United States* (1989).

Richard L. Wilson

Further Reading

Bischoff, Henry. *Immigration Issues*. Westport, Conn.: Greenwood Press, 2002.

Craig, Barbara Hinkson. Chadha: The Story of an Epic Constitutional Struggle. Berkeley, CA: University of California Press, 1990.

Legomsky, Stephen H. *Immigration and Refugee Law and Policy*. 3d ed. New York: Foundation Press, 2002. Legal textbook on immigration and refugee law.

LeMay, Michael C., and Elliott Robert Barkan, eds. *U.S. Immigration and Naturalization Laws and Issues: A Documentary History*. Westport, Conn.: Greenwood Press, 1999. History of U.S. immigration laws supported by extensive extracts from documents.

See also Deportation; Florida illegal-immigrant suit; Immigration and Naturalization Service; Immigration law; Mexican deportations during the Depression; Twice migrants; *Zadvydas v. Davis*.

IMMIGRATION "CRISIS"

Definition: Popular fear that began developing in the late twentieth century that the United States was in peril of being overrun by immigrants

Immigration issues: Demographics; Illegal immigration; Nativism and racism

Significance: Immigration to the United States increased steadily after 1965, reaching record levels during the 1990's and early twenty-first century. Between 1990 and 2000 alone, the U.S. Census reported a 57 percent increase in the number of foreign-born residents of the United States. Although earlier immigrants came chiefly from Europe, many of these more recent immigrants arrived from Latin America and Asia. This new trend in immigration increased ethnic diversity in the United States, and both the large numbers and the non-European origins of the immigrants created perceptions of an immigration crisis.

In 1965, the U.S. Congress passed an immigration act that did away with the European bias of the nation's immigration policy and made family reunification, rather than national origin, the primary qualification for admission. At first, it was thought that the Immigration and Nationality Act of 1965 would not greatly expand immigration. However, legal immigration increased from about 250,000 per year during the early 1960's to 1,827,167 in 1991. Illegal immigration, particularly from Mexico, also appears to have increased from the 1960's to the 1990's. A backlash against immigration began to develop among many segments of the American population.

A New Immigrant Population According to estimates of the U.S. Bureau of the Census, the legal immigrant population in the spring of 1997 was 25.8 million people. Immigrants, then, made up nearly one out of every ten people in the United States by the end of the 1990's. These were mostly relatively new immigrants: More than 80 percent had arrived since 1970, and more than 60 percent had arrived since 1980. In addition to these legal immigrants, approximately 300,000 to 400,000 illegal immigrants entered the United States each year. Although many of these illegal immigrants were in the United States only for seasonal or other temporary employment, the Immigration and Naturalization Service has estimated that the illegal immigrant population of the United States was about 4 million people during the 1990's.

Not only were immigrants entering the United States in large numbers, but they also were coming from places that had sent relatively few immigrants to America in earlier years. Heavy immigration from Latin America and Asia, combined with comparatively large family sizes among Latin Americans and Asians, began to change the racial and ethnic makeup of the United States. For most of U.S. history, the overwhelming majority of Americans were white Europeans, with a large minority of African Americans. The new immigrants and their children, however, brought a new cultural and racial diversity to the United States. According to projections of the U.S. Bureau of the Census, the white non-Hispanic component of the population could be expected to decline from about 72 percent to only 53 percent from the year 2000 to 2050. Black non-Hispanic Americans were expected to increase only slightly during this period, from 12.2 percent to 13.6 percent. Asians, who made up less than 1 percent of the U.S. population in 1970 had increased to almost 3 percent by 1990 ("Asians and Others" constituted 3.8 percent). By 2050, it was predicted that 8.2 percent of all Americans would be of Asian heritage. Hispanics, who were less than 5 percent of the U.S. population in 1970, had grown to 9 percent in 1990. By the year 2050, if ethnic trends in immigration and fertility continued as expected, almost one out of every four Americans would be Hispanic.

Although most Americans could not engage in the scientific projection of population trends, they were aware that large numbers of immigrants, both legal and illegal, were entering the country. They also were aware of the cultural changes brought about by immigration. In southern Florida, Texas, California, and other parts of the country, English-speaking Americans heard languages they could not understand and came into contact with unfamiliar cultures. Thus, both concern over the amount of immigration and reactions to cultural changes fueled the perception of an immigration crisis.

Economic Concerns over Immigration Many of those who feel that the flow of immigrants into the United States constitutes a crisis maintain that immigration poses serious economic problems. Immigrants, they argue, compete for jobs with people already living in the United States. Under U.S. immigration policy, there are two primary reasons that people from other countries can receive an immigrant visa that gives them permission to settle in the United States. The first reason concerns family: People who have family members who are citizens of or residents in the United States are given priority in the granting of immigrant visas. The second reason concerns employment: People with special professional abilities or workers arriving to take jobs for which Americans are in short supply are eligible for visas.

Roy Beck, a liberal activist and an advocate of limiting immigration, argued that those who receive permission to immigrate for purposes of employment do so at the expense of employees already in the United States. He pointed out that immigration lawyers, who help people find ways to enter the United States, frequently work for businesses that wish to employ foreign labor. These lawyers, according to Beck, help employers draw up job descriptions that make it appear that no qualified American workers are available so that the employers can import cheaper foreign workers.

Projected Changes in the Ethnic and Racial Composition of the United States, 2000–2050
(Percentage of total U.S. population)

Year	White, non-Hispanic	Black, non-Hispanic	Asian & Pacific Islander	Hispanic
2000	71.8	12.2	3.9	11.4
2005	69.9	12.4	4.4	12.6
2010	68.0	12.6	4.8	13.8
2015	66.1	12.7	5.3	15.1
2020	64.3	12.9	5.7	16.3
2025	62.4	13.0	6.2	17.6
2030	60.5	13.1	6.6	18.9
2035	58.6	13.2	7.1	20.3
2040	56.7	13.3	7.5	21.7
2045	54.7	13.5	7.9	23.1
2050	52.8	13.6	8.2	24.5

Source: U.S. Bureau of the Census, Current Population Reports, Series P25-1130, "Population Projections of the United States by Age, Sex, Race, and Hispanic Origin, 1995 to 2050." March, 1997. Washington, D.C.: U.S. Government Printing Office.

George Borjas, an economist specializing in immigration issues, maintained that high levels of immigration pose a problem for low-income American workers. Borjas observed that most immigrants enter the United States to join family members, and these immigrants tend to have few job skills and little educational background. Therefore, immigrants were more likely than other people to rely on public assistance, making them a financial burden, and they competed for jobs with low-skilled, low-income natives. In 1996, Borjas estimated that immigration had been the source of about one-third of a recent decline in the wages of less-educated American workers.

Cultural Concerns over Immigration Some of those alarmed over the influx of immigrants saw it as a cultural crisis. They claimed that immigrants were arriving in such large numbers, with cultures that were so foreign to the existing culture of the United States, that they could not be assimilated readily into American culture.

Journalist Peter Brimelow maintained that immigration posed a crisis for American political culture. The arrival of masses of immigrants who did not speak English, according to Brimelow and others, threatened the position of English as a language understood everywhere around the country. Moreover, cultural critics of immigration argued that newly arrived Mexicans, Dominicans, and Chinese identified with their own cultural backgrounds rather than with mainstream American culture. Therefore, critics such as Brimelow claimed that immigration endangered national unity. Some of those who believe that massive immigration could create a crisis for U.S. political culture argue that immigration is especially dangerous for African Americans. They point out that African Americans were likely to be replaced as the nation's largest minority and that this would decrease this group's political power. Many opponents of immigration also maintained that new immigrants would have little commitment to overcoming the racial inequality created by the history of slavery and discrimination in the United States.

Responses to Claims of Crisis Although no one denies that immigration increased greatly in the years following 1965, many political figures and scholars question whether this should be seen as an immigration "crisis." Economist Julian Simon argued that immigrants were frequently energetic and industrious and could create, not simply compete for, jobs. The economy of southern Florida, for example, boomed as a result of the activities of Cuban immigrants. Many supporters of immigration, including 1996 vice presidential candidate Jack Kemp, maintained that immigration was an economic blessing, since immigrants often performed work in areas that were experiencing labor shortages.

A number of observers believed that the influx of immigrants posed no threat to American culture. They pointed out that American culture had changed continually throughout its history. Moreover, the sociologist Alejandro Portes and other scholars cited evidence that the children of immigrants over whelmingly became fluent in English and were often weaker in their parents' languages than they were in English.

Carl L. Bankston III

Further Reading

Roy Beck's *The Case Against Immigration* (New York: W. W. Norton, 1996) presents an economic argument for seeing immigration as a crisis.

Immigration: Opposing Viewpoints (San Diego: Greenhaven Press, 2004), edited by Mary E. Williams, presents a variety of social, political, and legal viewpoints of experts and observers familiar with immigration into the United States.

Peter Brimelow's *Alien Nation: Common Sense About America's Immigration Disaster* (New York: Random House, 1995) provides a controversial but readable argument for drastically reducing immigration to the United States.

Leonard Dinnerstein and David M. Rimer's *Ethnic Americans: A History of Immigration* (5th ed; New York: Columbia University Press, 2009) traces the history of immigration in American, from 1492 to the present day, including changing public attitudes and legal approaches to immigration and immigrants.

The articles in *Immigrants Out! The New Nativism and the Anti-Immigrant Impulse in the United States* (New York: New York University Press, 1997), edited by Juan F. Perea, examine the backlash against immigrants and place it in the context of U.S. history.

Henry Bischoff's *Immigration Issues* (Westport, Conn.: Greenwood Press, 2002) is a collection of balanced discussions about the most important and most controversial issues relating to immigration.

For a balanced discussion of the economic impact of illegal immigration on American society, see *The Economics of Illegal Immigration* (New York: Palgrave Macmillan, 2005) by Chisato Yoshida and Alan D. Woodland.

See also Demographics of immigration; Immigration and Nationality Act of 1965; Immigration and Naturalization Service; Justice and immigration; Migration.

IMMIGRATION IN FILM

The Law: *O-1 Visas: Extraordinary Ability.* The O-1 visa obtainers are those foreign nationals who temporarily enter the United States and who display an exceptional ability in the sciences, education, business, athletics or arts or extraordinary achievement in the motion picture or television industry. To qualify, they must be coming to the United States specifically to work in their area or specialty. Currently, there is no annual cap on O visas.

Date: The O-1 visa legislation was drafted in 1990 by former Connecticut congressman Bruce Morrison.

Immigration Issues: Foreign nationals who come to the United States to fulfill their dream in the arts have options available to them depending on their level of skill in their area of expertise. According to the U.S. Department of State, Bureau of Consular Affairs, a temporary worker visas is available to those immigrants or aliens entering the United States for an employment period lasting a fixed period of time, and are not considered permanent or indefinite. In each case of these visa applications, it is required that the prospective employer first files a petition with U.S. Citizenship and Immigration Services (USCIS). An approved petition is required to apply for a work visa.

Significance: For decades, actors and films have brought a focus on immigration issues to the big screen.

Background: In order for an actor or actress to temporarily enter the United States to perform in the industry, they have to qualify for an O-1 Visa, which is for performers who exhibit extraordinary ability in the areas of arts or extraordinary achievement in the motion picture or television industry.

Films Movies such as *Sin Nombre*, which means "Nameless," the 2009 U.S.-Mexican adventure thriller film about a Honduran girl trying to immigrate to the U.S.A, and a boy caught up in the violence of gang life who also needs to escape, use the industry to portray immigration issues. Written and directed by Cary Joji Fukunaga, *Sin Nombre* was filmed in Spanish and won several awards, including the prizes for directing and cinematography at the 2009 Sundance Film Festival.

The Godfather, a 1972 American crime film directed by Francis Ford Coppola and produced by Albert S. Ruddy (based on a screenplay by Mario Puzo and Coppola), has left a long lasting impression on viewers for decade and remains one of the most popular films of all times. The Godfather became a film series consisting of three films, all directed by Francis Ford Coppola and based upon the novel of the same title by Italian American author Mario Puzo. The first two films were written, filmed, and released in the 1970s; however, the third was not released until 1990. The three films follow the fictional Corleone Mafia through the course of the family's history in both the United States and their homeland of Sicily.

The documentary *Who Is Dayani Cristal?* (2013) earned its title by referring to the tattoos on the body of an anonymous migrant found in the Arizona desert. In the documentary, Gael García Bernal attempts to identify the unknown man and to retrace his journey. The documentary was chosen to be shown at the 2014 Greater Washington Immigration Film Festival (see below).

Actors and Actresses Whether the film is about immigration or stars immigrants, such as Arnold Schwarzenegger when he first arrived from Austria, the film industry has left a significant motion picture impact on the topic of immigration for decades. Schwarzenegger, an Austrian-born American actor, film producer, activist, businessman, investor, writer, philanthropist, former professional bodybuilder and politician, is a great example of an immigrant coming to the United States to pursue their dream. He moved to the United States in September 1968 at the age of 21 and went on to become a United States citizen in 1983. Since then, he has served two terms as the 38th Governor of California from 2003 until 2011.

Actress, model, and philanthropist Charlize Theron was born in Benoni, Transvaal Province, South Africa, on August 7, 1975. After years of struggling to embark her dancing career, she successfully turned to modeling for a short while. After some time she decided to pursue acting instead, but soon learned that her heavy accent could hold her back from roles. Her luck changed in 1994 when she engaged in an argument with a bank teller, who refused to allow her to pull funds from a South African account. Her fit gained the attention of another bank customer,

John Crosby, who was a Hollywood manager who represented major talents such as John Hurt and Rene Russo. After watching Theron's interaction with the teller, he immediately offered to sign her and, within months, she made her acting debut in a small role in *Children of the Corn III* (1995). Other parts followed when she landed roles in *2 Days in the Valley* (1996) and *That Thing You Do!* (1996).

Later, Theron gave her Oscar-winning performance as serial killer Aileen Wuornos in *Monster*, and well-reviewed performances in both North Country and Young Adult. In 1999, Theron landed roles in notable films, including *The Astronaut's Wife* with Johnny Depp and *The Cider House Rules* with Tobey Maguire. Two years later, in 2001, she reteamed with Reeves in *Sweet November*. In 2003 she starred opposite Mark Wahlberg in the heist thriller *The Italian Job*. However, it was her performance in 2003's *Monster*—a biopic about serial killer Aileen Wuornos—that earned Theron the widespread respect she worked so hard for. She even gained almost 40 pounds for the role, which led to her Academy Award and Golden Globe awards. Theron is also a philanthropist and animal rights activist.

Actress Sandra Oh, the daughter of Korean immigrants, came to the United States from Canadian, where she was born in Nepean, Ontario on July 20, 1971. Oh decided on acting as a career, and in 1993 she graduated from Montreal's National Theatre School of Canada. Her ongoing success stemmed from both the Canadian stage and film roles that later led to her famed roles in *Under the Tuscan Sun* and *Sideways*. Oh's additional role as Cristina Yang on ABC's *Grey's Anatomy* earned her a Golden Globe, a Screen Actors Guild award, and four Emmy nominations.

Another *Grey's Anatomy* actor, Kevin McKidd, who plays Dr. Owen Hunt, is a Scottish actor, born on August 9, 1973. He studied engineering at the University of Edinburgh, but left school in order to pursue acting full-time. Prior to *Grey's Anatomy*, he played the roles of Lucius Vorenus on the HBO/BBC series *Rome*, his lead role in NBC's short-lived *Journeyman* and as Tommy in *Trainspotting*.

SAG/AFTRA According to SAG-AFTRA, they receive requests for opinion letters on foreign performers' applications for several types of visas that include: O-1, O-2, P-1, P-2 and P-3. In order for a visa to be granted, the application requires qualified petitioners, those who are the performer's representatives, to contact the labor union with jurisdiction over the work at issue, such as in the fields of television and radio broadcasting, sound recordings, and other recorded material, in order to seek an advisory opinion from the union on whether the visa should be granted.

Legislation According to the U.S. Department of State, Bureau of Consular Affairs, the petition document requirements are as the following:

A U.S. employer should file the petition with the following:
- A written advisory opinion, describing the foreign national's ability as follows:
- If the petition is based on the foreign national's extraordinary ability in the arts, the consultation must be from a peer group (including labor organizations) in the foreign national's field of endeavor; or a person or persons designated by the group with expertise in the alien's area of ability;

- If the petition is based on the foreign national's extraordinary achievements in the motion picture or television industry, separate consultations are required from a labor and a management organization with expertise in the alien's field of endeavor;.
- A copy of any written contract between the employer and the foreign national or a summary of the terms of the oral agreement under which the alien will be employed;
- Evidence the foreign national has received, or been nominated for, significant national or international awards or prizes in the particular field, such as an Academy Award, Emmy, Grammy or Director's Guild Award, or evidence of at least three of the following:
  - The foreign national performs or will perform services as a lead or starring participant in productions or events which have a distinguished reputation as evidenced by critical reviews, advertisements, publicity releases, publications, contracts or endorsements;
  - Achievement of national or international recognition, as shown by critical reviews or other published materials by or about the individual in major newspapers, trade journals, magazines, or other publications;
  - A record of major commercial or critically acclaimed successes, as shown by such indicators as title, rating or standing in the field, box office receipts, motion picture or television ratings and other occupational achievements reported in trade journals, major newspapers or other publications;
  - Achievement of significant recognition from organizations, critics, government agencies or other recognized experts in the field in which the alien is engaged, with the testimonials clearly indicating the author's authority, expertise and knowledge of the alien's achievements;
  - A high salary or other substantial remuneration for services in relation to others in the field, as shown by contracts or other reliable evidence; or if the above standards do not readily apply to the alien's occupation, the petitioner may submit comparable evidence in order to establish the alien's eligibility.

Films Festivals 2014 marks the fifth San Francisco Immigrant Film Festival. Throughout the year, the San Francisco Immigrant Film Festival offers free screenings of films and videos at different venues that are related to immigrant communities. www.sfimmigrantfilmfestival.com.

The Greater Washington Immigration Film Festival is one of the few festivals in the country devoted to films about immigration: 13 works over four days. www.immigrationfilmfest.org

Further Reading

Rubin, Rachel, and Jeffrey Melnick. *Immigration and American Popular Culture: An Introduction.* New York: New York University Press, 2007. A series of case studies about the influence of immigrants on American popular culture, including the film industry, popular music, literature, and fashion.

Santopietro, Tom. *The Godfather Effect: Changing Hollywood, America, and Me.*

New York: Thomas Dunne Books, 2012. An examination of the influence of Francis Ford Coppola's Godfather trilogy on both Hollywood and American society, including the portrayal of Italian Americans in the media, and the author's personal reflections on being an Italian-American.

U.S. Citizenship and Immigration Services. "O-1 Visa: Individuals with Extraordinary Ability or Achievement." http://www.uscis.gov/working-united-states/temporary-workers/o-1-individuals-extraordinary-ability-or-achievement/o-1-visa-individuals-extraordinary-ability-or-achievement Accessed Oct. 1, 2014.

See also European Immigrant Literature; Immigration and Naturalization Service; Latinos; Literature

IMMIGRATION LAW

Definition: Branch of federal law dealing with the entry and settlement in the United States of noncitizens

Immigration issues: Border control; Citizenship and naturalization; Civil rights and liberties; Discrimination; Government and politics; Law enforcement; Laws and treaties; Refugees

Significance: U.S. immigration laws have changed dramatically since the nation was formed during the late eighteenth century. These laws have directly affected tens of millions of people and have indirectly affected even more people in such areas as civil rights, the distribution of wealth, employment, labor policy, foreign relations, and freedom of association.

Immigration law is one of several areas of legal specialization, such as estate planning, domestic relations, tax law, or criminal law. Immigration lawyers serve two types of clients: individual immigrants and American businesses that have hired or wish to hire immigrants. They help their clients by providing advice on immigration law, by assisting them in choosing to apply for a particular immigration status, by providing appropriate forms, by helping clients complete and file immigration petitions, and by representing clients who must justify their claims to an immigrant status or appeal a decision of the Immigration and Naturalization Service (INS) or other agency.

Although persons need not obtain professional legal assistance in order to migrate to the United States, American immigration laws are complicated and expert advice can sometimes be helpful. Those whose applications for migration have been refused and who file appeals are usually well advised to turn to a professional immigration attorney. People who face deportation hearings need expert legal advice.

Laws regarding areas of lawyer specialization differ from state to state. Some states recognize specialization through self-designation. Under this system, attorneys who specialize in immigration law list themselves as experts in this area and can present themselves as such to the public. Generally, states that allow attorneys to designate themselves as specialists in a particular area require three years of practice and about thirty hours of legal education in the specific area before the designation can be recognized. Other states have certification systems. Under a certification system, an attorney who wishes to be recognized as an immigration lawyer must take an examination, similar to the bar examination, in this area of specialty.

Basic Immigration Legislation All American immigration law is set by the United States government, not the separate states. Therefore, although immigration lawyers must pass state bar examinations to practice law and the states set the conditions and qualifications that lawyers must meet to specialize in immigration law, these lawyers are chiefly concerned with federal legislation. The main outlines of immigration and naturalization law in the United States after World War II were set by the Immigration and Nationality Act of 1952, better known as the McCarran-Walter Act. The 1952 act continued the national origins system of granting visas that the U.S. Congress had adopted during the 1920's. Under this system, legal immigration was largely restricted to people from western European countries. Provisions of the McCarran-Walter Act barred from immigration communists, subversives, or anyone judged by the INS to have advocated communist ideas.

The "immigration" part of this act was largely replaced by the Immigration and Nationality Act Amendments of 1965, which abolished the national origins system in favor of a preference system based on family reunification, job skills of migrants, and refugee status. The McCarran-Walter Act, however, continued to be the basis of American naturalization policy. Under the conditions set forth in that act, before noncitizens can apply for U.S. citizenship, they must be at least eighteen years of age and have been legal residents of the United States for at least five years. Persons applying for citizenship must have lived in the state in which they file a petition for at least six months before petitioning the court. In most cases, petitioners for American citizenship must be able to speak, read, and write English. Moreover, applicants must demonstrate knowledge of American history and government.

The 1965 amendments greatly increased immigration law practice in the United States in several ways. First, they led to a wave of immigration to the United States, creating a large group of potential users of the services of immigration lawyers. Second, the complex system of preferences created a demand for experts who could provide advice on the best way to obtain permission to settle in the United

Work Performed by Immigration Lawyers

Immigration lawyers, who work with immigrants and with businesses employing or desiring to hire immigrants:

- Analyze the facts in the case of someone desiring to immigrate
- Explain all benefits for which immigrants may be eligible
- Recommend the best way to obtain legal immigrant status
- Complete and file appropriate applications
- Keep up with new laws affecting their clients
- Speak for clients in discussions with the Immigration and Naturalization Service (INS)
- Represent clients in court
- File necessary appeals and waivers

Adapted from: American Immigration and Lawyers Association, "A Guide to Consumer Protection and Authorized Representation," Washington, D.C.: AILA, 1998.

States. Third, increasing the importance of job skills as an avenue for immigration created incentives for American businesses to seek out the services of immigration lawyers. Businesses wishing to hire noncitizens often find it useful to obtain professional advice on how to get visas for prospective employees.

Concern over illegal immigration led to the Immigration Reform and Control Act (IRCA) of 1986. This act established fines for employers who hire illegal aliens and offered legal status to aliens who had entered the country illegally before January 1, 1982. The Illegal Immigration Reform and Immigrant Responsibility Act of 1996 was also primarily aimed at clamping down on illegal immigration. Among other provisions, the act streamlined deportation proceedings, making it easier and faster to deport foreigners who lacked proper documents. Persons seeking political asylum who arrived in the United States with falsified or borrowed documents could be held at the border and denied asylum unless they could demonstrate a "credible fear" of persecution in their homelands.

Each new piece of legislation has created new conditions and complications surrounding immigration and has therefore contributed to the growth of immigration law as a specialty. Immigration attorneys contributing pro bono services have assisted those seeking asylum in the United States, such as refugees from Central America, who are under threat of immediate deportation.

Essentials of American Immigration Law The basis of immigration law is a system of visa categories. A visa is a stamp placed in a passport by an American consulate outside the United States. In order to immigrate to the United States, persons' passports must contain a stamp indicating to which legal category they belong. Immigration attorneys or other knowledgeable persons can help immigrants identify the best category. There are two major classes of visas. The first class is the permanent residence visa. After entry into the United States, the

INS issues alien registration cards, commonly known as "green cards," to those who receive this type of visa.

Noncitizens who have permanent resident status have the right to live permanently and work in the United States. Usually, only people who have immediate family members residing in the United States or who have job skills demanded by U.S. employers can obtain this type of visa. The second class of visa is the non-immigrant visa. This type of visa is issued for vacations, study, or temporary employment. The U.S. government issues an unrestricted number of non-immigrant visas, but permanent residence visas are limited by quotas established by Congress.

Different groups of people have different chances of receiving permanent residence status in each annual quota. These groups are called preferences. The first preference consists of unmarried children, of any age, of U.S. citizens. Spouses of green card holders and unmarried children of green card holders fall into the second preference. This means that after the unmarried children of U.S. citizens who have applied for U.S. residence in a given year have been granted visas, quota slots begin to be filled by spouses and unmarried children of green card holders. The third preference goes to professionals and persons of exceptional ability in the arts and sciences who come to the United States to work for American employers. Married children, of any age, of U.S. citizens receive the fourth preference. The fifth preference goes to noncitizen sisters and brothers of U.S. citizens. Skilled and unskilled workers coming to take jobs for which American workers are in short supply are classified as the sixth preference.

Husbands and wives of citizens do not fall under the quota system. This means that marrying a U.S. citizen is one of the easiest legal ways to settle permanently in the United States. The 1986 Immigration Marriage Fraud Act Amendments amended the 1952 Immigration and Nationality Act, because it was believed that marriage fraud was a serious problem.

These amendments impose a two-year conditional residency requirement on alien spouses and children before they are eligible for permanent residency status on the basis of marriage. Couples must file a petition within the last ninety days of the conditional status period, after which the INS inter views them to establish that they have not divorced or had their marriages annulled and that they have not been married solely for the purpose of obtaining entry to the United States. Under the 1986 amendments, marriage fraud for the purpose of immigration may be punishable by up to five years imprisonment and up to $250,000 in fines. Marriage fraud can also be grounds for deportation and a bar to future immigration.

Refugees and political asylum seekers also do not fall under the quota system. These are people who have been forced to flee their native countries because of political oppression. A refugee is someone who has been granted permission to enter the United States before arriving. Political asylum is granted to persons only after they have entered the country. Those entering as refugees may apply for green cards one year after they arrive. Those who do not enter as refugees and receive political asylum may become eligible two years after asylum is granted.

Exclusion and Deportation Exclusion is the barring of noncitizens from entering the United States. Deportation is the prohibiting of noncitizens who have already entered the United States, either legally or illegally, from remaining and sending them back to their countries of origin. The United States government has decided that certain categories of people are undesirable and that these people should be excluded. Excludable aliens include those with tuberculosis, those with physical or mental disorders that may threaten others, those who have been convicted of committing certain crimes, those who are judged to be threats to national security, those who have previously violated immigration laws, those who practice polygamy, and those who engage in international child abduction.

As waivers are available in many exclusion cases, immigration attorneys can apply for and help persons obtain waivers. The INS decides when an individual falls into an excludable category and it is responsible for issuing or refusing to issue waivers. If a waiver application is denied or if a potential immigrant claims that a judgment of exclusion was a mistake, the decision of the INS may be appealed in a U.S. district court. As in all appeals cases, persons appealing should seek the representation of a qualified immigration attorney.

There are two broad categories of deportable aliens: those deportable for acts committed before or during entry to the United States and those deportable for acts committed since their entry. American citizens cannot be deported. Some aliens, including ambassadors, diplomats, public ministers, and members of their families, are also exempt from deportation. Aliens may be deported because they were excludable to begin with and misrepresented themselves in order to enter the country. A 1978 amendment to the Immigration and Nationality Act allowed the INS to deport aliens who participated in Nazi activities during World War II on the grounds that they committed acts before arriving in the United States that exclude them from remaining in the country. Immigrants who have entered the country illegally without inspection may be deported for illegal entry. Those deportable for conduct after entry include subversives, or people who advocate the violent overthrow of the government, and those who have committed serious crimes and have been sentenced to prison within five years after entry.

Persons who have crossed the border into the United States without proper documents are frequently deported immediately. However, persons who can reasonably claim to be seeking political asylum or contest their deportation may be granted a deportation hearing. Deportation hearings begin officially with the issuance of an order to immigrants to show why they are not deportable. Such hearings generally involve a judge, a trial attorney, immigrants' counsel, and sometimes an interpreter. Immigration judges are selected by the U.S. attorney general. The trial attorney has the job of showing why the immigrant should be deported and is therefore comparable to a prosecutor in criminal law. Immigrants' counsel is not necessarily an attorney, although attorneys are often the individuals best qualified to aid defendants in deportation hearings. According to the United States Code of Federal Regulations, various types of persons may serve as counsel for aliens in a deportation hearing: attorneys who are members of the highest court of any state, law students and law graduates under some circumstances who have not yet been admitted to the bar, representatives of organizations recognized by the Board of

Immigration Appeals, accredited officials of aliens' own governments, certain persons who meet criteria established by legal statute, attorneys outside the United States licensed to practice law in their own countries, and amici curiae, friends of the court whom the court recognizes as providing useful information. Under the law, the immigration judge at a deportation hearing must advise aliens of the availability of free legal services.

Major Organizations of Immigration Lawyers The largest and bestknown organization of immigration lawyers is the American Immigration Lawyers Association (AILA). Its more than 5,200 members are all lawyers specializing in immigration and nationality law. The AILA was founded in 1946 as the Association of Immigration and Nationality Lawyers and changed its name in 1981. Based in Washington, D.C., the AILA publishes a newsletter, the *AILA Monthly*, which has a circulation of 3,800, and the annual *Immigration and Nationality Law Handbook*.

The AILA has thirty-four local chapters in different regions of the country. It offers a mentor program, in which experienced immigration lawyers answer the questions of other members. Its Young Lawyers Division is open to all members aged thirty-six or younger or who have been members of the organization for less than three years. This division provides education and training for younger and newer members. The AILA holds an annual conference that offers panels, workshops, and professional education. Although the AILA exists primarily to promote the interests and professional development of its members, it also seeks to influence immigration policies. Staff and members at its Washington, D.C., headquarters maintain contact with the INS and other federal agencies involved in implementing immigration policies.

With only about fifty members, the Association of Immigration Attorneys (AIA), based in New York, is a much smaller organization. It was founded in 1983, and all of its members are attorneys specializing in immigration. In addition to representing the interests of immigration lawyers, the AIA is an advocacy group that seeks to assert the legal rights of aliens, lobbies the U.S. Congress on behalf of noncitizens, and attempts to bring about legislation to improve the position of legal aliens in the United States.

The National Immigration Project of the National Lawyers' Guild (NIP/ NLG), based in Boston, is an organization of five hundred members. Founded in 1973, its members include lawyers, law students, and legal workers. It seeks to defend the civil liberties of foreign-born persons living in the United States and to help noncitizens who have legal problems with immigration. The Project also holds seminars to improve the legal skills of its members.

Many local bar associations also sponsor volunteer legal services projects for immigrants. These provide legal representation to those facing deportation hearings or those who have other relevant legal needs. Bar associations often maintain referral services that provide the names of attorneys who do pro bono immigration work—that is, attorneys who provide their services free of charge. One of the most notable pro bono projects has been ProBAR in Texas. This is a project that provides free legal counsel, from lawyers and law students, to Central Americans in South Texas who are seeking political asylum.

Carl L. Bankston III

Further Reading
Perhaps the best tool with which to begin any study of immigration law is a basic glossary, such as Bill Ong Hing's *Immigration and the Law: A Dictionary* (Santa Barbara, Calif.: ABC-Clio, 1999).

Guidebooks provide information on American immigration law in a fashion that can be easily understood by nonlawyers. *U.S. Immigration and Citizenship: Your Complete Guide* (Rocklin, Calif.: Prima Publishing, 1997) by Allan Wernick, a top immigration lawyer, is one of the best guides for those interested in visiting or settling in the United States. Wernick explains the U.S. immigration system, details who can immigrate, and provides tips for dealing with the Immigration and Naturalization Service.

Aliza Becker's *Citizenship for Us: A Handbook on Naturalization and Citizenship* (Washington, D.C.: Catholic Legal Immigration Network, 2002) is another practical guide to immigration law written for nonlawyers.

Also useful is Carl R. Baldwin's *Immigration Questions and Answers* (3d ed. New York: Allworth Press, 2002).

A handbook for immigration attorneys that looks at immigration law in post-September 11, 2001, America is Iris D. Gomez's *Representing Non-citizens and INS Detainees: Resolving Problems in the Current Climate of Uncertainty* (Boston: MCLE, 2003).

Stephen H. Legomsky's *Immigration and Refugee Law and Policy* (3d ed. New York: Foundation Press, 2002) is an authoritative legal textbook on immigration and refugee law. Employment immigration, the other primary type of legal immigration, is handled in Bill Ong Hing's *Handling Immigration Cases* (New York: John Wiley & Sons, 1995), a guide for lawyers handling immigration cases related to employment.

Gerald L. Neuman's *Strangers to the Constitution: Immigrants, Borders, and Fundamental Law* (Princeton, N.J.: Princeton University Press, 1996) is an academic consideration of the problems involved in applying U.S. constitutional law to noncitizens and a discussion of case-law interpretations of immigrant rights.

For a general history of American immigration law, see *U.S. Immigration and Naturalization Laws and Issues: A Documentary History* (Westport, Conn.: Greenwood Press, 1999), edited by Michael C. LeMay and Elliott Robert Barkan, which is supported by extensive extracts from documents.

In *Immigration and the Politics of American Sovereignty, 1890-1990* (Ann Arbor: University of Michigan Press, 2001), Cheryl Shanks examines changing federal immigration laws from the late nineteenth through the late twentieth centuries, with particular attention to changing quota systems and exclusionary policies.

Leonard Dinnerstein and David M. Rimer's *Ethnic Americans: A History of Immigration* (5th ed; New York: Columbia University Press, 2009) traces the history of immigration in America, from 1492 to the present day, including changing public attitudes and legal approaches to immigration and immigrants, while Mae Ngai and Jon Gjerde's *Major Problems in American Immigration History: Documents and Essays* (2nd ed. Boston: Wadsworth, Cengage Learning, 2013) provides a collection of essays and documents covering the history of immigration in U.S. history.

See also Cable Act; Chinese Exclusion Act; Immigration Act of 1917; Immigration Act of 1921; Immigration Act of 1924; Immigration Act of 1943; Immigration Act of 1990; Immigration and Nationality Act of 1952; Immigration and Nationality Act of 1965; Immigration and Naturalization Service; Immigration Reform and Control Act of 1986; Naturalization Act of 1790; Page law; War Brides Act.

Immigration Reform and Control Act of 1986

The Law: Federal legislation on illegal aliens
Date: November 6, 1986

Immigration issues: Citizenship and naturalization; Cuban immigrants; Laws and treaties

Significance: The Immigration Reform and Control Act provided for the legalization of illegal aliens and established sanctions against employers who hire undocumented workers.

The Immigration Reform and Control Act (IRCA) was signed into law by President Ronald Reagan on November 6, 1986. The act amended the Immigration and Nationality Act of 1965 and was based in part on the findings and recommendations of the Select Commission on Immigration and Refugee Policy (1978-1981). In its 1981 report to Congress, this commission had proposed that the United States continue to accept large numbers of immigrants and enact a program of amnesty for undocumented aliens already in the United States. To deter migration of undocumented aliens to the United States, the commission also proposed to make the employment of illegal aliens a punishable offense.

Development of the Bill These proposals were incorporated into the Simpson-Mazzoli bill, a first version of which was introduced in 1982. In the five years between its introduction and its enactment, the bill ran into opposition from a variety of quarters. Agricultural interests, especially growers of perishable commodities, were concerned that the proposed employer sanctions would jeopardize their labor supply. Mexican American advocacy groups also opposed employer sanctions, while organized labor and restrictionists who were concerned about

446

the massive influx of foreign workers favored employer sanctions. Many liberals and humanitarians supported the notion of legalizing the status of undocumented aliens and expressed concerns over potential discrimination against them.

During the 1980's, the bill repeatedly was pronounced dead only to be revived again as various lawmakers, notably Representatives Leon Panetta, Charles Schumer, and Peter Rodino, introduced compromises and amendments to respond to their constituencies or to overcome opposition by congressional factions. Differences also developed between the House Democratic leadership and the Republican White House over funding the legalization program. On October 15, 1986, the House at last approved the bill, by a vote of 238 to 173; the Senate approved the bill on October 17, by a vote of 63 to 24.

Provisions The major components of the Immigration Reform and Control Act provided for the control of illegal immigration (Title I), the legalization of undocumented aliens (Title II), and the reform of legal immigration (Title III). Other sections of the act provided for reports to Congress (Title IV), state assistance for the incarceration costs of illegal aliens and certain Cuban nationals (Title V), the creation of a commission for the study of international migration and cooperative economic development (Title VI), and federal responsibility for deportable and excludable aliens convicted of crimes (Title VII).

A major objective of the IRCA, the control of illegal immigration, was to be achieved by imposing sanctions on employers. The IRCA made it unlawful for any person knowingly to hire, recruit, or refer for a fee any alien not authorized to work in the United States. Before hiring new employees, employers would be required to examine certain specified documents to verify a job applicant's identity and authority to work.

The act established civil and criminal penalties, and employers could be fined up to two thousand dollars per unauthorized alien, even for a first offense. Employers who demonstrated a pattern of knowingly hiring undocumented aliens could face felony penalties of up to six months' imprisonment and/or a three-thousand-dollar fine per violation. Employers also were required to keep appropriate records. Failure to do so could result in a civil fine of up to one thousand dollars. In order to allow time for a public education campaign to become effective, penalties against employers for hiring undocumented aliens were not phased in until June, 1987.

The second major objective of the IRCA, the legalization of undocumented aliens, was to be realized by granting temporary residence status to aliens who had entered the United States illegally prior to January 1, 1982, and who had resided in the United States continuously since then. They could be granted permanent residence status after eighteen months if they could demonstrate a minimal understanding of English and some knowledge of the history and government of the United States. After a five-year period of permanent residence, they would become eligible for citizenship.

The act also permitted the attorney general to grant legal status to aliens who could show that they had entered the United States prior to January, 1972, and lived in the country since then. Newly legalized aliens were barred from most forms of public assistance for five years, although exceptions could be made for emergency medical care, aid to the blind or disabled, or other assistance deemed to be in the interest of public health.

To assure passage of the bill, support of the growers in the West and Southwest was essential. After protracted negotiations, the growers succeeded in getting the kind of legislation that assured them of a continued supply of temporary agricultural workers. The new program differed from earlier bracero programs by providing for the legalization of special agricultural workers who could work anywhere and who could become eligible for permanent resident status or for citizenship. The IRCA granted temporary residence status to aliens who had performed field labor in perishable agricultural commodities in the United States for at least ninety days during the twelve-month period ending May 1, 1986, as well as to persons who could demonstrate to the Immigration and Naturalization Service that they had performed appropriate agricultural field labor for ninety days in three successive previous years while residing in the United States for six months in each year.

The act also revised and expanded an existing temporary foreign worker program known as H-2. In case of a shortage of seasonal farmworkers, employers could apply to the secretary of labor no more than sixty days in advance of needing workers. The employer also was required to try to recruit domestic workers for the jobs. H-2 also provided that during fiscal years 1990-1993, additional special agricultural workers could be admitted to temporary residence status as "replenishment workers." Their admission was contingent upon certification of the need for such workers by the secretaries of labor and of agriculture. Replenishment workers who performed ninety days of field work in perishable agricultural commodities in each of the first three years would be eligible for permanent resident status. They were, however, disqualified from public assistance. In order to become eligible for citizenship, they would have to perform seasonal agricultural services for ninety days during five separate years.

The IRCA also provided permanent resident status for a hundred thousand specified Cubans and Haitians who entered the United States prior to January 1, 1982. The law increased quotas from former colonies and dependencies from five hundred to six thousand and provided for the admission of five thousand immigrants annually for two years, to be chosen from nationals of thirty-six countries with low rates of immigration. Altogether, the Immigration Reform and Control Act led to the legalization of the status of three million aliens; however, IRCA was not as successful in curbing illegal immigration as had been anticipated.

Mindful of the potential for discrimination, Congress established an Office of Special Counsel in the Department of Justice to investigate and prosecute charges of discrimination connected with unlawful immigration practices. The act also required states to verify the status of noncitizens applying for public aid and provided that states be reimbursed for the implementation costs of this provision. To reimburse states for the public assistance, health, and education costs resulting from legalizing aliens, the act provided for the appropriation of one billion dollars in each of the four fiscal years following its enactment.

Although determining the specific effects of IRCA is difficult, an analysis by the Migration Policy Institute concluded that the good intentions behind the legislation were not always realized in practice. They conclude that employment rather than legislation remains, as of 2005, the primary driver in unauthorized immigration.

Helmut J. Schmeller

Further Reading

Bean, Frank D., Georges Vernez, and Charles B. Keely. *Opening and Closing the Doors: Evaluating Immigration Reform and Control.* Washington, D.C.: Rand Corporation and the Urban Institute, 1989. Scholarly study of the IRCA of 1986, its implementation, and its impact on illegal immigration.

Cooper, Betsy, and Kevin O'Neil. *Lessons from the Immigration Reform and Control Act of 1986.* MPI Policy Brief No. 3 (Aug. 2005). Available online from "http://www.migrationpolicy.org/sites/default/files/publications/PolicyBrief_No3_Aug05.pdf. An evaluation of the effects of the Immigration Reform and Control Act of 1986, written by analysts from the Migration Policy Institute.

Daniels, Roger. "The 1980s and Beyond." In *Coming to America: A History of Immigration and Ethnicity in American Life.* New York: HarperCollins, 1990. Brief, critical discussion of the IRCA, with special emphasis on the act's amnesty provision.

Fuchs, Lawrence H. *The American Kaleidoscope: Race, Ethnicity, and the Civic Culture.* Hanover, N.H.: University Press of New England, 1990. Concise, welldocumented discussion of the act by the executive director of the staff of the Select Commission on Immigration and Refugee Policy.

Hing, Bill Ong. *Immigration and the Law: A Dictionary.* Santa Barbara, Calif.: ABC-Clio, 1999. Useful general reference on immigration law.

Jacobs, Nancy R. *Immigration: Looking for a New Home.* Detroit: Gale Group, 2000. Broad discussion of modern federal government immigration policies that considers all sides of the debates about the rights of illegal aliens. Includes discussions of the immigration laws of 1986 and 1996.

Legomsky, Stephen H. *Immigration and Refugee Law and Policy.* 3d ed. New York: Foundation Press, 2002. Legal textbook on immigration and refugee law.

LeMay, Michael C., and Elliott Robert Barkan, eds. *U.S. Immigration and Naturalization Laws and Issues: A Documentary History.* Westport, Conn.: Greenwood Press, 1999. History of U.S. immigration laws supported by extensive extracts from documents.

Menjivar, Cecilia and Daniel Kanstroom, eds. *Constructing Immigrant 'Illegality': Critiques, Experiences, and Responses.* New York: Cambridge University Press, 2014. A collection of essays examining the concept of illegal immigration and how it is shaped by immigration law.

Ngai, Mae, and Jon Gjerde. *Major Problems in American Immigration History: Documents and Essays.* 2nd ed. Boston: Wadsworth, Cengage Learning, 2013. A collection of essays and documents on the history of immigration in U.S. history.

Shanks, Cheryl. *Immigration and the Politics of American Sovereignty, 1890-1990.* Ann Arbor: University of Michigan Press, 2001. Scholarly study of changing federal immigration laws from the late nineteenth through the late twentieth centuries, with particular attention to changing quota systems and exclusionary policies.

Zolberg, Aristide R. "Reforming the Back Door: The Immigration Reform and Control Act of 1986 in Historical Perspective." In *Immigration Reconsidered: History, Sociology, and Politics*, edited by Virginia Yans-McLaughlin. New York: Oxford University Press, 1990. Comprehensive, well-documented account of the genesis of the IRCA, with particular emphasis on the legislative history.

See also Cable Act; Chinese Exclusion Act; Immigration Act of 1917; Immigration Act of 1921; Immigration Act of 1924; Immigration Act of 1943; Immigration Act of 1990; Immigration and Nationality Act of 1952; Immigration and Nationality Act of 1965; Immigration and Naturalization Service; Immigration law; Naturalization Act of 1790; Page law; War Brides Act.

INDENTURED SERVITUDE

Definition: System whereby immigrants contract to work for specified periods for persons who pay the costs of their travel expenses

Immigration issues: Economics; European immigrants; Families and marriage; Labor; Slavery; Women

Significance: During the American colonial period, tens of thousands of people—mostly Europeans—sold their future labor in return for passage to the New World. Approximately 20 percent of these indentured servants were women.

During the early decades of Great Britain's North American colonization, the London Company needed workers to settle in its mid-Atlantic colony. At the same time, there were those in England who wanted to emigrate but did not have the funds. Meeting both needs, the system of indentured servitude brought tens of thousands of colonists to the New World, until the harsher system of slavery overtook it. The largest number of the indentured servants who came to North America came to the Chesapeake Bay Colony. Between the 1650's and the start of the American Revolution, some twenty thousand such servants arrived; of these, about four thousand were women.

Servants normally agreed to an indenture of three to seven years, with the average being four. Those with skills generally negotiated shorter periods, while the unskilled had to settle for the longest time. All indentured servants, regardless of skill, age, or gender, incurred the same debts emigrating to the colonies. To pay those obligations, they sold their future labor in the indenture contract.

The majority of indentured servants were between the ages of ten and forty. Younger children would have been more of a liability than an asset, and given the life expectancy of the time, workers beyond forty may well have died before the indenture was completed, thus costing the master more than they were worth. The peak age for indentured servants was between fifteen and twenty-five. While the men were generally in their teens, the women tended to enter an indenture in their early twenties. Most were done with service before their thirtieth birthday.

During the seventeenth century, most indentured servants came from England. In the eighteenth century, the majority came from Ireland or Europe as "redemptioners." Ship captains paid their passage, and the immigrants hoped that friends or relatives would pay for their passage and "redeem" them in the New World. Failing that end, the captain would sell them into servitude.

Whether they came from England or elsewhere, or whether they came in the seventeenth or eighteenth century, men were preferred as indentured servants over women. In the earlier time, as a result of the shortage of women in the colonies, a premium was paid for female servants, and perhaps as many as 25 percent of the servants were women; in the second century of colonialism, women made up only 10 percent of indentured servants. As the gender ratio equalized in the colonies, fewer women came as indentured servants.

Most servants signed their indentures—agreements that spelled out their rights and obligations, terms of service, and what was due upon conclusion of the contract—before they sailed. Some indentured servants were convicts, and a few were kidnapped or shanghaied. In return for providing food, clothing, and shelter, the master received the labor of the servant for the specified time. The master was to avoid cruel and unusual punishment, although servants could be whipped, branded, or even hanged for infractions.

Servants agreed to work, not to marry without their masters' permission, and not to run away. The servants, their labor, and all their possessions belonged to the masters, who could trade, lend, auction, or sell their servants. Servants could be separated from their families. They had few rights, and while the contracts were enforced in the courts, judgments generally favored the masters. In fact, during the time of the contract, most servants had no more rights than slaves. Once freed, if they lived that long, servants might rise to the rank of small landholders. Upon freedom, masters provided servants with their freedom dues, including clothes, tools, guns, and perhaps as much as fifty acres of land.

Indentured servants were cheaper for masters than hiring free labor. They performed all sorts of tasks, both skilled and unskilled. Most female indentured servants worked in their masters' homes, in contrast to the men, who worked in the fields and shops of their masters. Because the women worked in close proximity to the families, masters generally paid more attention to their references and their character.

Women generally had lower skill levels than men and were, therefore, restricted in the types of jobs that they were given. Most worked in domestic service, which included tasks ranging from emptying an overflowing chamber pot to starting the fire before the family arose to the more traditional feminine occupations of sewing, carding wool, and spinning. They also washed and ironed clothes and did other, similar types of domestic service. Child care occupied the largest amount of the female servant's time. Women worked as nursemaids and nannies, caring for children and adults alike. Occasionally, female servants did field work, although most worked in the house, often sleeping on the floor at the foot of the mistress' bed.

Abuses Women faced abuses that were different, and often harsher, than those of their male counterparts. Running away was one of the more common methods of coping with an abusive situation. Masters generally complained that female servants ran away either to rejoin a lover or because they were pregnant. In addition to the general penalties accorded all indentured servants, women bore the additional burden of pregnancy. A pregnant servant had additional time added to her indenture to cover her "crime." She then had to serve even more time to reimburse her master for time lost during her confinement and any expenses associated with the care and feeding of the infant, even though in many cases the master was the child's father.

A female servant's best hope was marriage. Two servants who married combined their freedom dues; marrying a freeman, however, improved her position more. A higher percentage of seventeenth century servants were women whose indentures were bought at a premium, likely with the intention of marriage.

A minority of indentured servants, both male and female, were convicts whose choice was death or imprisonment in England or transportation as indentured servants to the colonies. While some colonies would accept female convicts as house servants, others would take them only as field hands and still others had laws forbidding their introduction completely. Though part of the reason for transportation was reformation, there is no evidence that the process had any positive effects.

Upon conclusion of the indenture, success in the New World was far from guaranteed, and women had a harder time than men. During the late seventeenth century, two-thirds of Philadelphia's poor house residents were women. Furthermore, the long-term residents were more likely to be female. Generally, women who completed their indenture had few opportunities to support themselves and nowhere to go, and they often were forced into the poor house.

Duncan R. Jamieson

Further Reading

Brooks, Joanna. *Why We Left: Untold Stories and Songs of America's First Immigrants*. Minneapolis: University of Minnesota Press, 2013.

Galenson, David W. *White Servitude in Colonial America*. Cambridge, England: Cambridge University Press, 1981.

Hendrick, Veronica C. *Servants, Slaves, and Savages: Reflections of Law in American Literature*. Durham, NC: Carolina Academic Press, 2012.

Menard, Russell R. *Migrants, Servants, and Slaves: Unfree Labor in Colonial British America*. Burlington, Vt.: Ashgate, 2001.

Morgan, Kenneth. *Slavery and Servitude in Colonial North America: A Short History*. New York: New York University Press, 2001.

Salinger, Sharon V. *"To Serve Well and Faithfully": Labor and Indentured Servants in Pennsylvania, 1682-1800*. Cambridge, England: Cambridge University Press, 1987.

Smith, Abbot Emerson. *Colonists in Bondage: White Servitude and Convict Labor in America, 1607-1776.* New York: W. W. Norton, 1971.

Van der Zee, John. *Bound Over: Indentured Servitude and American Conscience.* New York: Simon & Schuster, 1985.

See also Asian Indian immigrants; British as dominant group; Chinese American Citizens Alliance; Chinese detentions in New York; History of U.S. immigration; Latinos; Racial and ethnic demographic trends; Women immigrants; Wong Kim Ark case.